A History and Philosophy of Sport and Physical Education

A History and Philosophy of Sport and Physical Education

From Ancient Civilizations to the Modern World

Second Edition

Robert A. Mechikoff
San Diego State University

Steven G. Estes
SUNY at Cortland

WCB
McGraw-Hill

Boston, Massachusetts   Burr Ridge, Illinois   Dubuque, Iowa
Madison, Wisconsin   New York, New York   San Francisco, California   St. Louis, Missouri

WCB/McGraw-Hill

A Division of The **McGraw·Hill** *Companies*

A History and Philosophy of Sport and Physical Education: From Ancient Civilizations to the Modern World

2 3 4 5 6 7 8 9 10   FGRFGR   9 9 8

ISBN 0–697–25883–1

Vice president, director of editorial: *Kevin Kane*
Publisher: *Ed Bartell*
Executive editor: *Vicki Malinee*
Project editor: *Theresa Grutz*
Senior marketing manager: *Pamela S. Cooper*
Managing editor: *Larry Goldberg*
Project manager: *Ann Fuerste*
Design freelance coordinator: *Mary Christianson*
Cover design by *Kay Fulton Design*
Cover photograph © Museo Nazionale Romano, Rome/Canali Photo Bank, Milan/Superstock
Photo research coordinator: *Rose Deluhery*
Art editor: *Joyce Watters*
Compositor: *Shepherd, Inc.*
Typeface: *10/12 Caslon*
Printer: *Quebecor Printing*

Library of Congress Catalog Card Number: 97–60303

Dedication

Books, like people, come and go. However, there are books and people that have achieved a "timeless and classic quality" in my life and have profoundly influenced it. I am grateful to the many students who have brought intellectual stimulation, rational debate (most of the time) and enjoyable conversation to my professional and personal life. Suffice it to say that I consider it a privilege to lead students on a journey through history and philosophy and, in part, dedicate this book to these students, past—present—and future.

Many textbooks and accounts on the history and/or philosophy of sport and physical education have been written throughout the ages. The works of these timeless and classic historians, philosophers, poets, and social critics have provided me with a revealing and illuminating account of the significance of sport. To the ancient and contemporary authors and athletes who leave to us their timeless legacies to debate, to ponder and to admire, my deepest respect, admiration, and at times, a major difference of opinion.

Last, my accomplishments would have likely not have happened without the support and encouragement of my parents, Alex and Aileen Mechikoff, daughter, Kelly, and wife, Kathryn. I would like to dedicate this book, in part, to them. My stepson Brad has just completed his second year of high school and competed in football and track. This book is dedicated in part to Brad and the generation of athletes he will compete against; may Brad and his fellow male and female athletes find as much joy and personal pleasure in athletic competition as did the preceding generations. The probability of this happening is great; after all, how many activities and institutions have a history that is as rich and timeless as is sport and physical education?

R. A. M
San Diego, California

Contents

s   e   c   t   i   o   n

Ancient Civilizations

s e c **2** i o n

From the Spiritual World to the Secular World: Changing Concepts of the Body

section 3

The Theoretical and Professional Development of American Physical Education

section 4

Historical and Philosophical Development of Sport in America

section 5

Modern Olympic Games

F o r e w o r d

Professional physical educators are often well-educated and dedicated to their work. They are consecrated to developing the holistic well-being of every single student. Knowledge of the preceding 150 years of sport and physical education history in the United States and of the brilliant thirty centuries of world physical education history is an important foundation for every professional.

Those physical educators who are unenlightened of the historical and philosophical developments that helped shape their profession will be prone to make needless mistakes. As the philosopher George Santayana observed, "Progress, far from consisting in change, depends on retentiveness. . . . Those who cannot remember the past are condemned to repeat it." Within the context of history and philosophy, the well-educated professional will have an appreciation and understanding of the trials, tribulations, and successes of those who preceded them. This fact is especially relevant as we approach the twenty-first century.

Physical education, also known as sport science, kinesiology and sometimes carelessly called sports and games, has been the target of frequent attacks. This situation has become increasingly evident during these last few decades of the twentieth century. Thousands of financially strapped school districts across the country look for programs to cut back or eliminate. More often than not, physical education is targeted for cutbacks or elimination. During these times, physical education teachers and coaches can support and defend their profession using the tools of history.

By reading this "benchmark" book by professors Mechikoff and Estes, students will understand the historical contributions that physical education has made to the citizens of the world. Many of these contributions are timeless and enduring. Philosophically, students will be engaged through the Socratic method to think about how societies and great philosophers have looked upon the body. The value of a mind and body education that incorporates the obvious health benefits are as timely today as they were during the Golden Age of Greece. The timeless contributions of physical education and sport, as well as its philosophical justification, is explained in this book.

No profession—law, medicine, engineering, physics, chemistry, biology, theology, or computer science—can possibly exist unless these specialists know a great deal about the pioneers that preceded them. At the foundation of my observations is that our undergraduate and graduate "majors" need to know as much history and philosophy as they do biomechanics, exercise physiology, and motor learning. Regrettably, as we approach the millennial year, this is not even close. Our universities and colleges find little time for instruction about the contributions of Homer, Marcus Aurelius, Galen, Per Henrik Ling, Oliver Wendell Holmes, Pierre de Coubertin, Amy Morris Homans, Eleanor Methany, and Roberta Park. Those who read this text by Mechikoff and Estes will have gone a long way in reducing this gap, enriching the whole education of our teachers and coaches and helping them (all of us) embrace the "Yin and Yang" . . . the interactive influences of human frailties and the multitudinous dimensions of greatness.

How wise it was for the energetic authors to recognize the magnificence of sport and physical culture in ancient and modern societies everywhere on the globe. Mechikoff and Estes see clearly the impossibility of any two researchers to adequately describe all of these contributions. They choose to concentrate almost all of their energies on Europe and North America (chapter two is entitled "Sumer, Egypt, and China"). It is one of the author's signal contributions that they take pride in America's heritage of organized physical activity and simultaneously acknowledge an even greater debt to earlier European societies. Such evenhandedness is not always found in the several scores of text books on "world physical education and sport" published this century and written in German, French, and English.

I've been reading physical education and sport literature for forty-five years . . . steadily and sometimes furiously. I have probably read twenty-five to thirty texts with similar titles to this book. A dozen of them are still around on our college campuses. Four or five or six of them are good. This Mechikoff/Estes text is the best that I have read.

Amidst the very important "gods of science," Mechikoff and Estes seem to be telling us that history and philosophy need to join hands and, in this book, make for a successful union, thus advancing the human condition. This can be achieved through energized, imaginative, wholly encompassing physical activity, for the several billion other "passengers" on this spaceship called planet earth.

John A. Lucas
Professor Emeritus of the Pennsylvania State University
Department of Kinesiology
Official Lecturer of the International Olympic Committee (IOC)
and 1996 Recipient of the IOC's Olympic Order

Preface

A large number of history and philosophy textbooks begin with a desire to create a vehicle for helping students understand the changes that have occurred in a defined area. This text is no exception. We have created a textbook that can be used to explain changes from several perspectives, particularly the way that cultures throughout Western civilization have viewed the relationship of the mind and body and the attendant impact on the development of sport and physical education.

Our Audience

Our belief that this text will be useful to contemporary undergraduate physical education and kinesiology students rests on the idea that this group has needs that are not met by much of the scholarship in the subdisciplines of sport history and sport philosophy. Simply put, undergraduate students whom we have taught have not had the methodological basis, theoretical grounding, or coursework in sport history or philosophy necessary to utilize contemporary scholarship. Our belief is born out of our experiences as teachers in the classroom and as players and coaches on the playing field. Because of our own experiences as athletes, as coaches, and as teachers, we have been in a unique position to observe that physical education and kinesiology students bring skills into the classroom that are experiential more than they are academic. The profound sporting and play experiences of physical education students are *experiential* more than they are *intellectual*. Clearly this is not the case with all students, but it has been the case often enough that we began developing course materials that could bridge the gap between experience and research.

As much as physical educators emphasize holistic thought, we believe most physical education research subscribes to the Cartesian and Platonic models of dualistic reality. Knowledge in these philosophical systems exists in a hierarchy of mind over body, where matters of the body are either unreal or inconsequential. We believe that when textbooks are geared toward a reality only of the mind, we are not taking advantage of the skills physical education and kinesiology students bring to the classroom. Furthermore, we are not addressing the substance of our discipline *by moving*. This irony does not escape us.

Our Approach

Most books in the West have the failing of being essentially mind oriented, and to the extent that this textbook is written in the dualistic traditions of the West, we admit our weakness. What we try to do, however, and what we believe is the major strength of this textbook, is to make physical education and kinesiology students aware of the metaphysical and ontological positions they bring to the classroom and relate these positions to their origins in Western civilization. By constantly referring to the relationship of the mind and the body, to the metaphysical and ontological positions of being that were developed through Western civilization and that can be used to help interpret the formation of the American character, we believe we can help today's students know the present by understanding the development of the past. We do not suggest, however, that any given culture's or philosopher's metaphysical position determines that culture's or philosopher's position of sport and physical education. Rather what we are doing is using metaphysics as an interpretive device, one that might help explain to today's students how and why sport and physical education developed the way it did. Our interpretation is not definitive, and we hope that our work will inspire both our students and critics to use this device. We have found it rewarding.

As a consequence of our approach, we do not list all the many sports and playful activities that have been developed since the beginning of Western civilization. There are many textbooks that do just this, and to create another textbook along these lines would be to continue the same problems we see in our history and philosophy of sport classes. Rather, we try to interpret, explain, and describe much of the development of sport in terms of how past cultures have viewed the human body. Clearly this is a subjective approach to understanding the changes that have occurred in the West, and we accept any criticism that this approach engenders.

We also hope that this approach humanizes the teaching process (always a goal in our positivistic times) and is more interesting to our students than those that merely list all the activities that constitute sport and play. We have had much success examining historical issues in sport and play through the interpretive lens of metaphysics and hope that other readers will find this approach as helpful as we have.

As professionals in the field (no pun intended), it is our hope that the second edition of this book will provide students and fellow educators with a comfortable and yet scholarly foundation to facilitate their understanding of how sport and physical education developed from a historical and philosophical perspective. In concert with the fine group of professionals at McGraw-Hill Higher Education Group, we have carefully considered the suggestions of the review team and, as a result, believe that we have produced a text that is "user friendly," accurate, appropriate, informative, and scholarly.

Changes to the Second Edition

There are several significant pedagogical changes in this edition. Unlike the first edition, we have formatted the second edition in a style that organizes the text into five separate sections that are chronologically and thematically sequenced. Prior to the beginning of the major sections, the prologue (chapter one) explains to the reader "how" history and philosophy are utilized to study sport and physical education. Naturally, each of the five major sections and its corresponding chapters are written to build on preceding chapters. By doing this, it is our intent that the reader will find that conceptually, the text is "user friendly." The new organizational format should enable students to identify salient contributions that sport and physical education have played in the development of various cultural institutions and civilizations that have shaped the course of history.

Each of the five main sections is identified by a title that reflects the significant historical and philosophical theme(s) that will be presented in the attendant chapters. Our intent was to chronologically sequence each of the sections to provide readers with a historical roadmap that takes them on a journey through time, from the ancient civilizations of Sumer, Egypt, China, and Greece, through the Middle Ages and on to the 1996 Atlanta Olympic Games and beyond. The book ends with the epilogue (chapter 17). We use the epilogue to close the text with a perspective that addresses sport and physical education as seen through the philosophical methods of existentialism and phenomenology which offer yet another view of the body and the value of physical activity.

Since this text has five major sections, faculty have the added flexibility of scheduling examinations and lectures around specific chapters or over a specific section. We also believe that the new format will strengthen the continuity of material.

Content has been significantly expanded in order to bring to the attention of the reader the role of sport and physical education within the cultural fabric of selected non-Western civilizations. We present information that enables the student to recognize the contributions of non-Western civilizations to the development of sport and physical education in Western civilization.

Section five, Modern Olympic Games, was re-organized and provides the reader with unique insight about some of the more prominent events that impacted the first 100 years of the modern Olympic Games. The mission of the International Olympic Committee as guardians of the Olympic Spirit is discussed, as are the many controversial political and social issues that have profoundly impacted the Olympic movement. Content has been expanded to include pertinent coverage of the 1992 Barcelona Olympiad, the 1992 Winter Olympics in Albertville, the 1994 Winter Olympics in Lillehammer, and the 1996 Atlanta Olympiad.

In addition, a prelude to the 1998 Winter Olympics in Nagano, Japan, is presented along with previews of the Summer Olympics in Sydney in 2000 and the Winter Olympics scheduled for Salt Lake City in 2002.

The Instructor's Manual is a new supplement that we designed for both student and professor. It contains chapter outlines and suggested test questions. The chapter outlines could be used as handouts as well as a guide in lecturing. The nature of history and philosophy tends to be viewed by many students and some faculty as overwhelming. In consideration of this view, we have devised examination questions that speak to the "big picture." We did not devise test questions that focus on issues and events that, while important, are not crucial to demonstrating understanding of the content and attendant ideas. This by no means suggests that the test questions provided are the final word in assessment. Like every other faculty member, we change our test questions from year to year and encourage the modification of these questions. (By all means send your modifications to us so we can share them with other faculty who use this book—we thank you in advance!) The Instructor's Manual is available in electronic format from McGraw-Hill Higher Education for IBM-PC users or for Macintosh users.

Acknowledgments

There have been a number of individuals who have been instrumental in assisting with the necessary research and suggestions that are of critical importance when undertaking a task of this magnitude. It is rare to count among one's best friends two professionals who are trained as historians and lawyers; enduring gratitude goes to John Cassidy of Austin, Texas, and Mitchell Haddad of Tustin, California, who critically examined pertinent materials throughout this book for historical accuracy and appropriate wording. John Haller has provided valuable insight and deserves a special note of appreciation for his contributions.

Steven Van Camp, M.D., who in 1996 served as President of the American Academy of Sports Medicine (ACSM), was a valuable source of information about the concept of health as described by Galen. Dr. Kenneth Greene was especially helpful in areas that fall within his expertise. Special appreciation is given to my mentor at San Diego State University, Professor Emeritus William H. Phillips, Jr. He has profoundly impacted my career at SDSU, and his words of encouragement and sage advice continue to serve me well.

I count myself among the thousands of students and professionals that have been fortunate enough to know Professor John A. Lucas of Penn State. As one of the leading sport historians in the world and the recognized authority on the Olympic Games, he graciously provided guidance and support to this book. The suggestions, comments, and opinions made known to me by Professor Lucas were the single most important source of information that helped me to shape the tone and content of this text. For this, I am eternally grateful.

The Museum of the International Olympic Committee located in Lausanne, Switzerland, is a magnificent resource devoted to the study of the Olympic Games, physical education, and sport. I was fortunate enough to spend time in Lausanne gathering information for this second edition. The professional staff working at The Olympic Museum are exceptional. I want to take the opportunity to express my sincere thanks and appreciation to Ruth Beck Perrenoud and Michele Veillard, who provided me with essential documents and access to the Olympic archives that contributed greatly to the new material in the second edition of *A History and Philosophy of Sport and Physical Education*.

If there was ever an individual professor who had the most profound impact on my early growth as teacher and professional, it has to be Professor Seymour Kleinman of Ohio State University. The philosophical positions of the body, which is the thematic approach of this book, are derived from my study with Dr. Kleinman. Many of the concepts, ideas, and positions presented in this book are a direct result of "the art of discovery" as taught by Seymour Kleinman. He is a fabulous teacher and a pretty fair tennis player.

We would like to thank the reviewers who critiqued the first edition of this text in order to provide suggestions on areas and aspects that needed attention: Dr. Shirley Houzer, Alabama A & M University; Dale

Campbell, Fresno Pacific College; John Lucas, Penn State University; and Mimi Haskel, Teikyo Loretto Heights University. My editor, Theresa Grutz is the consummate professional. She is a superb guide, and her support for this project is nothing short of phenomenal. I am personally grateful to her and to all the people associated with McGraw-Hill.

R. A. M.
San Diego, California

The changes in the second edition are the result of input from reviewers and conversations with students and colleagues that occurred over the past five years. Thanks go to all of those students at CSU Fullerton and SUNY Cortland who pointed out the strengths and weaknesses of the text, who learned from it and, perhaps more important, who helped me understand why learning did *not* occur. The points that I thought we made so eloquently sometimes were not points at all; and contradictions and errors of omission sometimes confused both student and author alike. We worked through these problems together once, and no doubt we will do so again! I look forward to the effort.

Help came in other, subtler, forms as well. In the big picture much of my work was facilitated by the faculty at CSU Fullerton, who taught me what it means to be a member of a faculty and of the Academy in general. A special thanks go to Ian Bailey and Ken Ravizza, my mentors at Fullerton whose conversations resonate implicitly in the ideas discussed in this text. I would like to thank John Lucas, who wrote the best review I've ever read, and whose example as a scholar in the field is truly inspiring. And I too would like to thank Sy Kleinman for both the ideas that inspired this book (his course *Concepts of the Body* and his work in *Physical Education: An Interdisciplinary Approach*) and his personal example as a member of a faculty. In the jive of our field, Sy, "Way to be."

Finally, to Erin, Katie, and Cheryl, for all the late nights, thanks.

S. G. E.
Cortland, New York

1

Doing History and Philosophy in Sport and Physical Education

Before describing the process of "doing" history, we need to answer a basic question: Why study history at all? The answer is that the study of history in any area, including sport and physical education, can lead to a better life. Indeed, many Americans argue that knowing history is irrelevant in their lives: one aspect of the American character is the prevailing belief that Americans are headed "into the future," and the most obvious aspect of history is that it is over and in the past. Making the study of history even more problematic is that the study of history (even sport history) is sometimes perceived as boring, repetitive, and not connected in any immediate way to the lives of those who read it. As the argument goes, since the players and events in history are behind us, then these events and people have no "say" in our lives.

This skeptical perspective relative to the study of history can be at least partially dismissed with a few observations. Students of history have found that it often provides an illuminating perspective of how we behave and think in the present, and offers a basis for predicting the future. History is not, however, *the only* answer to why we think and act as we do, nor is it *the only* manner in which we can predict what will happen. History provides a particular perspective—and when done well, a very enlightened perspective—of why we think and behave the way that we do and how we ought to think and behave in the future. This argument for understanding history was put most eloquently by philosopher George Santayana: "Progress, far from consisting in change, depends on retentiveness. . . . Those who cannot remember the past are condemned to repeat it."[1]

Assuming that the above arguments support the study of history, can these arguments be applied to sport and physical education? The answer would seem to be Yes: sport and physical education can be understood through the methods of history as can any other human activity. In so doing we understand how past events shaped the present and how the future events in sport and physical education will be impacted as a result of "current events." Furthermore, understanding how a culture plays tells us much about how a culture operates *outside* of sport and physical education. Play in the form of games and sport can be seen as serving certain functions in a given culture, from what Brian Sutton-Smith calls buffered cultural learning (learning necessary survival skills in a safe environment) to the expression of specific cultural values (such as discipline and teamwork).[2] Another quote summarizes this understanding: sociologist Jacques Barzun observed that, "Whoever wants to know the heart and mind of America had better learn baseball."[3] Barzun argued that baseball, its rules, how Americans interact with the game, and its importance to our culture over the past 130 years tells us much about how Americans think and behave today.

Having justified the study of history in sport and physical education, we are ready for a definition of history that can guide us in our studies. History is the study of change over time, or the lack of change over time, and sport history is the study of how sport has changed (or not) over time.[4] Looked at in this way, sport and play is the latest rendition of all of the changes that have occurred in the past. To study these activities as they have been practiced and viewed in the past is to understand what sport and play are now. This textbook can help kinesiology and physical education students understand our current attitudes and behaviors in sport and play by understanding how these attitudes and behaviors evolved over time. The following example of how sport has changed over time, and how we understand sport as a result of this change, will illustrate this point.

Michael Oriard in *Reading Football* tells the story of the development of the game of football and how our attitudes toward it came to be.[5] Students at American colleges played football for decades before the first intercollegiate game between Princeton and Rutgers in 1869. Students played football primarily because it was fun, but also because it served the purpose of hazing the new freshmen on campus and symbolized interclass rivalry. The game these students played, however, was more like the game of soccer than the game we now know of as football. Only Harvard used rules that we would recognize today as something like football; for example, allowing running with the ball and tackling.

In 1876 Harvard and Yale played each other using what they called the "Concessionary Rules," a game that was similar to the Harvard rugby style of football. In November of 1876, representatives of Harvard, Yale, Princeton, and Columbia met to formalize these rules and to create the Intercollegiate Football Association. These new, formalized rules distinguished American football from its rugby counterpart, a difference that remains to this day.

This change that occurred in the 1870s tells us a great deal about how football evolved from rugby and soccer, as well as about being an American in the nineteenth century. *Why* did Americans change the rules of rugby to make a distinctly American game? Specifically, Oriard asks why Americans ran with the ball from the line of scrimmage *instead* of playing rugby as our English ancestors did, and why we began to use judges and referees.

The interesting question is, why these most basic alterations? The evolution of football's rules has left a fascinating record that demands interpretation. Why American's initial preference for the running and tackling rather than the kicking game? (And) why our insistence on amending the Rugby Union code once adopted?[6]

The basic question Oriard asks, then, is why did these changes occur? Football changed from something like soccer or rugby to something like the contemporary American game. What can these changes tell us about Americans and American sport? Among other answers, Oriard argues that referees were needed because Americans had a very different attitude toward rules than did our English ancestors. English amateur athletes operated on a code of honor that was associated with the peculiarities of their elitist social class, and was as old as the games they played. Adherence among upper-class English boys to the code of honor was enforced by the captains of each team, thus supporting both the social nature of the contest and the social stations of the players.

Americans, in contrast, had no such social station—Americans argue to this day that they are of the "middle class," and as a consequence there is no code of honor to break. This difference in culture is reflected in our games, and Oriard argues that Americans wish to exploit the rules of the contest as much as they wish to adhere to them. The "American" attitude toward rules, then, is reflected in the change from the British games of soccer and rugby to the American game of football. Oriard concludes that

> . . . this attitude toward rules—a recognition of the letter but not the spirit, a dependence on rules in the absence of tradition yet also a celebration of the national genius for circumventing them—expressed an American democratic ethos, a dialectical sense of "fair play" (embracing both "sportsmanship" and "gamesmanship") that was very different from the aristocratic British version.[7]

Our point here is to show that studying sport history can help us understand how and why sport has changed over time. In so doing we understand a whole variety of changes that occurred: the evolution of football rules, the attitudes we have in America toward sport, and the nature of the American character.

The above example of how sport has changed over time utilizes a basic assumption that the changes that occurred can be *interpreted*. Not all histories are interpretive in nature, however. There are two basic types of historical research: descriptive and interpretive.[8] *Descriptive* history is just that: it describes, objectively and in as much detail as possible, what happened in the past. Descriptive history tries to provide the who, what, when, and where of the past, and it tries to do so without transposing ideas, values, and judgments from the present onto the events of the past. Many early historical works are descriptive and are quite literally records of the past.

Interpretive history seeks to explain the how and the why of events that happened in the past. The example above seeks to do just this: *how* did football change from its rugby origins, and *why* did it change in the manner it did? Unlike a descriptive history, the interpretive perspective introduces the narrator's subjective bias into the interpretation, and the history is no longer "just the facts." This subjective bias does not, however, make the interpretive history less valuable. On the contrary, the use of a subjective perspective allows much of the fullness and the richness of the history to come forth, and it makes the narrative much more open to discussion and understanding. In contrast, descriptive histories are not better or worse than interpretive histories; they are merely different kinds of accountings of what occurred in the past.

To write either descriptive or interpretive history, one must have access to different types of information, and there are two main sources used in historical research. The first is a primary source, one that was part of the actual event being studied. Examples of primary sources are an eyewitness account of an event, a newspaper story, a picture, a video recording of the event, or even a record of an event kept by an observer. Primary sources, then, are firsthand accounts of historical events. Secondary sources of historical research are those that did not participate in or observe the event being studied. Examples include magazine articles, history articles and books, and any other account of the event being studied.

As stated earlier, this textbook is an attempt to understand how and why sport has changed over time. As such, it is much more of an interpretive history than a descriptive one, although we use many who, what, when, and where descriptions of historical events. The perspectives we use most often to explain how and why sport and physical education have changed over time include premodern and modern culture, modernization theory, agrarian and urban living conditions, urbanization and industrialization, technological abilities, and finally and important for understanding the first half of this textbook, metaphysics. None of these perspectives provides a complete or perfect explanation for how and why behaviors and attitudes toward sport and physical education existed as they did. Rather, the variety of perspectives and the quality with which they are applied dictates the quality of the history and aids in students' comprehension of it.

Modernization Theory

One interpretive device we use is known as modernization theory, an organizational scheme that can be used to describe how culture tends to change from "premodern" or "traditional" characteristics to "modern" characteristics.[9] Premodern culture is stable, local, governed by people at both the family and political level, has little specialization of roles, depends on muscle power, views time as "cyclic" or by the seasons, and operates on myth and ritual. Modern culture is the polar opposite: it is dynamic, cosmopolitan, meritocratic, highly specialized, depends on technology, views time linearly or by the clock, and operates on the idea that it is rational. Historians who interpret history from the perspective of modernization theory use these characteristics to explain how and why a particular culture changed the way that it did. Sport and physical education, as part of culture, can be interpreted as either premodern or modern, and historian Melvin Adelman argues that sport changed from its "premodern" form into its current "modern" form between 1820 and 1870.[10]

Modernization theory is useful to explain many changes in American culture, including the manner in which sport and physical education changed. It should be noted, however, that modernization is not a *cause* of change. Americans did not want to become "modern" in the nineteenth century anymore than we want to be "premodern" right now; indeed, Americans did not know what "modern" is. This theory merely explains, from an artificially convenient perspective, the kinds of changes that took place more than one hundred years ago.

Urbanization and Industrialization

Another way of interpreting the changes in sport and physical education deals with where people live (in the country or the city), and how they go about providing for themselves (with muscle power or with technology). Like modernization theory, urbanization and industrialization patterns explain changes that happened primarily during the nineteenth century. In the early 1800s, most Americans lived in the country, providing for themselves by farming the land, and their farming practices utilized either their own muscle power or that of their livestock. In the 1820s cities in the United States began to grow faster than did the agrarian population, beginning the shift from a farming nation to an urban nation. Americans simultaneously experienced a technological revolution that radically changed the way they worked. These changes in living patterns had a significant impact on the sport and physical education patterns of Americans.[11] As historian John Betts noted,

> Telegraph lines went up all over the landscape, the railroad followed the steamboat from the East to the Midwest and the South, and by 1860 a network of over thirty-thousand miles of track covered the United States. An immigrant tide helped populate midwestern states, and Cincinnati, St. Louis, Chicago, Milwaukee, and Detroit gradually became western metropolises. The reaper and other new tools slowly transformed farm life; agricultural societies sprouted up; journals brought scientific information to the farmer; and the agricultural fair developed into a prominent social institution. (p. 31–32)

These changes facilitated a shift from an isolated farming lifestyle to a more city-oriented lifestyle, and the changes that occurred in sport and physical education correspond with this change. For instance, it was very difficult to have team games when people lived far apart because of their farming lifestyles. In addition, sporting activities could not be held at night until the invention of the electric light made possible large, indoor events. These and many other changes can be explained through interpretations that take into account urbanization and industrialization.

Doing History and Philosophy

Metaphysics

Metaphysics is an area of study in philosophy that concerns the nature of reality. Examples of metaphysical questions are, "Are ideas real?" "Where did the universe come from?" At first glance these questions seem silly. Many of us argue, "Of course ideas are real!" On the other hand, have you ever held an "idea" in your hand? And, can you prove that any answer to the origin of the universe is the "right" answer?

Whether or not these kinds of questions are silly, what do they have to do with the history of sport and physical education? The answer is that they have to do with how past cultures viewed the reality of the human body. Are we creatures composed of both mind and body? Or are we merely biological computers, organisms without a mind? Or are we all intellect, as the name *homo sapiens* (man the thinker) implies? Philosophers throughout the ages have debated the nature of our existence, and at one point or another all of the answers we describe, and many more, have been put forth. Important to our study, the "reality" of the human body has had a tremendous impact on how a given culture values sport and physical education. For example, the ancient Romans valued sport and physical education as both a mechanism for training young soldiers as well as a vehicle for entertaining and pacifying the masses. One thousand years later, the monks of the Middle Ages viewed the reality of the human body in very different terms. The ascetic behaviors that developed were a result of a philosophy that valued the eternal soul much more than the physical body, and as a result sport and physical education served completely different purposes.

These attitudes toward the human body still exist today, especially in the institution of education. In your experience, which is more important, the mind or the body? What would most of your teachers say? Which classes in your course of study are more valued, theory classes or laboratory courses? Is philosophy worth more credit hours than, say, an activity class in football? If so, why?

These and other questions can be answered when one uses metaphysics to interpret how sport and physical education have changed over time. The chart on page 7 will help make these changes more explicit.

To facilitate the process of interpreting history by focusing on the attitude toward reality and being, we will discuss briefly the process of "doing" philosophy, defining and discussing many of the terms commonly used in philosophy. An understanding of philosophy and its processes is important, for in our opinion the reality of the human body is one of the most important, if not the most important, factors in understanding how cultures have valued sport and physical education throughout history.

Philosophical Processes

Any discussion of history that is informed by the process of doing philosophy should begin with a discussion of ancient Greece. The magnificent

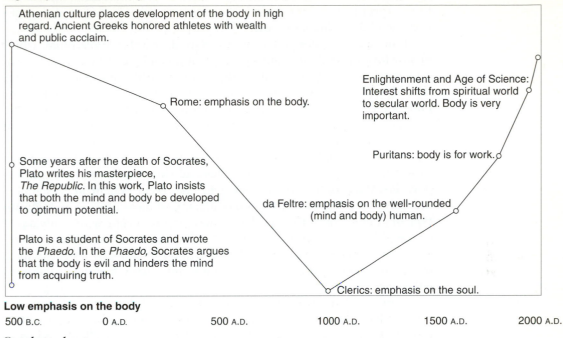

High emphasis on the body

Athenian culture places development of the body in high regard. Ancient Greeks honored athletes with wealth and public acclaim.

Rome: emphasis on the body.

Enlightenment and Age of Science: Interest shifts from spiritual world to secular world. Body is very important.

Some years after the death of Socrates, Plato writes his masterpiece, *The Republic.* In this work, Plato insists that both the mind and body be developed to optimum potential.

Puritans: body is for work.

Plato is a student of Socrates and wrote the *Phaedo.* In the *Phaedo,* Socrates argues that the body is evil and hinders the mind from acquiring truth.

da Feltre: emphasis on the well-rounded (mind and body) human.

Clerics: emphasis on the soul.

Low emphasis on the body

500 B.C.   0 A.D.   500 A.D.   1000 A.D.   1500 A.D.   2000 A.D.

Ontology chart

civilization that flourished and prospered during the Golden Age of Greece (480–338 B.C.) must have been spectacular indeed. Ancient Greek civilization is a primary source for the philosophical and historical forces that helped to shape and define Western civilization. Although most scholars look on Greece as the birthplace of Western civilization, the ancient Greeks also gave birth to Western ideas about physical education and athletic competition. They provided us with illuminating philosophical positions and commentary, and they attempted to provide rational explanations of the physical and spiritual nature of their existence and of the universe. For example, Anaximander (610–545 B.C.), generally recognized as one of the first philosophers,[12] provided us with a theory of evolution based on the process of adaptation that is very similar to Charles Darwin's theory of evolution developed more than two thousand years later! Plato (427–347 B.C.) described the nature of Purgatory in several of his works, and his ontology, or theory of being, is similar to that found in the Christian Bible. For our purposes, both Plato and the Bible explain the nature of reality as divided into two parts, matter and ideas, an approach to metaphysics that is known as "dualism."

This division of reality into two parts is of critical importance to students of sport history, for this concept can be used to explain many of the attitudes and behaviors we have in the twentieth century regarding sport and play. And if this claim is accurate, then other aspects of doing philosophy may be helpful as well. To understand fully the concept of dividing reality and being into different parts, and then using philosophy to interpret history, one must have a basic understanding of philosophy and the philosophical process.

Philosophy is derived from the Greek word *philosophia*, which means love of wisdom. Contemporary philosophy can be defined as the systematic investigation of reality, knowledge, and values, which should lead to the acquisition of wisdom. However, as we stated above, philosophy is concerned with much more than reality and being. Philosophy also provides the foundation on which virtually all other inquiries originate.

For most people, philosophy represents abstract ideas that originate from the minds of tortured academics and their more cerebral contemporaries. Philosophers often appear to take great delight in engaging in mental gymnastics that are often confusing to most of us. Although this type of philosophical inquiry does indeed go on, it represents only a part of the philosophical process. Physical education students should understand the links among religion, science, and philosophy, because in so doing an understanding of sport and physical education is greatly enhanced.[13]

Many students will find it surprising that philosophy, religion, and science have in common unprovable assumptions or starting points.[14] Indeed, most Americans tend to believe that science is "fact," whereas philosophy represents mere "opinion." However, if we look closely enough we will find that science, philosophy, and religion have their origins in "opinion." This does not, contrary to what one might believe, devalue any of the three. Rather, we describe the foundations of those areas of knowledge to point out that all of them can be discussed as human creations.[15] As the overall framework for our discussion is philosophical, the following points should help provide a basic understanding of the process of philosophy and how philosophy and religion differ from science:

1. Although philosophy and religion many times share similar purposes and common questions, religion is grounded in faith and belief, science operates from a set of rules called a "paradigm," and philosophy is grounded in reason and rationality. Some philosophers and theologians have tried to show a relationship between religion and philosophy, but by and large their efforts have been futile.[16]

2. Both philosophy and science analyze and examine phenomena, but each takes a different approach. Science strives for complete objectivity and rejects value judgments,[17] whereas philosophy studies the nature of values in an area known as "axiology." Unlike science, philosophy can assign and designate values to our experiences. So philosophy can be used to make value judgments, whereas science cannot.[18] Both science and philosophy employ the investigative process, even though their respective topics and evidence may be very different.

3. Questioning lies at the core of building a philosophy, but the answers are more a peripheral part of the process. Science, on the other hand, seeks to prove or disprove hypotheses.

4. The role of the philosopher traditionally has been to "raise and examine the more profound questions arising out of the human experience." Philosophers have sought to understand in rational terms the meaning of life. Scientists, however, are concerned with the material, observable universe and are less concerned with meaning than they are with measurement.

Basic Philosophical Terms

It is helpful to know the most used philosophical terms found in philosophical inquiry. Much of philosophical inquiry is concerned with reality, knowledge, and values. The following list describes these areas of study and their subtopics:

> Metaphysics: the study of the nature of reality
>> Ontology: the study of the nature of being
>> Theology: the study of the nature of God
>> Cosmology: the study of the nature of the universe
> Epistemology: the study of the nature of knowledge
> Axiology: the study of the nature of value
>> Ethics: the study of the nature of good
>> Aesthetics: the study of the nature of beauty
>> Politics: the study of the nature of the common good

One important area of philosophy not mentioned above is logic, the art and science of reasoning, and an area that describes the ability to think accurately and systematically. Our analysis, as well as any other historical process that uses a set of rules to interpret change over time, assumes that logic will be central to the process. Indeed, using logic is one of the central tasks of a liberal arts education, and it will be required on your part to understand both the process of doing philosophy as well as the process of interpreting history.

Some of the terms defined above will not be used much in this textbook, but they merit some discussion nonetheless. *Axiology*, the branch of philosophy that seeks to determine the nature of values, is central to understanding concepts like fair play. *Aesthetics* addresses the nature of art and beauty and can be applied to such forms of human movement as dance and other movement pursuits where beauty and grace of movement many times resemble art. *Ethics* is concerned with right and wrong, correct and incorrect behavior. The concept of fair play is representative of good ethical behavior. *Politics* is the study of the nature of the common good. The debate over moving professional sport franchises is a political issue, for it is concerned with how professional sport serves the common good.

Interpreting History Through Metaphysics and Ontology

Metaphysics, as we stated above, is the branch of philosophy that attempts to determine the ultimate nature of reality; that is, to distinguish between the real and the unreal. Metaphysical questions and inquiry are by their very nature profound and speculative. The ultimate nature of human existence, the nature of mind and soul, are metaphysical issues that have troubled philosophers, scientists, and theologians for thousands of years. The relationship of metaphysics and ontology is described in the following chart:

Area of philosophy	Metaphysics	Ontology
Deals with	Matter	Body
	Idea	Mind

For instance, in *The Republic* Plato told the "Allegory of the Cave" to illustrate his argument that reality was an idea.[19] Plato used his allegory to depict the relationship between the material world and the perfect, never-decaying ideal world.

In Plato's allegory, the prisoners chained to the wall of the cave could see only the shadows on the wall opposite them, and that is all they had ever seen. The prisoners believed that "reality" was the shadows on the wall. Given that this is all the prisoners had ever seen, it is understandable that they might think that the shadows are all that exists in "reality." However, we know there is more to reality than this, that there is a whole world outside the cave. Similarly, Plato argued that there is a whole world outside of the reality we experience with our bodies that is more "real" because it is perfect and never decays. This is the world of ideas, or in Plato's words, the "reality of forms," and of God. In this reality exist perfect knowledge, and souls that have access to and understanding of perfect knowledge.

There is a certain logic to Plato's argument. The idea that the material universe will change, but an idea will not and is therefore perfect and absolute, has a certain plausibility. A scientist, however, would probably argue that the material world is real and an idea is not. Who is right? It depends on one's metaphysical position.

A fundamental theme of this book is that metaphysics, especially ontology, has had and will continue to have an enormous impact on the value of physical education and sport. If one can understand the significant metaphysical and ontological positions of a culture, then one can gain perspective on that culture's views of sport and physical education. It follows from this position that if one studies the cultures that have significantly affected the development of Western civilization and helped determine our metaphysical position, then one also gains an understanding of how we view sport and physical education in contemporary culture. Consequently, a history of physical education and sport can be developed by examining the metaphysical and ontological positions of different cultures.

Epistemology

Epistemology is that branch of philosophy that examines the nature of knowledge and how we come to know things. Epistemology is relevant to physical education in that different ways of knowing have very different consequences for the mind and the body, and consequently for how we value the mind and body.[20] Epistemological questions would help answer the following questions: Are things more easily known through intellectual activity, or can we come to know better with our body and its senses? Is the information we acquire through the five senses valid or invalid? For example, is the information we obtain through sight and hearing completely reliable, or must this knowledge be subject to analysis in our mind in order to ensure that the knowledge is valid? This question is particularly important to physical education teachers, because if knowledge can be acquired only through the mind, or if the mind is the essential vehicle in the formation and acquisition of knowledge, then the body can be considered of secondary importance. Consequently, physical education, at least for all practical purposes, becomes of secondary importance to those areas of study that emphasize the mind, such as math or language.

Definitions

For our purpose, it will be helpful to present to the reader a brief definition of the concept of "sport" since the word will appear frequently throughout this book. As a word, sport is a modern term first used in England around 1440 A.D. The origins of the word sport, or its etymology, are Latin and French. In French, the word *de(s)porter* has its roots in the Latin word *deportare*, which means "to amuse oneself." Over time, the meaning of the term *sport* grew from merely "amusing oneself" to a term that was used extensively throughout England that meant competition in the form of games and individual exploits as well as hunting.

Sport cannot be understood, however, without understanding something about the nature of play and the nature of games. Play is a larger domain than sport. While it can be argued that all sport is play, it does not follow that all play is sport. Johan Huizinga, who wrote the classic *Homo Ludens*, developed the general hypothesis that play is precultural and permeates all facets of life.[21] Huizinga developed the view that play is a "significant function," that there is some sense to it and that this aspect of our existence—play—defines the nature of being human as well as the nature of culture. In short, the defining characteristic of the human being is that humans are playful and, in a word, seek activities that are simply *fun*. Huizinga's definition of play is that it is

> . . . a free activity standing quite consciously outside 'ordinary' life as being 'not serious,' but at the same time absorbing the player intensely

and utterly. It is an activity connected with no material interest, and no profit can be gained by it. It proceeds within its own proper boundaries of time and space according to fixed rules and in an orderly manner. It promotes the formation of social groupings which tend to surround themselves with secrecy and to stress their difference from the common world by disguise or other means. (p. 13)

Huizinga's work has generally withstood the test of time, and has been added to by Roger Caillois,[22] Brian Sutton-Smith,[23] and others.

A game is a somewhat more organized effort at play, where the organized and playful elements of the activity become more evident. All of us have "played games" in some point in our lives, so we have a good idea about what to expect when we play a game. This structuring of the playful impulse leads to the following definition of a game:

> . . . a play activity which has explicit rules, specified or understood goals . . . , the element of opposition or contest, recognizable boundaries in time and sometimes in space, and a sequence of actions which is essentially "repeatable" every time the game is played.[24]

Arriving at a definition of sport that is based on play and games, however, is not without its difficulties. This is because when factors such as religion, social class, and historical period are discussed, sport may not easily fit into a universally accepted definition. For example, throughout history, dependent upon one's socioeconomic status, one person's sport may be another person's work. Kings and nobility often hunted on their private reserves for the sheer enjoyment of the sport, whereas their peasant subjects worked at developing their skill as hunters to put food on the table and survive yet one more day. Another example of differing viewpoints is how sport was conceived and practiced by the ancient Greeks. The Greeks enjoyed competing with one another, whereas the Romans looked at these activities as work. The Romans, instead, enjoyed watching others compete.

For our purposes, a general definition of sport will include the following characteristics: continuity, division of roles, dynamic interaction with an audience, and a supporting sport establishment.[25] Continuity refers to the longevity of a particular game. For instance, American football has been played in its current form for more than eighty years, thus meeting the criteria of continuity. In philosopher Paul Weiss' words, a game is an occurrence; a sport is a pattern. The *pattern* of the game of football is one characteristic that defines it as a sport.

The division of roles in sport distinguishes it from games. A quarterback on a football team is different from a linebacker, and so on. This specialization of roles improves the quality of the performance and makes the game more competitive. The dynamic interaction with an audience also distinguishes sport from games. To a great extent the sport of football has been shaped by the spectators who *demand* to be entertained, and they turn off the television set if it is boring. Consequently, those who run "big-time" college football and professional football are very sensitive to the demands of the audiences who participate in the football games the NCAA and the NFL sponsor. By "supporting sporting establishment" we refer to those organizations that make possible these events: the NCAA, NFL, major network television, magazines, newspapers, and so on.

Summary

We have defined history as the study of change over time, and we have described the type of history that we will be doing: interpretive history that explains how and why change has occurred. We will also describe many of the people, events, times, and places that are important to our understanding of history. We will examine how history has moved from premodern to modern characteristics, how moving to the city and coming to rely on technology has changed sport and physical education, and how various cultures have viewed the nature of being and how these views have had an impact on sport and physical education. We have discussed briefly the process of "doing" philosophy and have introduced the idea that a critical examination of history can help explain how and why changes have occurred in sport and physical education. Finally, we defined play, games, and sport so that we can discuss these activities as they occurred throughout civilization.

The primary reason for presenting the information in this chapter, and the entire text for that matter, is to impress upon physical education and kinesiology students the revealing insights that history and philosophy provide to our discipline. Physical education and athletics have a rich and storied heritage which has existed for thousands of years. The athletic exploits of men and women athletes captured the attention of tens of thousands of fans in the ancient world in the same way that the feats of modern athletes leave us yearning for more. To study the scope and stature of sport and physical education through the medium of history and philosophy will enrich your personal and professional lives. After all, how many events have withstood the test of time as well as the Olympic Games? How many mere mortals have been glorified as much as athletes? Throughout history, what were the justifications that required men and women to develop such superb and aesthetic physiques? These and many other salient and illuminating discussions are presented in this book. We believe that you will find the study of history and philosophy of physical education and sport is well worth the effort.

Suggestions for Further Reading

Singer, R. N., D. R. Lamb, J. W. Loy, R. M. Malina, and S. Kleinman. *Physical Education: An Interdisciplinary Approach.* New York: Macmillan, 1972.

Swanson, R. A., and B. Spears. "History and the Study of Sport and Physical Education." In *History of Sport and Physical Education in the United States.* 3rd ed. Madison, Wis.: Brown and Benchmark, 1995.

Notes

1. George Santayana, "The Life of Reason," quoted in J. T. English, *A Garden Book of Profundities, Atticisms, and Smartaleck Sayings,* 9th ed. (Tacoma, Wash.: School of Education, University of Puget Sound, 1905), 60.

2. Brian Sutton-Smith, *The Folkgames of Children* (Austin: University of Texas Press for the American Folklore Society, 1972).

3. Jacques Barzun, "God's Country and Mine," quoted in J. T. English, *A Garden Book of Profundities, Atticisms, and Smartaleck Sayings*, 9th ed. (Tacoma, Wash.: School of Education, University of Puget Sound, 1905), 5.

4. N. Struna, "Sport History," in *The History of Exercise and Sport Science*, eds. John Massengale and Richard Swanson (Champaign, Ill.: Human Kinetics, 1996).

5. Michael Oriard, *Reading Football: How the Popular Press Created an American Spectacle* (Chapel Hill: The University of North Carolina Press, 1993).

6. Ibid., 27.

7. Ibid., 30.

8. J. Thomas Jable, "The Types of Historical Research for Studying Sport History," in *Getting Started in the History of Sport and Physical Education*, ed. William H. Freeman (Washington, D.C.: History of Sport and Physical Education Academy, 1980), 13–14.

9. Melvin Adelman, *A Sporting Time: The Rise of Modern Sport in New York City, 1820–70* (Champaign: University of Illinois Press, 1986).

10. Ibid.

11. John R. Betts, *America's Sporting Heritage: 1850–1950* (Reading, Mass.: Addison-Wesley Publishing Co., 1974).

12. The other two philosophers who are considered "founding fathers" are Thales (624–546 B.C.) and Anazimenes (585–528 B.C.).

13. S. Estes, "Knowledge and Kinesiology," *Quest* 46, no. 4 (1994): 392–409.

14. For a wonderful discussion of the assumptions that undergird science and how science is used in kinesiology, see R. Martens, "Science, Knowledge, and Sport Psychology," *The Sport Psychologist 1*, (1987): 29–55.

15. Religion, by definition, is a creation of God, but it can be discussed using rational discourse.

16. Perhaps the best known example of this, and one of the first, is that of Thomas Aquinas, who tried to reconcile the methods of philosophy with the dogmas of the Catholic Church.

17. R. Martens, "Science, Knowledge, and Sport Psychology," *The Sport Psychologist 1*, (1987): 29–55.

18. For example, the sociologist and political scientist can scientifically analyze and investigate the Nazi Holocaust. However, because the doctrine of science does not believe in making value judgments, the true social scientist would be discouraged from either approving or condemning Hitler's policies. In the social sciences, however, factions have arisen that have moved away from the value-free approach to research and discussion. Many sociologists have recognized the futility of value-free research.

19. Plato, *The Republic*, trans. Desmond Lee (London: Penguin Books, 1987).

20. S. Estes, "Knowledge and Kinesiology," *Quest* 46, no. 4 (1994): 392–409.

21. Johan Huizinga, *Homo Ludens: A Study of the Play-Element in Culture* (Boston: The Beacon Press, 1955).

22. R. Caillois, *Man, Play, and Games* (New York: Free Press, 1961).

23. Brian Sutton-Smith, *The Folkgames of Children* (Austin: University of Texas Press for the American Folklore Society, 1972).

24. L. P. Ager, "The Reflection of Cultural Values in Eskimo Children's Games," in D. Calhoun, *Sport, Culture, and Personality* (Champaign, Ill.: Human Kinetics, 1987), 47.

25. D. Calhoun, *Sport, Culture, and Personality* (Champaign, Ill.: Human Kinetics, 1987).

section 1

Ancient Civilizations

Sumer, Egypt, and China

General Events

Sumerian and Egyptian civilization mark beginnings of ancient western world

Sumer-ancient civilization that was established circa 4000 B.C.

Sumerians introduced cuneiform writing

Egyptian Civilization was established circa 3000 B.C.

Egyptians introduced writing in the form of hieroglyphics

First of Egypt's 30 dynasties was founded between 3200–3000 B.C. by Menes (also known as Narner), who ruled in the first dynasty

As the first Pharaoh, Menes founded the city of Memphis

From 3100–2686 B.C. is known as the Early Dynastic Period

With the rise of the Third Dynasty in 2700 B.C., Ancient Egypt is divided into the three prominent historical eras and some lesser ones:

1. The Old Kingdom: 2700 B.C.– 2200 B.C.—era during which the great pyramids were built

2. The Middle Kingdom: 2000 B.C.– 1800 B.C.—solidified economic and political power

3. The New Kingdom: circa 1600 B.C.– 1100 B.C.—reached the peak of power

The Late Dynastic Period Lasted from 1085–341 B.C.

Egypt became divided; Solomon's temple destroyed; invaded by Nubians and Assyrians

The Ptolemaic Period Lasted from 332–30 B.C.

Alexander the Great conquers Egypt

When Alexander dies, one of his generals establishes the Ptolemaic Dynasty

China

Chinese civilization predates Christianity by about 2,500 years

China's history began about 1500 B.C.

Over the course of 2,400 years, 10 major dynasties ruled China

Shang Dynasty: 1500 B.C.–1000 B.C.

Early Chou Dynasty: 1000 B.C.–600 B.C.

Late Chou Dynasty: 600 B.C.–221 A.D.

Ch'in Dynasty: 221 A.D.–206 A.D.

Han Dynasty: 206 A.D.–220 A.D.

Three Kingdoms Dynasty: 220 A.D.– 265 A.D.

Western Chin Dynasty: 265 A.D.– 316 A.D.

Northern and Southern Dynasties: 316 A.D.–589 A.D.

Sui Dynasty: 589 A.D.–618 A.D.

T'ang Dynasty: 618 A.D.–907 A.D.

Introduction

Athletic ability, physical fitness, competition, and play have been a significant cultural component of civilization since the dawn of time. Civilizations that perished long ago, as well as those civilizations that still exist today, share this characteristic. Historians, sociologists, and anthropologists who study our primitive ancestors and ancient civilizations have long noted the importance of physical ability and physical expression. It may manifest itself as play, dance, sport, or as a means of survival. One conclusion that we may draw from these observations is that the quest for survival during ancient times—and modern times—was and is in some way facilitated in our desire to play. In modern times, this desire to play serves as a catalyst for the current emphasis on physical fitness and explains our cultural attitude toward sports.

It is arguable, then, that the human race evolved because in part, the ability to adapt to our surroundings was facilitated by the playful characteristics that are manifest in human nature—our being. This play impulse is central to our ability to survive. During prehistoric times, dinosaurs ruled the earth. They were born with sharp fangs, ran very fast, were aggressive, and were large and strong. We know that these animals are extinct, yet we survived and, slowly but surely, grew stronger and faster with each successive generation. The English scientist Charles Darwin studied the evolution of plants and animals in the nineteenth century and popularized the phrase "survival of the fittest." From the dawn of time to the present, humans, like any other species, competed against the elements and each other for survival. Contemporary sport reflects this Darwinian maxim as athletes strive to defeat their opponent and emerge victorious, whether it is against the clock, another individual, or another team. In doing so they play out the contemporary version of learning life skills through play.

Initially humans hunted for food as individuals, but then found it more effective to form groups and hunt as a team. Once again, humans adapted to the environment and survived. Perhaps the individual that stood out as the best hunter was admired by those around him for his skill and bravery, and the activities that served to make one a better hunter were in all probability playful activities that emulated hunting. During the prehistoric era, honor and respect were given to those who had the courage and athletic skills that were necessary to insure victory over the elements. Each day was a contest for survival. Over time, the desire to survive, to compete for honor, and to claim victory has become a part of culture and is symbolized in many ways through games and sports.

Survival and the necessity to triumph over one's adversaries was a prominent theme in ancient times, when the lands were ruled by kings, queens, pharaohs, emperors, warlords, and tyrants.

Warfare was a routine occurrence. As one group sought to exercise dominance over another for political or economic gain, it became necessary to form an army that would conquer the enemy. This required a rigorous and demanding physical training program that would produce a warrior capable of defeating his enemy in hand-to-hand combat. This need for trained soldiers exists to the present day. In the twentieth century, physical skills such as endurance running, wrestling, swimming, and other related fitness activities that are required for military combat have been a curricular component of physical education programs for men during times of war.

In order to repel invaders, cities formed military units. Soldiers throughout the ancient world would receive roughly the same types of training. Skill with the bow and arrow, wrestling, boxing, riding horses, driving chariots, and racing across rugged terrain on foot required the ancient warrior to be in superb physical shape and possess athletic abilities that would insure his survival and the survival of his village or city.

As a consequence of the need for physical training, young men in the ancient world engaged in various combat sports, some of which are still evident in the contemporary world. These ancient sports manifest themselves in some of the events in track and field competition, wrestling and other martial arts, equestrian events, and dance. We know that the javelin throw originates from spear throwing contests, and ancient warrior athletes engaged in foot races which tested the speed of one athlete against another. In addition to foot races and spear throwing contests, archery contests and boxing and wrestling competitions were popular in the ancient world.

These same combat sports remain popular today and can be found in physical education and sports programs in schools, colleges, and the Olympic Games. For example, the modern pentathlon was developed to promote military skills needed in the late nineteenth and twentieth centuries. In the 1912 Olympiad held in Stockholm, Sweden, a young U.S. army officer named George S. Patton, Jr., placed fifth. He would later achieve fame as a tank commander in World War II.

Although combat sports have their genesis in ancient civilizations, they have endured and remain a significant activity in modern culture. Why have these ancient sports remained such a significant part of our culture? Perhaps it is because we still possess the innate need to persist and persevere, to compete against each other, to survive. The characteristics used to insure the survival of both the individual and his/her culture live on in these competitive sporting situations. However, the reason these contests and games survive may not be solely because they teach survival skills.

The children that lived long ago were not that much different than those of today. They played ball games, amused themselves with dolls, wrestled, and enjoyed rough-and-tumble activities. While the need to insure our survival, to compete, to emerge victorious and to play is a common thread that is woven through all civilizations, past and present, there may be other explanations about the nature of play. Perhaps Johan Huizinga, who defined play in his classic work, *Homo Ludens*, is right: the reason we play and partake in games is that we enjoy it; it is fun.

After reading Section One, ask yourself how much (if any) the direction of sport and physical education has changed when compared to the way it was practiced several thousand years ago. As you read the chapters, what do you believe lays at the core of our desire to compete or attend events where physical and athletic prowess is displayed?

To introduce the reader to some of the salient historical and philosophical themes that have shaped sport and physical education throughout the ages, we will present an important examination of other modes of thought, and philosophical positions that were present in the ancient non-Western world.

Sumer

The Sumerians lived in an area historians identify as Mesopotamia. We know it today as the country of Iraq. Mesopotamia is known as the "cradle of civilization" because over 5,000 years ago, the Sumerians created the world's first known civilization. The Babylonians and the Assyrians also established great cities in this region. Mesopotamia was situated between two great rivers, the Tigris and the Euphrates. Like the inhabitants of present-day Iraq, the inhabitants of Mesopotamia endured a climate that was very hot and dry. There are numerous references to Mesopotamia in the Old Testament. The prophet Jeremiah said of this land, "Her cities are in desolation, a dry land, and a wilderness, a land wherein no man dwellith, neither doth any son of man pass thereby."[1] Today the ruins of Sumer, Babylonia, and Assyria are buried in the harsh desert of the Middle East. Archaeologists work to uncover these civilizations that perished long ago, but other than their presence, it remains "a dry land, and a wilderness . . . wherein no man dwellith."

The Sumerians developed cuneiform writing that revolutionized the way people communicated. The age-old practice of committing ideas, conversations, and records to memory was replaced with a written form of record. Researchers have uncovered thousands of inscribed clay tablets written in the wedged-shape cuneiform style, and these records—primary sources for doing history—reveal a great deal about life in ancient Sumer. There were proclamations of Sumerian kings, inventories of the contents of a merchant's holdings, literary works, and a father's admonitions to his wayward son (some things never change).[2]

The issue of law and order was just as important to the people of Mesopotamia as they are in the 1990s. Among the best known collection of laws were those drawn up by Hammurabi of Babylon around 1800 B.C. Hammurabi's code consisted of close to 300 laws and reveals much about life in this era. For example, one law provides that, "If a builder constructed a house for a man, but did not make his work strong, with the result [being] that the house which he built collapsed and so has caused the death of the owner of the house, the builder shall be put to death."[3]

The city of Sumer was surrounded by villages, and an intricate economic and political system developed. Trade, travel, and entertainment were routine activities, as was warfare. The struggle to retain and extend power was important to the people of Sumer. As a result, skill as a warrior was important, and skill was largely dependent upon athletic ability and physical fitness. One of the most famous Sumerian kings was Gilgamesh, who is believed to have ruled during part of the twenty-seventh century B.C. Stories and legends have been uncovered about this man that relate epic feats. He slays lions, leads his armies into battle where he kills many of the enemy, and engages in contests with super-human opponents and wins. There is some speculation that Gilgamesh may have been the model for the Greek hero Heracles.[4]

Not to be outdone by Gilgamesh was the Assyrian warrior-king Assurbanipal, who reigned over an empire in 7 B.C. that extended from present-day Egypt to Iran. He led his own troops into battle and was quite a hunter. His palace was at Nineveh, and archaeologists have discovered a rich find that includes many reliefs and sculptures in addition to numerous odes and citations to his skill as a hunter and warrior:

> I am Assurbanipal, King of the universe, King of Assyria, for whom Assur, King of the Gods, and Ishtar, Lady of Battle, Have Decreed a Destiny of Heroism. . . . The God Nergal caused me to undertake every form of hunting on the plain, and according to my pleasure . . . I went forth. . . . On the plain savage lions, fierce creatures of the mountains rose against me. The young of the lions thrived in countless numbers. . . . They grew ferocious through their devouring of herds, flocks, and people. . . . In my sport I seized . . . a fierce lion of the plain by his ears. With the aid of Assur and Ishtar . . . I pierced his body with my lance.[5]

The inscription cited above reveals more than just a king with an ego; it demonstrates the connection that religion had with sport that existed into the 1800s: "The God Nergal caused me to undertake every form of hunting." Sport and spirituality will be connected until sport becomes "modern" and is governed by attitudes based more on reason than ritual. In a relief that illustrates the rituals of a lion hunt, King Assurbanipal is depicted wearing a ceremonial robe and pouring wine over the dead lions. This appears to be a religious ritual in which the King is able to exhibit his strength and virtue by removing the forces of evil (lions).

The archaeological evidence obtained from sights in Mesopotamia indicate that lions were a constant menace to the safety of the inhabitants. As sensational an athlete as King Assurbanipal appears to have been, one Assyrian king who preceded Assurbanipal must have been a better hunter because he claimed to have killed 1,000 lions![6] Lion hunting was a popular sport for the rulers. There were armies of huntsmen who accompanied the king because it was thought that lion hunting prepared men for the dangers and challenges that would be faced during war. Bravery in battle was expected, and the lion hunts enabled the king and his officers to instill bravery and other virtues. The process of teaching courage and bravery was simple but harsh: men were selected to form a circle around the lions in order to "fence them in" and prevent

Figure 2.1
*King Assurbanipal of Assyria demonstrating his skill as
an archer and hunter by slaying a lion. British Museum.*

them from escaping. The king could then enter the area and kill the
lions that had been trapped by the circle of men. It is not known how
many men were mauled by lions or the king and his men while attempting to escape. However, it seems logical that the men who survived this
ordeal were indeed courageous.

Archaeologists have discovered artifacts that provide evidence of
sports and games during the Early Dynastic period of Sumerian civilization (3000–1500 B.C.).[7] Artifacts that depict combat sports such as boxing and wrestling date from around 2,000 B.C.[8] With the ever-present
threat of war, it is understandable that combat sports existed and probably had many participants. The most well-known artifact of wrestling
is a copper statuette of two figures, heads interlocked and hands grip-
ping the belt on their opponent's hips.[9] On the head of each wrestler
appear to be large pots, and this has been the subject of much discussion. Some have maintained that the object of the contest was to knock
the pot off the head of the opponent, while others say that the pots
served as ornaments.

According to Howell, "Archaeological evidence related to warfare
allows the sport historian to make inferences about the possibility of
play activities. If an individual [Sumerian] is to master a chariot, it is
easy to envision challenge races. . . ."[10] Within this context, we can
also assume that there were contests in archery, running, swimming,
and other sports that would help insure one's survival in war.

The Sumerians fished and boated extensively.[11] This practice was a necessity to put food on the table; however, it may have been a form of recreation as well. Board games also were played in Sumer. Gaming boards with drawers to hold the pieces[12] have been discovered in the royal graves at Ur. In addition to these board games, children's toys have been found in the form of toy chariots and boats.[13]

Egypt

When we think of Egypt, pictures of pyramids, mummies, and giant statues come to mind. Egypt is a land that holds an extensive array of historical artifacts and enjoys a rich history. So prominent is the place of Egypt in the history of civilization that a significant part of the Old Testament is devoted to this land.

More than ten thousand years ago, people began to inhabit the land along the Nile River. Over time the villages grew in number and the collective population began to prosper. Geography favored Egypt as desert barriers ringed the Nile river valley, which discouraged invasion. In about 4000 B.C., Egypt emerged as a political and economic entity, ruled by pharaohs, that would last for the next twenty-seven centuries. According to Decker (1992), ". . . sports were a means by which the most famous Egyptian monarchs presented themselves to their people. . . . His obligatory and, in the ideal case, actual physical strength was that of a warrior, and a hunter as well as an athlete."[14]

To grasp the significance of Egyptian history, it will help to know that the ancient Greeks and Romans considered Egypt as "ancient." It was an established nation with grand palaces, monuments, streets, and commerce a thousand years before the Minoans of Crete constructed their opulent palaces. Moses would lead the Israelites out of Egypt nearly 900 years after Egypt became an imposing civilization. The Greek historian Herodotus toured Egypt in 5 B.C. and remarked, "wonders more in number than those of any other land."

The science of medicine may have its origins in Egypt. The ancient Egyptians used magic to cure disease because sickness was more often than not delivered by the gods. However, their skill as doctors and surgeons was known throughout the ancient world. The Greek physicians Hippocrates, considered the "father of medicine," and Galen, who some consider the "father of sports medicine," spoke about the work of the Egyptians.

Much of what we know about the ancient Egyptians and their lifestyle and sporting activities is revealed in the paintings found in tombs and in the countless artifacts that have been discovered. It appears that the paintings that exist in the tombs (the wealthy and the nobility were the only ones who could afford such a grand burial place) portray their expectations of life in the next world, which reflected those activities that they engaged in when they were alive. Death was considered to be merely another journey that they must prepare for.

The upper classes enjoyed a life of luxury, and their tombs were elaborately furnished. Paintings depict wealthy Egyptians boating on the

Nile, hunting fowl in the marshes, having picnics with their families, and enjoying beverages in the garden.[15] Interestingly enough, there is little evidence of ideas that reflected the beliefs of Hebrew ethics, Greek philosophy, or Roman law. The objective of the upper classes in Egypt was to become "socialites" and gain power and influence in the court. Success was measured in a material manner; how much land you owned and how many cattle you could call your own were the standards of material success. The most important statement that a wealthy Egyptian could make was constructing an impressive tomb that would be the envy of Egyptian high society.

To a degree, the good life was available for most Egyptians to enjoy. While the wealthy enjoyed festive parties and lavish surroundings, the less fortunate enjoyed life's little pleasures as well. Paintings show children engaged in playful activity while the adults work the fields or engage in other forms of commerce and trade. The Nile was the "highway" of Egypt. Skilled sailors navigated the Nile, moving people and commerce up and down the river where the great cities of Egypt were located. The Nile was a transit source as well as a source for food. Swimming is an activity that is depicted in many paintings. It appears that it was a recreational activity; however, the swimmer had to keep an eye out for the crocodiles who inhabited the area. The nobles did not have to worry about the crocodiles because it was not unusual for a member of the upper class to have his own swimming pool at home.

As advanced as Egyptian civilization was for its time, the demand for physical labor to build monuments, engage in trade and commerce, sustain agriculture, and for defense was neverending. Slaves were utilized for the most difficult labors, such as working the mines and moving heavy stones for monuments or public buildings.

Away from the large cities, life was unusually harsh, and maintaining the health and vigor of the individual was necessary to insure survival. Working the fields in the fertile Nile river valley required waking up before dawn and getting as much work done as possible before resting at noon when the heat became unbearable. After the rest break, work resumed again until the evening. Each day was more or less the same—time moved in endless cycles, seasons following each other as they always had in an endless, repeating pattern. Festivals and religious observations provided a break from the harsh demands of farming and fishing. Still, life was generally difficult as can be seen in the following account of life in an Egyptian village thousands of years ago:

> Mice abound in the field, locusts descend and animals eat the crop. . . . What remains . . . is taken by thieves. The hire of oxen is wasted because the animals have died. . . . Then the scribe arrives at the riverbank . . . to register the tax on the harvest.[16]

Survival depended in large part on physical fitness, health, and luck.

Like the Sumerians, the Egyptians were superb warriors. Ancient documents reveal that when the time for war came, the pharaoh could mobilize the entire land for battle. Scribes had records of soldiers; there were vast storehouses of food and armament. Conscription agents were sent into the land to draft men who were not yet on the roll of the army scribes. Reserve soldiers were called up from their jobs and families to join the fight. The following ancient account speaks of the daily routine of an Egyptian soldier:

> Come, I will speak to you of the ills of the infantryman. He is awakened while there is still an hour for sleeping. He is driven like a jackass and he works until the sun sets beneath its darkness of night. He hungers and his belly aches. He is dead while he lives. But frightened and calling to his god, "come to me that you may rescue me," he fought. He fought with maces, daggers and spears on fields filled with charging chariots and bronze-tipped arrows.[17]

This account, written by a scribe long ago, stirs our imagination. In order to endure such harsh conditions and physical demands, the physical training of the Egyptian soldier had to be severe. In the event that a young boy aspired to be a soldier, he was removed from his family and placed in the barracks, where he was "pummeled with beatings." After completing the necessary training, he was allowed to live with his family between campaigns. The Egyptians also relied on foreign mercenaries and captured slaves to fill the ranks of the army.[18]

The young men of the upper classes usually enlisted in the separately organized chariot corps. It was not unusual for a young, wealthy Egyptian man to show up with his own chariot, which he would take into battle. Contests among the chariot drivers enabled them to display their driving skills prior to battle.

The primary weapon of the soldier was the bow and arrow and his foot speed. Skill as an archer was very important for personal survival as well as assuring victory for the pharaoh. Archery contests were held to encourage young men to gain proficiency in archery, but the contests were probably very popular among the young men anyway. Archers were encouraged to be fit because of their place in the order of battle, and running contests pitted one archer against another. The archers along with the chariot drivers were the first wave to assault the enemy. The archers raced along with the speeding chariots and killed as many of the enemy as they could. They were followed by the infantry, who finished off the enemy in hand-to-hand combat. It is easy to understand why victory in combat sports was so important to the ancient Egyptian warriors.

The Egyptians were excellent bookkeepers, and scribes accompanied the warriors on their campaigns. Their purpose was to record every sheep, cow, ox, or other spoils of war taken in battle. The Egyptian army severed the hand of each captured enemy soldier for each item recorded by a scribe. In this way, believed the Egyptians, an exact count of the spoils of war could be made. The spoils of war were dedicated to the god Amon.[19]

Although life was difficult for the Egyptians, they also knew how to enjoy themselves. Hunting was a popular sport among the Egyptians. The nobleman rode into the country accompanied by trained hunting dogs to hunt gazelle and antelope. The peasants hunted also, but rarely for sport; it was a matter of survival. Skill with a bow and arrow was indeed a means of securing food as well as warding off the enemy. Music, singing, and dancing were popular activities among all classes of Egyptians. Among the wealthy, feasts were a frequent occurrence, and musicians and dancers provided entertainment. Sometimes, wrestlers would provide entertainment during the initial phase of a feast, followed by dancing girls selected by the host from his harem. The dancers were skilled athletes and delighted the guests by performing acrobatic stunts, pirouettes, cartwheels, the splits, somersaults, and backbends.[20] Archaeological finds have uncovered tops, balls, dolls, hoops, marbles, and other assorted amusements that are still used by children the world over. Wrestling and "games of chance" such as dice were played. Ball games were especially popular among men and women of all ages.[21]

China

The cultural history of China begins approximately 2,500 years before the advent of Christianity. Like the Egyptians, the Chinese enjoy a rich history that predates Christianity and continues in existence to this very day. From the Shang Dynasty (1500–1000 B.C.) through the T'ang Dynasty (618–907 A.D.), China enjoyed the status of the most civilized and influential country in East Asia. During the T'ang Dynasty, it was not unusual to find that from time to time, the standard of living and the cultural arts enjoyed by the Chinese surpassed those that existed in the West.[22] Archaeological evidence reveals that games and organized sport existed in China prior to the birth of Christ.[23]

The ancient Chinese political system was feudal in nature, and a consequence of this situation was a divided China composed of city-states that continually fought one another. One object of contention was the water routes through the Yellow River valley and Yangtze River valley that fostered trade and commerce. Early Chinese leaders waged territorial wars as well as repelled "barbarians," meaning anyone who was not Chinese.

Physical culture in China has been traced as far back as Peking Man, who lived over 500,000 years ago in the caves of Zhoukoudan. Archaeologists have discovered the skeletal remains of thousands of wild horses and deer. This is a strong indication that the ancient Chinese were swift runners and accomplished hunters. Cave paintings at Canhyuan, believed to be over 3,400 years old, show dancing and other physical activities. There is even historical evidence that portrays a dance identified as xiaozhongwu (reduce-swelling dance) used in ancient times to treat diseases of the legs and feet.[24]

Military training was a necessity for warlords and emperors to retain their turf as well as expand it whenever they could. The Chinese trained knights rode into battle on chariots while wearing bronze helmets. These knights, armed with axes, spears, and daggers, rode chariots that were weapons of war as well as expressions of wealth; they were lavishly decorated with bronze ornamentation. The extent of chariot ornamentation probably depended upon the wealth of the knight. Each chariot was manned by a driver, a spearman, and an archer. Following the chariots were the infantrymen, who were almost always drawn from the ranks of peasant farmers.

The farmer who was drafted into the army in time of war held out little hope of ever returning home. The ordinary infantryman could expect a miserable and harsh existence and would probably die on the hot sands of the northwestern deserts, repelling the barbarian hordes or in one of the many civil wars. His prowess as an athlete, level of physical fitness, and skill in using the tools of war (and some luck) was about all he had to depend on. If captured, the soldier or knight would probably be put to death because

> Victorious generals like to enhance their reputation for ferocity and to chill the hearts of future enemies by mass execution of prisoners. The First Century writer Wang Ch'ung reports that officers of the ancient state of Ch'in . . . buried alive 400,000 soldiers of a rival state.[25]

With the Mongol invasions came horses, and before long the Chinese developed a reputation as fine riders and fierce warriors. Hunting was a popular pastime as well. Falcons provided the nobility with an additional sport as these birds of prey were trained to hunt fowl. A royal hunt was a grand occasion. Men were sent in advance of the hunting party to act as "beaters"—people who flushed game into the open—in concert with hunting dogs. A commoner used falconry for purposes of survival and could take his trained hawk into the field with the hope that it would return with a rabbit or pheasant.

Captured slaves sometimes joined the court as servants, and women who danced were highly valued. Life in the court of Shih Hu, who reigned over the small northern state of Chao after the fall of the Han Dynasty, provides a revealing look at the opulence and flair of the ancient Chinese. Shih Hu was a violent man, a superb hunter, and a skilled archer. In his palace, he enjoyed the music of an all-girl orchestra, a battalion made up entirely of women who were clothed in sable furs and carried bows that were painted yellow. An interesting anecdote has it that as the years passed by, Shih Hu gained a lot of weight and could no longer walk to the hunting grounds. Yet he enjoyed the hunt so much that he was carried to the hunt on a litter by twenty men. Once he arrived, he sat on a revolving couch so that he was able to shoot in any direction.[26]

Just like the Sumerian and Egyptian nobility, the Chinese nobility enjoyed a life of luxury. By 9 A.D., wealthy families could enjoy a house equipped with baths, heaters, mechanical fans, water fountains, and rooms that were cooled with ice. One account tells of a guest who visited a monarch and was treated to a whirling fan that sprayed water behind the throne, which resulted in a cool breeze. The monarch invited the guest to sit on a stone bench that was cooled from within and enjoy an ice-cold drink![27] It seems clear that the ancient Chinese understood material comforts and from time to time indulged in corporeal delights!

Boxing became a popular sport after Buddhidharma came to China around 527 A.D. Initially eighteen movements were taught and focused the student on appropriate offensive tactics. Over time the system was refined and expanded, and in approximately 1070 A.D. a boxing teacher named Chio Yuan Shang Jen incorporated more than 170 movements and wrote a set of training rules which, among other things, espoused a vegetarian diet, self-discipline, and sexual control.[28]

The martial arts evolved from efforts like those of Chio Yuan Shang Jen's, and were a product of Chinese philosophy and the need for skilled warriors. According to Knuttegen, et al., the most recognized form of martial arts is currently known as wushu.[29] However, in earlier times, it was called wuyong, which meant military valor, or wuyi, meaning military skill. The ancient Chinese appear to have utilized military skills that were more complex than those traditionally practiced by their contemporaries in Western civilization. By the time of the Yuan and Ming Dynasties (A.D. 1279–1644), the movements and skills we in the West identify as martial arts had been refined and distilled into eighteen kinds of military skills. These skills reflected the various elements of Chinese philosophy such as the yin and yang, the negative and positive forces that exist in nature. Over time, martial arts incorporated jingluoxue, which is the science of attending to the main and collateral channels found in the body. This concept is a traditional mainstay of Chinese medicine. The result of all these influences is a system of martial arts that blends the physical aspects of existence with the philosophical, a highly sophisticated way of living that we who live in the West are only now coming to appreciate.[30]

Members of the upper class passed their time playing sports, parlor games, listening to music, and dancing. A form of football was played and was useful in military training. The game had rules of attack and was popular for centuries. During the T'ang Dynasty, the men and women of the aristocracy played polo, which was introduced by travelers from Persia (now known as Iran). The Chinese admired the equestrian skill of the Persians, and Persian horses were highly prized. Among the lesser sports were board and table games. Playing cards are believed to be a Chinese invention from the T'ang Dynasty, and games of chance were a popular activity in China, as was chess.[31]

Summary

The study of ancient civilizations reveals that the attitudes and behaviors found in Western civilization are similar to the modes of thought, cultural mores, and philosophical positions that reflect the beliefs and values of non-Western civilizations. These ancient civilizations flourished long before the birth of Christ, and appear to have influenced our Western ancestors in ways that we may never discover. Of interest to the student of history are both the similarities and the differences: certain aspects of these ancient civilizations that are similar to those found in the West reveal how all humans are similar. In contrast, those aspects that are manifest in these ancient civilizations that differ from what is believed and practiced in the West reveal the infinite variety of attitudes and behaviors that define our unique differences.

Although many of these ancient values and mores are very different from those which Westerners are comfortable with, there are common links that exist in all civilizations, past and present, that we all share. The ancient civilizations that inhabited Mesopotamia, Egypt, and China enjoyed many of the same sports and physical activities as we do today. Just like the people of today, the inhabitants of ancient civilizations linked sport and physical education with the spiritual as well as the secular world. Although long since vanished, these ancient civilizations left their mark on Western civilization in terms of science, architecture, thought, and in sport and physical education. One of these ancient civilizations, Egypt, was in contact with ancient Greece and Rome. Exactly how much the Egyptians influenced the Greeks and Romans is subject to debate. However, one thing is certain: the ancient Greeks and Romans were beneficiaries of Egyptian medicine, science, and sports and games.

Discussion Questions

1. Describe the association between the innate need in humans to survive and the growth of competitive sport in ancient civilizations.

2. In your estimation, why do the combat sports that were developed in ancient times continue to be practiced in modern times?

3. What were the similarities shared by the Sumerians, Egyptians, and Chinese concerning sport and physical activity?

4. How does martial arts training link the philosophical with the physical?

5. What types of sports and games do we engage in today that were just as popular in the ancient world?

6. Kings and other leaders in the ancient world involved themselves with manly pursuits that revolved around physical skill and athletic competition. To what extent do the leaders of modern industrialized countries continue this practice? What examples can you provide?

Suggestions for Further Reading

Breasted, J. H. *A History of Egypt.* New York: Charles Scribner's Sons, 1912.

Giles, H. A. *The Civilization of China.* New York: Henry Holt and Co., 1911.

Lexova, J. *Ancient Egyptian Dances.* Translated by K. Haaltmar. Prague: Oriental Institute, 1935.

Littauer, M. A., and J. H. Crouwel. *Chariots and Related Equipment from the Tomb of Tut'ankhamun, Tut'ankhamun Tomb Series 8* (Oxford, 1985).

Saad, Z. "Khazza Iawizza." *Annales du serivce des antiquites de l'Egypte. Cairo,* 37 (1937): 212–218; E. S. Eaton, "An Egyptian High Jump." *Bulletin of the Museum of Fine Arts, Boston* 35 (1937): 54.

Stumpf, F., and F. Cozens. "Some Aspects of the Role of Games, Sports, and Recreational Activities in the Culture of Modern Primitive Peoples," *Research Quarterly* 18 (October 1947): 198–218.

Notes

1. Jeremiah 51:43
2. Samuel Noah Kramer, *Cradle of Civilization* (New York: Time-Life Books, 1967), 12.
3. Ibid., 82.
4. Ibid., 36.
5. Ibid., 64, 66.
6. Ibid., 67.
7. Maxwell L. Howell and Reet Howell, "Physical Activities of the Sumerians" (paper presented to the Research Section American Alliance for Health, Physical Education and Recreation, Milwaukee, Wis., April 4, 1976), Denise Palmer, "Sport and Games in the Art of Early Civilizations" (master's thesis, University of Alberta, 1967), 3.
8. G. Contenay, *Everyday Life in Babylon and Assyria* (London: Edward Arnold, 1954), 3.
9. L. Woolley, *Mesopotamia and the Near East* (London: Methuen, 1961), figure 21.
10. Howell & Howell, "Physical Activities of the Sumerians," 6.
11. N. Kramer, *The Sumerians* (Chicago: University of Chicago Press, 1963), 25.
12. L. Woolley, *Ur Excavations: The Royal Cemeteries* Vol. 11 (Oxford University Press, 1934), 274–279.
13. *Iraq.*, Vol. VIII, 1946, Photo VIII; Howell & Howell, "Physical Activities of the Sumerians," 8.
14. Wolfgang Decker, *Sports and Games of Ancient Egypt* (New Haven: Yale University Press, 1992), 5. This book was originally published in German as *Sport und Spiel im Alten Agypten* by C. H. Beck'sche Verlagsbuchhandlung (Oscar Beck), Munich, 1987; C. E. DeVries, "Attitudes of the Ancient Egyptians Toward Physical-Recreative Activities" (Ph.D. diss., University of Chicago, 1960).
15. Lionel Casson, *Ancient Egypt* (New York: Time-Life Books, 1965), 35.
16. Ibid., 44.
17. Ibid., 63.
18. Ibid., 63.
19. Ibid., 68.
20. Ibid., 111.
21. Deobold B. Van Dalen and Bruce L. Bennett, *A World History of Physical Education,* 2nd ed. (Englewood Cliffs, N.J.: Prentice Hall, Inc., 1971), 11–12.
22. Edward H. Schafer, *Ancient China* (New York: Time-Life Books, 1967), 7.
23. Howard G. Knuttgen, MA Qiwei, and WU Zhongyuan, eds., *Sport in China* (Champaign, Ill.: Human Kinetics Books, 1990), 1.
24. Ibid., 4.
25. Schafer, *Ancient China,* 34.
26. Ibid., 40.
27. Ibid., 40.
28. Knuttgen et al., *Sport in China,* 5–6.
29. Ibid.
30. Van Dalen and Bennett, *World History Of Physical Education,* 15–16.
31. Schafer, *Ancient China,* 41.

c h a p t e r

Greece

General Events B.C.

c. 1600–c.1100 Mycenaean Period

c. 1184 Fall of Troy to Achaeans

c. 1100 Dorians and Ionians invaded
Greek peninsula, conquered
Achaeans; end of Mycenaean
Period, beginning of Hellenic
civilization

c. 950–c. 800 Period of Homeric epics

c. 800–c. 500 Archaic Period

c. 756 First Olympiad; all Greeks
competed in ceremonial games

c. 494 Persians under Darius invaded
Greece

c. 490 Athenians defeated Persians at
Marathon

480 Persians under Xerxes defeated
Spartans at Thermopylae

Athens sacked and burned

Athenians defeated Persian fleet at
Salamis

477 Delian League founded under
Athenian leadership

c. 461–429 Pericles (490–429) ruled
Athens

454 Delian League treasury moved to
Athens

437–404 Peloponnesian Wars between
Athens and Sparta

413 Athenians defeated at Syracuse,
Sicily

404 Athens fell to Sparta; end of
Athenian Empire

387 Plato founded Academy

335 Aristotle founded Lyceum

Architecture and Sculpture

c. 650 Ionic temple of Artemis built at
Ephesus

c. 600 Kouros from Sounion carved

c. 550 Hera of Samos carved

c. 530 Archaic Doric temples built at
Athens, Delphi, Corinth, Olympia

c. 489 Doric temple (Treasury of
Athenians) built at Delphi

c. 468–457 Temple of Zeus built at
Olympia

c. 460–440 Myron and Polyclitus active

450 Phidias appointed overseer of works
on acropolis

449–440 Temple of Hephaestus
(Theseum) built

447–432 Parthenon built by Ictinus and
Callicrates

Parthenon sculptures carved under
Phidias

437–432 Propylaea built by Mnesicles

427–424 Temple of Athena Nike built by
Callicrates

421–409 Erechtheum built by Mnesicles

c. 350–300 Lysippus active

A.D.

c. 100 Plutarch (c.46–c.125) wrote
Parallel Lives

c. 140–150 Pausanius visited Athens;
later wrote description of Greece

Philosophers

c. 582–c. 507 Pythagoras

500–428 Anaxagoras

469–399 Socrates

427–347 Plato

384–322 Aristotle

Historians

c. 495–425 Herodotus

c. 460–395 Thucydides

c. 434–c. 355 Xenophon

Sculptors

c. 490–c. 432 Phidias

c. 460–c. 450 Myron active

c. 460–c. 440 Polyclitus active

c. 390–c. 330 Praxiteles

c. 350–c. 300 Lysippus active

Dramatists and Musicians

525–456 Aeschylus

496–406 Sophocles

484–406 Euripides

c. 444–380 Aristophanes

Introduction

As we approach the new millennium, there are a number of "timeless" activities and pursuits that our society will continue to engage in. The scholarly study of sport and physical education will continue to mature. As a profession, we will endeavor to make profound discoveries that contribute to the growth and betterment of society and the individual. We will fine-tune our knowledge of diet and exercise to help achieve peak performance. We will continue to investigate the link between exercise and health and, in this regard, will seek additional information to develop a harmonious relationship between mind and body.

Our society will continue to build monuments to sport in the form of stadiums, gymnasiums, and arenas. Athletes will continue their quest to achieve victory, sometimes no matter what the cost. Their performances will inspire, entertain, and from time to time, disappoint us. All of these monuments, emotions, and achievements that take place in the 1990s have their origins in the legends and stories about the trials and tribulations of the athletes who lived in ancient Greece.

The timeless interest in athletes, sport, and physical development continues unabated. However, as far reaching as our current efforts in these areas are, we never cease to be amazed and humbled when we reflect upon the achievements made long ago by the ancient Greeks. The pursuit of individual excellence in mind and body that was emblematic of the Greeks during their Golden Age serves as an inspiration to the thousands of physical educators and athletes who follow in their footsteps today.

The Influence of the Jews and the Phoenicians upon Greek Culture

The Greeks developed, quite possibly, with Judaic and Phoenician influence, much of the Western world's philosophical orientation toward the body and physical education. Judaism predates the ancient Greeks. The Jews paid close attention to the care of the body as well as the significance of their corporeal existence. Their religion, culture, and philosophical views spread to some areas of the Greek world and could have been very influential. For example, during his trial, Socrates tells the court that he believes in a God that is far higher than any of the gods worshipped by the polytheistic Greeks. His reference to a single, supreme deity may have originated from interaction with Jews or through reading the works of Jewish theologians.

The close proximity of Greece to the Middle East enabled the Phoenicians to establish trade with the Greeks. These ancient seafaring people, who inhabited present day Lebanon, enjoyed sports and physical activity. Their influence upon the development of the Western world is significant. According to Boutros, ". . . the Phoenicians had developed in Antiquity a wide Civilization and had a significant role in the early development of European Culture."[1] Boutros states that

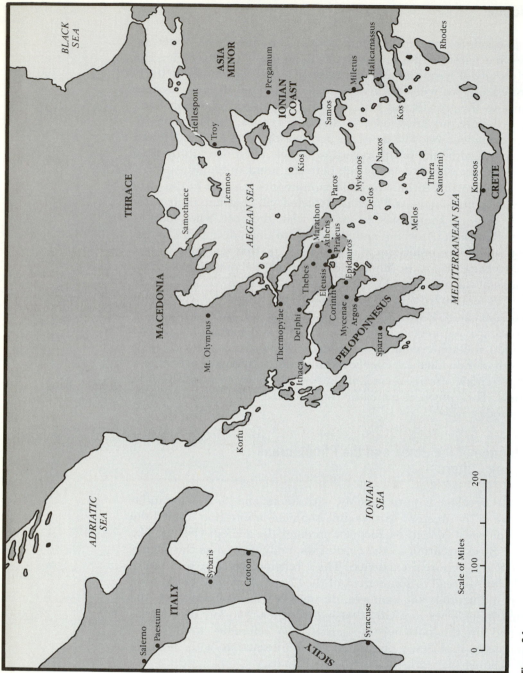

Figure 3.1

Map of ancient Greece. From Robert C. Lamm, Neal M. Cross, and Rudy H. Turk, The Search for Personal Freedom, Vol. 1, Wm. C. Brown, 1984.

Phoenician civilization was established prior to Greek civilization, which suggests that some of the rituals, sports, and physical activities enjoyed by the Phoenicians may have been adopted by the Greeks. According to Boutros,

> In fact, it appeared to me that Greek Sport was based on divinities and worship rites borrowed from the Phoenicians, and even the Greeks adopted Phoenician gods and rituals, almost completely, with only a change in the names of the divinities, which were clearly behind the establishment of the Olympic Games and other Athletic Festivals in Greece.[2]

The actual extent of the influence that the Jews and Phoenicians had upon the beliefs and practices of ancient Greeks remains unclear. There is evidence that these two cultures did play a role in the development of the Greek world, but historians are not sure how extensive this role was. However, one thing is clear; the idea that the Phoenicians are directly or indirectly responsible for the establishment of the Olympic Games and other Greek athletic festivals as reported by Butros is sure to result in lively debate. Nonetheless, the study of history is not an exact science. Over time, scholars in the field of sport history may uncover additional information that sheds more light on the development of sport and physical education in ancient Greece.

Philosophical Positions of the Body

There were two opposing ideas of physical education in Greece. According to Fairs, "Each idea of physical education was the end product of a specific world view, or metaphysical position, and its corresponding cultural mentality [and] sociocultural system."[3] These two opposing metaphysical schools of thought were naturalistic and antinaturalistic. The naturalistic approach believed man should have a balanced program that would incorporate both physical education and intellectual education, because the nature of man was perceived to function as both a spiritual and corporeal being. This approach necessitated achieving a harmonious balance among the spiritual, intellectual, and physical. The antinaturalistic view held that physical education was a servant to the intellectual process. The learning mind and a behaving body were the end product of a world view that rejected the material world in favor of the self-created world of pure thought.[4] The antinaturalistic view held the mind in higher esteem than the body; naturalistic philosophy held the body in higher esteem than the antinaturalistic school did. Both schools of thought held the mind in high esteem, but they differed on the position and subsequent importance of the body.

Dualism

The dualistic approach to the problem of being (ontology), whether humans are essentially spirit or body, was classically described by Plato in the *Phaedo*.[5] Two of the greatest philosophers of all time, Socrates and Plato of fourth century B.C. Athens, formulated philosophical positions of the body based on metaphysical dualism,[6] and this argument decisively influenced the purpose and status of contemporary physical education. The separation of our being or existence into two components—the mind and the body—is referred to as dualism and is a critical component in the history of metaphysical thought and remains very popular today. For example, the separation of mind and body in perhaps its most graphic form can be seen in the early philosophical and psychological orientation of ascetic dualism. Using a dichotomous approach, ascetic dualism held belief in (1) soul and (2) matter. Unlike the Greeks, who admired and strove to develop the mind and possess a magnificent physique, the ascetics of the Middle Ages (A.D. 476–1400) based their beliefs on the concept of the original sin and the attendant complete and total depravity of men, women, and children. The body was thought to be a tool of the devil that was to infect and pervert the soul. As a consequence, the training of the body—and the body as a mode of being and existing—was mortified, degraded, and so far as possible ignored and held as repugnant and repulsive. Had the ancient Greeks had the means to see into the future, they would have been truly discouraged by the beliefs and practices of the ascetic dualists. No doubt these same Greeks would have smiled and approved of the physical fitness movement that is sweeping across the United States today, and the devotion to health, exercise, and intellectual training that is emblematic of contemporary physical education majors.

Classical Humanism

Classical scholars, such as William Fleming, are comfortable identifying the ancient Greeks with the philosophy of humanism, which provides a system of human conduct among members of society. The philosophy espoused by Plato, however, may not lend itself readily to humanism. Throughout Plato's work, the importance of the mind or soul (that which is eternal) over the body (that which is temporal) is fairly clear, especially when his social class system is taken into account as told in the *Republic*. In his caste system, selected people who occupy the higher rungs of the caste hierarchy have less and less concern for earthly, humanistic concerns. The expressed humanistic qualities of the classical Greeks would be difficult to apply or merge with the caste system advocated in the *Republic*. Plato was not an advocate of classical humanism or democratic ideals, but instead believed that the masses should be ruled by philosopher-kings who have the wisdom, as a result of proper schooling, that ordinary citizens lack. Democratic voting as we know it in the United States would not be permitted in Plato's *Republic*.

The primary focus of the Greeks was on their existence as humans. They had the same concerns that we do today: what is one's place in nature and the universe, and what type of social relationships are we

Figure 3.2
Greek wrestlers.

best suited for? These questions and countless others helped form the foundation for humanism, the philosophical school that takes the position that concern for one's total welfare is central.[7] In this respect, the Greeks saw their gods as idealized human beings. This can be seen in their art, which uses the human form as a point of departure. The sculptures and artistic renderings of Apollo and Athena are often aesthetically depicted as perfect images of masculine and feminine beauty.

The Greeks were more thoroughly at home in the physical world than were the later Christian peoples, who believed in the separation of flesh and spirit. The Greeks greatly admired the beauty and agility of the human body at the peak of its development. In addition to studies in literature and music, Greek youths were trained from childhood for competition. Because it was through the perfection of their bodies that men most resembled gods, the culture of the body was a spiritual as well as a physical activity.[8]

Socrates' and Plato's View of the Body

If Socrates left any written material behind, it has yet to be discovered. The only knowledge of Socrates that is available is what his pupil Plato wrote. From all accounts, Socrates and Plato were not only accomplished

Figure 3.3

Plato and his students in the garden of the academy. From:
E. W. Gerber: Innovators and Institutions in Physical Education.
Philadelphia: Lea & Febiger, 1971.

philosophers but athletes as well. *Plato* in Greek means "broad shoulders," which may have been the reason for his success at the Isthmian
Games. He trained with the best wrestling coach in Athens, and it was
this coach, or *paidotribe,* who is credited with changing his name from
Aristocles to Plato.

Socrates' and Plato's metaphysical position regarding the nature
and reality of human existence is that of dualism, which divides us
into a corporeal (bodily) existence and a spiritual-mental existence.
This division culminates with the soul departing the body upon death.
Throughout Plato's writings (*Phaedo, Republic, Books II & III*) the
development and practice of philosophy (intellectual activity) that
will nourish the soul is always elevated over the cultivation and training of the body. The manner in which Plato argued for the division of
mind and body, or dualism, and the implications of his philosophy can
be seen in the following passage from the *Phaedo,* which is the story
of Socrates' last day in prison. During the course of the day, he discusses the immortality of the soul, the soul's capacity for pure knowledge, the establishment of the dualistic nature of existence, the gross-
ness of the body, and how the evil body infects and confuses the
mind/soul. The importance of death and the role of death is
explained, although only the true devotee of philosophy will understand that death will liberate the soul from the chains and limitations
of the body. Once rid of the evils of the body, the soul (mind) will

have the capacity to know that which is pure (unadulterated knowledge). The passage reads:

> And the true philosophers, Simmias, are always occupied in the practice of dying [in order to release the soul from the limitations of the body], wherefore also to them least of all men is death terrible. Look at the matter thus: if they have been in every way the enemies of the body, and are wanting to be alone with the soul, . . . how inconsistent would they be if they trembled and repined, instead of rejoicing at their departure to that place where, when they arrive, they hope to gain that which in life they desired—and this was wisdom [knowledge]—and at the same time to be rid of the company of their enemy [body].[9]
>
> What again shall we say of the actual acquirement of knowledge?—is the body, if invited to share in the enquiry, a hinderer or a helper? I mean to say, have sight and hearing any truth in them? Are they not, as the poets are always telling us, inaccurate witnesses? . . .
>
> Then when does the soul attain truth?—for in attempting to consider anything in company with the body she is obviously deceived. Then must not true existence be revealed to her in thought, if at all?[10]

This passage from *Phaedo* describes the epistemological position of Socrates as well as his contempt for the body. Plato presents us with an epistemological issue—can we come to "know things," acquire knowledge, while in the body? To Plato, the mind was eternal. In his concept of transmigration of the souls, he states that the eternal mind/soul had knowledge—knew things—which it forgot at birth. Knowledge (to Plato) was knowledge of the real (world of forms); belief was about the changeable, sensible world. Our earthly life is a process of rediscovering or uncovering all those things the soul/mind experienced as knowledge or truth before it inherited or was assigned to the body. The body, however, will constantly deceive us as to what is real or authentic. The body will fool us with inaccurate information; therefore, we should not trust our senses to reveal truth but rely completely on our mind/soul to reveal truth insofar as possible while in the company of the body. The ideas of truth and knowledge that are shaped by the mind/soul are far more accurate than the examples or representations of truth and knowledge represented in the physical-corporeal-material world, which, because of the ability of the body to deceive the mind, cannot be trusted.

This metaphysical position and attendant epistemology is very damaging to physical education because the body is not valued at all. In fact, the body is viewed as the enemy of the mind. If this extreme epistemological position were ever supported as the foundation of contemporary educational philosophy, physical education and sports would never be a component of the curriculum. The curriculum would be devoted to the exclusive training of the mind.

Socrates' and Plato's View of Physical Education

Although the *Phaedo* describes a philosophical position of the body that is clearly understood within the traditions of Western civilization, it is not their only position on this subject. The paradoxical nature of Plato becomes quite evident when we observe that although Socrates and Plato were both accomplished athletes and trained hard for competition and therefore cared for the body, they attacked the body as a "source of endless trouble" that prevents the mind and soul from attaining truth as long as "the soul is infected with the evils of the body."[11] However, in a radical departure, Plato provides us with yet another philosophical position of the body in *Books II* and *III* of the *Republic*. Although he continues to maintain his dualistic approach to the nature and reality of man, he argues in the following passage that there must be balance and harmony in the education of his citizens:

> Come then, and let us pass a leisure hour in story-telling, and our story shall be the education of our heroes.
>
> And what shall be their education? Can we find a better than the traditional sort?—and this has two divisions, gymnastic for the body, and music for the soul.[12]

In the *Republic*, Plato attempts to construct the first utopia in literature. The education and training of the citizens in his utopia was of critical importance to Plato. Gymnastics and music were the two components of the curriculum. Of interest to physical educators is that these components, identified as "physical education" and "academics," reinforce and perpetuate the dualistic approach to education that continues to remain in place today: one component educates the mind, another component educates the body. However, the logic Plato used to incorporate gymnastics into his educational curriculum elevates the philosophical position of the body. Although the body will never be equal to the mind or soul, the body is now in a position of importance, even though it continues to be subservient to the mind. In the *Republic, Book III*, Socrates states:

> Gymnastic as well as music should begin in early years; the training in it should be careful and should continue through life. Now my belief is . . . not that the good body by any bodily excellence improves the soul, but, on the contrary, that the good soul, by her own excellence, improves the body as far as this may be possible.
>
> Then, to the mind when adequately trained, we shall be right in handing over the more particular care of the body.[13]

Music is the term the Greeks used to encompass traditional academic subjects. Plato was concerned that the citizens of his utopia, especially its leaders (the philosopher-kings) and the warrior-athletes, receive a well-rounded liberal arts education. He recognizes that gymnastics can promote health, which is a significant departure from his views on health in the *Phaedo*. Perhaps more important, he realizes the problem of excess devotion to music or gymnastics, which can be seen in the following conversation between Socrates and Glaucon from the *Republic*, which uses the Socratic method of questioning. Socrates states:

> *Did you never observe, I said, the effect on the mind itself of exclusive devotion to gymnastic, or the opposite effect of an exclusive devotion to music?*

Figure 3.4
Under the watchful eye of his coach and rivals, a Greek athlete prepares to defeat his opponent in wrestling competition.

In what way shown? he said.

The one producing a temper of hardness and ferocity, the other of softness and effeminacy, I replied.

Yes, he said, I am quite aware that the mere athlete becomes too much of a savage, and that the mere musician is melted and softened beyond what is good for him. . . .

And so in gymnastic, if a man takes violent exercise and is a great feeder, and the reverse of a great student of philosophy, at first the high condition of his body fills him with pride and spirit, and he becomes twice the man that he was.

Certainly.

And what happens? if he does nothing else, and holds no converse with the Muses, does not even that intelligence which there may be in him, having no taste of any sort of learning or enquiry or thought or culture, grow feeble and dull and blind, his mind never waking up or receiving nourishment? . . .

And he ends by becoming a hater of philosophy, uncivilized, never using the weapon of persuasion,—he is like a wild beast, all violence and fierceness, and knows no other way of dealing; and he lives in all ignorance and evil conditions, and has no sense of propriety and grace. . . . And he who mingles music with gymnastic in the fairest of proportions, and best attempers them to the soul, may be rightly called the true musician and harmonist in a far higher sense. . . .

You are quite right, Socrates.

And such a presiding genius will be always required in our State if the government is to last.[14]

In summary, Plato provides us with two views of the body based on his metaphysical dualism: The argument in the *Phaedo* is for the development of the soul almost to the exclusion of the body, whereas in the *Republic* the argument is for the harmonic balance of the body and the mind/soul. The significance of Plato's dualism is tied into what knowledge is and how we acquire knowledge (epistemology).

Education Through the Physical versus Education of the Physical

Plato does not trust the body, which has a significant impact on the two historically divergent positions embodied in American physical education: that of *education through the physical*, and the opposing viewpoint represented by *education of the physical*. The impact of Plato's dualism can be best grasped by posing two questions:

1. Can "accurate" knowledge be achieved while in the body?
2. If the answer is no, how is it possible to become educated?

Philosophically, the discussion of physical education as "education of the physical" or "education through the physical" was and is a key distinction among approaches in physical education. These two positions were advocated by two of America's leading figures in physical education. Jesse Feiring Williams (1886–1966) in his excellent article "Education Through the Physical"[15] expressed his opposition to the dualistic nature of existence and instead supported the concept that viewed each individual as a unity of mind and body, with the soul seen as an essential element of the whole. As a result of the position taken by Williams, who obviously took exception to Plato's dualism, physical education had concern with not only physical fitness but also personal relationships, emotional responses, mental learning, group behavior, and related social, emotional, and aesthetic outcomes via education through the physical. Charles H. McCloy (1886–1959) was a contemporary of Jesse Feiring Williams, but he held fast to the position that physical education was education of the physical. The thematic emphasis in McCloy's work centered around the importance of physical characteris-

(a)

(b)

Figure 3.5a and b

(a) Jesse Feiring Williams. Courtesy Mary Pavlich Roby, University of Arizona. (b) Charles Harold McCloy. Courtesy of University of Iowa Photographic Service.

tics—physical development. Like Williams and physical educators of today, McCloy believed that the nature of men and women was that of an organic unity. McCloy's position was that the physical dimension was a significant aspect of our existence. In his book *Philosophical Basis for Physical Education*, McCloy states the classic position for supporting education of the physical:

> The psychological literature of late has spoken much of the fact of body-mind unity, but this same literature has usually gone on thinking and writing as though the child were all mind. We in physical education, with our growing overemphasis upon the educational aspects of physical education [education through the physical], are apt to fall in the same error. Our organism is more body than mind, and it is only through the adequate functioning of all of it that the most desirable functioning of even the brain occurs.[16]

McCloy believed that the development "of the physical," not education "through the physical," was the objective that should be the priority of physical education. It would be fascinating to speculate about the nature of a debate between Plato, Williams, and McCloy concerning their epistemological positions relative to the body: the dualism of Plato versus the organic unity of Williams and McCloy, and the "education through the physical" advocated by Williams vigorously opposed by the "education of the physical" espoused by McCloy.

Contemporary physical education professionals may look to Plato's *Republic* to articulate or defend the mission of physical education in the schools. The position that Plato argues for in the *Republic* is one that blends academics with movement. However, these same physical education professionals may be unaware of the philosophical position of the body presented in the *Phaedo*, in which the body is evil and subservient to the mind. The education of students in physical education is not complete without a basic understanding of the philosophical position of the body put forth by Socrates and Plato. The epistemology of Socrates and Plato relative to the body, their dualistic beliefs, and their views on the need for gymnastics/physical education continues to have a profound philosophical influence on physical education in particular and education in general. Plato viewed the world as an imperfect copy of the actual or "ideal" world that existed in the mind and would not trust his senses. His best pupil did not agree with him. Aristotle believed that the world of the senses is indeed real.

Aristotle

Aristotle (384–322 B.C.) was the son of the physician Nicomachus and went to study with Plato when he was eighteen. He spent the next twenty years with Plato and later became tutor to a thirteen-year-old boy who later became famous as Alexander the Great. In 335 B.C. Aristotle started his own school, the Lyceum, also known as the Peripatetic School of Philosophy. His students were called Peripatetics (from the Greek word that means to walk or stroll, which is the manner in which he taught). Aristotle would stroll around the grounds of the Lyceum while he lectured and engaged in philosophical discussions. In 323 B.C. the Athenian authorities accused Aristotle of impiety, and remembering what happened to Socrates when he was accused of impiety, he left Athens and the Lyceum twelve years after he opened the school. Aristotle moved to Chalcis, where he died at the age of sixty-three.

Aristotle is generally recognized as the preeminent philosopher of all time, as well as Plato's most gifted student. His influence on science and philosophy is profound. The works of St. Thomas Aquinas, René Descartes, Immanuel Kant, Georg Hegel, and others were profoundly influenced by Aristotle, who divided philosophy into three parts: (1) theoretical philosophy consisted of mathematics, physics, and metaphysics; (2) practical philosophy concerned itself with the theoretical practice of ethics and politics; and (3) poetic philosophy focused on aesthetics. According to Aristotle, logic enabled one to find truth rather than function as a compendium of truths. The study of logic prepared students to study philosophy. Aristotle believed logic would enable one to find truth, which meant that knowledge would agree with reality; truth will exist when mental ideals or representations concur with things in the objective world.[17]

The social and political philosophy of Aristotle is quite interesting. He believed that man must be extracted from the crude conditions he finds himself in by the State, which will then civilize him by providing him with the foundation of an ethical and intellectual life. The State is the mechanism that will allow man to achieve a life of virtue and happiness. Man is not capable of achieving this goal without the State, because man is a political animal by nature and therefore must exist within an organized society. The highest virtue for the individual is intellectual attainment and the pursuit of peace. Aristotle considered women, children, and slaves as inferior and therefore excluded them from government. However, he felt children should be provided with an education designed to instill virtue that would insure responsible citizenship and work toward the common good of the State. The educational curriculum Aristotle envisioned included grammar, gymnastics, music, and drawing.[18]

To Aristotle, it was important that the rational soul be educated because the health of the mind was dependent on the health of the body. Aristotle believed that athletics enables youths to develop as strong, healthy citizens who would defend Athens in time of war and serve her in times of peace. He held to the belief that because the health of the soul/mind was contingent on a healthy body, physical education (gymnastics) was necessary to insure the health of the mind/soul.

Historical Foundations of Sport and Physical Education

The Acropolis of Athens and the birthplace of the Olympic Games are familiar symbols that we associate with both ancient and modern Greece. The history of ancient Greece is a story replete with mythological tales, slavery, numerous wars, romantic poems, cultural activities on a grand scale, and the development of athletic competition and promotion of physical beauty that continue to fascinate us two thousand years later.

Funeral Games

The poet Homer provides us with an account of the Funeral Games in *Book XXIII* of the *Iliad*, which was written between 900 and 700 B.C. along with the *Odyssey*. The Funeral Games described by Homer is a story about Patroclus, a friend and fellow soldier of the legendary Achilles. Patroclus was killed during the battle of Troy, and Achilles, wishing to honor and mourn his friend, instituted Funeral Games in honor of Patroclus. The warriors were seated around the body of Patroclus and enjoyed a funeral feast.

The next day, Achilles placed Patroclus' body on an altar of wood surrounded by four slaughtered horses and twelve unfortunate Trojan prisoners who were executed for the occasion. The altar, horses, and Trojans were burned. After the cremation, the Funeral Games took place, consisting of chariot racing, discus throwing, archery, wrestling, footraces, spear contests, and boxing.

Funeral Games were not unusual, nor were they the domain of the Greeks. The Greeks, like other ancient cultures, were very religious and wanted to honor and appease their mythological gods such as Zeus (supreme god), Apollo (god of sun; patron of music, medicine, prophecy), and Athena (goddess of wisdom and the arts). In addition to honoring the deceased, Funeral Games were thought to give pleasure to the gods, who were believed to watch and enjoy athletic competition.

Figure 3.6
Minoan bull-jumping and acrobatics. From Repository at Knossos, Crete.

Influence of Crete

Environmental factors played a significant role in the development of athletics. Greece is located on the shores of the Mediterranean and is blessed with abundant sunshine and warm weather. These ideal climatic conditions enabled the Greeks to pursue a vigorous outdoor life throughout the year, as opposed to Scandinavian and Germanic peoples who stayed indoors much of the year because of the severe weather. Greece is a collection of numerous islands and the mainland, which has an irregular ragged coastline with beautiful harbors, serene bays, and villages. Historical ruins of the ancient Greeks are located on tiny islands and the mainland. The Mediterranean island of Crete, which flourished as a related but separate culture, also has magnificent ruins and monuments to sport, such as the frescoes and what would appear to be arenas in some of the major palaces where bull-jumping could have taken place. In Crete, major Minoan palaces occupied the sites of Knossos, Phaestos, and Mallia, and within the ruins remain works of art where athletes are depicted jumping over bulls, possibly using a vaulting device, in an arena setting that quite possibly may have been located in the central court of the palace. Boxing and dancing were other popular sports engaged in by the people of Crete during the Aegean Bronze Age (3000 B.C.–1100 B.C.).[19]

Some Historical Perspectives on the Development of Greek Sport

The origin of Greek sport has not been clearly established by scholars. There is an argument put forth by Boutros (1981) that the Phoenicians may have been largely responsible for the early development of Greek sport. However, this view does not represent the majority opinion. There are two predominant schools of thought on the development of Greek sport. The first explanation, which is the traditional view, is the rise-and-fall approach. Scholars who adhere to this romantic perspective believe that ancient Greek sports rose to glory during the fifth and sixth centuries and then endured a long decline due in part to the disdain the Romans had for Greek sports, the rise of Christianity, and the steady increase of professional athletes who ignored the original concepts of agon and arete. Arete is the ancient Greek concept of striving for excellence or quality, coupled with the concept of one's being as a unified whole. According to *Aetholon: The Journal of Sport Literature,* "Arete is possible only while one is striving; those who think they have attained arete have lost it, and have passed into hubris (excessive pride)." Agon, which is the origin of the word *agony,* represents the idea of the contest and the pain one experiences because of the desire to win. Although older cultures may have used and understood these concepts, the ancient Greeks popularized them.

According to the traditional view, Greek sports evolved primarily from the games described by Homer in the *Iliad* and the *Odyssey,* which eventually manifested itself in the concept of the amateur athlete. The primary goal of the athlete was to compete in a "circuit" of four major national competitions that were designated the Panhellenic Games. The Panhellenic Games were scheduled to ensure that one major contest was held every year. The Panhellenic Games consisted of the following:

1. Olympic Games—held at Olympia to honor Zeus. The oldest and most prestigious of the Panhellenic Games. First record of the Olympic Games appears in 776 B.C. Victors were crowned with an olive wreath.

2. Pythian Games—held in Delphi at the sacred site of Apollo. Victors were crowned with a wreath of laurel. Second in prestige.

3. Isthmian Games—held in Corinth to honor Poseidon, the sea god. Victors received a wreath of pine from a sacred grove.

4. Nemean Games—held in Nemea to honor Zeus every second year. Victors received a wreath of celery.

The traditional view holds that the rise of professional athletes gave way to an age of specialization, rewards, and all the attendant ills that money and glory bring about. By the fourth century, sport was nothing more than a spectacle, corrupted by money.

Modern sport historians view this traditional or romantic view as flawed, due in part to the influence of Baron Pierre de Coubertin, founder of the modern Olympic Games. The first modern Olympiad was held in 1896 in Athens, although the Greeks actually staged some "Olympic Games" in the nineteenth century prior to Coubertin's Olympics. The British Olympic Games predated the modern Olympics as well. Baron de Coubertin perpetuated the amateur ideal that, according to the traditionalists and romantics, epitomized the ideal of Greek athletic competition that was emblematic of agon and arete. However, the Greek ideal of "amateur" in fact may have been created by myth or self-serving groups that invented the concept as a means to an end.

Scholars who are not in agreement with the traditionalists suggest that Greek sport originated as a result of contact with the established sporting activities of Crete and Near Eastern civilizations such as the Phoenicians and the Egyptians. According to scholars who oppose the viewpoint espoused by the traditionalists, Greek sport did not develop along the ideal lines of amateurism described by the traditional school. H. W. Pleket, for example, maintains that our concept of amateur and professional and our beliefs about prizes and other rewards are often anachronistic with regard to Greek sport.[20] According to David C. Young, there was no Greek word for amateur and no word for games in the Greek language.[21] In support of Pleket, Slowikowski states that "the ancient Greeks never had a word which meant professional, and moreover, they did not distinguish between amateur or other athletes in their competition."[22] Young has also argued that the Greeks never considered themselves amateurs, and further that they never even developed the idea. Allen Guttman goes so far as to say that the idea of amateurism was a nineteenth-century invention by British historians and was perpetuated as a weapon of class warfare to keep the lower classes from beating their upperclass counterparts in athletic competition.[23]

There will continue to be different interpretations of history and general disagreement among physical education and sport historians over "what happened and why it happened" with regard to the development of sport in ancient Greece. However, like the walls of the ancient Acropolis in Athens, the foundation of the traditionalist/romantic interpretation of the origin of Greek sport is crumbling. Although crumbling, this view has not collapsed and remains popular with many physical education professionals. There is still more historical research to be done on Greek sport, and with time and new information, a clearer, more accurate picture will emerge.

Athens and Sparta: A Tale of Two Cities

Greece was composed of a series of city-states, which were a collection of regional cities and towns that formed together for mutual benefits such as business and defense. Greece was not a politically unified country; the city-states were ruled by kings who would often go to war against each other. Over time, these city-states merged into twenty major leagues or coalitions directed by the dominant city in each league. Athens and Sparta are the two most famous city-states and will be discussed here because the contrasting nature of the two most powerful city-states in ancient Greece provides an illuminating and revealing cultural analysis.

Athens was a city of immense culture, fabulous architecture, and the home of Socrates, Plato, Aristotle, Aristophanes, and other famous poets, playwrights, and philosophers. In addition, Athens had advanced the farthest toward democracy. Sparta, in contrast, was a military power whose primary purpose was to rule all of Greece. As a result, the citizens of Sparta had but one goal: to be warriors. Sparta imposed iron-fisted discipline over her own citizens and the lands she conquered. Because the Spartans were obsessed with military supremacy, they contributed minimally to the arts, sciences, literature, and philosophy of Greece. However, the physical education programs and athletic competitions were taken very seriously by Sparta, Athens, and the rest of the Greek world, which included colonies in Italy and Asia Minor.

As discussed earlier, the Greeks pictured their gods as perfect physical specimens. The artwork and literature of the Greeks is replete with pictures and tales that depict Zeus, Hercules, and other gods possessing incredible physical beauty and athletic prowess. For the Greeks to properly pay homage to their gods, they sought to resemble them through the attainment and cultivation of physical beauty.

The cultural nourishment and support of athletic competitions, along with the desire to resemble the gods through the perfection of physical beauty, promoted an athletic culture and sporting heritage of unprecedented proportions. Physical education reached a pinnacle in Athens, where it had the utilitarian purpose of preparing soldiers for war and exemplified the Greek idea of beauty and harmony. The Athenian physical education program was education through the physical, meaning that through physical education an Athenian was believed to acquire important virtues of citizenship, loyalty, and courage. The Athenians sought harmony of both mind and body, and consequently physical education occupied a prominent place in the education program. Athenians believed that if a person displayed an out-of-shape, flabby body, it was a disgrace and considered a sign of poor education.

Because the purpose of physical education was so different in Sparta than in Athens, their respective programs were not at all similar although their results, from a physical standpoint, compared favorably with each other. The Spartan approach of physical training (not physical education) was strictly education of the physical, meaning that the training of the body was for military purposes. The education of Spartan citizens was the responsibility of the state. Each newborn infant was examined by a council of elders who would determine if the infant would be of benefit to Sparta. Only the strongest and the healthiest babies were allowed to live; the rest were taken to Mount Taygetus to die. The child stayed at home until the age of seven, when he left home and was conscripted into military service and remained until he reached the age of fifty (if he lived that long). The seven-year-old boy was housed in primitive barracks under the watchful eye of the Paidonomous, who supervised the educational program called the Agoge. It was here that the Spartan character was developed that was personified by iron discipline, obedience to authority, indifference to pain and suffering, and obsession with victory in battle or any type of competition; defeat was unthinkable.

Gymnastics were the primary means of military and physical training. Spartan exercise did not take place in lavish gymnasiums or palaestrae that were available in Athens. Spartan facilities were, indeed, Spartan and functional. Spartan youths were instructed in swimming, running, fighting, wrestling, boxing, ball games, horsemanship, archery, discus and javelin throwing, field marches, and the pancratium (a combination of boxing and wrestling). When they reached the age of twenty, each male took an oath of allegiance to Sparta and then went into actual combat.

The physical education activities in Athens also commenced at about age seven and began with general physical conditioning. As in Sparta, physical education included boxing, running, wrestling, dancing, javelin and discus throwing, and the pancratium. If the family could afford it, chariot racing, choral training, and assorted ball games were also included.

Fitness Assessment in Sparta

Periodic testing and evaluations were done in Sparta by officials known as ephors. The ephors would observe the Spartan youths and comment on their progress, as can be seen in the following passage:

> And besides, it was written in the law that every ten days the youth stripped naked should pass in public review before the Ephors. Now if they were solid and vigorous, resembling the work of a sculptor or engraver, as the result of the gymnastic exercise, praise was accorded them; but if their physique displayed any flabbiness or flaccidity, with fat beginning to appear in rolls because of laziness, then they were beaten and punished.[24]

As can be seen, the well-educated Spartan was one that was physically fit and a good soldier. Spartan cultural mores were not broad based, as with Athenian culture, but were focused and directed to achieving military superiority, which their program of physical training reflected.

Athenian Education

In contrast, the education of Athenian youth was the responsibility of the family, not the state. Athens, like the rest of Greece, had a rigid class structure that placed citizens in certain classes depending on birthright, education, and financial resources. Depending on the resources of the family, the children would either receive an education centered in the home, with parents as the teachers, or a tutor would be retained who could provide a more enhanced and enriching educational experience. Nonetheless, Athenians believed that the education of both mind and body was absolutely essential, and a great deal of care was given to this area. The Athenians thought it necessary to perfect the military skills of the citizen and also to teach the appropriate values, virtues, and methods for the continued progress of the city through education and cultural enrichment.

Physical education was a prominent feature of Athenian education. According to Van Dalen and Bennett:

> The Greeks gave physical education a respectability that it has never since achieved. They accorded the body equal dignity with the mind. They associated sport with philosophy, music, literature, painting, and

Figure 3.7
Under the scrutiny of his coach, the athlete is victorious.

particularly with sculpture. They leave to all future civilizations important aesthetic ideas: the idea of harmonized balance of mind and body, of body symmetry, and bodily beauty in repose and in action.[25]

Athenian Physical Education

The athletic facilities in Athens and the rest of the Greek world consisted of gymnasiums and palaestrae. Located in Athens were three prominent gymnasiums: the Academy, the Lyceum built by Pisistratus, and the Cynosarges. Early gymnasiums were probably nothing more than a designated area located near water where the athletes could exercise and then bathe. Gymnasiums gradually evolved not only into elaborate centers of athletic training but also into places where intellectual pursuits were encouraged and supported. Plato's Academy is but one example. The palaestra is commonly referred to as a center where wrestling activity occurred. However, Robinson states:

> When gymnastic training was developed into a regular institution, subject to well-formulated rules, a slightly more elaborate athletic plant became necessary. A simple building, called Palaestra, seems to have been added to the exercise grounds' gymnasium. This afforded space for an undressing room, for the various steps in the care of the body, for storage of cloths and athletic implements as well as for 13 areas equipped for exercise used in training boxers and wrestlers.[26]

There were both public and private athletic facilities, and some of the wealthier Athenians had gymnasiums built for their personal use. If the family had enough money, they could hire a paidotribe, a physical education teacher who owned his own palaestra and charged a fee, similar to today's private health clubs. Music was very popular in the gymnasium and palaestrae of Greece, and flute music could often be heard. Pedagogues, or teachers, were trusted slaves who would accompany young boys as their guardian, tutor, servant, counselor, and when need be, disciplinarian. Formal educational training in Athens was limited to citizens. Slaves and other noncitizens did not have access to schools, although the gymnasium of Cynosarges allowed non-Athenian parents to enroll their sons. The comparison with the health fitness clubs and personal trainers available to us today is remarkably similar to the practices and beliefs of the ancient Athenians.

Athletic Participation of Greek Women

Spartan women also participated in gymnastic exercises. However, they never had to live in the public barracks as did the men. They received instruction in dance and were physically conditioned to give birth to strong, healthy children. Wrestling, swimming, and horseback riding were activities that were popular with the women of Sparta, and horse training was a specialty. This stands to reason as Spartan men were away from home much of the time, and women bore the responsibility of running the home and maintaining the Spartan way of life. Unlike Spartan women, Athenian women did not receive instruction in physical education. Athenian women kept the house, raised the children, and were excluded from the social and political activities enjoyed by the men.

Pausanias, who was the early predecessor of the modern-day travel agent, wrote a travel guide for second century A.D. travelers to Greece that described the Heraean Games for girls that occurred in approximately 175 A.D. The games he described consisted of footraces and were held at the Olympic Stadium, although the distance was shortened. The victors received crowns of olive, and a portion of a cow was sacrificed to Hera. Pausanias provides two accounts of the origin of the Heraean Games. The first account is traced back to Hipodameia, who instituted the games to pay homage to Hera on behalf of her marriage to Pelops. The second account revolves around conflict between the two cities of Elis and Pisa. The Eleans selected a wise old woman to settle disputes, and among her duties was weaving a robe for Hera and conducting games in her honor. Pausanias discusses Mount Typaeum, which was where women were taken and thrown to their death if they were caught observing the Olympic Games; however, later he states that women were not debarred from looking on at the games.[27]

Although women could not compete in the Olympic Games, women could own the horses that competed in the Olympics and other festivals. Toward the end of the pre-Christian era, girls competed in short-distance races in the Pythian, Isthmian, and Nemean Games.[28]

However, historical evidence indicates that when examined chronologically, the fact is that "little women's sport existed and that it was
insignificant."[29]

The Ancient Olympic Games

> There are enough irksom and troublesome things in life; aren't things
> just as bad at the Olympic festival? Aren't you scorched there by the
> fierce heat? Aren't you crushed in the crowd? Isn't it difficult to
> freshen yourself up? Doesn't the rain soak you to the skin? Aren't you
> bothered by the noise, the din, and other nuisances? But it seems to
> me that you are well able to bear and indeed gladly endure all this,
> when you think of the gripping spectacles that you will see.

These were the questions and observations made by Epictetus, who
lived in the second century A.D., to a friend who was about to begin the
trip to Olympia to watch the ancient Olympic Games (Dissertations 16,
23–9). For almost anybody who has attended the modern Olympic
Games as a mere spectator, the timeless questions of Epictetus remain
valid today.

There were numerous athletic festivals in Greece; nearly every city-
state and small town celebrated festivals where athletic competition was
the primary activity. Banned from the Olympic Games, women held
their own athletic contests in honor of Hera, the sister of Zeus, who
later became his wife as well. The Athenians held hundreds of festivals
over the years that were mainly religious in purpose, as are the probable origins of the Olympic Games.

Seven seventy-six B.C. provides the first recorded evidence of the
existence of the Olympic Games. Coroebus of Elis had the honor of
being recognized as the first Olympic champion. The games continued
to operate until 394 A.D. when Theodosius, Emperor of Rome, abolished
them as a pagan ritual. The last victor of the ancient Olympics was an
Armenian named Varastad.

The origins of the Olympic Games are based on mythology and religious festivals. However, it is known that around 1000 B.C. the small
town of Olympia became a shrine to Zeus who, according to legend, lived
on Mt. Olympus with eleven other gods who comprised the Olympic
Council. Religious festivals that honored their gods were very popular in
Greece, and Olympia was no exception. The athletes competed to honor
Zeus, the most important deity of the ancient Greeks, and had to take
an oath and swear to Zeus that they would play fair. In the second century A.D., Pausanias wrote the following account of the oath to Zeus:

> But the Zeus in the Bouleuterion is all of the images of Zeus most likely
> to strike terror into the hearts of sinners. He is surnamed Horkios
> [Oath god] and in each hand he holds a thunderbolt. Beside this image
> it is the custom for athletes, their fathers and their brothers, as well as
> their trainers, to swear an oath upon slices of boar's flesh that in noth-
> ing will they sin against the Olympic Games. . . .[30]

Figure 3.8
Entrance into the stadium at Olympia.

Figure 3.9
Ruins at Olympia.

Figure 3.10
Starting blocks. Athletes would set their feet or toes in the grooves and perhaps use a sprinter's start or upright start.

Figure 3.11
Bowl painting illustrating the Pentathlon.

When the athletes were caught breaking the rules or using other unsportsmanlike conduct, they were assessed fines that were spent to erect statues to Zeus. Although cheating was frowned upon, it did happen. In one instance, a father was so eager that his son emerge as an Olympic champion that he bribed the father of his son's opponent to "throw the match." They were caught and heavily fined. Over the years the religious festivals at Olympia became very popular and attracted athletes and spectators from around Greece.

Early Olympic Games had but one event, the Stade, a footrace of about 200 meters. By 724 B.C. another event was added, the meter race, and in 720 B.C. a "long run" of approximately 4800 meters was added to the program. Wrestling and the Pentathlon (which consisted of five events: jumping, the swift footrace, discus, javelin, and wrestling), were added in 708 B.C., chariot races in 608 B.C., followed by boxing in 623 B.C. and the race in armor in 520 B.C. The chronological order of Olympic events is listed in Table 3.1.

Athletic facilities during the early stages of development were rather primitive. Construction of permanent buildings began approximately 550 B.C. and culminated with a stadium (seating capacity 40,000), gymnasium, palaestra, and hippodrome. A temple dedicated to Zeus was erected, along with a Treasury building that housed the gifts brought to honor Zeus. There was even a hotel erected that housed the officials and visiting VIPs. It was known as the Leonidaion, named after Leonidas of Naxos, who built it in 4 B.C.

Table 3.1
Introduction of Events into Olympic Games

Olympiad	Year	Competition
1	776	Stade race
14	724	Diaulos or double stade
15	720	Dolichos or long race
18	708	Pentathlon and wrestling
23	688	Boxing
25	680	Chariot racing with teams of four
33	648	Pankration and horse racing
37	632	Footracing and wrestling for boys
38	628	Pentathlon for boys (immediately discontinued)
41	616	Boxing for boys
65	520	Race in armour
70	500	Chariot racing with mule (apene)
71	496	Race for mares (calpe)
77	472	Duration of Festival and Sequence of Events Legislated
84	444	Apene and calpe abandoned
93	408	Chariot racing with two horse teams
96	396	Competitions for heralds and trumpeters
99	384	Chariot racing for colts with teams of four
128	268	Chariot racing for colts with two horse teams
131	256	Race for colts
145	200	Pankration for boys

Source: Maxwell L. Howell, "The Ancient Olympic Games: A Reconstruction of the Program." *The Seward Staley Address of the North American Society for the History of Sport* (Boston, April 1975).

Every fourth year, three heralds left Olympia to travel all of the Greek world to announce the commencement of the Olympic Games. A sacred truce (together with a fine) by order of Delphic oracle, was to be observed that permitted athletes and spectators making their way to Olympia to travel in safety. Even Alexander the Great himself had to pay money to an Athenian who was robbed by some of his soldiers while traveling to Olympia. Only male citizens of Greece could compete in and watch the games. Women were not allowed to observe or participate as athletes, with the exception of the priestess Demeter, who observed the games. The rules of the Olympic Games were very explicit: Athletes and their trainers had to arrive in Elis, a short distance from Olympia, no later than one month before the start of the games. They had to prove that they were citizens without a criminal record, the athletes had to take an oath that they would compete fairly, and they had to swear to Zeus that they had trained for the previous ten months.

The most visible officials of the ancient Olympics were known as the Hellanodikai. Their preparations began some ten months prior to the start of the games. They lived in a complex called the hellanodikaion, located in the city of Elis, that was reserved exclusively for

Figure 3.12
Greek athletes embraced the concepts of Agon and Crete. They strove to perfect their bodies. The Greek who let his body deteriorate was a disgrace and was severely punished if he lived in Sparta. Photo courtesy of The Olympic Museum, Lausanne, Switzerland.

them. From the information available to us, we know that these officials were chosen by lot, and during most of the Olympics there were ten Hellanodikai on hand to oversee the games. One of them was selected to act as a general supervisor, and the others were assigned to the different events. According to Swaddling (1980), the first group of Hellanodikai were in charge of the equestrian competition, the second group was in charge of the pentathlon, and the third group was charged to oversee all of the remaining events. They were in charge of assessing fines and administering punishment for any infraction of the rules. These punishments could be very harsh. Both athletes and their trainers could be publicly flogged by the mastigophorai (whipbearers) if their failure to play by the rules was especially sinister.[31] These officials wore the purple robes of royalty because of their lofty position and authority. They took an oath to be fair in their judging and never reveal anything that they learned that would give one athlete an advantage over another.

For a minimum of one month prior to the start of the Olympics, the athletes were required to live in Elis and train under the watchful eyes of the Hellanodikai. These judges made sure that the athletes were indeed qualified to compete. Chariots and horses were examined to make certain they were within the rules. The training was harsh, for the ancient Greeks did not taper off or rest up immediately before competition as today's athletes do. The Greek athletes were careful to obey every command of the Hellansodikai and had to follow a strict diet as well.[32]

Two days prior to the start of competition, the Hellanodikai left Elis and, along with the procession of athletes, made their way to Olympia. Following the athletes were the coaches, trainers, horses and their owners, jockeys, and of course the chariots. This must have been an imposing and inspiring sight, watching all these Olympians march along the Sacred Way toward Olympia. Along the way, they stopped at the fountain of Piera, which was situated at the border between Elis and Olympia, to conduct religious rituals. At the end of the first day, the participants spent the night in Letrini.[33] The next morning they awoke and followed the Sacred Way through the valley of the Alpheios to Olympia, where they were greeted by thousands of spectators.[34]

With both opening and closing ceremonies, the atmosphere surrounding the Olympic Games was a spectacle itself. People sold food, businessmen arranged "deals," delegations from various city-states discussed political matters, and fortune tellers, souvenir sellers, musicians, dancers, along with pimps and prostitutes, did a brisk business.

In 472 B.C. the Olympics were reorganized into a five-day event[35] and remained virtually unchanged for the next eight hundred years. Two and a half days were devoted to competition, and the remaining days were primarily religious in nature. Table 3.2 shows a typical sequence of events.

The importance of athletic ability in Greek culture and the legendary display of athletic prowess at Olympia was a topic of conversation for centuries. In the second century A.D., Lucian writes:

> If the Olympic Games were being held now . . . you would be able to see for yourself why we attach such great importance to athletics. No-one can describe in mere words the extraordinary . . . pleasure derived from them and which you yourself would enjoy if you were seated among the spectators feasting your eyes on the prowess and stamina of the athletes, the beauty and power of their bodies, their incredible dexterity and skill, their invincible strength, their courage, ambition, endurance, and tenacity. You would never . . . stop applauding them.[36]

This timeless tribute to Olympic athletes by Lucian brings to us images of superbly trained ancient athletes taking part in a festival of sport that was as noble as it was religious. Lucien and Epictetus were not the only individuals who extolled the heroics of Olympic athletes. The Greek poet Pindar (518–446 B.C.) lived several centuries before Epictetus and Lucien attended the Olympic games, the Pythian games, the Nemean games, and the Isthmian games. Pindar relates the magnif-

Table 3.2

Ancient Olympic Festival (472 or 468 B.C.)

First Day

Morning
The Inauguration of the Festival
The Oath Taking Ceremony
The Contests for Heralds and Trumpeters
Afternoon
Contests for Boys

Second Day

Morning
Equestrian Events
Afternoon
Pentathlon (Discus, Jumping, Javelin, Running, Wrestling)

Third Day

Morning
Main Sacrifice to Zeus
Afternoon
Footraces (Dolichos, Stade Race, Diaulos)
Evening
Ritual Banquet?

Fourth Day

Heavy Events (Wrestling, Boxing, Pankration)
Hoplite Race

Fifth Day

Prize Giving Ceremony
A Service of Thanksgiving?
A Banquet?

Source: Ludwig Drees, *Olympia: Gods, Artists, and Athletes* (New York: Drager, 1968).

icent athletic feats in a series of lyric poems known as "odes." He wrote fourteen Olympic Odes, twelve Pythian Odes, eleven Nemean Odes, and eight Isthmian Odes.

Over the centuries the original purpose and spirit of the Olympics as a religious ceremony for Greek citizens gave way to athletes who competed for fortune and fame. Citizenship was no longer a requirement, and an athlete would often hire out to the city that paid him the most money and attendant luxuries.

The games deteriorated after the conquest of Greece by Rome, and the facilities at Olympia were neglected. The Roman Emperor Theodosius was converted to Christianity and could no longer tolerate the pagan athletic spectacles that the once-honored games had become and put an end to them in 394 A.D., 1,170 years after Coroebus was recorded as Olympic champion.

Summary

Perhaps no other civilization in the history of the world embraced athletic competition and intellectual development as did the ancient Greeks. The foundation for the tradition of athletics that is emblematic of the Hellenes was influenced in part by the Egyptians, the people of Crete, and quite possibly by the Phoenicians. Various athletic contests and games were carried to mainland Greece by merchant sailors from distant lands. We can assume that during the course of military expeditions, the Greeks adopted some of the ways of their conquered enemies, including games and sports that appealed to them.

As a general idea, the Greeks believed in the physical development of the body in a way that was aesthetic as well as athletic. Upon this concept there was agreement. Although athletics was a priority, intellectual nourishment and development as we know it was not uniform among the politically diverse Greeks. Although Athens was emblematic of cultural and political supremacy, Sparta in contrast was a cultural desert and politically represented a ruthless and repressive government. It was not unusual for the Greeks to wage war against each other or come to the aid of another Greek city-state when attacked by non-Greeks.

Athletic festivals emerged on both the local and national level and ultimately became institutionalized, which afforded a meeting place for all Greek men and, more important, provided an arena in which the city-states and their quasinationalistic athletes could compete. The earlier concept of the magnificent athletic festivals of the Panhellenic Games, based on honor to Zeus and athletic ideals of honesty and fair play, gave way to the era of professional athletes that represented the city that was able to pay the most money. In the early sixth century B.C., the Athenian King Solon offered the amount of 500 drachmae to Athenian athletes who were victorious at Olympia, and he offered smaller amounts of money and prizes to Athenian athletes who won at lesser athletic festivals. Under Roman rule the athletic festivals continued to operate but no longer served as an agency of physical education or in promoting individual excellence. The Greeks gradually started to place less and less importance on individual physical development, and by the fourth century A.D. the intellectual and athletic ideal of developing the all-around individual who was an educated citizen, an athlete, and a soldier in the Athenian sense had vanished.

Discussion Questions

1. Did the Greeks develop their own games and sports without outside influences, or does it appear that other cultures may have contributed to the development of Greek athletics?

2. What is meant by dualism?

3. Can dualism affect epistemological beliefs?

4. Generally speaking, where did Socrates and Plato place the development of the body in relation to development of the mind? What was their rationale?

5. Explain the two opposing ideas of physical education that existed in ancient Greece according to Fairs.

6. Describe the relationship of the military to physical education in ancient Greek culture. Does this same relationship exist today?

7. What role did religion play in ancient Greek sport?

8. What was the role of women in sport in ancient Greece? Were all the city-states the same in this respect?

9. How did the Greeks view the body? How, if at all, does their position (view of the body) affect contemporary society today?

10. Were the ancient Greek athletes "amateurs"? Where does this idea come from?

11. Describe the organization, training, rules, and events that were essential to the success and popularity of the ancient Olympic games.

12. Read some of the odes that Pindar devoted to Greek athletes. What are some of the themes that Pindar seems to stress?

13. What similarities can you identify in the way Greek athletes trained thousands of years ago with the way athletes train today?

14. In your opinion, were the athletes of ancient Greece better overall athletes than the athletes of today? Why or why not?

Suggestions for Further Reading

Balme, M. "Attitudes to Work and Leisure in Ancient Greece." *Greece and Rome* 1, no. 2 (October 1984): 140–152.

Cahn, J. L. "Contributions of Plato to Thought on Physical Education, Health, and Recreation." Doctoral diss., New York University, 1942.

Crowther, N. B. "Weightlifting in Antiquity: Achievement and Training." *Greek, Roman, and Byzantine Studies* 24 (1977): 111–120.

Dyson, H. G. Geoffery. "The Ancient Olympic Games." *Journal of the Canadian Association for Health, Physical Education, and Recreation* 42, no. 4 (March–April 1976): 3–7.

Fleming, W. *Arts and Ideas.* New York: Holt, Rinehart, and Winston, 1963.

Hyde, W. W. "The Pentathalon Jump." *American Journal of Philology* 59, no. 4, whole number 236, (1938): 405–417.

Lee, H. M. "Athletic Arete in Pindar." *Ancient World* 7, nos. 1–2 (March 1983): 31–37.

Mouratidis, J. "Games and Festivals as a Unifying Force in Ancient Greece." *Physical Education Review* 8, no. 1 (1985): 41–49.

Nagy, B. "The Athenian Athlothetai." *Greek, Roman, and Byzantine Studies* 19, no. 4 (1978): 307–313.

Pindar. *The Odes of Pindar. Including the principal fragments, with an introduction and an English translation by Sir John Sandys,* revised ed. (London: W. Heinemann; Cambridge, Mass.: Harvard University Press, 1937).

Raubitschek, A. E. "The Agonistic Spirit in Greek Culture." *Ancient World* 7, nos. 1–2 (March 1983): 3–7.

Romano, D. G. "The Ancient Stadium: Athletes and Arete." *Ancient World* 7, nos. 1–2 (March 1983): 9–16.

Seltman, C. "Life in Ancient Crete-II: Atlantis." *History Today* 2, no. 5 (May 1952): 332–343.

Sutts, A. "Our Greek Heritage." *Journal of Physical Education, Recreation, and Dance* 55, no. 1 (January 1984): 27–28.

Swaddling, J. "Olympic Glory." *Natural History* (June 1984): 60–74, 77.

Young, D. C. "Professionalism in Archaic and Classical Greek Athletes." *Ancient World* 7, nos. 1–2 (March 1985): 45–51.

Notes

1. Labib Boutros, *Phoenician Sport—Its Influence on the Origin of the Olympic Games* (Amsterdam: J. C. Gieben, Publisher, 1981), 1.

2. Ibid., 1–2.

3. John R. Fairs, "The Influence of Plato and Platonism on the Development of Physical Education in Western Culture," *Quest* IX (December 1968): 14–33.

4. Ibid., 14.

5. *Phaedo* and the *Republic*. All references are to B. Jowett, trans., *The Dialogues of Plato* (New York: Washington Square Press, Inc., 1966).

6. *Metaphysical dualism* is the philosophical division of existence into two components: mind and body. Dualism is evident in the very words *mind* and *body*, and is a tradition in the thought and languages of Western civilization.

7. This can be compared with asceticism, where one rejects the body in favor of the promise of spiritual salvation.

8. William Fleming, *Arts and Ideas* (New York: Holt, Rinehart, and Winston, 1966), 43–44.

9. B. Jowett, *Phaedo* and the *Republic*, 62.

10. Ibid., 78.

11. *Phaedo*, 80.

12. *Republic, Book II*, 253.

13. Ibid., 258–259.

14. Ibid., 262–264.

15. Jesse Feiring Williams, "Education Through the Physical," *Journal of Higher Education* 1 (May 1930): 279–282.

16. Charles Harold McCloy, *Philosophical Basis for Physical Education* (New York: F. S. Crofts and Company, 1940), 77–78.

17. William S. Sahakian, *History of Philosophy* (New York: Barnes & Noble, 1968), 63.

18. Ibid., 76–78.

19. James G. Thompson, "Clues to the Location of Minoan Bull-Jumping from the Palace at Knossos," *Journal of Sport History* 16, no. 1 (Spring 1989): 62–69.

20. H. W. Plecket, "Games, Prizes, Athletes, and Ideology: Some Aspects of the History of Sport in the Greco-Roman World," *Stadion* 1 (1975).

21. David C. Young, *The Olympic Myth of Greek Amateur Athletics* (Chicago: Ares Publishers, 1984).

22. Synthia S. Slowikowski, "Alexander the Great and Sport History: A Commentary on Scholarship," *Journal of Sport History* 16, no. 1 (Spring 1989): 73.

23. Allen Guttman, *From Ritual to Record: The Nature of Modern Sports* (New York: Columbia University Press, 1978).

24. *Variae Historiae Aeliani* 14:7, in Clarence Forbes, *Greek Physical Education* (New York: The Century Co., 1929), 33.

25. Deobold B. Van Dalen and Bruce L. Bennett, *A World History of Physical Education*, 2d ed. (Englewood Cliffs, N.J.: Prentice Hall, 1971), 47.

26. Rachel Sargent Robinson, *Sources for the History of Greek Athletics* (Cincinnati, Ohio: Author, 1955), 152.

27. Betty Spears, "A Perspective on the History of Women's Sport in Ancient Greece," *Journal of Sport History* II, no. 2 (Summer 1984): 32–47.

28. William J. Baker, *Sports in the Western World* (Totowa, N.J.: Roman and Littlefield, 1982), 22.

29. Spears, "Women's Sport in Ancient Greece," 46.

30. Descriptions of Greece v. 24.9; Judith Swaddling, *The Ancient Olympic Games* (Published for the Trustees of the British Museum by British Museum Publications, Limited, 1980), 41.

31. Swaddling, *Ancient Olympic Games*, 35, 41.

32. Ibid., 35–36.

33. Ibid., 36.

34. Ludwig Drees, *Olympia: Gods, Artists, and Athletes* (New York: Drager, 1968).

35. Anacharsis 12; Swaddling, *Ancient Olympic Games*, 79.

36. Swaddling, *Ancient Olympic Games*.

c h a *4p* t e r

Rome

General Events B.C.

100–44 Julius Caesar

29–19 Virgil wrote *The Aeneid*

27–A.D. 14 Augustus reigned

A.D.

c. 16 Maison Carrée at Nimes

c. 50 Pont du Gard at Nimes built

54–68 Nero reigned

70 Titus captured Jerusalem; temple destroyed

79 Eruption of Vesuvius; Pompeii and Herculaneum destroyed

81 Arch of Titus, Rome, built

82 Colosseum, Rome, finished

c. 93 Quintilian wrote *Institutes of Oratory*

96–180 Antonine Age; Roman Empire reached pinnacle of power and prosperity

96–98 Nerva, emperor

98–117 Trajan, emperor

c. 100 Suetonius wrote *Lives of the Caesars*

100 Pliny the Younger delivered Panegyric to Trajan before Roman Senate

100–102 Trajan's first Dacian campaign

105–106 Trajan's second Dacian campaign

110 Via Iraiana built between Benevento and Brindisi, Baths of Trajan built

113 Forum of Trajan built, Column of Trajan erected

114 Arch of Trajan built at Benevento

117–138 Hadrian, emperor

120–124 Pantheon, Rome, built

138–161 Antoninus Pius, emperor

161–180 Marcus Aurelius, emperor

217 Baths of Caracalla, Rome, built

Philosophers and Literary Figures

80 B.C.–A.D. 14 Golden Age of Literature

106–43 B.C. Cicero

c. 96–55 Lucretius

84–54 Catullus

70–19 Vergil

65–8 Horace

59–A.D. 17 Livy

43–A.D. 17 Ovid

A.D. 14–117 Silver Age of Literature

3 B.C.–A.D. 65 Seneca

23–79 Pliny the Elder

c. 66 Petronius died

c. 90 Epictetus flourished

35–95 Quintilian

40–c. 102 Martial

c. 46–120 Plutarch

55–c. 117 Tacitus

c. 60–c. 135 Juvenal

62–113 Pliny the Younger

75–c. 150 Suetonius

c. 160 Apulius flourished

c. 200 Tertulian flourished

Source: William Fleming, Arts and Ideas (New York: Holt, Rinehart, and Winston, 1963), 2.

Introduction

No one knows the precise date when Rome was given the status of the Eternal City. This title continues to reflect its location and historical position as the gateway both to Mediterranean culture and to civilizations that perished long ago. What was to eventually become one of the most legendary and prolific civilizations the world has known grew out of a small community known as Latuim situated near the Tiber River and the much acclaimed seven hills of Rome. In 509 B.C. these "Romans" defeated the Etruscans, a civilization of which we know very little even to this day.

After the Etruscans were defeated, the Roman Republic was formed, which was in effect an aristocratic oligarchy.[1] The Roman Republic lasted until 146 B.C., the year Rome finally conquered Greece by defeating and sacking the city of Corinth. Between 146 B.C. and 27 B.C. Rome survived a number of rulers and self-serving politicians until the establishment of the Empire in 27 B.C., which lasted until A.D. 476 when the Teutonic leader Odoacer ousted the last Roman emperor in the West. The Roman Empire was ultimately divided into two geographical regions: the Western Empire, centered in Rome, and the Eastern or Byzantine Empire, located in Constantinople (what is now Istanbul, Turkey). The Byzantine Empire survived the fall of Rome and lasted until 1453. The influence of the Greeks on Roman civilization was significant, and where appropriate will be discussed to provide the student with an informative cross-cultural comparison. We can illustrate this point by highlighting the Greek influence on Nero.

The influence of Greek culture upon the Emperor Nero, who reigned from 54–68 A.D., was very profound. He was more concerned about his achievements in the arts than with his achievements as a ruler. He preferred the company of Greeks to that of his fellow Romans because the Greeks could relate to his exquisite taste in art, literature, theater, music, and poetry. Nero had an enormous ego and believed that the Greeks alone were worthy of his genius, whereas his fellow Romans were unappreciative of his grandiose visions and cultural refinements. He enjoyed the company of Greeks so much that once, while in Greece, he received word that his presence in Rome was urgently required. He refused to return immediately, and instead he completed another one of his concert tours which, Nero was certain, were enjoyed by all who attended.[2]

The Romans had a fondness for size and spectacle, and the Colosseum, an arena used primarily for gladiatorial contests and other spectacles, provides us with a relevant example later in this chapter. Nero was no different in this regard. He was in need of a house worthy of his stature and position. The young emperor drew up plans and ordered that the construction on his Golden House begin as soon as possible. It was to be the largest and most opulent palace yet built by an emperor. Visitors to his house would have to pass in front of a statue of Nero that was more than 120 feet high! Once inside, the visitors must have been overwhelmed as they wandered among the many rooms adorned in ivory and other expensive accouterments. Panels could be removed from various rooms to release a perfumed mist or discharge a cascade of freshly gathered roses. The Golden House had a huge pool, artificial lake, gardens, and lawns upon which exotic animals roamed freely.[3]

Nero did not endear himself to his fellow Romans. He fancied himself as a gift to Rome from the gods; however, this feeling was not shared by everybody. Nero was so conceited about his many talents that he demanded that the Greeks hold a special Olympic Games so he could compete. He competed in the chariot race and to no one's surprise was declared the winner, adding the title of Olympic champion to his many accomplishments. Nero perceived himself as "larger than life." He died by his own hand when he was thirty-one years old.

The recipient of one of Nero's appointments was Vespasian. He served Nero as a soldier in Africa and was also sent to Palestine to subdue the Jews, who were causing trouble for Nero. Vespasian eventually became Emperor of Rome and began work on the vast amphitheater that would become known the world over as the Colosseum. This enormous monument was built upon the remains of an artificial lake that Nero had constructed to adorn his Golden House.

Cross-Cultural Analysis of the Greeks and Romans

In comparison, the Romans did not display the cultural genius and intellectual acumen of the Greeks, which we know bothered Nero. With the possible exception of Greek music, most Romans were not comfortable with the all-around development of the individual that emphasized the aesthetic and educated aspects of Greek culture. Nor did the Romans develop monumental philosophical or scientific contributions. The Romans were great civil engineers, however, and many Roman roads are still in use today.

Roman civilization had instead as its foundation a pragmatic, utilitarian focus that sought to emphasize the practical and purposeful. Romans were results oriented, deliberate, and methodical in their evaluation of civic responsibilities and duties. As a result, the aesthetic, abstract, and harmonious approach to life advocated by the Greeks had little appeal. Like the Greeks, the Romans were polytheistic. The Roman gods and goddesses were essentially the Greek ones, with a few name changes. For example, Zeus, the chief deity of the Greeks, became Jupiter, the chief god of the Romans; Hera, the wife of Zeus, became Juno; and Ares, who was the god of war in Greece, became the Roman god Mars. During the Empire a substantial number of "blue-collar" Romans rejected the mythological, businesslike gods of the state and began to embrace Christianity. Some chose life without religion and turned to the post-Aristotelian schools of philosophy for guidance and understanding.

In contrast with the Greeks, the Romans were not profound, speculative, or metaphysical thinkers. Metaphysical questions and speculations about the nature of things were not at all conducive to the utilitarian and pragmatic characteristics of Roman thought. Being purposeful and practical people, the Romans were quick to recognize and adapt the cultural, scientific, philosophical, architectural, and engineering achievements of the countries they conquered. Thus, the Romans imported, refined, and added their own signatures to science, philosophy, architecture, mathematics, and so on, that were acquired during their conquests.

Philosophical Orientation

During the fourth and third centuries B.C., the Roman Republic was emblematic of an ordered civilization where economic and political freedom was prevalent. The influence religion had on education was significant in that moral and military training took precedence over intellectual achievement, which no doubt must have pleased Mars, the Roman war god. Roman religion was relatively spiritless and practical:

> Their religion, both family and state, lacked the beauty and stately ceremonies of the Greeks, lacked the lofty faith and aspiration after faith that characterized the Hebrew and later Christian faith, was singularly wanting in awe and mystery, and was formal and mechanical in character.[4]

Prior to the establishment of the Empire, the early Romans were adamant that character formation was critical to the development of its citizens, and ultimately the survival of the Republic. However, when the ordered Republic collapsed, the Empire emerged, and it became the philosopher's task to provide the individual with a code of conduct that would enable him to "pilot his way through the sea of life . . . based on a certain spiritual and moral independence."[5] As a result, philosopher-directors were asked to serve the same tasks that spiritual directors, or priests, did in the Christian world.

The Roman concept of society was cosmopolitan. The Greeks, in contrast, believed that the cultures beyond their shores were inhabited by Philistines and barbarians who were culturally inferior. The cosmopolitan and "blended" world advocated by the multicultural Romans was anathema to the eugenics proposed by Socrates, Plato, Aristotle, and their Greek brethren. The cosmopolitan society that evolved under Roman leadership was bound to an idea of individualism in which philosophy would respond by focusing on the individual for providing guidance in life. This philosophical orientation dispensed by the philosopher-directors was based predominantly on ethical and practical doctrines advocated by the philosophers Zeno (Stoicism) and Epicutus (Epicureanism). These two philosophical schools competed with Christianity during the Empire and are compared to Christianity by Copleston:

> Insistence on ethics alone leads to an ideal of spiritual independence and self-sufficiency such as we find in both Stoicism and Epicureanism, while insistence on religion tends rather to assert dependence on a

Transcendental Principle and to ascribe the purification of the self to the action of the Divine. . . . both tendencies, the tendency to insist on the ethical, the self-sufficient perfection of the personality or the acquisition of the true moral personality, and the tendency to insist on the attitude of the worshipper toward the Divine or the need of the non-self-sufficient human to unite himself with God contributed to the same want, the want of the individual in the Greco-Roman world to find a sure basis for his individual life, since the religious attitude too brought with it a certain independence vis-a-vis the secular Empire.[6]

Liberally interpreted, the above passage states that Romans desired answers to metaphysical questions and a sure basis for the meaning of life, and that they used both philosophical and religious means to obtain answers to their questions. Both methods were encouraged in the Roman Empire, which *de facto* separated church and state.

The Cynics

To discuss Stoicism it is helpful to examine Cynicism, the philosophical school that preceded and influenced Stoicism. Prior to the arrival of Zeno in Athens sometime between 320 and 315 B.C., there appeared a group of disciples who were devoted to the teaching of Socrates and were known as Cynics because of their disdain for the common amenities of life. Both Plato and Zeno were decisively influenced by Socrates but were not enamored with the Cynics. The Cynics believed that Socrates' most important ideas were (1) his independence of character, and (2) his indifference to circumstances. Like Socrates, the Cynics believed that "no harm can come to a good man." However, they ignored one of the most fundamental beliefs of Socrates, that "Virtue is Knowledge." Jones provides a concise and insightful view of Cynic beliefs:

> Since poverty, pain, suffering, and death obviously can and do come to good men, the Cynics reasoned that none of these is really bad. The truly virtuous man will be indifferent to everything that happens to him. . . . Small decencies and proprieties of social intercourse, as well as the larger matter of political relationship, are without value and therefore should be ignored.[7]

This view differed considerably with Socrates, who in the *Crito* refused to escape from prison because his respect for "the laws" were without compromise. Although the Cynics did not influence Plato, traces of their ideas are evident in the ascetic ways of the Christians during the Middle Ages.

The Stoics

Initially Zeno was influenced by the Cynics but became uncomfortable with their anarchistic views. Zeno was concerned with the essence of political and social life, which not surprisingly were of paramount concern to both Plato and Aristotle. In approximately 300 B.C. Zeno established his own philosophical school, called Stoicism, which was derived from the site (*Stoa* translated into English means *porch*) from which Zeno lectured.

The Stoics, although influenced by Plato and Aristotle, rejected various beliefs put forth by Plato (the transcendental universal) and Aristotle (the concrete universal).[8] Through discussion and contemplation the Stoics concluded that only the individual exists, and what knowledge we do have is knowledge of specific objects. Interestingly, this belief is based on their epistemology, or how one acquired knowledge. Whereas Plato and Socrates did not trust the body and the subsequent acquisition of information and knowledge through sense-perception, the Stoics believed that *all* knowledge is based on sense-perception. As a result, the philosophical position of the body in Stoic doctrine was of significant importance, especially when compared with the position of the body in the *Phaedo*, in which Socrates condemns the evils of the body. As presented in the previous chapter, Socrates believed that the body deceived us, and while we are in company with the body we cannot know truth. Only after death, when we are no longer chained to the evils of the body, will the soul know truth in its purest form. In contrast, the Stoics emphasized personal conduct and the attainment of personal happiness in a world that required the Stoic to accept whatever life and body nature dealt him and to remain optimistic. The ethical function of the Stoics "consists essentially in submission to the divinely appointed order of the world and no doubt gave rise to the famous Stoic maxim 'Live according to Nature.'"[9]

The appeal of Stoicism to the Romans was grounded in this sense of individualism, its experiential basis, and also in part to the principle of conduct that was essential to Roman rule and organization. The great Roman Stoic Seneca looked on philosophy as the science of conduct. Self-development and an acceptance of the fate nature has dealt each person reflected Roman ideology as well. Copleston provides an illuminating look at the Stoic conduct: "Character, then, is the chief point stressed in truly virtuous conduct—which is fulfillment of duty (and) is performed only by the wise men. Moreover, he is lord over his own life, and may commit suicide."[10]

The Epicureans

Epicureanism was much like Stoicism in that it rejected metaphysical or religious claims on one's behavior. It rejected Plato's idealism by arguing that the body and its senses are "real" and are the best way of coming to "know" reality. Epicureanism, however, also promoted the development of cultured individuals who sought happiness and pleasure through the joys of the mind. The relationship of the mind and the body, then, was that we have greater control over the mind than the body, so we should concentrate on the friendship of gifted and noble men, the peace and contentment that comes from fair conduct, and good morals and aesthetic enjoyments to obtain pleasure and happiness.[11] One consequence of this philosophy was that the body and the senses are considered a viable way of knowing pleasure and happiness. As a result, the philosophical position of the body, as well as its role in the epistemological process, is more important to Epicurean thought than it was to

Platonic thought. What is important to remember, though, is that the ideas of friendship, peace, contentment, nobility, and pleasure are the objects of knowledge. The sensations of pleasure are not supposed to be the end result of Epicureanism; sensations are how we come to know these ideas. Indeed, Epicureanism is often incorrectly associated only with bodily pleasures. So while the body is definitely more important in this philosophy than in those philosophies that emphasize ideas, it is still the ideas that are important.

Marcus Tullius Cicero

Marcus Tullius Cicero (106–43 B.C.), the great Roman orator and philosopher, had a stormy career as a politician partly because of his disgust for the unethical politics engaged in by Julius Caesar, Pompey, and Crassus. These three rulers banished Cicero from Rome due to his social and political criticism of their activities. Because of the danger of attacking the rulers directly, Cicero became a social critic of arena sports because he believed they were representative of the larger social and political problems of Rome, Cicero's chief concerns. Cicero was very concerned with ethics and how man can attain the highest moral virtue. In this regard Cicero was heavily influenced by Antiochus of Ascalon and to a lesser extent Phaedrus the Epicurean, the Stoics Diodorus and Zeno, and the academician Philo.[12]

Antiochus

Antiochus' ethical system sought the achievement of ultimate good, which he interpreted as the ability to live in accordance with nature. To achieve this goal, one concentrated on the total development of all of one's capacities.[13] Antiochus stated that "wisdom's task was to perfect the whole man neglecting no side of him."[14] The optimum development of both mind and body was absolutely essential to Antiochus and his followers. To quote Antiochus, "The full and perfect philosophy was that which investigated the chief goal of man, left no part (of) either mind or body uncared for."[15] The impact of the Greek philosopher Antiochus, especially on the development of both mind and body, was attractive to the Stoic attitude of the Romans.

Sport and Physical Education

Over the course of a millennium the Romans went through a number of political and social changes. The Stoic and Epicurean philosophies had a profound impact on the social and political order of Rome during both the Republic and Empire. Eventually these philosophies gave way to a morally corrupt and hedonistic social and political order that collapsed from within. We shall examine the various forms of sport and physical education while keeping in mind that a number of social historians and sport sociologists adhere to the position that sport tends to reflect society and society reflects sport. In this framework the various forms of sport that dominate a society's existence are emblematic of its moral health or illness.

Under the Empire, the sporting activities of the Romans had evolved into massive spectacles of entertainment, debauchery, and carnage. However, this was not always the situation. During the early years of the Republic, physical exercise was enjoyed by the citizens of the fledgling Republic, although not nearly to the extent as was practiced in Greece.

As a culture, the Romans enjoyed ball games based on throwing and catching and a form of handball. The baths or thermae, as they were called, were very popular. Mild exercise, not the intensely competitive physical exercise of the Greeks, had great appeal to the Romans. It was a common sight to see men, in groups or alone, heading toward the baths after lunch where they might engage in mild exercise such as ball playing prior to entering the baths. The idea was to work up a sweat before entering the waters, not to engage in strenuous physical competition. Before the beginning of the Christian era there were two hundred baths available in Rome, and by A.D. 400 there were around nine hundred. Most of the thermae were privately owned, but some of the larger ones were public.[16]

The Romans were quick to accept the concept of health gymnastics because the maintenance of health was a worthwhile and natural goal for them, and to this end Greek physicians were used to instruct Romans in the benefits of health-related exercise.

As in Greece, the Romans paid homage to their gods to insure a bountiful harvest or curry their favor, offered prayers for prosperity, and made other similar requests. Physical activities such as footraces, ball playing, equestrian displays, and wrestling contests allowed mere mortals to exhibit their physical skills before the gods who were thought to be in attendance during religious holidays. Religion was of considerable importance to the Romans, and like the Greeks, they had numerous gods. The Romans believed they were selected by providence to rule the world. As a result the divinely inspired and guided Roman rulers became very pragmatic and utilitarian where physical training was concerned.

Military Training

The military was extremely important in both social and political contexts of Roman life. The Legion was the primary unit of the Roman army. Each Legion consisted of three to six thousand foot soldiers and one to two hundred mounted soldiers. The Roman Legion was legendary in the social fabric of Roman society and was supported by the Stoic and Epicurean virtues of honor and duty. In Rome the training of youth had but one purpose: to make them obedient, disciplined, and ready to be a warrior. With this in mind, the Romans developed their own system of physical training and did not borrow from the Greeks in military training techniques. Greek athletics were considered too individualistic for Roman tastes and did not promote the "team unity" that the Romans demanded.

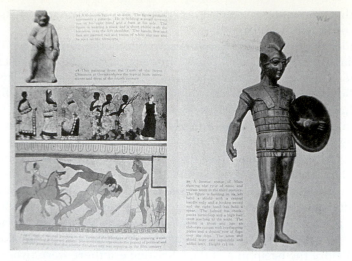

Figure 4.1

Mars, the Roman god of war.

The Campus Martinus was a large open area with a temple dedicated to Mars, the Roman god of war. It was here that fathers would bring their sons to teach them the necessary physical skills that were required prior to their induction into manhood, signified by the Roman Toga, and then into the military. Skills such as running, jumping, swimming, wrestling, horsemanship, boxing, fencing, archery, and complete obedience to commands were taught at the Campus Martinus in Rome and at other locations throughout the land. These physical activities had a dual purpose: basic military skills would be learned, and the benefits of healthful exercise could also be enjoyed. War was the prestige profession of the Romans, which necessitated brutal methods for training the body. For instance, twenty-mile, forced marches were made about three times per month at four miles per hour carrying packs that weighed up to eighty-five pounds.[17]

Claudius Galen

Galen (A.D. 130–200) began the study of medicine when he was seventeen; he also studied under the Stoics, the Epicureans (which he rejected), the Academicians, and the Peripatetics. Traveling throughout the Mediterranean, Galen became knowledgeable in the healing arts, the surgical procedures of the day, and the use of drugs. He developed a reputation in Alexandria for his ability to treat gladiators. Due to his success, Galen believed himself to be the most accomplished physician of his time: "No one before me has given the true method of treating disease."[18] Galen was one of the first to incorporate medicine and biomechanics into the science of exercise. He was opposed to the professional athletes that were worshipped as heroes, because in his way of thinking they were the antithesis of a healthy citizen. In his work titled "Exhortation on the Choice of a Profession," he states his opinion about the professional athlete as follows:

> In the blessings of the mind athletes have not. . . . Beneath their mass of flesh and blood their souls are stifled as in a sea of mud. . . . Neglecting the old rule of health which prescribes moderation in all things they spend their lives in overexercising, in overeating, and over-sleeping like pigs. . . . They have not health nor have they beauty. Even those who are naturally well proportioned become fat and bloated.[19]

Galen's concern is astonishingly similar to a contemporary issue that today's parents, coaches, physical educators, and others are deeply concerned about: that talented youth will follow the often ill-fated road to perceived quick riches and rewards when the prospects of a career in athletics lures them away from completing their education and eschewing "moderation in all things" as Galen had prescribed. These same youths in Galen's day were apparently only too quick to abandon the halls of education and medicine for the shallow and short lives of the arena and coliseum.

Galen had considerable knowledge about diet, exercise, and the kinship between mind and body and provided this information to the general populace. Galen believed that

> Mental exertion, alone, makes a person thin; but if it is combined with some physical exercise and rivalry ending with pleasure, it very greatly assists the body to health and the mind to intelligence. There is no unimportant advantage of an exercise, if it can help both the body and the mind toward the perfection innate in each.[20]

In "Exercise with the Small Ball" Galen states, "Now I maintain that the best gymnastic exercises of all are those which not only exercise the body but also bring delight to the mind."[21] Galen believed that this type of exercise (with the small ball) was convenient and that it required that all of the body be in constant motion to achieve a conditioning effect. Exercises could be violent (strenuous) ball exercises or of a mild type. In "Maintenance of Health" he identified wrestling, the pancratium, running, and boxing as forms of gymnastic exercises.[22] Galen believed the Greek athletics and gymnastics system to be more beneficial than the Roman approach to conditioning. He advocated both vigorous (performed with strength, not speed), and violent (combining both strength and speed) exercises. For example, the exercise of digging was classified by Galen as a vigorous and strong exercise but one that did not require quick motion. The practice of rope climbing required strength. Jumping continuously without rest was a form of exercise, like hurling the discus, that would develop strength and speed.[23] Galen was the chief fitness expert of his time and one of the first to practice sports medicine. He stressed the development of the body in a harmonious way and, like the orthopedic surgeons and fitness professionals of today, questioned the benefits of running. Galen discouraged running because it wears a person thin, furnishes no training in bravery, and causes some parts of the body to be overtaxed.[24]

Greek Athletics

Galen continued to embrace the Greek ideals of harmoniously proportioned bodies that made them alert and physically fit for both civil and military duties, which was in contrast with the Roman approach that demanded a severe and harsh training program that would produce a disciplined and obedient warrior. In general, the Romans that lived during the Republic were not interested in the formal athletic competitions of the Greeks that demanded, in their view, excessive athletic training. The athleticism of the Greeks was not valued militarily by the utilitarian Romans. Another factor in the Roman disfavor for Greek athletics was the Roman prejudice against the nudity of the Greeks. What little appeal for Greek athletics that did exist was found primarily in the leisured and literate classes. However, Greek athletics (athletik) did enjoy popularity during the era between the late Republic and early Empire. The emperors of this period played a significant role in advancing the benefits of Greek exercise by establishing public facilities such as the Imperial Thermae or baths that also had palaestrae. Nudity was no longer a problem, and the Roman youth enjoyed Greek gymnastics (gymnastik). In contrast to the Roman Republic, Greek athletics fared well during the early Roman Empire, in part because of the changing attitudes of the pragmatic Romans who appreciated the value of exercise and good health that was available through the practice of Greek gymnastics.[25]

Women and Sport

The role of women in athletics as spectators and athletes is not nearly as well documented as that of the men. There is no doubt that athletics were the primary occupation of males due in no small part to the social and political system of both the Republic and the Empire that was based on a system of patriarchy and class stratification. During the first century A.D. the Emperor Domitian instituted races that featured young women during the Capitoline Games in Rome; one hundred years later, during the "Romanized" Olympic Games at Antioch in Syria, girls were attired in shorts and participated in wrestling and running.[26] There is general agreement that the participation of women in sport during both the Empire and Republic was for entertainment and not taken seriously.[27] Swimming and dancing, along with tossing balls back and forth, were activities that women engaged in along with visits to the thermae. Some evidence shows that fashionable women of Rome included weight-training exercises to tone muscles. The account provided by Juvinal of Tome is quite revealing:

> It is at night that she goes to the baths, at night that she gives orders for her oil-flasks and other impediments to be taken there; she loves to sweat among the noise and bustle. When her arms fall to her sides, worn out by the heavy weights, the skillful masseur presses his finger into her body, and makes her bottom resound with his loud smack.[28]

Figure 4.2
The Colosseum was the scene of bloody spectacles and brutal gladiator contests.

Games and Spectacles

Holidays during the era of the Republic emerged from simple religious occasions and agricultural offerings and eventually evolved into elaborate games and festivals that were financed and administered by the government. The government introduced official sporting events during which all businesses were closed, and admission to the games was generally free. Apparently, only during the early period of the Republic did Romans actually participate in games and sports like their counterparts in Greece. Aside from the warriors, the Romans grew into a nation of spectators, not participants, who enjoyed watching slaves and professional athletes perform as competitors while the less fortunate Christians, criminals, and political prisoners were unwilling participants. Roman games and sporting events did not serve as a catalyst for physical education, as happened in Greece. Spectacular gladiatorial fights in the Colosseum between slaves and prisoners, along with horse and chariot races at the Circus Maximus, provided large-scale entertainment and was immensely popular with the Romans. The individual athletic contests of the Greeks had little appeal for the Romans because these athletic activities were boring by Roman standards and did not prepare men for war as well as the Roman method. To the Greeks, the games were great events in which every man aspired to compete; they were contests between citizens to demonstrate their physical fitness. The Romans, however, regarded the games as spectator entertainment.

During the Empire as well as the Republic, the politicians encouraged and produced games and spectacles for blatant political purposes. Politicians would sometimes use their own money to produce spectacular and often bloody events to curry favor with their constituents, who often behaved like thrill-hungry mobs. This process of pandering to the masses came to be known as "panem et circenses" or "bread and circuses," where the people of Rome were fed and entertained in exchange for their support.

J. Carcopino, in *Daily Life in Ancient Rome*, maintains that the Romans were guilty of despicable behavior as a result of the capital executions that occurred in the Colosseum, which was turned into a torture chamber and human slaughterhouse.[29]

The bloody "games" and "despicable behavior" that occurred within the confines of the Colosseum and other venues around the Roman Empire may have been in part the result of the religious rituals of the Etruscans, who we know were conquered by the Romans in 509 B.C. The utilitarian mentality of the Romans resulted in an opportunist approach, which means that they would borrow ideas from people they conquered. For example, when the Etruscans were finally vanquished, the Romans appear to have adopted some of the Etruscan religious customs and other cultural elements that they found to their liking.

The Etruscans enjoyed life's pleasures, feared death, and were cruel and very superstitious. In order to curry favor with the spirits who inhabited the dark and forbidding world of the dead, the Etruscans offered up human sacrifices to the spirits of the underworld. During the time that the Romans were at war with the Etruscans, captured Roman soldiers knew that death was imminent. This was because the religious beliefs of the Etruscans required human sacrifices, and Etruscans preferred to sacrifice Roman prisoners of war to the underworld instead of one of their own. Also, from time to time, the prisoners of the Etruscans were ordered to fight among themselves to the death, like gladiators. The utilitarian nature of the Etruscans seems to be very evident in some of the methods employed by the Romans. Like the Etruscans, the Romans wanted to appease their gods with sacrifices. Like the Etruscans, if it just so happened that along with the sacrifice another problem could be solved (what to do with the prisoners), so be it.

The Etruscan and Greek religious influence on Roman sport continued to manifest itself during the gladiatorial contests conducted during the Empire. When it appeared that a gladiator had been slain, an attendant ran to the lifeless body and determined if death had indeed occurred. The attendant was dressed to resemble Charon, the Etruscan god of fate, or as the Greek deity Hermes Psychopompos. These characters were believed to lead the spirits of the dead to the underworld.

In Chapter 1, we discussed the definition of the term "sport" and noted how the term is subject to debate. It is clear that the Greeks practiced a style of sport that was not at all similar to the Roman version. Noted historian H. A. Harris, who extensively researched sport in the ancient world, wrestled with the issue of a proper definition of sport. He equated sport with the Hellenic (Greek) athletic activities and limited the concept and scope of Roman sport to those aspects of Greek sports that survived or were adopted by the Romans. The bloody and gruesome entertainment spectacular that took place in the Colosseum and other venues throughout the Empire to entertain thrill-hungry mobs were not "sport" by his definition. Harris presents a vivid description of the Greek and Roman concept of athletics:

> In Greece, athletics were the traditional sport, hallowed by centuries of experience. It had links with religious observance; it had enjoyed a Golden Age when it had been the leisure occupation of the wealthy. Even before the first impact of the Romans on the Greek world, it had become public entertainment provided by well-paid professional

performers. . . . In the Roman world, Greek athletics had no tradition of centuries and no belief in a Golden Age to lend a romantic glow. Athletics meetings were introduced by ambitious politicians as an amusement to gratify the people.[30]

Harris clearly sees more differences than similarities between Greek and Roman sport. Politicians during the Republic instituted games and spectacles on a frequent basis to divert the attention of a nation weary and depressed by constant warfare. Roman emperors designated one official holiday after another, and by 173 B.C., fifty-three public holidays existed. This already large number of holidays was added to until A.D. 300, when 200 days were set aside as public holidays, 175 of which were devoted to spectacles and games. Roman games and spectacles served the utilitarian function of pacification, a way for the masses to spend their idle time and to keep from being bored. Roman leaders feared that a bored citizenry could lead to revolution. In addition, the Roman emperors kept the masses entertained to preserve their political fortunes. During the reign of Emperor Marcus Aurelius, 135 days out of the year were devoted to festivals, and during one point in time 17 of the 29 days in April were spent at the circus, amphitheater, or theater.[31]

The Circus Maximus in Rome was the premier hippodrome in the Roman Empire. Situated in the heart of Rome, the Circus was a long rectangle adorned with statues, obelisks, and elaborate arches. One end of the Circus was rounded to facilitate the chariots and horses that raced before as many as a quarter of a million spectators. The Circus Maximus was a 2,000-foot long, 600-foot wide, 3-tiered stadium that appealed to men and women of all social classes, as well as some Christians. Van Dalen and Bennett provide an illuminating look at the chariot races that took place in the Circus Maximus:

> Hours before the games people placed bets while the poor eagerly waited to see if the sponsor of the games would have presents thrown among the audience. Everyone gradually found a seat, the emperor, magistrate, and Vestel Virgins occupying special places. With much ceremony, the sponsor of the game and a procession of men proceeded to an altar to make sacrifice, paid their respects before the imperial box, and then the games commenced.
>
> In vaulted stalls with barred doors, the charioteers awaited the starting signal. There were usually four chariots in each race and in later days as many as twelve. . . . Each driver controlled as many as seven horses although a team of four was the most common. . . . The charioteers struggled for the lead in the seven lap race around the SPINA, a distance of about three miles. Speed alone was not the decisive factor in those races, for a driver had to negotiate sharp turns around a sandy track and avoid the other driver as well. Charioteers employed every device to keep the lead and upset the carts of their competitor. The intense rivalry often resulted in arguments, riots, and bloodshed.[32]

During the era of the Republic, it was unthinkable for men of class and wealth to take part in chariot races, gladiatorial contests, and Greek

Figure 4.3

Chariot race. Notice the strewn bodies under the chariots.

Figure 4.4

The start of the race.

athletics. However, during the Empire, Nero and Caligula, two infamous emperors, participated in these activities.

Between chariot races, riders on horseback displayed their courage and athletic ability by jumping from one galloping horse to another. However, these equestrian feats and the occasional footraces and wrestling matches were not as popular as the well-timed wrestling/ boxing matches. In these contests each pugilist protected his hands by wearing crude leather straps. On the outside of these "gloves" were jagged pieces of metal that would rip the flesh of his opponents to shreds, much to the delight of the spectators.

For sheer carnage, nothing exceeded the gory gladiatorial combats, the slaughter of Christians and criminals, or the staged naval battles made popular by Julius Caesar, Augustus, Claudius, and Nero. In A.D. 52, Emperor Claudius ordered 19,000 slaves onto ships and sent them into battle against each other. Because the slaves were outfitted in armor, more perished by drowning than by bloody combat. The crowds, however, who were not in an ideal location to actually see this spectacle up close, soon lost interest in the slaughter and turned their attention elsewhere.[33]

The most famous landmark in Rome, the Colosseum, was begun under the direction of the Emperor Vespasian (A.D. 69–79) and completed during the reign of his son Titus in A.D. 80. Titus was so proud of the magnificent structure that the opening ceremonies lasted for 100 days. He issued orders that the mint strike a new coin to commemorate the occasion.[34]

The Colosseum, an engineering marvel, is a four-tiered oval with eighty entrances that permitted the giant structure to be emptied in minutes. Awnings protected the approximately 90,000 onlookers from the scorching sun while they enjoyed streams of scented water that spewed from numerous fountains to cool them. The floor of the Colosseum was made of wood and covered with sand, and could be lowered and then flooded to provide yet another venue for deadly naval battles. The Colosseum could be lit at night by torches so those attending the events could escape the oppressive heat of the day.

Around the arena, behind the wall that separated the spectators from the participants, were various types of seating arrangements. Close to the action was an elaborate and beautiful marble terrace where members of the aristocracy would sit in regal splendor. Above this section rose tier after tier of marble seats that were divided into two main sections and several secondary ones. The first section was reserved for wealthy Romans and their guests. The second section was reserved for members of the Roman middle class. Another section was set aside for foreigners and slaves, while a fourth section high above the floor of the Colosseum was for women and the poor, who sat on wooden benches.

A typical agenda of events in the Colosseum began with animal fights in the morning and included elephants, bulls, tigers, lions, panthers, bears, boars, apes, and crocodiles. During the reign of Nero, four hundred tigers lashed into bulls and elephants during one day! As disgusting as the animal fights were, however, they paled in comparison to the frequent slaughter of men and women who were mauled and eaten by lions, tigers, and panthers. Criminals were condemned to death, dressed in animal skins, and thrown to the starved lions much to the delight of the crowd. In this manner the pragmatic Romans were able to dispose of criminals and other undesirables, especially Christians, and provide entertainment at the same time.[35] No doubt this practice had an impact on how Christians viewed sport, and as Van Dalen and Bennett note, "Small wonder that the Christians, themselves often thrown to the lions, developed a fanatical antipathy to the cruelty of the games and carried a general aversion to sport well into the Middle Ages."[36]

The most popular event was the gladiatorial fights, which were generally held in the afternoon after the animal fights. The gladiators were criminals, slaves, and occasionally the adventurous volunteer.[37] They trained in schools especially designed to train gladiators and were taught to kill using swords, spears, daggers, and their hands. These men were required to perform as gladiators for three years and then released into slavery for yet another two years. Needless to say, very few gladiators survived three years. The gladiatorial combats were brutal, and the

Figure 4.5
Moving the animals to the Colosseum.

Figure 4.6
Man against beast.

Figure 4.7
Gladiators train for combat.

Figure 4.8
Roman gladiators in action.

crowds would eagerly bet on their favorites. The gladiators always fought each other, never against animals.[38]

The gladiators entered the Colosseum through one of two tunnels assigned exclusively for them. One of the entry tunnels was given the name **Porta Libitinaria** after the Roman goddess of death, Libitina. This same tunnel was used to remove the bodies of the slain gladiators from the bloodsoaked sands of the Colosseum floor to an unmarked grave somewhere in the vicinity.

Frequently two gladiators were pitted against each other, while at other times mass combats were held in which many men hacked each other to pieces before thousands of screaming spectators seated a safe distance away, enjoying the perfumed mists and refreshment of the Colosseum. According to Baker,

> In the most brutal of all gladiatorial contests, only one of a great number escaped alive at the end of the day. The slaughter began with two men facing each other. When one fell, the other took his place, more often than not slaying the original victor who was now fatigued. On and on, a succession of gory fights filled an entire afternoon. Admittedly, this form of combat was exceptional. Usually it was held when a good number of murderers, robbers, and incendiaries were on hand, having been sentenced, literally, to "death in the games."[39]

Clearly this was one event where being last in line was a definite advantage!

Pompeii, buried during the eruption of Mt. Vesuvius in A.D. 79, contains the remnants of the best-preserved gladiatorial training school and amphitheater. The excavation of Pompeii uncovered the skeletons of four gladiators who were in chains and shackles when Vesuvius erupted. Within the same compound seventeen gladiators were uncovered, along with a woman who was ornamented in expensive jewels and in all probability was engaging in a business or amorous transaction that involved pleasures of the flesh. This might suggest that the gladiators were either pampered slaves or a desirable commodity, or perhaps both.

Sport and Christianity

The growth of Christianity had a profound impact on sport. In much the same manner as the Jews, the early Christians came into contact with adherents of Greek and Roman sport. Christian writers were quite knowledgeable about sport. Their literature went from using metaphors from Greek sport to emphatic denunciations of Roman sport. The early church leaders were not opposed to the care of the body or health promotion and were tolerant of Greek sport; however, Roman sport was condemned.[40] The Christian writers targeted both Christians and non-Christians alike relative to the immoral and hideous displays of Roman sport because Christians were still attending the games. DeVoe in "The Christians and the Games: The Relationship Between Christianity and the Roman Games from the First Through the Fifth Centuries, A.D.," provides revealing insight into the relationship between the Roman games and a "Christianized Rome." His research indicates that the impact and influence of Christianity on Rome was significant both politically and socially with regard to Christian participation in the games. Christianity was definitely Romanized.[41] The extent and scope of Christian participation as spectator and athlete in Christian Rome has yet to be subjected to extensive research and will no doubt provide the basis for much debate.

Christians were the dominant force that opposed the carnage of the games and spectacles of ancient Rome. The Christians were more often than not the victims of the Roman penchant for bloody spectacles and obviously had a great deal to gain when these atrocities ended. Ignatius, Bishop of Antioch (A.D. 108), stated that the Roman spectacle was one of the most "cruel tortures of the devil" with which Christians had to contend.[42] The conquest of Christianity over the pagan worship of the Romans and Greeks did not immediately put an end to sports. The Greek athletic festivals and carnage that was associated with the Roman gladiatorial and animal slaughter eventually came to an end. However, the real irony is that the Roman tradition of chariot racing was so popular that it was adopted by the Christian (Byzantine) Empire and remained popular for centuries.[43]

Greek Reaction to the Introduction of Roman Sport

There was some opposition to Roman sport in Greece; however, by the first century A.D., gladiatorial contests were staged in Athens and Corinth.

In Corinth, however, riots began when the Roman proconsul attempted to force the Greeks to accept Roman sport on a mass scale. The Greeks had no love for the Romans, who were their masters, and Greek criticism of Roman sport was largely the reaction of people who believed they were watching the demise of their sporting heritage at the hands of the Romans.

Summary

The conquering Romans, ever utilitarian and pragmatic, were quick to adopt those aspects and practices of their vanquished victims that were compatible with their culture. The Romans incorporated sport from both the Etruscans and the Greeks with varying degrees of success. The events associated with the circus and arenas were derived from the Etruscans due to their preoccupation with death. The massive displays of brutality and carnage that occurred with monotonous regularity in the Colosseum and gladiatorial arenas differed sharply from the Greek form of athletics, which focused on individual physical excellence and attendant health. Yet, the Romans found room for both even though the practitioners of Greek athletics were in the minority. The Romans blended the features of conquered nations to their liking. Sport in Rome was a significant part of Roman life, as it was in Greece, and as it is in the United States. When possible, comparisons have been made between Rome and Greece to provide the student with an appreciation and understanding of the role, scope, and nature of sport in a cross-cultural context.

The impact and influence of the Greeks on Roman civilization cannot be underestimated. Romans assimilated the philosophy and religious deities of the Greeks in addition to athletics. The ethos of the Romans accepted cruelty, slavery, patriarchy, class stratification, obedience to authority, and an educated elite, which is but a mirror image of Greek society except for the cruelty that seemed to personify itself in the Roman Colosseum and elsewhere. Both Romans and Greeks shared a common enthusiasm for sport. Sport was imbedded in the cultural fabric of Rome as it was in Greece, although their respective views of the body were dichotomous, as were their methods of physical education/training. The scientific exercises advocated by Galen, along with his promotion of health through fitness, did much to help the average Roman appreciate the benefits of physical activity and Greek gymnastics. Galen's skill in attending to the injuries of Roman athletes has earned him the distinction of being the "Father of Sports Medicine."

The Emperor Constantine, sensing the inevitable collapse of Rome by both internal and external forces, left Rome in A.D. 330 and moved the capital of the Empire to Byzantium, which he renamed Constantinople. By the fifth century, Rome was in economic chaos, and the once-mighty Roman Empire collapsed in 410 at the hands of Alaric and the Goths. The Circus Maximus was torn down and the Colosseum was abandoned and left to decay.

Discussion Questions

1. How did the Romans differ from the Greeks in their feelings toward sport?

2. Did the Romans believe in physical education? If so, for what purposes did the Romans use it?

3. How did the Romans use sport as a means of social control?

4. How is Roman sport similar to sport in the United States today?

5. What contributions did Galen make to the health of Romans? According to Galen, what were the benefits of exercise?

6. In general, how did Romans view the body? Was it an asset to be cared for? If so, what were some of the methods used by the Romans to care for their body?

7. What possible influence did the Etruscans have upon the development of Roman sport?

8. What were the philosophical positions of the body as espoused by the Stoics, and Epicureans? How did their beliefs about the body in an epistemological sense differ from that of Platonic thought?

9. How did Marcus Tullius Cicero use sport as a forum for his views?

Suggestions for Further Reading

Bonfante, L. "Human Sacrifices on an Etruscan Funerary Urn." *American Journal of Archaeology* 88, no. 4 (October 1984): 531–539.

Bury, J. B. *A History of the Roman Empire.* New York: American Book Co., 1927.

Crowther, N. "Nudity and Morality: Athletics in Italy." *Classical Journal* 75 (1980–81): 119–123.

Fowler, W. W. *Roman Festivals of the Period of the Republic.* London: Macmillan, 1899.

Lee, H. M. "The Sport Fan and Team Loyalty in Rome." *Arete: The Journal of Sport Literature* 1, no. 1 (Fall 1983): 139–145.

Norman, N. J. "Excavations at Carthage, 1982." *American Journal of Archaeology* 87, no. 2 (April 1983): 247.

Pascal, N. "October Horse." *Harvard Studies in Classical Philology* 85 (1981): 261–291.

Notes

1. An oligarchy is a government in which political power rests in the hands of a few people.

2. Peter Quenell and the Editors of Newsweek Book Division, *The Colosseum* (New York: *Newsweek* 1971), 15.

3. Ibid., p. 15.

4. Ellwood P. Cubberly, *The History of Education* (Boston: Houghton-Mifflin, 1920), 58.

5. Frederick Copleston, *A History of Philosophy,* Vol. 1 (Westminster: The Newman Press, 1966), 380.

6. Ibid., 381.

7. W. T. Jones, *The Classic Mind—A History of Western Philosophy,* 2d ed. (New York: Harcourt, Brace and World, 1969), 326.

8. A transcendental universal, according to Plato, is the perfect idea that is poorly imitated in the material world, whereas the concrete universal, according to Aristotle, is the idea predicated on or induced from the material world. In both cases the

material world is secondary to the world that "transcends reality." As a consequence the body is believed not as important as the mind.

9. Copleston, *A History of Philosophy*, 395.

10. Ibid., 398.

11. P. H. De Lacy, "Epicurus," *The Encyclopedia of Philosophy*, Vol. 3 (New York: Macmillan and The Free Press, 1972), 3–5.

12. Lawrence W. Fielding, "Marcus Tullius Cicero: A Social Critic of Sport" (University of Louisville, KY).

13. Ibid.

14. Cicero, *De Finibus*, 339–341.

15. Ibid.

16. William J. Baker, *Sports in the Western World* (Totawa, N.J.: Rowman and Littlefield, 1982), 29.

17. Deobold B. Van Dalen and Bruce L. Bennett, *A World History of Physical Education*, 2d ed. (Englewood Cliffs, N.J.: Prentice Hall, 1971), 77.

18. Robert Montraville Green, *A Translation of Galen's Hygiene* (Springfield, Ill.: Charles C. Thomas, 1951), XXII.

19. E. Norman Gardiner, *Athletics of the Ancient World* (Oxford University Press, 1930), 115.

20. Rachel Sargent Robinson, *Sources for the History of Greek Athletics* (Cincinnati: Author, 1955), 187.

21. Ibid., 177.

22. Ibid., 178.

23. Ibid., 188.

24. Ibid., 188.

25. Don Kyle, "Directions in Ancient Sport History," *Journal of Sport History*, 10, no. 1 (Spring 1983): 24–25.

26. Harold Arthur Harris, *Sport in Greece and Rome* (London: Thames and Hudson, 1972), 41.

27. Ibid.

28. Ibid., 150.

29. J. Carcopino, *Daily Life in Ancient Rome* (Harmondsworth: Penguin, 1941), 267.

30. Harris, *Sport in Greece and Rome*, 73.

31. Van Dalen and Bennett, *A World History of Physical Education*, 78.

32. Ibid., 81.

33. Baker, *Sports in the Western World*, 33.

34. Quenell, *The Colosseum*, 36.

35. Ibid., 33–34.

36. Van Dalen and Bennett, *A World History of Physical Education*, 82.

37. Baker, *Sports in the Western World*, 34.

38. Ibid.

39. Ibid.

40. Kyle, "Directions in Ancient Sport History," 30.

41. Richard Franklin DeVoe, "The Christians and the Games: The Relationship Between Christianity and the Roman Games from the First Through the Fifth Centuries, A.D." Doctoral diss., Texas Tech University, 1987.

42. Ibid., 37.

43. Kyle, "Directions in Ancient Sport History," 30.

section 2

From the Spiritual World to the Secular World: *Changing Concepts of the Body*

Philosophy, Sport, and Physical Education During the Middle Ages: 900–1400

General Events That Occurred During the Dark Ages (A.D. 476–900) and the Middle Ages (A.D. 900–1400)

Dark Ages

402–476 Ravenna was capital of the Western Roman Empire

476 Odoacer sacked Rome, conquered Ravenna; end of Western Roman Empire

476–540 Ravenna was capital of Gothic kingdoms

476–493 Odoacer, king

493–526 Theodoric the Great

527–565 Justinian, Eastern Roman Emperor

533 *Digest of Laws*

534–540 Justinian's general Belisarius conquered Italy

540 Belisarius entered Ravenna; end of Theodoric's Ostrogothic kingdom

546 Maximian appointed Archbishop of Ravenna and Byzantine Exarch

556 Archbishop Maximian died

590–604 Gregory the Great, pope; liturgy of Roman Catholic Church codified; Gregorian chant established

768–814 Charlemagne, king of the Franks

800 Charlemagne crowned Holy Roman emperor by pope

841 Vikings invaded northern France and colonized French territory

Middle Ages

910 Abbey of Cluny at Burgundy, France, founded

927–942 Odo, abbot of Cluny, reputed author of musical treatises

962 Otto the Great (936–973) crowned Holy Roman emperor

994–1049 Odilo, abbot of Cluny

c. 995–c. 1050 Guido of Arezzo, author of musical treatises, inventor of staff notation

c. 1000 Leif Eriksen, Viking navigator, believed to have reached coast of North America

1000–1150 Romanesque Period at height

1035 William succeeded his father Robert as Duke of Normandy after the latter's death on pilgrimage to Jerusalem

1049–1109 Hugh of Semur, abbot of Cluny

1050 Holy Roman Empire at height; ascendancy of papal power

1056 Westminster Abbey

1063 Pisa Cathedral begun

1066 William, Duke of Normandy, conquered England; reigned as king of England

1066–1087 Death of Edward the Confessor, King of England

Coronation of Harold as his successor

Invasion of England by William the Conqueror

Battle of Hastings: English forces defeated; Harold killed

William crowned king of England

1073–1085 Gregory VII (Hildebrand), pope

1077 Emperor Henry IV bowed to Pope Gregory VII at Canossa; Abbot Hugh of Cluny was intermediary

1078 Tower of London begun by William the Conqueror

c. 1088 Bayeux Tapestry completed

1088–1099 Urban II, Cluniac pope

1088–1130 Great third church at Cluny built

1095 Urban II preached the First Crusade

1098 Cistercian order founded; opposed Cluniac order; St. Bernard of Clairvaux was its principal spokesman

1109 Pontius became abbot of Cluny

1122 Peter the Venerable became abbot of Cluny

1096–1291 Crusades: European Christians fought Moslems and Saracens; extended Christianity as well as opened up trade routes

1140 Guelph and Ghibelline wars began

1163–1235 Cathedral of Notre Dame in Paris built

1198–1216 Innocent III, pope; church reached pinnacle of power

Source: William Fleming, Arts and Ideas (New York: Holt, Rinehart, and Winston, 1963).

Introduction

The period beginning with the tenth century and ending with the birth of the Italian Renaissance in the fourteenth century has been termed the Medieval Period, or more commonly the Middle Ages. For the student of physical education the Middle Ages represents an intriguing time, with events ranging from the athletic feats of knights during the Age of Chivalry, to the use of sport in preparation for the Crusades, to the ascetic views of monks. The latter were represented by self-denial and even bodily mortification (i.e., self-inflicted pain and mystical punishment that were supposed to inhibit bodily lusts and desires, and in so doing prepared one's soul for heaven).

Generally speaking, the philosophical position of the body during the Middle Ages reflected theological beliefs. Most early Christians did not glorify the body, and held it in contempt. There were some notable exceptions, however, which will be presented later in this chapter. While the ancient Greeks were tremendous athletes who admired the human form and consequently sought to develop great physiques, they were pagans in the eyes of the early Christians. Greek athletes competed nude in the Olympic Games to honor a pagan god, Zeus. Athletics became a symbol tied to pagan rituals. To the early Christians of the Middle Ages, this ancient Greek practice of worshiping pagan gods by way of athletic prowess and the achievement of physical perfection was seen as paying too much attention to secular concerns (the glorification of the human body), and not enough attention to spiritual concerns (the nurturing of the eternal soul). In the *Phaedo*, Socrates voiced similar concerns; that his fellow Athenians spent too much time attending to their secular/material needs and too little time improving the soul.

The majority of Christians believed that to participate in athletics or engage in physical training to glorify the body would contaminate the body, which "housed" the soul, and would make the soul impure. It comes as no surprise that the negative attitude that Medieval Christians had toward the body was in no small part the result of a reaction to paganism.

Although the Christians' negative attitude about the body stemmed from a reaction to paganism, many of the same Christian theologians would come to embrace the ideas of Plato and Aristotle, who were "pagan Greeks." It is important to understand that philosophy during the Middle Ages was mixed with religion, and many times emerged as a vague collection of ideas that were difficult to grasp and explain. For example, some of the ideas that originated with the Greeks (particularly Plato's and Aristotle's metaphysical dualism), were accepted, while others (such as physical education), were to a great extent ignored.

The Impact of Christianity

The Christian church was one of the few remaining institutions left intact by the barbarian hordes that overran Europe after the fall of

Ravenna, the capital of the Western Roman Empire. Is it important to understand that, in addition to the Christian influence on European civilization, Judaism and the religion of Islam also had a profound impact upon the development of European civilization as well. Europeans were exposed to new "ideas" and unique cultural aspects that were essential elements in Jewish and Moslem society as a result of expanding opportunities for trade and military campaigns that brought Europeans to the Middle East. The Crusades provide an example of how Europeans came to the Middle East as soldiers. If they were fortunate enough to survive the bloody battles and returned home, they brought back with them "new" foods, weapons, garments, medicinal cures, and an expanded insight into Middle Eastern philosophy and religion.

The collapse of Rome in 476 A.D. resulted in a state of chaos that drove many people to seek protection from powerful aristocrats who demanded complete allegiance and subjugation. As many people left Rome, the advances made by the Roman Empire in commerce, trade, and public administration were eventually forgotten. Instead of going forward, civilization deteriorated and entered a bleak period known as the Dark Ages (476–900). Europe regressed into kingdoms that were similar to tribal societies. Society gradually became feudalistic, with castles and walled cities designed by desperate people for protection and self-preservation. Wars and armed conflict between knights and feudal armies, who would often lay siege to the walled cities, were the order of the day in the Dark Ages. Organized sport and physical education during the Dark Ages was, for the most part, nonexistent.

With the inception of the Middle Ages around 900, people began to emerge from the cultural and intellectual "darkness" that epitomized the Dark Ages. Although it was still dangerous to travel and wars were still common, the Middle Ages were an improvement over the Dark Ages. Trade and commerce began to be revived, and a market economy began to emerge. Metaphysical questions began to surface once again, and these questions were almost always linked to the religious beliefs of the time. So where did people turn to for guidance and answers during the Middle Ages? In general, it depended upon the religion one practiced. For Christians, the church was the lone cultural institution that, through intellectual and spiritual leadership, provided a symbol of stability and order amidst fear and chaos. Jews continued to seek spiritual leadership and guidance in their temples, while Moslems found comfort and spiritual leadership by praying in the Mosques and following the teachings of Mohammed. Judaism and Islam were practiced in the Middle East and parts of Spain and northern Africa as part of thriving economies and rich cultures. However, while these religions played significant roles in shaping the thoughts and ideas found in Western Civilization, the dominant cultural and religious force in Europe during the Middle Ages was the Christian church.

Christianity spread throughout the ruins of the Roman Empire. The Roman Catholic Church in particular felt obligated to convert all those who were not Catholic to Catholicism. It did not matter if you were a

Jew, Moslem, or a mere pagan: conversion to Catholicism was a serious goal of the Roman Catholic Church. This religious decision eventually resulted in the Inquisition, a religious movement designed to convert nonbelievers to Christianity—by force if necessary—and to root out the heretics within the Catholic Church. In hindsight, the inquisition is viewed by historians as a tragic and brutal episode in the history of the Catholic Church.

The Inquisition was a medieval court that was based in part on the belief of St. Augustine, who interpreted the biblical passage found in Luke 14:23 as permission to use force against heretics. Heretics were identified as those individuals who held controversial beliefs and were not in agreement with the official teachings of the Roman Catholic Church. The papal Inquisition was used by Pope Gregory IX in 1231. He issued a papal decree that ordered heretics to be burned at the stake. If an individual was accused of being a heretic, that person could either confess or deny the charge. If a confession was made immediately, the church authorities could issue sentences that ranged from flogging to simple prayers. However, if the charge was denied and there was reason to believe that the person was not telling the truth, it was necessary to "extract" a confession. Since the church was not supposed to shed blood, secular authorities were given the task of obtaining the necessary confession through the use of torture. The most severe practice was physical torture on "the rack," and then a sentence of death was handed down. To add insult, the condemned person's property was confiscated as well. In most cases, death by burning was carried out almost immediately after the sentence was announced.

Among the most infamous of these medieval church tribunals was the Spanish Inquisition. The impetus for this most cruel of Inquisitions was at the insistence of Ferdinand II of Aragon and Isabella I of Castile. Under pressure by these two rulers, Pope Sixtus IV authorized the Spanish Inquisition in 1483. The primary targets of the Spanish Inquisition were the Marranos (Jews who converted to Christianity), and the Moriscos (Moslems who also converted to the Christian faith). The Spanish Inquisition was headed by Tomas de Torquemada, who was as sinister as he was cruel. He believed that the Marranos and Moriscos were still secretly practicing their original faiths. The Marranos and Moriscos who denied the charges were subjected to the cruelest of tortures and then burned to death. Clearly this was a corrupt and violent period in the history of the church.

The church gradually and deliberately became both the source of all spiritual solutions for Christians and an enormous political and economic power. Within the realm of the Catholic Church, this control was exercised through various popes. The theology of the church was based on absolute faith and belief in the certainty of *divine revelation*. Divine revelation is a way of knowing that argues that "truth" is obtained through prayer and directly from God. This epistemology, along with scripture, was the philosophical basis of the early Christian church. From a political perspective, all Christians were gradually brought under complete church control through a kind of carrot-and-stick philosophy, which was by no means reserved for the exclusive use of Christianity. Failure to comply with church authority was to risk eternal damnation, which the enemies of the church would most surely suffer. On the other hand, by obeying church laws, or dogma, one could hope to bask in the infinite glory of God for eternity in heaven. Because life during the Middle Ages was relatively difficult, the prospect of infinity in heaven looked pretty good![1]

Christianity and Greek Philosophy

The early medieval philosophies did not have access to a wealth of literary sources. What they did come to possess were the ancient works of Greek philosophers, especially those of Plato and Aristotle. Both Plato and Aristotle were interested in the metaphysical questions that form the foundation of Christianity: the existence of the soul, the personification of and belief in God, the nature of being/existence, and the purpose and codes by which people should conduct their lives. Early Christian writers were compelled to embrace specific attitudes about the philosophy of the ancient Greeks in order to reconcile Greek philosophy with Christian theology.[2]

Not all Christians were eager to embrace the merging of Christianity with Greek philosophy, however. Tertullian, for instance, demanded bodily mortification and was adamant in his opposition to recognizing and admitting the pagan philosophy of the Greeks. Tertullian, however, and those who believed as he did were in the minority. Platonism not only was recognized by Christian theologians but also "was commonly regarded by Christian thinkers as having been an intellectual preparation for Christianity."[3]

Christian theologians attempted to use philosophy to prove their theological Christian dogma. This means that medieval theologians, who were also men of philosophy, tried to prove the actual essence and nature of God using philosophical methods. This task, to say the least, is quite difficult. The Schoolmen, or Scholastics, as they were known, spent their life formulating philosophical positions that would prove and support the existence of God and divine revelation. To this end St. Augustine, Boethius, John Scotus Erigena, St. Anselm, Peter Abelard, St. Bonaventure, and the greatest Scholastic of all, St. Thomas Aquinas, resurrected the philosophical traditions of the past and embarked on a metaphysical quest that was tempered by their beliefs as theologians and Scholastics.

The attempted marriage of theology and philosophy was at best quite cumbersome. Although philosophers and theologians both use reasoned inquiry and rational thought, they differ in their presuppositions. Philosophy requires one to accept starting points that cannot be substantiated, a practice found in metaphysics. In contrast, theology is based on faith. Theologians accept the existence of God on faith alone—not necessarily by philosophical deductions based on reasoned and rational inquiry. Indeed, it is the "leap of faith" that makes religion the unique and powerful way of life that it is.

Philosophical Position of the Body in the Middle Ages

With the exception of the work of Jewish and Islamic philosophers, the home of medieval philosophy was the Catholic Church. As mentioned earlier, Christian theologians recognized and incorporated the works of Plato and Aristotle into a philosophy that was uniquely Christian in purpose. The Arab world had preserved the works of Plato and Aristotle and passed them on to Christians during the twelfth century and first half of the thirteenth century.[4] The works of the original Greek writers were translated from Arabic and Greek into Latin, and translations were also made of works by Islamic and Jewish philosophers. All of these works were of considerable importance to the development of theology and philosophy in Western Christendom.[5]

The portrayal of Jesus in these translated works was one of perfection in body, mind, and soul. An interesting dilemma that occurred in the philosophical positions of the body was the idea that when God made heaven and earth and added man and woman, he approved of his work. This would certainly imply that both the body and the soul are good, and that God would not purposely create something that was harmful or evil. Logically, then, the human body is a good thing.[6] This discussion regarding the body of Jesus became quite confused during medieval debates, however, and the metaphysical arguments that ensued ultimately led to the splitting of Christianity into Eastern Orthodox (centered in the Eastern Roman Empire in Byzantium), Roman Catholic, and Protestant religions. According to Fleming, during the early medieval period of the late fifth and early sixth centuries,

> . . . the main doctrinal battle centered on the nature of the Trinity. . . . The ostrogoths believed that since Jesus was created by God the Father, he was subordinate and not of one substance with God. . . . The Arians revered Christ as the noblest of created beings, but as human rather than divine. In Byzantium, it was held that Christ as the Incarnated Word was of one single substance with the Father and hence of divine nature only. The Roman Papacy found a middle ground between the two extremes and took the position that since the Word was made flesh, Christ possessed both divine and human natures and was a full member of the Trinity.[7]

Some Orthodox Christians consistently rejected contentions that the body was evil; however, they were in the minority. The minority view believed that because God was omnipresent, He was in all things, including the body. The body, filled with God, was good.[8] However, this position of the body held by some of the Orthodox Christians was not without controversy. Elements of the early Christian church, along with various powerful and influential "streams" of Roman Catholicism during the early Middle Ages, looked upon the human body as vile, corrupt, and beyond redemption.

The subject of the corporeal nature of Christ, the influence of Neoplatonism, and the position of the church combined to create a distinct but inconsistent Christian view of the worth of the body. The beliefs of

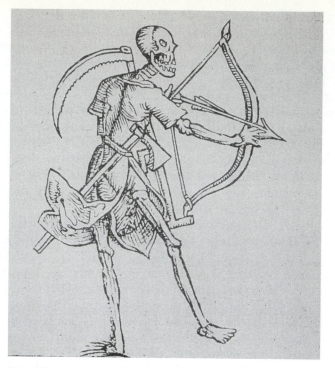

Figure 5.1
The bow and arrow was often used by medieval artists to symbolize death and destruction. This skeletal bowman, in a German wood cut of 1514, reminded the devout of the Middle Ages to reflect on the inevitability of man's mortality.

those Christians who were ascetic dualists was the result of the combination of Platonic philosophy, early Christian history, Islamic, and Jewish influences. Ascetic dualism is the belief that the human body should be denied any kind of pleasure in order to purify the soul. This concept is not necessarily the position put forth in the Old and New Testaments. Biblical concepts of the body, soul, and flesh describe man as a whole being, as opposed to having a dualistic existence.[9] Not all scholars are in agreement on this point, however. There were, and continue to be, confusing and contradictory views of scripture, especially on the position and role of the body. Important to our discussion is the understanding that the various interpretations of scripture can have a significant impact on the perceived worth or value of the body, which directly impacts the nature, development, and scope of sport and physical education.

One perspective of the body is that "the enfleshment of God" is the cardinal belief of Christianity.[10] By "enfleshment" Bottomley means that human beings are "bodily images" of a perfect God, and therefore the "body" part of our existence is, in some profound way, good. The merging of the corporeal with the native of God as a result of "enfleshment" resulted in a heightened respect for the body. Hebrew writers insisted that man—the only true image of God himself—was a psycho-somatic entity of both body and soul. Had this concept been accepted by the Western world it could have effectively ended the dualism of body and spirit. However, the bubonic plague devastated Europe during the fourteenth century, leaving in its wake an obsession with death that eventually compromised the positive view of the body held by a minority of Christians. Instead, an attitude of despair and futility relative to one's fate dominated, and the result was that the body became viewed as the "messenger of sin."[11]

Another perspective on the value of the body during the Middle Ages appears to be a result of the merging of Eastern Orthodox religion and Greek philosophy. This can be seen in the monastic life of early Christian monks, which was "ascetic." The monks sought enlightenment through bodily mortification, vows of silence, prayer, and the renouncing of material possessions. The consensus among some medieval historians is that, with the exception of ritual dancing and manual labor, Christians were encouraged to avoid the pleasures and temptations of the flesh. Van Dalen and Bennett explain:

> The Christians eventually came to regard the body as an instrument of sin. The body was mortal and of little consequence to a man seeking eternal salvation. . . . Many men came to accept the premise that life in the world to come could best be secured by rising above all thoughts of the body, even to the extent of ignoring and neglecting essential physical needs. In such an atmosphere, even the most worthy ideals of physical education could not exist.[12]

While physical education could not exist from such a perspective, this does not mean that the early Christian monks were not "aware" of the body. Indeed, the monks were *extremely* aware of the body, and argued long and hard against the pleasures of the flesh, temptations, and the meaning of these concepts. Their attitude toward the body, and the consequences of this attitude, was a matter of choice: these early monks *chose* to deny themselves the pleasures of the flesh. In so doing they "proved" to themselves that they were, from the perspective of their Christian faith, worthy of eternal salvation.

From both theological and philosophical positions, then, physical education and sporting activities would appear to be all but absent from the Middle Ages, except for the military activities of the time. This, however, was not entirely the case. Although most early Christians who lived during the Middle Ages did not glorify the body as did the ancient Greeks, there did exist some noted individuals and groups that did not abandon the body. In fact, the Scholastics saw value in physical activity, and instead of emphasizing the differences between mind and body, the Scholastics actually saw a close relationship between the two.[13]

The Body and Physical Fitness According to St. Thomas Aquinas

The greatest of the medieval Scholastics, St. Thomas Aquinas (1225–1274), embraced the idea of physical fitness and recreation as a positive force in promoting social and moral well-being. In his classic work *Summa Theologiae*, Aquinas argued that

> . . . in order to achieve happiness, perfection in both the soul and body are necessary. Since it is natural for the soul to be united with the body, how is it credible that perfection of the one (soul) should exclude the perfection of the other (body)? Let us declare, then, that happiness completed and entire requires the well-being of the body.[14]

In what was no doubt a bold statement for his time, Aquinas stated what many physical educators have argued for years: intelligence depends in part on the physical fitness level of the individual. He noted that "because some men have bodies of better disposition, their souls have a greater power of understanding."[15] He went on further to say that

> . . . a man is rendered apt of intelligence by the healthy disposition of the internal powers of the organism, in which the good condition of the body has a part. Consequently intellectual endowments can be in the powers of sense, though primarily they are in the mind.[16]

From an epistemological perspective, Aquinas believed that we can come to know things through our bodies as well as through our mind, although the mind was to remain superior to the body. A healthy mind and a healthy body were desirable qualities for all to have.

Why did Aquinas believe that physical fitness was of benefit to the physical, mental, social, and moral well-being of Christians at a time when most medieval Christians renounced the body? For example, the heretical Manicheans and Albigensians denounced the body and matter in general as evil. An evil and perishable body could never be integrally united with a noble and immortal soul. The body imprisoned the soul and, as a result, did not contribute in a positive way to man's mental, social, and moral well-being.[17] Plato's position of the body, as stated in the *Phaedo*, was embraced by the Manicheans and Albigensians.

Aristotle, however, did not agree with his teacher (Plato) and put forth a much different view. The Greek philosophers, especially Aristotle, had a profound impact upon the Scholastics. Aquinas and others approved of Aristotle's position—that man is an integral composite of body and soul—and that the soul needs a body to acquire knowledge. As a result of Aristotle's influence, the theory of the unity of man was adopted by the Scholastics of the thirteenth century.[18] Scholasticism also received support from Orthodox Christians who believed that because God was omnipresent, he was in all things, including the body. The body was filled with God, and therefore the body was good and not an instrument of sin.[19] Under the tutelage of Aquinas, the Scholastics were able to establish for the first time in Western civilization a philosophical and religious justification for cherishing the body and valuing physical fitness and recreation for man's physical, mental, social, and moral well-being.[20] Aquinas clearly saw the relationship between physical well-being and mental and biological health.

Moses Maimonides and St. Bonaventure

Although most intellectuals in the Middle Ages were dualists, Aquinas was not alone in his view that the body was important to the mind and spirit. The noted Jewish philosopher and physician Moses Maimonides (1135–1204) observed that "nothing is more useful for the preservation of health than physical exercise."[21] Similarly, at the University of Paris, perhaps the best university of the time, St. Bonaventure (1217–1274) wrote that the body does not imprison the soul but is actually a friend and companion, and therefore the individual exists as a natural union of body and soul.[22]

Even though Aquinas, Maimonides, and Bonaventure understood the relationship of the mind, body, and spirit to be a close one, the understanding of the majority of Catholic monks was very different. And the views of these monks about the role of the body led to some ambiguous attitudes toward sport and physical education. Generally, the church tolerated fun and games because it could not stop them, yet the church never really condoned these types of activities.

Linking the Spiritual with Secular Sport

Change is a difficult thing to accept, especially if it necessitates that an individual or an institution tolerate a practice or new idea that was at one time discouraged. This was the situation that the Christian church had to deal with as it related to sport and games. The negative attitude toward sport and other secular activities evident with the early Christian monks was changing. These changes started to take place in the eleventh and twelfth centuries.[23] During this time many nobles elected to become monks, primarily because of the manner in which property was inherited. Generally speaking, the oldest son inherited the lands of his father, leaving the younger brothers either to a life of warring as a knight, or as a member of the priesthood. In the case of the young priest, secular habits such as hunting, falconry, and perhaps even the combat sports used to train knights, remained popular. Young nobles who became priests introduced these activities into the ecclesiastical community, and with the passage of time these playful activities were slowly accepted by the church.[24] Perhaps the best example was Bishop Odon of Bayeux (1049–1097). The Bayeux Tapestry (figs. 5.2 and 5.3) is very explicit in its secular portrayal of Bishop Odon. He is depicted as a noble knight and served in the army of his half-brother, William the Conqueror. Bishop Odon is also depicted participating in hunting. Bishop Odon was able to blend his spiritual virtues with the secular athletic skills of a knight.[25]

The popularity of sports and other physical activities in Medieval England, both aristocratic and servile, is depicted on the scenes found on the Bayeux Tapestry. It is a unique source that helps us to understand the extent of sporting activities during this historical period as they existed in England. The tapestry is a multicolored cloth made

Figure 5.2
Bishop Odon encourages the soldiers to emerge victorious over the Saxon Army led by Harold.

Figure 5.3
In a bloody battle, the Saxons are defeated on October 14, 1066, and William is crowned King of England.

Figure 5.4
Games and amusements.

around 1070 A.D., that is nineteen and one-half inches wide and about 230 feet long. This embroidered work of art was supervised by Bishop Odon of Bayeux (hence the name), the half-brother of William the Conqueror. The tapestry contains numerous sporting activities such as archery, hunting, hawking, fishing, make-up games, cock-fighting, fencing, jousting, bear-baiting, bull-baiting, riding, and assorted ball games, and is a primary source of information about sporting activities in England during the Middle Ages.

Holidays and Ball Games

The agrarian life of the peasant-serf was particularly hard. The serf of the Middle Ages was not a slave; he owned his own home and worked a plot of land as a tenant (renter). Rent and taxes went to the lord of the estate in the form of crops, other agricultural products, and services in return for protection. Primitive farming techniques (which improved during the tenth century with the invention of the plowshare and the horse collar) required long and hard workdays. The only regular opportunity for peasant recreation came on Sundays after church services. With the permission of local church authority, serfs participated in games and amusements.

Major holidays such as May Day, Shrove Tuesday, and Whitsuntide celebrations were considered pagan holidays.[26] Such seasonal agricultural holidays extended over several days and were associated with generous amounts of food, wine, entertainment, and games. Fine points of etiquette and genteel manners were not required of peasant behavior, and it was therefore not uncommon for these festivals to degenerate into drunken free-for-alls that resulted in property damage, injury, and sometimes even death.

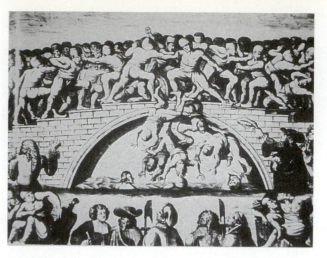

Figure 5.5
The free-for-alls.

Rugged Ball Games, Equestrian Events, and English Football

Ball games that were popular during Roman times continued to be popular during the Middle Ages and often took place on church land if a common area was not available. A ball game called *soule* was popular among the peasantry, and it often contributed to property losses and personal injury. The game resembled the modern game of soccer and was played with an indeterminate number of men each side. Possession of a stuffed leather ball was the goal, and two teams played the game between two set points. During the heat of competition the achievement of this goal sometimes left the "playing field" (and often someone's private property) in ruins. Most accounts of the game describe it as a violent affair, and one scholar noted that the players engaged in "a veritable combat for the possession of the ball for which they fought like dogs battling for a bone."[27] King James noted that the game was "meeter for the maiming than making able the (players) thereof."[28] As one can imagine, soule was quite violent, and this contributed to the church's ambivalence about its association with the game. Local customs governed the rules of play, and there were many versions of the game throughout Europe.

There were other ball games as well, some that employed the use of sticks and were precursors to modern versions of hockey and baseball. Another game, kegels, was similar to bowling. Although the legacy of some ball games were distinctly Roman, there is evidence to suggest that ball games were being played by Germanic tribes and by the Irish and the Scots before Roman occupation. The Moors also introduced their own ball games to Spain in the eighth century.

William Fitzstephen, a noted writer and clerk for Thomas Becket, the Archbishop of Canterbury, lived in London during the twelfth century. The London described by Fitzstephen was a dynamic city that assimilated immigrants from the continent into the social classes that were the staple of British society. Fitzstephen provided an account of nobles and nonnobles assembling at a smooth field every Friday for the local horse show: "It is plesant to see the nags, with their sleek and shining coats. . . ."[29] He reports that part of the reason for attending was to watch the horses race: "The horses . . . are eager for the race . . . upon the signal being given, they stretch out their limbs, hurry over the course, and are borne along with unremitting speed."[30]

English football was gaining popularity in London, and the following account written by Fitzstephen in *Descriptio Londoniae* helps one visualize the athletes and spectators who enjoyed the game in medieval London:

> After dinner, all the young men of the city go out into the fields to play at the well known game of football. The scholars belonging to several schools have each their ball; and the city tradesmen, according to their respective crafts, have theirs. The more aged men, the fathers of the players, and the wealthy citizens, come on horseback to see the contests of the young men, with whom, after their manner, they participate, their natural heart seeming to be aroused by the sight of so much agility, and by their participation in the amusements of unrestrained youth.[31]

The apparent universality of ball games, their popularity with the peasant-serfs, the interest of the tradesmen and upper classes, their association with Christian holidays, and the long tradition of quiet acceptance of such games by church authority made it extremely difficult for the church to end its association with these games. Yet it became increasingly difficult to tolerate the rising mayhem that surrounded peasant recreations in the last centuries of the Middle Ages. Outraged by the number of incidents of damage to property and persons by widespread drunkenness and by openly lewd conduct, the church intervened with prohibitions against games that involved gambling, specific festivals, and immoral behavior. Such condemnations were only partially successful, however. Time, traditions, and human nature mitigated against any permanent solution to the church's dilemma—that of teaching moral introspection and spiritual self-examination to illiterate peasants who lived and worked on the farm day after day.

Medieval Social Structure: Knights, Nobles, and Worthy Pursuits

As the Middle Ages moved from the early centuries to its close around 1400, a complex hierarchy of aristocratic privilege and power was established. From the beginning, feudal relationships were based on military and political responsibilities. These responsibilities were primarily military allegiance to the local monarch for his personal protection. The tradition of a personal bodyguard was a customary practice of both Germanic and Roman ruling classes. In return for the pledge of these personal military services, the lord or vassal was given land (a fief) and servants and peasants sufficient to supply the needs of his family. These vassal lords then had the right of taxation over their serfs. The control of wealth (feudalism) of the upper classes was based on land ownership and the labor of the serfs.

This system also provided another essential quality that distinctly separated the nobility from the serfs. Because the wealth of the aristocracy came from the labor of others, leisure became the unique commodity of nobles. Even if a peasant could afford the horse and the arms required of a knight, he would not have the necessary time to practice the skills of war. Leisure became the signature of European aristocracy from the Middle Ages until the twentieth century. It is this one quality of wealth, established during the Middle Ages, that has led to many of the differences between the recreational pursuits of upper and lower classes.

By the tenth century, the titles, property, and privileges of the nobility, as well as the feudal subordination of the serfs to an overlord, came to be considered a hereditary right. This greatly restricted the opportunities of warriors to move into the nobility, opportunities that had been available in the eighth and ninth centuries. Although it happened rarely, even serfs who could save and buy additional land had the chance of upward social mobility from the fifth to the ninth centuries. The increasing costs of personal armor, weapons, and horses provided another barrier to upward mobility. A horse cost five times as much as an ox, and the most important piece of armor, the cuirass, cost 100 shillings, which was a considerable amount of money at that time. Full armor cost several pounds, and to give you an idea of the worth of a pound, it would sometimes take years for a serf to save just a few pennies (one-twelfth of a shilling) due to the lack of paying jobs and an economy largely based on the barter system, which traded food, chickens, or services for work. By the last centuries of the Middle Ages wealth, leisure, and the hereditary rights had made the warrior class quite exclusive.

The feudal system was also strengthened by Christian belief. Loyalty was viewed as a basic Christian ideal, with Christ being the embodiment of this ideal loyalty. Christians believed that God gave his Son for the salvation of man through his loyalty to humanity, and similarly the lord of the fiefdom was loyal to and protected his vassals. Thus was born the concept of *noblesse oblige*, which required persons of high social rank to be the epitome of honorable and generous conduct. In turn, the vassal had to give his complete loyalty to his overlord for the salvation of both, and he trusted in his lord to protect him from outside forces.

Loyalty within a hierarchy of political power was perfectly in tune with the medieval world view of social order. The entire concept of heavenly order was based on Christian hierarchical concepts. God, the ultimate overlord, presided over well-defined levels of heavenly grace. Even the angels had nine tiers of importance, with the archangel at the top level and cupids at the lowest level. Entry into heaven was seen in terms of stages of acquiring grace; only saints went directly to heaven. In this manner Christian idealism reinforced and perpetuated the existing social structure.

Sport of the Aristocracy

Because military obligations were the main function of the noble classes, it is not surprising to find that the most popular sporting events were war games and demonstrations of military skills. The most famous of the war games was the medieval tournament, or joust. Such events were gala affairs that served several important recreational and social functions. Recreationally, the tournament allowed all levels of society to rest from the duties and work of everyday life. Peasants enjoyed the gaily colored tents and banners erected for the occasion. They also enjoyed feasting, wine, games, and perhaps a brawl or two! The warriors could display their military prowess and receive kudos from their fellow warriors.

Medieval Tournaments

Socially, the tournament was a celebration of the social order of feudal society. The overlord or king presided over the festivities in which his vassal lords participated with their warrior knights. Historically, the tournament grew out of the realities of war, where winner took all—property, armor, horses, and people. These early tournaments were very rough free-for-alls on horseback, with no concept of chivalry acknowledged by the participants. Played on a field bounded by ropes, it was not uncommon for several knights to gang up on another, single knight. After subduing him they ransomed him back to his family for all they could get. In this way fortunes were made and lost, all for the thrill of the battle. There was no such danger of this type of exchange in the carefully planned tournaments of the late Middle Ages.[32]

Notable events in the tournament were the joust and the melee. The joust was between two mounted horsemen who charged at each other with long, wooden lances. The object was to knock the opponent from his horse. In the melee, groups of opposing knights engaged in hand-to-hand combat with dull swords. Contestants could fight from horseback or on foot. Although the purpose of these contests was not to kill the opponents, injuries were inevitable, and deaths occurred as a matter of course. Eventually social pressures, the dominant force being the church, transformed both chivalry and the tournament. The church had always been in opposition to the carnage and brutality of the melee, and during the twelfth century, popes had issued Papal Bulls, or laws made by the pope, that forbade the savage and abominable tournaments from being held. The participants were threatened with eternal damnation. Caesarius of Heisterbach, a Cistercian monk of the early thirteenth century, warned: "For there is no question but such as are slain in tournaments go down to Hell, if they be not helped by the benefit of contrition."[33] However, for utilitarian reasons the church did embrace chivalry and the knightly sports of the tournament and melee during the era of the Crusades (1096–1291). By the fifteenth century, changes in warfare, the brutality of the events, and the disapproval of the church made the tournament an obsolete curiosity of the nobility.

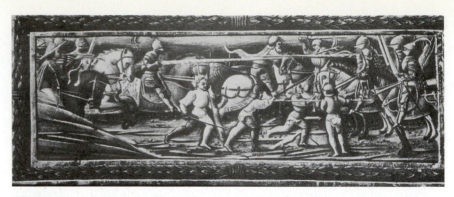

Figure 5.6
The melee. The British Library.

Figure 5.7
Game board. Note that the figures are of the church, aristocracy, and knights. The British Library.

Hawking, Hunting, and Other Pastimes

Other recreational pastimes of the nobility were longer lived. Hawking and hunting were particularly popular and were exclusively the sports of the nobles. The privilege to hunt and hawk were denied the lower classes by both cost and legal restrictions. Ladies often accompanied the men on these hunting outings. Such games as *le jeu de paume* (a form of handball), and royal tennis, which was played within an enclosure (and has only modest resemblance to modern lawn tennis), were widely enjoyed. Shuffleboard, billiards, and board games such as chess and backgammon were more sedentary forms of recreation.

Medieval Concepts of Health and Hygiene: Galen Revisited

The tradition of medical knowledge during the Middle Ages reflected the classical Greek knowledge of Hippocrates, which was codified and amplified by Galen, the Greek physician of second century Rome. Galen's major contribution to the theoretical concepts of medicine was in the area of anatomy. He developed his body of knowledge through the dissection of animals, particularly apes, and, when permitted, human dissection. Galen's principle work, *De Medicina*, became the undisputed authority of medical knowledge during the Middle Ages. In it he developed an understanding of human physiology, which he believed was composed of four essential humors: blood, phlegm, yellow bile, and black bile. These humors resided in certain primary areas of the body.

Blood was to be found in the veins and arteries, although it was also partially located in the heart and liver. Phlegm was seated in the brain, but was also evidenced in the bladder and chest. When these humors blended in certain ways within the body, the person would be in a state of health. The concept of health was seen as a state of balance, which was further complicated by the four qualities associated with each humor: moist, dry, cold, and warm. The natural state of blood was warm and moist; yellow bile was warm and dry; black bile was cold and dry; phlegm was cold and moist.

In addition to the qualities, each humor was associated with characteristics that predominated at different stages of life and during different seasons of the year. Blood was bitter, phlegm was salty and sweet, black bile was strong, and yellow bile was sharp. In this way, there was an explanation for the exuberance of children, the strength of youth, the maturity of middle age, and the slowness and weakness of old age.

Human moods, personality, and disease were controlled by the disposition of the humors. Blood could make a person happy, kind, fat, or sleepy, whereas phlegm could move a person to thoughtfulness and prudence. An overabundance of one or more of the humors brought on physical maladies. Too much yellow bile caused mental worry; too much blood brought on mental disorders that were identified by laughing and singing. An overabundance of phlegm caused anorexia.

A large part of medical treatment was therefore focused on correcting the humoral imbalance. One of the most common treatments was phlebotomy (bloodletting). It was believed that phlebotomy could clear the mind, restore the memory, improve digestion and sleep, cleanse the stomach, and stop tears. The amount of blood taken was dependent on the age and physical condition of the patient. The removal of any blood, however, was done with the intent of restoring the humors to a state of healthy balance.

Other means used to restore the humoral balance of the body included a vast array of plants (herbs), minerals, and animal materials. Many times the belief in the therapeutic value of these materials commingled with local superstitions, magic, and astrology. Along with such mundane treatments as herbal teas and poultices, medical prescriptions included some quite disgusting preparations. Drinking one's own urine or the boiled extract of cow's dung was recommended as a cure for the plague. Hemorrhoids were treated by boiling a particular type of worm in linseed oil and applying the oil to the affected area. A fresh ram's lung placed on the forehead would cure a headache. Apparently, precious metals and jewels were highly therapeutic for almost any ailment.

In addition to the belief in classical humoral medicine, the strength of Christian faith was an additional dimension to the treatment of disease, which was viewed as punishment by God or the work of evil forces. Invoking the help of God through the saints became as important a therapy as humoral treatments. Pilgrimages, relics of saints, amulets, and incantations were clearly as popular as other therapies. Certain saints were identified with specific diseases, and the possibility of miracle cures through saintly or heavenly intervention was widely accepted. This was reinforced by the belief that miracles did not have to occur immediately but could be accomplished over time.

Summary

The church had a significant impact on the nature and purpose of sport, and this impact was based on the position and worth of the body. The early church was profoundly influenced by the Greek philosophers, and the position of the body in classical Greece, as well as within some segments of the Christian church, occupied a prominent and respected position. The Greek gods and the Christian concept of God assumed human form, which in Christianity is expressed as the "enfleshment." The corporeal nature of human existence was of serious importance that necessitated proper care.

Physical fitness and health were advocated by the Scholastics, because perfection in both the soul and the body were necessary to achieve happiness. The early Christian monks, however, sought enlightenment through bodily mortification and denounced all forms of sports and physical activities that were designed to promote health. This difference in opinion reflected the majority position in the church, that the body was vile and corrupt and beyond redemption. Needless to say, the early Christian monks (majority viewpoint) and Scholastics (minority viewpoint) were in disagreement concerning the worth of the body and the value of physical activity.

The church tolerated the games and amusements of the peasants and the aristocracy as well. There was not much the church could do to suppress the natural instinct for people to play and frolic, but it intervened when the games deteriorated into drunken brawls and lewd behavior. No doubt a strong sermon and reminder of proper behavior, along with other appropriate chastisements, were used. The brutality and carnage that were often present during the aristocratic sports of the medieval tournament and melee were opposed by the church. During the Crusades the church did permit the contests associated with the tournament and melee to be practiced in preparation for war.

The body was an object of medical research during this era. Galen's principle work, *De Medicina*, was the undisputed authority of medical knowledge. Galen was also one of the first physicians to "specialize" in sports medicine and was very interested in the training of athletes. He wrote about the necessity of proper exercise and warned against the dangers as a result of "jogging."

The treatment of disease was multitherapeutic. Christians believed that bodily diseases were punishment from God. The body was a mechanism by which mortal sins were punished by God. This belief was devastating to the earlier views of some Christians that held the philosophical and theological position of the body in high regard.

Discussion Questions

1. What was the prevalent concept of the body during the Middle Ages? Where did this concept come from, and what impact did it have on sport and physical education?

2. What were the main types of sport and physical activity during the Middle Ages? Which social group participated, and what did they gain from their efforts?

3. Who in the church was in favor of physical education? Were there any in the church who were against physical education? Why?

4. What was the connection between the tournaments and the Crusades?

5. Was St. Thomas Aquinas able to reconcile church dogma with philosophy? What was Aquinas' position on the body, and how did it conflict, if at all, with church dogma?

Suggestions for Further Reading

Ballou, R. "Early Christian Society and its Relationship to Sport." *National College Physical Education Association for Men 71st Proceedings* (1968): 159–165.

Boulton, W. B. *The Amusements of Old London.* London: J. C. Nimmo, 1901.

Bretano, R., ed. *The Early Middle Ages 500–1000.* N.P.: Free Press of Glencoe, 1964.

Carter, J. M. "Sport in the Bayeaux Tapestry." *Canadian Journal of History of Sport and Physical Education* 11, no. 1 (May 1980): 36–60.

———. *Ludi Medi Aevi: Studies in the History of Medieval Sport.* Manhattan, Kans.: Military Affairs/Aerospace Historian Publishing, 1981.

———. *Sports and Pastimes of the Middle Ages.* Columbus, Ga.: Brentwood Communications, 1984.

———. "A Medieval Sports Commentator: William Fitzstephen and London Sports in the Late Twelfth Century." *American Benedictine Review* 35, no. 2 (June 1984): 146–152.

———. "Muscular Christianity and its Makers: Sporting Monks and Churchmen in Anglo-Norman Society, 1000–1300." *British Journal of Sport History* 1, no. 2 (September 1984): 109–124.

Cheyette, F. L., ed. *Lordship and Community in Medieval Europe.* New York: Holt, Rinehart, and Winston, 1967.

Clepham, T. C. *The Tournament: Its Periods and Phases.* London: Methuen, 1919.

Cripps-Day, F. H. *The History of the Tournament in England and France.* London: Bernard Quartich, 1918; AMS Reprint, 1980.

Dahmus, J. *The Middle Ages: A Popular History.* Garden City, N.Y.: Doubleday, 1968.

Davis, R. H. C. *A History of Medieval Europe: From Constantine to Saint Louis.* London: Longmans, Green, 1957.

DeAneslev, M. *A History of Early Medieval Europe 476 to 911.* London: Methuen, 1956.

Evans, J. *The Flowering of the Middle Ages.* New York: McGraw-Hill, 1966.

Henderson, R. W. *Ball, Bat and Bishop: The Origin of Ball Games.* New York: Rockport, 1947.

Hoskins, C. H. "The Latin Literature of Sport." *Studies in Medieval Culture.* New York: Redereick Ungar, 1958.

Hoyt, R. S., ed. *Life and Thought in the Early Middle Ages.* Minneapolis: University of Minnesota Press, 1967.

MacKinney, L. C. *Early Medieval Medicine: With Special Reference to France and Chartres.* Baltimore: Johns Hopkins University Press, 1937.

———. *The Medieval World.* New York: Farrar & Rinehart, 1938.

Morrall, J. B. *The Medieval Imprint: The Foundation of the Western European Tradition.* London: C. A. Watts, 1967.

Painter, S. *French Chivalry.* Baltimore: Johns Hopkins University Press, 1940.

———. *A History of the Middle Ages.* New York: Alfred A. Knopf, 1953.

Pole, A. L. "Recreation." *Medieval England,* Vol. II. Oxford: Clarendon, 1958.

Reynolds, S. *Kingdoms and Communities in Western Europe 900–1300.* Oxford: Clarendon, 1984.

Riesman, D. *The Story of Medicine in the Middle Ages.* New York: Paul B. Hoeber, 1935.

Rubin, S. *Medieval English Medicine.* New York: Barnes & Noble, 1974.

Ruhl, J. K. "German Tournament Regulations of the 15th Century." *Journal of Sport History* 17, no. 2 (Summer 1990): 163–182.

Sandoz, E. "Tourneys in the Arthurian Tradition." *Speculum* 19, no. 4 (October 1944): 389–420.

Savage, H. "Hunting in the Middle Ages." *Speculum* 8, no. 1 (January 1933): 30–41.

Strutt, J. *The Sports and Pastimes of the People of England.* London: Methuen, 1893.

Thiebaux, M. "The Medieval Chase." *Speculum* 27, no. 3 (April 1967): 260–274.

Walsh, J. J. *Medieval Medicine.* London: A & C Black, 1920.

Notes

1. The "carrot" was the bliss obtained by living in a state of Christian grace; the "stick" was the punishment meted out by the Inquisition and the fear of going to hell. This explanation is a social and political one, and stops short of an endorsement of any religious explanation for the rise of the Catholic Church during this period of time. We do not wish to discount the legitimacy of the Catholic Church from a theological perspective, nor are we qualified to do so. Whether the Catholic Church, or any other church, is the sole repository of the will of God requires a "leap of faith" that we leave to each reader.

2. Frederick C. Copleston, *Medieval Philosophy* (New York: Harper & Row, 1961), 10.

3. Ibid.

4. Ibid., 60.

5. Ibid., 62.

6. David Sanderlin, "Physical Education in the Medieval Universities," unpublished paper, San Diego, 7.

7. William Fleming, *Arts and Ideas* (New York: Holt, Rinehart, and Winston, 1966), 136.

8. Sanderlin, *Physical Education in Medieval Universities,* 7.

9. D. R. G. Owen, *Body and Soul* (Philadelphia: Westminster Press, 1956); Wheeler H. Robinson, *The Religious Ideas of the Old Testament* (London: Duckworth, 1913); Daryl Siedentop, "A Historical Note on the Concept of Organismic Unity," typewritten manuscript, Hope College, 1989.

10. Frank Bottomley, *Attitudes to the Body in Western Christendom* (London: Lepus Books, 1979).

11. Ibid.

12. Deobold B. Van Dalen and Bruce L. Bennett, *A World History of Physical Education* (Englewood Cliffs, N.J.: Prentice Hall, 1971), 90.

13. Sanderlin, *Physical Education in Medieval Universities,* 1.

14. St. Thomas Aquinas, *Summa Theologiae,* trans. Blackfriars (New York: McGraw Hill, Vols. 1–60, 1964–66. First part of the Second part, question 4, article 6 (Abbrev. S. T., I–II, 4, 6).

15. Saint Thomas, I, 85, 7, trans. from the edition by the Fathers of English Dominican Province (New York: Benziger Bros., 1947), I, 439.

16. Thomas Gilby, ed., *St. Thomas Aquinas: Philosophical Texts* (London: Oxford University Press, 1951); S. T., I–II, 50, 4, reply obj. 3. Trans. from Gilby, Philosophical Texts, 203, no. 548.

17. Sanderlin, *Physical Education in Medieval Universities*, 6.

18. Maurice deWulf, *An Introduction to Scholastic Philosophy: Medieval and Modern*, trans. P. Coffey (New York: Dover Publications, 1956), 124–125.

19. Sanderlin, *Physical Education in Medieval Universities*, 7.

20. Ibid., 8.

21. Moses Maimonides, "Treatise on Asthma," in *The Medical Writings of Moses Maimonides No. 1*, ed. Suessman Munter (Philadelphia: Lippincott, 1963), 26.

22. Matthew M. de Benedictis, O.F.M., *The Social Thought of Saint Bonaventure: A Study in Social Philosophy* (Washington, D.C.: Catholic University of America Press, 1946), 46.

23. John Marshall Carter, *Ludi Medi Aevi: Studies in the History of Medieval Sport* (Manhattan, Kans.: MA/AH Publishing, Eisenhower Hall, Kansas State University, 1981), 62–63.

24. Ibid., 63.

25. Ibid., 63.

26. The pagan nature of these games led the Calvinists/Puritans of the seventeenth century to denounce both the amusements associated with these holidays and the Catholic Church for permitting these pagan celebrations to occur.

27. Allen Guttmann, *Sports Spectators* (New York: Columbia University Press, 1986), 49.

28. Ibid.

29. William Fitzstephens, *Descriptio Londoniae*; see J. M. Carter, *Ludi Medi Aevi*, 1981; F. M. Stenton's Norman London (Historical Association Leaflets, nos. 93, 94, 1934); English Historical Documents, 1042–1189, ed. D. C. Douglas and G. W. Greenaway (New York, 1953); Stow's Survey of London (London, 1965), 500–509.

30. Carter, *Ludi Medi Aevi*, 82.

31. W. Fitzstephens in Stow, *Descriptio Londoniae*, 501.

32. Stephen H. Hardy, "The Medieval Tournament: A Functional Sport of the Upper Class," *Journal of Sport History*, vol. 1, no. 2, 91–105.

33. Hardy, *Medieval Tournament*, 102.

The Renaissance and the Reformation

General Events

1270–1347 William of Occam, Scholastic philosopher

1309–1376 Popes resided at Avignon, France

1314–1321 Dante Alighieri writes *Divine Comedy*

1338–1453 100 Years War

1348 Black Death sweeps Europe

1370–1444 Petrus Vergerius

1378–1417 Great Schism between rival popes

1378–1446 Vittorino da Feltre

1400–1468 Johann Gutenberg and moveable print

1405–1564 Aeneas Silvio Piccolomini

1452–1519 Leonardo da Vinci

1453 Fall of Constantinople to Turks

1462–1525 Pietro Pomponazzi

1469–1517 Desiderius Erasmus

1469–1527 Machiavelli

1475–1564 Michelangelo

1478–1529 Baldassare Castiglione

1483–1531 Martin Luther

1490–1546 Thomas Elyot

1492 Columbus discovers new world

1508–1512 Michelangelo paints Sistine Chapel

1509–1564 John Calvin

1515–1568 Roger Ascham

1517 Protestant Reformation begins with Luther's *95 Theses*

1528 Castiglione's *The Courtier* published

1530 Henry VIII breaks with Rome

1532 Machiavelli's *The Prince* published

Introduction

The influence of the Catholic Church on European culture in the late Middle Ages cannot be overestimated. It permeated every aspect of culture—scholarship, politics, economics, and even one's private life. The periods of time following the Middle Ages are known as the Renaissance and the Reformation, and these periods stand out as a time of cultural change with respect to the Church. The Renaissance was in part caused by the reintroduction of Greek and Roman thought in intellectual circles, and as a result the Church had to compete with the philosophies, literature, and the paganism of ancient Greece and Rome. The Reformation was an effort to reform the Church itself and return it to the ways of the original Christians. One way to distinguish the Renaissance from the Reformation is that the Renaissance was an intellectual reawakening confined primarily to the upper class and nobility, while the Reformation was a religious reawakening that affected all of Western civilization. In both cases, however, the authority of the Catholic Church was diminished, and this change had a significant impact on how Western civilization viewed the body.

Different theories of how one should view the human body were developed during the Renaissance and the Reformation, and as a consequence the groundwork was laid for different attitudes toward sport and physical education. The Renaissance was heavily influenced by the classics—the great works of literature written during the times of the Greeks and Romans—especially the philosophies of Aristotle and Plato. These arguments were adopted by the humanists.

"Humanists" were philosophers who believed in the concept of "humanism," a philosophy that placed its focus on "humans" as opposed to the "other worldly" or heavenly concerns of earlier philosophies.

The ancient Greeks believed that the human body played an important role in every day life, and their philosophies accounted for this belief. Eventually Renaissance arguments evolved into the ideal of the "universal" or "Renaissance Man": one who is well-rounded, a philosophy that includes the use of the body to develop discipline and character. The Reformation was more complex; religious reformers argued that the body "housed" the soul. As such, the body could not be denigrated because it was the temple of God, and eventually it was argued that the "quality of the soul" could be determined by observing one's behaviors. Implicitly, then, the body was considered by scholars and leaders of the Renaissance and the Reformation to be more important than it was in the Middle Ages. How these positions developed is what makes the Renaissance and the Reformation interesting to physical educators.

Cultural Changes of the Renaissance

The Renaissance occurred roughly between 1300 and 1550, and was a time of radical change in European culture as it emerged from the Middle Ages. The word *renaissance* means rebirth or revival of "classics," which was how European culture described the writings of the ancient Greeks and Romans. Intellectuals during this period of time considered themselves enlightened because of their return to the classics. Indeed, the idea that the Middle Ages were "dark" began with the Renaissance scholars who were so critical of that period. In the previous chapter we discussed how the Middle Ages were characterized by feudalism and an agricultural economy, and were dominated politically and intellectually by the Church. The Renaissance, by comparison, was characterized by secular influence on thought and culture, the development of nations, and urban economies based on trade and commerce. These changes were considered an improvement and occurred for a variety of reasons like war, disease, and an influx of new ideas. None of these changes came easily to those who endured them.

Because the Renaissance fostered a rebirth of classical thought, it helped end Medieval ways of thought associated with the Church. Prior to the Renaissance, the Church was the arbiter of secular authority, and this allowed the Church a significant amount of religious, political, and economic control over the lives of Christians.

"Secular" is a word that describes matters of this world like politics and education. It can be contrasted in this case with matters of the church that were concerned with "other worldly" or heavenly matters.

Church leaders, from the pope down, told Christians how to live in this world so that they could gain entrance to heaven in the next world. Ignoring the authority of the Church could result in excommunication, a threat that implied enduring the fires of hell for eternity. Similarly, the Church also promised a life of eternal bliss in the presence of God if one obeyed its ways. This approach facilitated Church control over how people lived their every day lives.

The Renaissance undermined the philosophical basis used by the Church to control its members by creating an environment in which competing philosophies were read and discussed. These philosophies were those of the Greeks and Romans. In intellectual circles during the Renaissance, the classical philosophies of Plato and Aristotle rivaled Christian theology. While several scholars had previously attempted to reconcile the classics with the dogma of the Church (most notably Thomas Aquinas and Aristotle's philosophy), this proved very difficult to do. The classical philosophies emphasized how to live in this world, while Christian religion emphasized life in the next. Many intellectuals began to differ with the Church as to what was "reality," and a consequence of this change was the view that the material world and our bodily experiences were "real" and important. These differences led to important educational changes. As a consequence of its worldly concentration, Renaissance philosophy laid the groundwork for the justification of physical education and sport in Western civilization. It is no accident that the leading educators of the Renaissance incorporated physical education into their educational curriculums.

The rise of the nation-state also took control away from the Church. Kings and the nobility gained political power throughout the Renaissance, and developed the idea that a nation could exist separate from the Church. This change was made easier by the "schisms," or divisions, that developed within the Church (1378–1417). Basically, the schisms were competing political groups within the Catholic Church that fought for power among themselves, power that would give these groups more control over the material wealth of the church. Perhaps the best measure of these divisions was the simultaneous election in 1409 of three popes, all of whom had their own secular goals![1] Ironically, as the popes consolidated their power in the secular, material world, they came under increasing attack for abandoning their role as spiritual guides. These divisions were major causes of the Reformation, a movement that sought to "reform" the Catholic Church and return it to its original mission.

Politics and philosophical/religious factors were not the only causes of the development of the nation-state. Europe experienced several vicious wars, particularly the Hundred Years' War (1338–1453). Initiated by the English King Edward III, the war was fought over the interests of English and French royalty, economic factors like the control of the wool industry in Flanders, and the decades of prejudice and animosity that existed between the French and the English going back to the Norman Conquest in 1066. It appeared that the English would win for much of the war, controlling large parts of France including the entire northern half and the southern west coast in 1429. Eventually, however, the French were able to cast the English from their lands with the development of military technology that included gunpowder and cannon.

Another war that had a significant impact on the Renaissance was the ongoing battle between Christian Europe and the "infidel" Turks. Christians banded together throughout the late Middle Ages and the early Renaissance to travel to the East in "Crusades," the purpose of which was to free Constantinople, the capital of Eastern Christianity, from the influence of the Islamic Turks. The Turks, however, surrounded Constantinople in the early 1400s and finally took control in 1453.

Since the fall of Rome a thousand years earlier, the center of the Roman empire had been in Constantinople. Many of the great works of ancient Greece and Rome were there, and as the Turks came closer to conquering the city, many scholars left for the relative safety of the West. Indeed, while the fall of Constantinople was a disaster from the perspective of Europeans during the Renaissance, its fall caused an infusion of teachers and classical ideas into European intellectual circles that jolted philosophers and educators out of their old ways. In addition, the war caused the movement of armies, the trading of goods that supplied the soldiers, and the travel of many people to distant lands. The considerable amount of travel helped break down feudal culture and led Europe into a period of economic and cultural growth. So while war had its obvious devastating consequences, it also had the effect of shaking Europe out of its feudal traditions and providing the opportunity for the exchange of philosophical ideas.

War was not the only destructive force that changed European culture. Europe was ravaged by bubonic plague, known to contemporaries as the "Black Death." An often fatal disease carried by flea-infested rats, it reached a peak in 1348–50 and is estimated to have killed almost *one-third* of Europe's population. There were several causes of the plague, among them famine, a poor understanding of hygiene, and a complete misunderstanding of the causes of the plague itself. By 1300 it was difficult to grow enough food for Europe's increasing population, and most people faced at least one period of famine in their lives. Life during the Renaissance for the average person was very difficult. Indeed, the life-span of the average European in the late Middle Ages was only thirty-five years! Famines followed the population explosion, hitting newly developed urban areas extremely hard. In addition, Europe experienced an economic depression, making food that much harder to come by. As a result of all of these factors, Europeans in the early fourteenth century were in generally bad health. This led them to be highly susceptible to the plague.

In sum, there is no one single cause of the end of the Middle Ages and the beginning of the Renaissance and the Reformation. War, intellectual curiosity, plague, religion, overpopulation, famine and a variety of other factors all combined to cause great changes in the fabric of European culture. Every institution was forced to change, and education was no exception.

The Reformation

While the Renaissance was stimulated by the idealism of the classics and the concept of the "universal man," the Reformation was stimulated by religious zeal. As a consequence, the end of the Middle Ages looked quite a bit different in northern Europe than it did in the south. The Renaissance in Italy was at its height when the ideas it fostered came to northern Europe, and as far as the intellectuals of fifteenth- and sixteenth-century England and northern Europe were concerned, the Reformation was the Renaissance.

The Reformation had as its goal the "re-forming" of the Catholic Church. By the time of the Reformation the Catholic Church as a political institution was corrupt, and its agents at every level sought money for the Church accounts. Money-seeking had an impact on the truly devout, as monks pestered people in the street with their begging in hopes of gaining entrance into heaven. The clergy was skilled at getting tithes and perquisites from the parishioners, and they noted that the popes no longer looked like the Apostles when they wore their fine clothes. According to Desiderius Erasmus, a famous critic of the Catholic Church, the popes sought riches, honors, jurisdictions, offices, dispensations, licenses, indulgences, ceremonies and tithes, excommunications, and interdicts![2] Popes lusted for legacies, hoped to be worldly diplomats, and fought bloody wars. It was very difficult to argue with Erasmus when he argued that this was no way to run a Church . . . unless you were the pope!

Religious reform was not the only reason for removing the pope and the Church from political power. In 1530 Henry VIII broke with the Catholic Church and formed the Anglican Church because the pope would not, or could not, help the political interests of England. There were two reasons for Henry and the pope to be at odds. First, Henry, who was married to Catherine of Aragon, intensely desired a son. When Catherine did not bear a son, Henry tried to divorce her and sought an annulment from the pope. However, politics intervened. In the early 1500s Rome was controlled by the troops of Charles V, a Spaniard who was also Catherine's nephew. As long as Charles' troops surrounded the Vatican, the pope would not grant an annulment. Second, Henry resented the pope because he believed that since 1511 England had fought Continental wars for the pope without reward.[3] The only recourse left to Henry was to make a national Church of England, of which Henry would be the head.

Political interests aside, those who sought to reform the Church for religious reasons wanted to go back to the beginning of Christianity. They claimed for themselves the label of "Christians" and sought to differentiate themselves from "Catholics" (formerly all believers in Christ were known as "Christians"). The Reformation, from a religious perspective, moved the Catholic Church from the role of "middle man" and placed the authority of one's religiosity in the hands of that individual. From social and political perspectives, the Reformation caused the creation of the various Protestant (from "protest") sects and a new, rebuilt version of the Catholic Church. Furthermore, the Reformation strengthened the newly developed idea of nationalism by undermining the authority of the Catholic Church and helped develop the idea of a middle class. As Bronowski noted,

> The Reformation, at least in its Calvinist version, made religion a thing of this world and achieved the miracle of identifying good works with the accumulation of riches. The shame of profiteering was wiped away and what was formerly the lust for wealth became the fulfillment of God's purposes on earth.[4]

All of these ideas came together during the Reformation. For our purposes, the combination of changes in culture and Reformation ideas regarding the nature of the human body, the soul, and the mind had a radical impact on education. Indeed, many ideas from the Reformation are alive and well in American education today in our attitudes toward sport and physical education.

The Philosophers and Educators of the Renaissance

Unlike the Middle Ages, the Renaissance did not produce philosophers who had a lasting impact. The most studied philosophy of the Renaissance was scholasticism, a highly intellectual philosophy that emphasized the mind and that tried to reconcile the theology of the Christian church with rational thought. In other words, the scholastics tried to prove that reason and faith are consistent with each other. This effort lasted through the Reformation before waning during the eighteenth century, succumbing to attacks from philosophers like William of Ockham, who argued that the senses and the material world are all one can know. The influence of the scholastics has lasted to this day, however, and is evident in the emphasis placed on intellect and mind in our educational institutions. The emphasis on the mind by the scholastics can be seen by the connotations of the words *scholar* and *scholastic*, two words derived from scholasticism that even today emphasize intellectual learning.

Philosophers of the Renaissance spent a considerable amount of time resurrecting the philosophies of antiquity, especially Plato and Aristotle. These philosophies were compared to and contrasted with the teachings of the Church. Like Aquinas, these philosophers hoped to show that the classic philosophies went hand in hand with the teachings of the Church. Instead Renaissance philosophers paved the way for the philosophical undermining of the Church. This occurred because the link that the Renaissance philosophers tried to find between medieval Christian virtues and the classical philosophies did not exist. The Church of the Renaissance emphasized the ascetic and monastic virtues of self-denial and even bodily mortification. Those "pleasures of the flesh" that the Christian church allowed, like sex, eating and drinking, were necessary to one's bodily survival. Furthermore, the Church accepted these vices as proof that humans are by nature weak. In contrast, the classical philosophies of the Greeks and Romans accepted the human body. Indeed, so different were scholasticism and the classic philosophies that a new group of Renaissance philosophers developed. This group eventually attacked the monastic virtues as having been falsely imposed on the true structure of Christianity.

This new group of Renaissance philosophers was known as "humanists." Humanism is a philosophy that placed its focus on "humans" as opposed to the "other worldly" concerns of Medieval philosophy. Humanists disagreed with the monastic, ascetic approach to daily life emphasized by the scholastics, and refused to think of the human body as evil. Indeed, humanists rejected the idea of original sin, "the belief that the soul and the body are sharply divided and that, because man cannot express his soul except through his body, he carries an unavoidable sin."[5] Instead humanists believed in the doctrine of original goodness, the Greek belief that ". . . the soul and the body are one, and that the actions of the body naturally and fittingly express the humanity of the soul."[6]

Humanism had as its ideal the "universal" man, also known as *l'uomo universale*. The universal man cultivated interests in the arts, the sciences of the day, languages, was well traveled and well mannered, and skilled in the martial arts, games, and sports. Ideally he was able to function in all possible settings of contemporary life, and his ability to do this would be given to him through schooling. Consequently, schooling reflected this well-rounded approach and provided the necessary instruction to meet its goals. Certainly, physical education became more valued because of the focus of humanism.

The Italian scholars, in particular, used the humanistic approach and emphasized three main ideas. First, humanists admired the ancient Greeks and Romans, and sought to understand the philosophy and history of the classics. This approach to education was adopted by the Church in the late Middle Ages and did not draw any criticism from the Church. Second, the humanists emphasized the joy of living and sought to enjoy their corporeal lives.

> "Corporeal" is another word for "bodily" or "material." It is used to emphasize an idea that is clearly not "spiritual" in nature.

Third, the humanists argued that one's corporeal life was worth contemplating. These two ideas existed in sharp contrast to the ways of the Church and represent a significant difference between humanism and scholasticism.

Aeneas Silvio Piccolomini's *De Liberorum Educatione* (The Liberal Education), Pietro Pomponazzi's *De immortalitate animae* (The Immortal Animal), and Baldassare Castiglione's *The Courtier* are some of the most famous books of the Renaissance and represent the culmination of the humanist train of thought. Based on the work of the humanists who preceded them, all of these books were similar in that they told the universal man how to live and think. The writings of Piccolomini, Pomponazzi, and Castiglione in turn influenced many of the leading intellectuals of the Renaissance, who helped the philosophy of humanism come to life in the shape of the universal man.

The universal man valued knowledge for its ability to expand his awareness of the world. He was as interested in knowing about the world as much as in being an interesting individual, and as a result the universal man was well read in many fields of study rather than a specialist in a few narrow fields. Many of the things he studied would never be used, but this generalization helped make him the interested and interesting person of the Renaissance ideal.

Petrus Paulus Vergerius

Petrus Paulus Vergerius (1370–1444) was one of the first of the great Italian humanists, and his contribution was that of the "true founder of the new education." His *De Ingenuis Moribus* was written for Ubertinus, the son of the lord of Padua, and described the basic ideas upon which humanist education was built. Influenced by Plato, Vergerius believed that education was a matter of public interest and should create a good citizen of the state. However, Vergerius' idea of education was aimed primarily at the sons of the wealthy, and not just any citizen. He believed that the best way to develop the good citizen was to start teaching children at an early age, emphasizing morals along with activities suitable to the age of the student.

Vergerius' model was that of Sparta, and he tried to adapt the methods of contemporary warfare to the Spartan model of training young men for war. He believed that the purpose of physical education was that of preparing one for the military. Vergerius' attitude toward sport in this respect was not significantly different from that of an educator during the Middle Ages, when military matters were of utmost importance. The main difference with Vergerius was that physical education was incorporated into the education of the total individual. Examples of Vergerius' program were the Greek pentathlon, swimming, horsemanship, and use of the shield, spear, sword, and club.

Vittorino da Feltre

The most famous of the Italian humanists was Vittorino da Feltre (1378–1446). Like Vergerius, Vittorino was educated at Padua where he studied grammar, mathematics, and Greek. He became a professor of grammar and mathematics at Padua, and he remained there until 1415 when he resigned, as one scholar put it, because of the undisciplined and decadent life of the university town.[7] Da Feltre was offered the chance to teach the children of the Marquis Gonzaga of Mantua, and the school that he developed, La Giocosa, was the first to blend the spirit of Christianity with both the classics and Greek concepts of physical education for the sons of the wealthy. La Giocosa, or Pleasant House, was an ideal setting for a school. Because it was surrounded by meadows and bordering a river, students were able to exercise freely. Indeed, Vittorino eventually adopted the name Gymnasium Palatinum, or Palace School, in imitation of the ancient Greek gymnasiums. This was a radical departure from schools of the Middle Ages, where education was only for the mind.

Da Feltre believed in educating the mind, but he also believed in educating the body and the soul. So while Renaissance education was, to a certain extent, separated from the Church compared to Medieval education, da Feltre serves as an example of how Christian values continued to be taught. Da Feltre believed that he could create the Renaissance version of the philosopher-king: educated princes who would rule with wisdom and justice. Da Feltre believed that the development of the ideal citizen required a combination of the classics and Christian morality. As W. H. Woodward noted,

> He brought with him to Mantua a desire to combine the spirit of the Christian life with the educational apparatus of classical literature, whilst uniting with both something of the Greek passion for bodily culture and for dignity of the outer life.[8]

It was da Feltre's commitment to this combination that made him so effective. Starting with only three students, he soon had as many as

Figure 6.1
Vittorino da Feltre. From: E. W. Gerber: *Innovators and Institutions in Physical Education.* Philadelphia: Lea & Febiger, 1971.

seventy. His fame as an educator spread through all of Europe and had an impact that has lasted through today. Woodward called da Feltre the first "modern schoolmaster."

One reason for his excellence as a teacher was that he could do everything he taught. Da Feltre could teach all of the "Arts" (grammar, dialectic, rhetoric, history, and moral philosophy), as well as mathematics and languages (primarily Latin and Greek). Together these areas of study came to be known as the "liberal arts"; it was argued that studies in these areas literally "liberate" the educated person from the chains of ignorance and prejudice. Da Feltre believed that these subjects disciplined and educated the mind. Yet he also believed that the body had to be disciplined and educated, and he practiced what he preached. Apparently a small, thin man, he subjected himself to the cold in order to endure it better. He exercised regularly and never ate or drank too much. His regimen must have been very effective, for he was never sick until the final illness that took his life. He was also deeply religious, going to Mass and confession regularly. No wonder his students learned; da Feltre led his students as much as he instructed.

For our purposes, Vittorino da Feltre was one of the first, if not the first, to institute physical education as an important part of an educational curriculum during the Renaissance. He may have been emulating Plutarch's *Education for Boys*, a text that was translated in 1411 and was very popular in Renaissance Italy. Da Feltre's goal was to develop the health of his students, and he did this by having them participate in two or more hours daily in physical activities including games, riding, running, leaping, fencing, and ball games—all watched by teachers skilled in these activities. During the summer he moved his school to the Castle of Goito, where the students went hiking and camping for days at a time. Da Feltre also sought to educate future rulers in military skills that might be needed to defend their lands. To this end his students practiced archery, fencing, and riding.

Vittorino da Feltre was the first to effectively bring together the humanist ideals of mind, body, and spirit in order to develop the ideal citizen. He believed that each part of the individual needed cultivation, and that education was the means to do this. Clearly influenced by Plato's ideas, he may have gone one step further than Plato by putting these ideas into practice and living by them as well. La Giocosa became the model upon which subsequent physical education programs were based.

Aeneas Silvio Piccolomini

Most humanist philosophers were commissioned by the aristocracy and courts of the Italian princes, and it was for these students that the Renaissance concept of the universal man was established. Aeneas Silvio Piccolomini (1405–1464), also known as Aeneas Sylvius and later Pope Pius II, wrote *De Liberorum Educatione* for Ladislas, King of Bohemia and Hungary. Like Vergerius and da Feltre, Piccolomini's ideas on education were reserved for the children of the rich. In *De Liberorum Educatione*, Piccolomini argued that children should be taught to use the bow and sling, throw spears, ride horses, and swim in order to be good soldiers. Yet Piccolomini was also interested in the general well being of students:

> As regards a boy's physical training, we bear in mind that we aim at implanting habits which will prove beneficial through life. . . . A boy should be taught to hold his head erect, look straight and fearlessly before him and to bear himself with dignity whether walking, standing, or sitting. . . . Games and exercises which develop the muscular activities and the general carriage of the person should be encouraged by every teacher.[9]

Piccolomini, one of the earliest Renaissance writers, emphasized military proficiency because he believed these skills were necessary for Christians to defend themselves from the Turks.

Baldassare Castiglione

Baldassare Castiglione's (1478–1529) *The Courtier* was written to teach young members of the aristocracy how to behave in the court. Castiglione did not attach as much importance to military training as did Piccolomini, although he still rated it important to the universal man. Castiglione did not believe the courtier should be a professional soldier. Indeed, he was as at home in the court (hence the name *courtier*) as much as he was on the battlefield. This emphasis on the well-rounded individual can be seen when Castiglione makes fun of a man who refused an invitation to dance with a gentlewoman because he does not think it is "professional." In this conversation the gentlewoman asks the would-be courtier:

> 'What then is your profession?' 'To fight.' Then said the gentlewoman, 'Seeing you are not now at war nor in place to fight I would think it best for you to be well smeared and set up in an armory till time were that you should be occupied, lest you wax more rustier than you are.'[10]

The well-rounded nature of the courtier can be seen by the many different types of activities he should have experienced in school:

> It is fitting also to know how to swim, to leap, to run, to throw stones. . . . Another admirable exercise, and one very befitting a man at court, is the game of tennis, in which are all shown the disposition of the boys, and quickness and suppleness of every member, and all those qualities that are seen in nearly every other exercise. Nor less highly do I esteem vaulting on horse, which, although it be fatiguing and difficult, makes a man very light and dexterous more than any other thing; and besides its utility, if this lightness is accompanied by grace, it is to my thinking a finer show than any of the others.[11]

By the time of Castiglione, a soldier's life was seen by socialites as a very specialized career. Castiglione encouraged courtiers to be more well rounded. Ironically, the rise of the professional soldier gave the courtier time to practice his social skills, and therefore made the courtier possible. Castiglione was criticizing the very profession that made his courtier possible.

The Philosophers and Educators of the Reformation

As we stated above, the theme of the Reformation was that of the reform of the Christian Church. Many other changes occurred as well during this time: commerce and industry expanded as trade increased, people moved from the country and into the cities, and an emphasis on education became evident as its benefits were seen among the nobility and the upper class. Important to our discussion, education came to be seen as a necessity in a changing world where trade and commerce was becoming more common as a way of life. Since physical education was part of the total educational package of many philosophers of both antiquity and of the Renaissance, it became more common in the curriculum in the Reformation than it was in the Middle Ages. By and large, however, physical education was a small part of the total curriculum, and where it did exist it was usually associated with the education of the wealthy.

This emphasis on education did not occur without some resistance. In 1391 English feudal landowners petitioned Richard II to enforce a rule that forbade the children of serfs to attend school without their lord's permission. Richard refused, and the next king decreed that any child could go to school. While the change toward public education proceeded slowly, the change from education for only the elite to mass education was begun.

As in the Middle Ages, most teachers were priests. Priests had always been trained in reading and language, but during the Renaissance and more in the Reformation the curriculum expanded to include the catechism, the Creed, the basic prayers, reading, writing, arithmetic, singing, and flogging.[12] During the Reformation the body was often seen as a tool that could be used to pry a reluctant mind into learning. Flogging was often the method of choice, but all methods of corporal punishment relied on the same idea: use the body to get to the mind. As Durant noted,

> Even in secondary schools flogging was the staff of instruction. A divine explained that 'the boys' spirits must be subdued': the parents agreed with him; and perhaps 'tis so. Agnes Paston urged the tutor of her unstudious son to 'belash him' if he did not amend, 'for I have lever he were fairly buried than lost by default.'[13]

The main emphasis on education through secondary school was religious training, but grammar and composition were added during this time that included classic literature from ancient Rome. In 1372 the first of England's "public" schools was formed to provide college preparatory training for a limited selection of boys.[14] In 1440 Henry VI established Eton School to prepare students for King's College, Cambridge. The public schools became famous in the 1800s for their use of sport to teach desirable virtues such as discipline and courage. Eton School in particular is famous for this practice, as can be seen in the saying, "The Battle of Waterloo was won on the playing fields of Eton." This saying describes the belief of nineteenth-century Britons, who argued that those traits necessary to winning wars were learned not in the classroom but on the playing fields.

The education of women continued, for the most part, to be scattered and incomplete by modern-day standards. Many women of the middle class learned to write English, and a few women learned literature and philosophy. After elementary school, however, women were confined largely to the home and were responsible for raising the children and keeping the house.

The sons of the aristocracy were educated differently from the children of the middle class. Until the age of seven, male children of the nobility were taught by the women of the house. After this they often served as pages for relatives or for neighboring nobles. At the age of 14 they became squires, a kind of adult assistant to the lord of the manor in which they served. At this stage their education was primarily physical education: they learned to ride, shoot, hunt, joust, and practice those physical skills that were necessary to wage war. No doubt this life of sport was more enjoyable than the intellectual exercises practiced by their social lessers, and indeed, the sporting life to a certain extent distinguished the upper class nobility from those who worked for them. As Durant notes, "Book learning they left to their inferiors," indicating that the intellectual skills learned by the middle class were to be put to use by the nobility to preserve the social order.[15]

The early part of the Reformation witnessed the development of one of the great institutions of the Western world, the modern university. Oxford and Cambridge both grew significantly, adding "halls," or places of residence for selected students. While there was much growth, these colleges were not quite recognizable as such. Most classes were held in schoolrooms or auditoriums scattered throughout the town. Still, some of the great philosophers of the fourteenth century came out of Oxford, including Duns Scotus and William of Ockham.

Sport was not yet part of the life of the college student, indicating that the education of the mind was still the only important task of schooling. Furthermore, the influence of the Church curtailed sporting activities for the same reasons as it had for the last several centuries: the body was meant to be disciplined, not used for pleasure. Durant notes that without sport, students were left to other, less wholesome pursuits:

> Forbidden to engage in intramural athletics, they spent their energy in profanity, tippling, and venery; taverns and brothels throve on their patronage. Attendance at Oxford fell from its thirteenth-century peak to as low as a thousand; and after the expulsion of Wyclif academic freedom was rigorously curtailed by episcopal control.[16]

While attendance at Oxford fell, it grew at Cambridge until by the 1400s both colleges were roughly equal in size and prestige. During this century classes became more structured, beginning at six in the morning and continuing until five in the afternoon. Courses were strictly intellectual in nature, and physical activities were largely prohibited.

The dominant philosophy of the Reformation was that of scholasticism. As we noted earlier, scholasticism as a philosophy attempted to show the consistency of reason with religious faith. In such an environment, with the noted exceptions of St. Bonaventure and St. Thomas Aquinas, the use of the body and its senses was not encouraged. However, it is during this time that certain philosophers began to undermine the scholastics, and in so doing paved the way for the acceptance of the human body and the senses as a way of knowing reality in the modern world.

For our purposes, philosophers like William of Ockham developed a philosophical foundation for the use of the body and sensations in the education of children, and in so doing anticipated the philosopher John Locke by almost 300 years. It is upon these types of philosophical arguments that the field of physical education is based. However, while the philosophical arguments that justify the existence of physical education became more frequent during the Reformation, the practice of physical education itself was not evident for several centuries to come. Indeed, the theologians of the Reformation argued against sport and physical education as, at best, a waste of time, and at worst proof that one's soul was doomed for hell! It is our position that the arguments that developed during the Reformation continue to burden physical educators in that we have to continually justify playful activities as being educational.

The value in understanding these arguments, and knowing how they came about, is that Reformation arguments are in direct contrast to the extreme intellectualism that existed at the time, and to a great extent still exists in the modern-day institution of education. The philosophical arguments that were used against overintellectualism are as potent now as they were then. Furthermore, understanding the arguments against the value of play enables physical educators to overcome prejudices that are centuries old. Indeed, the bias against play as a valuable educational tool reached new heights during the Reformation, and this bias still exists among educators who do not know the history of the Reformation and its consequences in the modern world. Understanding Luther and Calvin can help modern physical educators justify the existence of their profession in the modern institution of education.

William of Ockham

One of the most famous philosophers of his time was William of Ockham. Born at the end of the thirteenth century, Ockham was raised in a Franciscan order until the age of twelve, when he was sent to study at Oxford. Ockham did not address physical education directly. However, he argued against the layers upon layers of philosophical abstractions that were the hallmark of medieval philosophy. Ockham did not like strictly intellectual arguments over strictly intellectual issues (How many angels can dance on the head of a pin?). Ockham developed a philosophical method now known as "Ockham's razor," which, simply stated, is the argument that the correct answer to any question is probably the correct one. He used his razor on epistemology, and instead argued for the use of the body and sensations as a way of knowing reality. "Applying the principle to epistemology, Ockham judged it needless to assume, as the source of material knowledge, anything more than sensations."[17] From sensations arise memory, perception, imagination, anticipation, thought, and experience.

Ockham's philosophy was a controversial one in his day, and it is hard to understand, from the modern worldview, just why Ockham created such an uproar in his own time. In short, Ockham attacked both the intellectualism of his times as well as the philosophical foundation upon which the Christian church rested. Ockham attacked the style of philosophy that was used to support the Christian church for centuries, and an attack on the philosophy was seen as an attack on the Church itself. Since during Ockham's time the Church was associated with a kind of antiphysicalism, Ockham can be seen as one who made it possible for physical education to exist in the future even though he was not an advocate for it in his own time.

Desiderius Erasmus

Desiderius Erasmus (1469–1517) is a pivotal figure, representative of the humanists of the Renaissance yet central to the Reformation in northern Europe. Indeed, while Erasmus can be considered a figure of the Renaissance, he was famous for his use of the humanistic methods of scholarship and literature to criticize the Catholic Church as a political institution, and consequently he helped usher in the Reformation. Many contemporaries of Erasmus believed that he was the cause of much of the religious struggle during the Reformation, that he "laid the eggs which Luther . . . hatched."[18] Erasmus, however, disassociated himself with the reformer Martin Luther because he felt Luther's revolutionary zeal was too extreme. Still, his attitude toward the human body reflects that of many Reformation theorists.

Trained as a priest, Erasmus was fluent in Greek and Latin. He used his knowledge to interpret ancient texts, but he became famous for his satirical portraits of anyone who boasted of their knowledge, power, or piety. Erasmus' *The Praise of Folly*, his most famous work, argued that the human race owed its existence to folly rather than the methods of reason. In 1516 he wrote *Education of a Christian Prince*. In this book he argued for lower taxes, less war, fewer monasteries, and more schools. Erasmus' work helped to undermine the absolutist powers of the Church and to justify an approach to religion that relied on an individual's interpretation of the Bible rather than the official Catholic Church version of the Bible. In so doing he helped make education a part of every person's life, regardless of social class.

While Erasmus was an advocate for education, he appears to have argued against physical education in education curriculum. He believed that after age six the intellectual demands on a child were so great that they precluded much time spent on the sport and games. This can be seen in his dualistic position on the body, in which he separates mental powers from physical condition:

> We have to meet an argument against early training drawn from the superior importance of health. Personally I venture to regard the mental advantages gained as outweighing some slight risks in the matter of physical vigour.[19]

As can be seen, Erasmus was somewhat ascetic, which can be explained by his strong beliefs regarding the proper role of religion in culture. His ambivalence regarding the virtues of health and physical education in favor of one's intellect was manifest in the colleges and universities of northern Europe during the Reformation.

Martin Luther

Perhaps the best known figure of the Reformation was Martin Luther (1483–1546). Luther's famous *95 Theses*, posted on the door of the Whittenberg Church, condemned the selling of indulgences.

> *"Indulgences" were the remission of punishment granted by Catholic priests. Upon hearing confession, a priest would grant a sinner "indulgence," which placed the sinner's soul in the state of grace necessary for entrance into heaven. In the Reformation indulgences were sold by priests, and in many cases the holy act of confession was perverted into a form of extortion used to enrich the bank accounts of corrupt church officials.*

Briefly put, Luther argued that the selling of indulgences was wrong, that one should be forgiven for his or her sins through one's faith and the acceptance of the merits of Christ. This removed the Church as "middleman" and put the responsibility for religion directly on the shoulders of the individual. Luther's intention was to remove the Catholic Church from its perceived role of arbiter of heaven and hell. The effect, however, was far more dramatic. Luther helped make practical the ideas of democracy that were to follow in the Enlightenment, that each individual, rather than some other power, chooses his or her beliefs. He also paved the way for the idea that each individual, no matter what social class, needs to be educated.

Luther studied theology and philosophy in the university at Erfurt and, after a brief stint in law school, became a monk. Eventually he was ordained a priest. Luther believed that man could be saved only by complete faith in Christ, and this led him to believe in the power of individual faith. As a consequence of his belief that each individual must interpret the word of God, Luther was a strong advocate of education.

In the time of Luther, however, many parents began to reject the type of education that was commonly available because it was too oriented toward developing priests and nuns. In other words, education was strictly intellectual and taught primarily religious dogma. And since they were not in school, children spent their time as children will—playing. To Luther the idea that children were playing rather than learning how to read and commune with God was wrong. Instead, Luther argued that boys and girls should spend an hour or two a day in school learning how to read, rather than

> . . . spend tenfold as much time in shooting crossbows, playing ball, running, and tumbling about. In like manner, a girl has time to go to school an hour a day . . . for she sleeps, dances, and plays away more than that.[20]

It can be seen by this statement that Luther believed play could not take the place of education, and that playing games was in direct conflict with "real" education.

Having been raised in a family that believed in both superstitions and religion, Luther struggled with matters of the body and of the spirit. He attempted to practice the monastic virtue of self denial as a young man, but he rejected this idea in adulthood and came to believe that complete subjugation of the body was impossible. Consequently he advocated music, games, and dancing as acceptable pastimes for adults because they were not in themselves evil, and that these activities were better than the entirely unwholesome and sacrilegious alternatives that were available at the time. Luther believed that people should be able to engage in

> . . . honorable and useful modes of exercise . . . so that they might not fall into gluttony, lewdness, surfeiting, rioting, and gambling. Accordingly, I pronounce in favor of these two exercises and pastimes, namely, music, and the knightly sports of fencing, wrestling, etc., of which, the

one drives care and gloom from the heart, and the other gives a full development to the limbs, and maintains the body in health.[21]

Clearly Luther believed that the human body should be taken care of for both spiritual and physical reasons. He argued that a Christian should take care of his own body because, in so doing, it enabled him to be a hard worker. This argument was quite different from the Medieval view that the body was to be denied in order to obtain spiritual purity. Indeed, Luther helped change the focus of spirituality from the next world (heaven or hell) to this world, and consequently helped change the attitude of Christians toward the human body. But to say that Luther was an advocate for physical education and sport would be a grave error, for Luther saw these activities as, at worst, a waste of time and at best, an alternative to the sin of seeking physical pleasure. To summarize, while Luther did not endorse physicality in the same way as did the humanists, he was more favorable toward it than the monks of the Middle Ages.

John Calvin

While Luther helped change attitudes toward the use of our bodies, John Calvin (1509–1564) may have had the most impact on modern attitudes toward sport. At the age of only 26 he composed, in the words of one scholar, ". . . the most eloquent, fervent, lucid, logical, influential, and terrible work in all the literature of the religious revolution."[22] *The Principles of the Christian Religion* was a brilliant treatise that rejected the humanist concern with earthly excellence and turned men's thoughts again to the after world. As such, Calvin was a dualist who wished to spend time on the spirit and none on the body. Eventually his ideas were accepted by millions of Protestants in Switzerland, France, Scotland, England, and North America. As a Puritan Calvin resisted the idea of gentle birth, and like Luther, Calvin helped democratize religion by making each individual more important.

One major difference between Luther and Calvin was that Calvin accepted the idea of "predestination." During his studies Luther came across the idea of predestination, the belief that God destined some souls to salvation and the rest to hell. Only God knew where one's soul was bound. This idea, accepted by Calvin and many later Protestant Reformers, was considered absurd by Luther. Calvin argued that by a simple act of faith one could believe that one was *predestined* to go to heaven, the "divine election." This concept must have been of tremendous relief to those who could not afford to buy indulgences from Catholic priests during the Reformation. Another belief of Calvin's was that most people were destined to burn in hell because God, who was seen as an angry, vengeful being, created people as sinners. It was left to the individual to elect to believe that one was predestined to go to heaven, and of course those who elected to believe were members of Calvin's church. If one did not choose, then one would burn in hell.

While it appears that one could merely choose to go to heaven, it was not that simple. One's behaviors were continually observed, and only those with souls that were predestined to go to heaven would behave in the proper way. Only God knew for sure where one's soul was headed; people could only guess at their destination as measured by their habits and disposition toward prayer and work. Proper behavior included a good work ethic, abstinence from gambling and drinking, and in general an avoidance of any type of observable, physical pleasure. This avoidance included many of the playful pursuits of Calvin's time, so many of the activities that were associated with physical education and sport were prohibited by Calvin's theology. Those whose behaviors tended toward drinking, gambling, and the pursuit of physical pleasure through play were seen as destined to go to hell.

Of importance to physical educators are the consequences of how predestination affected attitudes toward work and play.[23] Simply put, if one believed in Calvin's doctrine of predestination, one's behaviors were disposed toward work and prayer. Those who enjoyed work were destined for heaven. In contrast, those who were disposed toward play were predestined for hell. The logical conclusion of this theological formula is that physical education and sport are the activities of those who are destined for hell. Clearly, John Calvin was no friend of physical education and sport!

Central to Calvin's argument was a different concept of how people viewed time. Before the Reformation, time was viewed cyclically; each day, season, or year would renew itself. Using this logic, people believed that each day the sun would rise just as it had the day before, after each winter there was spring, and every year was a copy of the year before. Prior to Calvin, people believed that time went in a circle, or accepted a view that historians describe as "cyclic time."

Calvin argued for a concept historians call *linear time*, which is the way that people view time in the modern world. Each moment was considered "God given" and not to be wasted. Once a moment was gone, it could never be used as God saw fit. Consequently, to waste this God-given gift was a sin, and those who wasted God's time were sinners. Calvin argued that the best use of God's time was to be productive and to pray, and that the few people elected by God to go to heaven were disposed toward using God's time well and could be observed as having the necessary character to use his time well.

Calvin's ideas about time, work, and prayer had a negative effect on participation in sport and physical education that has lasted well into the twentieth century. While his rationale was very different from that of the early Christian monks, Calvin's theology had the consequence of working against participation in physical education, sport, and other playful activities. The monks believed that denying the body purified the soul; Calvin believed that work and prayer were a good use of God's time. Both interpretations of the Bible, however, had the same consequence: sport, play, and physical education were to be avoided. Calvin's ideas eventually evolved into Puritanism, where the way to tell the difference between those saved and those condemned could be seen in one's discipline and good deeds. Those destined to be saved were industrious and hard working; those who were not used their time poorly by, among others, playing. Besides forbidding activities like dances, playing cards, or singing, people were forbidden to *enjoy* sensual pleasures like sex, drinking, and gambling because these activities eventually would seduce an individual away from God.[24] In Calvin's words:

> . . . it is clear that this conseration means that licentious abuse is to be curbed, and confirms the rule of St. Paul that we should make no provision for the flesh to fulfill its lusts (Rom. 13:14), which, if they are given too much scope, boil over furiously out of control.[25]

Calvin's argument put an emphasis on the value of the body in that what one did with his or her body determined where one's soul was bound. In so doing, Calvin argued against the ideas of the early monks that the body is evil or to be denied. The only saving virtue of this position is that the body is, at least, good for physical work. This position can be used to argue for concepts like healthful living, for a healthy person can work harder than one who is not. Yet at the same time his ideas sought to remove play and games from the lives of everyday people. Simply put, if you were not working, you were wasting God's time. A saying that would reflect Calvin's theology is, "Idle hands are the Devil's workshop." Eventually Calvin's position evolved into the "Protestant work ethic," where one's measure of inner moral goodness could be measured by observing his or her work habits. In this situation, if you are playing, you are showing that you are a sinner. Clearly, if one were a follower of Calvin's religious beliefs, it was very difficult to partake in any sporting activities.

Thomas Elyot

Like the educators of humanist Italy, many involved in education in northern Europe were associated with the monarchy. However, the universities and schools in England were much more influenced by Erasmus, Luther, and Calvin than they were by the humanists of Italy. As a consequence there developed two different "schools" in England: those associated with the monarchy and those associated with the public schools and universities. Those who sided with the monarchy and the ways of the Court favored a more sporting life. The curriculum of the public schools and universities was similar to that of the monasteries in the Middle Ages in that the body was to be denied in order to purify the soul.

Thomas Elyot (1490–1546) was much more like the Italian humanists. The ideal of the "universal man" dominated the English royal court, and to this ideal the English added the notion of the "governor." Elyot's *The Book of the Governor* argued that the Tudor gentleman should be versed in literature, science, and philosophy; he should be educated in both writing and fighting, be able to read Greek and to know modern languages, to dance and to make music, and to read and write poetry. In addition to these humanist skills, the "governor" should know something of law so that he might serve England in the capacity of a magistrate, an officer, or an administrator. This concept of citizenship was very popular in England, and was influenced by a strong tradition of local government.

Unlike his Reformation counterparts, Elyot's concept of education concerned primarily the nobility. Elyot believed that gentle birth was necessary to a gentleman, whereas Puritans argued that one could be made a gentleman. Elyot supported his view by arguing that society was composed of inherited "degrees." A person was born into one of these "degrees," and according to Elyot, one should stay in this social position throughout life. To alter this system was to shake the order of society. This put Elyot at odds with the Puritans, who disagreed with the idea that those who were born in the nobility were distinctly different from those who were not.

Sir Walter Raleigh, famed English explorer, was a good example of the English ideal. A younger son in his family, Raleigh was expected to "make it in the world" on his own. After studying at Oxford, Raleigh fought in France with the Huguenots, the French Protestants, and demonstrated his military skills. Returning to England, Raleigh then studied law. Fluent in Greek and Latin, Raleigh also read French and Spanish fluently. He was an excellent poet at a time when advancement in Queen Elizabeth's court depended on such things. A skilled sailor, he participated with notable heroism in a number of military actions on both land and sea. Indeed, he became such a favorite of the Queen that she held him back from the more risky ventures, which really amounted to high seas piracy! He was one of the initial proponents of the colonizing of America, and did so with the idea of making money. As a poet, a military man, a sailor, and a business man, Raleigh represented the ideal of English humanism.

Elyot devoted several chapters of his book to physical education. In so doing he tried to educate the sons of the nobility as to how to conduct themselves in contemporary England. The games and sports Elyot recommended came from his time as well as that of the classics: running, swimming, and hunting were easily defended. But not all sports were considered good by Elyot, and in this respect one can see the influence of Luther and Calvin. Some exercises were more acceptable for English gentlemen than others. Football in particular was frowned upon because it left the body beaten and the spirit inflamed. No doubt Puritan ideas of restraint had some impact on Elyot's thinking. Dancing was acceptable, but not if it was associated with idleness and sexual pleasure. In sum, Elyot's program of physical education supported Calvin's and Luther's ideas that pleasure is not at the heart of physical education and sport. This position eliminated fun games like football because one played football because of the pleasure one derived from playing it.

Elyot is notable for his efforts to improve physical education because he was familiar with the latest medical teaching of his time. He claimed six physiological benefits that could be derived from exercise.

Exercise aided digestion, increased one's appetite, helped one live longer, warmed the body, raised one's metabolism, and cleansed the body of its wastes. And by following this physical education program, one was healthier. Consequently, because of improved health one could do God's work better. In sum, Elyot was concerned with several objectives, the most important of which had to do with health and physiological efficiency in order to do God's work. His book was the first to use the science of his day to achieve his objectives. Were Elyot to be judged by today's standards, however, he would be considered more of a health educator than a physical educator, for he was not concerned with playful skills as much as he was concerned with doing God's work.

Roger Ascham

Like Elyot, Roger Ascham (1515–1568) was an English humanist. A professor at Cambridge University, Ascham is famous for his book *The Schoolmaster*, in which he advocated the study of Latin and Greek as a means of obtaining a liberal education. From these sources he recognized the importance of physical education. Ascham urged young men to

> . . . engage in all courtly exercises and gentlemanly pastimes. . . . All pastimes joined with labor, used in open place and in daylight, containing either some fit exercise for war or some pleasant pastime for peace, be not only comely and decent but also very necessary for a courtly gentleman to use.[26]

Ascham also appreciated the value of exercises as a means of resting the mind, so that it may be sharper at a later time. This idea fit nicely with the coming of the first industrial revolution and became the justification for recreation where it was recognized that people had to rest in order to work harder. Influenced by the Puritans, Ascham's educational values lent themselves to the work ethic that was developing in the sixteenth century.

The activities that Ascham believed necessary involved riding, running, "to run fair at the tilt or ring," to be able to use all weapons and to shoot a boy and gun, to vault, leap, wrestle, swim, dance, sing, play musical instruments, to hawk, hunt, and play tennis. Ascham also wrote a treatise, *Toxophilus*, on the art of shooting the bow.[27] In it Ascham discussed everything from how to choose and care for the bow to how to shoot it properly. Indeed, it was one of the first "how to" books in sport in the Western world.

Summary

The Renaissance was an intellectual reawakening that helped change Medieval attitudes toward the human body. With the reading of the classic Greek and Roman philosophers, scholars began to re-examine all aspects of their lives in classical perspective. Eventually this led to the discussion of the Catholic Church in terms of the classic philosophers, and this discussion helped lead the Western world out of the Middle Ages. While the Renaissance was primarily an upper-class movement, it laid the groundwork for those who followed.

Like Plato and Aristotle, the intellectuals of the Renaissance placed an emphasis on living in this world as opposed to living in the next world, or heaven. This philosophy, known as humanism, emphasized our "human-ness" rather than our spiritual selves. As a direct consequence of this type of thinking, affairs of the human body were considered much more acceptable. Sport and physical education were direct beneficiaries of this type of thought.

While the Reformation was primarily a religious movement, it had a lasting impact on Western civilization in all aspects of life and for every social class. After the Reformation, the Catholic Church no longer had a hold on matters of political, national, or intellectual importance. Indeed, the very nature of how people interacted with religion was different. Because of the Reformation, religion was relegated to one's private or "inner" life and was to be determined by each individual. So even though the Reformation focused more on social and religious reform than it did on individual growth, a consequence was that each individual had to read and interpret the Bible for him- or herself. The impact on education was significant. All people, no matter what social class, needed to learn to read. From this position it was a short step to the development of an educational system for all people that was sponsored by the state.

In addition, the Reformation encouraged the rise of the middle class, and in its Calvinist version made religion a tool with which we could judge people's behavior. The Reformation caused people to identify good works and prayer with hard work and industriousness, and as a consequence caused Protestants to concentrate on the affairs of the soul in this world rather than the state of the soul in the next world. These changes had a significant impact on how one viewed the activities of play and work.

The Reformation, especially Calvin's version, emphasized what one did with his or her body, because how one used the body was a measure of the quality of one's soul. A good soul was predestined to go to heaven, and a bad soul was predestined to go to hell. To work and to do good deeds was clearly the best use of one's time, and was the mark of one bound for heaven. Indeed, after the Reformation, Western civilization viewed time in a completely different manner than it did before the Reformation.

Luther's and Calvin's version of the Reformation sought to remove play and games from the lives of everyday people. Eventually this argument evolved into the "Protestant work ethic," where one's measure of inner moral goodness could be measured by observing one's work habits. In this situation, if you are playing, then you are showing that you are a sinner. This attitude toward work and play, in its more modern form, is still evident in America today. Luther and Calvin undermined the medieval belief that the body should be denied in order to purify the soul, and replaced it with the idea that the body is here to do God's good work and to use God-given time in the appropriate manner. But the effect of the Reformation with respect to play and physical education was much the same as the philosophy of the early monks: both theologies worked against play, sport, and physical education. It falls to a later time to justify the activities that we have come to accept as acceptable in physical education and sport.

Discussion Questions

1. What was the Renaissance? How did it differ from the Middle Ages? Did this difference affect sport and physical education?

2. What was the Reformation? How did it differ from the Middle Ages? Did this difference affect sport and physical education?

3. What ideas from the Renaissance and the Reformation are with us today in sport and physical education?

4. The theology of the Reformation differed from that of the early Christian monks with respect to the value of the body, yet the consequence for sport and physical education is much the same. Why?

Suggestions for Further Reading

Bronowski, J., and Mazlish, B. "The Expanding World: From Leonardo to Galileo, 1500–1630." In *The Western Intellectual Tradition: From Leonardo to Hegel*. New York: Harper & Brothers, 1960.

Calhoun, D. "From Fun to Business: Sport in Modern Society." In *Sports, Culture, and Personality*. Berkeley, Calif: Leisure Press, 1981.

Hackensmith, C. W., "The Renaissance" and "Realism in Education." In *History of Physical Education*. New York: Harper and Row, Publishers, 1966.

Rice, E., J. L. Hutchinson, and M. Lee. "The Renaissance" and "Realism." In *A Brief History of Physical Education*. New York: John Wiley & Sons, 1969.

Van Dalen, D., E. Mitchell, and B. Bennett. "Physical Education in the Middle Ages and Early Modern Times." In *A World History of Physical Education*. Englewood Cliffs, N.J.: Prentice-Hall, Inc., 1953.

Notes

1. J. Bronowski and Bruce Mazlish, *The Western Intellectual Tradition: From Leonardo to Hegel* (New York: Harper & Brothers, 1960).

2. Ibid.

3. Ibid.

4. Ibid., 106.

5. Ibid., 62

6. Ibid.

7. W. H. Woodward, *Vittorino da Feltre and Humanist Educators* (Cambridge: The University Press, 1921).

8. Ibid., 27.

9. Ibid., 137–38.

10. Baldassare Castiglione, *The Book of the Courtier*, trans. Sir Thomas Hoby (New York: Dutton, 1959), 37.

11. Castiglione, *The Book of the Courtier*, 29–31.

12. Will Durant, *The Reformation* (New York: Simon and Schuster, 1957).

13. Ibid., 235.

14. England's public schools are quite different from those that exist in contemporary America. "Public" in 14th century England meant that the school existed outside of the home of the nobility, and that professional teachers who were paid through tuition taught the children.

15. Ibid., 236.

16. Ibid., 236.

17. Ibid., 247.

18. Bronowski and Mazlish, *The Western Intellectual Tradition*, 74.

19. Desiderius Erasmus, *The Education of a Christian Prince*, trans. Lester K. Born (New York: Columbia University Press, 1936), 27.

20. Martin Luther, "Letters to the Mayors and Aldermen," *Classics in Education*, ed. William Baskin (New York: Philosophical Library, 1966), 376.

21. Frederick Eby, *Early Protestant Educators* (New York: McGraw-Hill, 1942), 176.

22. Durant, *The Reformation*, 460.

23. This interpretation is developed by Max Weber, *The Protestant Ethic and the Spirit of Capitalism*, trans. Talcott Parsons (New York: Scribner, 1906). See also Don Calhoun, "From Fun to Business: Sport in Modern Society," *Sports, Culture, and Personality* (Berkeley, Calif.: Leisure Press, 1981).

24. Ellen Gerber, "John Calvin," *Innovators and Institutions in Physical Education* (Philadelphia: Lea and Febiger, 1971), 36–39.

25. Albere-Marie Schmidt, *John Calvin and the Calvinist Tradition*, trans. Ronald Wallace (New York: Harper and Brothers, 1960), 142.

26. Roger Ascham, "The Schoolmaster," *The Whole Works of Roger Ascham*, ed. Rev. Dr. Giles (New York: AMS Press, 1965), III, 139.

27. Roger Ascham, *Toxophilus, the Schole of Shootinge* (New York: Da Capo Press, 1969).

c h a p t e r

7

The Age of Science and the Enlightenment

General Events
Age of Science

1561–1626 Francis Bacon

1562 and 1594 French Religious Wars

1564–1642 Galileo Galilei

1588–1679 Thomas Hobbes

1596–1650 Rene Descartes

1619–1622 Great Depression

1618–1648 Thirty Years War in Germany

1630–1632 Plague in France

1642–1727 Isaac Newton

1647–1649 Plague in France

1642–1648 English Civil War

1660 Return of English Monarchy

1665 Plague in England
    Invention of the Printing Press

1685–1753 George Berkeley

Enlightenment

1688 English Revolution

1715 Death of Louis XIV

1715–1723 Period of the Regency

1723–1774 Reign of Louis XV

1723–1790 Adam Smith

1748 Hume's *Inquiry Concerning Human Understanding* and Montesquieu's *The Spirit of the Laws*

1751 Appearance of the first volumes of Diderot's *Encyclopedia*

1754 Diderot's *On the Interpretation of Nature*

1756 Treaty of Versailles signed by France and Austria

1756–1763 Seven Years War

1759 Voltaire's *Candide*

1762 Rousseau's *The Social Contract* and *Emile*

1762–1796 Catherine II (the Great) of Russia

1763 Peace of Paris signed by Britain, France, and Spain

1774 Accession of Louis XVI

1776 American Declaration of Independence, Adam Smith's *The Wealth of Nations*

1778 The Death of Voltaire and Rousseau

1781 Kant's *Critique of Pure Reason*

1788 Kant's *Critique of Practical Reason*

1789 French Revolution and *Declaration of the Rights of Man and of the Citizen*

Sport and Physical Education

1483–1553 Francois Rabelais

1530–1611 Richard Mulcaster

1553–1592 Michel de Montaigne

1592–1671 John Comenius

1608–1674 John Milton

1618 King James issues Declaration of Sport

1632–1704 John Locke

1633 King Charles Reissues Declaration of Sport

1712–88 Jean Jacques Rousseau

1723–90 Johann Bernhard Basedow

1759–1839 Johann Friedrich GutsMuths

Introduction: From Heaven to Humanity
The Age of Science and the Enlightenment

From the mid–1500s to 1789 the Western world was, philosophically speaking, turned upside down. The orientation toward what is real and how one comes to know it changed radically, and the corresponding view of the human body changed as well. In short, the changes argued for by philosophers in the Renaissance and the Reformation became reality during the Age of Science and the Enlightenment. The consequence of these philosophical changes were that people no longer lived in this world by rules that would get them into heaven. The Ten Commandments, the Bible, and the influence of the various Christian faiths became less important in the Western world, while medicine, science, and technology came to dominate the thoughts and behaviors of all people. People began to live, more and more, according to rules that would serve them well in this world. Consequently, the Age of Science and the Enlightenment are perhaps best known for the change in style of political governance, of a movement from the rights of divine governance through kings to the rights of individuals to govern themselves.

Broken down into roughly 100-year increments, the Age of Science (1560–1688) and the Enlightenment (1688–1789) have in common an emphasis on living in the "here and now." This change from an emphasis on the next world to an emphasis of on living in this world did not come easily. Indeed, this 230-year period was one of the most contested in the history of civilization. Yet while religion, politics, science, law, and other institutions changed radically, people still enjoyed their recreational and sporting activities. Indeed, to a certain extent these activities were legitimized by the actions and arguments of prominent philosophers and educators. While physical education and sport continued to become a larger part of the lives of Europeans and Americans, they were still a minor part of Western culture even as the arguments for these activities became more substantial and widely accepted. Important to our discussion, the arguments for physical education and sport that were used in the Age of Science and the Enlightenment are still valid today and are those that justify the use of science to understand human movement as a way of making people healthier.

The Age of Science: 1560–1688

The seventeenth century witnessed explosive changes in Western culture. On the one hand, this period of time continued the change in thinking, begun in the Renaissance and Reformation, from "other-worldly" concerns to those of the observed, natural world. On the other hand, philosophers sought to understand the natural world in terms that were theoretical and timeless by developing rules and laws that could be used to explain particular experiences. Added together, these changes continued the march begun in the Renaissance toward what is now called "modern" culture: the idea that humanity can understand life in terms of scientific laws. This change in thinking led to major advances in science, such as Galileo's astronomical discoveries and Newton's explanations of the physical universe. And the use of science to create new laws led historians to call this period of time both the Age of Reason and the Age of Science.

These changes did not come easily, nor did they occur at a leisurely pace. In many respects they were responses to contemporary problems. After a relatively unbroken economic expansion in the sixteenth century, Europe experienced a large-scale economic downturn in the seventeenth century. By 1600 Spain was losing its political influence, along with her loss of control of the South Atlantic and therefore her silver supply. There was a depression from 1619 to 1622, and as international trade dropped off and unemployment increased, a pool of mercenaries was created to fight the many religious wars that wracked Europe: the Thirty Years' War (1618–1648) in Germany; the Civil Wars (1642–1648) in England, and the two religious wars in France (1562 and 1594).

The religious wars pitted one religion against another and all religious faiths against nonbelievers. As one scholar noted, the early seventeenth century looked like a scene from the Middle East in our times, where people had a fair chance of having their throats cut and their houses burned down by strangers who merely disliked their religion![1] In Central Europe the German states were in constant battle, Protestants against Catholics. The Thirty Years' War (1618–1648) was started over religious disagreements and concluded with both sides agreeing to tolerate one another's religion. France divided along religious lines between the Huguenots and the Catholics, and England experienced a civil war between Catholics and Anglicans.

Among other factors, the English civil war was precipitated by the Declaration of Sport, an edict issued by King James in 1618 and reissued by his son Charles in 1633.[2] The Declaration stated that sport could be played on Sunday after church services. The Puritans, however, strongly disagreed with this edict and believed that Sunday should be a day spent in worship. This position, known as "Sabbatarianism," and various "Blue Laws" remained popular in the United States until the 1930s.[3]

"Blue Laws," or laws that prohibited certain acts, gained their name from having been printed on blue paper. Most frequently Blue Laws prohibited drinking, gambling, and many playful activities associated with drinking and gambling.

The seventeenth century was marked by increasing religious intolerance that manifested itself in all aspects of life. One was forced to commit to one religion or another, and critical discussion of religious doctrine became increasingly rare throughout the century. To a great extent the philosophies developed during the Age of Science were an attempt to avoid the emotional intensity that accompanied religious debate. By being "objective" one could discuss an idea, religious or otherwise, on its own merits and come to a solution that was reasoned. From this perspective the development of reasoned inquiry based on the experienced world was a reaction to religious turmoil.

On top of the economic and religious crises were recurrences of the plague. France suffered from 1630–1632 and 1647–1649, while England experienced her final serious outbreak in 1665. In addition, western Europe experienced a period of lower than normal temperatures that we now call the Little Ice Age. Whole rural areas were depopulated, causing city slums to grow. This population shift caused further outbreaks in disease and poverty. The combination of profound religious disagreement, economic depression, global cooling, plague, rural depopulation, and urban growth had an incredible impact on life in Europe in the seventeenth century. The philosophies that were developed during this century reflect these historical conditions.

On a more positive note, the seventeenth century witnessed the continued growth of books in print and an increasingly educated group of lay people. Since the invention of the printing press in the 1300s, cheaper books were available, and more people could afford to buy them. This allowed more people to read and led to more schools where people could learn how to read. Some argue that printing led to the Age of Science and paved the way for the Enlightenment, for the American and French revolutions, and for democracy.[4]

Lay Person: Roughly defined, "lay people" were educated but were not explicitly tied to the church as was a brother or a priest. As a consequence, a lay person could use his education for means other than those of the church. Eventually this concept of an educated person not associated with the church became commonplace.

As a result of the increased number of lay people, educated citizens were no longer as strongly influenced by church dogma. It is not an accident, then, that the growth of science occurred at a time when the church was losing its hold on education. One consequence was the growing away from the concentration on the afterlife, and the acceptance of one's existence in the present on earth.

The emphasis on science was probably the most explicit measure of this concentration on the present, and the tools of science were developed to expand the limitations in our observational powers. Microscopes and telescopes, thermometers, barometers, hydrometers, better watches, and finer scales all enhanced humanity's ability to observe the material universe, and these instruments to a great extent affected the manner in which philosophers in the Age of Science explained the nature of reality.

It was during this time that science came to be seen as a separate area of study from philosophy. What we now call "science" was formerly called "experimental philosophy" or "natural philosophy," and those who practiced "science" considered themselves philosophers. These men had a tremendous impact on philosophy. Seeking to overcome the otherworldly concerns of the Church, science turned its face from metaphysics to Nature and developed its own distinctive methods. The goal of science was to improve the quality of life on earth, and this goal was in direct contrast to the medieval idea of asceticism or self-denial.

The Age of Science, then, was a continuation of the philosophies of the Humanists developed during the Renaissance. But the Age of Science was not limited to the use of the classics and "pure reason." Reason and tradition could be balanced by methodical investigation based in the material world. Science accepted as its realm only that which could be measured and quantified, mathematically expressed, and experimentally proved. It was up to the philosophers to explain this radical shift in thinking.

The change from otherworldly concerns to the here and now had a direct impact on education generally and physical education specifically. Sport and physical education were more easily justified as philosophers came to accept the material world and the place our bodies occupy in it. Scientists and philosophers used new ways of thinking to understand our bodies and explain how they function. This approach led to advances in medicine, improved educational techniques, and a variety of ideas that were believed to better our earthly existence.

The Enlightenment: 1688–1789

What was the Enlightenment? We can learn much from the term itself. Enlightenment literally means the process of making bright that which is dark. Applied to eighteenth-century Western civilization, the term describes how a relatively large, well-educated public believed that a new way of thinking would "enlighten" the thoughts and behaviors of the civilized world. "Enlightenment" tells us that the old ways of Europe were "dark," while the new, scientific ways of Newton, Galileo Galilei, Hobbes, Locke, and Descartes were the "light" that would guide humanity toward a basic harmony of interests in the long run. Indeed, much of our attitude toward the "Dark Ages" of Medieval Europe, which modern historians have shown were not really so "dark," comes from the attitudes of intellectuals who argued for change during the Enlightenment. Many disagreed with the philosophers and intellectuals who advocated this new way of thinking, but there is no doubt that the Enlightenment had an incredible impact on the modern world.

Many ideas that had their genesis during the Enlightenment are taken for granted in contemporary education, and it is helpful to physical educators to know how and why these educational ideals came about. Indeed, education is intimately connected to the Enlightenment tradition. Perhaps the most powerful advocates of the Enlightenment were the educators who organized the public schools and had ready access to printing and publishing. Their views are well represented in books from the eighteenth century and have had a significant impact on subsequent educators. Physical education and sport were similarly affected by the Enlightenment, especially since the many Enlightenment critics had so much to say about the virtues of human movement as a means of creating the ideal individual and community.

In historical terms, "Enlightenment" describes the changes in attitude among an increasingly well-read European and American population during that period, especially with respect toward the common person. It was during this time that Enlightenment intellectuals began to argue for the rights of free men, an idea that manifested itself in the American and French wars of independence. The use of science to improve humanity was combined with a sense of egalitarianism, and was manifest in the writings of Jean Jacques Rousseau, Francoise Voltaire, and Jacques Diderot. Perhaps the best examples of Enlightenment thinking occurred in the documents supporting the American Revolution in 1776 and the French Revolution in 1789, both of which were described and justified by declarations and constitutions advocating the rights of all citizens: the *Declaration of Independence*, the *Constitution*, and the *Bill of Rights* in the United States, and the *Declaration of the Rights of Man and Citizen* in France.

These changes did not occur out of the blue. The late seventeenth and early eighteenth centuries witnessed significant shifts of power and influence among the states of Europe. Nations that were once strong—Spain, the United Netherlands, Poland, Sweden, and the Ottoman Empire—lost their dominant status to Great Britain, France, Austria, Russia, and Prussia. Europe was a political conglomeration based on international rivalry, and warfare was regarded as the ultimate court of appeal. As a result there were extended periods of general warfare. The result of these wars was the establishment of Prussia and Russia as powers to be reckoned with, the creation of America, the decline of Sweden and the Ottoman Empire as major powers, the replacement of Austrian influence in southern Italy with that of Spain, Lorraine became a French province, and Britain became a great colonial empire.[5]

With the exception of Great Britain, which had become increasingly "democratic" from the time of the Magna Charta (1288) to the English Revolution (1688), the model of political organization for nations was that of the French monarchy. Yet the French monarchy came under increasing attack, largely because of the conflicts generated by the changes in Europe in the eighteenth century. These changes included the rise of empirical science, the writings of scientists like Galileo, Bacon, and Newton, and the writings of philosophers Descartes, Locke, and Hobbes. Writers like Rousseau, Voltaire, Montesquieu, and Condorcet advocated new social theories that redefined the traditional role of kings, parliaments and citizens. These ideas conflicted with the actual social and educational structures that remained unchanged in France. France was still a Catholic country controlled by the monarchy, the clergy, and the noble class. Seen in this way, too many unstoppable forces collided in France in the eighteenth century, and the result was the bloody French Revolution of 1789.

Philosophers of Science

Prior to the seventeenth century, science, philosophy, and education were not distinct academic areas as they are to twentieth-century America. Indeed, scientists during the seventeenth century considered themselves philosophers.[6] Perhaps the most important of these scientist-philosophers were Galileo Galilei, Isaac Newton, and Francis Bacon, all of whom had a lasting impact on both science and philosophy. All of these men, however, had in common the goal of understanding the world in a systematic and reasoned way. The impact of these philosophers is that they helped move the Western world from a type of thinking that emphasized strictly intellectual processes to a type of thinking that emphasized the examination of the material world. Included in the material world, of course, is the human body. Questions from the new perspective included: How do bodies in motion work? What are the rules that guide all matter? These questions and others like them can be applied to the study of the human body, which explains why we discuss their contributions to the Western mentality. While Galileo, Bacon, and Newton had nothing to say about the study of physical education, the type of thinking about the material world that they initiated is assumed in modern-day science. And modern science is one of the cornerstones of contemporary kinesiology and physical education.

Galileo Galilei

Galileo Galilei (1564–1642) was an Italian astronomer and physicist who made famous the Copernican view of the universe.

> The "Copernican" view of the solar system argues that the sun is at the center of the solar system, which is in contrast to the Ptolemaic system in which the earth is at the center.

Although he created no systematic philosophy, his influence on the trend of modern philosophical thought is considerable. Scholars credit Galileo, along with Descartes, for much of the philosophical foundation on which modern culture operates. To Galileo we owe much of the drive to separate the physical sciences from philosophy, and his work lent credibility to the idea that what we observe through our senses is real and important. This approach legitimized the use of the senses (the human body) instead of Catholic dogma as a means of acquiring knowledge. What was so important about Galileo's work was that it removed humanity from the "center of the universe" and made the corporeal world more important. Galileo's influence can be seen especially in the writings of Thomas Hobbes and Isaac Newton.

We can learn much about the spirit of the Age of Science by looking at how well Galileo's ideas were received. While modern culture appreciates his scientific views, his religious contemporaries did not appreciate their religious and political implications. The attitude of the Inquisition is summarized by this historic edict:

> The view that the sun stands motionless at the center of the universe is foolish, philosophically false, and utterly heretical, because (it is) contrary to Holy Scripture. The view that the earth is not the center of the universe and even has a daily rotation is philosophically false, and at least an erroneous belief.[7]

Galileo was convicted of heresy by the Inquisition and forced to repudiate the Copernican theory in 1633. He was sentenced to prison but was allowed to live in his villa near Florence, where he died in 1642. There he was free to study and teach, write books, and receive visitors. Even his "imprisonment" had an impact. Many scientists sought to avoid the philosophical implications of science on religion, and philosophers were careful to avoid the wrath of the Church. It was not until 1835 that the Church withdrew the works of Galileo from her Index of Prohibited Books.

Francis Bacon

Francis Bacon (1561–1626) was a contemporary of Galileo's and was a versatile man, if not the "universal man" so desired during the Renaissance. He was well read in politics, law, literature, philosophy, and science, and he achieved the office of Chancellor in England, where he ruled in the absence of the King. Bacon's most lasting contribution was to the philosophy of science, where he utilized the methods of philosophy to justify and legitimize the use of science. Bacon called for the support of colleges, libraries, laboratories, biological gardens, museums of science and industry, for the better payment of teachers and researchers, and for the funding of scientific experiments.

Most important, though, was that he developed an organizational scheme of science of what could be learned. Denis Diderot, the French encyclopedist, once said of Bacon, "when it was impossible to write a history of what men knew, he drew up the map of what they had to learn."[8] Bacon attempted to classify the sciences in a logical order and to determine their fields of inquiry in order to obtain answers to major problems awaiting solutions. This type of thinking is evident in physical education today with the division of the physical education profession into the various subdisciplines like exercise physiology, sport history, motor learning, and so on. Bacon believed in the betterment of life through the good use of knowledge and thereby connected science to the lives of everyday people.

Bacon believed that this betterment of humanity could be done best through the methods of induction, the process by which one draws conclusions based on many observations.

> *Induction is the process that allows one to draw a conclusion based on many observations. Put differently, one might describe induction as "finding the common denominator" among a group of situations.*

According to Bacon, induction is the process by which one moves from particular facts or observations to a more general knowledge of forms, or generalized physical properties.[9] Bacon sought mastery over the human condition through the expansion of what is known, and this goal has had a tremendous impact in all areas that use science as a means of acquiring knowledge. This method of developing rules and standards from particular experiences is widely used by physical education researchers today.

Isaac Newton

Isaac Newton (1642–1727) was an English mathematician and physicist whose work revolutionized the study of the physical world. In short,

Newton's mechanical theory was used to support the view that God created the world as a perfect machine. All physicists had to do was to discover the laws that governed the machine, and one had the keys to the universe. His most famous work was *Mathematical Principles of Natural Philosophy* or, in short, *Principia*, published in 1687. In it were the three "laws" of motion from which theorems and corollaries are subsequently deduced. These are required reading in any biomechanics class in physical education today:

1. Every body continues in its state of rest, or of uniform motion in a right (i.e., straight) line, unless it is compelled to change that state by forces impressed upon it.

2. The change of motion is proportional to the motive force impressed; and is made in the direction of the right line in which that force is impressed.

3. To every action there is always opposed an equal reaction; or, the mutual actions of two bodies upon each other are always equal, and directed to contrary parts.[10]

Eventually Newton's work was used to argue that the universe is guided by laws that are timeless and unchanging. The *Principia* became the model of scientific knowledge and had a significant impact on all subsequent scientific inquiry in all fields.

The Philosophers

The influence of Galileo, Bacon, and Newton was felt by all in their day, especially the philosophers who tried to explain the impact of these new scientists. The Age of Science coincides with the beginning of "modern" philosophy, a period when philosophers began to break from the traditional methods of philosophy that were used in the Middle Ages and during the Renaissance. While most philosophers of this time still considered God the creator and conserver of the universe, some philosophers began to argue that Nature could be studied and expressed as a dynamic system of bodies in motion without any immediate reference to God, and the intelligible structure of the universe could be expressed mathematically. This is due in large part to the influence of science, particularly the work of Galileo and Newton, who stimulated the mechanistic conception of the world. In addition, many prominent philosophers worked outside the prestigious European universities. As a result, they were able to develop their own ideas free from the influence of the Church and the great Greek philosophers who had inspired the Renaissance, and were able to break with the traditions of the Church and scholasticism.

This approach to understanding the world caused quite a stir among the intellectuals of the seventeenth century. The problem of reconciling the scientific approach that emphasized the material world, with the traditional approach that emphasized God and one's spiritual soul, divided many philosophers. The traditional approach argued that man is a material being that possesses a spiritual soul, is endowed with the power of free choice, and partly transcends the material world and the system of mechanical causes. The scientific approach argues that the material universe includes all that one is, that one's psyche is material and that there is no free will.[11] Indeed, the Age of Science was well represented by many philosophical extremes, yet most of them emphasized the development of the individual. The two extremes discussed here, represented by Rene Descartes and Thomas Hobbes, are evident in many of the philosophical writings of the Age of Science.

The ideas of the Enlightenment were to a great extent influenced by philosophers like John Locke, George Berkeley, and David Hume.[12] Locke lived in the seventeenth century, and the impact of his writings was felt well into the eighteenth century in the work of Berkeley and Hume. All of these philosophers contributed theories of knowledge that came to be accepted in their own time, and are still debated in their contemporary forms today. In their most basic sense, these theories hold that people come to know something through their experiences, particularly through their senses. Humans are considered to be of "nature," that is, they are as much of this world as are the plants, animals, and the elements. This idea is important to education, for it means that the body can and should be used as a learning tool. Indeed, if the body is not used, then a person cannot learn in a "natural" way. Clearly the epistemologies of Locke, Berkeley, and Hume differ from those that say learning occurs only in the mind or soul through reading, rote memorization, and repetition. It is important for our purposes in that these epistemologies do not eliminate physical education from the educational spectrum as do the ways of knowing of other metaphysical positions.

By understanding the metaphysical positions of Hobbes, Descartes, Locke, Berkeley, and Hume one can also understand how the philosophers of the Age of Science and the Enlightenment believed humans learned, what their relationship to nature was, and for our purposes, what they believed the role of physical education was in developing an individual.

Thomas Hobbes

Strongly influenced by Galileo's and Newton's mechanical conception of Nature, Thomas Hobbes (1588–1679) applied the basic idea of mechanics to all reality.[13] He argued that the realm of philosophy is only that which can be observed, and that reality is composed solely of bodies and motion. This removed the idea of God from philosophy, but not from religion or theology. Put differently, Hobbes removed philosophy from religion, and it is this change that angered his critics. Hobbes considered humans to be purely material beings and was not concerned with their immortal souls or minds, because they cannot be directly observed or measured. The question can then be asked, "What do we call consciousness?" Hobbes believed that mind was the product of atoms and chemicals interacting with each other, and nothing more.

Hobbes was severely criticized for this approach, for it has several implications. Religious critics branded Hobbes a heretic and banned his work, and for some time he lived in France for fear of his life. This was a practical consideration, to say the least! Philosophically, however, Hobbes' philosophy is revolutionary because it states that humans are composed of only one thing: the body. There are no confusing concepts of mind or soul to worry about because, if one cannot observe them, they are not the concern of philosophy. Indeed, Hobbes argued that philosophy and science could not be used to prove whether or not the mind or soul even exists. This monistic approach relies on the idea that all there is to Nature is matter in motion. If one has enough knowledge about the composition of matter and the forces that act upon it, then one can predict what will happen in the present and the future. This philosophy can be applied to human bodies, where each person is considered to be only the sum of all the different chemical components that make up our physical being.

This is a plausible idea in many respects, and it makes sense in an age of machines (like computers) that can predict to a high degree of certainty how objects will have an impact on each other. However, this philosophy is criticized on the grounds that it is deterministic, or that one's actions are determined only by the physical forces that affect the individual.

Determinism is the doctrine that every fact in the universe is guided entirely by law. Applied to people, determinism holds that all the actions of an individual are determined by previous causes and not by free will. Indeed, there is no such thing as free will in a deterministic philosophy.

Put another way, what one has done in the past combined with one's environment determines how an individual will behave. According to Hobbes' argument, even though an individual *believes* that he chooses to behave as he does, there really is no choice in the matter. According to determinism, thoughts are *determined* by one's past actions and one's environment.

Hobbes' materialism is evident in the field of behavioristic psychology, in which concepts of mind are abandoned and the psychologist concentrates only on behavior. Behaviorists argue that this is all that a psychologist can observe, and that behavior is all that can be influenced. Behaviorism has been an important part of research in physical education and has had much success in shaping behavior both in the physical education classroom and in the sport environment, where one is concerned strictly with performance. Hobbes' philosophy is perhaps most evident in the subdiscipline of sport psychology.

Critics of behaviorism argue that since determinism does not accept the idea of free will, it is very difficult to explain new ideas and creativity. Furthermore, determinism does not explain one's sense of being. So while Hobbes' philosophy can be used to explain the material world and human behavior in a logical and systematic way, it can be criticized by those who believe in free will.

Rene Descartes

Rene Descartes (1596–1650) epitomized the dualistic approach of mind and body. Descartes contributed two concepts to the modern world. His philosophy argues that knowledge can be created from simple ideas and developed into more complex ideas, and that knowledge is not valid unless we are absolutely certain of its authenticity. The process of creating knowledge step by step has been called the "building block theory of knowledge," in which subsequent theories rest on simpler, previous theories. He also argued that what is certain is only that which can be inferred or rationalized since we cannot trust our body or our senses. Descartes believed that the material world could be described in terms of mathematical theories, identified with geometrical extension (Descartes developed "Cartesian coordinates" in geometry), and motion.[14] He believed that all bodies, including living bodies, are in some sense machines.

But Descartes also believed that our being cannot be reduced only to that of a member of a mechanical system. This was due to his belief in the spiritual mind or soul that transcends the material world. Indeed, Descartes believed that one's soul is the essence of one's being, which can be seen in his famous statement, *Cogito, ergo sum*, or "I think, therefore I am."[15]

> *"Cogito, ergo sum." Perhaps one of the most powerful statements ever made in philosophy, the "Cogito" came out of an attempt to prove the existence of God and to develop a way of coming to know reality with absolute certainty. Out of this argument came Descartes' method of rationalism, a way of knowing reality through purely intellectual means.*

Descartes, in a powerful argument, claimed to doubt everything, even the fact that he was awake. He eliminated all of his experiences and senses as a means of acquiring absolute knowledge through the argument that they are unreliable sources. As a result he both reduced man's state of being to an act of mind and advocated a way of knowing called rationalism. Ironically, Descartes' argument had the result of emphasizing the existence of humanity. By putting the word "I" in the statement "I think, therefore I am," Descartes inadvertently placed humans in a position of importance. Before Descartes, one might have said, "God thinks, therefore humans are."

Descartes emphasized the use of mathematics to construct new knowledge by starting with simple theorems and moving to the more complex. He viewed the process of constructing new knowledge as being completely the function of reason, and believed that this method could be used in any of the sciences to continue to add to the knowledge already developed. Important to education, Descartes' approach implies that the body is less important than the mind as a way of knowing anything.[16] Rationalism argues that absolute knowledge can only be generated through inference or other processes of the mind.

Once one begins from this position, this argument is very powerful, and it is still prevalent in educational systems today where matters of the mind are considered more important than matters of the body. One consequence of this position, important to physical educators, is that it becomes very difficult to account for the interaction between mind and body. Descartes did not adequately explain how this process occurs, at least to the satisfaction of those involved in the study of human movement.[17] These scholars argue that from a Cartesian perspective it is very difficult to justify human movement as an educational experience.

George Berkeley

George Berkeley (1685–1753) was an Irish philosopher and Anglican bishop and is known for his theory of idealism. Unlike many philosophers, Berkeley was not "godless." He sought to reconcile his religious ideals with the empirical basis of science, and he argued that this could be done if one understood the relationship of the perceiver and that which is perceived. Berkeley believed that all that exists is that which either perceives or is perceived. In Berkeley's words, "Their *esse* is *percipi*."[18] This means that the existence of something depends on its being perceived. Put differently, if you cannot perceive something, it cannot exist. Nothing can exist except active beings that experience with their senses (perceive), and those things that are experienced (perceived) by those active beings. Berkeley's argument has been outlined in the following way:

1. Sensible qualities of objects are nothing but "ideas" in the mind.
2. Physical objects are nothing more than their sensible qualities.
3. Therefore, physical objects are nothing but "ideas" in the mind.[19]

Berkeley used his famous analogy of the falling tree in the forest to illustrate his argument. Berkeley asked a simple question: If a tree falls in the forest, does it make any sound if there is no one there to hear it fall? If one accepts Berkeley's philosophy at face value, the answer would be no. Since no one was around to perceive the noise made by the tree falling, then that sound never existed. However, Berkeley used his argument to prove the existence of God, and in so doing he arrived at a different answer. The noise generated by the tree would be perceived by God, the ultimate perceiver. Since God perceives everything, then the noise exists whether a human hears it or not.

This argument was a necessary one for Berkeley because it "proves" the existence of both humans and God. In so doing Berkeley rejected the "Godless" approach of Hobbes and his strict materialism where everything is "body." By arguing for the primacy of perception, Berkeley argued that the existence of the world depends entirely upon the perceptive abilities of the mind or spirit. Consequently the body is not necessary to our existence.

Berkeley's metaphysical position was that of a monist: since all of reality depends on perception, there is no division between the mind and the body. Everything is of the mind. Yet Berkeley's argument had one consequence that he could not have foreseen. An end result of his chain of reasoning is that our senses, which are associated with our bodies, are a more viable mechanism for knowing reality. Berkeley's philosophy is important in that it bridges the division between mind and body with a coherent argument that makes the body more important. One can easily argue that physical education benefits from any epistemology that places the body in an important position of dealing with reality.

While Descartes' approach would seem to reject physical education as education, Hobbes' approach would seem to say that all education is physical education. Yet one must be very careful when drawing this conclusion. It has been noted that the positions of Hobbes and Descartes are *metaphysical positions* attempting to establish the nature of reality.[20] It does not follow that a certain metaphysical position constitutes a specific plan for a physical education program. However, understanding the metaphysical positions of Hobbes and Descartes yields many insights into what kinds of activities were thought to be of most benefit to people. And understanding these same arguments helps us understand attitudes toward sport and physical education in the twentieth century. Educators and social critics were significantly affected by these new concepts of mind and body, and these ideas were manifest in their educational philosophies and curriculums.

The Educators

In spite of the differences between the above scientists and philosophers, all of them shared assumptions about the place of rationality in culture. This consensus is what marks the Age of Science and the Enlightenment as different from the Middle Ages and the Renaissance, and this difference was manifest in the views of educators. Simply put, these new, or "modern," educators accepted the idea that being human is "natural" and not necessarily evil, and that an individual can change his or her life on earth for the better. These educators are known as "realists" for their advocation of the study of the "real" things of life.

Realism was a radical change from the Middle Ages and the Renaissance, where one's life on earth was guided by the hope for bliss in heaven. During this time education consisted of learning to read and write in Latin and Greek, and the texts were those of the Bible and the classic Greek and Roman authors. Methods of instruction were authoritarian and discipline oriented, and students were not encouraged to concentrate on the present.

Realists sought to change this educational situation and emphasized three main approaches: humanist realism, social realism, and sense realism. The humanist realists used Latin, Greek, and classical literature as a basis for their educational curriculum but rejected the idea that this is the only means of education. They added physical education as a means of creating a well-rounded individual. The social realists accepted a modified curriculum of classical literature and added to this approach instruction in the social graces and political affairs. The sense realists were the most radically different from the old style. Sense realists argued that students should be taught in their own language and should learn useful arts and sciences that are based on scientifically sound principles. All three approaches emphasized the "here and now" approach of their philosophical contemporaries, resulting in an emphasis on skills that can help in everyday life. So while philosophers paved the way for the modern world to think about nature in a new and "scientific" way and to use more "rational" methods to deal with the problems of human life and society, educators put these ideas in practice. Physical activities thus became a means of improving one's life on earth.

Francois Rabelais

Francois Rabelais (1483–1553) was a French educational theorist and is considered a humanist realist because of his emphasis on the development of the whole person. He published his views in *The Life of Gargantua*, a book that contrasted the style of education of the Renaissance and the Latin grammar school with a new, improved version based on the revolutionary ideas of his times.[21] The former style of education was marked by rote memory drills, reading, and prayer, and concentrated on the spiritual development of the pupil. Rabelais was a critic of this old style of education and called for an educational program that would facilitate the social, moral, spiritual, and physical aspects of life. While he believed that books were the source of all education and that mastering these texts provided for the education of the student, he believed physical activities would help him reach his goal of the well-rounded individual. These activities ranged from horsemanship, martial arts, and hunting to ball playing, running, and swimming. By concentrating on many different types of activities, Rabelais hoped to develop an individual capable of adapting to the many different problems in the real world.

Richard Mulcaster

Richard Mulcaster (1530–1611), an English schoolmaster, was one of the sense realists. Strongly influenced by the growing sense of democracy in Europe, sense realists believed that all people, no matter their gender or income, should have an education. In so doing they could contribute to their society in a manner up to their potential. The position of the sense realists differed from their predecessors, who by and large believed that education was necessary only for the nobility.

For Mulcaster, education was to develop both the mind and the body, and it was believed that the senses were the best means of doing so. This meant that experience was more important than studying or reading, and that to learn one's native language well was as valuable as learning Greek or Latin. Mulcaster also believed that the teaching process should be adapted to the learner, rather than the formal method of lecture and reading used by the traditional schools.

Mulcaster was among the first educators to emphasize the student rather than the subject that was being taught. This was a radical shift in education and reflects the change in philosophy from concentration on the afterlife to concentration on the present. His thoughts on education were described in his book *Positions*, which dealt specifically with physical education.[22] Schoolmasters who proposed an extensive program of physical activities appear to have been rare, and it is this distinction that makes Mulcaster important to the history of physical education. For indoor activities he recommended reading and speaking out loud, talking, laughing, weeping, holding one's breath, dancing, wrestling, fencing, and climbing. For outdoor activities he recommended walking, running, leaping, swimming, riding, hunting, shooting, and playing ball. Mulcaster believed that school was better than a tutor, and this facilitated some of the activities he used for physical education. To this end Mulcaster may be considered the "father" of the modern educational practice of including sport in the schools.

Michel de Montaigne

Michel de Montaigne (1553–1592) preceded Descartes and Hobbes and was strongly influenced by the humanist movement of the Renaissance that argued for the well-rounded individual. Montaigne, like Hobbes, believed that our experiences are valid, and that our senses are an important means by which we learn. And like Descartes, he believed that we have a mind that can be "experienced" when we think. As a monist Montaigne argued against the view that the mind and the body are separate, and that to try to separate the mind from the body is to try something that cannot really be experienced. For Montaigne, the mind

> has such a tight brotherly bond with the body that it abandons me at every turn to follow the body in its need. I take (the mind) aside and flatter it, I work on it, all for nothing. In vain I try to turn (the mind) aside from this bond. . . . There is no sprightliness in (the mind's) productions if there is none in the body at the same time.[23]

Montaigne believed that the two are closely connected and to separate them is a philosophical convenience:

> He who wants to detach his soul, let him do it . . . when his body is ill, to free it from the catagion; at other times, on the contrary, let the soul assist and favor the body and not refuse to take part in its natural pleasures.[24]

Montaigne came to this position because he believed that philosophers who advocate dualism are uncomfortable with their bodies, and as a result they take refuge in the purity of the mind.

Michel de Montaigne is identified as a social realist for his emphasis on the development of character, right habits, manners, morals, and citizenship. A skillful writer and essayist, Montaigne described his educational theories in "Of Pedantry," "Of the Education of Children," and "Of the Affection of Fathers to Their Children."[25] Montaigne was trained in the humanist tradition, but he disagreed with the soft lifestyle this sort of education promoted. As a result he advocated "manly exercise," where the child experienced the rougher life in the outdoors. His rejection of the dualistic nature of humans led him to promote physical education as a means of achieving his goals.

> It is not enough to fortify his soul; you must also make his muscles strong. . . . It is not the mind, it is not the body we are training; it is the man and we must not divide him into two parts. Plato says we should not fashion one without the other, but make them draw together like two horses harnessed to a coach. By this saying would it not indicate that he would rather give more care to the body, believing that the mind is benefited at the same time?"[26]

The mind and the body should act as one unit, and this could be done by acclimating the student to heat and cold, wind and sun. The student should not fear danger, and should not have any effeminate characteristics. Montaigne's views were somewhat elitist in that he was trying to develop citizens of the upper classes, which are easily explained given his own upper-class background. However, many of his ideas have been accepted in modern education, which attempts to make them available to everyone.

John Comenius

John Comenius (1592–1671) believed in many of the same ideas as Mulcaster. Comenius differed in that he did not include knightly sports as a means of physical development or even recreation, for he believed that to do so was expensive and useless for the type of students he had. Most people did not need to know sword play, courtly dances, and riding skills because they could not afford this style of living. Like other sense realists, Comenius believed that exercise served as a rest from other parts of the learning process. Indeed, the use of the argument that physical education exists to refresh the body and enable one to work and study more efficiently can be traced back to Comenius, and this argument is widely used by contemporary physical educators. Sense realists were strongly influenced by Descartes' "building block theory of knowledge" and developed a curriculum that moved from the simple to the complex and from present knowledge to the unknown. As a result, classes were taught in a certain logical order, a practice that exists in contemporary curriculum development.

Among the three schools of realism, the sense realists were particularly interested in educating girls, although most of the realists were interested as well. Interestingly enough, educational opportunities for girls were limited since it was believed that women would never have an opportunity to use the skills they would develop. In addition, women in the Age of Science were considered inferior, and there was some debate as to whether or not they could be educated at all. What is important to remember about the realists is that they laid the foundation for the public education of women during a time when women were educated only in the home or in the convent for a life of devotion to the church. In so doing the realists broke away from the traditional treatment of women, and their contemporaries considered them quite liberal even though their programs were very tentative by today's standards.

John Milton

John Milton (1608–1674) was an English poet and wrote *Paradise Lost*.[27] Strongly influenced by the English civil war, Milton sided with the Puritans and argued against play for the sake of play, especially on Sunday. He was angered when Charles I reissued the Declaration of Sport, believing that sport should serve some utilitarian purpose. For example, Milton believed that the martial arts should be practiced in school because they were useful in a time of war. Given the violent time in which he lived, his idea had some merit. However, he believed that warfare was only one aspect of daily life and that education should prepare the student for all possibilities. His "Tractate of Education" articulated the ideas of humanism, which argue for a well-rounded educational curriculum. Milton called for ". . . a complete and generous education that which fits man to perform justly, skillfully, and magnanimously all the offices, both private and public, of peace and war."[28]

John Locke

John Locke (1632–1704), also a social realist, is better known as a philosopher than as an educator. Thomas Jefferson and the framers of the United States Constitution were strongly influenced by his ideas of "life, liberty, and property," which were adapted in the Constitution to read "life, liberty, and the pursuit of happiness." Trained as a physician, he wrote extensively on philosophy, where his ideas on nature and epistemology influenced the philosophers of the eighteenth century.

In his *Essay Concerning Human Understanding* Locke developed the philosophical foundation on which many other philosophers and educators based their arguments for reason over revelation.[29] Locke believed that the mind was a *tabula rasa*, or "blank slate," on which the senses of the body acted. Consequently, Locke argued that the body was of much more importance than in other epistemologies that emphasize the soul or the mind. Locke believed that if you can control a person's experiences, then you can control the formation of the mind, the character, or any other aspect of what a human can become. The end result of this chain of reasoning is that the body becomes a means to train all aspects of a person: mind, body, or soul. He went so far as to argue that physical education was of primary importance in developing an educational foundation. Locke's reasoning influenced the philosophers who followed him. While they may not have agreed with him, they at least had to refute him or risk ridicule for not recognizing the logic of his ideas.

While Locke believed that the body is the vehicle by which the other aspects of the whole person could be educated, he was definitely a dualist. Mind and body were considered to be separate, as can be seen by the following quote: "A gentleman's more serious employment I look on to be study; and when that demands relaxation and refreshment, it should be in some exercise of the body, which unbends the thought and confirms the health and strength."[30] Our point here is not to criticize Locke for his dualistic approach to education as much as it is to show what dualism looks like in practice. Physical activity is used here to *refresh* the individual in order to pursue more important intellectual pursuits. This understanding of the role of human movement is prevalent in contemporary education, and it can be contrasted with a monistic view of activity that explains movement as a function of the *union* of mind and body. Locke's understanding does not preclude enjoying the activity, however. Locke defined a good recreational activity as one that is inherently enjoyable and will leave the participants refreshed and relaxed, an idea in keeping with the Puritan work ethic.

Locke also had an impact as an educator in his own time. His "Some Thoughts on Education" was written for the sons of the wealthy, whom he considered spoiled and soft.[31] Locke argued for the health of the student, which could be enhanced through proper diet and exercise. He believed that "a sound mind in a sound body" was a good rule of thumb for maintaining a happy state in the world and a foundation for moral and intellectual training. In so doing one could develop the knowledge and social skills necessary for a "Man of Business, a Carriage suitable to his Rank and to be eminent and useful to his Country, according to his Station."

Philosophes and Physical Educators

As the eighteenth century progressed, one social class in particular grew in size and hostility to the privileges claimed by the monarchy and the aristocracy. This social class was called the "bourgeoisie" and was composed of the well-educated middle class that was strongly influenced by the new writers of the eighteenth century. The bourgeoisie believed that a free society could be achieved in which each person would be allowed to create his life in the manner he saw fit.

These new writers were known as the *philosophes*. It was in an environment of war, social change, and economic growth that the philosophes developed and advocated a new way of thinking to solve age old problems.

> The philosophes *were educators, politicians, journalists, and men of letters who were dedicated to the use of "human reason, science, and education as the best means of building a stable society of free men on earth."*[32] *They differed from "philosophers" in that they did not develop an entire coherent philosophy as did Plato or Aristotle. Rather they were much more concerned with practical changes that would occur during their own lives.*

The philosophes were not separated from the philosophers. The distinction between the two groups is arbitrary, based on modern scholarship's interpretation of the types of work the two groups did. The philosophes were social critics rather than academic philosophers, and they can be compared to popular social critics of our time, such as newspaper columnists, television editors, and so forth.

The Enlightenment was marked by the suspicion of any epistemology, or theory of knowledge, based on simple authority, religion, tradition, custom, or faith. It was a secular movement, or one that was divorced from religion, and was subsequently attacked from many quarters because of its "godless" nature. The philosophes rejected much of what the Church stood for in terms of education and the development of society and the individual. As one scholar noted,

> The philosophes, could they have been polled in the modern way, would probably have ranked the Roman Catholic Church—indeed, all Christian churches—as the greatest single corrupting influence of their times. According to the philosophes, priests were selfish, cruel, intolerant. . . . But at bottom the great evil of the church, for the enlightened, was its transcendental and supernatural base, which put faith and revelation above reason.[33]

The position of the philosophes can be contrasted with that of the aristocracy, which relied on tradition, custom, and religion for its authority. The philosophes sought to undermine the Old Guard to improve their lot, and they developed arguments for a freer society in order to do so. They offered the first model of how to build a community out of completely "natural" ideas, or those ideas that are generated by humans through their powers of reason. Out of the ideas of the philosophes one can note four common principles:

> (1) Man is not natively depraved; (2) the end of life is life itself, the good life on earth instead of the beatific life after death; (3) man is capable, guided solely by the light of reason and experience, of perfecting the good life on earth; and (4) the first and essential condition of the good life on earth is the freeing of men's minds from the bonds of ignorance and superstition, and of their bodies from the arbitrary oppression of the constituted authorities.[34]

The philsophes believed that the newly created society based on these principles would then be more responsive to the immediate needs and desires of every individual. The literate classes of Europe, with the exception of those who stood to lose power like the Church and the monarchies, promoted the ideals of the Enlightenment. These groups believed that the realization of Enlightenment ideals could not fail to benefit them in the way that each desired.[35] What made the philosophes so different was that they were effective social and educational critics in their own time, and that no such group had existed since the sophists in ancient Greece. It should be noted that they did not lead the changes in eighteenth-century Europe as much as they represented them. The ideas they articulated were expressed by many intellectuals.

As educators the philosophes had several positions in common. First was their faith in nature as the guide by which humans should live. Another commonality was that children should be allowed "childrenly" activities since the philosophes did not wish to limit natural play expression. Play was felt to be a natural activity that could be used to develop other human faculties, and therefore those activities children seem to inherently enjoy should be encouraged. Eighteenth-century educators accepted Locke's idea of how children should be taught: "They must not be hindered from being children, or from playing, or doing as children; but from doing ill. All other liberty is to be allowed them."[36] The end result of this type of thinking was that physical activity was of primary importance to these innovative educators. What their specific programs were like is the subject to which we now turn.

Jean Jacques Rousseau

Jean Jacques Rousseau (1712–1788) was born in Switzerland, the child of a Swiss mother and a French father. He had a troubled childhood. His mother died shortly after he was born and his father neglected him, a situation that may explain his failure to care for his own five children (Rousseau's family situation was ironic, for while his classic work *Emile* is one of the most famous books on education, Rousseau's children became workers and peasants because of their lack of education.) He held a variety of odd jobs throughout his youth: notary, engraver, lackey, secretary, and tutor. Rousseau even studied for a short time to enter the priesthood. This varied experiential background may explain Rousseau's sympathy for the plight of the peasantry, who worked hard yet who had little hope of material gain in eighteenth-century France. These experiences, combined with years of self-study, led Rousseau to write an essay that was one of the single greatest literary influences on the French revolution: *The Social Contract*.[37]

Rousseau believed that the will of the people constitutes a kind of social contract that is the basis of society. Like Locke and Hobbes, Rousseau believed that society was composed of autonomous individuals, and that each person needs to be educated in a way that will make him a good citizen. Therefore, how each citizen is educated is important to the determination of what society looks like. This is one of Rousseau's great contributions to modern education: that the individual and the corresponding relationship to the community are strongly influenced by the educational process. While this idea was not new (Plato understood this relationship and described his corresponding educational ideas in the *Republic*), Rousseau reiterated it in a way that is now taken for granted in modern education.

The educational philosophy of Rousseau can be summarized by the first sentence of *Emile:* "Everything is good as it leaves the hands of the Author of things; everything degenerates in the hands of man."[38] In short, "nature" should determine what is good education, not the traditional methods used by civilization. Rousseau differed from contemporary educators in that he believed individuals are essentially good, that the corrupting influence on individual character was civilization and not original sin. Consequently, Rousseau argued that to develop the ideal educational curriculum one should follow the whims of nature, and make the educational process as "natural" as possible.

With his emphasis on nature, Rousseau argued that the mind and the body work in harmony with one another. Yet one would not call him a monist, for he recognized the differences between mind and body and ascribed to each a separate function, with the mind directing the body:

> It is a most pitiable error to imagine that the exercise of the body is harmful to the operations of the mind, as if these two activities ought not to move together in harmony and that the one ought not always to direct the other.[39]

Direction was the function of the mind, yet it was to work in harmony with the body. So close was this unity that the quality of one affected the performance of the other. Indeed, the ability of the mind to direct was directly related to the wellness of the body:

> Thus his body and his mind are exercised together. Acting always according to his own thought and not someone else's, he continually unites two operations: the more he makes himself strong and robust, the more he becomes sensible and judicious. This is the way one day to have what are believed incompatible and what are united in almost all great men: strength of body and strength of soul; a wise man's reason and an athlete's vigor.[40]

In *Emile*, Rousseau describes this ideal education process for both boys and girls. The child should be educated continuously from birth through adulthood, an idea we now take for granted but which was new with Rousseau. Rousseau's first requirement in the education of the child was for the development of the child's health. If this could be facilitated, then the child had a strong foundation upon which to build other aspects of his being. Rousseau believed, then, that the body is of primary importance in learning, not of secondary importance as argued by many of his contemporaries. It was only after the body was developed and made healthy that one could develop the properties of the mind:

> Do you, then, want to cultivate your pupil's intelligence? Cultivate the strengths it ought to govern. Exercise his body continually; make him robust and healthy in order to make him wise and reasonable. Let him work, be active, run, yell, always be in motion. Let him be a man in his vigor, and soon he will be one in his reason.[41]

The powers of reason were not of secondary importance, however. They were to be developed after the physical aspects of the individual. Rousseau's logic was powerful and persuasive, and he sought to elevate physical education to a position not seen since the time of the ancient Greeks.

Rousseau began with the idea that children should be outdoors and active. In so doing the child would develop his senses through his own experiences. The senses would then provide the background against which ideas take shape. By moving and touching everything, seeing and hearing, tasting and smelling, the child would begin to associate the objects of the external world with the five senses. "It is only by movement that we learn that there are things which are not us."[42] Emotions follow, along with the concepts of extension and motion.

As the child aged, Rousseau wished to develop the senses through specific physical activities:

> There are purely natural and mechanical exercises which serve to make the body robust without giving any occasion for the exercise of judgment. Swimming, running, jumping, spinning a top, throwing stones, all that is quite good. But have we only arms and legs? . . . Do not exercise only strength; exercise all the senses which direct it. Get from each of them all they can do.[43]

And,

> In the morning let Emile run barefoot in all seasons, in his room, on the stairs, in the garden. . . . Let him know how to jump long and high, to climb a tree, to get over a wall. Let him learn to keep his balance; let all his movements and gestures be ordered according to the laws of equilibrium. . . . If I were a dancing master . . . I would take him to the foot of a cliff. There I would show him what attitude he must take, how he must bear his body and his head, what movements he must make, in what way he must place now his foot, now his hand, so as to follow lightly the steep, rough, uneven paths and to bound from peak to peak in climbing up as well as down. I would make him the emulator of a goat rather than of a dancer of the Opera.[44]

It would seem from this quote that Rousseau had the physical educator in mind when he created the ideal teacher! Rousseau hoped by performing a variety of tasks, the child would develop the skills necessary for performing well in life, and it was the role of the teacher to provide the appropriate experiences:

> When a child plays with the shuttlecock, he practices his eye and arm in accuracy; when he whips a top, he increases his strength by using it but without learning anything. I have sometimes asked why the same games of skill men have are not given to children: tennis, croquet, billiards, the boy, football, musical instruments. . . . To bound from one end of the room to the other, to judge a ball's bounce while still in the air, to return it with a hand strong and sure—such games are less suitable for a grown man than useful for forming him.[45]

Rousseau was one of the first modern educators to promote the education of women. Yet his model is not what we would use today:

> Men's morals, their passions, their tastes, their pleasures, their very happiness also depend on women. Thus the whole education of women ought to relate to men. To please men, to be useful to them, to make herself loved and honored by them, to raise them when young, to care for them when grown, to counsel them, to console them, to make their lives agreeable and sweet—those are the duties of women at all times, and they ought to be taught from childhood.[46]

To say the least, by contemporary standards Rousseau was a "chauvinist pig." But by his own standards he was a daring educational revolutionary arguing that women have been endowed by nature "to think, to judge, to love, to know, to cultivate their minds as well as their looks."[47]

These goals were developed very early on, and like boys, girls should develop their bodies first:

> Since the body is born, so to speak, before the soul, the body ought to be cultivated first. This order is common to the two sexes, but the aim of this cultivation is different. For man this aim is the development of strength; for woman it is the development of attractiveness. Not that these qualities ought to exclude one another; their rank order is merely reversed in each sex: women need enough strength to do everything they do with grace; men need enough adroitness to do everything they do with facility.[48]

While we cannot learn much from Rousseau with respect to specific physical education programs for girls, we do know that he was ahead of his time. This implies that his attitude toward the education of women, as "barbaric" as it appears, was better than that of his peers! And in knowing this we know much about that which Rousseau reacted against. Education for girls must have been stifling by today's standards, emphasizing those qualities in women that would make them desirable in marriage. Rousseau argued that women, too, were human beings, and should develop their human qualities in addition to their looks.

Rousseau did not live to see the revolutions he advocated in either politics or in education. He died one year before the French Revolution and before his ideas could take root in educational institutions. His impact lived on, however, in the acceptance of his ideas by the most progressive schools of the eighteenth century.

Johann Bernhard Basedow

If Rousseau was the educational innovator in theory, Johann Bernhard Basedow (1723–1790) was the educational innovator in practice. More of an educator than a social critic like Rousseau and the philosophes, Basedow was a radical in the actual implementation of the ideas of the philosophes. Basedow founded the Philanthropinum in 1774, which was modeled on the theories of Rousseau. Ironically, *Emile* was more influential in Germany than it was in France, where the book was used as a guideline for developing a new "aristocracy of worth" based on the dignity of man and the rightness of nature.[49] Basedow was an intellectual in his own right, having published several books on educational theories and methods. After the publication of *Address to Philanthropists and Men of Property on Schools and Studies and Their Influence on the Public Wealth*, he was able to secure funding for his school from the Duke of Anhalt, Prince Leopold Franz. Basedow opened the Philanthropinum in Dessau, which was later renamed the Dessau Educational Institute.

Basedow combined the educational ideas of Rousseau with those of Francis Bacon and John Comenius. He emphasized the use of the senses in the learning process and used nature as a guide. This approach led Basedow to treat children as children rather than as small adults, an idea we take for granted in modern education. In Basedow's time children dressed as adults did: with formal coats, powdered wigs, rouged cheeks, and small swords. Basedow rejected this and instead believed children should "act their age" and engage in activities appropriate for them according to nature. Children at the Philanthropinum dressed in simple uniforms that allowed for the freedom of movement called for in Rousseau's *Emile*, and they were encouraged to act like children instead of like adults. This led to the first physical education classes in modern education.

According to the Philanthropinum's prospectus, approximately half of each ten-hour school day was to be spent in intellectual activities and the other half in bodily activities. For the physical activities, three hours were allotted to recreational activities like fencing, riding, dancing, and music. Two hours were to be spent in manual labor such as carpentry, masonry, and other crafts. Once the children were of the proper age they were taught the appropriate martial arts, and for two months in the summer they lived in tents to facilitate hunting, fishing, boating, and swimming activities.[50]

It is not surprising, given the innovative nature of the Philanthropinum, that the teacher responsible for the physical education activities is considered by many to be the first "modern" physical educator. The program was developed by Johann Friedrich Simon, who had students of different ages engage in activities appropriate to their "natural" abilities and desires. Younger students, for instance, engaged in "Greek gymnastics" (contests in running, wrestling, throwing, and jumping) that were similar to the activities of the ancient Greek games. The older students practiced the "knightly exercises" that included dancing, fencing, and riding, and vaulting on live horses. Other activities included shuttlecock, tennis, skittles, and playing with a large, air-filled ball.[51]

While many of the ideas put into place in the Philanthropinum are accepted today, such as specialists in physical education, outdoor activities, and specialized equipment and facilities, these ideas were not nearly as accepted in Basedow's time. At most the Philanthropinum had fifty-three students, and it closed in 1793 because it was not financially solvent. In addition Basedow was a difficult man to work with. He was described as "coarse, arrogant, argumentative, vulgar in his language, and given to drunkenness. It is amazing that a school could be entrusted to such a man."[52] Basedow resigned in 1778, and the school closed fifteen years later in 1793. Yet the school had an impact on education in Europe both because of its innovative nature and the quality of the teachers associated with it.

Johann Friedrich GutsMuths

While Simon may be credited with being the first "modern" physical educator, Johann Friedrich GutsMuths (1759–1839) legitimized the profession of physical education with the quality of his work. While he also taught geography, French, and technology, physical education was his favorite. GutsMuths was the second physical education teacher at the Schnepfenthal Educational Institute. The first, Christian Andre, duplicated nearly all of the exercises that he had seen at the Philanthropinum. GutsMuths continued the program Andre established and continued to develop it for the next fifty years. His teaching techniques and writings became the standard by which subsequent physical educators were judged.

When visitors looked at the Schnepfenthal Educational Institute, one of the first things they noticed was the tremendous location of the school. Situated on an estate near Gotha, Germany, the campus was in an ideal location for outdoor activities, and when weather did not permit, indoor facilities were available. Many of the activities needed to be outdoors to be performed: climbing ropes, masts, rope ladders, and swinging required the use of trees and other large apparatus. In addition students balanced rods on their fingers or performed exercises while standing on one foot. Swimming was a highly valued exercise, and GutMuths wrote a book, *Manual on the Art of Swimming* (1798), on how to perform the activity and how to teach it. In another book, *Gymnastics for the Young* (1793), GutsMuths classified his exercises according to how they developed the individual: (1) walking and running; (2) jumping, free and with apparatus; (3) lifting and carrying exercises of the back muscles, pulling, pushing, thrusting, and wrestling; (4) fencing; (5) climbing; (6) exercises to maintain equilibrium, or balancing with the aid of apparatus; (7) throwing and archery; (8) bathing and swimming; (9) exercises of suppleness, to train the aesthetic sense, will power, and organs of speech; (10) dancing; and (11) exercises to train the senses. GutsMuths led camping expeditions, some of which lasted four days. In so doing the students were at one with nature and developed as they should. Schnepfenthal became famous for its well-lit and well-ventilated rooms, and the wholesome but simple food gave the students an attitude of health that impressed those who came to visit.

GutsMuths used several ideas to develop his physical education programs. He believed that many educational institutions were not aware of the value of gymnastics, or what we call physical education. He argued that a nation should promote the health of its people and in so doing would be a stronger nation as a result. GutsMuths believed that the best way to develop health was through his gymnastics program. This idea was very attractive to Germans, who argued that the separate German states should be united in one strong nation. He also believed that exercises should be fun and should have as their purpose the harmonizing of the mind and the body. This monistic idea of the union of mind and body was very different in practice from most other educational institutions that emphasized the development only of the mind through reading and oral repetition. Like Rousseau, GutsMuths argued that the development of the body should come first, and only after the body is developed can the mind and its processes be developed. And like Rousseau, GutsMuths argued that girls and women should engage in light gymnastics and games, but not in the heavy work of men. In so doing they would be healthy, refined, and pleasing.[53]

GutsMuths had an immediate impact on physical education in the more progressive schools of his time. Perhaps most significant is that people began to place their children in programs that taught gymnastics. With more demand schools began to teach it, and universities began to study gymnastics in a manner we would recognize today.[54] Although he was not the first modern physical educator, he is considered the real founder of physical education because of his fifty years of service and the books he wrote. *Gymnastic for the Young* and *Games* (1796) were the first manuals published by an experienced professional in physical education and were based on the accepted medical and physiological principles of his time. GutsMuths also published *Book of Gymnastics for Sons of the Fatherland* (1817), and *Catechism of Gymnastics, a Manual for Teachers and Pupils* (1818).[55]

Summary

The Age of Science and the Enlightenment witnessed the growth of a belief in the powers of human beings to understand and manipulate their environment. This belief was at first limited primarily to small groups of intellectuals, but as time passed these ideas came to represent the dominant belief system in the Western world. The philosophers, scientists, educators, and an increasingly larger, well-read public began to live in the eighteenth century according to the new philosophies developed during the seventeenth century. With the colonization of North America, a new country was formed whose leaders were well versed in Enlightenment ideas, and these ideas eventually found their home in *The Declaration of Independence* and the *Constitution.*

The Enlightenment was a period of time during which the methods of science were applied to many other aspects of life such as politics, social thought, and philosophy. During the Enlightenment the new, scientific ways of Newton, Galileo, Hobbes, Locke, and Descartes were the "light" that guided humanity toward a basic harmony of interests that we are comfortable with today. As a consequence, many of our attitudes in contemporary times stem from the attitudes of intellectuals who argued for change during the Enlightenment.

Significant ideas that had their genesis during the Enlightenment are taken for granted in contemporary education, such as democratic education. Indeed, education is intimately connected to the Enlightenment tradition. Physical education was similarly affected by the Enlightenment, especially since the many Enlightenment critics had so much to say about the virtues of human movement as a means of creating the ideal individual and community, and the role that "nature" had in the development of the whole human being. It is no accident, then, that the first physical educators in "modern times" lived during the Enlightenment, and many of their ideas are still with us today.

Discussion Questions

1. How did Hobbes' materialism have an impact on the development of physical education? How did Hobbes view free will and concepts of the mind and spirit?

2. How did Descartes' rationalism have an impact on the development of physical education? How did Descartes view the body?

3. How did Isaac Newton have an impact on how we view the body? How are his "Three Laws of Motion" used in physical education today?

4. What is Michel de Montaigne's metaphysical position? How is it different from that of Hobbes? Of Descartes?

5. What types of physical education programs evolved during the Enlightenment? What were the major influences on this evolution?

6. How was Rousseau's *Emile* representative of Enlightenment thinking? How does *Emile* differ from educational philosophies that preceded it?

Suggestions for Further Reading

Brailsford, D. "Puritanism and Sport in Seventeenth Century England," *Stadion* I, 2, 316–330.

Burke, R. K. "Naturalism and Physical Education." In Elwood Craig Davis, *The Philosophic Process in Physical Education*. Philadelphia: Lea and Febiger, 1971, 56–80.

Gerber, E. "Francois Rabelais," "Michel de Montaigne," "Richard Mulcaster," "John Amos Comenius," "John Locke." In *Innovators and Institutions in Physical Education*. Philadelphia: Lea and Febiger, 1971, 54–75.

Kleinman, S. "The Classic Philosophers and Their Metaphysical Positions." In *Physical Education: An Interdisciplinary Approach*, by Robert Singer, David Lamb, John Loy, Robert Malina, and Seymour Kleinman. New York: The Macmillan Company, 1972.

Ross, S. "Cartesian Dualism and Physical Education: Epistemological Incompatibility." In *Mind and Body: East Meets West*, edited by S. Kleinman. Champaign, Illinois: Human Kinetics Publishers, Inc., 1986, 15–25.

Rousseau, J. J. *Emile*. Translated by Allan Bloom. New York: Basic Books, Inc., 1979.

Struna, N. L. "The Declaration of Sport Reconsidered."

Notes

1. Stephen E. Toulmin, *Cosmopolis: The Hidden Agenda of Modernity* (New York: The Free Press, 1990).

2. J. Bronowski and Bruce Mazlish, *The Western Intellectual Tradition: From Leonardo to Hegel* (New York: Harper & Brothers, 1960). As Bronowski noted, the economic and social issues that led to the Puritan Revolution were expressed in religious and political terms. This terminology is indicative of how economics, social class, politics, religion, and of course, sport, were interwoven in sixteenth-century England.

3. Dennis Brailsford, "Puritanism and Sport in Seventeenth Century England," *Stadion* I(2): 316–30.

4. Will Durant, *The Reformation* (New York: Simon and Schuster, 1957).

5. Robert Anchor. *The Enlightenment Tradition* (New York: Harper and Row, 1967).

6. The association of science and philosophy has survived to this day at the older universities like Oxford, where a chair of Experimental Philosophy still exists. This person is engaged in what we now know as science, not philosophy.

7. Abraham Wolf, *History of Science, Technology, and Philosophy in the Sixteenth and Seventeenth Centuries* (London: Allen & Unwin, 1960), 36.

8. Maurice Cranston, "Francis Bacon," *The Encyclopedia of Philosophy*, vol. 1 (New York: Macmillan Publishing Co., Inc. & The Free Press, 1967), 235.

9. Dagobert D. Runes, ed., "Francis Bacon," *The Standard Dictionary of Philosophy* (New York: Philosophical Library, 1983).

10. Dudley Shapere, "Newtonian Mechanics and Mechanical Explanation," *The Encyclopedia of Philosophy*, vol. 5 (New York: Macmillan Publishing Co., Inc. & The Free Press, 1967), 491.

11. Frederick Copleston, *A History of Philosophy*, vol. IV, (London: Burns & Oates Ltd., 1969).

12. Philosophers differed from the philosophes only in that the philosophers developed more formal, rigorous systems of thought. Some contemporary philosophers no longer differentiate between the two groups. See Crane Brinton, "Enlightenment," *The Encyclopedia of Philosophy*, vol. 3. (New York: Macmillan Publishing Co., 1967), 519–25.

13. Bronowski and Mazlish, *The Western Intellectual Tradition*.

14. John Dewey, *Types of Thinking* (New York: Philosophical Library, 1984).

15. Rene Descartes, *Meditations*, trans. Laurence J. Lafleur (New York: Liberal Arts Press, 1951).

16. Saul Ross, "Cartesian Dualism and Physical Education: Epistemological Incompatibility," in *Mind and Body: East Meets West*, ed. Sy Kleinman (Champaign, Illinois: Human Kinetics Publishers, Inc., 1986), 15–25.

17. Ibid.

18. George Berkeley, *The Principles of Human Knowledge* (Cleveland, Ohio: The World Publishing Co., 1963), 18.

19. Seymour Kleinman, "The Classic Philosophers and Their Metaphysical Positions," *Physical Education: An Interdisciplinary Approach*, by Robert Singer, David Lamb, John Loy, Robert Malina, and Seymour Kleinman (New York: The Macmillan Co., 1972), 337.

20. Kleinman, "The Classic Philosophers."

21. Francois Rabelais, *The Five Books of Gargantua and Pantagruel* (New York: The Modern Library, 1936).

22. Richard Mulcaster, *Positions: Wherein Those Primitive Circumstances Be Examined, Which are Necessary for The Training Up of Children, Either for Skill in Their Booke, or Health in Their Bodies* (London: Thomas Vautrollier, 1581).

23. Michel de Montaigne, quoted in Toulmin, Cosmopolis, 37–38.

24. Ibid.

25. Michel de Montaigne. The Essays of Michael Lord of Montaigne (Vol. I and II), John Florio, Trans. (New York: E. P. Dutton & Co., 1927).

26. Ibid.

27. John Milton, English Minor Poems: Paradise Lost, Samson Agonistes, Areopagitica (Chicago: Encyclopedia Britannica, 1948).

28. John Milton, *Milton on Education, the Tractate of Education* (New Haven: Yale University Press, 1928).

29. John Locke, *Essay Concerning Human Understanding*, 5th ed., ed. J. W. Yolton (London: Cambridge University Press, 1970).

30. John Locke, "Some Thoughts Concerning Education," *Essays by John Locke* (London: Ward Lock and Co., 1883), 153.

31. Robert H. Quick, *Some Thoughts on Education by John Locke* (Cambridge: The University Press, 1880).

32. Anchor, *The Enlightenment Tradition*, ix.

33. Ibid., 520.

34. Ibid., 7–8.

35. Ibid.

36. Locke is quoted in Deobold Van Dalen, Elmer Mitchell, and Bruce Bennett, *A World History of Physical Education* (Englewood Cliffs, N.J.: Prentice-Hall, 1953), 194.

37. Ellen Gerber, "Jean Jacques Rousseau," *Innovators and Institutions in Physical Education* (Philadelphia: Lea and Febiger, 1971), 76–82.

38. Jean Jacques Rousseau, *Emile*, trans. Allan Bloom (New York: Basic Books, Inc., 1979), 37.

39. Ibid., 118.

40. Ibid., 119.

41. Ibid.

42. Ibid.

43. Ibid., 132.

44. Ibid., 139–40.

45. Ibid., 146–47.

46. Ibid., 365.

47. Ibid., 364.

48. Ibid., 365.

49. Ellen Gerber, "The Philanthropinum," *Innovators and Institutions in Physical Education* (Philadelphia: Lea and Febiger, 1971), 83–86.

50. Ibid.

51. Ibid., 85.

52. Ibid.

53. Emmett A. Rice, John Hutchinson, and Mabel Lee, *A Brief History of Physical Education*, 5th ed. (New York: The Ronald Press Co.), 1969.

54. Ibid.

55. C. W. Hackensmith, *History of Physical Education* (New York: Harper and Row, 1966).

Philosophical Positions of the Body and the Development of Physical Education: Contributions of the Germans, Swedes, and Danes in Nineteenth-Century Europe

General Events

1780 Pestalozzi's *Evening Hours of a Hermit*

1798 France annexes Switzerland

1800 Pestalozzi establishes Institute at Burgdorf

1804 Pestalozzi leaves Burgdorf, starts school at Yverdon

1806 Prussia defeated by Napoleon

1807 Peace of Tilsit

1813 Beginning of German wars of liberation

1814 Carlsbad Decrees

1816 Froebel establishes Universal German Institute; publishes *Education of Man*

Sport and Physical Education

1746–1827 Johann Heinrich Pestalozzi

1776–1839 Per Henrik Ling

1777–1847 Franz Nachtegall

1778–1852 Friedrich Ludvig Jahn

1800 Physical education program at Yverdon

1810 Jahn promotes German League

1811 Beginning of German turnverein movement

Introduction

In the Western world the philosophy of idealism can be traced back to the beliefs and logic articulated by two sages of ancient Athens, Socrates and Plato. Idealism has competed with naturalism for adherents since ancient times. Naturalism believes that all events, human and natural, share the same character and can be explained as a process inherent in nature; that is, nature is reliable and dependable. In this chapter we will discuss the general parameters of idealism with initial concentration on the German idealists of the nineteenth century and the role they had in developing the philosophical position that had an impact on the concepts of the body and the consequent impact on physical education. Then we will turn our attention to the historical role of education during this era, concentrating on the development of physical education under the watchful eyes of (1) Johann Pestalozzi, (2) Friedrich Froebel, (3) Franz Nachtegall, (4) Per Henrik Ling, and (5) Friedrich Ludwig Jahn. However, we must first turn our attention to idealism and the proponents of German idealism, namely Immanuel Kant, Georg Wilhelm Friedrich Hegel, and Johann Gottlieb Fichte.

The position of idealism relative to the body and purpose of education and corresponding epistemological beliefs are very significant to physical education. Idealism, as are other philosophical schools, is very interested in ethics; how we treat others and the importance in establishing a code of conduct that helps us determine the proper course of action as opposed to an improper or unethical course of action (determining right from wrong). Ethics traditionally has manifested itself in physical education and sport as sportsmanship.

Idealism

Idealists have focused their energy and effort in investigating three specific topics: (1) the existence of God, (2) the self, and (3) knowledge. These issues comprise the fabric of the metaphysical (God and self) and epistemological (knowledge—how we come to know things) positions that help form the major components of idealism. These components are not limited to idealism but form the basic tenets of all philosophies. Two other components of idealism are logic and axiology, which address ethical, aesthetic, religious, and social values, and which also are manifest in other philosophical schools.

According to idealism, reality is mind. (If this statement appears to be abstract and somewhat "mind boggling," don't panic!) Idealists believe that the entire universe is that which is conceived by mind. The world of material objects is secondary. In other words, what the mind or spirit experiences and perceives as real is essentially authentic. For example, idealism holds that the world we actually exist in is an imperfect world. However, our mind is able to visualize or conceive of a perfect world, which according to idealism also must exist and is real. According to idealism, the fact that we have an *idea* of a perfect world is evidence that it exists. The use of logic is essential to idealism. Since the idea is conceived by the mind, idealistic logic dictates that in all probability it exists, because according to idealism, reality is mind.

The mind, to an idealist, is composed of a spiritual quality, which logically results in the view that *ultimate reality*, as it exists, is beyond the phenomenal sensory perceived world. By contrast, the *basic fundamental nature of reality* to the idealist is mind or reason, which manifests itself in everyday consciousness. At this point it will be helpful to distinguish between two philosophical views inherent in idealism: metaphysical idealism and epistemological idealism.

Metaphysical idealism analyzes the universe as a psychic or mental reality; all "things" in the universe are linked by an ideal element that can be logically deduced. Plato, St. Augustine, and to a lesser degree Aristotle, were proponents of metaphysical idealism. The difficulty with metaphysical idealism, like most metaphysical inquiries, is that the facts or evidence in support of their positions are obtained through deductive and subjective logic, which delights the skeptics who oppose metaphysical inquiry. Epistemological idealism, on the other hand, approaches the study and indeed the actual identification of reality with "mentally knowable" data, which are perceptible truths.[1] Whatever is "out there" beyond our minds, all we can know is what is in our minds. Idealism can use both inductive and deductive reasoning.

In general, what do idealists actually agree on and believe? To reiterate, the three primary subjects that idealism investigates are: the existence of God, the personal self, and the acquisition of valid knowledge.

The Self

The reality of our existence, in philosophical terms, rests with the acknowledgment that the *self* is a certainty. This question about self as a certainty is abstract philosophizing. We refer back to Descartes, discussed in chapter 6, because he is able to provide insight and resolution about the reality of the self. Kleinman analyzed Descartes' beliefs as follows:

> The nature of the body and that of the soul have nothing in common. Thus, these two entities or substances may be regarded as substances distinct in kind. Therefore . . . the soul, or mind, needs no knowledge of, nor must it have dependence upon the body, in order to exist.[2]

In his *Meditations on First Philosophy* Descartes decided that if he really is going to "know things" as they truly exist, he must rid himself of all that he has been taught and even doubt his own existence or self.[3] Descartes, as you remember, eventually concludes through deduction that he cannot have faith in what his physical senses reveal to him and therefore cannot rely on prior experiences to be real or authentic. Descartes continues his logic and inquiry in the *Meditations* to the point where he starts to doubt his own existence or self: What am I (body, mind, soul)? Do I actually exist? It is the doubt that Descartes has about his existence that actually rescues him from his quandary. Doubt became one of the most direct routes to the discovery of the self.

Butler states that "in doubting everything, as Descartes did, even to the point of questioning if the world about us is any more real than our dreams, we can scarcely fail to observe before long that there is someone who is doubting. Doubt is thought and thought involves a thinker."[4] In Descartes' classic statement "I think, therefore I am," Descartes' "self" was mindful activity, thereby confirming the logic of idealism that reality is mind.

On Knowledge

Idealists make the statement that understanding the nature of knowledge will logically clarify the nature of reality. In other words, ideals that are accepted as true and authentic must be derived from evidence. The *evidence* can be established by the process of logic using both inductive and deductive reasoning. Like anything else, the initial data that our sensory experiences provide us must be interpreted and validated as authentic and true or unreliable and inaccurate. Zeigler describes truth for the idealist:

> (T)ruth for idealists is orderly and systematic. A test for truth is its coherence with knowledge that has been previously established. An individual, therefore, attains truth for himself by examining the wisdom of the past through his own mind. Everything that exists has a relationship to something else and is intertwined. Reality, viewed in this way, is a system of logic and order—a logic and order that has been established by the Universal mind. Experimental testing helps to determine what the truth really is with the chips falling where they may.[5]

The German Idealists: Kant, Fichte, and Hegel

The idealist believes that the world and the universe are primarily spiritual (spiritual being part of the perfect ideal). Pure idealists do not accept the theory of evolution, which in part portrays humankind as high-grade monkeys. Humans are composed of more than just the corporeal; they each have a soul and this fact alone places them in a higher order than any creature inhabiting the earth. The soul is the "link" to the spiritual nature of reality, which to the idealist is the only true reality—ultimate reality is spiritual, which may be manifest in mind. Bishop George Berkeley (1685–1753), one of Ireland's major contributors to philosophy, believed that the world has meaning because our minds are able to discern it. Because worldly experience allows us, through the mind, to assimilate and extract quality and meaning from our existence, "something" must exist that actually provides the elements of quality and meaning. Berkeley identified this "something" as the universal mind or God that provides quality and meaning as a process. Ever the idealist, Berkeley supported the idealistic concept that reality is mind; in this case ultimate reality is universal mind. German idealists did not necessarily identify their belief in ultimate ideals with traditional Western belief in God.

Having presented some general ideas about idealism, we now turn our attention to the German idealists. Before we begin our discussion of Kant, Fichte, and Hegel, it is historically relevant to provide a brief account of the relationship between these three giants of philosophy. Without question, Immanuel Kant is revered as one of the greatest philosophers who ever lived. From an idealistic position he addressed epistemological and metaphysical questions such as personal freedom, the reality of the self, moral law, God, and immortality. Kant's interest in ethics was of considerable importance. He developed the concept known as the "categorical imperative," which will be presented later in this chapter. Sport philosophy has tied Kant's categorical imperative to the ideal that serves as the foundation of sportsmanship. It is interesting to note that he did not identify with any form of organized religious worship during adulthood because of his disgust with the primitive forms of religion he encountered in his younger days.

Kant received his education at Königsberg University, where he later returned to teach and achieved full professorship after fifteen years of service. Johann Gottlieb Fichte was an admirer and disciple of Kant. Fichte was so spellbound by and in awe of the great master that early on he traveled to Königsberg to discuss philosophical issues with Kant. However, Kant dismissed Fichte as yet another student who obviously did not know the first thing about the philosophical process. Fichte was not to be denied. He stayed around long enough to produce an article that examined an area of Kant's philosophy that even eluded and perplexed the great master himself. Kant was so impressed by the article that Fichte was proclaimed a "philosopher" by none other than his idol, Kant. Fichte later became the Chair of Philosophy at the University of Berlin, which was eventually occupied by Hegel. It was Fichte who was able to link the philosophy of Kant with that of Hegel.[6]

Immanuel Kant

The work of Kant (1724–1804) is difficult to comprehend, and therefore the student of Kant must exercise patience and persistence. As Butler states: "Because of the great comprehensiveness and caliber of his thought, it often seems that there is no end to the detailed excursions on which he takes the reader."[7] He did not publish his first major book until he was fifty–seven years old. Kant asked one of his friends to read *Critique of Pure Reason*,[8] and the friend replied that he was sure he would indeed lose his ability to reason (along with his mind!) if he read it through to the end.

Kant can be very pedantic. In *Critique of Pure Reason* he makes a complete and thorough analysis of the reasoning process and presents his theory of knowledge. His examination and analysis concludes, in part, that conscious reason is the catalyst or genius for all of humankind's experience. It is our conscious experience (mind) that provides unity and order. According to Kant, the world is represented (not presented) to us by way of our physical senses and the sensory input we receive. Sensations are actually chaotic and therefore unrelated. Kant believed that these sensations we perceive are manufactured and *caused* by "something out there." It is the act or mechanism of conscious thought (mind) that can actually describe and order these sensations into two perceptible components of space and time. Simply put, Kant believed that we can link and therefore unify our sensory input by placing sensations in time and space and categorizing them, which is made possible by mindful activity (consciousness). As a result, we will examine and catalog these sensations as reliable and unreliable. Butler states that "It is reason . . . that fits perceived objects into their respective classes and thus supplements perception in giving us the perfectly integrated experience we will normally possess. Kant spoke of this aspect of mind as the understanding; the classes in which we group objects according to similarities and differences as conceptions."[9] Kant believed that there exists but only twelve kinds of conceptions, which he calls categories. What Kant attempted to get across is that knowledge and reason constitute an interactive process that in general has its origin and direction from the mind toward the world (interactive) and not from the world toward the mind (passive). Thus, our ability to understand allows us to categorize and relate/link things logically.[10] Epistemologically speaking, we can come to "know things" in this fashion.

We now return to the "thing out there," as Kant described it, as the source in the external world that manufactures and gives us sense impressions and assigns a quality to them. Kant referred to this "thing" as the "Thing in Itself," which is so great and omnipresent that it defies our knowledge and therefore can never be known. Some scholars believe that the "Thing in Itself" is God or universal reason. Kant, however, based his belief in God on moral grounds and not necessarily on supernatural phenomena. As such he appears to be agnostic in defining the "Thing in Itself." Perhaps another way to approach the question is from the following perspective. As humans we have a finite existence and finite capacity for knowledge. Logic dictates that because we are indeed finite, we can never comprehend or know something that is infinite. An infinite "thing" can know us; however we do not have the intellectual capacity or ability to "know" the infinite "Thing in Itself." This form of logic suggests that God in the Judeo-Christian sense is unknowable beyond what God chooses to reveal to us.

What did Kant actually believe? The following five beliefs are recognized as central to his inquiry into philosophy:

1. *Moral Law.* There exist universal moral laws. The only acts/behaviors that we can do are those acts or behaviors that are practiced by all of us. For example, if someone were to murder another person, the actual taking of a life may be indeed justified because of the circumstance. However, if "casual" murder became an accepted and universal practice, it would result in the eventual annihilation of the human race. Thus, there exists a universal moral law that eliminates this possibility from ever happening.

2. *Categorical Imperative.* In addition to the existence of moral laws, Kant believed that each and every person has a feeling of obligation

to obey these moral laws. Because this obligation and sense of duty to *obey* moral laws are grounded in reason (not in experience), Kant refers to this sense of duty and obligation as a categorical imperative. According to Kant, the categorical imperative is the one duty which everyone must regard as sacred or universal. It acts as a universal ethical mandate that says, "treat others as an end in themselves rather than using people to serve your own ends." This ethical belief would act as a guide for all decisions. In contrast, an unethical individual who ignored Kant's categorical imperative would use individuals as a means to an end; tools to achieve some personal goal.

3. *Freedom.* He believed in freedom. It is quite possible for us to do good purely out of the desire to do good (we are free to act in this way) and not because we are motivated by an extrinsic reward. According to Kant, to do good will just for the sake of doing good for its own sake is the only unqualified (not dependent on motivation by ulterior motives) good in the world.

4. *Immortality.* Kant believed in the immortality of the soul.

5. *God.* Kant believed that the categorical imperatives and the lack of moral guarantees in the natural world make the existence of God a certainty. "It is necessary that there be a Supreme Intelligence as the cause of the moral obligation in us."[11]

Kant's philosophy is quite relevant to physical education and sport. Human existence to Kant manifests itself as a unified consciousness that participates (1) in a sensory/corporeal world by which we are defined/determined and (2) in the world of reason in which we are free. As a result, we have both a sensuous (natural) and a rational aspect to our existence.[12] The sensuous aspect compels us to the particularity of idiosyncratic inclination, caprice, and desire. The reasoned and rational aspect impels us to the universality of moral obligation and the acceptance of the categorical imperative which can be equated with "sportsmanship." Kant argues from his categorical imperative position that the moral law, unlike the natural law which is sensuous and capricious, commands unconditionally or categorically to "act only according to that maxim by which you can at the same time will insure that it should become a universal law."[13] Kant adds clarity to this belief as he continues his line of reasoning, "act so that you treat humanity, whether in your own person or in that of another, always as an end and never as a means only."[14]

Robert Osterhoudt is an eminent scholar in the field of sport philosophy. He provides a revealing look at Kant's categorical imperative and the significant relationship it has with sport and physical education:

The imperative commands that we universalize our respect for each person as a free moral agent, and so withhold regarding him as a mere object externally found to, and thereby exploited by our sensuous or egoistic inclinations. This notion entails extending to others what we, as free, self-determining, rational beings, would have extended to ourselves. Kant therefore proposes a union of all rational beings in a realm of common law (a 'realm of ends') in which the general ends of all become the ends of all others. In this the individual and common goods coalesce. Accordingly, it follows that a willful violation of this principle is humanistically self-destructive in a general fashion, let alone in a fashion particular to sport.

The use of the imperative in sport secures an internal relationship with those laws (rules and regulations) which define and govern it, and with those other persons who also freely participate in it. A regard for these laws as self-legislated, and an intrinsic respect for those others is nonetheless presupposed by a free entry into the sporting activity . . . this is what is meant by such an entry; that is the taking on of the laws of sport as one's own, and the cultivation of a divining sympathy for all others who have also made such a choice. The categorical imperative commands that we abide by the laws for their own sake (for they are expressions of our most fundamental nature), and that we consequently treat others with a regard that we ourselves would prefer—that is, treat others as ends-in-themselves. Only insofar as persons make such a treatment, do they stand in a positive and viable relation to reason, and so to one another.[15]

The categorical imperative of Kant is an ethical belief that remains timely and has tremendous potential for physical education and sport. Sportsmanship and moral conduct in athletic competition and physical education represents an ideal situation in which to instill and teach the humanistic qualities espoused by Kant.

Some people claim that the traditional concept of sportsmanship that espouses fair play and the need to instill positive core values have become obsolete, replaced by the philosophy that believes in "win at all cost." What are your thoughts about the way contemporary sport and physical education is practiced?

Johann Fichte

Johann Gottlieb Fichte (1762–1814) devoted most of his writing to the ethical issues that challenge human life. He described reality as a morally purposeful will and believed that the phenomenal world in which we live was actually designed to nurture and develop the "will" of men and women and thus bring their character into being. Fichte and Kant parted company when the subject of the "Thing in Itself" surfaced. Unlike Kant, Fichte believed the "Thing in Itself" (Kant's description) was indeed knowable. There are, of course, evils in the world over which people have no control but that are part of the overall plan; that is, evil is necessary. According to Butler, Fichte would say that

these apparent evils in the very texture of the natural world are the prods for awakening the human spirit and spurring it to active achievement. Man's relation to nature could not be altogether soothing and comfortable, or the human spirit would be allowed to sleep on and never awaken to achieve consciousness. . . . Health of the body is essential to vigor of mind and spirit.[16]

The philosophical position of the body and the corresponding association between mind, body, and spirit, which is a fundamental component of idealism, enables physical education to look upon Kant and Fichte as providing a philosophical position (as did Aristotle) that demanded a healthy and fit body for each person to reach his or her full potential. Philosophically, the body and physical education are accorded a position of critical importance within the educational scheme advocated by Kant and Fichte. The mind would be at a disadvantage without a healthy and fit body. Also, evil appears to occupy an intentional and purposeful place relative to our existence.

Georg Hegel

Georg Wilhelm Friedrich Hegel (1770–1831) grew up in Stuttgart and enrolled at the University of Tübingen. He went on to the University of Jena, where he was awarded a professorship in 1805. Unfortunately for Hegel, a year later Prussia suffered a crushing defeat defending Jena, and Hegel was ousted from his position at the university. He was not able to obtain another professorship until 1816 when the University of Heidelberg hired him. He stayed at Heidelberg for two years, and he left to occupy the Chair at the University of Berlin made famous by Fichte. During his tenure at Berlin, where he remained until his death in 1831, Hegel was the preeminent philosopher in all of Germany.

The metaphysical positions espoused by Kant were the epitome of classic idealism. On the other hand, contrary to his predecessors, Hegel believed that war was necessary to develop and fortify the idealist concept of man's spiritual being beyond the position adhered to by Kant. Hegel developed the ideal that ultimate realities that affected man must be within the realm of man's reason to comprehend them. Kant believed man did not have the capacity to comprehend ultimate realities. Hegel asserted that reason could fathom all aspects of human experience. Philosophy, therefore, had but to determine all the laws by which reason functions within man.[17] Hegel assigned a greater value to the ability of humankind to "know things" than did Kant and other idealists.

Arthur Schopenhauer (1788–1860), a pessimist to be sure, and Herbert Spencer (1820–1903), a true independent thinker and nonconformist, took exception to Hegel's philosophy of man having the capacity to reason the nature of ultimate reality. Hegel's idealism states that the parts must always be viewed as they relate to the whole, not as independent entities; man (part) must be viewed as he relates and interacts with the universal (whole). To extend Hegel's thesis further, he believed that we can indeed "know" ethical and spiritual realities through reason, and as previously stated, this was unthinkable to Kant and his contemporaries. Hegel's philosophical process was a trial of (1) thesis—the idea; (2) antithesis; (3) synthesis. The thesis and antithesis are opposite and contradictory to each other; the synthesis combines the positive and affirmative elements of both. To illustrate this process, Hegel believed that the history of the human race is a story of successive contradictions and conflicts that have been resolved only by successive synthesis that cause new trades to arise in the social process. Progress is made through the long ages by the external pendulum swing of thesis and antithesis in human affair.[18]

Hegel believed there is unity throughout the universe. Karl Marx later applied Hegel's principles to economic history, arguing that the thesis of capitalism met by the antithesis of revolution would result in a new synthesis of communism. For Hegel, thought operates according to the dialectical process whereby the act of reasoning involves a systematic analysis of concepts that will be in conflict, and the resulting synthesis will result in truth. His Absolute Idea is the grand synthesis, an inclusion of the truths of philosophy into an all-inclusive global conformity. Hegel is the consummate idealist who places the physical corporeal world as a limited or finite idea and rests near the bottom of his hierarchy. According to Hegel, the body, although recognized and dealt with, occupies an inferior position to that of Mind, Spirit, and the Infinite idea, which, as you may logically conclude, occupies the top of his hierarchy. Man's finite existence in this temporal, corporeal, and imperfect world is part of the process that will eventually be realized as the Absolute End, which is a reflection of the Absolute Mind.

In general, idealists believe that within the educational process, growth will occur through self-activity. Self-activity facilitates and nourishes the mental development and corresponding mental maturity. The vast majority of physical educators agree with contemporary idealists who believe that the ultimate responsibility to learn is with the student.

The Application of Idealism to Physical Education

The self-activity that idealism embraces is not an abstract process that ignores the physical. To develop the self includes the development of the body. Idealism embraces and supports the inclusion of physical education. The physical educator who incorporates the philosophical beliefs of idealism starts from the premise that the educational process is ideal-centered as opposed to child-centered or subject-matter centered.[19] The nature of idealism allows us to arrive at an opinion of what all that is "good" embraces. The "ideal good" may be based on the beliefs contained in scripture or a profound sense of moral duty and obligation. The moral bases for classic sportsmanship or the concept of "Muscular Christianity" are additional possibilities that can form the basis for determining "ideal good."

Student

Idealism will not support an educational process that views our existence as purely corporeal, "a biological organism responding to 'natural forces.'"[20] Idealism views our existence as one of body and soul; in general, that is reality for the idealist. As a result, if physical educators are indeed dedicated professionals who are committed to doing the greatest good for the students, they must not look on them as simply bodies that are to be trained and made physically fit; they must do more! They must teach moral values and, where appropriate, spiritual values as well. The body, to the idealist, is the physical expression of the nature of the soul. The weight-training and cardiovascular programs in contemporary physical education must be understood by themselves; according to idealists, they are not end products and therefore have no true significance to the student.[21] This aspect of "education of the physical" ignores the moral and spiritual bases of our existence and therefore has blatantly omitted a significant component of the self. Physical education students must ask whether they will aspire to become educators or mere technicians who simply train and mold the body without regard to the personal, moral, and spiritual development of their students.

Values

Delbert Oberteuffer was without question one of the most prolific scholars in the history of American physical education. Oberteuffer makes the point that "idealism believes in only two values which are rooted in existence: persons, and the moral imperative."[22] Put simply, athletes and students do not represent to the coach or teacher a means to an end. They are not "meat on the hoof" or commercial products that can be exploited by capitalizing on their athletic ability for the benefit of the coach, school, university, or team. Athletes and students in the care of physical educators represent individual and unique personalities that consist of mind, soul, and body. In this respect, the coach and physical education professional must understand that athletes and students in physical education classes are "ends," not a means to an end. The ruthless exploitation of high-school and college athletes by coaches, agents, and some educational concerns are reprehensible to idealists. The shocking graduation rates of college athletes at many of our well-known, sports-oriented colleges and universities point to the fact that the system has lost sight of the athlete as a person. The moral imperative that Kant spoke of, "act so that in your own person as well as in the person of every other you are treating mankind also as an end, never merely as a means," does not fit with the sports-as-big-business approach so pervasive today. The abysmal graduation rates of athletes, especially minority athletes, from big-time athletic programs offer proof that athletes are often used as a means to an end. The end is money, glory, a perception of power, and the egotistical satisfaction that participants in the process appear to live for. Working from the position of idealism, what positive values, ethical progress, and "ideal good" actually occur as a result of big-time college athletics and high-school athletics? Realistically, does Kant's moral imperative have a place, a future, in highly competitive sports and physical education programs of today?

Objectives

Idealism holds that achievement of a superior life is the objective for the student. For the student to achieve a superior life, the idealist does his or her best to ensure that every opportunity is available for the student to grow physically, intellectually, morally, and spiritually.[23] The objectives of physical education must benefit the development of the whole person. The development and nurturing of an individual's personality and corresponding character is an important objective of the physical educator who adheres to idealism in the cultivation of health because "it enhances and makes surer and richer the realization of the social, moral, and spiritual-mental aims."[24]

Curriculum

Instruction in social, moral, and spiritual values occupies a prominent position in the curriculum. The idealist has formed an opinion of the "ideal good" on the basis of belief in God and/or moral obligations and responsibility. The idealist believes in the importance and necessity of being a positive role model, which enables him or her not only to articulate social, moral, and spiritual values but also to be emblematic of these values. The curriculum is ideal-centered, with emphasis on the development of the self toward perfection insofar as this is possible. The idealist is suspect of curricular innovation and fads and prefers a stable curriculum that is based on the tried and true. The *ability* and *potential* of the student is of primary importance to the idealist when determining how best to provide for each student to realize his or her potential. Self-improvement will manifest itself in opportunities for students to develop self-reliance, self-responsibility, self-direction, self-examination, and other related personal improvement.[25] Both Plato and contemporary adherents of idealism believe that the unexamined life is not worth living.

Evaluation

How the student changed with regard to the self is what interests the idealist. The outcomes in physical education are analyzed as to the extent they contributed to the development and subsequent enhancement of the student in areas of social interaction, self-confidence, social and psychological maturity, physical growth, skill development, and moral and spiritual growth, which is considered character development in many circles. Because the idealist strongly believes in a developmental process that is indeed subjective with regard to the perspective of the evaluator, subjective grading is quite acceptable. The teacher is interested in not only what each student does but also in "what each student knows, thinks, feels, and is. . . . Students will be evaluated with regard to appropriate behavior, citizenship, and sociomoral conduct."[26] The idealist would not accept purely statistical evaluation, nor would he or she rely completely on objective tests to determine the worth and subsequently the grade assigned to each student. Idealists do not rely on quantitative measures but wait to see (subjectively) what changes are made in the self.[27]

The Educators

Johann Heinrich Pestalozzi

Perhaps the greatest educational reformer of all time was Johann Heinrich Pestalozzi (1746–1827). His father was an established surgeon in Zurich but died when Pestalozzi was only five years old. He was raised by his mother and a faithful servant, who were dedicated to shielding the young boy from inappropriate influences, and as a consequence, young Pestalozzi had no male role model or association with boys his own age while growing up. He remained shy, weak, and awkward for the remainder of his life as a result of his overprotective mother and limited association, at best, with his peer group. When he attended school, Johann was a social outcast and avoided by his classmates to the point where he was cruelly nicknamed "Harry Oddity of Foolborough." Although always frail and weak, his views on education included the necessity of mandatory physical education.

Prior to becoming an educator, Pestalozzi tried his hand at a number of different professions. He studied theology, practiced law, and eventually became a farmer. Pestalozzi was influenced by the writings of Rousseau and may have become a farmer because of the return-to-nature advocacy espoused by Rousseau. Fortunately for educators everywhere, Pestalozzi was not a success on the farm, so he converted his house into a place where children from poor families and other unfortunates could receive an education and perform manual labor, a form of early vocational and physical training not to be confused with physical education as we know it. Five years later, in 1779, Pestalozzi was out of money and was forced to abandon his efforts at educating children. The following years found Pestalozzi in utterly wretched conditions of poverty and despair. Although he wrote articles and opinions during his student days while attending the Collegium Humanitatis in Zurich, he had abandoned his writing after leaving the Collegium. He started writing again during the eighteen years he lived in Neuhof after closing his school, but his early writings were largely ignored.

In 1780 he published "The Evening Hours of a Hermit," which reflected the influence of Rousseau. The article focused on what Pestalozzi perceived as the natural aptitude of man and the necessity for this natural aptitude to be developed: "The pure and beneficent powers of mankind are not the gifts of art or of accident . . . their development is the fundamental need of mankind . . . nature develops all the powers of mankind through exercise, and their growth results from use."[28] One year later Pestalozzi published his very successful and much acclaimed *Leonard and Gertrude*, which told the story of a humble peasant woman and her contributions to her village by way of devotion and dedication. *Leonard and Gertrude* made Pestalozzi famous because in this work he wrote about something he was quite knowledgeable in (peasant life and its attendant hardships), and provided a format whereby peasant life can be improved. Pestalozzi believed that education is of value only if the knowledge gained through education could be put to use.[29]

Even though Pestalozzi was famous, he still lived in poverty. In 1798 France annexed Switzerland, and Pestalozzi embraced the newly arrived French government, which had earlier honored him with the title "Citizen of the French Republic." During the French occupation, Pestalozzi occupied a number of celebrated educational positions. In 1800 he established an Institute at Burgdorf where he taught teachers how to teach in addition to providing instruction to his beloved pupils. He left Burgdorf in 1804 and moved to the Castle of Yverdon near Lake Neuchatel, where he established the most celebrated school in the annals of education.[30]

The school at Yverdon had a fabulous reputation, and students and educational reformers from all over the world came to Yverdon to study and observe the methods of Pestalozzi and his staff. Pestalozzi left Yverdon in 1825 because the school was torn apart by internal dissension. Pestalozzi's theory of education stated that three elements or aspects comprise the education of the young: intellectual education, moral education, and practical education. His views on practical education were of great benefit to physical education. Like Fellenberg (with whom he briefly worked in 1804 at Hofwyl), Pestalozzi believed in the necessity of providing vocational training along with the primary focus on intellectual training. This approach necessitates the development of all the identified capacities of our abilities as students. Pestalozzi developed the physical capacities of his male students through physical work, which was also called manual labor in the educational jargon of the era. He advocated gymnastics and games in addition to physical labor.

Besides the development of strength and dexterity, Pestalozzi believed that physical education could also develop healthy and cheerful children, which in his moral education of children were two very important goals. Gymnastics promote a spirit of union and brotherly association as well as habits of industry, openness and frankness of character, personal courage, and manly conduct when one suffers from pain. Slightly ahead of his time, Pestalozzi also was adamant that women, especially mothers, should become knowledgeable in gymnastics so they can direct their children's activities in a way that will be beneficial and helpful.[31] However, education for women, although unusual and therefore seemingly progressive, was not intended to expand women's options but to help them do their restricted options better.

The physical education program at Yverdon included gymnastics as part of the daily curriculum. Additional activities included hiking, swimming, sledding, skating, dancing, and fencing. Military drill was also practiced. According to Gerber, "The kind of Physical Education done at Yverdon under the direction of Pestalozzi was not particularly well developed or unique. The significance of the work at Yverdon lies in its connection with the great educational reforms. Finding new theories of education which influenced both the new and old world, he included as part of the course of study, gymnastics exercises. Pestalozzi's 'imprimatur' gave an important impetus to the general progress of physical education as a school subject which has a part in the fulfillment of educational goals."[32]

Although both Pestalozzi and his contemporary, Friedrich Froebel, undisputedly had an important impact on educational theory in the nineteenth and early twentieth centuries, they were both inept organizers and administrators. Both had great ideas but were hard pressed to see their ideas and schools remain free of internal strife and financial problems. Froebel's greatest contributions to education in general and physical education in particular were the establishment of the kindergarten and his theory of play. Play, according to Froebel, is the highest phase of child development.

Friedrich Wilhelm August Froebel

Froebel (1782–1852) was the son of an Orthodox Protestant minister who was a strict and rigid role model. When he was ten years old, Friedrich left the small German village of Oberweissbach and went to live with his uncle and his family at Stadt-Ilm, where life was far more pleasant and enjoyable. He became a forester at age fifteen and later enrolled at the University of Jena for two years, where he was profoundly influenced by the philosophical works of Kant, Fichte, and Hegel. Unfortunately for Froebel, he could not pay his debts and was placed into a debtors' prison. After his release, he held many different jobs until he arrived in Frankfurt to study architecture. It was in Frankfurt that Froebel made the acquaintance of Anton Gruner, whose mentor was none other than Pestalozzi. Gruner was using the methods he had learned from Pestalozzi at the Model School of Frankfurt, where he served as Director. Gruner urged Froebel to become part of the teaching staff, and Froebel wrote his brother that he had at last found his niche in life. He stayed on at the Model School for approximately one year, during which time he visited Pestalozzi's school at Yverdon.

After leaving the Model School, he hired out as a private tutor to three pupils. He later took his pupils to study at Yverdon for two years. In his autobiography, Froebel states,

> the boys play . . . games in the open air, and learned to recognize their mighty power to awake and strengthen the intelligence and the soul as well as the body. . . . The games, as I am now fervently assured, formed a mental bath of extraordinary strengthening power.[33]

His belief in physical education was further strengthened when he met Friedrich Jahn, who will be discussed later in this chapter, while teaching at the Plamann's School in Berlin. Like Jahn, he fought in the Teutonic War of 1813 against Napoleon. Froebel enlisted in Baron Von Lutzow's army and became a member of the Black Hunters led by Jahn.

In 1816 Froebel established the Universal German Institute in Griesheim and a year later moved the school to Keilhau, where he remained for twelve years. During this time he experienced great difficulty in keeping the school financially solvent and administratively cohesive.[34] Froebel published *The Education of Man*, which provided him with the forum to present his theories on the education of children. According to Gerber, the book "reflected the influence of Kant's 'new' philosophy as applied by Schelling and Hegel."[35] The influence of the German idealists on Froebel was obvious. Froebel stressed that his students appreciated the unity or oneness in all things through self-activity that sought to encourage (1) observation, (2) discovery, and (3) creativity because these three activities would use and benefit those aptitudes and talents we possess.[36] In *The Education of Man*, Froebel supports the place and purpose of physical education when he establishes his theory of play:

> Play is the highest form of child development—of human development at this period; for it is self-active representation of the inner-representation of the inner necessity and impulse.

Play is the purest, most spiritual activity of man at this stage, and, at the same time, typical of human life as a whole—of the inner hidden natural life in man and all things. It gives, therefore, joy, freedom, contentment, inner and outer rest, peace with the world. It holds the sources of all that is good. A child that plays thoroughly, with self-active determination, perseveringly until physical fatigue forbids, will surely be a thorough, determined man, capable of self-sacrifice for the promotion of the welfare of himself and others.

Play at this time is not trivial, it is highly serious and of deep significance . . . to the calm, keen vision of one who truly knows human nature, the spontaneous play of the child discusses the future inner life of the man.[37]

Froebel believed that play in the form of physical education was a wonderful mechanism for stress reduction and what we would call "character and moral development." He believed physical education would help nourish the intellectual faculties and developed the idea of giving five specific toys to a child in sequence that would teach space, mass, and basic movement patterns. The first gift was a ball, the second was a cube and sphere, the third, fourth, and fifth items in progression were "complicated divisions of the cube into a series of rectilinear solids, oblong prisms, and obliquely divided component cubes."[38] These toys could challenge and help develop the mental and physical components of the child. His work in education was insightful and enlightening and remains with us today in the kindergarten, which is nothing less than an institution in America, and in his belief in the purpose and value of physical education. In his *Education of Man* Froebel said, "without such cultivation of the body, education can never attain its object, which is perfect human culture."[39] He believed that when teachers and students participate together in physical education activities such as play and organized games, children will come to understand the world of humanity through self-activity in the form of physical education.

Figure 8.1
*Friedrich Ludwig Jahn. From: E. W.
Gerber:* Innovators and Institutions in
Physical Education. *Philadelphia: Lea &
Febiger, 1971.*

Friedrich Ludwig Jahn

After Napoleon was crowned Emperor of France in 1804, sixteen South
and West German princes seceded from the "Holy Roman Empire of the
German Nation"[40] to support him. They established the Confederation
of the Rhine, which ended the Empire and began more than a decade of
occupation, wars, and uprisings.[41]

Prussia, which was one of the German states that did not collabo-
rate with the Confederation, was defeated by Napoleon in 1806, at the
Battle of Jena and Auexstedt during the Fourth Coalition War. After
the resulting Peace of Tilsit in 1807, Prussia lost its Western and Polish territories, and Napoleon stationed his Ninth Corps in Berlin.
Introduction of several domestic reforms after 1807 established in
Prussia a new society that ended the old feudal and legal order. The
populist concept of nationalism became the driving force behind the
Prussian resistance to French rule and the wars of liberation that
began in 1813.[42]

One of the principal patriots behind the growing nationalist movement in Prussia was a Berlin gymnastics teacher, Friedrich Ludwig Jahn
(1778–1852). Jahn was an orthodox monarchist who firmly believed
that Prussia was destined to become the leader of all the German states.
This belief eventually led to Jahn's hatred of anything foreign, and his
goal was to eliminate foreign influences from Prussia that "might corrupt the purity of the German Volk."[43]

Jahn was born at Lanz, the son of a Prussian clergyman. He spent his early years studying at various gymnasia throughout Prussia. He attended the university at Göttingen around 1800. Although he never obtained a degree, Jahn pursued an eclectic course of study that included physical education.

Jahn's physical education studies were based on the work of GutsMuths, who has been called "the most important philanthropic physical educator and establisher of systematic physical exercise at school."[44] GutsMuths believed that

> body and intellect . . . [exerted] a reciprocal influence on one another and [were] in need therefore of being exercised as a unity. The senses had to be schooled so as to train the intelligence . . . [and] health was the precondition for moral fitness. Reason and strength were united in his educational ideal.[45]

Jahn applied these beliefs to his own work, which would become, ultimately, the pursuit of national unity for all of Germany and freedom from French rule.

With his formal but incomplete education behind him, Jahn spent several years writing and teaching gymnastics. He observed the Prussian defeat and concluded that it had resulted from the cultural influences of the French occupation. These French impurities, as Jahn perceived them, had caused a loss of German national pride. Jahn felt that the basis for reviving patriotism in Prussia was to be found, in part, in the study of German language and customs. Furthermore, the concept of national democracy, which originated in the French Revolution, resulted in Jahn's belief in the

> [propagation] of a national education devoted to the training of responsible citizens and [he] called for the abolition of aristocratic privileges, development of a People's Army in place of an army of mercenaries, and elimination of bondage and all forms of oppression including the corporal punishment then still usual in the army.[46]

To achieve his objectives of national unity in the German states and the liberty of Prussia, Jahn first moved to Berlin in 1809. There he became an auxiliary teacher at the Friedrich Werdescher Gymnasium and got involved with other Prussian patriots whose goals matched his. Because Prussia had remained resistant to French rule during Napoleon's occupation, it became a haven for German patriots and the center of the "all-German movement for national freedom."[47]

Sometime during the following year, Jahn and two other patriots, Karl Friedrich Friesen and Wilhelm Harnich, established the German League. This secret society was composed mainly of army officers and teachers who sought "the spiritual renovation of Germany at the moment of its deepest humiliation."[48] The constitution of the German League called for a nationwide program of physical education and spiritual renewal in all German universities. According to Treitschke, "the conspirators assembled at night in the woods near Berlin and consecrated themselves to the struggle for the fatherland."[49] This organiza-

Figure 8.2

Exercising on a turnplatz. From: Charles Beck. A Treatise on Gymnastiks. *Taken chiefly from the German of F. L. Jahn. Northampton, Mass., Simeon Butler, 1828.*

tion provided the patriots with little more than a means of expressing their anger concerning the French occupation. Its main contribution to the cause for freedom became apparent later, when the Burschenschaft [student societies] were formed in 1815. The constitutions of these societies contained the same basic concepts as those found in the constitution of the German League. In 1813, at the start of the wars of liberation, the German League was dissolved.

Shortly after the formation of the German League, Jahn became a member of the Grauen Kloster Gymnasium in Berlin, where he started teaching at Johann Ernst Plamann's school. Twice each week, on Wednesday and Saturday afternoons, he taught gymnastics and general physical exercise to his pupils. They practiced outdoors, in a yard near the school. These afternoons were the precursor of Jahn's turnen (gymnastics) programs, which he started the following year.

The spring of 1811 marked the beginning of the German turnverein movement. Coining what he believed to be an extinct Teutonic word— *turnen* (to perform gymnastic exercises)—Jahn established the first *turnplatz* (outdoor gymnastics field) on the Hasenheide just south of Berlin. He organized the first *turnfest* (outdoor gymnastics festival) on June 19, 1811, which was a popular success. By Christmas of the same year, Jahn had left the Plamann school to devote all his time to the Turners.[50]

Turnvater [father of gymnastics] Jahn, as his pupils called him, worked hard at instilling a sense of national pride in his gymnasts. He reorganized the Hasenheide Turnverein during 1812 and increased the number of exercises offered at the turnplatz. During the summer, Jahn and Friesen set up the Gymnastics Association in an effort to spread their program throughout Prussia. They also won the support of School Inspector Wilhelm Schroder, who called publicly for schools to accept gymnastics as part of their curricula.[51]

The wars of liberation against France started in 1813 and would last until 1815. Jahn and a group of his gymnasts joined the Lutzow Free Corps, which fought as a unit throughout the war. By the time they returned, assured of France's defeat and confident of the German states' future unity as a nation, the Turners had acquired a sense of nationalistic pride, and Jahn was their acknowledged hero. The Turners' marching song made their feelings abundantly clear:

> When for the people's old and sacred rights
>
> Bravely the Turnermeister, Friedrich Jahn,
>
> Strade to the field where man for freedom fights,
>
> A warlike generation followed on.
>
> Hey, how the youths leapt after him,
>
> Fresh and joyful, godly, free!
>
> Hey how the youths sang after him:
>
> Hurrah![52]

The Turners returned from war, and Prussia's newly found freedom also served to rejuvenate the popularity of gymnastics.

After the wars of liberation ended in 1815, the goals of the Turners became less clear. Prussia had been liberated from French oppression; domestic reforms since 1807 brought about a new tolerance for more liberal views; and the gymnastics societies were popular throughout the Germanies. As a result, the Turners concentrated on the internal nature of their societies, becoming, in effect, a self-contained nation. Jahn refused to acknowledge the possibility that the army or the schools had any part in the development of German youth. Instead, "his gymnastic grounds were to constitute a world apart, a nursery of Germanism, inspired by his spirit alone."[53] Jahn believed that the only true German was a Turner—"virtuous and vigorous, continent and courageous, pure and prepared, manful and truthful," whereas all others were "false Germans."[54] He exhorted his gymnasts to

> immediately report the discovery of anything which friend or foe of the turncraft may say, write, or do for or against the said craft, in order that at the fit time and place all such fellows may be thought of the praise or blame![55]

The Turners had found a new cause—themselves—and they believed that they would bring about the unity of the Germanies by fighting anyone who stood in their path, including their fellow countrymen, if necessary.

In their zeal, the Turners overlooked the fact that the German states had become more unified since the wars of liberation. The French had brought about some positive changes during their various European campaigns. Specifically, they had generated the spirit of a democratic state among many nations in Europe. This spirit provided the foundation for social reform and the establishment of constitutional freedom. In the German states, this foundation took the form of popular demands for certain rights, including "the separation of justice and administration, public and oral court proceedings, trial by jury, freedom of the press, and equality before the law for all citizens."[56]

At the University of Jena in 1815, a group of student patriots, advocating the adoption of these rights, formed the first Burschenschaft (student society). The students adopted the constitution of Jahn's German League, and the societies soon appeared on many German university campuses. The purpose of the Burschenschaft was the pursuit of freedom and constitutionalism, and gymnastics was the symbol and means by which the students would reach their goal. The "student gymnasts at universities would prepare the way for German unity that had not been achieved in the political sphere."[57]

What started out as peaceful protest, however, soon turned into chaos and violence. The Burschenschaft, also known as the Patriotic Students, became gradually more involved with the Nationalist Gymnasts, an activist group that Jahn had formed in 1816. These two groups brought the nationalism so typical of the nineteenth century to university lecture halls and influenced what had initially been idealistic endeavors in a way that later turned out to be most dangerous.[58]

Alarmed at the vandalism and increasing violence perpetrated by members of the Burschenschaft in Austria and Prussia, King Friedrich Wilhelm III sought an end to the problems. Two violent events precipitated his actions. First, the Wartburg festival that occurred on October 31, 1817, which started as "a great festivity of romantic and patriotic uplift and of religious reflection,"[59] turned rapidly into a chaotic rout; and second, the Breslau feud, which was based on the objectives of gymnastics, also became a heated political confrontation. The king was forced to close the Breslau gymnastics field, and he directed the universities to more closely supervise their students. The king later found, however, that his tactics were not adequate.

By 1819, the liberal movement had gained strength, and the king was rapidly losing control over the situation. He was scared into more drastic action when a gymnast and theology student named Karl Sand murdered Alexander von Kotzebue, a dramatist who had made the fatal error of writing critically about gymnastics. The king turned reluctantly to Austrian Chancellor Metternich for assistance. Metternich proceeded to meet secretly with Prussian Chancellor Hardenberg to find a solution to the problems caused by the liberals. Together these men drafted a set of decrees that allowed authorities to investigate the universities and impose political censorship throughout the German states.[60]

In July 1814, a conference of German Confederation Ministers approved the decrees at Carlsbad. Known as the Carlsbad Decrees, they caused the almost immediate disappearance of the liberal movement, especially in Prussia. Their issue brought about the surveillance of student activity at the universities, caused the banning of student organizations, and encouraged the harassment of those suspected of leading the liberal movement.[61]

King Friedrich Wilhelm III was relieved by the suppression of the liberal movement, although he was not fully aware of some of the actions that were taken. Unbeknownst to the king, Chancellor Metternich took matters into his own hands and ordered the arrests, in both Austria and Prussia, of anyone whom he or Prussian Chancellor Hardenberg suspected of treasonous acts. On July 13, 1819, Jahn was arrested "on suspicion of secret, treasonable connections"[62] (which were never specified) and sent to Spandau fortress. He was transferred to Kustrin prison a short time later. Although he was released on May 22, 1820, Jahn was then forced to live under house arrest in the town of Kolberg until 1825.

The fate of Turner gymnastics appeared bleak during the period between 1820 and 1848. The Prussian government had originally planned to assume control of gymnastics by including it in the schools' curricula. As a result, in March 1819, the government banned gymnastics in Turner societies. On January 20, 1820, however, a Prussian royal decree was issued, banning all gymnastics in the state and ordering the closure of more than one hundred gymnastics fields. They would not reopen in any form until 1842, when a younger and more liberal King Friedrich Wilhelm IV assumed the throne.[63]

Jahn was acquitted and released from house arrest in 1825. He moved to Freyberg/Unstrut, where he lived until his death in 1852. As a condition of his release from imprisonment, Jahn was not allowed to live in a town with a university or gymnasium. Because he could not practice his beloved gymnastics, his career appeared to be over. Jahn remarried in 1825 (after the death of his first wife in 1823), and he focused on domestic life for the next several years.[64]

During the period that Jahn was imprisoned and gymnastics was banned in the German states, the lives of three of Jahn's followers took turns that ultimately led them to the United States as the pioneering teachers of American physical education.

Charles Follen

One of the results of the ban on gymnastics in Prussia was that some of the more patriotic rebels formed secret societies in which they kept alive their political zeal. One of these societies, known as the Blacks,[65] was a particularly subversive group formed in 1816 that worked hard at annoying the Prussian authorities, especially Metternich. The Blacks believed that they were divinely guided to "direct the emancipation of the enslaved peoples"[66] of all Germans. Late in 1819, one of the Blacks considered to be most dangerous by Prussian authorities, a lawyer named Charles Follen (1795–1840) and a follower of Jahn, escaped to Strassburg. Earlier that year, he had been found guilty of providing money for the journey taken by Karl Sand to murder Kotzebue. He was not convicted of the act, however, because Prussian laws at the time did not provide any grounds for legal action against him. Follen managed to escape to Strassburg before the Prussian authorities could detain him.

Follen left Strassburg during the summer of 1820, when he moved to Basel, Switzerland, to take up a position teaching jurisprudence at that city's university. For three years he lived and worked in Basel under the constant fear of being deported back to Germany. He was a political refugee and, like all political refugees, feared for his safety. When the danger became too great, Follen fled to Paris, where he met Charles Beck. Together they sailed from Le Havre to New York, where they arrived as emigrants on December 19, 1824.

Charles Follen secured a teaching position at Harvard University, where he taught German. Follen requested permission from the Harvard administration to construct a turnplatz on the campus where he could teach German gymnastics to the students on a voluntary basis. He was allocated an area on campus known as the Delta, where he built the turnplatz and taught gymnastics. His efforts were not too successful, and interest died out after a few years. He later taught gymnastics at the Boston Gymnasium.

Charles Beck

Charles Beck (1798–1866), another of Jahn's followers, was a classical scholar who had also trained in theology. He had worked for many years to establish a student society based on Christianity, but he soon found that he could not pursue a career and survive politically in his native country. As a result, Beck moved to Basel in 1823, where he taught classical literature for a year. By late 1824, Beck also found that his proximity to Prussia was too dangerous, and he sailed with Follen from Le Havre to New York. He secured a teaching position at the Round Hill School in Northampton, Massachusetts. The school was founded by Joseph Cogswell and George Bancroft, who had studied in Germany and while there, became familiar with the gymnastics of the Turners. Upon returning to the United States, Cogswell and Bancroft instituted a required program of daily physical education and hired Charles Beck, who is credited for being the first physical education teacher in America. Round Hill School is historically significant as the first school that required mandatory physical education in the form of German gymnastics.

Francis Lieber

The third member of the group of German emigrants who provided the basis for American physical education was Francis Lieber (1800–1872), an ardent follower of Jahn since the early days of the Hasenheide in 1811. Lieber was arrested shortly after Jahn in 1819 but was released after four months. He completed his doctorate in 1820, after which he left the continued persecution of the Burschenschaft era by fighting for

Figure 8.3

Vaulting the Horse. From: Charles Beck. A Treatise on Gymnastiks. *Taken chiefly from the German of F. L. Jahn. Northampton, Mass., Simeon Butler, 1828.*

the Greeks in their attempt to overthrow their Turkish oppressors in 1821. Lieber wanted to return to Prussia in 1823, and he was assured by both the Prussian king and that state's minister of police that it was safe to do so. When he arrived in Berlin in August 1823, however, Lieber was subjected to the beginnings of three years of harassment and imprisonment by the state police. In May 1826, Lieber escaped to London, where he lived and taught the German language for a year. In April 1827, Lieber accepted an offer as Follen's successor at the Boston Gymnasium, and he arrived in New York on June 20, 1827.[67]

The turnverein movement served as an important instrument of social change in the German states. The Turners led the drive toward a unified democracy of those states during the period between 1811 and 1819. Encouraged by the ideals of freedom and independence from French rule, the Turners practiced their unique form of physical activity, gymnastics, in order to be physically and mentally ready to liberate their nation.

Another significant contribution of the Turners was the export of their gymnastics methods. In America, the turnverein movement catalyzed the emergence of physical education as an important area of study. Charles Beck succeeded in establishing the first recognized, school-sponsored physical education program in the United States. The

Turners were, in fact, the pioneers of modern physical education in America in the nineteenth century.

Franz Nachtegall

The acknowledged father of physical education in Denmark is Franz Nachtegall (1777–1847). He was born in Copenhagen, the son of an immigrant German tailor, and was educated at a private school and later entered the university to study theology. During his university days he earned a reputation as a formidable fencer and was quite skilled in vaulting in the gymnastic sense. Unfortunately he quit the university when his father passed away, and he became a tutor to support and care for his mother. It was during this time that he read "Gymnastik fur die Jugend," by Johann GutsMuths (1759–1839), whom many historians refer to as the grandfather of physical education.

Nachtegall was so inspired by GutsMuths' gymnastics that he began to teach it in addition to his private tutorials in Latin, geography, and history. He is credited for establishing and operating a private gymnasium, which he started on November 5, 1799, and which was "the first institution for physical training to be opened in modern times."[68] The gymnasium was so successful that by 1804 he had an enrollment of 150 children and adults along with six assistants.

In addition to operating his own gymnasium, Nachtegall provided instruction in gymnastics in the public and private schools scattered throughout Copenhagen. The equipment employed by Nachtegall included hanging ladders, climbing poles, balance beam, vaulting horses, and rope ladder. As his reputation grew, Nachtegall began to attract notice from a number of influential and powerful people, including none other than the King of Denmark and Per Henrik Ling, the founder of Swedish medical and pedagogical gymnastics, who attended Nachtegall's gymnasium.

In 1804 the king appointed him Professor of Gymnastics at the University and Director of the Military Gymnastic Institute, which remains in existence to this day. An avid swimmer, Nachtegall launched the Society for Promoting the Art of Swimming, which provided free swimming lessons and organized competitive meets for children from poor families.

Fortune continued to smile on Nachtegall when one of his former students, Prince Frederick, ascended the throne in 1808 and became one of Nachtegall's primary supporters in his efforts to introduce compulsory physical education into the schools. In 1809 a law was passed that required, whenever possible, secondary schools to provide gymnastics; five years later in 1814 the law was modified to also include instruction in the elementary schools, albeit only for boys. To ensure that elementary and secondary school teachers were able to provide physical education instruction, a law was passed in 1818 that made gymnastics a required course in the teacher training colleges (Seminarier) in Denmark.[69] However, with all the work of Nachtegall and the support of the Danish government, physical education programs ranged from substandard to nonexistent. In spite of the mandatory physical education requirement in teacher training colleges, few teachers were actually trained in gymnastics or schooled in the importance of physical education. This situation was mitigated to some degree in 1821, when Nachtegall was appointed Gymnastic Director with authority of the entire civilian and military gymnastics program. He focused his efforts on ensuring that gymnastics was taught in all the schools in Copenhagen, public as well as private. Although Nachtegall did not create a new system of physical education, he did introduce and champion the system of gymnastics developed by GutsMuths.

Nachtegall emphasized the need to train physical education teachers and provide instruction for the students. To this end he turned to the Military Gymnastic Institute and established a cooperative arrangement between the Institute and the public school, which later became the Normalskole for Gymnastikken where military and civilian teachers could conduct classes. The Normal School opened its door in 1828 with 160 students and 200 teachers, all working to perfect their knowledge and expertise in gymnastics. Women were included in 1838 when Nachtegall helped to establish an experimental school for girls. The girls received instruction in gymnastics three times a week, with the dubious distinction of being subjected to the method of instruction provided by three army sergeants and two women. This suggests that the educational and military orientation as taught to boys was similar for girls as well. One year after the establishment of the experimental school for girls, the Normal School of Gymnastics for Women (Normalskole for Kvindegymnastik) was established in 1839. The curriculum consisted of teaching methods and exercises that reflected the methods advocated by GutsMuths, which was the curriculum for men.

Danish gymnastics received a boost when Nachtegall and four of his associates wrote a "Manual of Gymnastics for the Village and Town Schools of Denmark" in 1828. The manual was distributed to all the schools in Denmark by authority of the king, who simultaneously decreed that instruction in gymnastics immediately begin in each and every school in Denmark. By 1839 most of the schools in Denmark were in compliance with the law; however, the need for physical education teachers to come into compliance with the law necessitated that the primary source of gymnastic teachers was from the military. The military presence and influence in Danish physical education was not objectionable to the Danes. As in Germany and Sweden, gymnastics was appreciated for its military application rather than its educational contribution.

As a tireless champion of physical education, Nachtegall was the driving force behind the promotion and inclusion of gymnastics in the schools of Denmark. He resigned as Director of the Military Gymnastic Institute when he turned sixty-five, but he returned to his position as Director of Gymnastics for Denmark and visited schools and colleges in Denmark, forever encouraging and promoting gymnastics. However, military gymnastics eventually was the dominant program in Denmark brought on in part when the Normal School that trained gymnastic teachers for the schools closed its doors. Beginning in 1859, the stu-

Figure 8.4
Per Henrik Ling. From: E. W. Gerber.
Innovators and Institutions in Physical
Education. *Philadelphia: Lea & Febiger,*
1971.

dents in the teacher training college received their instruction in gymnastics from military men who were assigned to the college or physical education teacher. As a result, Nachtegall's school physical education program, consisting of the gymnastics of GutsMuths, began to disappear and was soon replaced by military gymnastics.

Per Henrik Ling

The originator of Swedish gymnastics was a consummate scholar and athlete. Per Henrik Ling (1776–1839) was born in the south of Sweden in the town of Smaland, where his family had lived for generations. Life was not easy for the future member of the Swedish Academy (a distinguished body of eighteen of Sweden's most noted leaders) and champion of physical education. His father died when he was four, and his mother passed away when he was only thirteen. He attended high school and in 1793 matriculated at the university in Lund, where he stayed for two semesters. He then moved to Stockholm, where he worked as a clerk and privately tutored students in French and German. From 1799 to 1804 he lived in Copenhagen, where he participated in Nachtegall's gymnastics program and enrolled in the university. While Ling was enrolled in the university in Copenhagen, he was introduced to the Danish poet Oehlenschläger and the philosophy of Schelling by one of his countrymen who happened to be teaching at the university. He began to study the literary and ethnic heritage of his ancestry and eventually was profoundly influenced by both the poetry and philosophy of Sweden and Denmark.

Ling also began to take fencing lessons and noticed that fencing and the associated exercises had a wonderful therapeutic effect on his arthritic arm, and this began his life-long interest in the medical effects of exercise. In 1804 he returned to Sweden and the university in Lund, where he became the fencing master and student of anatomy and physiology.

During this time Sweden's once mighty empire crumbled all around him, primarily to the military assaults by the French and Russians. In 1805 Gustavus IV of Sweden attempted to stop Napoleon by entering into a military agreement with England, Russia, and Austria. This was a major mistake for Gustavus. By entering into an alliance with England and opening ports to English ships, the king incurred the wrath of the Russian czar who conquered Finland in 1808 (Finland was part of Sweden), which resulted in reducing Sweden's empire by one-third. Napoleon conquered Swedish Pomerania in 1807 along with Stralsund and Rugen, the last Swedish possession south of the Baltic.[70] The citizens of Sweden were outraged and beaten; King Gustavus was subsequently dethroned, and eventually the Swedish Diet appointed the distinguished French general Jean Baptiste Jules Bernadotte as king in 1818 and designated him Charles XIV. After suffering humiliating military defeats at the hands of the French and Russians, the French-General-turned-King-of-Sweden was anxious to proceed with a rapid military buildup and supported Ling's idea to build and administer a physical training institute because of its obvious military application.

Ling was appointed fencing master in 1813 at the Royal Military Academy, and the king approved and financed his plan to make Stockholm a center for physical training. In 1814 the Royal Gymnastics Central Institute, as it was named, was where Ling developed his system of gymnastics, which was to become known worldwide as the Swedish system. Thulin describes the basis of Ling's system as follows:

> Physical exercise must be based on the laws of the human system, and influence not only the body but also the mind. The fundamental principles can be briefly comprised in the following four clauses:
>
> 1. The aim is all-around harmonious development of the body.
> 2. The attainment of this is sought by means of biologically and physiologically grounded physical exercises in definite form and, as far as possible, of known effect.
> 3. The exercises must have developmental and corrective values, be easily understood, and satisfy our demand for beauty.
> 4. The exercises must be carried out with a gradually increasing degree of difficulty and exertion.[71]

What Per Ling did was to ground his system in the science of the day, and as a result he incorporated (1) aesthetic, (2) military, (3) pedagogical, and (4) medical aspects of exercise. He believed that these four components were linked with each other and in concert enabled his pupils to achieve a unifying relationship of mind, body, and duty to Sweden; health was a harmony between the nervous, circulatory, and respiratory systems. Ling's system was designed to help achieve this end. Ling did not enjoy notoriety because, ironically, his scientific foundation of exercise received criticism because his theory of gymnastics was said to be inconsistent and illogical.

Ling did not accept Jahn's work or approach because he believed German gymnastics were too complicated; Ling wanted exercise to result in a "demonstrated effect." Gymnastic apparatus was designed to revolve around specific exercises that would have certain results. He invented stall bars, Swedish broom, Swedish box, window ladder, and the oblique rope.[72] His gymnastic equipment did not require complicated movements, unlike those used by the German Turners under the leadership of Jahn. Ling preferred free exercises without hand-held dumbbells or wands. He concentrated on body position as opposed to movement sequences and was quite exact with regard to actual location/position of the trunk, head, arms, and legs. Gerber states that "Ling gymnastics began to consist of positions retained for the length of time it took the teacher to observe and correct the faults. This meant that an entire class was often held for a long time in the artificial and strained position specified."[73]

The sad truth is that Ling's Swedish gymnastics was nothing less than a bore and did not achieve popularity, even in Sweden. His system did gain some respect in the northeastern United States, especially the Boston area, but never did catch on in the United States the way that German gymnastics did. Ling's gymnastics were based on the scientific and medical knowledge of the day (albeit at times untenable), which is more than we can say of its chief rival, Jahn's German gymnastics.

Summary

Philosophically, the German idealists believed in the development of the self. The body, soul, and intellect as the primary mode of being must be educated in the fashion required by idealism. The overall development of each person is based on the idea of perfection as found in scripture. Moral and ethical development can be found in Kant's categorical imperative, which can provide the moral fabric for sportsmanship and fair play.

The justification and development of physical education benefited greatly from the philosophy of idealism and the tireless efforts of physical educators in Germany, Sweden, and Denmark. The use of physical education as a political tool was at the foundation of the Turner movement in Germany. The Turners sought to fan the flames of nationalism and patriotism under the direction of Friedrich Jahn, the architect of the turnverein. The political situation that resulted from the activities of the Turners was partly responsible for the importation of German gymnastics to America. During their student classes in Germany, Joseph Cogswell and George Bancroft were heavily influenced by German gymnastics as practiced by the Turners. Upon their return to the United

States, they opened the Round Hill School in Northampton, Massachusetts, and hired Charles Beck, a political refugee due to his activities in support of the Turners, as the first physical education teacher in America.

Franz Nachtegall was the father of Danish gymnastics and is credited for promoting a physical education program based on the work of GutsMuths. He influenced Per Ling during Ling's stay in Copenhagen. Nachtegall saw the need for the inclusion of physical education into the Danish school system and was very successful in achieving his goal.

The work of Per Ling established the basis for grounding physical education in the medical and scientific aspects of exercise. Swedish gymnastics did not enjoy the popularity that German gymnastics did when it was brought to America.

The promotion of physical education in Germany, Sweden, and Denmark was for military purposes rather than for its educational and health value.

Discussion Questions

1. What are the three basic topics that are fundamental to Idealism? How do these three tenets of Idealism manifest themselves in contemporary sport and physical education?

2. According to Kant, we should "act so that you treat humanity, whether in your own person or in that of another, always as an end and never as a means only." How could you incorporate this idea into contemporary sport and physical education?

3. Idealism has as a basic tenet the development of the "self." How could this be achieved through participation in sport and physical education?

4. Does the body play a prominent role in the epistemology of Idealism? Why or why not?

5. Johann Fichte believed evil was necessary in order for the individual to reach his or her potential. Do you agree with him? Explain your answer.

6. How did Friedrich Jahn use the gymnastics programs of the Turners to further German nationalism?

7. What was the initial impact of the Turners on the development of American physical education?

8. How can one reconcile the philosophy of Idealism, especially its metaphysics, and physical education?

9. Potentially, what is the impact of Kant's philosophy on physical education?

10. Compare and contrast Ling's Swedish gymnastics with Jahn's German gymnastics. Which was the better system to actually promote physical education?

Suggestions for Further Reading

Bair, D. E. "An Identification of Some Philosophical Beliefs Held by Influential Leaders in American Physical Education." Doctoral dissertation, University of Southern California, 1956.

Clark, M. C. "A Philosophical Interpretation of a Program of Physical Education in a State Teachers College." Doctoral dissertation, New York University, 1943.

Hackensmith, C. W. *History of Physical Education*. New York: Harper and Row, 1966.

Hocking, W. E. *The Self, Its Body and Freedom*. New Haven, Conn.: Yale University Press, 1928.

Hoernle, R. F. A. *Idealism as a Philosophy*. New York: Doubleday, 1927.

Kleinman, S. "The Nature of Self and its Relation to an 'Other' in Sport." *Journal of the Philosophy of Sport* II (1975): 45–50.

Leonard, F. E., and G. B. Affleck. *A Guide to the History of Physical Education*. Philadelphia: Lea & Febiger, 1947.

Pfister, G. "The Medical Discourse on Female Physical Culture in Germany in the 19th and Early 20th Centuries." *Journal of Sport History*, Vol. 17, No. 2 (Summer 1990): 183–198.

Royce, J. *Lectures on Modern Idealism*. New Haven, Conn.: Yale University Press, 1919.

Savage, H. J. et al. *American College Athletics*. New York: Carnegie Foundation for the Advancement of Teaching, 1929.

Schopenhauer, A. "The World as Will and Idea." In *Masterworks of Philosophy*. New York: Doubleday, 1946.

Weiss, P. "Some Philosophical Approaches to Sport." *Journal of the Philosophy of Sport* IX (1982): 90–93.

Zeigler, E. "In Sport, As in All of Life, Man Should be Comprehensible to Man." *Journal of the Philosophy of Sport* III (1976): 121–126.

Zwarg, L. F. *A Study of the History, Uses, and Values of Apparatus in Physical Education*. Philadelphia: Temple University, 1929.

Notes

1. William S. Shakian, *History of Philosophy* (New York: Barnes and Noble, 1970), 369.
2. Seymour Kleinman, "The Classic Philosophers and Their Metaphysical Positions," in *Physical Education, An Interdisciplinary Approach*, ed. Robert N. Singer (New York: Macmillan, 1972), 331.
3. *Descartes' Philosophical Writings*, selected and translated by Norman Kemp Smith (London: Macmillan, 1952). See Meditations I, II, and VI.
4. Donald J. Butler, *Four Philosophies and Their Practice in Education and Religion*, 3rd ed. (New York: Harper & Row, 1968), 148.
5. Earle F. Zeigler, *Philosophical Foundation for Physical, Health, and Recreation Education* (Englewood Cliffs, N.J.: Prentice Hall, 1964), 174.
6. Butler, *Four Philosophies*, 132.
7. Ibid., 128.
8. Immanuel Kant, *Kritix der reinen Vernunft, English. Critique of Pure Reason*, Abridged ed., Translated, with an Introduction, by Norman Kemp Smith (New York: Modern Library, 1958), 335 pgs.
9. Butler, *Four Philosophies*, 130.
10. Ibid.
11. Ibid., 132.
12. Robert G. Osterhoudt, "In Praise Of Harmony: The Kantion Imperative and Hagelian Sittlichkeit as the Principle and Substance of Moral Conduct in Sport," *Journal of the Philosophy of Sport*, Vol. 3 (September 1976): 65–81.

13. Immanuel Kant, *Foundations of the Metaphysics of Pure Morals*, trans. Lewis W. Beck (Indianapolis: Bobbs-Merrill, 1959), 39.

14. Ibid., 47.

15. Osterhoudt, "In Praise of Harmony," 67–68.

16. Butler, *Four Philosophies*, 161.

17. Zeigler, *Philosophical Foundation*, 37.

18. Butler, *Four Philosophies*, 137.

19. Delbert Oberteuffer, "Idealism and Its Meaning to Physical Education," in Elwood Craig Davis, ed., *Philosophers Fashion Physical Education* (Dubuque, Ia.: Wm. C. Brown, 1963), 17.

20. Ibid., 18.

21. Ibid.

22. Ibid., 19.

23. William A. Harper et al., *The Philosophic Process in Physical Education* (Philadelphia: Lea & Febiger, 1977), 133.

24. Ibid.

25. Ibid., 135.

26. Ibid., 137.

27. Oberteuffer, 23.

28. Lewis Flint Anderson, *Pestalozzi* (New York: McGraw Hill, 1931), 13.

29. Ellen W. Gerber, *Innovation and Institution in Physical Education* (Philadelphia: Lea & Febiger, 1971), 88.

30. Ibid., 89.

31. Ibid., 91–92.

32. Ibid., 92.

33. Friedrich Froebel, *Autobiography*, translated and annotated by Emile Michaelis and H. Keatley Moore (Syracuse: C. W. Bardeen, 1889), 82.

34. Gerber, *Innovation*, 95.

35. Ibid.

36. Friedrich Froebel, *The Education of Man*, translated and annotated by W. N. Hailman (New York: D. Appleton, 1896).

37. Ibid., 54–55.

38. Gerber, *Innovation*, 97.

39. Froebel, *Education of Man*, 250.

40. Horst Ueberhorst, *Friedrich Ludwig Jahn and His Time, 1778–1852* (Munich: Heinze Moos Verlag, 1978), 102.

41. The authors are grateful to Alida J. Moonen for permission to quote extensively from her Master's thesis, "The German Turnverein Movement in San Diego, 1873–1913," San Diego State University, 1987.

42. Ueberhorst, *Jahn*, 32–35; and Heinrich Von Treitschke, *History of Germany in the Nineteenth Century*, 7 vols. (New York: Ams Press, 1968), 1:358.

43. R. R. Palmer and Joel Colton, *A History of the Modern World to 1815* (New York: Alfred A. Knopf, 1978), 403; and Treitschke, *History of Germany*, 1:358.

44. Ueberhorst, *Jahn*, 22.

45. Ibid.

46. Ibid., 36.

47. Palmer and Colton, *History of Modern World*, 404.

48. Ueberhorst, *Jahn*, 39.

49. Treitschke, *History of Germany*, 1:354.

50. Treitschke, *History of Germany*, 1:359; and Ueberhorst, *Jahn*, 103.

51. Ueberhorst, *Jahn*, 103.

52. Treitschke, *History of Germany*, 3:6.

53. Ibid., 3:8.

54. Ibid., 3:6.

55. Ibid., 3:11.

56. Ueberhorst, *Jahn*, 38.

57. Ibid., 42.

58. Ibid.

59. Ibid., 105.

60. Treitschke, *History of Germany*, 3:168.

61. Treitschke, *History of Germany*, 3:135–233; see also, Ueberhorst, *Jahn*, 44–46.

62. Ueberhorst, *Jahn*, 106.

63. Ibid.

64. Ibid., 106.

65. Treitschke, 3:73.

66. Ibid., 4:73.

67. Fred E. Leonard, *Pioneers of Modern Physical Training* (New York: Association Press, 1915), 77–81.

68. Gerber, *Innovation*, 178.

69. Ibid., 179.

70. Ibid., 156–157.

71. J. G. Thulin, "The Application of P. H. Ling's System to Modern Swedish Ling Gymnastics," *Mind and Body*, no. 38 (November 1931): 625–631.

72. Gerber, *Innovation*, 159.

73. Ibid., 161.

s e c 3 *i o n*

The Theoretical and Professional Development of American Physical Education

c h a p t e r 9

Science, Medicine, and the Concept of Health: The Theoretical and Professional Development of Physical Education, 1885–1930

General Events

1886 Haymarket riot and bombing in Chicago; Geronimo surrendered; American Federation of Labor (AFL) organized

1889 Johnstown, Pennsylvania, flood; 2,200 people perished

1890 Battle of Wounded Knee; Ellis Island opened as immigration depot; Sherman Antitrust Act enacted

1893 Nationwide financial depression

1896 Supreme Court ruled in *Plessy v. Ferguson* to allow "separate but equal" treatment of people

1898 U.S. battleship Maine blown up in Cuba; U.S. declared war on Spain; U.S. annexed Hawaii

1899 John Dewey published *School and Society*

1900 Boxer Rebellion in China, U.S. sent troops

1901 President William McKinley assassinated by Leon Czolgosz

1903 Panama Canal agreement signed; first airplane flight by Orville Wright

1906 Great San Francisco earthquake and fire

1907 Nationwide financial depression

1909 Admiral Robert E. Peary reached North Pole; National Conference on the Negro held, led to establishment of the National Association for the Advancement of Colored People (NAACP)

1910 Boy Scouts of America founded

1911 First transcontinental plane flight

1912 U.S. sent Marines to Nicaragua

1913 U.S. blockades Mexico

1914 President Wilson declares neutrality re: war in Europe

1915 First telephone conversation coast to coast; Lusitania sunk by Germans, 128 American passengers perished

1916 Jeanette Rankin, first woman member of Congress, from Montana; John Dewey published *Democracy and Education*

1917 U.S. enters World War I

1920 19th Amendment ratified, giving women right to vote

1924 Law approved by Congress making all American Indians citizens of the U.S.

1925 Scopes trial in Tennessee regarding teaching evolution in the schools

1927 Charles A. Lindbergh flew nonstop from New York to Paris

1928 Amelia Earhart was first woman aviator to cross the Atlantic Ocean

1929 St. Valentine's Day massacre in Chicago; stock market crash; Depression began

1931 Empire State Building opened

1933 Prohibition ended; U.S. abandons gold standard

1935 Will Rogers killed in plane crash; Senator Huey Long (La.) assassinated

Sport and Physical Education

1885 American Association for the Advancement of Physical Education founded

1887 First National Women's Singles tennis championship

1888 Amateur Athletic Union founded

1889 Boston Conference in the Interest of Physical Training

1891 Basketball invented by James A. Naismith

1899 Committee on Women's Basketball; American Association for the Advancement of Physical Education (AAAPE) formed

1900 Davis Cup tennis competition began; American League of Professional Baseball Clubs formed

1903 First baseball "World Series" played

1905 Intercollegiate Athletic Association of the United States founded, would later evolve into the NCAA

Sport and Physical Education Time Line from: Betty Spears and Richard A. Swanson, History of Sport and Physical Education in the United States (Dubuque, Ia.: Wm. C. Brown, 1988), 150, 206.

Introduction to the Nineteenth-Century Concept of Health

One of the major concerns of nineteenth-century Americans and Europeans alike was the issue of health. Health was the subject of books, lectures, articles, and pamphlets, all of which extolled the virtues and pitfalls of an endless variety of health enhancement techniques and benefits. It should not be surprising that health was considered so important to Americans in the early half of this century when we consider the routine occurrence of disease. American cities were ravaged by cholera, typhus, typhoid, scarlet fever, influenza, diphtheria, smallpox, measles, and whooping cough. Illnesses such as tuberculosis, or consumption, were common. The state of medical knowledge during the nineteenth century was poor. As a result, physicians and other "healers" were not very effective in treating disease.

As we head for the new millennium, physicians, physical educators, and other allied health professionals continue to investigate the link between health and its relationship with the mind and body. This dualistic relationship and its impact upon health and well-being has been an area of interest for centuries. This concept is especially significant in the history and philosophy of physical education. It was during the nineteenth century that a dialogue between physicians and physical educators began over the relationship between mind and body with regard to health. This common interest remains very strong today as health promotion and disease prevention remains an essential philosophical component of both physical education and medicine.

Although Louis Pasteur's germ theory of disease was proposed in 1860, it was not widely accepted by the medical profession until the end of the nineteenth century. Instead, medical knowledge was based on the dualistic idea that health consisted of a balanced constitution (the body) and temperament (the mind and spirit). Known as humoral medicine, the medical diagnosis and treatment of illness consisted of "heroic" procedures, which many times resulted in tragic consequences for the patient. Treatments included bleeding, leeching, and cupping. Large doses of medicine were administered that contained such toxic substances as arsenic, strychnine, emetics, and mercurial compounds.[1]

In addition to these invasive methods of purging the body to restore it to a state of health, which meant a balanced constitution, medical experts believed that the mind could predispose the body to disease. Health was believed to be a matter of moral character. Such characteristics as diligence, integrity, honesty, hard work, and right action were demonstrable traits of the mind and spirit operating in a state of harmony. The belief that a healthy mind resided in a healthy body—the translation of the old Roman saying, *mens sana en corpore sano*—was the foundation of what constituted health.[2]

Orthodox Medicine

Physicians have not always been considered the exclusive guardians of health. This may be hard to believe given the status of medicine in the twentieth century, but such was the case in the nineteenth century. During this era, several concerns emerged that focused public attention on the training and accepted authority of physicians, lawyers, and even the clergy. There was an absence of educational standards in the training of lawyers and doctors. Depending upon what region of the country you lived in, your education as a physician or lawyer could have been credible or it could have been abysmal. To compound this problem, standards for professional licensure as a doctor or lawyer varied greatly around the country, which served to erode confidence in these professions. New scientific ideas and discoveries raised suspicion about conventional medical treatments. Perhaps the most profound societal impact upon the profession of law and medicine was the growing antielitist feeling in America that served to undermine occupational professionals. Professional designation was accorded to anyone who claimed special status by right of education, protective legislation, or licensure, such as doctors and lawyers. The election of President Andrew Jackson in 1828, who ran on a platform of the "common man," demonstrated both an expansion of democratic enfranchisement and an essential distrust of the intellectual and economic elite who had traditionally provided social and political leadership. In the world of health this meant that a doctor was not necessarily an authority because of his training.

Doctors and lawyers were especially mistrusted because of the special protections they had received under state or local licensing standards, which effectively created professional monopolies. The idea of monopoly or special protection was in direct contradiction to the existing notion of democratic participation. Interestingly, this prodemocracy attitude extended to all parts of life. People increasingly believed that they had the right to oversee all aspects of their affairs, whether that be business, legal matters, or health, without the aid of (or payment to) a professional. In the wake of these antielitist feelings, which emerged between 1820 and 1840, states began to repeal existing licensing laws. Physicians and lawyers were very concerned about the repeal of licensing laws because they were directly affected. The general public, with support from President Jackson, cast a suspicious eye on the lack of quality control and educational standards that, in general, reflected the professions of law and medicine.

At the same time, interest in health and periodic scientific discoveries combined to provide a fertile environment for alternative (irregular) medical theories and treatments. This should come as no surprise because the "cure rate" of doctors during this era was poor. Americans began taking some steps to take care of their health and well-being because a visit to the doctor cost money and the treatment, especially in rural America, was highly suspect. As a result numerous health and hygiene reforms emerged, many of which attempted to merge moral and social reform with health promotion. One example of a popular dietary reform that blended current theories of chemical vitalism with generous amounts of Christian morality was vegetarianism. Medical treatments such as homeopathy, chemopathy, electropathy, and hydropathy all had their adherents. Homeopathy, which was the most popular and well-known alternative to orthodox medicine at the time, attempted to restore the body's balance with infinitesimal doses of medicine. This was in direct contradiction to the "heroic" dosing and purging approach used by traditional physicians. Chemopathy, electropathy, and hydropathy are general terms referring to various chemical treatments, electrical treatment, and water cures, respectively. All these cures were popular throughout the century.[3]

Thomsonianism, created by American Samuel Thomson, was another nontraditional approach that claimed every man or woman could be his or her own physician. Based on herbs and spices, Thomsonianism appealed to the democratic, egalitarian trends of the time. Playing on these sentiments, Thomson hawked books, pamphlets, botanical preparations, and Thomsonian medical credentials.

Medical education itself suffered from democratization. The antielitest sentiment directed against institutions that set admission standards for medical school and trained doctors were attacked because of their traditionally elitest approach. Although a few medical schools maintained what must be considered a relatively stringent education for the period, for-profit institutions sprang up throughout the United States. Weak entrance requirements, inadequate facilities, unqualified teachers, and less-than-rigorous curricula—sometimes as short as thirteen weeks—swelled the ranks of marginally trained medical graduates. Orthodox physicians continually warned against unqualified medical graduates. These same Orthodox physicians tried to improve medical education standards, but generally Americans did not support these efforts. Doctors had lost the "public trust" and were no longer accorded the title of "guardians of health." However, for the remainder of the nineteenth century, the professions of law and medicine would work very hard in an effort to restore their professional credibility with the public. Today, the profession of medicine is a highly respected profession and the level of health care in America is the best in the world.

The Preeminence of Biological Science

The nineteenth century was the age of science, and biology became the premier science of the period. Concerned with the study of living organisms, biology engaged the interest of some of the best scientific minds of the period. These scientists tried to unlock the mysteries of the functional processes of organic life, and by doing so they assisted both physical educators and medicine in preventing disease and restoring health.

Form, function, and transformation were the three general concepts that dominated biological study during the nineteenth century. Form referred to the shape and structure of the organism and its various parts. Function was concerned with understanding the vital processes of an organism. Transformation referred to how organisms change over time. The study of each separate concept resulted in monumental discoveries that radically changed ideas about organic life.

For example, the study of form was manifest in the theory of the cell as the structural basis of plant and animal life. Proposed by German scientists Matthias Jakob Schleiden and Theodore Schwann in the late 1830s, the cell theory soon led to the belief that the cell was also the center of functional (metabolic) activity as well. Cell theory was of critical importance to the study of transformation because it provided the basis in which science was able to explain individual organic development through progressive cell division and diversification. Put another way, each organism develops from the fertilized egg to adulthood through successive cell divisions. The cells take various forms according to the function they are to accommodate within the organism. This led to the widely accepted belief that "form follows function." This discovery is also central to Darwin's work, that the human mind has a biological rather than metaphysical basis. The organic development of each individual was grounded in science and provided a great deal of impetus in defining the role and scope of physical education.

Social and Institutional Change in Nineteenth-Century America

As described in the previous chapter, the nineteenth century was one of radical change. Seemingly, all aspects of American society were in flux. One of the consequences of this change was the development of a middle-class, bureaucratic society based on specialization and expertise. The field of physical education experienced this change in that it reflected the more general social and institutional changes that occurred in every other aspect of American culture. Specifically, specialists and organizations were developed to determine the needs and direction of the emerging profession.

The development of the "professional" is a phenomenon of the nineteenth century. In the early part of that century, practitioners of law, medicine, and religion served as mediators between the public and their fields of expertise. Schooled in classical absolution (the belief that their knowledge was absolute, unchanging, and the "truth"), these self-designated experts explained and interpreted both the mysteries of the world and classical knowledge to the everyday person.

However, the epistemological belief in an unchanging "truth" eroded late in the nineteenth century because of the expansion of knowledge. The experimental sciences and the needs of the new, urban society advocated the idea that a new epistemology that focused on new "truths" could develop as new knowledge was gained. By the end of the nineteenth century the exclusive professional authority once given to experts in law, medicine, and religion was gone forever, and new disciplines were developed to house the evolving bodies of knowledge. These new disciplines would create new epistemologies that provided additional "ways of knowing" that would augment and sometimes replace older epistemologies.

Some of these new disciplines found a home in the American university system. Prior to the nineteenth century, universities focused primarily on the liberal arts (literature, language, history, and philosophy). During the nineteenth century this changed as the American university began to cater to pragmatic, career-oriented students through an elective system centered around specific disciplinary departments. For those fields wishing to achieve professional status, acceptance into the academic community was absolutely essential. College degrees came to be valued by the middle class and equated with social status and material success.

Universities became increasingly "professional," and during the 1880s and 1890s the new, young professionals sought to create communities of academic interest through professional associations. Examples of these were the American Historical Association (1884), the American Economic Association (1885), the National Statistical Society (1888), and the American Political Science Association (1889). Medicine, closely allied at this time to physical education, was represented by the American Medical Association (1847). Furthermore, medicine began to specialize into subdisciplinary groups such as the American Neurological Association (1875).

One such subdisciplinary group was physical education. On November 27, 1885, a group of forty-nine people came together at the invitation of William G. Anderson, M.D., to discuss their common interest in physical education. An important issue that received a great deal of interest was the debate on the Battle of the Systems, which centered on the advantages and disadvantages between German gymnastics and Swedish gymnastics. The growth of physical education was reflected in the fact that by 1885 there were already teacher-training institutions, gymnasiums, and physical education programs in nonschool settings such as the YMCA. These early physical education programs used, in general, the Swedish system, the German system, or a combination of both. In addition, physical educators were incorporating exercises that were not identified with either system, such as the system of calisthenics developed by Catharine Beecher (1800–1878), and the gymnastics system favored by Dioclesian Lewis (1823–1886). Both Beecher and Lewis devoted their efforts to promoting health and exercise for women. They were not advocates of the German system primarily because

Figure 9.1

Catherine Beecher. From: E. W. Gerber. Innovators and Institutions in Physical Education. *Philadelphia: Lea & Febiger, 1971.*

German gymnastics were considered too physically demanding for the women of this era.

Of particular interest is Beecher's system of calisthenics. Her system was based on a physical education program structured around twenty-six lessons in physiology and two courses in calisthenics, one designed for school and the other to be done in exercise halls. Her system used "light exercises," which were sometimes performed with the use of light weight.[4] She wanted her students to develop beautiful and strong bodies and believed her calisthenics would serve "as a mode of curing distortions, particularly all tendencies to curvature of the spine, while at the same time, it tends to promote grace of movement, and easy manners."[5]

The composition of those who attended the meeting called by Anderson reflects the medical orientation of these early physical educators: twenty-five were medical doctors, most of whom were associated with a college or university. The large proportion of doctors provided a beginning point for the body of knowledge in physical education. Becoming a legitimate and recognized profession was essential if physical education was going to be accepted by the public and other recognized learned professionals. One of the accomplishments that came out of the meeting called by Anderson was the formation of the American Association for the Advancement of Physical Education (AAAPE). In

1903 AAAPE was renamed the American Physical Education Association (APEA). The formation of AAAPE was an important step in developing professional standards and to identifying the theoretical basis for the emerging profession of physical education.

The Theoretical Basis of American Physical Education

Interest in health, hygiene, exercise, and physical education had been growing unevenly in America since the 1830s. New programs emerged between 1830 and 1860 that became much more focused and formalized from 1870 to 1900. Terms such as gymnastics, physical culture, physical training, and physical education were used more or less synonymously to describe the systematic exercise programs that emerged during this time. Of these, physical education survived as the name that became most closely identified with the professional field and the academic discipline. When the AAAPE formed in 1885, any of these four terms might have been used to describe an organized system of physical exercise. All these terms supposedly related to some type of theoretical understanding of the nature and operations of the human body.

Just what this theoretical base was, however, was the subject of a good deal of disagreement. The newness and flexibility of the profession of physical education accommodated many different ideas that were advanced as physical education's theory base. However, this same flexibility caused much concern among the leaders of the field. Basically they felt it would be most difficult, if not impossible, to achieve harmonious relationships among members who held radically different ideas as to what physical education was.[6] The term *theory* is not used here in a strict, scientific sense. For our purpose, the term refers to both tested and untested assumptions that were used to explain physical activity.

The mixture of ideas, opinions, and verified facts that composed the theoretical base of early physical education was derived from a variety of sources. The findings in experimental science, particularly anatomy and physiology, were especially important. Physical education drew heavily on medicine to establish its body of knowledge. It is not surprising, therefore, that a large percentage of the founders of the AAAPE, as well as directors of college gymnasia at the turn of the century, were holders of an M.D. degree. Being strongly influenced by medicine, however, posed its own problems. Physical educators often had a hard time deciding on their own unique focus or territory of research. This "identity crisis" complicated the establishment of physical education's theory base.

Cultural values, especially those of the middle class, also played an important part in influencing the theory base. Physical educators demonstrated a high degree of sensitivity to the ideologies and attitudes that defined the nature of health and hygiene, the development of character, and the improvement of society. Physical education was also deeply influenced by the nineteenth-century social reform movements that connected physical and moral perfection, and the movements that connected the individual to society.

A strong social reformist attitude was one of the hallmarks of professional physical educators in the late nineteenth century. Simply put, many physical education professionals believed that physical education should be used to affect the health, moral, and intellectual development of the individual in much the same manner espoused by the philosophy of idealism. However, not all members of the AAAPE agreed on how this should happen. For example, Dioclesian Lewis blended ideas about physical exercise and hygiene to promote temperance and women's rights.[7] Lewis tied his work in physical education to a social agenda that sought to advance the rights of women as well as to ban the sale and consumption of alcoholic beverages.

In 1864 he hired Catharine Beecher (his system was actually an adaptation of Beecher's) to teach at his school for girls located in Lexington, Massachusetts. His school attracted "mostly girls of delicate constitution sent there for their health." Lewis was a self-promoter and charlatan; he presented himself as a physician, even though the title was an honorary one from Cleveland Homeopathic College, which underscores the mistrust and questionableness of the medical profession during this era. Lewis not only was an advocate of social reform and a health crusader; he also helped organize the Woman's Crusade, which later evolved into the Woman's Christian Temperance Union. Others, such as Dr. Edward Mussey Hartwell, demanded a cautious, measured, and objective approach.[8] However, even the scientific and objective Hartwell became convinced that a proper program of physical education could make a boy into a better man and enable him to transmit to his children an aptitude for better thoughts and actions. Character development would soon become an essential part of the emerging profession of physical education.

Still others expressed the opinion that physical education should not be limited to the strict approach of training the body. The U.S. Commissioner of Education, William T. Harris, declared, "We wish to discuss physical training in view of hygiene, and to avoid . . . all narrow interpretations of our subject." In observing that "the old physical education had thought that muscular education was all that was necessary to the training of the body," Harris argued that the new physical education was much broader in scope.[9] In so doing Harris touched on a debate that would become central to twentieth-century physical education.

The conviction that physical education was good for both the individual and the community was a major component of physical education's theory base. For a large number of practitioners this conviction was the entire basis for physical education, yet there was no scientific basis for this belief. Such was the case of William Blaikie, a prominent New York attorney. Blaikie wrote a popular book on physical exercise, *How to Get Strong and Stay So.*[10] This book perpetuated the myth that exercise was a cure for tuberculosis, even though the work of Pasteur, Koch's work in bacteriology, and the germ theory of disease showed that exercise had nothing to do with the cure. Still, Blaikie was influential in popularizing physical training and was an active member and officer of the AAAPE. Blaikie is also a good example of how educated men were concerned with matters of health and physical activity.

Three Distinct Periods

Three rather distinct periods occurred between 1885 and 1939 during which the theoretical framework of physical education was developed and modified. The first period was characterized by distinctive nineteenth-century beliefs that viewed health as a balance or harmony between the mind, body, and spirit. Science was felt to be the provider of knowledge and truth, and the tools of science (experimentation, observation, and measurement) were the symbols of learned authority.

The second period was a transitional one occurring between 1900 and 1917. During this period physical education was engaged in a debate regarding the appropriate methods and goals of the field. In addition, physical education would accommodate sports (1906–1939) as a signif-icant component of its theoretical and philosophical base. The accommo-dation of sports by physical education will be discussed in the next chapter. The third period occurred from 1917 to 1930 and was charac-terized by the acceptance by physical education of the psychosocial and behavioristic principles as a major part of its theoretical foundation.[11] This is not to say that these new developments were unopposed. How-ever, physical education accepted these new trends and ideologies while it also used popular notions regarding the virtues of physical activity, and in so doing tried to legitimize itself in the eyes of both the public and other professionals.

During the post-Civil War years interest in exercise increased for a variety of reasons: changing concepts of work and leisure, the desire of individuals to improve themselves, popular literature that stressed the relationship between health and exercise, an expanding body of knowl-edge about human physiology, and the influence of evolutionary theory on concepts of race regeneration. Interest in exercise and health was also influenced by the athletic craze that swept the country between 1870 and 1900.[12] In addition, some medical doctors treated physical deformities and chronic conditions with exercise, a treatment known as the Swedish Movement Cure[13] (not to be confused with Swedish gymnastics).

One reason for the increased interest in health was a personal sense of anxiety. Americans continued to move to the city in the late 1800s, and this urban growth caused the need to reaffirm a sense of commu-nity in a physical, social, and psychological sense. The loss of the tradi-tional, rural lifestyle left many Americans with a desire for a new lifestyle that would meet their new urban needs. Consequently many Americans favored an energetic style of living that would minimize the impact of their urban environment.[14] Americans pragmatically sought a connection between ideas and action, and in this social and psycholog-ical environment the body became the means by which this connection could take place.[15]

All this turmoil occurred at the same time that a significant number of Americans began to lose faith in the ability of religion to solve social and moral problems. Sin was no longer seen as the single cause of moral, social, and health problems. Many Americans believed that individuals were at the mercy of a possibly amoral social environment. Yet although many believed they were powerless to control this environment, they still wanted control over their own bodies. Consequently, health was seen as analogous to personal philosophy, law, order, government, self-reliance, and initiative. Whether the search was for personal order, social order, or communal identity, it was believed that exercise and the corresponding enhancement of health was necessary to insure total wellness and equilibrium of the whole person—mind, spirit, and body.

Biological and Philosophical Issues

The approach that identified the whole as the sum of its parts was influenced by the rapidly expanding body of knowledge in the biological sciences. This type of thinking related easily to the concept of the "social organism," which made each individual a "cell" in the body of society. With the interest and discoveries in the biological sciences influenced by Darwin, humans were increasingly viewed as an organismic part of social body. Health was seen as a balance between the organic systems of the body and those systems that set us apart from other creatures. We are part of the biological world; however, we are also unique.

What made humans unique were those qualities associated with the human mind. Will, volition, cognition, emotion, and character were unique to humans, yet these characteristics were increasingly studied as physiological phenomena. One example of this is William James, who turned psychology from the study of mind to the study of behavior (see chapter 10). Scholars studied how the mind and body were related and functioned. The success of the biological sciences influenced the manner in which the unique qualities described above were studied.

The relationship between mind and body has occupied the agendas of scientists and philosophers alike. The identification of the nerve pathways from the brain and spinal cord to the muscles and organs of the body, and returning back to the spinal cord and brain, lent evidence to the possibility that mental processes were biological functions. This idea was not a new one. If you recall, Thomas Hobbes' materialistic notions of reality are very similar to this idea.

Biological concepts, however, could not completely accommodate notions of the will. The concept of biological determinism called for the will to be a product of the body. In application this meant that willpower was genetically predetermined and was therefore a product of one's parentage rather than other mental factors. To many nineteenth-century Americans this idea was preposterous, almost sacrilegious! Most believed that will was one aspect of being human that separated man from the lower animals. As the foundation of character, will separated the superior individual from the inferior individual. If will was a product of biology, then individuals would have little control over who was superior.

This discussion of the nature of the will and its relationship to the body was the focus of much scholarly work. One example is William B. Carpenter, author of *Principles of Mental Physiology*.[16] Carpenter wrote that he could explain will strictly in terms of physiology. Wilhelm Wundt gave considerable thought to the subject of will. He investigated the physiological basis of sensory perceptions, instinctive and involuntary action, and sense feelings. Wundt believed that these aspects of our bodies are necessary to the development of higher mental processes. Yet Wundt also recognized that certain psychic processes could never be fully understood and that these processes lie outside individual consciousness.[17] For Wundt, will was related to character in that it was both physically inherited and socially acquired. This was significant to physical education; physical education would develop strong and healthy people and contribute to the formation of character and will. These desired traits would then be passed on to generation after generation through heredity. Needless to say, the work of Wundt was popular in physical education during this time.

There were two rationales for the development of physical education in the latter part of the nineteenth century: (1) that the mind is in part a product of our biology, and (2) that character can be acquired through the exercise of the will. The identification of neural pathways was used to build a strong case for exercise as essential to the healthy, integrated self.[18] For instance, Edward Hartwell, a leading nineteenth-century physical educator at Johns Hopkins University, stated that a single muscle is not a simple organ. Rather it is made up of two clearly distinguishable, yet intimately related, parts: the contracting muscle and the stimulating nerve. If the two parts were to disassociate, or if either part atrophied for any reason, the dual organ was "thrown out of gear" and ceased to function as a muscle. This process was felt to be similar to the human body when it was treated as two parts and trained to function separately as "fractions"; i.e., mind and body.[19]

The impact of science on nineteenth-century thought was profound. The epistemology of dualism was increasingly challenged by the epistemologies of science. However, this is not to say that dualism was abandoned. Questions about the nature of our existence and the role of physical education in enhancing life was a popular topic to discuss and remains so today. Is human existence divided into two separate but interrelated parts, mind and body? Or, is our existence as humans explained as a unified biological organism as opposed to one-part body and one-part mind? Contemporary physical educators seem to identify with the unity of mind and body as opposed to a dualistic approach. However, this choice or belief is not as clear cut as science would like. Although scientific inquiry provides the basis for research and teaching in physical education, the philosophy of idealism which strives to improve the "self" remains very popular with physical educators and coaches. The "self" includes physical improvement, cognitive improvement, moral and character development, and in many cases, spiritual development. More importantly, idealism lends itself to dualism more than it lends itself to a unified approach. Most physical educators and coaches utilize an eccletic approach which incorporates several epistemologies. Do you use more than one epistemology, more than one way of knowing?

Evolution

Evolution theory was combined with physiological assumptions about the relationship between mind and body to justify physical education.[20] However, much of the early theory base of physical education was based on assumptions about its virtues, and not on scientific evidence. This *a priori* approach to physical education was therefore the cause of both the successes and the failures of the discipline.

Exercise was thought to be one of the measures of biological improvement of the species. Anthropomorphic measurement revealed that changes in the body could occur in as little time as a few weeks, and the logic of the day believed that improvements in physical stature were symbolic of mental and moral improvement as well. As the theory went, individual improvements would enhance the evolutionary process of the entire human race, and therefore physical education was of benefit to the race.[21] This was a strong statement and enabled physical education to work in a direction that would continue to link its theoretical base with established scientific theory, in this case, evolution.

Exercise was felt to be critical to the normal evolutionary development of man. Early physical education theory dictated that it not only improved the human form but also was essential to building nerve centers and a sound mind. The often repeated *mens sana en corpore sano* was truly part of physical education's belief system. Jay Seaver, a physical educator at Yale University, reiterated the dependence of the functioning of the mind on the health of the body: "We may have fine intellectual powers and attainment in persons whose condition is like 'sweet bells jangled out of tune and harsh' whose central nerve power may be grand, but whose peripheral ganglia may be so morbidly out of tune as to make every process pathological."[22] Seaver's statement represented the antidualistic view of intellectuals who felt that proper physical exercise facilitated the functional unity of the individual. As such, exercise promoted harmony within the individual.

Evolution provided a strong scientific basis for the emerging theoretical basis of physical education. In the normal development of the species, evolution demonstrated that the ability to adapt and change was the key to survival. The species that did survive were stronger than those who became extinct. Exercise and its attendant health benefits helped to insure that men and women would continue to grow stronger and thus increase their ability to adapt to change and to survive. Strength was also equated with health, which could be handed down from one generation to the next. Women were identified by physical educators as being especially helped by evolutionary theory, as we shall see later in this chapter. It is certain that nineteenth-century physical education benefited from evolutionary beliefs.

The Disease—Neurasthenia: The Cure—Exercise!

Although physical educators argued for the unity of mind and body as opposed to a dualistic separation, they continued to wage a campaign against nervous disorders. Known as neurasthenic disease, this kind of dysfunction was thought to be of epidemic proportions in the late nineteenth century. For instance, George M. Beard published a book, *American Nervousness*, that contributed to the belief that nervous disorder was widespread.[23] It was felt that the urban environment, which cloistered workers in offices and factories, made everyone susceptible. The emphasis on brain work and fine motor movements, such as writing, placed stress on the brain and nerve centers, and it was felt that exercise would restore the balance. Randolph Fairies, a medical doctor and physical educator, argued that exercise was therapeutic with respect to the "brain overwork" brought about by too much studying, overanxiety, and the many moral decisions and responsibilities nineteenth-century Americans were faced with.[24] Dr. Fairies felt that the organs of "thought" (the brain, spinal cord, and nerves) were stimulated through exercise, and new blood was sent to the nervous system and the old blood was carried away.

Students were thought to be especially susceptible to this condition and more vulnerable to mental overstrain because young scholars were still developing physically. Exercise for students was therefore viewed as a therapeutic and as a developmental agent. The preoccupation with neurasthenia and the influence of Fairies may have been among the impetuses for offering physical education opportunities to students during the nineteenth century.

Exercise Builds Brain Power

In the late nineteenth century, questions arose regarding how intelligence developed, how it could be improved, and how it could be measured. Randolph Fairies reported to the AAAPE in 1894 that men who exercised their limbs had well-developed convolutions of the cerebral mass. His research stated that intelligent men have highly convoluted brains, whereas the cerebral mass of "idiots" was almost smooth. The conclusion reached by Fairies was startling: intelligence could be physiologically observed and controlled through exercise. Apparently Fairies missed the obvious conclusion: if his theory were true, all great athletes would be Phi Beta Kappas!

If, as Fairies argued, exercise actually stimulated willpower, character, and other mental attributes, then it had tremendous potential for the rehabilitation for deviant classes. Hamilton D. Wey, a doctor from a state reformatory in New York, believed exercise could rehabilitate "criminals and dullards." Wey reported to the AAAPE the astonishing benefits of exercise with his patients: gains were made in weight, posture, and general vigor. With these gains came an improvement in their mental capacities never before manifested in their prison life.[25]

Furthermore, Wey concluded that social deviants could be "exercised" into an acceptable level of moral behavior.[26] This concept remains popular today and can be observed in prison camps and other correctional institutions that use physical training in the form of boot camps as a means of establishing "correct" moral behavior.

Women: Mothers of the Race

The influence of evolutionary principles in the latter part of the nineteenth century affected attitudes about exercise, health, and the bodily development of women. Health was important for everyone, but it was particularly important for women in their role as progenitors and nurturers of new life. As the argument went, defective women produced defective children, whereas healthy women strengthened the race through their offspring. The procreative function of women gave them a special need for physical education.

The prevailing attitude toward women was that their unique biological function required exercises that would cater to their special physiology. This type of thinking implied that exercise for men and women should not be the same. Dr. Angelo Mosso, a professor of physiology in Italy, stated that the muscles used in respiration and those of the abdomen are much more important for women than for men because those were the muscles used in giving birth.[27] He also believed that exercise for men and women should not be the same.

Exercise for women, viewed within the parameters of nineteenth-century thinking, was enthusiastically endorsed by both men and women physical educators. However, Victorian attitudes of the nineteenth century did not permit women to dress in a fashion that allows the freedom of movement that is necessary if calisthenics and exercises are to be done as intended. On the contrary, women could often be seen "layered" in undergarments, blouses, and skirts that no doubt made any sudden movement difficult to say the least! This style of dress carried over into the gymnasium and compounded the problem. Needless to say, the "workout attire" of the nineteenth century did not permit for a vigorous program of physical education for women when compared with the high-intensity fitness programs of today's physical education.

An additional justification for women's physical education was that it made women more attractive. For instance, in 1894 physical educators argued over the virtues of heavy apparatus in exercise programs for women. Many believed that heavy apparatus could detract from the womanly form by making the shoulders too wide and the hips too narrow. Most physical educators believed that "heavy work" was permissible if it was used for the overall development of health, but it should not be used for increasing strength. The object of physical education was to perfect the female body, both in its outward contours and in its ability to resist lifelong wear and tear. Physical education prepared women for motherhood, and health was essential to that role.

Figure 9.2
Mount Holyoke Seminary students in early 1860s at exercise.
Courtesy of Mount Holyoke College Library/Archives.

In 1894 Mary E. Allen, owner of the Allen Gymnasium in Boston, summarized the benefits of exercise for late nineteenth-century women. She argued that healthy women could maintain their equilibrium, sick women could restore their health, depressed women could be cheered, fat women could reduce, thin women could build up, mature mothers could maintain their youth to meet the needs of growing children, young mothers could make their bodies "the sound and holy temple it should be" for the creation of life, and all young women could increase their vigor and make their figures supple.[28] Although gender differences were recognized and maintained, many nineteenth-century physical educators actively supported physical education opportunities for women, and women benefited from the social and biological imperative to good health during this period. Many of the attitudes and justifications of physical education articulated by Mary Allen are still manifest in contemporary physical education.

Women, Higher Education, and Physical Education

Physical educators supported higher education for women, and nowhere was the health of women more of an issue than in women's colleges. The growth of higher education for women was a phenomenon of the post-Civil War years, and dissenters to the experiment believed that women were too frail to withstand the rigors of academic study. The physical constitution of women was not something administrators could dismiss easily. Nervous disorders were believed to be particular to American culture, and American women were believed to be the most susceptible.

The female nervous system received much attention from the medical community in the last half of the nineteenth century and was a major argument against higher education for women. Dr. Edward Clarke suggested that intellectual education would unduly tax the nervous system of women by redirecting the nervous energy necessary for reproduction toward intellectual development.[29] Many of Clarke's contemporaries who supported higher education for women strongly disagreed. The inclusion of physical education programs in college curricula was the response in many cases.

The Golden Age of Anthropometric Measurement: 1885–1900

The emphasis on form was manifest in the new academic area of anthropometry, the study of the measurements of body segments, girths, and lengths. Anthropometry was used by many different disciplines, particularly anthropology, to prove or disprove all kinds of theories that dealt with the nature of humans. For instance, Dr. Charles Roberts, an English M.D., measured the heights and weights of men of the artisan class and compared these measurements with those of the "most favored," or upper, class. Roberts' study showed the artisan class to be inferior in height, weight, and chest girth, and he concluded that height differences were probably due to inherited characteristics whereas weight was more influenced by the conditions of life.[30]

This kind of work had a significant impact on physical educators in the late nineteenth century. Roberts' *A Manual of Anthropometry* was cited by Dudley A. Sargent in his address on anthropometry before the AAAPE in 1890.[31] Dr. Henry P. Bowditch studied the growth of Boston schoolchildren, and William T. Porter initiated an anthropomorphic study of thirty-three thousand schoolchildren in St. Louis. Porter concluded that children with less-than-average mental ability were lighter, shorter, and smaller in the chest than children of average or better mental ability.[32] Such physical measurement was tremendously important in the minds of physical educators in the latter part of the nineteenth century. In 1891 Roberts and Bowditch were made honorary members of the AAAPE; Porter was already an active member of the association.

Anthropometry was a particularly popular research tool during this period and was particularly well suited to the research needs of physical educators who sought to both quantify their scientific status as well as legitimize their claim to professional status. Anthropometry suited research, pedagogical, and status needs, lending an aura of science to physical education.

As were all academic questions, those generated by physical educators were influenced by post-Darwinian thought. Darwinism emphasized inheritance and health as the mechanisms of social progress. One sign of health was the attainment of the ideal form for humans—a shape that had symmetry and harmony of proportion. Physical educators used anthropometry to determine the ideal proportions of man and woman. However, "ideal" to nineteenth-century physical educators did not mean what it does today: the concept of ultimate bodily development. Interestingly enough, physical educators defined "ideal" as an average, or a norm, of the measurements of large numbers of people.

This norm, according to scientists, could be improved by changing the environment, and one of the best ways to change the environment was to provide students with the opportunity to exercise. Influenced by the studies of contemporary anthropometrists on the inheritance of mental and physical traits, Dudley Sargent stated his conclusions regarding the improvement of the human race through exercise during an address to the AAAPE in 1890:

> Both the intellectual and physical supremacy of a people are dependent upon the intellectual and physical condition of the masses. In other words, the only way to produce the highest specimens of the individual, improve the condition of the race and better the quality of future humanity, is to raise the normal or mean standard of mental and physical development.[33]

Clearly, according to physical educators, the means to improve the physical, mental, and moral aspects of the race was through exercise. By associating themselves with the goal of race improvement through the mechanism of science, primarily through anthropometry, physical educators attempted to establish themselves as the new arbiters of racial supremacy.

During the late nineteenth century the most honored physical education researchers were those men and women who directed programs at the college level. Edward Hitchcock, M.D., Professor of Physical Education and Hygiene at Amherst College, was the epitome of what physical education professionals aspired to be. Anthropometry was at the cutting edge of physical education research, and Hitchcock collected anthropomorphic measurements from 1861 to 1901 as part of the mandatory physical examinations of all students. Dudley Sargent was Professor of Physical Training and Director of the gymnasium at Harvard, and in a similar manner he collected measurements from which he devised his anthropometric chart of the ideal: a graph that plotted the norms of symmetrical development of college-aged men. Sargent concluded that the closer a student was to the fiftieth percentile, the more symmetrical the individual.[34] Men were not the only subjects for anthropometric research. Delphine Hanna, M.D., at Oberlin College; Lucile E. Hill and Mary Anna Wood at Wellesley; Carolyn C. Ladd, M.D., at Bryn Mawr; and others routinely collected anthropomorphic measurements of women students as a part of scientific gymnasium work.[35]

Social prejudice and the homogeneous nature of college student populations of both genders acted as parameters for physical education research. The thousands of measurements that were collected were of a generally homogeneous socioeconomic group of upper- or middle-class Anglo-Saxon college students. These students routinely were shown to be taller, heavier, and larger in girth than those whose economic and social status made attending college difficult. Unfortunately, and against the methods that we now use in the scientific world, the information gathered from anthropometric studies was erroneously used to validate nineteenth-century prejudices. It was not until the twentieth century that many of these incorrect uses of anthropometry were understood and discounted.

Although some anthropometrists claimed to offer proof of racial superiority, this claim was not really the point of anthropometric research. The purpose of these studies, according to Hitchcock, was to understand the physical data of the typical or ideal college student. By observing every student possible with the most modern of anthropometric measuring devices, Hitchcock hoped to compute the "average" student and then to instruct students to achieve the average. What needed to be determined and agreed on, then, was what constituted "perfection," or the average.[36]

Defining the Scope of the Discipline

The assumptions, theories, and scientific evidence that made up the theoretical base of physical education supported the conviction that exercise was good for the individual and good for society. The arguments and rationales drawn from the related disciplines of physiology, psychology, and medicine came together as a combination of ideas that related individual health, public hygiene, race improvement, physical and moral rehabilitation, and educational reform through the science of physical education.

Founded on these beliefs, physical education had both strengths and weaknesses. The blend of theory, assumption, and knowledge congruent with contemporary beliefs provided the enthusiasm and reformist zeal during the initial growth period of physical education. However, this same blend also provided the basis for possible contradictions within the theoretical foundation of the field. Physical education attempted to gain acceptance with groups that had different world views concerning the nature of "truth." If, for instance, physical educators catered to the needs of the public and condoned popular ideas not based on scientific evidence, then the academic world would not respect the work done in the discipline. If, however, physical education attempted to define itself solely in the strict terms of scientific empiricism, it might not have the base needed to attract a popular following.

Dr. George Fitz, a research physiologist at Harvard's Lawrence Scientific School, was one of the first to understand the paradigmatic problems of the new discipline. Admonishing his colleagues on the lack of high-quality research, Fitz cautioned the AAAPE that physical education must not rely on general assumptions that are not based on the findings of science. He felt that the basis of many theories were valueless as working hypotheses because they were not based on experiments or experience, but instead were accepted *a priori* (on assumptions or other theories).[37]

Although he continued to press his fellow physical educators to test the assumptions that they promoted and perpetuated, Fitz was in the minority. His promptings went largely unheeded for several reasons. One was that other physical education leaders disagreed with Fitz on the scope of physical education. For instance, Dr. Edward Hartwell had a larger vision of physical education, one that accepted the integrated person as the legitimate sphere of physical education. He believed that almost all human actions could be understood as the union of the body moving under the control of the mind, and that bodily actions demand first consideration because without them mental power, artistic feeling, and spiritual insight cannot occur. His definition covered almost all facets of human existence and therefore made physical education central to being human.[38] Fitz eventually became exasperated with these lofty characterizations of the field of physical education and left it to study physiology.

Most physical educators, however, continued to concentrate on anatomical and anthropometric studies. Unlike today, few physical educators paid attention to physiological research, mainly because physiology was changing during this period. Most physiologists were interested in cellular function, whereas physical educators were interested in the functioning of the human body as a whole. Strength was seen as both a dynamic indicator of functional efficiency and a measurement of bodily integration, and measuring strength became a part of anthropomorphic testing. Physical educators such as Dudley Sargent, Jay Seaver, and Watson L. Savage agreed that one of the principal objects of physical training was the development of muscular power, and as a consequence anthropometry remained the dominant research topic throughout the 1890s.

Efforts to be the professional standard bearer of anthropomorphic research caused the AAAPE to create the Committee of Anthropometry and Vital Statistics at its first meeting in 1885. A major task of this committee was to establish a chart of anthropometric measures that would become the recommended standards of the organization. Before such a standard was achieved, however, the annual AAAPE meetings evolved into a political battle over procedural protocol, measurement sites, and equipment. For example, the matter of whether to measure height with the shoes on was of considerable concern during a discussion at the 1891 AAAPE Annual Meeting. Both Hitchcock and Sargent had developed their own anthropomorphic charts that they had used in their college work, and each felt that his method was superior. Sargent vigorously promoted and campaigned for the adoption of his system.[39] Eventually a standard of fifty measures were agreed on as the recommendations of the AAAPE.[40]

The Contributions of German Gymnastics, the Swedish System, and Dio Lewis to Teacher Training

The theories discussed by physical educators in colleges and universities were supposed to be applied in primary and secondary schools, and during the late nineteenth century the primary pedagogical methods of physical education were gymnastics, calisthenics, and exercise programs. The best known of the various systems was the German system of Friedrich Jahn, which, as you remember, was introduced into the U.S. in the latter part of the 1820s. The most notable feature of the German system was the use of heavy apparatus, including jumping horses and horizontal bars, and light equipment such as dumbbells and wands. German gymnastics was quite popular in Massachusetts between 1830 and 1860. It was not unusual to see devotees of German gymnastics marching in formation or doing calisthenics and other similar drills by command.

The revolutionary unrest in Germany in 1848 and 1849 caused a large number of Germans to immigrate to the United States. This infusion of Germans led to the formation of several Turner societies, and in 1850 a turnerbund was created in New York. Modeled after Turner societies in Germany, these new societies in the United States continued to offer gymnastics work in addition to being social societies for the German-American community. The Turners believed in the value of physical education, in the form of German gymnastics, and actively campaigned for mandatory physical education instruction within the schools. They volunteered to provide instruction free of charge and were especially successful in the Midwest, where there was a large concentration of German immigration. By 1867 there were 148 Turner societies consisting of 10,200 members.[41] Their influence was considerable as noted in Ohio, when in 1892 a law was passed there stipulating that physical culture be taught in the larger schools; in 1904 the law was changed to include all schools. Anton Leibold and John Molter, both of whom were Turners, introduced the law in the Ohio state legislature.[42]

The Turners of the New York City turnerbund began a seminary in 1866 for training teachers of German gymnastics. Nineteen men enrolled in 1866 and attended class primarily during the evening hours and on Saturday, which enabled the students to hold jobs. Only Turners could enroll, and a per capita tax of ten cents a year was levied on the membership to support the teacher-training program. The one-year curriculum included classes in history, anatomy, first aid, aesthetic dancing, theory of physical education systems, terminology, and the practice of gymnastics with emphasis on teaching methods. Five faculty members taught the courses; nine men finished the coursework and took the final exam, but only five were awarded diplomas.[43] Three more classes were offered, two in New York in 1869 and 1872, and one in Chicago in 1871. Each class was six months long, but results were very discouraging.

The Turners decided that their efforts in training teachers would be more successful in the West. The North American Gymnastic Union, the formal name for the Turner society, voted in 1874 to move the Normal School for the teaching of gymnastics to Milwaukee, where it operated under the direction of George Brosius from 1875 to 1888 and awarded 103 diplomas.[44]

Figure 9.3
Baron Nils Posse was the leading proponent of Swedish gymnastics in the United States. From: E. W. Gerber. Innovators and Institutions in Physical Education. Philadelphia: Lea & Febiger, 1971.

In 1860 Dioclesian Lewis introduced his own system of light gymnastics to men, women, and children in the Boston area. He opened a private gymnasium and offered normal courses (teacher training) for those who wished to teach gymnastics. Another system of gymnastics was the Swedish system of Ling. This system was first introduced to the U.S. at the Swedish Health Institute in Washington, D.C., and by 1887, Swedish gymnastics were being used at Johns Hopkins University. The Swedish system used light equipment such as dumbbells and chest weights, but to a lesser extent than the German program.

During the nineteenth century physical training was associated with some form of systematic exercise regimen and was no doubt influenced by the European style of calisthenics, primarily German or Swedish. These systems reflected contemporary thinking, which sought to develop bodily symmetry through disciplined, well-ordered, and progressively graded exercises. In the first fifteen years of the AAAPE, physical educators engaged in debate over the most appropriate exercise system that would best serve the needs of the American people. The German system and the Swedish system were often promoted by their respective adherents as the "correct" system of physical education, and the controversy surrounding the two approaches is known as "The Battle of the Systems." Physical educators called for an

American system tailored to American needs, needs that could not be met by foreign systems.

Physical Education the American Way

A conference on physical training was held in Boston in 1889 to develop an American system of gymnastics. Influential educators and the leading physical educators of the day attended, and the meeting was chaired by William T. Harris, United States Commissioner of Education. The purpose of the meeting was to discuss the various systems of training in an effort to decide what method of exercise would be most suitable for educational institutions. Spokesmen for the German system and the Swedish system presented what they felt were the unique contributions of each. Both systems graded their programs as to age, sex, and physical condition of the individual and proceeded to more difficult work as physical conditioning improved. Dudley Sargent provided information about his programs at Cambridge, as did Hitchcock about his program at Amherst. Sargent's program, which prescribed an individual program of exercises for each student, differed from the Swedish and German, which emphasized class groups. Hitchcock conducted his program in class groups, although he did examine each student and suggest further work to correct deficiencies.[45]

The notable feature of this conference was the openness and willingness to learn and develop a method of gymnastic exercise based on the best available knowledge and methods. The concern for understanding the underlying principles of movement and how they related to hygienic and educational issues was very much in evidence in the discussions that followed the formal presentations.

Changing Concepts of Health

While physical educators conducted research in anthropometry and debated the various gymnastic systems, the very concepts on which their work was based began to change. The nineteenth-century concept of health, as a balance among mind, body, and will, became inappropriate and impossible to sustain in the face of new biological and medical evidence. Specifically, the understanding of germs and their connection to disease undermined the idea that health is a balance of mind, body, and will. New medical techniques such as inoculation, purification of water and milk, new surgical techniques, and asepsis led to a new faith in invasive medicine's ability to control, cure, and restore health. It became increasingly difficult to blame moral indiscretions on physical capacity, and vice versa. By 1900 the conceptual foundation of health began to shift away from the old paradigm, and the constitution of a healthy human being was beginning to be defined in terms of social interaction and behavioral action.[46]

A Changing Profession

Even the nature of the reform movement in the United States was changing as a new and growing middle class came to accept, and even welcome, the opportunities of an urban, industrial, specialized, and professional society. The progressive movement used both the philosophical foundations of the pragmatists and the organizational techniques of business and industry.

This attitude toward reformism manifested itself in almost every aspect of American culture including physical education. The reform of physical education will receive additional emphasis in chapter 10. The reform movement and the desire for professional status and recognition was very important to the nature and development of American education. Physical education found itself adjusting its focus and purpose in the light of these changes, and although some welcomed these changes, others did not. Those who did not welcome change were those who continued to promote gymnastic exercise as the pedagogical heart of physical education and anthropometry as its research core. Those who sought change did so through the adoption of play theory as the rationale for physical education and the pedagogic use of play, games, and sport as the methodology of physical education.[47] We will elaborate on these issues in the following chapter.

One of the major end products of the health-reform movements of the nineteenth century was the creation of career opportunities. Jobs that facilitated the practice of physical education became available for both men and women in the form of gymnasium directors, physical training instructors, playground leaders, and hygiene teachers. Before 1885 most of those who were employed in these jobs did not have the benefits of formal training in college or university programs. When William G. Anderson founded the Association for the Advancement of Physical Education (AAPE) in 1885, one of the most important goals of the organization was the desire to improve and professionalize the teaching of physical education. The 1885 meeting was the beginning of a systematic attempt to develop physical education instructors.

The Professional Preparation of Teachers

The debate between the promoters of gymnastics and the play theorists was not the only one important to the direction of teacher preparation. In a debate that is very familiar to physical educators today, a difference in opinion as to how teachers should be trained existed between administrators of the AAAPE and the teachers who worked in the schools. The national executive council, which was made up entirely of college men and women, state superintendents of physical education, city directors of physical education, and other administrators, judged teacher behavior by standards that were more applicable to higher education (colleges

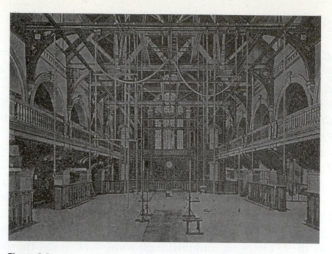

Figure 9.4
*Dudley Sargent's laboratory: Hemenway Gymnasium,
Harvard University, 1885. From: E. W. Gerber.
Innovators and Institutions in Physical Education.
Philadelphia: Lea & Febiger, 1971.*

and universities). The problem with their goals was that what was professionally necessary to enhance the authority of people in administrative and college-level positions was quite different from the needs of teachers in elementary and secondary education.

The majority of men and women who held leadership positions in the AAAPE held medical degrees, whereas others had college degrees and/or graduate training. Medical training continued to be seen as necessary for college physical educators as well as for those men and women who wanted administrative or college positions.[48] This position makes sense in the light of the strong health influence that existed in physical education at this time. In opposition to this group were the practitioners who were the frontline workers in playgrounds, summer camps, and physical education programs. The preparation programs that developed to provide trained workers for these positions were limited by the desire to put qualified teachers into the marketplace as quickly as possible.

One institution that facilitated the needs of the teacher/practitioner was the "normal school." During the nineteenth century, private normal schools offered certificates of completion for one- or two-year courses and were under the direction of well-known physical educators. Normal schools were well respected before World War I, and the Sargent Normal School of Physical Education is an example of this. Until the 1890s, these private normal schools were the only programs available for training for physical educators. Sargent's proposed curriculum was an ambitious one that emphasized anatomy and physiology along with practical gymnasium experiences. In 1891 the program was lengthened to two years, and in 1902 the school merged with Boston University to become the Sargent College of Physical Education.

The YMCA International Training School, which would later be named Springfield College, was established in 1887 in Springfield, Massachusetts. The school offered a two-year course in professional physical education, which enabled the YMCA to staff its gymnasium with qualified teachers. Luther Halsey Gulick, M.D., was appointed as an instructor in the Department of Physical Training. One of the great leaders of physical education, Gulick remained at the YMCA Training School from 1887 to 1902. In 1889, after the resignation of Robert J. Roberts, Gulick was appointed superintendent. He remained superintendent until 1900. From 1887 to 1902 he served as the YMCA's first Secretary of the Physical Training Department of the International Committee of the YMCA of North America.[49] His contributions to the field of physical education were of such magnitude that the American Alliance for Health, Physical Education, Recreation and Dance (AAHPERD) has made the Gulick Award the highest honor to be given a member.

Dr. Gulick started a summer school course for the training of physical education teachers who were already in the field. The first graduate coursework in physical education was started in 1891. Courses were offered in (1) physiological psychology, (2) history and philosophy of physical education, (3) anthropometry, and (4) literature of physical education. Completion of the coursework culminated in a thesis of 3,000 words. Upon successful completion of the graduate program of study, a graduate diploma in physical education (not a graduate degree) was awarded. Three men completed the work necessary for a diploma between 1891 and 1900.[50] The first graduate degree program in physical education was offered at Teachers College–Columbia University; it was started in 1901 and led to the master's degree.

The Chautauqua Summer School was operated by William G. Anderson, M.D., who later turned administrative duties over to Jay Seaver, M.D. Founded in 1888, the school offered a teacher preparation (normal school) program in gymnastics, playground supervision and management, first aid, sports skills, and aquatics instruction. Completion of the normal course required attending three six-week terms. Classroom instruction was given in anatomy, physiology, anthropometry, psychology, medical gymnastics, orthopedics, Swedish and German gymnastics, and storytelling.[51]

Dudley Sargent operated the Harvard Summer School of Physical Education, which he opened in 1887. The school "was probably the most important source of professional training in the United States during the early part of the twentieth century."[52] The alumni totaled 5,086 students from the United States and abroad. Coursework consisted of anatomy, physiology, hygiene, anthropometry, applied anatomy, and lectures on the various gymnastic systems, including their history and philosophy. Course offerings were later expanded to cover calisthenics, first aid, physical diagnosis, testing for normal vision and hearing, and treatment of spinal curvature. Sports were added in 1900 for men and women.[53] The school closed in 1932 because a bachelor's degree was required by the state to teach physical education, which forced potential educators into a four-year program.

Figure 9.5

John Swett. From: E. W. Gerber. Innovators and
Institutions in Physical Education. *Philadelphia:
Lea & Febiger, 1971.*

Always a leader in curriculum reform and innovation, California
passed a state law in 1866 requiring physical education in the schools.
John Swett was Superintendent of Public Instruction for the state of
California and the person responsible for implementing the law requiring mandatory exercise. Signed on March 24, 1866, by Governor Lou,
the law stated:

> Instruction shall be given in all grades of schools, and in all classes,
> during the entire school course, in manners and morals, and the laws
> of health; and due attention shall be given to such physical exercises
> for the pupils as may be conducive to health and vigor of body, as well
> as mind; and to the ventilation and temperature of school rooms.[54]

There are two important points in the California legislation: (1) The
1860s was a period in the history of America that evoked concern about
the nation's youth relative to their physical condition and ability to use
arms in defense of the country. California made physical education
mandatory in an effort to promote health and vigor. (2) The concern of
the physical readiness of the nation's youth to provide the means for the
military defense of America's interests abroad and at home resulted in
most educators favoring mandatory military drill, not gymnastics, in the
schools. In 1863 the Teacher's Institute favored the teaching of military
drill in the public schools.[55] John Swett was able to successfully argue in
behalf of mandatory gymnastics rather than military drill. As a result,
Swett enabled California to lead the nation in requiring mandatory

physical education in the public schools at a time when many people throughout the country were concerned about the health and physical ability of our nation's youth. These concerns continue to be voiced today, however, not enough is being done to insure the health and physical well-being of the nation's youth. Enhancing health and prevention of disease is a national issue and at the foundation of effective physical education programs. Physical educators are the best trained professionals to deliver information about the benefits of developing a healthy and active lifestyle in order to prevent disease and promote health and wellness. However, why do you think physical education, with so much to offer students and the general public, continues to be underfunded?

As discussed earlier in this chapter, Ohio passed a law in 1892 requiring that physical culture be taught in the state's larger schools. This law was a popular victory for the large population of German Turners living in Ohio, who were advocates of mandatory physical education in the schools. The state legislature modified the law in 1904 to include the amendment that all schools, not just the larger ones, require physical education. Louisiana in 1894, Wisconsin in 1897, and North Dakota in 1899 were other states that passed laws requiring physical education. With state legislation mandating physical education, the professional preparation of physical education teachers was at the top of the political and professional agenda.

Concern over the training of new practitioners was typical in the professionalization process. It had to be addressed successfully if the profession was to grow in stature, prestige, and authority. From the beginning of the AAAPE there was constant pressure to improve training, and in 1896 Jakob Bolin argued for the improvement of teacher preparation programs:

> It is deplorable that, in matters pertaining to physical education, the gymnastic teacher, who, from the nature of the avocation ought to be considered as experts, have far less influence than the pedagogue (regular teacher) . . . the insufficient general and special education of our gymnastic teacher, I see (as) the cause of the lost state of physical education in our land. Our teachers are not thoroughly acquainted with the fundamental principles of their work.[56]

Even though professional preparation programs were steadily improving, professionals were concerned with the quality of instruction and sought to improve it to legitimize their positions.

Four-year major courses were introduced between 1892 and 1911 at Stanford (1892), Harvard (1892), University of California (1898), University of Nebraska (1899), Oberlin (1900), Teachers College–Columbia University (1901), and the University of Wisconsin (1911). Yet there was considerable diversity among these degree programs. The blend of personalities involved in the development of each school and the place that new physical education departments assumed within the structural organization of the college affected the manner in which the programs developed. The program at Stanford reflected the interests of

Thomas D. Wood, the first chairperson of the Department of Physical Training and Hygiene. Health and hygiene were the strength at Stanford, whereas Harvard, under the leadership of George Welk Fitz, emphasized physiology.[57]

As teacher preparation courses developed in other colleges and universities, many departments were placed within schools of education. One reason for this was that many states legislated mandatory physical education, and colleges and universities responded to the increased need to prepare physical educators. Michigan, for example, passed mandatory physical education laws in 1911 and 1919, and the University of Michigan added a four-year teacher-training course in physical education to the curricula of the School of Education in 1921.

In spite of these improvements, some physical educators felt that standards within the profession remained weak. In 1914 it was noted that:

> Professional standards should be established which would elevate the profession. In time the license to practice gymnastics will be as thoroughly regulated by state laws as the license to practice medicine.[58]

Until 1919, however, there were no state licensure laws for a teaching specialty in physical education. Although certain similarities in program content existed in both private and public college curricula, standards and emphasis depended on the personalities, motivations, and interests of those involved. Without state licensure teachers could claim a specialty in physical education by taking a summer school course, a normal course that varied from one to three years, or a four-year degree program in a college or university that offered such a specialty. Until standards could be developed and agreed on, practitioners of physical education were able to certify themselves with little, if any, professional instruction.

Due to World War I and the poor physical condition of many of the nation's men, interest in physical education increased. The sense of national emergency after the war created a sympathetic attitude toward physical education, and by 1921 there was compulsory public school physical education in twenty-eight states.[59] By 1930 some type of certification was required for teaching in thirty-eight states.[60] A four-year course leading to the bachelor's degree became the standard of training in the 1920s, and as this trend continued, private institutions such as the Sargent School of Physical Education began to merge with degree-granting colleges.

In spite of increases in the number of schools offering physical education curricula in an effort to license practitioners, physical educators continued to express feelings of professional inadequacy over what constituted a trained physical educator. Two factors were attributed to this condition. Some felt that physical education was unable to attract competent recruits, particularly men.[61] The quality of recruits was not as high as in other disciplines, and a corresponding loss of professional prestige was the result. Another problem was that physical educators were seen as those who merely organized play activities. Even though teacher-training curricula was based on natural sciences such as anthropometry, physiology, anatomy, kinesiology, biology, and hygiene, the actual practice of physical education teaching did not demonstrate the body of knowledge gained through the training process. Physical education teachers did not teach physiology or kinesiology, they taught games. They may well have called on their knowledge of these sciences to organize activities and evaluate student progress, but this was not a daily, demonstrable element of their work.[62] This argument, first held in the early 1900s, continues today in contemporary physical education.

The tremendous need for teachers in the wake of state legislation made it possible to teach physical education courses with a minimum of training. This may have been the most devastating blow to the prestige of the profession. Also, the qualifications of physical education practitioners already in the field undermined the claims of needed improvement called for by the AAAPE and other professional organizations. In the end, it was probably a combination of all these factors that led to feelings of professional inadequacy on the part of physical education leaders.

Summary

During the nineteenth century, one of the major concerns of Americans and Europeans was health. During this era, disease was a routine occurrence, and the ability of medicine to cure the sick and prevent disease was very poor. The nature of health, according to the medical authorities, was manifest in a balanced constitution (the body) and temperament (the mind and spirit). The relationship between mind and body with regard to health continued to be an important area of concern. Although physicians attempted to treat disease and restore health, their methods frequently did more damage to the patient. As a result, Americans began to search for alternative medical treatments that would not only cure whatever it was that ailed them but also prevent disease. One example is Thomsonianism, which claimed that every man and woman could be his or her own doctor. There were books, pamphlets, botanical preparations, and Thomsonian medical credentials that could be purchased.

Biology became the preeminent science of the day and the discovery of the cell theory was central to the work of Charles Darwin. Science focused on the organic development of the individual, which provided a great deal of impetus in defining the role and scope of physical education.

The nineteenth century was a period of radical change. One of the most notable developments was the establishment of a middle class, bureaucratic society based on specialization and expertise. The field of physical education experienced this change in that it reflected the more general social and institutional changes that occurred in society. As a result, specialists and organizations were developed to determine the needs and direction of the emerging profession. On November 27, 1885, a group of forty-nine people came together at the invitation of William G. Anderson, M.D., to discuss their common interest in physical education. The majority of those in attendance were trained as physicians. Out of this meeting came the first serious effort to develop physical education as a legitimate profession. The large proportion of doctors who attended this meeting provided a beginning point for the body of knowledge in physical education that was based on health and the prevention of disease. The new professional organization was called the American Association for the Advancement of Physical Education.

Physical education was concerned with health promotion and the prevention of disease. Its methods were based primarily on exercise in the form of gymnastics and calisthenics. The concept of health changed. The understanding of germs and their connection to disease undermined the idea that health is a balance of mind, body, and will. Medical science had redeemed itself and developed sound scientific methods that earned the public's trust in its ability to control, cure, and restore health. As a result, it became increasingly difficult to blame moral indiscretions on an individual's physical capacity or lack thereof. The concept of health now included social interaction and behavioral aspects. This social reform movement that included social interaction and behavioral outcomes as significant components in the development and promotion of health for all Americans was very strong. Physical education adjusted to these changes and sought to reflect social interaction and behavioral objectives through the expansion of the curriculum to include play, games, and sports. However, not all physical educators were going along with this change. These people continued to promote gymnastic exercises and anthropometry as the core of physical education.

The development of the theoretical base of nineteenth-century physical education was grounded in the medical and scientific knowledge of the day. The trend in contemporary physical education is once again toward medicine. It is not unusual to have physicians on the faculty of physical education departments today, as was the custom during the nineteenth century. The professional preparation of teachers continues to stimulate debate in the twentieth century as it did during the nineteenth century, when the Battle of the Systems was raging. The content of physical education majors in the nineteenth century was similar to that of today. Anatomy, physiology, health, first aid, history and philosophy, educational psychology, and sports skills were essential parts of the fledgling physical education curriculum during the era when colleges were introducing the bachelor's degree in physical education. Prior to the four-year college major, normal schools were the primary source of physical education teachers and offered a similar, but shorter, curriculum. Physical education programs for women focused on matters of health, beauty, posture, and movement. The Swedish system was better suited for women when measured against the content and methods of German gymnastics. Dio Lewis and Catharine Beecher were the leaders in promoting the benefits of exercise for women and advocating women's political and social rights. This was an era in which science was at the cutting edge regarding research efforts in physical education, and pioneers such as Dudley Sargent, George Fitz, Luther Gulick, Mary Allen, Delphine Hanna, and Catharine Beecher shaped the future of American physical education.

Discussion Questions

1. What influence did medicine have on the emerging profession of physical education?

2. How did science have an impact on the metaphysical positions of leading educators during the late nineteenth and early twentieth centuries?

3. What was the Battle of the Systems?

4. What role did physical education play in enhancing the health of women?

5. What impact did anthropometry have on the theoretical development of physical education?

6. Describe the early teacher-training programs available from 1885 to 1930.

7. Identify those individuals and social forces that had a profound influence on the direction of physical education?

8. How did the work of Charles Darwin influence physical education?

Suggestions for Further Reading

Ainsworth, D. *History of Physical Education in Colleges for Women.* New York: A. S. Barnes & Co., 1930.

Aller, A. S. "The Rise of State Provisions for Physical Education in the Public Secondary Schools of the United States." Doctoral diss., University of California, 1935.

Eastman, M. F., and C. C. Lewis. *The Biography of Dio Lewis.* New York: Fowler and Wells Co., 1891.

Haverson, M. E. *Catharine Esther Beecher, Pioneer Educator.* Lancaster, Penn.: Science Press Printing Co., 1932.

Kindervater, A. G. "Early History of Physical Education in the Public Schools of America." *Mind and Body* 33 (June 1926): 97–103.

Leonard, F. *Pioneers of Modern Physical Training.* New York: Association Press, 1919.

Lewis, D. *New Gymnastics.* Boston: Ticknor and Fields, 1862.

Rice, E., J. Hutchinson, and M. Lee. *A Brief History of Physical Education.* New York: The Ronald Press, 1969.

Schwendener, N. *History of Physical Education in the United States.* New York: A. S. Barnes & Co., 1942.

Stecher, W. A., ed. *Gymnastics, A Textbook of the German-American System of Gymnastics.* Boston: Lee and Shepard, 1895.

Wacker, H. M. "The History of the Private Single Purpose Institutions Which Prepared Teachers of Physical Education in the United States of America from 1861–1958." Doctoral diss., New York University, 1959.

Notes

1. John S. Haller, Jr., *American Medicine in Transition, 1840–1910* (Urbana: University of Illinois Press, 1981). See also John Duffy, *The Healers: A History of American Medicine* (Urbana: University of Illinois Press, 1979).

2. Paula Rogers Lupcho, "The Professionalization of American Physical Education, 1885–1930" (Ph.D. diss., University of California, Berkeley, 1986).

3. See examples in William Alcott, *The Laws of Health* (Boston: John P. Jewett, 1857); Idem, *The Young Woman's Book of Health* (New York: C. M. Saxton, 1859); Catharine Beecher, *Physiology and Calisthenics for Schools and Families* (New York: Harper and Brothers, 1856). See also Haller, *American Medicine*, 100–149; and James C. Whorton, *Crusaders for Fitness: The History of American Health Reformers* (Princeton University Press, 1982).

4. Catharine Beecher, *Educational Reminiscences and Suggestion* (New York: J. B. Ford and Co., 1874).

5. Catharine E. Beecher, *Treatise on Domestic Economy*, rev. ed. (New York: Harper and Brothers, 1870), 56. See also Ellen W. Gerber, *Innovators and Institutions in Physical Education* (Philadelphia: Lea & Febiger, 1971), 252–258; Mabel Lee, *A History of Physical Education and Sports in the USA* (New York: John Wiley & Sons, 1983), 46.

6. Lupcho, "Professionalization," 28.

7. Ibid., 29.

8. Ibid., 30.

9. William T. Harris, "Physical Training," in *Physical Training: A Full Report of the Papers and Discussions of the Conference Held in Boston in November, 1889* (Boston: Press of George H. Ellis, 1890), 1.

10. William Blaikie, *How to Get Strong and Stay So* (New York: Harper and Brothers, 1884).

11. Lupcho, "Professionalization," 32.

12. John A. Lucas and Ronald A. Smith, *Saga of American Sport* (Philadelphia: Lea & Febiger, 1978), 123–266.

13. George H. Taylor, *An Exposition on the Swedish Movement Cure* (New York: Fowler and Wells, 1860); Charles F. Taylor, *Theory and Practice of the Movement Cure* (Philadelphia: Lindsay and Blakiston, 1861).

14. William B. Carpenter, *Principles of Mental Physiology* (London: Henry S. King & Co., 1875).

15. For a more detailed analysis of this view, see Anita Clair Fellman and Michael Fellman, *Making Sense of Self: Medical Advice Literature in Late Nineteenth Century America* (Philadelphia: University of Pennsylvania Press, 1981).

16. Carpenter, *Mental Physiology*.

17. Wilhelm Wundt, *Lectures on Human and Animal Psychology*, trans. J. E. Creighton and E. B. Titchener (New York: Macmillan, 1901).

18. Lupcho, "Professionalization," 38.

19. Edward M. Hartwell, *On the Philosophy of Exercise* (Boston: Cupples, Upham & Co., 1887), 22.

20. Lupcho, "Professionalization," 40.

21. Ibid., 40–41.

22. Jay Seaver, "Military Training as an Exercise," in *Proceedings of the American Association for the Advancement of Physical Education, Third Annual Meeting* (Brooklyn: Rome Brothers, 1887), 18.

23. George M. Beard, *American Nervousness* (New York: G. P. Putnam, 1881).

24. Randolph Fairies, "The Therapeutic Value of Exercise," in *Proceedings of the American Association for the Advancement of Physical Education, Eighth Annual Meeting* (New Haven, Conn.: Press of Clarence H. Ryder, 1894), 30–37.

25. Hamilton D. Wey, "Physical Training for Youthful Criminals," in *Proceedings for the American Association for the Advancement of Physical Education, Fourth Annual Meeting* (New Haven, Conn.: L. S. Punderson and Sons, 1889), 17–35.

26. Lupcho, "Professionalization," 47.

27. Angelo Mosso, "Training of the Human Body," in *Proceedings of the American Association for the Advancement of Physical Education, Eighth Annual Meeting* (New Haven, Conn.: Press of Clarence H. Ryder, 1894), 39.

28. Harriet I. Ballentine, "Should Physical Education in Colleges be Compulsory," in *Proceedings of the American Association for the Advancement of Physical Education, Ninth Annual Meeting* (New Haven, Conn.: Press of Clarence H. Ryder, 1894), 114.

29. Edward Clarke, *Sex and Education: Or a Fair Chance for the Girls* (Boston: Osgood & Co., 1873).

30. Hartwell, *Philosophy of Exercise*, 17.

31. Dudley A. Sargent, "The Physical Test of Man," in *Proceedings of the American Association for the Advancement of Physical Education, Fifth Annual Meeting* (Ithaca, N.Y.: Andrus and Church, 1890), 44; Charles Roberts, *A Manual of Anthropometry: Or, A Guide to the Physical Examination and Measurement of the Human Body* (London: J. & A. Churchill, 1878).

32. Roberta J. Park, "Science, Service, and the Professionalization of Physical Education: 1885–1905," *Research Quarterly for Exercise and Sport Centennial Issue* (April 1985): 13.

33. Sargent, "Physical Test," 50–51.

34. John F. Bovard and Frederick W. Cozens, *Tests and Measurements in Physical Education, 1861–1925: A Treatment of their Original Sources with Critical Comment* (University of Oregon Publications, Physical Education Series, 1926), 15.

35. Edward Hitchcock, "A Comparative Study of Average Measurements," in *Proceedings of the American Association for the Advancement of Physical Education, Sixth Annual Meeting* (Ithaca, N.Y.: Andrus & Church, 1891); Delphine Hanna and Nellie A. Spore, "Effects of College Work Upon the Health of Women," *American Physical Education Review* (known hereafter as APER) 4:3 (September 1899): 279–280; Gerber, *Innovators and Institutions*, 329.

36. Hitchcock, 40.

37. George W. Fitz, "Psychological Aspects of Exercise With and Without Apparatus," in *Proceedings of the American Association for the Advancement of Physical Education, Eighth Annual Meeting* (New Haven, Conn.: Press of Clarence H. Ryder, 1894), 14–15.

38. Hartwell, *Philosophy of Exercise*, 3.

39. Sargent, "Physical Test," and idem, "The System of Physical Training at the Hemenway Gymnasium," in *Boston Physical Training Conference* (Boston: Press of George H. Ellis, 1890), 62–76.

40. Bovard and Cozens, 6.

41. Henry Metzner, *History of the American Turners* (Rochester, N.Y: National Council of American Turners, 1974), 25.

42. Emil Rinsch, *The History of the Normal College of the American Gymnastic Union of Indiana University, 1866–1966* (Bloomington: Indiana University, 1966), 139.

43. W. K. Streit, "Normal College of the American Gymnastic Union," *The Physical Educator* 20 (May 1963): 51–55.

44. Gerber, *Innovators and Institutions*, 268–69.

45. Lupcho, "Professionalization," 69.

46. George Herbert Mead, *Mind, Self, and Society*, ed. Charles W. Morris (University of Chicago Press, 1974); John Dewey, *Democracy and Education* (New York: The Free Press, 1966); Donald J. Mrozek, *Sport and American Mentality, 1880–1910* (Knoxville: University of Tennessee Press, 1983).

47. Dominick Cavallo, *Muscles and Morals: Organized Playgrounds and Urban Reform* (Philadelphia: University of Pennsylvania Press, 1981).

48. Carl Ziegler, "The Preparation of the Director of Physical Education," *APER* 21:8 (November 1916): 462–471.

49. Gerber, *Innovators and Institutions*, 349.

50. Ibid., 349.

51. Lupcho, "Professionalization," 276.

52. Gerber, *Innovators and Institutions*, 298.

53. Ibid., 299.

54. John Swett, ed., *Second Biennial Report of the Superintendent of Public Instruction of the State of California, 1866–1867* (Sacramento: D. W. Gelincks, State Printer, 1867), 265.

55. Gerber, *Innovators and Institutions*, 101.

56. Jakob Bolin, "Presidential Address at the Annual Meeting of the Physical Education Society of New York and Vicinity, December 4, 1896," *APER* 2:1 (March 1897): 6–7.

57. Lupcho, "Professionalization," 278.

58. "Editorial," *APER* 19:6 (June 1914): 479–480.

59. S. Lyman Hillby, "Statutory Provisions for Physical Education in the United States from 1899–1930," (master's thesis, Stanford University, 1930).

60. K. M. Cook, "State Laws and Regulations Governing Teachers Certificates," Bulletin No. 19 (Bureau of Education, 1927): 280–285.

61. Elmer Berry, "Problems in the Recruiting of Teachers of Physical Education," *APER* 25:6 (June 1920): 233–239.

62. Frank A. North, "Working Conditions of Teachers of Physical Training," *APER* 28:10 (December 1923): 469.

Toward the Reform of Physical Education: 1900–1939

General Events

1900 Boxer Rebellion in China, U.S. sent troops

1901 President William McKinley assassinated by Leon Czolgosz

1903 Panama Canal agreement signed; first airplane flight by Orville Wright

1906 Great San Francisco earthquake and fire

1907 Nationwide financial depression

1909 Admiral Robert E. Peary reached North Pole; National Conference on the Negro held, led to establishment of the National Association for the Advancement of Colored People (NAACP)

1910 Boy Scouts of America founded

1911 First transcontinental plane flight

1912 U.S. sent marines to Nicaragua

1913 U.S. blockades Mexico

1914 President Wilson declares neutrality re: war in Europe

1915 First telephone conversation coast to coast; Lusitania sunk by Germans, 128 American passengers perished

1916 Jeanette Rankin, first woman member of Congress, from Montana; John Dewey published *Democracy and Education*

1917 U.S. enters World War I

1920 19th Amendment ratified, giving women right to vote

1924 Law approved by Congress making all American Indians citizens of the U.S.

1925 Scopes trial in Tennessee regarding teaching evolution in the schools

1927 Charles A. Lindbergh flew nonstop from New York to Paris

1928 Amelia Earhart was first woman aviator to cross the Atlantic Ocean

1929 St. Valentine's Day massacre in Chicago; stock market crash; Depression began

1931 Empire State Building opened

1933 Prohibition ended; U.S. abandons gold standard

1935 Will Rogers killed in plane crash; Senator Huey Long (La.) assassinated

Sport and Physical Education

1885 American Association for the Advancement of Physical Education founded

1887 First National Women's Singles tennis championship

1888 Amateur Athletic Union founded

1889 Boston Conference in the Interest of Physical Training

1891 Basketball invented by James A. Naismith

1899 Committee on Women's Basketball; American Association for the Advancement of Physical Education (AAAPE) formed

1900 Davis Cup tennis competition began; American League of Professional Baseball Clubs formed

1903 First baseball "World Series" played

1905 Intercollegiate Athletic Association of the United States founded, would later evolve into the NCAA

1906 Playground Association of America founded

1910 Jack Johnson/James J. Jeffries boxing match

1916 American Tennis Association founded by black tennis players

1919 Chicago Black Sox baseball scandal

1919–20 Man O'War won twenty of twenty-one horse races

1922 Paris track meet sponsored by Federation Sportive Feminine Internationale (FSFI)

1923 White House Conference on Women's Athletics

1929 Carnegie Foundation's investigation of men's college athletics

1930 Bobby Jones won Grand Slam in golf

1931 Mabel Lee first woman president of the American Physical Education Association (APEA)

1932 Babe Didrikson starred in 1932 Olympics

1934 Madison Square Garden hosts Men's Collegiate basketball tournament

Sport and Physical Education Time Line from: Betty Spears and Richard A. Swanson, History of Sport and Physical Education in the United States (Dubuque, Ia.: Wm. C. Brown, 1988), 150, 206.

The Transformation of Physical Education and the Adoption of Sports Programs

Significant reform in the composition of physical education took place during the early part of the twentieth century. Among the more significant reforms that occurred was the move toward social development objectives, the adoption of sports by physical education, and the development of play theory.

For almost a century, physical education was focused on making the greatest possible contribution to the health of students. Early pioneers in physical education were doctors and educators who provided students with information and lifestyle orientations that were supposed to contribute to their personal health and well-being. The medium they used to deliver the message revolved around course work in hygiene, physiology, and instruction in fitness activities. For the most part, the fitness activities that were utilized prior to 1900 were gymnastics and calisthenics.

American education was undergoing reform. The new educational philosophy believed that the education of students should include social development objectives. In order to articulate these new ideas, physical education adopted new activities and introduced additional objectives. According to Lewis, the transformation of physical education began with the "athletics are educational" movement, 1906–1916, and was consummated during the age of "sports for all," which began in 1917 and ended in 1939. The result of this transformation was that the traditional health and fitness objectives of physical education were subjugated to the social development objectives. Physical fitness exercises were relegated to a position of importance that was secondary to providing instruction in sports.[1] The important question is whether this change in the focus and scope of physical education was the result of a philosophical reorientation by members of the profession or the result of external forces which physical educators had little or no control over.[2] According to Lewis, "In response to outside forces and developments within education between 1906 and 1916, physical educators began seriously to consider the place of sports instruction in the basic curriculum and gave some thought to extending the program to include supervised competition for highly skilled students."[3]

During the early part of the twentieth century, the American public was very interested in athletic competition. The sports pages of the daily papers were just as popular then as they are now. Physical educators capitalized on this high interest in sports and began to reform their philosophy in order to accommodate sports into the curriculum. According to Bennett and Lee, the addition of sports was the result of a determined effort by the American Physical Education Association to put athletics into education and education into athletics.[4] Apparently, what physical educators failed to realize at this time was that very soon serious athletic competition and intramural sports would challenge traditional physical education activities like gymnastics and calisthenics.

By 1930 almost all of the instructional activities in physical education were devoted to sports and intramural programs. Lewis (1969) states that there were several developments that led to the adoption of sports programs in physical education. These developments occurred in three areas: competitive athletics, physical education, and social reform.[5]

Prior to 1906, physical education programs in the nation's colleges were administered by the faculty, but this was not the case with athletic competition. Athletic competition was governed by athletic associations that were controlled by students and alumni. This created many problems. There was no national governing body that effectively oversaw intercollegiate athletic competition. Students of questionable character appear to have enrolled in colleges and universities just to play football, baseball, basketball, and other sports. Faculty became outraged at the practices of some of these athletic associations who would field teams in the name of the university. It was not too long before the faculty finally achieved control over athletic competition at both the high school and college level.

At the secondary level, this control was solidified in the form of merging athletics and physical education into a single entity. Both the public and private secondary schools hired more athletic directors and coaches (not necessarily physical educators) to teach physical education and provide instruction in sports. During this time, interest in physical education grew and became quite popular. There was a significant increase in the number of physical education programs, along with changes in how physical educators were academically prepared. This was seen in the philosophical shift away from the medical orientation that was emblematic of the early professional preparation in physical education. Physical educators no longer received their professional preparation in schools of medicine. Instead they were trained as educators and soon began to replace doctors in positions of leadership within the field.

Women dominated the ranks of physical educators, and while there were male physical educators, most men preferred to become coaches instead of physical educators. From 1900 to about 1920, most physical education programs did not offer course work in coaching. However, there was a need to train coaches, and many coaching schools were created to do this. In 1919, George Huff developed the first degree program in coaching at the University of Illinois. Other established universities soon developed similar programs to train coaches. While these expanded curricular offerings that focused on coaching were needed, it was not necessary to have a college degree to coach in the high schools or colleges. Unfortunately, we will see that the practice of hiring coaches who were not properly trained would serve to undermine the profession of physical education.

Recreation was a new area of study, and this emerging profession promoted the adoption of directed play as an answer to the problems that were created by the impact of economic forces upon society and attendant social structures. It appeared that the emerging profession of physical education was undergoing constructive reform and would soon become a respected professional member of the educational establishment. Unfortunately this did not happen as expected. Lewis (1969) believes that the most important factor in the transformation of physical education was the existence of highly organized, well-established, and popular varsity athletic competition.[6] Although physical education and athletics share a common history and a common interest, there are distinctive differences. These distinctive differences are what concerned physical educators in the early part of the twentieth century. Would their professional identity be compromised by including serious athletic competition and coaches within the domain of physical education? Was the transformation of physical education in the best interests of the profession?

From 1906 to 1916, the theme of "Athletics are Educational" was a dominant factor in physical education. In order to build upon this concept, college presidents and administrators in the nation's public and private schools assumed responsibility for intercollegiate and interscholastic athletic programs. From 1917 to 1939 the theme changed from "Athletics are Educational" to "Sports for All" which Lewis (1969) calls the final stage in the transformation of physical education.[7]

Athletic competition was heavily promoted. The National Committee on Physical Education and the National Amateur Athletic Federation (NAAF) were charged with increasing sports participation throughout the land.[8] In 1918, The National Collegiate Athletic Association (NCAA) authorized a resolution that called for colleges to make adequate provisions in their schedule of classes that would allow students to participate in physical training and sports. The NCAA worked closely with the National Committee on Physical Education to promote athletic participation in the nation's schools and colleges.[9]

By this time, most states had passed legislation that mandated that physical education be taught in the schools. The nation's public schools were in need of qualified physical educators to fill teaching positions, but there was a shortage of teachers. In answer to the demand for qualified physical educators, colleges and universities soon established physical education departments where students could earn a degree in the field and become employed in the schools. However, there was a significant problem. There was a dearth of qualified physical educators who would qualify for academic rank. In their zeal to meet the demand for physical educators, unqualified individuals were given administrative appointments by colleges and universities as directors of physical education programs. In 1929, a survey was published that found that out of 177 physical education directors surveyed, only twenty-three had majored in physical education in college. Only four had earned master's degrees in the field of education. Success as a football coach was the lone requirement for many of these "directors."[10] One observer remarked that, "Of all the fields of higher education, physical education shows the largest number of members with the rank of professor who have only a bachelor's degree or no degree whatever."[11]

This did not bode well for a profession that worked so hard to establish a credible theory base and to create high professional standards. However, there was no doubt that sports were becoming the dominant focus in the curriculum of most physical education departments. This is understandable. The American public was excited about athletic competition more so than they were about physical education. In addition, many coaches without a degree in physical education (or any other subject for that matter), were offered jobs in physical education departments because of their background as an athlete or as a coach. These individuals could provide instruction in sports skills and little else. By the 1930s, coaching courses had become the primary focus of many physical education departments that offered an undergraduate degree. The Carnegie Foundation released the results of a study in 1929 that said physical education had been used to turn colleges and universities into giant athletic agencies.[12] Lewis (1969) provides additional insight to the Carnegie study: "opinion favoring sports so pervaded society that few saw the need to question the value system which supported it, but there was evidence that physical education had been reconstructed not for the purpose of fulfilling the ideal of education for all through sports and athletics but to serve the interests of intercollegiate athletics."[13] Many physical educators were very concerned with the erosion of the profession that was caused by hiring unqualified coaches to provide instruction in physical education.

As athletic competition and related interests assumed a dominant role in most physical education programs at both the interscholastic and intercollegiate level from 1906 to 1939, it became necessary for the profession to modify its philosophy and accommodate these interests. Jesse F. Williams managed to convince those physical educators who were opposed to accommodating sports that it was the responsibility of the profession to make participation in competitive athletics an educational experience for students. Williams was so successful in this effort that the author of the 1929 Carnegie study that identified physical education as the servant of athletics remarked that education as mind and body "gave currency to a definition of physical education that includes all bodily activity—even sport itself."[14] The legacy of Williams and the accommodation of sport by physical education is alive and well as we head toward the twenty-first century.

Today, physical education programs at the K–12 level incorporate "all bodily activity": sports, lifetime fitness activities, developmental-directed play, and appropriate games. Physical education teachers in the public schools are highly trained professionals who usually wear two hats, one as a physical education teacher and one as a coach. Small colleges and universities continue to employ faculty who both teach physical education and coach intercollegiate athletic teams. Within institutions of higher learning, there continues to be a chasm between coaches and physical educators. In the larger colleges and universities, faculty in physical education departments rarely coach. They devote their professional efforts to teaching, research, and community service. Big time athletic programs that exist in the nation's colleges and universities hire coaches, and the expectation is that these coaches will devote their time and energy to develop strong athletic teams. These coaches rarely teach courses in the physical education department. While many of these coaches have degrees in physical education, it is not that unusual to find coaches with degrees in other fields like English or history.

Physical education, like all professions, undergoes periodic reform. The reform that physical education underwent in the early part of the twentieth century did result in a number of significant outcomes. We have already seen how physical education was transformed by sport. We will now turn our attention to the development of play theory, which was one of the more profound changes that shaped the development of physical education in the twentieth century.

The Development of Play Theory: 1900–1915

Between 1900 and 1930, physical educators debated appropriate methods and goals for research and teaching. This debate was a result of changing beliefs and trends in science, broad social changes in American life, and changing developments in education. Perhaps the most powerful change that occurred was the acceptance of play, games, dance, and sport as methods for imparting educational goals, a trend that reflected a growing interest in the phenomenon of play that was evident even before the turn of the century.

Herbert Spencer

One of the earliest champions of play was the Englishman Herbert Spencer (1820–1903). As early as 1855 Spencer conceived of play as an instinctual, natural, and enjoyable activity essential for physical welfare and development.[15] An advocate of Darwin's theory of evolution, Spencer believed that play could be used to expend excess energy. This aspect interested Spencer because he believed that excess energy was that which was not necessary for survival.[16] In *Principles of Psychology* (1890), William James agreed that play behavior was instinctual, but he did not believe, as Spencer did, that instinctual behavior was simply a reflex in more complex animals. Instead James believed that habits and impulses combined with one's capacity to reason and therefore helped determine human behavior.[17]

Karl Groos

One of the more influential play theorists was Karl Groos. In 1898 Groos hypothesized that humans played as preparation for life through imitating others. He believed that play behavior was instinctual, but it was an imperfect instinct and needed to be added to through one's life experiences. His logic was that if, for some reason, certain kinds of detailed instincts were needed for more serious acts of survival, then humans would have these specific instincts at birth. Play would provide the necessary experiences and prepare the individual for the coming tasks of life.[18] Groos' theory of play as an educational vehicle that could lead to improved adult behavior was important to physical educators because play was considered the exclusive domain of physical education. Play eventually became a critical component of educational theory, and consequently Groos' theory was used to promote physical education as essential to individual development.

G. Stanley Hall

Another important contributor to play theory was G. Stanley Hall, who taught at Clark University in Worcester, Massachusetts, and was a leader in the child study movement. Hall popularized the saying "ontogeny recapitulates phylogeny," a concept of recapitulation that sees childhood as a rehearsal for the evolutionary process.[19] In Hall's theory each individual must replay the prehistory of the species. Each stage of human hereditary development is recorded in the phyla of nerve cells of the individual. From birth, an individual mimics the development of the species by assuming a type of behavior that was required in the development of the species.[20] Play was felt to be a fundamental form of the history of the human species, unlike gymnastics, which was not fundamental but only recently invented by humans. According to the theory "ontogeny recapitulates phylogeny," each stage of development promotes the acquisition of the necessary motor skills and psychosocial growth to move on to the next stage of development.

In Hall's view, play and its natural extensions—games and sport— were the ideal mechanisms for development. "This is why, unlike gymnastics, play has as much soul as body, and also why it so makes for unity of body and soul that the proverb 'man is whole only when he plays' suggests that the purest plays are those that enlist both alike. . . . Thus understood, play is the ideal type of exercise for the young, most favorable for the growth, and most self-regulating in both kind and amount."[21] This quote expresses his belief that play had as much "soul as body" and helped make for the unity of the soul and body. His belief in the proverb "man is whole only when he plays" implies that the purest play was that which used both soul and body equally. This saying reflected the nineteenth-century belief in the unity of the mind and body, yet brought physical education into the twentieth century because it used theories of evolution and science. Hall believed that 811 human characteristics could be learned in the developmental play activities of children. He further believed that muscles were the organs of expression and that they were the vehicles of imitation, obedience, character, and even of manners and customs.[22] Hall envisioned physical education as the educational process that could connect matters of the body and the mind.

Hall's educational philosophy provided enthusiastic support for play as an essential component of education and thus provided a theoretical basis to physical educators who desired to incorporate play, games, and sport in physical education classes.

Luther Halsey Gulick

As discussed in chapter 9, Luther Halsey Gulick (1865–1918) was one of the most important physical educators of the nineteenth and twentieth centuries. Gulick was an early adherent of play as a major component of physical education and made significant contributions to the growing literature on play theory. In *A Philosophy of Play*, published posthumously in 1920, Gulick emphasized the benefits of play for the development of both the private (sense of self) and social aspects (social self) of the individual.[23] Play developed the social conscious on which democratic civilization was dependent.

John Dewey

Preeminent among educators and philosophers and important to play theory and physical education was John Dewey (1859–1952). Dewey believed that education was necessary for democratic citizenship, social efficiency, and social experience. Dewey considered mind and body to be integrated parts of the human whole, and he believed that the body or physical aspect of humans served as the conductor of experience. Once again, the philosophical position of the body relative to epistemological considerations and the nature of our existence becomes an important issue. Dewey's philosophy is in contrast with the tradition of classical realists and dualists who believe that the world of the mind is more important than the world of experience. Dewey believed that the socialized mind shared with others a sense of similar experiences and that the agreement among people based on their common experiences produces a better, more efficient society.[24] Dewey believed that we should learn how to think and act based on our experiences rather than on some predetermined set of rules. A collection of experiences that were shared could be used to create "consensual" knowledge, and the human condition would therefore be improved. Dewey's pragmatic philosophy, based on the work of Charles Peirce, William James, and other pragmatist philosophers, was a radical departure from traditional philosophies, and it had a profound impact on the theory of play.

Dewey believed play to be a purposeful activity that directed interest through physical means. Play was not a physical act that had no meaning. Rather it was an activity that integrated mind and body. This approach gave the play act meaning, and therefore it became an argument for play as an important educational tool. Play became a "quality" experience valuable for its educational possibilities rather than an activity in and of itself. The ultimate product of Dewey's educational process would be an individual who participated fully as a member of a democratic society.

These kinds of discussions might seem irrelevant to an understanding of physical education, yet they are important in the early twentieth century because they justify entirely new activities in physical education. Before Dewey, playful group activities such as football and baseball were considered poor choices to develop health and community. The philosophy of Dewey and his colleagues was used to justify team sports in physical education because they promoted democratic activities and social interaction. The societal benefits derived from participation in physical education were very significant and did much to insure strong support for physical education and athletic programs.

Advocates and Adversaries: The Promotion of Play

Play as a natural developmental tool was increasingly recognized by physical educators, yet it was accepted with varying amounts of enthusiasm. Physical educators, like many Americans, viewed the usefulness of play with some ambivalence. As early as 1887 Jay Seaver spoke against the use of military drill in physical education programs, arguing that the lack of play in such exercises was not beneficial to the student.[25] The rationale for his program was that the young of every species is fond of play and that play fosters the muscular development necessary for self-preservation.[26]

Yet most physical educators believed that play, games, and sport should play a secondary role in physical education rather than a primary role. In 1889 Edward Hartwell presented the consensus viewpoint of the profession. Hartwell recognized the usefulness of play but upheld the educational superiority of gymnastics. As a proponent of gymnastic activities, Hartwell believed that the essential difference between sporting activities and gymnastics was the nature of the products of the activities. The goal of sporting activities was one of recreation, whereas the goal of gymnastics was discipline, training for pleasure, health, and skill. Hartwell believed that gymnastics was more comprehensive in its aims, more formal, more elaborate, and more systematic in its methods. Furthermore, one was able to gain more significant, or measurable, results. Sporting activities during this era were marked by their "childish" origins, and as a result were considered inadequate for physical education.[27]

Play and Popular Culture

The general public began to take an interest in play between 1890 and 1900, and this phenomenon was noted by physical educators. In 1886 sandgardens (piles of sand in which children could play) were built in Boston to provide a place for wholesome play for children who lived in crowded city neighborhoods. In 1889 the Charlesbank Outdoor Gymnasium opened in Boston as part of a large park system that was initiated ten years earlier. Similarly, New York City opened several school playgrounds for recreational use in 1889, and Chicago opened the South Park Playgrounds in 1903. Luther Gulick organized the Public School Athletic League in New York City in 1903, and in 1906 the Playground Association of America was founded. Play captured the interest of the public, municipal government, foundations, and reform groups, and as a consequence the interest in play education grew.[28]

Play versus Gymnastics

The popularity of play with the public at large and among the ranks of physical education professionals between 1900 and 1915 increasingly put advocates of gymnastics exercise on the defensive. Gymnastics advocates found it necessary to acknowledge the perceived benefits of play, games, and sport while at the same time tried to make a case for gymnastic programs. William Skarstrom, M.D., of Teachers College, Columbia University, wrote a series of articles arguing for the use of gymnastics to correct improper posture and development.[29] Skarstrom believed that the function of physical education was to promote community, social success, efficiency, management of self, physical efficiency, and business success.[30] Accomplishment of these goals required a variety of physical activities, among them gymnastics exercise. Skarstrom also acknowledged the usefulness of sporting activities in developing quick perception and judgment.

In spite of the efforts of men like Skarstrom, gymnastics continued to diminish in popularity as the primary component in physical education programs. By 1915 those who favored gymnastics programs sought equal time with sporting activities in physical education programs. By this time play was the primary method of physical education, and gymnastics was used primarily to correct posture problems. In 1912 the editorial opinion of the American Physical Education Review stated that "athletics, properly conducted, are one of the strongest social and moral forces we can use in the development of manhood."[31] In the same year Paul Phillips wrote:

> [The] importance of play in the physical development and education of the individual has become better recognized and appreciated year by year. . . . It has been shown that normal play is not only important but also absolutely necessary to the normal development of boys or girls both physically and mentally, and morally as well. Play and the play spirit constitute perhaps the most important single element in growth and education: in fact, looked at broadly, play is the most serious thing in life.[32]

Although gymnastic enthusiasts like Skarstrom kept the gymnastics issue in print, by 1915 the number of educators who believed in the virtues of play was overwhelming. New members to the field of physical education such as Clark Hetherington, and playground leaders such as Joseph Lee and Henry Curtis, took up the cause of play and influenced their colleagues through their writing, lectures, and association work.[33] These men pressed for the general acceptance of play with the same fervor and intensity with which early nineteenth-century physical educators promoted gymnastics. Play became the dominant method of physical education, replacing gymnastics by 1915. The spirit of sportsmanship, which began in England, occupied a position of importance when the objectives of physical education were discussed.

Play in Physical Education: 1900–1915

According to leading physical educators in the early 1900s, play had several distinct advantages over gymnastics. Henry Curtis stated that a team game was one in which individual players substituted individual goals for team goals and blended their individual identities into a new unity. Individuals played as a team because the game required group consciousness, loyalty, and leadership. Curtis felt that team games were the highest form of play and one of the highest forms of human activity.[34] We can see the influence of Dewey on the thinking of Henry Curtis regarding the advantages of play over gymnastics. The inability of the proponents of gymnastics to put up a unified front to defend their interests added to the demise of gymnastics. In addition, the visibility and popularity of intercollegiate and professional sport help propel play, games, and sport to the forefront of physical education, much to the detriment of gymnastics.

Luther Gulick was another strong supporter of play activity and used the biological rationale of recapitulation in his explanation of the play instinct. Gulick believed that sport activities played a critical role in the development of boys, because sports were an inherited activity from a bygone era. Humans needed to survive through the skills of running, throwing, and striking, and sport activities arose because of a need to practice these skills. Gulick concluded that humans of his day were the survivors of those whose lives depended on their ability to run, strike, and throw.[35]

In addition to their physical skills, however, were the mental and moral qualities of endurance, pluck, teamwork, and fair play. These qualities were developed in connection with play, and because these qualities were the same as those that defined manhood, athletics became both a measure of manhood and a rite of passage for many.

One of the most important and far-reaching effects of the early twentieth-century debate regarding play in physical education was its association with arguments of manliness. Most believed that if athletics, especially team games, were a measure of manliness, then there is little rationale for the use of athletics for the development of women. Luther Gulick used the manliness argument to show that athletics were gender-defined activities and were therefore inappropriate as a means of developing femininity. However, Gulick did approve of basketball for girls.[36] Drawing from the idea that form follows function, Gulick stated that prepubescent girls could be very athletic because they had not yet begun the maturing process into womanhood.[37] Sport activities supervised by school officials provided women with the exercise and recreation that was necessary in the urban environment. Of great concern to parents and school officials, however, was the fear that women who participate in sport activities might assume masculine qualities. This same logic still exists today, although it is not as pervasive.

In summation, advocates of play were in general agreement about the desired outcomes of play, games, and sport. Play developed health and vigor; it developed character and the associated habits of loyalty, sportsmanship, friendliness, honesty, and leadership; it developed ideals such as democracy through group cooperation; it developed moral and ethical values; and it promoted worthy group membership. Finally, because play was instinctive and natural, it was educative. These were the primary concepts in the minds of physical educators and formed the theoretical base of twentieth-century physical education. The evolutionary scope and content of physical education would be shaped by the efforts of a new generation of physical education, resulting in a paradigmatic basis that incorporated new ideas from education, psychology, and sociology. The results of their effort and commitment became manifest in the form and content of twentieth-century concepts of physical education.

The Paradigmatic Basis of the New Physical Education: 1915–1930

The Architects of the New Physical Education: Clark Hetherington, Thomas D. Wood, and Rosalind Cassidy

The period from World War I to 1930 was characterized by the acceptance of the social development objectives in the form of psychosocial and behavioristic principles as a major part of the theoretical foundation of physical education. These changes in theory were similar to those that occurred in other disciplines such as education, psychology, and sociology, and also changes in society. The three architects for the "new physical education" were Clark Hetherington, Thomas D. Wood, and Rosalind Cassidy. Hetherington, who studied with G. Stanley Hall, successfully integrated into written form the new theoretical position of physical education. His seminal work, *School Program in Physical Education*, provided the direction for the discipline early in the twentieth century.[38] Although there have been semantic changes over the years, the conceptual structure has remained virtually unchanged.

Components and Goals of Physical Education

Hetherington divided physical education into four separate but cooperative areas: organic, psychomotor, character, and intellect. These four areas were blended together in varying degrees to produce five stated objectives. The first objective was the "organization of child life as expressed in big-muscle or physical training activities."[39] This organization required adult leadership. Only through adult leadership could a child's natural play instinct be guided to its full and complete end, and the necessity of adult supervision meant that the use of play was a legitimate function of education. The adult role was to make the play act efficient and to aid in the democratic organization of play.[40] Reflecting the thinking of Dewey, Hetherington considered physical education an excellent vehicle for imparting democratic skills because of the ability of the teacher to observe the student in action and to provide appropriate guidance.

The second objective of physical education was the development of social adjustment skills based on the customs of society. Hetherington felt that play activities were economic, defensive, domestic, communicative, civic, interpretive, artistic, and recreative.[41] Although big-muscle activities did not directly teach adult adjustment skills, play activities provided the proper developmental foundation for acquiring such skills in later life. This objective reflected the thinking of Luther Gulick and his recapitulation theory: proper use of play created the foundation for the development of skills that are necessary in adult life.

Hetherington's third objective of physical education was that of developing latent powers and capacities, and this objective used the theories of psychologist Edward L. Thorndike. Thorndike's stimulus-response theory stated that learning was the result of repeated positive responses to specific stimuli. Each student would either try to gain satisfaction from the stimulus or try to remove the annoying stimulus altogether.[42] Physical education could be used to create certain kinds of stimuli in play so that children could practice those skills that would aid them as adults.

The fourth objective was the development of character, and this objective remains one of the justifications for the inclusion of physical education in school curricula. Character was the appropriate and desirable combination of desires, impulses, habits, ideas, and ideals. Sport activities were particularly important to this objective, yet Hetherington objected to the idea that sport activities automatically instilled students with a long list of virtues. Leadership provided the crucial element in meeting the objective of building desirable character traits, and therefore without proper leadership the desirable character traits could not be developed. This is where properly conducted physical education was necessary. The idea that sport builds character remains a popular expression in the late twentieth century. The advantages and disadvantages of this type of thinking underwent serious discussion in the early twentieth century, and the same debate continues as we approach the twenty-first century.

Hetherington's fifth and final objective was to use big-muscle and fine motor movements to improve thinking. Big-muscle activity was superior because it developed what he called "strategic judgments." These were defined as alertness, quick response, and rapidity of movement. Hetherington believed that team games were filled with opportunities to learn these skills, and the proof of learning was in the "safety first motor efficiency" of athletes, who, as Hetherington noted, "are not run down by automobiles and street cars."[43] To Hetherington, the abilities acquired by athletes clearly had utility in the urban life of the early twentieth century. He contended that the strategic judgment that physical education could develop was essential for industrial productivity and adult recreation. If physical education could impart big-muscle skills into children and these skills had social benefits, then physical education should be an important component of the educational curriculum.

Promotion of Physical Education

Hetherington championed the educational and socially oriented objectives of physical education over the health objectives that were used to justify physical education in the nineteenth century by arguing that physical education required special faculties and leadership; that physical education was the only vehicle to condition self-directed health habits; and that exercise was necessary for adult health maintenance. Children needed four to five hours of physical activity daily, adolescents needed two to three hours daily, and adults needed only twenty minutes. The differences between these groups were due to the differences between the requirements of big-muscle activity. Children and adolescents needed big-muscle activity for development, whereas adults needed it for health maintenance.[44] Development was an outcome of physical activity and was differentiated from the term *growth*, which was the outcome of heredity. This line of thought identified development as the fundamental process of education, which was first built on the quality of play and work experience.[45]

The strong evolutionary, biological, and psychological influence on physical education thinking was extensive. It imparted a credibility and worthiness to physical education that demanded the attention of educated people. Play was very serious business. Gymnastics had only health benefits and, to Hetherington, was useful only as a rainy-day activity. Hetherington used such words as irksome, artificial, fatiguing, and uninteresting to describe gymnastic exercise. Play, on the other hand, could be systematically developed to achieve the objectives Hetherington outlined.[46] According to Hetherington:

> The natural physical-training (big muscle) activities are educationally more valuable than gymnastic drills. They give a certain development of intellectual, emotional, nervous, and organic powers not given in the same degree by any other kind of activity in child life, and it is impossible to gain the broad and more significant phases of these values through drills. A comparison of values makes apparent the greater importance of these natural activities.[47]

Hetherington's program provided the basis for the argument that physical education is an essential component of education. Eventually almost all physical educators came to enthusiastically embrace play, games, dance, and sport as the primary mode of physical education. Hetherington's rationale justifies the use of sport activities in the educational realm. Athletic teams exist in the United States at a level not seen anywhere else in the world. The justification of this system is best articulated by Clark Hetherington.

Physical Education Literature in the Early Twentieth Century

The publication of Hetherington's work marked the beginning of a time when views about the nature and methodology of physical education crystallized. During the 1920s many textbooks and manuals were written for physical education teachers and teacher-training programs. These publications reflected the directional scope that committed physical education to the physical, social, emotional, and intellectual development of the individuals. In 1927 Thomas Wood and Rosalind Cassidy published an influential text representative of this trend. Titled *The New Physical Education: A Program of Naturalized Activities of Education Toward Citizenship*, this book became one of the leading texts in physical education training programs.[48] *The New Physical Education* was an extension of Hetherington's aims and objectives of education, accepting intact that the concerns of physical education were organic, psychomotor, intellectual, and character building.

Science and the Quantification of Physical Education

Tests and Measurements

From 1915 to 1930, physical education reflected the work that was done in psychology and also the establishment of the science of teaching, or pedagogy. These trends were part of the progressive movement in American education, and they had a monumental effect. One example was the intelligence scale devised by Alfred Binet and Theodore Simon. The concept behind this particular scale led to the general conception of scale indexing for characteristics other than intelligence. It was a small step to develop indexed standards of performance in physical education.

The measurement of ability became the focus of much research in education, a movement that is rekindled every few decades.[49] Between 1908 and 1916, Thorndike and his fellow researchers at Columbia developed ability tests for arithmetic, spelling, reading, drawing, language ability, and handwriting. By 1918 hundreds of ability tests were devised. This enthusiasm for measurement and quantification, which had been largely a professional matter within psychology and education, gained in popularity.[50]

The quantification offered by intelligence and ability testing became a means toward a science of education. The goal was efficient education that would teach those essential skills that would enable the student to perform and contribute to society. This type of thinking stimulated a sweeping reexamination of curricula in physical education, which sought to define minimum competencies known as essentials. Measurement of essential skills (and defining what those skills were) became a major part of the science of education.

Physical educators engaged in defining motor ability and physical efficiency. Cardiac function was only one criteria. Tests that evaluated strength were pioneered by Dudley Allen Sargent. Work on motor ability tests and physical efficiency tests became popular around 1914 with the beginning of efficiency testing in Michigan, New Jersey, and New York. The California Decathlon Test was begun in 1918 under the supervision of Clark Hetherington, the first State Superintendent of Physical Education. Other work on physical ability testing came out of university departments of physical education such as the University of California, Berkeley (1917), the University of Oregon (1924), the University of Illinois (1919), Ohio State University (1920), and Oberlin College (1922). Most of these tests included such skills as running, jumping, throwing, and climbing. Some included proficiency in such gymnastic skills as marching, Indian clubs, vaulting, and rope climbing. Some required swimming proficiency. The science of physical education, which was reflected by anthropomorphic work in the nineteenth century, now manifested itself in tests of physical efficiency.

The Relationship Between Physical Ability and Mental Ability

The second major concern of physical education during the 1920s was the idea that physical ability is correlated to mental ability. Many physical educators of the late nineteenth century believed that physical activity promoted cognitive development. Yet this long-held belief was not widely accepted outside the physical education field, so in 1923 Landis, Burtt, and Nichols tested the idea "that physical prowess, especially as manifested in athletic achievement, implies inferior intellect."[51] Put differently, Landis, Burtt, and Nichols tested the idea that athletes are "dumb jocks." Their correlation study used four physical tests to measure physical ability: the hundred yard dash, the running broad jump, the baseball throw, and the fence climb. The Ohio State University intelligence test was used to determine mental capacity. Not surprisingly, no significant correlation was found between mental ability and physical ability, and other researchers validated their findings.[52]

Interest in these subjects remained high throughout the decade, yet several problems were noted in the studies that tried to correlate physical efficiency to mental capacity. Problems ranged from the lack of clearly defined criteria as to what constituted physical efficiency to the different populations used in the studies.[53] Perhaps the most serious problem with this type of research, however, was the desire on the part of physical educators to obtain the answers they wanted regardless of what their measurements were. This type of error in research is known as an artifact, which means the researcher commits a fundamental error in his or her research that invalidates the study.

Physical educators have long desired to demonstrate that a positive relationship exists between physical and mental ability. The persistence of this belief despite evidence to the contrary reflects the bias of physical educators. A conclusion by Vern S. Ruble in 1928 shows his desire to achieve specific results and serves as an example of a research artifact:

In no instance do we have a sufficient number of cases to establish norms, and, as has been suggested, it is impossible to draw any definite conclusions from a single test, but the foregoing data are very significant and indicate strongly that there is an important relationship between athletic ability and mental strength as measured by standardized psychological or intelligence tests.[54]

Cozens' work also contains this bias. He was certain that the physically well-developed child was brighter than the poorly developed child, and he believed that the level of physical ability of bright children was distinctly superior to that of dull and retarded children. He then asked why a correlation between intelligence and physical ability could not be found. Cozens concluded that the fault lay not with the premise but with the tests, specifically the physical efficiency tests.[55] In short, Cozens looked for a test that would prove his theory, rather than induce theories that were supported by the data. Both Cozens' and Ruble's work are examples of poor science in that their data did not change their opinions. However, they were much improved in one respect over the scientists who preceded them.

In spite of the desires of physical educators to prove that physical education improved intellectual performance, the quality of their research prevented them from doing so. So even though Cozens and Ruble tried to prove their pet theories, they honestly reported that they could not positively correlate intelligence and physicality. This condition was a significant change from the pseudoscience of the late nineteenth century, which allowed physical educators to connect physical education to any theory deemed desirable.

Physical Fitness Assessment

The purpose of physical ability testing was twofold: to create a measurement tool that could classify students according to ability, and to predict future achievement. Two of the leading persons in the area of tests and measurements in physical education were Frederick Rand Rogers and David Kingsley Brace, both trained at Teachers College, Columbia University. Teachers College was at the center of the educational testing movement during the 1920s.[56]

Rogers' book *Test and Measurement Programs in the Redirection of Physical Education* was one of the most interesting texts published during the 1920s.[57] Rogers resurrected strength testing as a major variable in measuring physical ability. From strength testing he derived a Strength Index represented by a single numerical value. Rogers' assumption was that strength was the major component of physical ability, especially in adolescent boys engaged in team games. From the Strength Index score an individual could be classified into a group with like ability. This homogeneity of groups was a necessary condition for Rogers' "redirection" of physical education. It was his opinion that inequality in competitive team games "misdirected" individuals from the goals that could be achieved in those types of activities. Social efficiency—defined as courage, perseverance, self-respect, self-confidence, fair play, cooperation, courtesy, and sympathy—could only be achieved when equality of competition was maintained. Unequal or mismatched teams served neither the loser (whose unabashed failure produced frustration) nor the winner (whose victory was too easily acquired). Using statistical procedures, the author converted the strength test score into an Athletic Index, which was interpreted as a numerical expression representing the total athletic ability of a subject.[58]

Rogers also used the Strength Index to determine a student's health and progress. Although Rogers believed that the function of the heart, digestion, and elimination could not be accurately measured, he assumed an indirect correlation between muscle strength and vital functions. The Physical Fitness Index was therefore a quotient that the physical educator could use to determine individual fitness needs.

The final index presented by Rogers was a refined statistical quotient for use by coaches of competitive athletic teams. Rogers explained the need for the index, along with its uses and limitations, when he said that it was a highly valid test of general athletic ability. Rogers noted that although it was adequate for most physical education situations, it was not an accurate measure of endurance and had no correlation with intelligence, two essential attributes of the competitive athlete. It could also be used to discover potential physical educators. To determine the Athletic Index, Rogers provided the following formula:[59]

Strength Index divided by 10

plus

Physical Fitness Index

plus

Intelligence Quotient

equals

The Athletic Index.

The more complex Athletic Index was designed to determine outstanding athletic potential. Intelligence represented by the Intelligence Quotient (IQ) score was added to the statistical analysis.

Much to the chagrin of many physical educators, Rogers cited literature that revealed a negative correlation between mental and physical ability. As for the athletic program, which Rogers viewed as a separate program, the purpose of athletics at any level was not the winning of the contest, but to make athletes live morally.[60]

Summary

Physical education underwent significant reform during this era. According to Lewis, the transformation of physical education was due to several developments. Among the most important was the existence of a highly organized, well-established, and very popular varsity athletic competition. Sports soon challenged traditional physical education activities. Social development objectives which could be taught through the medium of sports overshadowed physical education's traditional focus on health-related activities. Physical education expanded its scope and content to provide instruction in varsity athletic competition and the promotion of intramural sports. However, it appeared that physical education had been used to justify and create "giant athletic agencies" in the nation's colleges and universities. Many physical educators felt that their profession was being undermined by coaches who had little or no training in physical education but were employed in schools and colleges to both coach and teach physical education.

During the 1920s physical educators were significantly influenced by general trends in education. These trends blended considerations of child interest and motivation with desired social outcomes such as democratic citizenship and the measurements movement. Play, games, and sport were the natural activities of childhood, and if properly organized and directed they would develop desirable character traits and qualities that could be defined in physical, social, and psychological terms.

The development of physical education from 1900 to 1930 reflected the belief system of the larger society and the major trends in other academic disciplines. The nineteenth-century concept of health as a balance of mind, body, and will gave way to a more physical integration of mind and body that could be expressed in social and behavioral terms. Play theory provided the theoretical vehicle that enabled physical education to redefine itself in these social and behavioral terms.

Three elements of the theory remained unchanged. First, physical education contributed to the health of the individual. Second, physical activity was a major component of character development. Third, physical education was committed to the development of research theory and methodology. Play theory reinforced the idea that gross motor exercise through play developed those positive qualities that were called character.

From a philosophical and theoretical position, physical education focused on the development of the entire being. This was the objective of early nineteenth-century educators who wished to build body and will (character) through regulated exercise. Physical educators throughout the 1920s reinforced this same view. By 1930, the holistic view of physical education championed by Hetherington, Wood, and Cassidy had become the standard concept in physical education. The development of health, citizenship, moral conduct, and social growth was of most importance, and research increasingly focused on pedagogical methods that could facilitate this development. Physical education was committed to the whole being, yet had to separate and fragment the various aspects of the individual for analysis and measurement. The problem then became, how do we achieve reintegration of the whole person?

Discussion Questions

1. What arguments did the concept of "play" have to overcome before being taken seriously as a method of physical education?

2. Who were the major play theorists? What were their positions?

3. What influence did John Dewey have on the development of physical education?

4. How were athletics supposed to contribute to character formation, and what types of games supposedly did this the best?

5. What were the cooperative areas of Hetherington's physical education program? How did they work?

6. Describe the promotion of physical education between 1900 and 1930. What were the outcomes of physical education?

7. What impact did tests and measurements have on physical education? What was the relationship between physical ability and mental ability?

Suggestions for Further Reading

Betts, J. "Organized Sport in Industrial America." Doctoral diss., Columbia University, 1951.

Boyle, R. *Sport—Mirror of American Life.* Boston: Little, Brown, and Company, 1963.

Cozens, F. W., and F. S. Stumpf. *Sports in American Life.* Chicago: University of Chicago Press, 1953.

Dean, C. F. "A Historical Study of Physical Fitness in the United States, 1790–1961." Doctoral diss., George Peabody College for Teachers, 1964.

Lee, M., and B. L. Bennett. "This Is Our Heritage." *Journal of Health, Physical Education, and Recreation* 31 (April 1960): 25–33, 38–47, 52–58, 62–73, 76–85.

Petroskey, H. "A History of Measurement in Health and Physical Education." Doctoral diss., University of Iowa, 1946.

Rainwater, C. E. *The Play Movement in the United States.* Chicago: University of Chicago Press, 1922.

Zeigler, E. F. "History of Professional Preparation for Physical Education in the United States, 1861–1948." Doctoral diss., Yale University, 1950.

Notes

1. Guy M. Lewis, "Adoption of the Sports Program, 1906–39: The Role of Accommodation in the Transformation of Physical Education," *Quest* 12 (1969), 34.

2. Ibid., 34.

3. Ibid., 36.

4. Bruce Bennett and Mabel Lee, "This is Our Heritage," *Journal of Health, Physical Education, and Recreation,* XXXI (April 1960); Lewis, *Adoption of the Sports Program,* 35.

5. Lewis, *Adoption of the Sports Program,* 35.

6. Ibid., 35.

7. Ibid., 38.

8. Ibid., 38.

9. Ibid., 38.

10. Harry A. Scott, "A Personal Study of Directors. . . ," 1929, in *Athletics in Education* by Jesse Williams and William Hughes, (Philadelphia: Bureau of Publications, Teachers College, Columbia University, 1930), 119–125.

11. Howard J. Savage, *American College Athletics.* New York: Carnegie Foundation, Bulletin #23, 1929; Lewis, *Adoption of the Sports Program,* 39.

12 Ibid.

13. Lewis, *Adoption of the Sports Program,* 40.

14. Lewis, *Adoption of the Sports Program*, 42; Savage, *American College Athletics*.

15. Herbert Spencer, "Thoughts on Education," *American Journal of Education* 11:27 (June 1862): 491.

16. Herbert Spencer, *Principles of Psychology*, vol. 2, 3d ed. (New York: Appleton, 1896, first published in 1855).

17. William James, *Principles of Psychology*, vol. 2 (New York: Holt, 1890).

18. Karl Groos, *The Play of Animals*, trans. E. L. Baldwin (New York: Appleton, 1898).

19. Ontogeny recapitulates phylogeny was not an original discovery by Hall; it emerged from work being done by nineteenth-century embryologists who noted remarkable similarities between developing embryos of different animal species. Hall's contribution was the emphasis he placed on postnatal development. Paula Rogers Lupcho, "The Professionalization of American Physical Education, 1885–1930" (Ph.D. diss., University of California, Berkeley, 1986), 117.

20. G. Stanley Hall, *Adolescence: Its Psychology and Its Relation to Physiology, Anthropology, Sociology, Sex, Crime, Religion and Education*, vol. 1 (New York: Appleton, 1907).

21. Ibid., 203.

22. Ibid., 113.

23. Luther H. Gulick, *A Philosophy of Play* (New York: Association Press, 1920), 11, 32–33.

24. John Dewey, *Democracy and Education* (New York: The Free Press, 1966).

25. Jay Seaver, "Military Training as an Exercise," in *Proceedings of the American Association for the Advancement of Physical Education, Third Annual Meeting* (Brooklyn: Rome Brothers, 1887).

26. Ibid.

27. Edward Hartwell, "The Nature of Physical Training, and the Best Means of Securing its Ends," in *Boston Physical Training Conference* (Boston: Press of George H. Ellis, 1890), 112–115.

28. Stephen Hardy, *How Boston Played* (Northeastern University Press, 1982), 65–123; Allen V. Sapora and Elmer D. Mitchell, *The Theory of Play and Recreation* (New York: Ronald Press, 1961), 57–63; and Foster Rhea Dulles, *A History of Recreation: America Learns to Play* (Englewood Cliffs, N.J.: Prentice-Hall, 1965).

29. William Skarstrom, "Kinesiology of the Trunk, Shoulders, and Hip Applied to Gymnastics," *American Physical Education Review* (known hereafter as APER) 13:2 (February 1908): 69.

30. Ibid.

31. "Editorial Note and Comment," *APER* 17:5 (May 1912): 187.

32. Paul C. Phillips, "The Extension of Athletic Sports to the Whole Student Body of Amherst," *APER* 17:5 (May 1912): 339.

33. See Gulick, *Philosophy of Play*; Clark Hetherington, *Normal Course in Play* (New York: A. S. Barnes & Co., 1925); idem, *School Program in Physical Education* (New York: World Book Co., 1922); Joseph Lee, *Play in Education* (New York: Macmillan, 1917); Thomas D. Wood and Rosalind F. Cassidy, *The New Physical Education* (New York: Macmillan, 1927); Henry S. Curtis, *The Practical Conduct of Play* (New York: Macmillan, 1915); and idem, *Education through Play* (New York: Macmillan, 1917).

34. Curtis, *Practical Conduct of Play*.

35. Luther H. Gulick, "Athletics Do Not Test Womanliness," *APER* 11:3 (September 1906): 158–159.

36. Lupcho, "Professionalization," 82.

37. Gulick, "Athletics," 139.

38. Hetherington, School Program.

39. Ibid., 22.

40. Ibid., 24.

41. Ibid.

42. Ibid., 26.

43. Ibid., 31.

44. Ibid., 39.

45. Lupcho, 91.

46. Ibid., 93.

47. Hetherington, *School Program*, 43–44.

48. Wood and Cassidy; *New Physical Education*. See also Thomas D. Wood and Clifford L. Brownell, *Source Book in Health and Physical Education* (New York: Macmillan, 1925).

49. As this book goes to press, the debate about "indexing" and intelligence rages, especially surrounding the reliability of the Scholastic Aptitude Test (SAT).

50. Lupcho, "Professionalization," 95.

51. M. H. Landis, H. E. Burtt, and J. H. Nichols, "The Relation Between Physical Efficiency and Intelligence," *APER* 28:5 (May 1923): 220.

52. R. A. Schwegler and J. L. Engleshardt, "A Test of Physical Efficiency: The Correlation Between Results from Tests of Mental Efficiency," *APER* 29:9 (November 1924): 501–505.

53. Frederick W. Cozens, "Status of the Problem of the Relation of Physical to Mental Activity," *APER* 31:3 (March 1927): 147–155.

54. Vern S. Ruble, "A Psychological Study of Athletes," *APER* 33:4 (April 1928): 221–222.

55. Cozens, "Relation of Physical to Mental Activity," 154–155.

56. Frederick Rand Rogers, *Test and Measurement Programs in the Redirection of Physical Education* (New York: Teachers College, Columbia University Bureau of Publications, 1927); David K. Brace, *Measuring Motor Ability: A Scale of Motor Ability Tests* (New York: A. S. Barnes, 1927).

57. Rogers, *Test and Measurement*.

58. Ibid., 27.

59. Ibid., 128.

60. Ibid., 131.

section 4

Historical and Philosophical

Sport in the Colonial Period

General Events

1492 Columbus discovers America

1500–1700 Colonization of America

1607 Virginia colonized

1609 Pilgrims land at Plymouth Rock
Spanish found Santa Fe

1618 King James Issues *Declaration of Sports*

1619 First Africans landed in America

1620 First permanent colony in Massachusetts

1633 King Charles reissues *Declaration of Sports*

1636 Harvard College founded

1641 English civil War
Puritans take control of Parliament

1660 Restoration of British monarchy

1664 English assume control of New York from the Dutch

1776–1783 War of Independence

1776 *Declaration of Independence, Articles of Confederation*

1789 United States of America formed; *Constitution of the United States of America*

Sport and Physical Education

1647 General Court in New England outlaws shovelboard, bowling, and gaming

1665 First organized horse race in New York City

1733 Schuylkill Fishing Company, Philadelphia

1734 Students at Harvard playing "baseball"

1736 First known admission fee charged for a sporting event, a horse race in New York City

1766 First Jockey Club founded, Philadelphia

1768 Horse racing begins on Long Island

Sport in the Colonial Period

When Christopher Columbus sailed from Europe in 1492 to explore a new route to India, he instead discovered America. For the next century Europeans struggled to grasp the significance of an unexplored New World, and toward the end of the 1500s settlements were established on the eastern shores of the American continents. As far as the explorers and colonists of this new land were concerned, the American continent was new and empty, and the native American "Indians" who already lived there were considered to be uncivilized, primitive, and "lower" than the European colonists.[1] That the land was both empty and settled by "savages" is a contradiction the European settlers never really considered, and it has been left to twentieth-century Americans to come to grips with the manner in which our country was developed in the image of Europe.

The development of America from 1500 to 1700 witnessed the importation of the ideas of Western Civilization that began with the ancient Greeks, and reflected the ideas that composed the Catholic Church, Renaissance, Reformation, the Age of Science, and the Enlightenment. The attitudes of the colonists toward sport and recreation were representative of the regions of Europe from which the settlers came, and during the first two hundred years of American colonization these attitudes were most strongly influenced by religion. This stands to reason in that many of the colonists were motivated to make the perilous journey to the New World because of religious persecution in the Old World.

Sport in England: A Tale of Two Cultures

To understand the development of sport in Colonial America, it is helpful to begin with the role of sport in England during the same period. Sport in England was influenced significantly by the Reformation, especially John Calvin's brand of religion. During the 1550s hundreds of English converts fled from the Catholic reaction to Protestantism under Queen Mary Tudor ("Bloody Mary," 1554–57).[2] While three hundred of their brethren were executed, those reformers in Geneva studied Calvin's theology and then eventually they returned to England. This story represents the conflict in England during the 1500s: the English monarchy, along with the common people of England and the Catholics, were allied against the Puritans and Parliament. These alliances were about the changing nature of the Western world. The English monarchy, Catholics, and the common people of England were for a style of living that was primarily agrarian, land based, viewed time cyclically, was patriarchal and ascriptive in terms of family and position, and generally represented the way that Europeans had lived for centuries. In contrast, the reformers represented the world that was to come: meritocratic, bourgeois or business oriented, viewed time in a linear fashion, and sought to change the nature of English culture.

These differences manifested themselves in business, religion, politics, and for our purposes, sport. The most significant religious group in England were the Puritans, who wanted to make God's kingdom come alive here on earth. Puritans wanted to utilize God's time in the most efficient manner possible. Idleness was the most serious of sins, for wasting the gift of time was a sin for which one could never atone. Once time was gone, it could never be brought back and used more efficiently.

One can see how this type of thinking fits with a newly industrialized society. While sixteenth-century England was not "technological" in the terms with which we are comfortable today, the advent of water and steam power in the lives of the English revolutionized the manner in which products were refined and brought to market. This new technology could be used twenty-four hours a day, and to fail to use this time was both unprofitable and a sin against God. It is easy to see how industry and religion combined to create a culture that was urban and technological rather than rural and agrarian, and that the new ways of life were radically different from the old ways and required very different ways of looking at the world.

Sport in England was similar to that of other areas in Europe. Football was a very popular game, yet city administrators had tried to put an end to the game even before the Puritans. Football was a violent affair, usually taking place after church on Sunday, and was accompanied by drinking and many bumps, bruises, and broken bones. Drunken boys and men chased one another through fields, on roads, and through towns and villages, all in pursuit of an inflated pig bladder in a manner that was more like "king of the hill" than any modern game. In the process of pursuit, windows were broken, furniture smashed, and bodies were rendered incapacitated through drink or injury.

> In the cities, especially, football was considered a disruptive game best prohibited. . . . Urban footballers not only interfered with commerce but also destroyed property. In 1608 the town council of Manchester complained that 'a company of lewd and disordered persons' annually broke 'many men's windows and glass at their pleasures.'[3]

No doubt the participants had a lot of fun, but the next day they were probably not fit to work, to say the least!

While town fathers tried to put an end to the game because of the civic disorder it created, the Puritans hated the game because of the drinking, waste of time, and the general disrespect the game seemed to have for the "Lord's Day," the Sabbath. Puritans objected to football primarily because of religious concerns.[4] Any playful activity that removed the chosen few from "Godliness" was considered wicked, especially if it occurred on a Sunday. Football, and most other recreational activities, were wicked because they did just this.

There were a variety of reasons that playful activities were considered wicked. The keeping of the Sabbath, or "sabbatarianism," represented Puritan ideas toward work and rest. Sunday was the Lord's day, a day of rest, and was not to be used for the selfish and sinful reason of indulging in physical pleasure. Other games were sinful as well: stoolball, quoits, bowling, dancing; boxing and wrestling contests; running, jumping, and throwing contests; and blood sports such as the cockfight, bear and bull baiting. All of these games had in common the seeking of physical pleasure (an association with the "paganism" of Catholicism) and gambling.

Gambling was associated with games, and both winning money without toil as well as wasting money earned were sinful activities. Gambling was also associated with taking delight in carnal pleasures, and the association with drinking, gambling, and sex made traditional pastimes off limits to Englishmen. "In the Puritan equation, the active pursuit of pleasure meant a first step down the path of immorality, away from the portals of heaven."[5] In sum, there were many arguments against the old ways of play and recreation, all of which both facilitated profitability and religiosity in the new industrial world as well as mitigated against idling away one's time seeking physical pleasure.

This conflict in cultures came to a head in 1618 when King James was petitioned to support the "common folk" and their traditional dancing and playing after church on Sundays. James issued a royal proclamation entitled the *Declaration on Lawful Sports*, ordering that

> . . . after the end of divine service our good people be not disturbed . . . or discouraged from any lawful recreation such as dancing, either men or women, archery for men, leaping, vaulting or any other such harmless recreation.[6]

James ordered that his *Declaration* be read from the pulpits in churches all over England, and those who refused were punished. However, this did not stop the Puritans from pressing for their position on play, and after James died in 1625 his son Charles had to deal with the same issue. In 1633 Charles had the *Declaration* expanded and reissued, which led to still more distrust between the monarchy and the Puritans. Eventually the Puritans rose in violent rebellion, initiating the English civil war, which led to the Puritans taking control of Parliament and the country. In 1641 Charles was executed, and the Puritans took control of England and imposed their brand of religion on the rest of England.

The Puritans were not entirely successful, however, even though they won the war. Traditional pastimes continued, and maypoles, football games, drinking, and other activities continued, although they were significantly curtailed. In 1660 the monarchy was restored, which allowed for some of the traditional games to be held again. However, the peculiar British Sunday continued on and was exported to the United States, where Puritans sought to create the perfect society in a land unblemished by the paganism of old Europe.

Sport in New England: The Puritans

New England Puritans were strongly influenced by the Puritan movement in seventeenth-century England and for the most part were cool toward playful activities. The initial generation of Puritans in Massachusetts tried ". . . to establish a society dedicated to the preservation of the visible church and bound by a philosophy which clearly defined man's role and niche in the world."[7] This philosophy included God's values of hierarchy, inequality, mutability, variety, and order.[8] The New England Puritans believed that all men, as descendants of Adam, were corrupted by Original Sin. This position meant that all human beings were born "flawed" in the eyes of God, and consequently it was necessary to build a community that could restrain the evil impulses of the sinner. As Perry noted,

> . . . without a coercive state to restrain evil impulses and administer punishments, no life will be safe, no property secure, no honor observed. Therefore, upon Adam's apostasy, God Himself instituted governments among men. . . . He enacted that all men should be under some sort of corporate rule, that they should all submit to the sway of their superiors, that no man should live apart from his fellows, that the government should have full power to enforce obedience and to inflict every punishment that the crimes of men deserved.[9]

New England Puritans, like their English ancestors, were extremely concerned with the religious life, and their interpretation of what was the good religious life determined how they should behave on this earth. Seen this way, Puritanism in New England was a throwback to the Middle Ages and the Reformation, during which the way one lived life on this earth played a role in whether one's eternal soul went to heaven.

Since this idea was so important to the Puritans, they developed governments that would fulfill God's will here on earth. Government to the Puritans was quite a bit different from that which we experience today. Indeed, government to the Puritans was an active vehicle to promote the good religious life:

> The state to them was an active instrument of leadership, discipline, and wherever necessary, of coercion; it legislated over any or all aspects of human behavior. . . . The commanders were not to trim their policies by the desires of the people, but to drive ahead upon the predetermined course; the people were all to turn out as they were ordered . . . there was no idea of the equality of all men. There was no questioning that men who would not serve the purposes of the society should be whipped into line. The objectives were clear and unmistakable; any one's disinclination to dedicate himself to them was obviously so much recalcitrancy and depravity.[10]

Salvation could be had only through the control of both one's emotions and behaviors, so the Puritans debated extensively just what the proper emotions and behaviors for a saved soul were. The Puritans were God-fearing people who left their legacy in the form of the Protestant work ethic, which personified the principals of hard work, sobriety, and piety. Although men and women were believed to possess a natural desire for play and recreational activities, Puritans also believed that play and games could also be the "workshop" of the devil. The Puritans were very utilitarian, and the climate in New England required that if one was going to survive the harsh winters and short agricultural season, then an enormous amount of hard physical work had to be completed. This efficient use of time left little time for amusements. However, this efficient use of time was enormously profitable and undoubtedly led to the success of the early Puritan colonists. Had it not been for their thrifty and hardworking attitude, it is arguable that they would never have survived the harsh New England winters. Consequently, the environment of New England played an important role in confirming the Puritan lifestyle of hard work and efficient use of time.

What free time that was available was, according to leading Puritans, supposed to be spent in church or in an appropriate recreational activity. The Puritans adhered to a classical religious dualism that separated soul and body. Puritan dogma argued that spiritual nourishment was provided for the soul while the body was made for work and prayer, and not play. The early Puritan mentality with respect to work and play can be illustrated by the Puritan saying, "idle hands are the devil's playground."

Puritans recognized, however, that an absolute ban on recreation was impossible, and two extremes in Puritan attitudes eventually evolved toward recreation. The first extreme was that sport in the right form was beneficial if pursued in the appropriate manner and if it was helpful in maintaining civic order. John Downame, a New England minister, argued that moderate recreation might even be necessary so as to keep one refreshed in order to work and pray. Similarly, John Winthrop, the first governor of the Massachusetts Bay Company, found that abstention from recreation created disorder in his life. Moderate activities of the body were necessary in order to refresh both the body and an overworked mind. In so doing, order was maintained by achieving the balance between mind and body that was ordained by God. Acceptable recreations like fishing, hunting, and walking became acceptable because it was believed that they improved one's health and would renew one's spirit so that one could return to work refreshed.[11]

The other extreme was negative and dealt with the response by the New England magistrates. The magistrates wrote laws that insured both sanctity of the Sabbath and the promotion of the public good, demonstrating the integrated nature of New England government and the Puritan church. In 1630 a man named John Baker was ordered to be whipped for bird hunting on the Sabbath.[12] What concerned the magistrates was Baker's failure to keep the Sabbath, and not his bird hunting.

Still, the primary means of recreation in seventeenth-century New England were sporting, and as a consequence it was sporting recreation that frequently was condemned. By 1635 all persons absent from church meetings faced fines or imprisonment. Activities that detracted from the economic success of the colony were also condemned, and sport was one means by which one could shirk his obligations. But it was not the only one. Inns and common houses of entertainment were felt to disrupt the orderly arrangement of society, and in 1647 the General Court outlawed shovelboard, and soon after bowling and gaming in general. But it was not the games as much as it was the drinking, gambling, and wasteful use of time associated with the games that threatened the magistrates' sense of social order. As one historian notes, "The delay in banning these games, as well as the emphasis on unprofitability and drunkenness, suggest that the magistrates did not intend to denounce the nature of the game, but rather to attack overspending and inebriation."[13]

The influence of Puritanism reached its peak during the mid-1600s, yet even at this time many colonists ignored the sermons that argued against play and games. Only one in four colonists in New England was a church member, and once the colonists were firmly established in New England the urgency of the Puritan message was lost.[14] The exceptions to this rule were the "Great Awakening," a period in which Puritan ideas enjoyed a powerful resurgence during the middle of the eighteenth century; the pockets of Puritanism that lasted well into the nineteenth century; and the admonishments against playful activities on Sunday, which lasted well into the twentieth century in the form of various Blue Laws.

If an individual who lived in Massachusetts or Pennsylvania wanted to leave the Quaker or Puritan sphere of influence for some ale or other forms of entertainment, he did not have to travel very far. Two days or less on horseback heading west from Boston or Philadelphia would put the traveler in an area where taverns and inns were beyond the reach of most religious authorities. It was in the taverns that the playful amusements of the Colonial period were held.

Amusements in New England

In all probability, the taverns and inns that the magistrates tried to manage were the American version of English pubs, German beer halls, and European inns. People needed a place to stay when traveling, and they would also gather at taverns and inns for amusements, conversation, drink, and friendly competition. Taverns were built about a day's ride by horseback from each other, extending from Canada to the south, and from the east to the western frontier. Frontier taverns provided amusements and lodging for the weary traveler and sports fan alike.

It was not unusual for the tavern keeper to arrange contests and promote them by offering prizes, charging fees, and selling food and drink. Darts and cards were popular games, and marksmanship, boxing, cockfighting, and horseracing were among the most popular contests. The nature of the contests tell us much about colonial culture. In shooting contests, a nail was partially driven into a tree, fence, or post, and each contestant attempted to finish driving the nail by actually shooting it with his rifle from a pre-set distance. Turkey shoots were also popular. In this contest the unsuspecting turkey was tied behind a tree stump so that only its head would pop up. The victor was the marksman who could literally blow the turkey's head off at a distance of 80 yards or more.

Puritan influence in New England gradually eroded under the wave of non-Puritan immigrants who settled in New England. In addition, third- and fourth-generation Puritans began to question the practices of the church. However, rampant recreation did not spring up overnight. The Puritans remained politically powerful in New England, and over time socially accepted amusements such as hop scotch, horse racing, ice skating, and sleigh riding became more acceptable.

Sport in the Mid-Atlantic Region

The Quakers of Pennsylvania influenced sport in much the same way as the Puritans did. Dutch Calvinists in the New York area, in contrast to the Quakers and the New England Puritans, were somewhat more friendly toward playful activities. Dutch immigrants ". . . smoked their pipes, played at bowls, and skated on the wintry ice."[15] Eating, drinking, and gambling were common activities of the Europeans who settled in what was originally known as New Amsterdam. The Dutch immigrants continued to observe their traditional European customs as much as their lives in the New World permitted, and this included their sporting activities.

Horse racing was popular from the beginning, ostensibly for the improvement of the breed but also because New Yorkers loved to watch and gamble on the outcome. During the 1700s horses were imported from England to improve the American breed, and as soon as this occurred, rivalries soon arose. As early as 1768, a race was held between Figure, an English horse, and the American horse Salem. The English horse prevailed, but the interest generated from the race eventually led to intersectional rivalries in America.

New Yorkers also enjoyed bowling, golf, early versions of croquet, tennis, and cricket. Shooting matches were popular, and in the winter many New Yorkers enjoyed sleigh rides and skating. It seems clear that the sporting life that is evident in New York City in the late twentieth century can trace its origins back to the early days of the city in the seventeenth and eighteenth centuries.

Sport in the South

The American South was still different from its northern counterparts. The growth of sports in the south was facilitated by favorable climate considerations, the absence of Puritan reformers, and the importation and practice of sports, games, and amusements by the various immigrant groups, especially the English. Catholicism was a fixture in the deep south and was considerably more tolerant of sports activities than the New England Puritans. Unlike the New England colonists, southern settlers immigrated more for adventure and opportunity than for the pursuit of religious freedom.

Figure 11.1

Black jockeys, dominant in this period. Courtesy of the Library of Congress.

The southern gentlemen of Virginia were extremely competitive, individualistic, and materialistic, all elements that reflected the economic conditions of the South. As one scholar notes, the wealthy planters enjoyed wagering money and tobacco on horse races because ". . . competitive gaming was for many gentlemen a means of translating a particular set of values into action. . . ."[16] Indeed, gambling reflected the core elements of seventeenth- and eighteenth-century gentry values. The great plantations occupied huge areas of land, and the planters lived far away from one another and sought to aggressively acquire more land to increase their income. This led the plantation owners to develop attitudes of rugged individualism and competitiveness, and these attitudes manifested themselves in their playful pastime of wagering on horses. "In large part, the goal of the competition within the gentry group was to improve social position by increasing wealth."[17] There were a number of prominent American politicians, including many of the Founding Fathers, who enjoyed horse racing. George Washington, Thomas Jefferson, James Madison, John Marshall, Henry Clay, and Andrew Jackson, among others, loved to wager on the races.

The first horse races were a quarter mile long, a distance that eventually led to the name of the Virginia quarter horse. During the early days of horse racing it was not unusual for races to be held on the town streets. Race tracks were built in Virginia, Maryland, and South Carolina. Wagering was often heavy, and both women and men placed bets. The big races were often followed by elaborate social festivities attended by those who could afford to participate. Horse racing, however, was not the only popular sport. Southerners also enjoyed fox hunts, county fairs, hunting, fishing, rowing, lawn bowling, dancing, cock fighting, boxing, and fencing. Shooting matches were popular throughout all of Colonial America, and the South was no exception. One story illustrates the meaning of the contests to the participants. The legendary Daniel Boone described an encounter between himself and some of his Indian friends.

> I often went hunting with them, and frequently gained their applause for my activity at our shooting matches. I was careful not to exceed many of them in shooting; for no people are more envious than they in this sport.[18]

During the antebellum era, and afterwards as well, social class often dictated appropriate sporting behavior. Southern gentlemen from proper families were expected to exhibit requisite social and athletic skills that included riding, dancing, fencing, and conversation. Southern gentlemen were more often observers and producers of sports rather than actual participants, especially in boxing and horse racing, where the athletes were slaves.

The vast majority of slaves were subject to a hard life of either field work or domestic services. Slaves often endured harsh conditions and punishment and were purposely kept ignorant by their masters. It was illegal in many parts of the south to teach a slave to read and write, although many whites risked their lives to do just this. Yet slaves were also participants in southern sport as jockeys and boxers, providing entertainment and betting opportunities for whites.

Although boxing contests originated in ancient Greece, American boxers, or "pugilists" as they were known, were strongly influenced by the English. Eighteenth-century Elizabethan England is recognized as the birthplace of modern boxing. According to Lewis:

> With the decline of fencing, boxing became increasingly popular in England. Fighters were called 'bruisers.' They lost a fight only if they failed to come up to 'scratch,' a line drawn in the middle of the ring. Since there was not time limit, fighters took a tremendous beating. A round was considered over only when a man went down. Gouging and hair pulling were allowed and since no gloves were worn, broken bones were common. . . . There was no medical supervision and most fighters died young.[19]

America's first well-known pugilist was Tom Molyneux, who gained his freedom from slavery by fighting on the Southern Plantation Circuit. After beating the best that the North was able to offer, Molyneux went to England in 1810 to fight the British champion, Tom Cribb. The fight took place in a pouring rain, and for twenty-nine rounds Molyneux was beating Cribb. When the partisan British fans were able to stop the fight briefly on a technicality, Molyneux caught a chill and was eventually beaten by Cribb in the fortieth round.

While this particular fight caught the attention of many Colonial Americans, boxing as a sport did not attract a following until the latter part of the nineteenth century. Boxing's early years were spent in obscure and questionable surroundings, for boxing was outlawed in most of the states and territories. Fights took place in barns, river barges, and secluded remote locations.

Figure 11.2

*Tom Molyneux, early United States boxer.
From: Betty Spears and Richard Swanson.*
History of Sport and Physical Education in
the United States, *Third Ed., Dubuque:
Wm. C. Brown, Publishers, 1988.*

Figure 11.3
*Early American boxing match. Photo courtesy of Department
of Library Services, American Museum of Natural History.*

Figure 11.4
Playing lacrosse.

Figure 11.5
*Ball playing among the Choctaw Indians, from an
engraving after a drawing by George Catlin,* North
American Indian Portfolio. *London, 1844.*

Native American Indians originated the game of lacrosse in the
Northeast. The Iroquois, which was actually an Indian Confederacy of
the Cayuga, Oneida, Mohawk, Senaca, and Onondaga tribes of New
York, were known for their Lacrosse skills. With the introduction of
horses to North America by the Spanish, the Indians of the Great Plains
and Far West soon became expert riders and would engage in horse racing and tribal dances. The courage and athletic prowess of Native Americans and slaves soon spread throughout the various geographical
regions of North America.

Summary

Sport in America developed largely along regional lines and was influenced by the cultural, political and religious agendas of the era. Quakers in Pennsylvania, Puritans in New England, the regional cultures of the South and West, and Native American contributions of lacrosse and ballgames exerted a significant influence during sport's formative years.

The link between sport and religion in Colonial America was significant. The Quakers in Pennsylvania and the Puritans in New England believed the path to salvation was through prayer and work. Time was "God given," and what you did with your time on earth would determine, to a large degree, your prospects for salvation. Generally speaking, engaging in play, games, and sports simply did not constitute the wise use of time. While Puritans and Quakers realized that they could not stop people from engaging in play and games, they did their best to discourage it with some notable exceptions.

As time went by, immigrants began to settle in New England and Pennsylvania who were not Puritans or Quakers. These immigrants, along with second- and third-generation Puritans, softened their position against recreational activities, in large part because of the hard work that their ancestors did. Third- and fourth-generation Puritans and Quakers were quite prosperous and had the time and resources to enjoy games and sports. With the exception of the Great Awakening, Puritanism as a theology declined in popularity from the mid 1600s. All that was left were some of the more explicit measures of the religion, such as the keeping of the Sabbath and Blue Laws.

The Dutch Calvinists settled an area they called New Amsterdam, which is now New York. Just like the Quakers and Puritans, the Dutch left Europe for religious freedom and the promise of a better life. However, the Dutch were not opposed to play, games, and sport. They enjoyed horse racing, bowling, golf, and other activities which would be frowned upon by the Quakers and Puritans. Religious beliefs did not affect the Dutch in the same way it affected the Quakers and Puritans in regard to sports and related activities.

In the southeastern part of Colonial America, the Catholic Church was the dominant religious institution. Catholics enjoyed games and sports, unlike their counterparts in Pennsylvania and New England. The English who settled in Virginia brought with them their passion for horse racing, which flourished in the south. Boxing was also a popular sport. Tom Molineaux was a former slave who was the first prominent boxer in America. He traveled to England to fight the British champion Tom Cribb in 1810 and lost the fight in the fortieth round.

The Native American contributions of lacrosse and ball games exerted a significant influence during sport's formative years. The game of lacrosse is still popular in many regions of the country. Lacrosse and ball games have a rich legacy that is grounded in the culture of Native Americans.

The attitudes of the early colonists, then, were influenced by a variety of factors including the attitudes toward sport they brought with them from Europe, the nature of the early American economy, and religion. These attitudes for the most part remained unchanged throughout the colonial period, although each area continued to experience growth through immigration. For instance, the population of New York quadrupled between 1790 and 1820, and this growth brought with it the attitudes of the immigrants who settled there.[20] Yet New Yorkers generally continued to enjoy their recreational pastimes as they had since the early 1500s, and it was not until the 1800s that American attitudes toward sport experienced any significant change.

Discussion Questions

1. How did Puritanism have an impact on the development of sport in New England? Are any ideas of the Puritans with us today in contemporary sport?

2. What were the popular sports in colonial America? Why were many of these sports so violent by today's standards?

3. How did sport in the South differ from sport in New England? What factors contributed to the growth and popularity of sport in the South?

Suggestions for Further Reading

Baker, W. J. *Sports in the Western World*. Urbana, Illinois: University of Illinois Press, 1988.

Betts, J. R. "Mind and Body in Early American Thought." In *The American Sporting Experience*, edited by Steven A. Riess. New York: Leisure Press, 1984.

Struna, N. "Puritans and Sport: The Irretrievable Tide of Change." In *The American Sporting Experience*, edited by Steven A. Riess. New York: Leisure Press, 1984.

Swanson, R. A., and Betty Spears. *History of Sport and Physical Education*, 4th ed. Madison, Wisc.: Brown & Benchmark, 1995.

Notes

1. James Oliver Robertson, *American Myth, American Reality*, (New York: Hill and Wang, 1980).

2. W. J. Baker, *Sports in the Western World*. (Urbana, Illinois: University of Illinois Press, 1988).

3. Ibid., 75.

4. Ibid., 75

5. Ibid., 77.

6. Ibid., 79.

7. Nancy Struna, "Puritans and Sport: The Irretrievable Tide of Change," in *The American Sporting Experience*, ed. Steven A. Riess (New York: Leisure Press, 1984), 16.

8. Ibid.

9. Perry Miller, *Erand Into the Wilderness* (New York: Harper and Row, 1956), 142–43.

10. Ibid., 143.

11. Betty Spears and Richard A. Swanson, *History of Sport and Physical Education*, 3rd ed. (Dubuque, Iowa: William C. Brown Publishers, 1983).

12. Ibid.

13. Ibid., 19.

14. Baker, *Sports in the Western World*.

15. John R. Betts, "Mind and Body in Early American Thought," in *The American Sporting Experience*, ed. Steven A. Riess (New York: Leisure Press, 1984), 62.

16. Thomas Breen, "Horses and Gentlemen: The Cultural Significance of Gambling Among the Gentry of Virginia," *William and Mary Quarterly*, 34 (1977), 243.

17. Ibid., 245.

18. Daniel Boone, "The ADVENTURES of Col. Daniel Boone; Containing a NARRATIVE of the WARS of Kentucke, 1798," in *The Discovery, Settlement and Present State of Kentucke*, ed. John Filson (New York: Coring Books, 1962), 65.

19. William A. Lewis, "Man to Man—A History of Boxing," *Mankind*, vol. 3, no. 6 (April 1972): 32–41.

20. Melvin L. Adelman, *A Sporting Time: New York City and the Rise of Modern Athletics 1820–70* (Chicago: University of Illinois Press, 1986).

Changing Concepts of the Body Sport and Play in Nineteenth-Century America

General Events

1803–1882 Ralph Waldo Emerson

1809–1882 Charles Robert Darwin

1812 War of 1812

1817–1862 Henry David Thoreau

1821 First public high school, Massachusetts

1833 Oberlin College founded; first coeducational college

1837 Telegraph invented by Morse

1839–1914 Charles Sanders Peirce

1840 2800 miles of railway tracks in United States

1842–1910 William James

1844 First telegraph in regular operation

1846 Sewing machine invented

1859 Darwin publishes *Origin of the Species*

1860 30,000 miles of railroad track in United States

1861–1865 Abraham Lincoln president

1861–1865 Civil War

1876 Telephone invented by Alexander Graham Bell

Sport

1819 John Stuart Skinner writes articles on sport in *American Farmer*

1823 Henry v. Eclipse horse race

1825 "The Sporting Olio," the first column on sport deals with horse racing

1829 *American Turf Register* and *Sporting Magazine*

1831 *Spirit of the Times*

1852 First intercollegiate competition, Harvard–Yale crew race

1853 Caledonian Games first held

1858 Formation of the National Association of Base Ball Players

1868 Formation of the New York Athletic Club

1869 Cincinnati Red Stockings are undefeated and national champions in baseball

1871 Formation of the National Association of Professional Base Ball Players

1872 National Amateur Regatta, Philadelphia; formation of the National Association of Amateur Oarsmen

1883 Joseph Pulitzer starts what was probably the first separate sports department in a newspaper, the New York *World*

1888 Formation of the Amateur Athletic Union

A Changing America

The nineteenth century was a time of rapid change. These changes occurred so quickly and are very different from one another, yet at the same time they all contributed to a colorful and complex tapestry of historical change. Viewed from the perspective of over 100 years, it is still difficult to say which changes were the most significant. These changes do seem to have one characteristic in common, though, in that all of them have some basis in an awareness of the material aspects of life. And this awareness of the "here and now" remains a characteristic of the contemporary American character.

Changes in the United States of America can be described from a variety of perspectives: demographic, technological, modernization, and philosophical. No one view can adequately describe all of the different kinds of changes that occurred, and the use of many perspectives helps the student of history understand the plurality of American culture. In short, America is not only a big "melting pot" as so many historians have described her in the past. Rather, America is also a nation created by a variety of peoples and cultures living through changes upon which each group has a unique perspective. What these peoples and cultures had in common in nineteenth-century America was an understanding that the material world was real and important to their lives. While religion and spiritual matters maintained an important role in the lives of Americans, the emphasis on the material world was manifest in a growing awareness of the use of technology to make life better, the gradual movement from the country to the city to facilitate industry, a use of rationality to understand how to live better, and the use of philosophy to understand the material world. The four perspectives we use that take into account this commonality and to describe these changes are urbanization, industrialization, modernization theory, and how all of these changes were coincident with philosophical changes among intellectuals.

In the 1820s cities grew faster than did the agrarian population, beginning the shift of America from a farming nation to an urban-industrial nation. Americans simultaneously experienced a technological revolution that radically changed the way they lived. As historian John R. Betts noted,

> Telegraph lines went up all over the landscape, the railroad followed the steamboat from the East to the Midwest and the South, and by 1860 a network of over thirty-thousand miles of track covered the United States. An immigrant tide helped populate midwestern states, and Cincinnati, St. Louis, Chicago, Milwaukee, and Detroit gradually became western metropolises. The reaper and other new tools slowly transformed farm life; agricultural societies sprouted up; journals brought scientific information to the farmer; and the agricultural fair developed into a prominent social institution.[1]

These changes facilitated a shift from an isolated farming lifestyle to a more city-oriented lifestyle. Railroads facilitated the shipping of goods from east to west and made travel much faster, easier, and safer. Telegraphs made the exchange of information much more rapid than anyone at that time could have dreamed possible. Telegraphs combined with the business of newspapers and magazines, and the institution of modern journalism developed. Americans had access to inexpensive information, and this change had an impact on every facet of American life. This ability to assimilate large amounts of information reflected the fact that more Americans than ever before were able to read and write, and the level of literacy in turn encouraged the development of communication technologies in a kind of snowball effect.

Early Technological Innovations and Their Impact on Sport

Other technological changes affected American society as well, and many of these made possible sport as we know it. The concept of mass production gained popularity during the eighteenth century and made possible cheap athletic equipment like bats and balls. The sewing machine made possible more uniform equipment toward the end of the nineteenth century. Vulcanized rubber made tires for bicycles possible, as well as the development of elastic and resilient rubber balls for golf and tennis. The incandescent light bulb, developed by Thomas A. Edison in 1879, started a new era in the social life of the cities. Electric light eventually replaced the smokey, dim gas lamps that made large indoor events difficult to hold. Electrification allowed for the development of home appliances that made everyday life easier and helped create more leisure time. The replacement of horsedrawn carriages with mass transit electric streetcars directly affected the development of sport by transporting large numbers of people who wished to see professional baseball games.[2] As Betts noted,

> Numerous inventions and improvements applied to sport were of varying importance: the stop watch, the percussion cap, the streamlined sulky, barbed wire, the safety cycle, ball bearings, and artificial ice for skating rinks, among others. Improved implements often popularized and revolutionized the style of a sport, as in the invention of the sliding seat of the rowing shell, the introduction of the rubber-wound gutta-percha ball which necessitated the lengthening of golf courses, and the universal acceptance of the catcher's mask.[3]

After the Civil War, cameras were used to capture sporting experiences. In 1872 Edward Muybridge made one of the first "moving pictures" of a trotting horse, a principle that was eventually applied to celluloid film. The telephone, the typewriter, the phonograph, the automobile, and many other inventions all were developed in the nineteenth century, and all in one way or another had an impact on sport. Betts summarized these changes by noting that

> While athletics and outdoor recreation were sought as a release from the confinements of city life, industrialization and the urban movement were the basic causes for the rise of organized sport. And the urban

movement was, of course, greatly enhanced by the revolutionary transformation in communication, transportation, agriculture, and industrialization.[4]

These examples represent some of the more significant technological changes that affected the way Americans lived and played. There were many more changes that could be listed, but suffice it to say that the patterns of life that we enjoy took shape in the nineteenth century. It was left to the philosophers and historians to explain these changes, to provide a systematic and rational set of explanations of how to understand a rapidly changing world.

Nineteenth-Century American Philosophy: Transcendentalism and Pragmatism

During this era, two major philosophical movements developed in the United States: transcendentalism and pragmatism. The New England transcendentalists were a very influential group of writers, critics, philosophers, theologians, and social reformers who lived in and around Concord, Massachusetts, from about 1836 to 1860.[5] Transcendentalism was more of a literary phenomenon than a philosophical movement, a passionate outcry on the part of a number of brilliant and articulate young Americans who were influenced by the spirit of European philosophers like Immanuel Kant, Johann Fichte, and Georg Hegel. Basically, this group rejected the narrow rationalism, pietism, and conservatism of American intellectual leaders of the eighteenth century and developed a "philosophy" that was eclectic, individualistic, and relevant to almost every aspect of nineteenth-century American life.

While transcendentalism was representative of a strain of thought that was developed in Europe, it had its own characteristics that were very attractive to Americans in the early nineteenth century. Transcendentalists believed in the godlike nature of the human spirit and insisted on the authority of the individual. They rejected the idea of metaphysical dualism, a characteristic that led them to believe that all aspects of being human are somehow connected. This meant that individuals should not be seen as separate from society, that humans are a natural part of the universe, and that the mind and the body are as one. Transcendentalists believed that imagination was better than reason, that creativity was more important than theory, that the creative artist was the epitomy of civilization, and that action was more important than contemplation. This last characteristic, that action is more important than contemplation, manifested itself in an awareness of the importance of physicality. Indeed, the transcendentalists were physical in a contemporary sense of the word. They were reformers who sought to change the way nineteenth-century Americans lived, and who believed that nature is "real" and that humans are a very important part of nature. In making these arguments, transcendentalist values helped make many types of sport and physical education necessary and important.

Ralph Waldo Emerson

Ralph Waldo Emerson (1803–1882) was born in Boston, Massachusetts, where he was raised and educated. Like many philosophers, Emerson initially studied to become a preacher. After completing his studies he accepted a pastorate in Boston, but he left after the death of his wife of tuberculosis in 1831. He eventually sailed for Europe, a trip that was crucial to the development of the "philosophy" of transcendentalism.

Emerson was not really a philosopher, however, as much as he was a writer and poet. Like the *philosophes* of Enlightenment Europe, Emerson was concerned with the nature of the self and the universe, of the mind and nature. Emerson believed that religion as he had been taught it was inadequate to explain his personal relationship with reality, but he still wanted an explanation that could accommodate his religious beliefs and satisfy his intellectual needs. What he developed was an expression of his individuality and the admiration of the hero, both traits that fit well with ideas that were popular with his contemporaries. Emerson was the first of the American transcendentalists and was perhaps the most influential of the group. His optimism infected those who followed him, and his ideas of overcoming, or "transcending," the dichotomies that were used to describe American life were readily accepted by Americans. Those who read Emerson's essays saw themselves as intimately connected, both physically and mentally, with both nature and the city. This helped lead Americans out of the dualistic lifestyles advocated by the New England Puritans that preceded Emerson.

Henry David Thoreau

While Emerson was the first American transcendentalist, Henry David Thoreau (1817–1862) may be the best known. Born in Concord, Massachusetts, Thoreau was a brilliant student who was described by his teachers and friends as a moral and intelligent man. Early in life Thoreau was infected with the ideas of the New England transcendentalists and gave up all plans of having a regular profession in life. As such, he "dropped out" and made a life of making pencils and surveying, jobs that enabled him to earn a living for the rest of his life. But his best hours were spent trying to understand his relationship to his fellow man and to nature, and many of these hours were spent in the wilderness alone near Concord at Walden Pond.

For two years Thoreau lived with Emerson in the Massachusetts countryside, absorbing Emerson's ideas and developing his own. Nature, for Thoreau, represented an "absolute freedom and wildness" that was superior to anything that humans could create. Therefore humans were at their best when they lived as one with nature. This idea fit well with Americans who were moving west, developing farms, and "carving civilization" out of the wilderness. Thoreau's ideas regarding the human spirit and the wilderness are described in one of his most famous works, *Walden, or Life in the Woods,* an experiment in which Thoreau tried to live in the most "natural" manner he could.[6] Thoreau believed that true freedom was to be found in the western frontier, and this idea was in step with the pervasive American attitude toward the civilization of the wilderness.

Thoreau was not only concerned with nature, though. His essay "Civil Disobedience" has been the most influential of his works because of its use as a guide for peaceful revolution. Thoreau's belief in individualism led him to argue that on certain occasions resistance, and even active rebellion, against the state is a valid moral choice. Gandhi developed his own doctrine of passive resistance from a reading of Thoreau's essay, and the Rev. Martin Luther King, Jr., was also influenced by his reading of Thoreau. In Thoreau, then, we see the philosophy of American individualism at its peak: each person has the right and a moral obligation to protect his or her individuality with respect to the state.

Pragmatism

Another perspective on the way that America changed in the nineteenth century was provided by a group of late nineteenth-century American intellectuals who developed the American philosophy known as pragmatism. The philosophy of pragmatism evolved from the desire to do two things: to determine the differences between the many philosophies that were developed in the preceding 2500 years, and to develop a practical method for dealing with the social unrest generated by the rapid changes in American society. Consequently, pragmatism can be seen as a philosophical response to changes that occurred earlier in the nineteenth century. As philosopher Philip Smith noted,

> Old ways (philosophies) were unable to deal with this situation. The result was that people found themselves in a vacuum on many significant matters, matters that were of intellectual as well as practical concern. The progressive movement originally gained in public support because it appeared to fill this void on both counts. And, truly, it was suited for the American scene. Born and bred in the United States, it had none of the shortcomings of imported schemes from Europe. From the start it was designed to reintegrate American culture, and by 1900 had been finely fitted out specifically for this purpose.[7]

The importance of pragmatism as a philosophy in American culture, or, perhaps more boldly, the philosophy *of* American culture, cannot be overestimated. Pragmatism evolved at the same time as, and is a product of, the demographic, technological, and philosophical influences described above. It is also a product of one of the most powerful scientific advances of all time, the seminal work on genetics by Charles Darwin. The value of Darwin's work to physical education may not be obvious at first, yet his influence on the modern mind is unquestioned in historical and philosophical circles. In short, Darwin revolutionized thinking by arguing that biological systems are the *response* to some change in the environment. Consequently, the moving human body can be seen as a response to a changing environment.

The Influence of Charles Darwin

Charles Darwin (1809–1882) had a profound impact on both scientific investigation and philosophical inquiry, primarily through two works:

Origin of the Species (1859) and *The Descent of Man* (1871). Darwin's work is of particular historical importance to physical educators, for it was only after *Origin* was written that our physical selves were studied as a consequence of our environment. To a great extent this is a goal of physical education today.

In *Origin* Darwin established beyond reasonable doubt that all living things, including man, have developed from a few extremely simple forms. His theory contradicted the prevailing explanation for the origin of each species, known as the "doctrine of special creation," which held that each species was created independently from every other species.[8] Monkeys, for instance, were believed to have always been monkeys and had no genetic link to any other species. Darwin's scientific explanation of the origin of the species was applied to the disciplines of philosophy, science, and biology. In so doing the explanations each discipline used for the nature of humanity were turned, literally and figuratively, upside down.[9]

Prior to Darwin, philosophers, theologians, teachers, and many other Americans believed that the capacity to think was a result of a special gift of some type. Most accepted a religious answer for this phenomena, that God somehow gave the gift of intelligence to humans. Interestingly, Americans living prior to Darwin did not believe that religion and science were incompatible. Rather, it was believed that the findings of science would reinforce the relevations of the Bible.[10] For instance, it was common to take a class in the colleges of the day titled "Evidences of Christianity," in which students were taught to view the wonders of the scientific world, and specifically the biological world, as evidence of God's incredible power.

After Darwin, however, popular explanations for the nature of the universe, along with romantic and transcendental explanations, were questionable. Darwin provided a scientifically convincing explanation for the genesis of humans, one that contradicted popular beliefs generally and the Bible specifically. Darwin's work, then, had important consequences for how intellectuals perceived our ability to think. As Smith noted, ". . . what was once seen as a unique philosophical faculty for perceiving abstract truths is now seen more simply as an ability to recognize empirically significant possibilities."[11]

What Darwin's work meant is that the ability to think is a product of our biology, and not a special gift. This scientific explanation for the ability to think was, both literally and figuratively, world shattering, and the debate about whether or not it is a correct explanation of our intelligence rages today. To understand how the emotional impact of this argument must have affected Americans in the nineteenth century, one needs only to examine the heated contemporary debate between "creationists" and "evolutionists" over content in school biology curriculum. Basically, creationists believe the Biblical version, described in the Book of Genesis, of how humans were created by an act of God. Evolutionists, in contrast, believe that humans evolved from primates, and that the ability to think is a product of adapting to the environment. Each argument is believed to be true by its proponents, and neither side will submit to the authority of the other.

Darwin's research, in 1859, legitimized the theory of evolution in a manner that seriously differed with the Biblical story of Genesis. Furthermore, it legitimized the use of our senses and our power to reason to understand the material world. Darwin's doctrine of natural selection said that change must be supported by natural forces that can be observed, and that extranatural forces, like religious miracles, were simply irrelevant to physical changes. Specifically, his work promoted the idea that our environment—both the material world around us and the social world in which we live—is the cause of the changes we experience, not other forces that we cannot observe. It is no coincidence that physical education in the modern world, which can be described as an attempt to control students' environment to promote skill acquisition and physical, social, spiritual, and psychological growth, began after Darwin's research was published.

The Pragmatists

Shortly after the publication of *Origin of the Species*, a group of intellectuals around Harvard University began to talk about the impact of the book on philosophical issues. This group called itself "The Metaphysical Club" and was composed of what later became the preeminent group of "progressives" in America. Yet as Smith notes, the name "Metaphysical Club" was selected more as a joke than anything else. None of the members of the club believed in metaphysics as the term was defined by contemporary philosophers. These men had as a goal the undermining of traditional metaphysics as a means of knowing reality.[12] Charles Peirce and William James were its most famous members, but men like Oliver Wendell Holmes, Jr., later a well-known member of the Supreme Court, also attended the discussions. Out of the meetings of the Metaphysical Club came the ideas that are known in philosophy as "pragmatism."

Charles Sanders Peirce

Charles Peirce (1839–1914) was the principle organizer of the Metaphysical Club and one of its more notable members. He was the founder of pragmatism and formulated the first tenets of the philosophy. His first step was to reject everything Descartes said about the nature of reality: that all we can know absolutely are ideas. Descartes' philosophy began by doubting everything, even his own existence. Peirce said that this is a silly thing to do. He further argued that we do not doubt everything that is logically possible to doubt, and, furthermore, there is no reason why we should. Peirce argued that it is rational to accept some things as true even if we are not absolutely certain of their truth. In arguing this way, Peirce discredited Descartes' dualistic concept of mind and body as the best way of coming to know something.

Peirce argued that there is no reality outside of nature where ideas exist. Rather, he argued, we come to know ideas by using our senses. In so doing Peirce unified the physical world and the ideal world and is therefore a monist. Peirce argued that by empirically investigating the material world we could create ideas, and that ideas that are induced in this manner are "real" in a philosophical sense. What Peirce argued is that human beings create ideas and that the best way to do this is to use the scientific method. Peirce hoped that, for the first time, the ideas used to understand the world could be experimentally developed, tested, and laid to rest.

Peirce's hopes rest easily with most Americans. It makes sense to try to discover the nature of the universe by using the methods of science. One part of his philosophy has not been borne out, however. Peirce believed that the rules and generalizations we use to describe the world would be unchanging and universal. Yet in the history of science there has not been one law that does not have an exception. Even the "Law of Gravity" has been found by physicists to have exceptions. In any event, Peirce's contribution to the development of pragmatism is significant to physical educators. For our purposes, Peirce's pragmatism connects the human body with the mind in a way that makes them both one and the same: a unity. And if there is no division between mind and body, then there is no placing of one over the other in an educational hierarchy.

William James

William James (1842–1910), the other well-known member of the Metaphysical Club, was formally trained as a scientist. Beginning with physiology and anatomy, James eventually earned a degree as a medical doctor. However, he never practiced medicine, turning instead to psychology and then to philosophy. James taught at Harvard (1872–1907) during a time when the methods of science were applied to every field of study, including psychology. James is best known for shifting the interest in psychology from the study of consciousness to the study of behavior. This move was made because James believed that one cannot observe consciousness, but one can infer the states of consciousness by observing one's behavior.

It should not be surprising that James approached philosophy from the perspective of a psychologist. Critics of his philosophy argue that James' pragmatism was too subjective, that it was whatever the individual wanted it to be. As Smith notes of James,

> 'Truth,' he argued, is 'what works' or 'what pays,' or more precisely, that if the results of accepting a particular belief are 'good' or 'satisfactory,' then that belief must 'so far forth' be counted as true.[13]

Truth, according to James, is relative to the individual. Each individual could create "truth" by applying his or her own experiences, which may be different from anyone else's. Peirce hated this definition of pragmatism because, as stated above, he believed that there is only one truth for everyone that would be created by the methods of science. Another contribution of James and the pragmatists was that he argued that many previous philosophers debated questions that were essentially unprovable. James said that this was a foolish thing to do. Rather, he argued, we should use philosophy to improve our daily lives in ways that are tangible. In so doing James represented a characteristic popular with many Americans.

Both Peirce and James were monists in that they rejected the idea that the mind and the body are separate in any way. Both believed that one begins with observations in the creation of knowledge, and in so doing developed a philosophy that was friendly to the human body. Yet they did not reject the concept of mind. Rather their philosophies tried to unite the ideas of mind and body into an integrated whole. Their philosophies affected popular ideas of sport and physical education in the late nineteenth and early twentieth centuries by influencing the leading educators of those times.

Sport in the Nineteenth Century

As stated earlier in the chapter, a number of perspectives can be used to explain the rise of sport in America in the nineteenth century. American culture became increasingly urban and technical, providing both the necessary numbers of people as athletes and spectators, and the technology necessary for sports as we know them today. Throughout the century Americans became less resistant to the idea that adults could use their spare time for recreational activities, and among their leisure pursuits were both playing and spectating. American culture underwent a period of modernization in which the roles of individuals and institutions with respect to all types of activities were viewed in radically different ways. On the whole, America experienced a cultural revolution, and sport changed along with everything else.

Justifying Sport in the Nineteenth Century

As has been the case in the past 2500 years in the Western world, attitudes toward sport in America changed as Americans changed their attitudes toward religion. As in the sixteenth through the eighteenth centuries, nineteenth-century Puritans generally frowned on sport involvement. Certain activities were acceptable that "re-created" an individual, but for the most part physical activity was frowned upon. What is interesting about the nineteenth century is how, for the first time in our discussion, religion was used to *justify* participating in sport. How this came about takes us back to England, where a movement known as "muscular Christianity" developed.

Other arguments were used as well. The idea that competitiveness is a desirable virtue developed during this time. In addition, health issues associated with living in the city justified participation. Sport was seen as a "man builder," an activity that would turn boys raised by mothers into men when fathers were in the factory. All of these arguments were used by the newly developed press with great effectiveness, and at the end of the nineteenth century attitudes toward participation were turned around completely from where they were early in the nineteenth century.

Religion as an Argument for Sport

During the early 1800s in England an attitude toward physicality developed known as "muscular Christianity," and this attitude had a positive effect on the popularity of sport in America. The doctrine of muscular Christianity argued that there is something innately good and godly about brute strength and power. Physical weakness was considered to be unnatural because it was only a reflection of moral and spiritual weakness. Consequently, an effort to overcome physical weakness could also be construed as an effort to be Christian and therefore moral and good. Sport activities came to be seen as an effort to be a good Christian. In addition to this justification, muscular Christians believed that the "body was a temple," and consequently muscular Christians believed that they were obligated to care for and develop one's physical being.

Developed in England by Bishop Fraser, Thomas Hughes, Charles Kingsley, and Charles Wordsworth, muscular Christianity associated godliness with manliness. Perhaps the most influential argument for muscular Christianity was made in *Tom Brown's Schooldays* by Thomas Hughes.[14] Published in 1857, the book was incredibly popular among both English and American students and went through six editions in its first year of printing. Many of the teachers and students who read the book were associated with the English public schools (which Americans would call private schools), and the ideas of muscular Christianity permeated these educational institutions.

The particular effect of muscular Christianity on education has been spelled out by Gerald Redmond:

> The sentiments of the muscular Christian gospel—i.e., that physical activity and sports (especially team games like cricket and football) contributed significantly towards the development of moral character, fostered a desirable patriotism, and that such participation and its ensuing virtues were transferable to other situations and/or to later life (such as from the schoolboy playing-field to the military battlefield).[15]

These ideas were readily accepted by Americans who were developing education in the late 1800s. In addition, Baron de Coubertin, the French founder of the modern Olympic Games, was very influenced by the ideas of muscular Christianity. Clearly the ideas of muscular Christianity have been one of the most significant factors in the development of sport in educational systems.

Other Arguments That Justified Sport Participation

The ideas of muscular Christianity combined nicely with other philosophies. Transcendentalists sought a return to nature and promoted ideas of rugged individualism. Physicality became a desirable image during the 1850s, and as one scholar noted, "Winning in athletics gave colleges visibility in a physical form. The physical nature of the individual and of American society appeared to be a desired quality in the age of Darwin."[16]

Specifically, after Darwin the idea of being competitive was important, and sport was seen as the tool with which to teach young children the necessary virtue of being competitive.

Another argument that justified activity was the idea that "manliness" was a necessary characteristic in the "modern" world.[17] Families moved from the country to the city so that fathers could work in factories and offices. Fathers became concerned that when their sons could no longer work with them in the fields, mothers would cause their sons to grow up to be "feminine." The physicality associated with sports was seen as a desirable counterbalance to the influence of women in the life of young boys.

All of these justifications were used at one time or another in the nineteenth century, and all served to overcome the influence of Puritanism that had mitigated against playful activities for over 200 years. While this strategy was successful, it was not without its drawbacks. For every argument put forward to justify sport, a limitation has been found in the twentieth century. For instance, as the logic goes, if sport builds men, then women who play sport must be . . . *men!* In the twentieth century women have had to fight to overcome this stereotype, and it has not been easy for either men or women. Similarly, not all agree with the idea that competitiveness is a virtue. Indeed, cooperation is just as much a virtue as competitiveness.

Still, these arguments appear to have been necessary to overcome centuries of arguments that limited adult sport participation. It should come as no surprise that it may take more time still to overcome centuries of anti-play attitudes.

Sport Develops in the Nineteenth Century

As a generalization, playful recreations in the early 1800s tended toward games and less competitive activities, while the concept of competition and sport as we know it became more prevalent in the late 1800s. This does not mean, however, that Americans were not competitive in the early 1800s and that less competitive games were nonexistent in the late 1800s. Americans had both characteristics throughout the nineteenth century; the difference is one of degree.

The beginning of sport as we know it today began in the early 1800s, where "sport" can be distinguished from the activity of "games" and "play."[18] Most definitions of play describe it as a free or voluntary activity, one that stands outside ordinary life and is not "serious."[19] Games add the element of competition and always involve a struggle to win.[20] Sport can be both play and a game, and is also characterized by a demonstration of skill and often occurs within an institutional framework.

Examples of "play," "game," and "sport": A group of friends can "play" a "game" of football on a Sunday afternoon, where they enjoy themselves immensely by involving themselves in a playful activity and where the recreational activity is ". . . not necessarily oriented to outcome or production as (the) primary objective. . . ."[21] They can then watch a "game" of football on television. The game they watch represents "sport," where the teams are members of the institution that organizes professional sport: the National Football League. The rules are highly organized, the level of play is very high, the players highly skilled, and the purpose is to win. The first game of football, as we have defined it, is more a "game" than "sport," while the second game is more "sport" than "game"; This distinction does not devalue either activity. On the contrary, there is a large body of literature that argues that both activities are valuable. Rather, the purpose of the distinction is to describe how sport, as we know it now, has many different characteristics.

A perspective that describes how play and games evolved into sport is provided by the concept of modernization theory. Modernization theory is actually an organizational scheme used by historians to describe how a culture changes from a set of "premodern" characteristics to "modern" characteristics.[22] Applied to sport, modernization theory argues that sport tends to change from a set of premodern sporting characteristics to a set of modern sports characteristics. To understand how sport changed in the United States in the nineteenth century, one needs to understand how American society changed in the nineteenth century. Sport "mirrored" this change, and in fact sport may have been a tool in teaching Americans how to make the transition from traditional beliefs and practices to more contemporary or "modern" ways.

Traditional society is stable, local, governed by men at both the family and political level, has little specialization of roles, and depends on muscle power. Historian Mel Adelman goes on to say that

> [t]he past, present and future are the same, and time moves in endless cycles. Traditional society is further characterized by the weaving together of family and community in labor, leisure, and religion. Ritual flows through the entire experience of traditional society, and no precise boundaries exist between the secular and religious life, or between work and leisure. The prevailing outlook is one of actual acceptance or of resignation toward life as it is; the repetition of past ways rather than innovative action is encouraged. By contrast, modern society is dynamic, cosmopolitan, technological, and marked by a functional social structure that conforms to shifting political and economic structures; most of all, it is rational. The desire for change and the belief that it can be achieved through the application of rational analysis is central to modern society.[23]

Adelman concludes that the assumptions of modern life, especially the belief that we can use rational methods to manipulate objects, the environment, people, and ideas undergird the way that we see the world today. Sport changed in a similar manner, and the characteristics of premodern and modern sport can be described and applied to all sorts of sporting situations. The characteristics of premodern and modern ideal sporting types can be seen in table 12.1.

Modernization theory is useful because it can be used to relate all kinds of changes to one another. Used properly, the theory can explain

Table 12.1

"The Characteristics of Premodern and Modern Ideal Sporting Types"[24]

Premodern Sport

1. *Organization*—either nonexistent at best informal and sporadic; contests are arranged by individuals directly or indirectly (e.g., tavern owners, bettors) involved.
2. *Rules*—simple, unwritten, and based on local customs and traditions; variations exist from one locale to another.
3. *Competition*—locally meaningful only; no chance for national reputation.
4. *Role differentiation*—low among participants; loose distinction between playing and spectating.
5. *Public information*—limited, local, and oral.
6. *Statistics and records*—nonexistent.

Modern Sport

1. *Organization*—formal; institutionally differentiated at the local, regional, and national levels.
2. *Rules*—formal, standardized, and written; rationally and pragmatically worked out and legitimated by organizational means.
3. *Competition*—national and international, superimposed on local contests; chance to establish national and international reputations.
4. *Role differentiation*—high; emergence of specialists (professionals) and strict distinctions between playing and spectating.
5. *Public information*—reported on a regular basis in local newspapers, as well as national sports journals; appearance of specialized magazines, guidebooks, etc.
6. *Statistics and records*—kept and published on a regular basis; considered important measures of achievement; records sanctioned by national associations.

Melvin Adelman, *A Sporting Time: New York City and the Rise of Modern Athletics, 1820–70* (Urbana, Ill.: University of Illinois Press, 1986), 6.

many changes in American culture, including the manner in which sport and physical education changed. It should be noted, however, that modernization is not a *cause* of change. Americans did not want to become "modern" in the nineteenth century any more than we want to be "traditional" right now; indeed, Americans then did not know what "modern" was. This theory merely explains, from an artificially convenient perspective, the kinds of changes that took place over 100 years ago.

How sport developed from play and games can be explained within the framework of modernization, and examples of modernization are the development of horse and harness racing, baseball, and some of the supposedly "amateur" sports. It should be noted that "modern" is not necessarily better than "premodern." Those who raced horses or trotters before those sports were modernized no doubt enjoyed themselves just as much as those who raced after those sports were modern. Yet the setting in which these different participants raced were very different, and modernization theory describes what these differences were.

Sport and Play in Nineteenth-Century America

The forces that changed the manner in which nineteenth-century Americans participated in sport are evident in the sports themselves. The sports that we enjoy in the twentieth century developed in the nineteenth century, and the story of how these sports evolved helps one understand why they look the way they do. The development of sports such as horse and harness racing, baseball, rowing, boxing, and track and field, evolved into sporting institutions that shaped the organization of all subsequent sports. In the twentieth century a sport *must* look like these nineteenth-century leaders in terms of organizations, written rules, the easy availability of public information and statistics, or we do not even recognize the activity as a sport at all. So the story of the development of certain sports provides a model for the development of any sport in our time.

Horse and Harness Racing

One of the most popular American pastimes during the nineteenth century was horse racing. While the North tried, with limited success, to ban horse racing (in 1802 New York State legislated an antiracing law), Americans of all social classes would gather to see which of two horses was the faster. Southern Americans, particularly the wealthy, enjoyed horse racing as far back as the mid-1600s. Racing horses served as amusement and to distinguish the upper classes from other social groups. As one scholar noted,

> By promoting these public displays the great planters legitimized the cultural values which racing symbolized—materialism, individualism, and competitiveness. These colorful, exclusive contests helped persuade subordinate white groups that gentry culture was desirable, something worth emulating. . . . The wild sprint down a dirt track served the interests of Virginia's gentlemen better than they imagined.[25]

This activity was more "game" than "sport" as we have defined it. Southern planters wagered on the contests and no doubt enjoyed them as playful diversions, but the contests were unorganized, informal, and sporadic. The justification for racing horses was to "improve the breed," to find out which horses were faster, stronger, and had more endurance, and then to breed them to one another. In so doing the main means of transportation during the early nineteenth century would be improved.

Legalized racing resumed in New York in 1821 when the antiracing law was modified. Racing was deemed acceptable on two days a year on Long Island as long as the public was safeguarded by the sheriff and that attempts would be made to eliminate gambling and the undesirable elements that accompanied it. Races ranged from one to four miles in distance, and usually between only a few horses. Wagering was common, and prizes by the New York Association for the Improvement of the Breed (NYAIB) varied from $1,000 to $1,900. While horse racing was legal, then, it did not capture the hearts of Americans until the famous

Figure 12.1

*Maryland Jockey Club, Pimlico, 1802. Courtesy of
the Enoch Pratt Free Library, Baltimore, Maryland.*

Figure 12.2

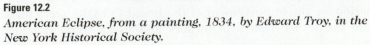
*American Eclipse, from a painting, 1834, by Edward Troy, in the
New York Historical Society.*

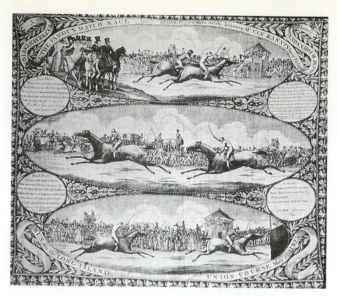

Figure 12.3

Great North–South horse race took place in 1823 on the Union Course on Long Island. A crowd of 60,000 turned out to watch the Northern horse, Eclipse, defeat the pride of the South, Sir Henry. Eclipse won 2 out of 3 four mile heats.

race between Eclipse and Henry, in which Eclipse represented the North and Henry represented the South.

Eclipse defeated Henry two out of three races over four miles to the delight of tens of thousands of spectators. The following passage describes what it must have been like to be part of one of the first major sporting events in America:

> Those who had not attended the contest waited anxiously for the results. The *Post* came out with a special edition, probably the first sporting extra in American journalism, while the *American* did not go to press until informed of the winner. The coverage of the race in subsequent days was extraordinary, especially given the four-sheet format of local newspapers and the limited space allocated to news. The picture drawn by the New York newspapers was generally favorable. They noted that numerous men of wealth and taste were present and that the ladies' stands were nicely filled. Although the match attracted a large crowd, perfect decorum was evident among a gathering of good losers and subdued winners.[26]

While the popularity of horse racing rose and fell through the early 1800s, the race between Eclipse and Henry served as a model throughout the 1820s. In the 1830s more horses raced in each event, and tracks were built throughout America. Jockey clubs, such as the New York Association for the Improvement of the Breed (NYAIB), were formed to facilitate the social desires of owners and to facilitate the logistical

Figure 12.4
Trotting.

needs of races by standardizing the rules that governed the sport. Magazines like the *American Turf Register* and *Sporting Magazine* provided summaries of races and documented the history and breed of American horses. All of these changes are characteristics of modern sport.

Harness racing, or trotting, began in the cities. Early on it consisted of impromptu contests between individuals who merely wanted to race their carriages. More formal matches were a natural outgrowth and were conducted on tracks and city streets with the prize being the wager between the two contestants. In 1824 interested racers formed a trotting club, with the NYAIB as the model. They built a racecourse on Long Island, met twice a year, and used the same arguments (improvement of the breed) to justify their interests. As horse racing declined in popularity in the late 1830s, trotting became more popular, perhaps because many people owned trotters while only the very wealthy could bet on a thoroughbred race horse. Furthermore, the egalitarian bent of harness racing overcame the aristocratic trappings of horse racing. This difference manifested itself in the commercialization of trotting, making it available to almost everyone. Harness racing was the leading American spectator sport by the early 1850s, and as Adelman noted,

> The founding of the National Trotting Association in 1870 symbolized the transformation of harness racing from a premodern sport to a modern sport. In contrast to the informal road contests that took place in the Northeast half a century earlier, harness racing had evolved into a highly organized, national sport with relatively uniform rules. The emergence of a trotting literature . . . and developments in the breeding industry . . . in the 1870s further demonstrated the centralizing and modernizing forces at work in the sport.[27]

In sum, horse racing and harness racing changed significantly between 1820 and 1870. Initially contests between a few participants

Figure 12.5

Opening Day on the Fashion Course, from a drawing in Frank Leslie's Illustrated Newspaper, June 28, 1856.

and of local interest, horse and harness races met all of the criteria that describe modern sport. For better or for worse, a pattern was established that was emulated in many other sports.

Ball Games: Cricket, Baseball, and Football

The modern game of baseball is the culmination of a variety of simple bat, base, and ball games that were played as early as the colonial period. However, these games did not capture the hearts of Americans until the early to mid-1800s. Several bat, base, and ball games, among them rounders, town ball, and "base-ball" (as it was known in its early forms), evolved into the modern game of baseball between 1840 and 1870. Many have argued that baseball is the "national game," yet the status of baseball as any kind of American game was, during the early and mid-1800s, problematic. How and why baseball developed the way it did is the subject of both American mythology and historical study.

It has been argued that in order for ball games to be attractive to Americans, a tradition of spring and summer rituals that involved bat and ball games was needed.[28] However, Americans did not have this tradition, and as a consequence it took longer to develop ball games than it did in England. In addition, Americans were much more individualistic than their English counterparts. Americans enjoyed sports that were individual in nature, like hunting, racing, or boxing. Furthermore, ritualistic games were considered "pagan" by Puritans, who associated ball games with the rituals of the Catholic Church. Finally, ball games were not considered "manly" activities because those who played were generally children and did not have well developed skills. As a consequence, the quality of play was low and did not attract much attention.

Cricket. The various games of baseball in the early 1800s included the English game of cricket, a slightly older and more formalized ball game. Interestingly, cricket was initially more popular than baseball between 1840 and 1855.[29] Cricket received more attention in the press than any other sport other than horse and harness racing. However, it was a sport that was played primarily by English immigrants and was not as easily accepted by Americans for a variety of reasons.

Cricket was popular in England for nearly a century, and it benefited from an English tradition of playing ball games. As one scholar notes,

> Unlike other sports which sprang from day-to-day activities, ball games originated in religious and magical functions and were closely associated with fertility rites. The Church adopted these ritualistic ball games and used them for Christian purposes, with some modification in their meaning. In Europe various ball games became part of the Easter observance and other springtime customs. . . . (T)he subsequent development of the bat and ball games so familiar to us hinged on the adoption of the pagan ball rites into the Easter Christian ceremonies.[30]

Cricket was the first sport to try to overcome these obstacles to popularity in America, but it had several "strikes" against it.[31] First, cricket in England was a highly evolved, competitive sport relative to the simple ball games played by American children. It was too hard for Americans to play, and as a consequence it had a difficult time catching on. Second, it was highly organized and had the basic characteristics of a modern sport with standardized rules and a central governing authority, the Marleybone Cricket Club in England. For cricket to be played properly it had to be played the Marleybone way, and this was difficult to do in an America that was, for the most part in the early and mid-1800s, rural. Third, cricket was closely associated with gambling, an association that was distasteful to many Americans who had the time to play. Fourth, cricket in England had a tradition of allowing the lower social classes to play with the upper classes. But this tradition did not exist in America, where those with time to recreate would not associate with those of lower class. But perhaps the most important reason that cricket did not catch on was that it had no "manly" virtues, and therefore men would not spend the time to develop the skills necessary to playing cricket. Instead they would play the game of their youth: base-ball.

Around 1855 the popularity of baseball began to overtake that of cricket. One reason was that cricket was associated with its English origins, while baseball was the "American" game that was familiar to its schoolboys. In addition, the outbreak of the Civil War in 1861 had a dramatic and immediate impact on the popularity of baseball. Baseball was a much easier game to play than cricket and was taught to fellow soldiers in both the North and the South. After the War, soldiers returned home and continued to play baseball. Finally, baseball was a much faster game. Cricket matches could last days, while baseball could be played in a matter of hours. Eventually these characteristics of the game came to be associated with nationalistic claims. Baseball became the "American" game, while cricket was the "English" game.

Perhaps most important, however, was that Americans were playing any kind of ball game at all. As stated earlier, games were associated with children and were not considered a good way for adult men to spend their time. Cricket and baseball did much to undermine this argument, and the arguments that were used to promote these two sports still resonate with Americans today:

> The character value argument had profound importance for the development of ball games in general, and it was especially critical to the acceptance of ball playing as a manly activity. Claims that ball playing promoted healthful exercise were important but did little if anything to overcome the charge that ball playing was for children; hence, statements that cricket and baseball were manly often accompanied claims that they were healthy activities. . . . The argument concluded that if ball games called these virtues into play—and in fact they were critical to doing well at such sports—then ball playing was obviously one way of demonstrating manhood.[32]

If one played ball, then, one was either "manly" or could become so. It should not be surprising, then, that women had such a difficult time breaking into sport in the twentieth century. The very argument that justified the inclusion of sport in American culture precluded women because it would make men out of them!

Baseball. Many myths surround baseball, and to the extent that they create the flavor of the game they do much good. One of them has to do with baseball's origin. As the story goes, Abner Doubleday created baseball in 1839 in Cooperstown, New York. In reality this story was created by Albert Spalding, the former major league pitcher and sporting goods magnate, who had formed a commission to investigate the origins of the American game. At the time Spalding was trying to promote baseball, and Spalding must have believed that the acceptance of this story was critical to popular acceptance of baseball.

Baseball evolved from the games of rounders and town ball and was known to be played in various forms as early as 1734 at Harvard.[33] A dozen or so clubs sprang up in New York City between 1845 and 1855 and were composed of middle-class, white-collar workers who lived in the city. One of the most popular of these clubs was the Knickerbocker Base Ball Club, and one of its members, Alexander Cartwright, helped develop the rules that we use today. By 1860 there were over 100 clubs in the New York area alone, and contemporary newspaper reporters were stunned by the popularity and the growth of the sport.

This sudden growth and the competition between the teams caused a need for consistent rules of the game. It was difficult to play a game when the two teams involved used different rules. For instance, some of the rules that were debated were the adoption of the nine-inning game over the 21 run rule, caught fly balls that would put out a batter, and the elimination of throwing the ball at the runner to get him out. In 1858, twenty-six clubs banded together to form the National Association of Base Ball Players, an organization that would govern baseball for thirteen years. This organization was weak and ineffective, but it marks the beginning of an era in which players would meet to revise the rules, settle disputes, and try to control the game.

Figure 12.6
1869 Cincinnati Red Stockings. Courtesy Spalding Archives, Chicopee, Massachusetts.

In 1871 the National Association of Professional Base Ball Players was formed. This organization represented a variety of changes in America relative to sport in general and baseball in particular. Prior to 1871 professional athletes existed in fact, but their status was problematic because of American attitudes regarding wagering, play, and sport. Consequently, most "professionals" prior to 1871 were paid "under the table." Also, professional athletes could not exist unless spectators were willing to pay them, indirectly at least, to compete. Finally, that men were willing to play baseball for money and were paid to do so meant that Americans no longer believed sport to be the domain of children.

> More than any other sport in America baseball came to symbolize the
> increasing tendency of Americans to watch athletic contests. . . . The
> rise of spectator sports permitted onlookers to enjoy 'vicariously what
> they would have liked to do themselves. . . .'[34]

In the end, the emergence of baseball as a professional sport legitimized sport participation in sport generally. Sport advocates argued that it had health and recreational benefits; it served as a counterbalance to the evils of the city; it developed character through the exercise of discipline, self-control, and teamwork; and that it was a valuable educational tool as a teacher and tester of manhood.

Football.   Long before the first collegiate football game between Rutgers and Princeton on November 6, 1869, men have made a contest of moving an object between two goals by brute force. The English played rugby, primarily an upper-class sport, and for centuries had ball games somewhat similar to the goals of American football. English ball games were often a contest between two towns or villages, with the abled bodied men of the towns squaring off on the adjoining Green or Commons. Mass brawls often occurred that caused many an injury among the commoners of seventeenth- and eighteenth-century England. The origins of American football are primarily derived from soccer and rugby and were gradually modified until the modern game of football emerged during the early part of the twentieth century.

Early American football was characterized by the violent nature of the sport, a characteristic which is emblematic of the sport today. The first games were adaptations from the rules and format established by the London Football Association. The ball was round and the athletes wore no protective clothing or equipment. Players would work the ball toward their opponent's goal by a series of short punts, relying on the team's ability to keep the opposing players from gaining control of the ball. This was usually accomplished by using mass formations which proved to be brutal and injurious. Carrying the ball was not allowed, and the forward pass was also prohibited. Goals were scored by kicking the ball into the opponent's goal.

Football in the early 1800s resembled soccer more than rugby. The students at Harvard modified the game, and by 1871 the modified rules permitted picking up the ball at any time, much like rugby. In 1873 Princeton, Yale, Columbia, and Rutgers formed the Intercollegiate Association for Football, which allowed the members to refine and codify the rules of the game. Perhaps no one person gave more to the game of football than Walter Camp. While coaching at Yale in 1879, he began to change the game from rugby to American football. He was a member of every football rules convention in college football's early years, and many consider Walter Camp the "father" of American football. Contributions by Camp include:

1. replacing the rugby "scrummage" with the scrimmage;
2. using a system of downs tied to yards gained as a means to advance or relinquish the ball;
3. eleven players on a team with specific positions; and
4. tackling below the waist, elimination of the arms while blocking.[35]

The evolution of football from a kind of rugby to a distinctly American game, using the basic rules outlined above, was not a smooth transition. The rule changes were debated extensively, yet as Oriard argued, these changes were necessary to make the American game:

> First the creation of the scrimmage, as a substitute for the rugby scrummage (players from both teams massed about the ball, all trying to kick it out to a teammate), gave the ball to one team at a time; then the five-yard rule guaranteed that the team possessing the ball either advanced it or gave it up. Later revisions—rules on scoring, on blocking and tackling, on movement before the ball was snapped, on the number of offensive players allowed behind the line of scrimmage, most crucially on forward passing—were necessary before American football assumed a form in 1912 that we would recognize today as our game. Nonetheless, in the evolution of American football from English rugby, the distance from 1882 to 1993 is less significant than that from 1876 to 1882.[36]

The study of football reveals much about how Americans feel about rules. It was necessary in America to have referees to enforce the rules that were developed, for American coaches and players continually sought to use the rules *to win the game* rather than to penalize *ungentlemanly conduct*, as was the case in Victorian England. The "American character" differed from its English counterpart in that, since the beginning of modern sport, Americans valued the *outcome* of the game more than *how* the game is played. In contrast, English sportsmen valued the *style* of play and the way the games supported the British social class system. The two approaches to sport are made explicit by the following quotes. Oriard noted that an English gentleman objected to the imposition of rules because of the assumptions that support their need:

> It is a standing insult to sportsmen to have to play under a rule which assumes that players intend to trip, hack and push their opponents and to behave like cads of the most unscrupulous kind. I say that the lines marking the penalty area are a disgrace to the playing field of a public school.[37]

In contrast was the American attitude that *applauded* tripping, hacking, and pushing opponents if it served to win the game. This strategy was evident in early baseball, where rules were regularly circumvented in order to give a team an advantage and included such situations as

> . . . a manager substituting himself as a foul ball sails toward the dugout, just in time to catch it; a catcher throwing his mask a few feet down the first-base line to trip the runner; an outfielder juggling the ball as he trots toward the infield, preventing a runner from advancing on a sacrifice fly. Buck Ewing, a baseball manager early in the twentieth century, summed up this spirit: 'Boys . . . you've heard the rules read. Now the question is: What can we do to beat them?'[38]

Football was similar in this respect, and many applauded the "brainy" nature of the college athlete who could figure out a way around the rules to take advantage of them. The scrimmage line was continually redefined because players used tricks to interfere with the center snap. Rules on blocking, mass plays, scoring, holding, and so on, were developed through the late nineteenth century. "Until a rule made it impossible, a clever team discovered that it could score repeated touchdowns simply by bunting the after-touchdown goal kick to its own man, who then touched the ball down behind the goal line."[39] In sum, Americans would do anything to win, and they needed rules to limit behavior so that all could play the "game."

Another characteristic of American sport is revealed in the role of the modern coach. English tradition limited the role of the coach to that of an active "team captain," but Americans sought the help of more seasoned leaders who, because of their knowledge of the game, could lead a team to victory with more frequency. Initially sideline coaches were banned, as team captains led their squads from the field, but attempts to circumvent this rule were made as soon as the rule was in place. The next step toward the professional coach was the unpaid graduate student who had played the game. Paid professional coaches originated at western colleges such as Minnesota and Chicago, and eventually they held positions at all colleges that had football. Professional coaching was considered a "shady practice," however, and was only grudgingly accepted. By the beginning of the twentieth century, paid professional coaches were here to stay. But the debate over the role of professionals in sport had only just begun.

"Amateur" Sports

One of the movements that developed in American sport during the 1800s was amateurism. The popular definition of an "amateur" is one who competes for the love of the sport, and as a consequence receives no money for his or her athletic efforts.[40] Nineteenth-century historians, primarily English but also American, sought to identify their athletic efforts with the ancient Greeks. Their interpretation of the ancient Greek Olympic athletes, who competed only for the "wreath" that symbolized victory, called for them to disassociate with those who would earn money through athletic pursuits. More recent scholarship, however, shows that amateurism developed in the 1860s and 1870s, when upper-class athletes refused to compete against their middle- and lower-class counterparts, primarily on the track and on the water in rowing.[41] The social clubs that were formed to house these two sports remain to this day, although the concept of amateurism is no longer accepted as a valid distinction between athletes. For over one hundred years, however, the idea of who and what an amateur is has dominated many American sports.

Rowing. Rowing was one of the most popular sports in the early to mid-1800s. Rowing races began as simple, unorganized races conducted by working class "watermen," rowers who lived in port cities who made a living by rowing. In the 1800s rowers were needed to quickly reach incoming sailing ships with news and supplies, and they also made a living by rowing customers across rivers and bays where there were no bridges. In both cases the speed of the rowers was critical to their making a living, and racing was a natural byproduct of their desire to prove they were the fastest (not to mention that racing was fun!). In both cases rowers would race for bets, and occasionally outsiders would also bet for the fun of it. In the early 1820s several races were held in New York that drew large crowds and large wagers. One race, between a crew from the English frigate *Hussar* and a New York rowing club composed of watermen called the Whitehallers, drew between 20,000 and 50,000 spectators. The Whitehallers' victory was a source of national pride and elevated the popularity of rowing for several years after the race.

In contrast to the watermen were the young men from prominent families who rowed for social diversion rather than for a living or for competition. The first clubs were formed in the 1830s and 1840s in New

York, Boston, and Philadelphia, and as far back as 1837 we know that they had rules against competing for money. The Undine Barge Club, formed in 1856, had one rule that stated that any member who raced against another boat for a wager would incur a fine of twenty-five dollars, and furthermore, for "tyrranical or ungentlemanly conduct (one) was liable to a fine of five dollars."[42]

Rowing clubs became more numerous following the Civil War and continued to try to distinguish themselves from their lower-class counterparts. The reason for this distinction is fairly clear in retrospect: members of the upper class did not want to look bad by losing to members of lower classes in sporting contests, which in rowing were highly visible. At the same time, however, rowing races were becoming increasingly popular, and members of the exclusive rowing clubs wanted to be a part of these races. Between the years 1845 and 1865, professional rowers dominated rowing, and crowds of up to 10,000 people watched the biggest races. By 1870 over 200 rowing clubs had been formed, and there was a corresponding increase in the number of regattas.

In 1872 an event was held that marked the beginning of amateurism.[43] In June of that year the Schuylkill Navy Rowing Association held the National Amateur Regatta, and among its "Special Rules" was the following:

> Amateur Oarsmen only, will be admitted. We define an Amateur Oarsman to be one who has never rowed for money, and who has never depended upon rowing for his livelihood.[44]

For the first time an athletic event excluded those who were not "amateur." The problem with this definition was that it could not be fairly applied, and in hindsight scholars have called amateur rules a "weapon of class warfare."[45]

The National Amateur Regatta was considered quite a success, and in August of that year twenty-seven clubs formed the National Association of Amateur Oarsmen (NAAO). This association, like the NAPBBP, was formed to develop uniform rules and to govern the sport. Unlike the NAPBBP, however, one of the rules was to exclude professionals, and in taking this step rowers were the first to clearly separate amateurs from professionals. This separation was widely criticized at the time, and it supports the contention that no accepted view of amateurism or professionalism had emerged by the 1870s.[46]

Amateurism during this period of time, by our standards, was a type of social discrimination. Basically it was a rule that separated athletes by social class, specifically working men from "gentlemen." Begun in England as an effort to separate noblemen in sport from the common man on the basis of right of birth, amateurism looked much different in America, where there was no acknowledged "nobility." Therefore, instead of using nobility as a means of distinguishing social class, the leaders of the amateur movement in the United States used racing for money as a means of distinguishing social class. This idea eventually became intertwined with the concept of "sport for the love of sport" and

Figure 12.7
Single sculler.

in practice was used to separate those who did physical work for a living from those of the higher social classes.

While rowing was one of the most popular sports in the mid-1800s, by the late 1800s it was limited to the amateur clubs and elite universities in the East. It no longer attracted the large crowds that it once did, and the idea of betting in rowing was limited to college oarsmen racing for the shirts of their opponent. The reason for the decline in popularity of professional rowing is subject to debate. One theory has it that rowing was difficult to commercialize because rowing races do not lend themselves to good spectating. Another is that spectators became disgruntled after several races that were "thrown" by the contestants in order to collect on their wagers. At any rate, by 1870 amateur rowing was a "modern" sport, with "a higher level of modern structure than any other sport in America, with the exception of harness racing and baseball."[47]

Track and Field. Much like rowing, track and field competition was affected by the amateur movement. Sometimes called "pedestrianism" in its early days (from the walking contests that were part of early track and field contests), track and field athletics were stimulated by the initiation of the Caledonian Games.[48] Organized by the Scottish community that immigrated to the United States, the Caledonian Games continued a tradition of informal annual gatherings that included athletic competition. The first games were held in 1853, and Caledonian Clubs were organized in Boston, New York, and Philadelphia in the next few years.

The games included throwing the heavy hammer and light hammer, putting the light stone and the heavy stone (both precursors to the shot put and the hammer throw of modern athletic competition), tossing the caber, wheelbarrow races (which was conducted blindfolded), sack races, the standing high jump, the running long jump, a short running race, and dancing.[49] These initial contests sometimes offered cash prizes and quickly became highly organized and popular contests that drew large crowds.

While the Caledonian Games were popular, they were clearly not amateur in their intent. Track and field took on these characteristics through the influence of the New York Athletic Club (NYAC), formed in 1868. Three men, William Buckingham Curtis, John Babcock, and Henry Buermeyer, were involved in sports in the New York City area and were attracted to the English model of track and field that they had been exposed to when traveling in that country. Curtis, a noted sports enthusiast, was especially influential in the formation of the NYAC. A successful weightlifter, a track and field enthusiast, and also a champion rower, Curtis was also influential in the formation of the National Association of Amateur Oarsmen. In 1868 the NYAC sponsored its first indoor meet in the Empire Skating Rink, and among the innovations Curtis introduced were spiked running shoes imported from England.

By 1879 there were over 100 athletic clubs in New York City, and many other cities followed the amateur model. Influenced by both the success of the NAAO and the NYAC, these clubs promoted athletics in conjunction with the concept of amateurism. In 1879 an organization was formed that would hopefully settle all disputes regarding amateurism and help organize national championships in amateur sports. The National Association of Amateur Athletes of America (NAAAA) attempted to do just this but was largely ineffective. In 1888 fifteen clubs, led by the NYAC, joined together to form the Amateur Athletic Union (AAU). The AAU was a much stricter organization that banned athletes from their competitions if they competed in any open race they did not sanction. By the 1890s the AAU had control of all amateur competition in the United States.

Summary

Horse and harness racing, cricket and baseball, and rowing and track and field were obviously not the only sports that were practiced in the 1800s. Boxing and golf developed as professional sports during this time period, while football, yachting, tennis, bicycling, and many other sports began on an amateur basis. Sporting competitions were held between the colleges as early as 1852 with the Harvard–Yale crew race. Furthermore, not all sport activities were competitive. Americans continued to practice traditional recreations like hunting, fishing, dancing, bowling, and many other pursuits.

The 1800s mark the time when Americans came to be more comfortable with physical activity for its own sake, and this can be associated with a significantly more favorable view of the human body. They were much more health conscious with the change from the "healthy" agrarian lifestyle to the "unhealthy" urban lifestyle, and sports were one of the means to overcome this change. Furthermore, the idea that one developed desirable social and personal skills came to be associated with sport. Manliness, character building, discipline, and many other virtues were associated with sport to legitimize it as an activity worthy of adults. The association of sport with our educational institutions meant that Americans believed these activities were in some way educational.

Almost every organized sport underwent a process of modernization that helped them develop governing institutions, organize rules, and keep statistics. Organized sports were exposed to the various media, and their competitions became meaningful on a national level. Athletes developed the specialized skills necessary to be competitive. Clearly the 1800s were a time of rapid change for sport, and many of the changes we witnessed during this century are still with us today.

Discussion Questions

1. What is modernization theory? How does modernization theory explain the changes in sport in the nineteenth century?

2. What was the metaphysical position of William James and Charles Peirce? How did their views of the mind/body relationship reflect the changes in American sport?

3. How did the characteristic of "manliness" affect the evolution of baseball in America?

4. How influential were English sporting traditions upon the development of sport in America?

Suggestions for Further Reading

Betts, J. R. "Mind and Body in Early American Thought." In *The American Sporting Experience,* edited by Steven A. Riess. New York: Leisure Press, 1984, 61–79.

Betts, J. R. *America's Sporting Heritage: 1850–1950.* Reading, Mass.: Addison-Wesley Publishing Co., 1974.

Gutmann, A. *From Ritual to Record: The Nature of Modern Sports.* New York: Columbia University Press, 1978.

Oriard, M. *Reading Football: How the Popular Press Created an American Spectacle.* Chapel Hill, N.C.: University of North Carolina Press, 1993.

Struna, N. "Puritans and Sport: The Irretrievable Tide of Change." In *The American Sporting Experience,* edited by Steven A. Riess. New York: Leisure Press, 1984, 15–33.

Young, D. C. *The Olympic Myth of Greek Amateur Athletics.* Chicago: Ares Publishers, Inc., 1984.

Notes

1. John R. Betts, *America's Sporting Heritage: 1850–1950* (Reading, Mass.: Addison-Wesley Publishing Co., 1974).

2. Stephen Riess, *Touching Base: Professional Baseball and American Culture in the Progressive Era* (Westport, Conn.: Greenwood Press, 1980).

3. Betts, *America's Sporting Heritage,* 78.

4. Ibid., 84.

5. Michael Moran, "New England Transcendentalism," in *The Encyclopedia of Philosophy,* Vol. 7, edited by Paul Edwards (New York: MacMillan Publishing Co., Inc., & The Free Press, 1967), 479–80.

6. Henry David Thoreau, *Walden, or Life in the Woods* (Boston, Mass.: Houghton Mifflin, 1906).

7. Philip Smith, *Sources of Progressive Thought in American Education* (Lanham, Md.: University Press of America, 1981), 4–5.

8. Cynthia Eagle Russett, *Darwin in America: The Intellectual Response 1865–1912* (San Francisco: W. E. Freeman and Co., 1976).

9. Goudge describes the impact of Darwin in intellectual circles as being ". . . more far reaching than that ushered in by Copernicus." T. A. Goudge, "Charles Robert Darwin," in *The Encyclopedia of Philosophy*, Vol. 2, edited by Paul Edwards (New York: MacMillan Publishing Co., Inc., & The Free Press, 1967), 294.

10. Ibid.

11. Russett, *Darwin in America*, 18.

12. Smith, *Sources of Progressive Thought*, 21–22.

13. Ibid., 108.

14. Gerald Redmond, "The First Tom Brown's Schooldays: Origins and Evolution of 'Muscular Christianity' in Children's Literature, 1762–1857," *Quest*, 30 (1978): 4–18.

15. Ibid., 7.

16. Ronald A. Smith, *Sport and Freedom: The Rise of Big Time College Athletics* (New York: Oxford University Press, 1988), viii.

17. Melvin Adelman, *A Sporting Time: New York City and the Rise of Modern Athletics, 1820–70* (Urbana, Ill.: University of Illinois Press), 1986.

18. The definition we use is, of course, an arbitrary one, but it does serve to distinguish between types of activities in a manner that serves the purposes of this book.

19. Allen L. Sack, "Sport: Play or Work?," in *Studies in the Anthropology of Play: Papers in Memory of Allan Tindall*, edited by Phillip Stevens (West Point, N.Y.: Leisure Press, 1977), 186–95.

20. John Loy, "The Nature of Sport," in *Sport, Culture, and Society*, edited by John W. Loy and Gerald Kenyon (London: The MacMillan Co., 1969), 43–61.

21. Adelman, *A Sporting Time*, 11.

22. Ibid.

23. Ibid., 5.

24. Ibid., 6.

25. T. H. Breen, "Horses and Gentlemen: The Cultural Significance of Gambling Among the Gentry of Virginia," *William and Mary Quarterly*, 34 (April 1977): 329–47.

26. Adelman, *A Sporting Time*, 36.

27. Ibid., 73.

28. Ibid.

29. Ibid.

30. Adelman, *A Sporting Time*, 98.

31. Ibid.

32. Ibid., 106.

33. Smith, *Sport and Freedom*.

34. Ibid., 149.

35. Ibid., 140.

36. Michael Oriard, *Reading Football* (Chapel Hill, N.C.: University of North Carolina Press, 1993), 26–27.

37. Quoted in Oriard, *Reading Football*, 27.

38. Oriad, *Reading Football*, 29.

39. Ibid., 29.

40. Steven G. Estes. "The 1872 National Amateur Regatta: The Definition of an Amateur Oarsman" (unpublished master's thesis, San Diego State University, 1985).

41. David C. Young, *The Olympic Myth of Greek Amateur Athletics* (Chicago: Ares Publishers, Inc., 1984).

42. Louis Heiland, *The Undine Barge Club of Philadelphia: 1856–1924* (Philadelphia: Drake Press, 1923), 14–15.

43. Estes, "The 1872 National Amateur Regatta."

44. Ibid., 67.

45. Allen Gutmann, *From Ritual to Record: The Nature of Modern Sports* (New York: Columbia University Press, 1978).

46. Adelman, *A Sporting Time.* Indeed, even today there is no agreed upon definition of an amateur. This is one of the reasons that amateurism has been removed from the Olympic Charter, and that professional athletes will be allowed to compete in the Olympics based on eligibility requirements of the national governing body of their sport.

47. Adelman, *A Sporting Time,* 197.

48. Gerald Redmond, *The Caledonian Games in Nineteenth-Century America* (Cranbury, N.J.: Associated University Press, 1971).

49. Betty Spears and Richard Swanson, *History of Sport and Physical Education in the United States,* 3d ed. (Dubuque, Iowa: Wm. C. Brown, 1983).

c h a p 13 t e r

Sport in the Twentieth Century

General Events

1891 James Naismith invents basketball

1892 Biddle University v. Livingston College: first intercollegiate football game between Black colleges

1895 William Morgan invents volleyball

1899 Uniform rules for women's basketball developed

1902 First Rose Bowl

1905 Football crisis, mediated by President Roosevelt; Intercollegiate Athletic Association of the United States founded

1910 National Collegiate Athletic Association founded

1915 Joint Basketball Committee makes uniform basketball rules

1917–1918 United States in World War I

1917 Athletic Conference of American College Women formed; National Committee on Women's Sports established

1920 American Professional Football Association formed in Canton, Ohio

1922 Chicago Bears formed

1925 New York Giants formed; Red Grange signs with Chicago

1941–1945 World War II

1960 American Football League formed

1966 First Super Bowl

1970 AFL and NFL merge

1971–1983 Association for Intercollegiate Athletics for Women active

Introduction

The model for sport as we know it in contemporary America was firmly in place by the late 1800s. The demographic, technological, and philosophical changes that occurred in American culture in the nineteenth century were reflected in the ways Americans behaved and thought about sport and play. America continued to become more urban as the economy reflected its increasingly industrialized basis. The trend of Americans moving to the cities led to a continued push for sport and recreational activities that could both accommodate urban lifestyles and mitigate against the unhealthy effects of living in the city. Technological innovation continued at an increasing rate, and these innovations were used in the sports world as much as in any other cultural arena. Sports information was increasingly easier to come by with telegraphs, then radio, then television. Sports journalism, developed in the nineteenth century, is more than ever a fact of American life.

Americans continued to become more comfortable with the human body throughout the twentieth century. One consequence of this was that sport and playful activities, which were associated with the body, were seen as increasingly acceptable. Religion has come to be seen as more of a personal guide than a public one and is no longer used as a reason for participating, or not participating, in public activities.[1] Consequently, sport and play, for better or worse, became increasingly free of religious restrictions. By the mid-1900s religion and sport were rarely associated in conversation in America. Religion was related to the spiritual aspects of a person; sport was related to the physical.

Yet in a country as large as America many different sets of attitudes and behaviors about sport can be found. Indeed, America is as pluralistic and multicultural as it has ever been, and the attitudes and behaviors of Americans toward sport and play are as varied as ever. This is so much the case that, although there are trends that can be studied, making any generalizations regarding the current status of sport in any given part of America is difficult. Sport and play are practiced in rural as well as urban America, exist in premodern as well as modern form, and are seen both as the exercise of only the body and as a means of achieving the integration of one's being. Sport and play, as we know these activities, are the summation of how an individual has experienced these activities in his or her own past.

Given the plurality of sport and playlike conditions that exist in American sport and play, a short discussion of some of the more significant changes in the twentieth century is in order. We have chosen to address football, basketball, volleyball, and women's sports to illustrate some of the trends evident in the twentieth century.

College Football

By the turn of the century, football was the most popular sport on American college campuses. Many "big games" emerged during the early part

Figure 13.1
Fielding Yost, Glenn "Pop" Warner, Amos Alonzo Stagg, and John Heisman.
Famous early football coaches. Courtesy of the University of Michigan.

of the century; for instance, Stanford–California, the Army–Navy game, and the Rose Bowl, which was first played in 1902. Football was clearly the "King of Intercollegiate Athletics," with Eastern teams having considerable success over teams from the South, Midwest, and West. Coaches became legends and national heroes. Among the greatest was Amos Alonzo Stagg, who was hired to coach at the University of Chicago in 1892, and who coached at Chicago for the next forty-nine years. Other coaches included Glenn "Pop" Warner, who coached Jim Thorpe at Carlisle Indian School and then coached at Stanford. John Heisman, for whom the Heisman Trophy is named, coached at Georgia Institute of Technology. Fielding Yost coached at the University of Michigan, and the immortal Knute Rockne at Notre Dame.

The first reported game between two black colleges involved Biddle University, currently known as Johnson C. Smith, and Livingston College. The game was played on Thanksgiving Day in 1892. By 1894,

KNUTE ROCKNE

Figure 13.2
Knute Rockne, legendary football coach at Notre Dame.

Figure 13.3
Coach Eddie Robinson with Grambling State University football team at Houston's Astrodome.

Tuskegee Institute, Lincoln University of Pennsylvania, Atlanta University, and Howard University were playing intercollegiate football. College football programs began to integrate in the late 1800s. In 1890, Amherst's football team had two black players, William H. Lewis and William Tecumseh Sherman Jackson.

The growth of intercollegiate football did not go smoothly. In 1905, eighteen football players were killed, and countless others were seriously injured. The brutality of the game caused Columbia and Northwestern to drop the sport, and Stanford and California reverted back to rugby. Mass formation plays, the most infamous being the "flying wedge," made the game into a devastating contact sport that could injure as well as kill.

Safety was not the only issue in college football, however. The positive changes that occurred did so because of the popularity of the game, yet many of the problems that developed as a consequence of football's popularity are still with the game today. Beginning in the early 1900s, huge stadiums were constructed on college campuses, and football rapidly became a big business. Alumni and fans began demanding winning seasons from their universities, and because of the demand for victories and the large amounts of money involved, football became a victim of its own success. The recruiting of players included promises of money, cars, and other gifts, and "tramp" athletes evolved. Tramp athletes would play for one school and then attend another under an

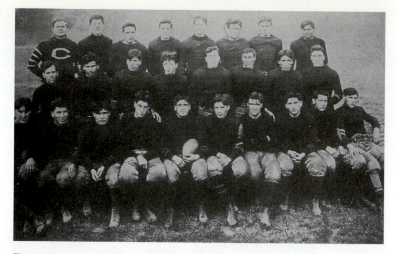

Figure 13.4

One of Carlisle's best teams—1907—with Jim Thorpe next to Coach "Pop" Warner in third row. Photo courtesy of Cumberland County Historical Society, Carlisle, PA.

Figure 13.5

Jim Thorpe, All American. Photo courtesy of Cumberland County Historical Society, Carlisle, PA.

assumed name as long as the "price was right." Eligibility rules were nonexistent in some colleges and loosely enforced in others. Players began to miss classes due to road games and injuries, and faculty control was minimal. For instance, in 1905 Yale's outstanding athlete, James D. Hogan, was accused of accepting a suite in Vanderbilt Hall, free meals at the University Club, and an all-expenses-paid, ten-day vacation to Cuba courtesy of the Yale Athletic Association. In addition, he held a job as a cigarette agent for the American Tobacco Company.[2] Scandals were familiar to college football fans in the 1990s, which is an indication of how little the game has changed. The accusations of the early 1900s, like most accusations made during the 1990s, were made by educators, who believed that college football perverted the goals of higher education. In 1918, Shailer Mathews, Dean of the Divinity School at the University of Chicago, stated:

> Football today is a social obsession—a boy killing, education-prostituting gladiatorial sport. It teaches virility and courage, but so does war. I do not know what should take its place, but the new game should not require the services of a physician, the maintenance of a hospital, and the celebration of funerals.[3]

As a result of the deaths and injuries that occurred in 1905, President Theodore Roosevelt met with the administrations and coaches of the leading football universities to reform the rules of the game in order to make it safer. Walter Camp and other football coaches who sought to change the game for the better attempted to control the changes, but it was President Roosevelt, an avid football fan, who exerted enough pressure on the college presidents to take the necessary steps for reform. It should be mentioned that President Roosevelt's son was injured while playing football. As a result, the president took a personal interest in this issue. In 1905, Henry McCracken, Chancellor of New York University, called a meeting of college presidents and other interested parties to discuss whether college football should be allowed to exist.[4] Thirteen colleges were represented at the first December meeting, and these colleges agreed to keep football and meet several weeks later to form a governing agency for college football.

The second December meeting was attended by sixty-two colleges, and the result of this meeting was the formation of the Intercollegiate Athletic Association of the United States, composed of thirty-eight colleges. This organization was re-named the National Collegiate Athletic Association (NCAA) in 1910. The NCAA saw its role as an educational one, and not one of enforcement or administration as is the case today. Minimum eligibility rules were adopted by the thirty-eight charter members, but there was no mechanism to enforce the rules. It was during this meeting that the new organization adopted a new rule that was to revolutionize the game of football: the forward pass.

Football grew at a slower rate during World War I. College officials were invited to attend a meeting in Washington convened by the NCAA to discuss the effect of the war on intercollegiate athletics. The position taken by the Secretary of War encouraged college students to participate in college athletics, and the NCAA passed resolutions that encouraged colleges to continue to offer athletics programs for all men. In spite of the efforts of the NCAA and the Secretary of War, however, sports were dropped by a number of colleges and high schools. In their place colleges offered physical education programs that emphasized military drills and such programs as the Reserve Officer Training Corps (ROTC).

Although intercollegiate athletics programs were dropped in some colleges, the war had a generally positive effect on athletics and physical education. Men were strongly encouraged, even required, to participate in the programs that were offered to prepare them for military service. Thus began a pattern that existed through the 1980s: during periods of war in which the United States is involved, athletic participation in both the schools and the military increases. The competitive atmosphere of athletics coupled with the physical and mental demands of actual training and competition were believed to prepare young men for the military. Football and wrestling in particular were believed to be of benefit to those who will have to fight in a war.

Professional Football

Professional football was played as far back as 1894, when the teams consisted of blue-collar workers and former college football players from the mill towns of Ohio and Pennsylvania. During the mid-1890s and early 1900s, teams practiced a few times a week and played primarily on weekends. These games were not held in high regard, however, and professional football struggled to gain the legitimacy of professional baseball. Connie Mack, one of the greatest baseball legends of all times, also managed the Philadelphia Athletics football team. Philadelphia's two major league baseball teams sponsored two professional football teams as rivals to the powerful Pittsburgh football team, and these three teams were the most financially sound. If an athlete was fortunate enough to sign with one of these professional teams, he could expect to earn between four hundred and twelve hundred dollars per season. Smaller teams usually paid less.

The popularity of college football and the lure of thousands of paying spectators ushered in the era of organized professional football in 1920. At Ralph Hays' Hupmobile Automobile dealership in Canton, Ohio, representatives from eleven football clubs gathered on September 17, 1920, to form the American Professional Football Association (APFA).[5] The APFA's charter teams in 1920 paid one hundred dollars for a franchise and agreed not to recruit college athletes who still had eligibility remaining or to attempt to induce players who were bound by contract to other teams in the APFA. The APFA's first president was Jim Thorpe, at that time America's greatest all-around athlete. He oversaw the teams that were the first of modern professional football: Chicago Cardinals, Massillon Tigers, Dayton Triangles, Cleveland Indians, Rock Island Independents, Akron Steels, Canton Bulldogs, Rochester (New York) Kodaks, and teams from Decatur, Illinois, and Muncie, Indiana.

Figure 13.6
In the New York Giants offices, in 1913, Jim Thorpe posed for the signing of his contract. Photo by Culver Pictures, Inc. Courtesy of Cumberland County Historical Society, Carlisle, PA.

In Jim Thorpe the APFA had a "big name" and public recognition, but unfortunately Thorpe's administrative ability was minimal at best.[6] Several of the clubs that started the APFA were in financial difficulty and eventually folded. Joe F. Carr of Columbus, Ohio, became the new president and changed the name of the APFA to the National Football League (NFL) and lowered the franchise fee to fifty dollars. Teams from Muncie, Massillon, and Hammond withdrew and were replaced with franchises in Green Bay, Detroit, Buffalo, Cincinnati, and Columbus. The Decatur team was sold to a young man by the name of George E. Halas, who changed the name of Staley Athletic Club to the Chicago Bears in 1922.

Interestingly, during the 1920s most college coaches discouraged many players from turning professional after graduation. During its formative years professional football struggled to gain the respect of the public, whereas college football remained much more popular. Two events occurred in 1925 that helped professional football gain the same respect as college football enjoyed. Tim Mara formed the New York

Giants and publicized the team in the newspapers of New York City. Football fans were treated with exciting accounts of professional football teams in the biggest media center in the country. Second, and perhaps more important, Harold "Red" Grange, the Galloping Ghost from the University of Illinois, signed with the Chicago Bears. Fans turned out by the tens of thousands to see him run, and his status was such that it gave the NFL an aura of legitimacy.

Professional baseball and college football remained more popular than professional football through the end of World War II. After the war professional football enjoyed enormous growth, with the establishment of the American Football League (AFL) in 1960, the Super Bowl in 1966, and the eventual merger of the AFL and NFL in 1970. The World Football League and the United States Football League attempted to compete with the NFL for fans and money, but both efforts were short lived. The World Football League (WFL) played one season, 1974, and the United States Football League (USFL) spring football season lasted just three seasons, from 1983 to 1985. Most recently football has moved indoors, known as Arena Football, and to Europe with the World League of American Football (WLAF). Time will tell if these two efforts will be successful.

In 1946, Kenny Washington and Woody Strode, both out of the University of California, Los Angeles, became the first black football players to play professional football when they joined the Los Angeles Rams. Although much less heralded and less publicized than Jackie Robinson, the first black baseball player, these men faced the same discriminating practices that Jackie Robinson endured during his professional career. That these two athletes are not as well known as Robinson for breaking a color barrier in sports tells us much about the popularity of football relative to baseball in the 1940s. Clearly football was not the national game it was to become twenty years later.

Basketball

Springfield College, originally established as the Young Men's Christian Association (YMCA) Training School, enjoys a proud tradition of physical education excellence and athletic success. Perhaps the most noteworthy achievement to have occurred at Springfield was the invention of basketball by Dr. James A. Naismith. In 1891 the Director of the Gymnasium, Dr. Luther Gulick, asked Naismith to develop a game that could be played indoors during the winter. At this time winter athletic activities revolved around formal gymnastics, calisthenics, and similar pursuits that were considered by the participants to be very boring. Gulick hoped to develop a game that would be more fun and therefore have more participation.

It is difficult to say for certain where Naismith came up with the concept of basketball, although he may have been aware of the early forms of the game played by American Indians and Central Americans between A.D. 1000 and 1500. Naismith tried modified versions of lacrosse, water

Figure 13.7
Dr. James Naismith, inventor of basketball. From:
Betty Spears and Richard Swanson, History of Sport
and Physical Education in the United States, *3rd ed.,*
Dubuque: Wm. C. Brown, Publishers, 1988.

polo, field hockey, soccer, rugby, and football, but he was apparently unsuccessful. He finally devised a game incorporating a soccer ball and two goals, often described as peach baskets, that were placed ten feet high at opposite ends of the gym floor. Participants were supposed to pass the ball back and forth and ultimately to "score" by tossing the ball into one of the baskets.

On December 21, 1891, Naismith and future football legend Amos Alonzo Stagg faced each other in what was probably the first basketball game, no doubt wondering how successful the new game would be. Naismith need not have worried. The game was an instant success, and news of the new game called basketball spread quickly. As the traveling ambassador for basketball, Naismith introduced the game in northeastern cities, and soon the YMCAs became the "hotbed" of basketball. High schools and colleges adopted the sport, and women played the game as well. Senda Berenson, a physical education teacher at Smith College, modified the game for her students. She reconfigured the rules and other aspects of the game to conform with the prevailing nineteenth-century medical, psychological, and social concepts of women's physical capabilities.[7] Basketball played by men was a rough and tumble sport, not at all consistent with the appropriate behavior of women athletes of that era. As a result, basketball rules for women varied from place to place and tended to be

Figure 13.8

Senda Berenon tossing up ball for game, 1904. Smith College Archives, Smith College. Photo by Katherine E. McClellan.

much more cooperative in nature than competitive. For instance, oftentimes women's rules did not allow players to travel the full length of the court. Consequently passing was emphasized over dribbling.

Leading women physical educators and coaches convened in 1899 at Springfield, Massachusetts, to develop a uniform set of basketball rules, sixteen years before the men had a similar meeting. It was decided that the women would use the current YMCA rules for men's basketball with several modifications: (1) the court was divided into three equal zones; (2) stealing the ball from an opposing player was prohibited; (3) teams were to consist of no fewer than six players and no more than nine. This last rule was based on the belief that women could not play at the pace or intensity of their male counterparts, and it also allowed more athletes to play the game. By 1928 ten states held state basketball tournaments for high-school girls. These tournaments, however, operated outside the control of women physical educators. Most women were opposed to interscholastic competition for girls and instead favored large-scale participation in intramurals.

The men were no better off with regard to rules. By 1900 all that leading men's coaches could agree on was that each team should consist of five players. Beyond that, colleges had one set of rules, the YMCA had yet another, and the AAU had still another. In 1915 the Joint Basketball Committee was established with representatives from the NCAA, AAU, and YMCA to reach agreement on uniform rules. However, the professional teams that appeared during the early part of the twentieth century had their own rules, and still do today.

High schools in Denver formed the first basketball league in 1896, and five years later in 1901 Eastern colleges formed the Intercollegiate League. By the start of World War I, basketball was second only to football in popularity in high schools and the colleges where the game was played. The American military introduced the game around the world, and missionaries such as Robert Gailey introduced the game to China in 1898. In Indiana, Kentucky, Kansas, and New York City, basketball enjoyed enormous popularity in both the schools and the playgrounds. However, only in the era of World War I did basketball begin to enjoy widespread public attention.[8]

Volleyball

During the noonday lunch hour, a group of businessmen gathered at the Holyoke, Massachusetts, YMCA under the watchful eye of William Morgan. Perhaps sensing a need to provide a more stimulating recreational activity that was less demanding than basketball, he developed the game of volleyball in 1895. Originally called "minonette," Morgan believed that volleyball would fulfill the needs of his clientele. Initially the game incorporated the entire gymnasium and used a basketball bladder that was hit over a 6'6" tennis net. Each game was composed of nine innings, and the size of each team depended on who showed up to play. According to the first published account of the game in July 1896,

> The ball was volleyed back and forth without hitting the floor or the net. A player could dribble by bouncing the ball on the hand while moving but could not go within four feet of the net. A serve had to go at least ten feet and could be helped over the net by a player of the same side.[9]

Volleyball, although popular with the YMCA followers, had a difficult time gaining acceptance in school physical education curriculum because, like basketball, it was believed that the sport did little to develop the upper body. In addition, participation in volleyball did not lend itself to a scientific knowledge base in the way that formal gymnastics did. The result was that volleyball was opposed by those physical educators who were adherent to the regulated and "scientifically established benefits" of gymnastics. Volleyball was promoted by the YMCA and, like basketball, was adopted by the American military. Although women's volleyball currently is one of the most popular sports in high school and on college campuses, the game was not embraced by women in its early stages. Volleyball was initially promoted as a men's game, and it was not until later that the YWCA and college women played the game.

Figure 13.9

Mabel Lee, Blanche Trilling, and Agnes Wayman. Courtesy of American Alliance for Health, Physical Education, Recreation, and Dance.

Women and Sport

Athletic activities for girls and women during the later part of the nine-teenth century and much of the twentieth century reflected the beliefs and biases of many Americans regarding play and sport. One of the argu-ments used by early sport advocates was that sport built "manliness." Clearly, then, if one believed that sport built men, then one probably would believe that women should have nothing to do with it! Additionally, the early twentieth century witnessed a transition from gymnastics to athletics and dance, with dance becoming a popular and integral component of women's physical education programs, especially in the colleges. The efforts of Melvin Ballou Gilbert, Luther Gulick, Elizabeth Burchenal, Isadora Duncan, and others led to dance being a part of the physical education curriculum. Dances such as clog, tap, aesthetic, folk, natural, modern, social, and square dancing became important curricu-lar offerings in physical education departments.

Several women's colleges provided athletic programs for their stu-dents. In 1901, Vassar College began playing field hockey, and Wellesley College played lacrosse. Smith College promoted volleyball in 1907, and at Bryn Mawr students played cricket, soccer, and water polo.[10] Coedu-cational colleges were slow to provide athletic opportunities for women, and high schools were slower still in providing conventional physical education and athletic programs. Much of the problem had to do with the shortage of qualified teachers.

Illinois became a leader in the conduct and promotion of girls' ath-letics when it established the State League of Girls' Athletic Associa-tions in the early 1920s. According to the association, its purpose was to "promote programs of athletics for all girls to offset the undesirable program of interschool athletics maintained in many schools by male coaches for the highly skilled few."[11] Colorado and Nebraska, following the lead of Illinois, formed similar associations. These early organiza-tions promoted and sponsored intramural programs encouraging mass participation, as opposed to participation by a few highly skilled athletes. Awards were given for achievement and participation.

In spite of the efforts by women physical educators to discourage the competitive environment of interscholastic athletics, men promoted championships for girls' high-school basketball teams that were highly successful. In 1928 the Ohio tournament had fifty-five hundred girls entered; four thousand girls entered in Texas, and two thousand girls participated in the Oklahoma basketball championship tournament.

Blanche M. Trilling (1876–1964) provided much of the leadership for women's athletics during its formative years. Because of her position as Director of Physical Education for Women at the University of Wisconsin, she was able to convene a meeting in 1917 to discuss athletic participation for women. It was during this meeting that the Athletic Conference of American College Women was formed. From the very beginning, the organization denounced intercollegiate athletics for women and vigorously promoted intramural programs in the high schools and colleges.

As women became more interested and involved in sports, William H. Burdick, president of the American Physical Education Association, established the National Committee on Women's Sports in 1917 to determine rules and standards for athletic participation for women and girls. The general philosophy of women's athletics during the early twentieth century was "A sport for every girl and every girl in a sport." During the 1920 meeting of the Conference of College Directors of Physical Education, members justified their opposition to intercollegiate athletics for women for the following reasons:

1. it leads to professionalism;

2. it emphasizes the training of the few at the expense of many;

3. it is unsocial;

4. the necessity of professional coaches;

5. physical educators, both men and women, of our leading colleges find the results undesirable;

6. the expense; and

7. unnecessary nerve fatigue.[12]

The control of women's athletics was fought over by the Amateur Athletic Union (AAU), the National Amateur Athletic Federation (NAAF), the National Federation of High School Athletic Associations (NFHSAA), and the State Leagues of High School Girls' Athletic Association. Eventually the AAU became the most influential organization for girls' and women's sports. Women physical educators, however, resisted AAU efforts to control and coordinate women's athletics. In 1922 the first Women's Olympic Games were to take place in Paris, and the AAU had every intention of sending a track and field team. However, the AAU did not have jurisdiction over track and field and was opposed by many women physical educators. The AAU ignored pleas from women physical education professionals and sent the team to Paris under the direction of Dr. Harry Stewart.

Figure 13.10

Mildred "Babe" Didrikson on her way to victory in the 80-meter hurdle event at the 1932 Olympic Games. From: Betty Spears and Richard Swanson. History of Sport and Physical Education in the United States, *3rd ed., Dubuque: Wm. C. Brown, Publishers, 1988.*

It was during this time that members from the NAAF asked the wife of President Herbert Hoover to assist them in organizing and promoting women's participation in competitive athletics. Mrs. Hoover convened a conference in 1923 to discuss the proposal and invited leading men and women to participate. Sixteen resolutions were adopted, among them Resolution IV, which is indicative of the NAAF position on women in athletics:

> IV. Resolved, in order to develop these qualities which shall fit girls and women to perform their functions as citizens:
>
> (a) that their athletics be conducted with that end definitely in view and be protected from exploitation for the enjoyment of the spectator, the athletic reputation, or the commercial advantage of any school or other organization.
>
> (b) that schools and other organizations shall stress enjoyment of the sport and the development of sportsmanship and minimize the emphasis which is at present laid upon individual accomplishment and the winning of championships.[13]

It was not until the 1932 Olympic Games in Los Angeles, when the legendary Mildred "Babe" Didrikson Zaharias won two gold medals and one silver in track and field, that the critics of women's athletics were silenced. Didrikson later went on to become a stellar golfer who won every major golf tournament she competed in between 1940 and 1950. She was honored once again in 1950 as the greatest woman athlete in the first half of the twentieth century. Most of these critics, among them women physical educators, believed that women were frail and physiologically not suited for intense athletic competition. The opinions of these educators, however, were based on the best evidence available at the time. It was only after the basis for these opinions was undermined by the continued success of women athletes like Didrikson that women began to enjoy more opportunities for participation. Still, women physical educators opposed the participation of women in the 1928 and 1932 Olympics.

The NAAF Women's Division and Committee on Women's Athletics adhered to a philosophy that guarded against exploitation and stressed the availability of a broad sports program, medical supervision, and women coaches. They continued to oppose intercollegiate athletics competition for women and collected data and wrote articles to support their position. The type of approved and appropriate athletics for college women were in the form of play days or sports days, which were popular with women students who attended Stanford and California-Berkeley during the 1920s. Informal games such as archery, swimming and running relays, and ball games were the norm, and the more participants, the better! The event was more a social affair than a competitive experience. More often than not, invitations were sent out to potential spectators, and men were discouraged from attending.

The decade preceding World War II was a significant era for women's athletics. The Committee on Women's Athletics reorganized in 1932 into the National Section on Women's Athletics (NSWA), which consisted of a number of sports committees that oversaw rule changes, rated officials, provided educational information, and published the results of athletic contests. In 1936 women's basketball was modified from the three-court configuration to the current two-court (meaning front court and back court) configuration. Four major trends in women's physical education and sport occurred during this time:

1. an increase in opportunities in sport for women and an increase in the number of participants;
2. a growing use of research as a basis for planning and improving sport and athletic programs;
3. a greater acceptance in society of the concept of women in sport; and
4. a reexamination of the position limiting intercollegiate athletics.[14]

The gradual acceptance of high-level athletic competition for women was facilitated by the performances of Babe Didrikson Zaharias, but compared with the opportunities available to her male counterparts, opportunities for competitive athletics for girls and women were limited. The prevailing attitude of the era continued to be influenced by conservative thinking, which held that sports developed character and helped turn boys into men. Consequently, girls and women were expected to refrain from participating in sports that detracted from their femininity. Interest in women's athletics occurred during the Olympic Games but continued to take a back seat to the men regarding financial support, training opportunities, and press coverage.

During the 1950s, high schools provided opportunities for participation through the efforts of the Girls' Athletic Association (GAA), and colleges continued to offer play days and began to schedule contests against other institutions in field hockey, fencing, basketball, volleyball, softball, gymnastics, swimming, and track and field. The atmosphere was as much social as competitive, and practice and preparation for these athletic competitions were not at the same level of intensity as the respective men's teams.

In 1957 there was enough interest in women's intercollegiate sports to establish a committee to investigate the growing interest in athletic competition. The National Section on Girls' and Women's Sports (NSGWS) was formed under the auspices of the American Alliance for Health, Physical Education, and Recreation (AAHPER). This organization, after several name changes, evolved into the Association for Intercollegiate Athletics for Women (AIAW) in 1971.

The AIAW was administered by women for women athletes, and from the beginning it pledged to avoid the "evils" of men's athletics. Initially the AIAW was opposed to awarding athletic scholarships, recruiting gifted athletes, and a win-at-all-cost philosophy that seemed to reflect the philosophy of men's intercollegiate athletics. The AIAW sponsored championships in gymnastics (1969), track and field (1969), volleyball (1970), badminton (1970), and basketball (1972). For a team to qualify for the AIAW tournament or championship, the college was required to hold AIAW membership and abide by the organization rules. Membership in the AIAW grew steadily and by the late 1970s had reached 970 colleges and universities.[15] On July 1, 1979, the AIAW broke away from the auspices of the National Association for Girls' and Women's Sports and the American Alliance for Health, Physical Education, and Recreation.

If there was one event that changed the nature of women athletes forever, it was Title IX of the Educational Amendments Act of 1972. Title IX was an antidiscrimination provision of a federal statute of the Civil Rights Acts of 1964. It was brought about by the efforts of the Department of Health, Education, and Welfare (HEW) and contains language that specifically addresses physical education and athletics. All physical education and athletic teams in high schools and colleges were open to members of both sexes, with the exception of contact sports. Equal opportunity had to be provided for facilities, coaching, and financial support. If an institution that received federal money failed to provide equal opportunity, then those monies would be withheld.

The NCAA filed suit against the provisions of Title IX as it related to athletics because of the belief that the money required to fund women's athletic programs on par with the men's would threaten the financial stability of intercollegiate athletics. The NCAA suit was not successful, and athletic departments in colleges and universities across the nation were forced to fund women's athletic programs at the same level as the men's, relative to coaching, facilities access, travel, scholarships, and so on. In retrospect, Title IX has had a greater impact on sport in the educational arena than any other federal legislation.

After losing its suit, the NCAA decided that it would be in its best interests to control women's athletics. The NCAA and the AIAW entered into discussions about the governance of women's athletics but met with little success. The NCAA decided to hold championships for women and enticed membership in the NCAA with financial support and incentives that the AIAW was unable to match. In 1975 the NCAA proposed national championships for women and did so again in 1978 and 1979. The AIAW filed an antitrust suit against the NCAA over the control of women's intercollegiate athletics in 1981, the same year that the NCAA began offering women's championships. The NCAA prevailed in court, and the AIAW disbanded in 1983. It is ironic that just seventeen years before, in 1964, the NCAA went on record stating, "Acting upon the request of female college sports leaders, the NCAA Executive Committee amended the executive regulation to limit participation in NCAA championships to undergraduate male students."[16]

Women in the 1990s enjoy many more opportunities in sport than their sisters before 1970. Many programs in today's high schools and colleges are similar to those of men. Indeed, the similarities are striking in that the problems found in men's sports are also manifest in women's sports. The next battles to be fought would seem to deal less with discrimination than with individual athlete abuse, but this remains to be seen.

Summary

Most of the sports that developed in the nineteenth century grew and continued to do well in the twentieth century. The process of modernization can explain many of the changes that occurred in each sport as it was developed, and this pattern of change helps us understand, and even predict, how these sports will be organized. Yet not all activities follow this pattern, and no one can say whether sport is better off because of these kinds of changes.

For instance, the new sport of triathlons, developed in San Diego in the 1970s, began as a premodern sport. Races were informal in nature, there was no organizational structure, race distances and rules were different between races, and the sport was unheard of outside of San Diego. By the early 1980s triathlons were fully modern, with the United States Triathlon Federation sanctioning and organizing races. Standard distances had evolved, athletes were specialized as to distance, the races were highly competitive, statistics and records were kept, and results were nationally and internationally communicated. Yet there are those who long for the simpler days of triathlons, when one could organize a race and not worry about insurance or traffic control. One knew all the competitors, and winning and losing were not as important as having fun swimming, riding, and running. Which is better? Who can say?

One pattern does seem to be evident, however. There are more opportunities to participate in a wider variety of sports and playful activities than ever before, and there is no indication that this trend will stop. Americans seem to be more comfortable with their bodies with respect to sport and play than at any time since the 1500s. One even hears arguments that there is too much time spent on these kinds of activities. Whether this is true or not depends on one's perspective. What seems clear is that in one shape or form, Americans will continue to participate in sport and play.

Discussion Questions

1. How is sport in the twentieth century different from that in the nineteenth century? Is the difference one of degree or one of kind?

2. Are there examples of the modernization of sport in the twentieth century? Are there examples of activities that represent premodern sport? Which is better?

3. How have women's sports evolved in the twentieth century? Will these changes continue, and if so, what will sport look like for women in the twenty-first century?

4. What contributions did the YMCA make to sport?

5. What impact did Mildred "Babe" Didrikson Zaharias have upon the development of women's athletic participation?

6. What impact did Jim Thorpe have upon the development of professional sports?

Suggestions for Further Reading

Betts, J. R. *America's Sporting Heritage: 1850–1950*. Reading, Mass.: Addison-Wesley, 1974.

Lewis, G. "Theodore Roosevelt's Role in the 1905 Football Controversy." *Research Quarterly* 40 (1969): 717–724.

Smith, R. A. "Harvard and Columbia and a Reconsideration of the 1905–1906 Football Crisis." *Journal of Sport History* 8 (Winter 1981): 5–19.

Spears, B., and R. A. Swanson. *History of Sport and Physical Education*, 3d ed. Dubuque, Ia.: William C. Brown, 1983.

Notes

1. Michael Harrington, *The Politics at God's Funeral* (New York: Holt, Rinehart, and Winston, 1983).

2. John R. Betts, *America's Sporting Heritage: 1850–1950* (Reading, Mass.: Addison-Wesley, 1974), 127.

3. Shailer Mathews, *Nation*, XCV (August 24, 1918): 198.

4. Guy Lewis, "Theodore Roosevelt's Role in the 1905 Football Controversy," *Research Quarterly* 40 (1969): 717–724. See also Ronald A. Smith, "Harvard and Columbia and a Reconsideration of the 1905–1906 Football Crisis," *Journal of Sport History* 8 (Winter 1981): 5–19.

5. Betty Spears and Richard A. Swanson, *History of Sport and Physical Education*, 3d ed. (Dubuque, Ia.: William C. Brown, 1983).

6. Ibid.

7. Ibid., 176.

8. Betts, *America's Sporting Heritage*, 132.

9. Deobold Van Dalen, Elmer Mitchell, and Bruce Bennett, "Physical Education in the Middle Ages and Early Modern Times," in *A World History of Physical Education* (Englewood Cliffs, N.J.: Prentice-Hall, 1953), 421.

10. Mabel Lee, *A History of Physical Education and Sports in the USA* (New York: John Wiley & Sons, 1983), 58.

11. Ibid., 146.

12. Bulletin (1920–21), Mary Hemenway Alumnae Association, Department of Hygiene, 48. Wellesley College Archives, Wellesley, Mass.

13. Alice A. Sefton, *The Women's Division, National Amateur Athletic Foundation* (Stanford: Stanford University Press, 1941), 77–79.

14. Ibid., 245.

15. Lee, *History of Physical Education and Sports*, 313.

16. Ibid., 312.

s e c t i o n **5**

Modern Olympic Games

A Selected Political and Social History of the Modern Olympic Games, 1896–1936

Introduction

From its humble origins in Athens during the spring of 1896 to the media and athletic extravaganza that spellbinds a global audience for several weeks during designated Olympic years, the Olympic Games have evolved into one of the most significant social forces of the twentieth century. The concept of an international athletic festival to act as a social force enables

1. athletes from all over the world to meet and compete against athletes representing all colors, races, creeds, and political beliefs.

2. athletes to travel to other countries to establish communication and dialogue with fellow athletes that will foster and promote international understanding and the appreciation of cultural diversity.

3. athletes to test themselves against the best athletes in the world in the supreme physical and mental challenge.

4. the ideals of fair play and character formation through athletic participation to be promoted throughout the world for all the youth of the world to enjoy.

5. the ideals of peace, harmony, and cooperation to transcend political barriers, which would allow the Olympics to act as a force for world peace and cooperation.

The Olympic Games are a timeless legacy. The enduring qualities that personified Agon and Arete as developed by the ancient Greeks are preserved and perpetuated as an essential component of Olympism. Under the auspices of the International Olympic Committee (IOC), the spirit of Olympism transcends borders and has become a viable social force that encourages and supports change in a positive and constructive fashion. Within the modern Olympic Movement,

Olympism seeks to create a way of life based on the joy of effort and on mutual respect. Its aim is to place sport at the service . . . to bring about a world of peace in respect for human dignity. This ideal was proclaimed with fervour at the festivals celebrated every four years by the ancient Greeks at the Olympic Games, in which they devoted themselves to the pursuit of harmonious development, not only of the body and moral sense, but also of . . . cultural and artistic qualities.[1]

The Olympic Games are unlike any of the existing "mega sports" that have flourished in the twentieth century. The Super Bowl is one of the most watched and followed sporting events in modern history. It is broadcast all over the world. However, participation in the Super Bowl is exclusively limited to American professional football teams that belong to the National Football League (NFL). The World Series is another phenomenon of the twentieth century. It is closely followed around the world, especially in Latin America and Japan. However, this great sporting championship is exclusively limited to professional baseball teams in the United States and Canada that belong to the American League or the National League. The same situation exists with the National Hockey League (NHL) and the National Basketball Association (NBA) championships. The Super Bowl, World Series, Stanley Cup, and the NBA championship are *exclusive* events that are currently limited to teams from North America. However, the Olympic Games are *inclusive*, in that they belong to the world. This is of enormous benefit. More athletes, male *and* female, participate in the Olympics, where they promote peace and understanding throughout the global community.

As the world's premier international sporting event, the Olympic Games host a multicultural athletic festival that includes thousands of athletes from every continent. Men and women representing different political and social systems and worshipping different religious dieties gather to represent their country in a glorious atmosphere of athletic competition where Agon and Arete occupy center stage. The inclusive nature of the Olympic Games lends itself to a multiplicity of faces. While the spirit of Olympism embodies the essence of athletic competition and all that it reflects, significant political and social events have also left their mark on the Olympics. Athletes who represent their country are understandably patriotic and proud. However, one of the more pervasive problems that has surfaced is how to balance patriotism with the ideal of internationalism.

Along with the accomplishments of selected athletic performances, we have chosen to highlight selected political and social events that have impacted the Olympic Games. The Olympic Games are complex, inspiring, disappointing, and exhausting. Partly because of their intent to include participants rather than exclude participants, the Olympic Games frequently become embroiled in turmoil. Differences of opinion and disagreements are to be expected when such a monumental event unfolds. As a result, the modern Olympic Games (as were the ancient

Figure 14.1

Baron de Coubertin. From:
E. W. Gerber. Innovators and
Institutions in Physical Education.
Philadelphia: Lea & Febiger, 1971.

Olympic Games) are from time to time subject to significant problems. However, what is truly inspiring is that with all the controversy that has surrounded Games, the International Olympic Committee has remained steadfast to the spirit of Olympism. The Olympic Movement continues to grow each year; its creed of inclusivity as opposed to exclusivity is an ideal that should be considered by other organizations that promote sport.

The Architect: Baron Pierre de Fredy de Coubertin

The Olympic ideals were the product of one man, Baron Pierre de Fredy de Coubertin, whose tireless efforts and enthusiasm made the modern Olympic Games possible.[2] Coubertin was born on January 1, 1863, to Charles Louis Baron Fredy de Coubertin and his wife Agathe Gabrielle de Crisenoy. The family was a well-to-do member of the French aristocracy and had impeccable social and political connections, which would later open many doors to the young Baron in his quest to (1) revitalize the youth of France, and (2) establish the modern Olympic Games. The Coubertin family was proud, patriotic, and very nationalistic, and the family, as well as the entire nation, was devastated by France's defeat in the Franco-Prussian War. This event was very significant in the early years of the young Baron's life. The Prussians achieved an overwhelming victory, which did not inspire confidence in the character and manly ability of the French youth. This fact greatly disturbed the young Coubertin, whereby he made a decision to devote his life to bringing about pedagogical change and improving the national character of the youth of France. He was not about to sit idly by and watch his beloved France being trampled by the dreaded Prussians, or the English for that matter.

Young French aristocrats of this era had several occupational paths available to them: the clergy, political office, and finance were among the more popular selections. Baron de Coubertin chose pedagogy. Pedagogy, although a noble and honorable profession, was not the first choice of most young men of the aristocracy. England was the world power during this historical period, and after completing his formal schooling in France, Baron de Coubertin traveled to Great Britain to study the success of the British system and learn more about the stoic and manly character of the British. As a boy, he read *Tom Brown's School Days*[3] and came away very impressed by the system of sports and games that formed a large part of the social and educational fabric at Rugby School under the direction of Dr. Thomas Arnold, one of the foremost advocates of muscular Christianity of the era. The family's impeccable social connections enabled the Baron to be wined and dined in the best supper clubs in London, as well as to have access to the English leadership, which he questioned and studied. All the while Coubertin was looking for that elusive factor that developed the manly character and stoic courage for which the English leadership was famous and of which the youth of France were in desperate need.

While touring the English Public Schools, which in reality are private and elite institutions that have educated many of Britain's leaders, Coubertin found the elusive but obvious catalyst for character development that he had been searching for: athletic competition.

During the afternoons, the students at Rugby School, Eaton, Winchester, and other elite institutions engaged in rough-and-tumble games such as rugby, soccer, boxing, and races. Pride and honor were on the line during these afternoons of sporting competitions, and the result was the character formation that was emblematic of the English and so admired by Coubertin. Coubertin had to "sell" the idea of character development through athletic participation to his countrymen, who historically did not covet or embrace anything that the island across the channel held dear.

When he returned to France, Coubertin used his political and social connections to gain control over amateur sport in France, although he was strongly opposed by the Gymnastic Union. He invited politically powerful and socially well connected people to his villa, where he entertained them by showcasing the talents of athletes, both national and international. The majority of the spectators came for the lavish displays of food and drink and were only mildly interested in the athletic competition. However, Baron de Coubertin was able to enlist their support for his efforts to promote athletics throughout France, especially in the schools. The Baron believed that by inviting foreign teams in for athletic competition and exhibition, much could be learned that would benefit French athletes and his pedagogical goal of securing a place for athletics in the schools. In addition, the gathering of athletes from other nations would certainly promote good will and foster understanding; it would thus provide an activity that would promote peaceful cooperation among the youth of the world through fair sporting behavior. Pierre de Coubertin was an idealist; he truly loved sports, and to him the Olympic ideals of amateurism, fair play, and good competition were emblematic of all that was good and honorable.

Although he knew that sports were the vehicle to attain his goals, he was not sure how until he visited the United States and came into contact with William Sloane, a professor of history at Princeton who had expertise in the classics, especially the ancient Greeks. Professor Sloane invited Coubertin to his home to watch as his students reenacted the athletic festival of ancient Olympia in Professor Sloane's backyard. Although Coubertin was well schooled in the classics and the history of ancient Greece, the idea of the Olympic Games had evaded him until he watched in fascination as the answer to his problems unfolded before his very eyes! If he could reestablish the Olympic Games, the means to his end of the reinvigoration of French youth would be achieved.

Coubertin returned to France, and during the meeting of the Unions des Sports Athletiques held at the Sorbonne in November 1892, he proposed his idea to renew the Olympic Games almost fifteen hundred years after the Roman Emperor Theodosius I terminated them in A.D. 393. The assembled delegates were very cool to Coubertin's proposal, much to his disappointment. Although discouraged, he would try again. The second opportunity arose in June 1894, when Coubertin organized the International Congress of Paris for the study and the propagation of the Principles of Amateurism held at the Sorbonne. He planned his second proposal very carefully and enlisted the support of the British and Americans for his revival of the Olympic Games. Invitations were sent to sports associations the world over, and Olympic discussion was placed as the last agenda item of the Congress, which lasted one week. Baron de Coubertin used the week of meetings to politic, lobby, and nurture his proposal for reestablishment of the Olympic Games, and he designated himself as president of the newly created International Olympic Committee (IOC). Coubertin then selected the fourteen charter members of the IOC and began preparation for the first modern Olympiad to be held in Athens in 1896.

Although Baron de Coubertin is credited for reestablishing the modern Olympic Games, there were earlier versions of the games. The English celebrated the "Olympic Games" of England from 1610 to 1860. The English Olympics were conducted at Dover's Hill and lasted for two days. The originator of the games, Captain Robert Dover, initiated the athletic festival as a protest against the Puritans, who sought to suppress games and sports as works of the devil. The athletic events consisted of wrestling, field hockey, fencing, jumping, and throwing the pole, hammer, and javelin.[4] The Greeks initiated the National Greek Olympics in

1859 and again in 1875 and 1889. Gymnastic exercises, shooting, and athletic competition were the events of the National Greek Olympics.[5]

Baron de Coubertin was not in favor of allowing women to compete in the Olympic Games, due as much to cultural beliefs as anything else. The IOC has been primarily a body of elected aristocrats from member nations, and it was not until 1981 that the IOC admitted women to membership.

The Ist Olympiad: Athens, 1896

Baron de Coubertin had an enormous task ahead of him once support for the Olympic Games was obtained. The games were only two years away, and much had to be done to prepare for them. Greece was enthusiastic about Athens hosting the first modern Olympiad but was financially ill prepared to contribute to the effort. Construction of the stadium was the major hurdle, and it was only after Prince Constantine, Honorary President of the organizing committee, contacted George Averoff, that the construction of the stadium could begin. Averoff donated over one million drachmas, and additional monies were raised by issuing postal stamps, ticket sales, and commemorative medals.[6]

Another task, equally as difficult, was convincing the world and major sporting associations that the Athens Olympiad was indeed legitimate. The New York Athletic Club, the premier athletic club of the era, scoffed at the suggestion of sending a team to represent the United States. The Boston Athletic Association accepted the challenge and, along with athletes from Princeton University, traveled to Athens. The American team was organized by Professor Sloane and consisted of five members of the Boston Athletic Association and four Princeton students. Participation in the first modern Olympiad was limited to twelve track and field events, eight gymnastic competitions, five target shooting events, and three fencing matches.

James Connolly, an American, was the first athlete to win a medal in the Athens Olympiad. He won the triple jump. However, the most inspirational athlete was a twenty-one-year-old Greek shepherd, Spiridon Louis, who won the marathon in two hours, fifty-eight minutes and fifty seconds. He prepared for the marathon by fasting and praying. Three hundred and eleven male athletes representing thirteen National Olympic Committees (NOCs) competed in the Athens Olympiad.

The IInd Olympiad: Paris, 1900

The games grew in scope and popularity throughout the years, but they were not without problems. The success of the 1896 Athens Olympiad, as the Greeks perceived it, demanded that all successive Olympiads be held at Athens and not awarded to a new city as envisioned by Coubertin. He successfully defeated the Greek efforts, and the second Olympiad was held in Paris.[7] These games were full of promise, but they fell apart from an organizational standpoint. The Union des Sports Athletiques of France, the governing body of French sport, had no desire to cooperate with the newly created International Olympic Committee (IOC). The Union des Sports Athletiques of France did not want to share power with the IOC and did not have much confidence in the Olympic movement to begin with. The management of the Paris Exposition, where the 1900 Olympic Games were to be held, did not share Coubertin's enthusiasm, nor did they attribute much significance to the Olympic movement.[8] The French were indifferent, at best, to the 1900 Olympiad and preferred to marvel at the Eiffel Tower and the customary amusements and entertainment that were available at the Exposition. Baron de Coubertin was thoroughly frustrated and discouraged. Facilities were difficult to obtain, and his beloved Olympics were relegated to sideshow status, which pleased both the organizer of the Paris Exposition and the Union des Sports Athletiques of France. In a situation that must have been humiliating, Coubertin reluctantly agreed to include motorcar races, competition between firemen, free balloon races, and trials of carrier pigeons.[9] Tug-of-war turned out to be the highlight of the games, whereas track and field meets were the low points; the American team defeated the French in the tug-of-war. The problem was that there were official and unofficial Olympic events. Promoters would claim to be staging Olympic competitions that were not sanctioned or supported by the IOC. During the Paris Olympiad, fifteen women representing five countries took part in two sports, tennis and golf.[10] A total of 1,319 athletes representing twenty-two National Olympic Committees (NOCs) participated in the Paris Olympiad. The Paris Olympiad was a major disappointment to Baron de Coubertin; however, it paled in comparison to the politics and Olympic program of the 1904 St. Louis Olympiad.

The IIIrd Olympiad: St. Louis, 1904

The IOC had received proposals from both Chicago and St. Louis. When the IOC met in Paris in May of 1901, Chicago sent a representative to secure the 1904 Olympic Games. St. Louis failed to send a representative, and under such circumstances, the IOC was left with a seemingly simple decision: award the 1904 Olympic Games to Chicago, which they did. The IOC then offered the presiding of the 1904 Olympiad to President Theodore Roosevelt. President Roosevelt accepted the presidency of the 1904 Olympic Games on May 28, 1901.[11]

The city of Chicago celebrated the announcement from the IOC and began preparation for the games. What appeared to be a "done deal" was far from over. St. Louis continued its efforts to secure the games. The Louisiana Purchase Exposition, commemorating the purchase of the Louisiana Territory by the United States from France in 1803, was scheduled to open in 1904 in St. Louis. The promoters of the exposition were eager to add the Olympic Games to the exposition program and, when confronted with the fact that Chicago had been awarded the

Olympic Games, threatened to organize a rival athletic exhibition if the games were held in Chicago.[12] James Sullivan, secretary of the Amateur Athletic Union (AAU), was appointed Chief of the Department of Physical Culture of the Louisiana Purchase Exposition by D. R. Francis, president of the St. Louis Exposition. Sullivan was politically powerful and very well connected with the nation's leader. If there was a person capable of organizing a rival athletic festival that would overshadow the 1904 Chicago Olympiad, it was James Sullivan. As secretary of the AAU, he would have enormous influence on whether America's best athletes should compete in St. Louis or Chicago.

The Chicago Organizing Committee realized their fate and proposed to postpone the Olympic Games until 1905, after the St. Louis Exposition was over. Besides having James Sullivan to contend with, Chicago did not have the financial resources to upstage St. Louis.

President Roosevelt let it be known to the IOC that it was his desire that the Olympic Games be held in conjunction with the St. Louis Exposition. On February 10, 1903, the IOC met and voted to transfer the games to St. Louis. The political character and nature of subsequent Olympiads was all but ensured.

The St. Louis organizers assigned the term Olympic to all phases of competition, which caused considerable confusion as to exactly which events were truly Olympic. The following "Program of Olympic Events" was published by the St. Louis Post-Dispatch:

May 14	Interscholastic meet, for St. Louis only
May 21	Open handicap athletic meeting
May 28	Interscholastic meet for schools of Louisiana Purchase Territory
May 30	Western college championships
June 2	AAU handicap meeting
June 3	AAU Jr. championship
June 4	AAU Sr. championship
June 11	Olympic college championships, open to colleges of the world
June 13	Central Assoc. AAU championships
June 18	Turner's mass exhibitions
June 20–25	College baseball
June 29, 30	Interscholastic championships
July 1, 2	Turner's international and individual team contest
July 4	AAU all-around championships
July 5, 6, 7	Lacrosse
July 8, 9	Swimming and water polo championships
July 11, 12	Interscholastic basketball
July 13, 14	YMCA basketball championships

July 18, 19	College basketball
July 20–23	Irish sports
July 29	Open athletic club handicap meeting of the Western Assoc. AAU
Aug. 1–6	Bicycling
Aug. 8–13	Tennis
Aug. 18	YMCA gymnastic championships
Aug. 19	YMCA handicap meeting
Aug. 20	YMCA championship meeting
Aug. 29–Sept. 3	Olympic Games
Sept. 8–10	World's fencing championships
Sept. 12–15	Olympic cricket championships
Sept. 19–24	Golf
Sept. 26–Oct. 1	Military athletic carnival
Oct. 14, 15	AAU wrestling championships
Oct. 27	Turner's mass exhibition
Oct. 28, 29	AAU gymnastic championships
Nov. 10, 11	Relay racing, open to athletic clubs, colleges, schools, and YMCAs
Nov. 12	College football
Nov. 15–17	Association football
Nov. 17	X-country championships
Nov. 24	College football and local x-country championships: East vs. West[13]

The Olympic Games of 1904, held in St. Louis, sank to its lowest point. The U.S. team competed primarily against itself because there was little representation from around the world. Germany, Canada, Britain, Greece, Hungary, and Cuba sent athletes, but it was purely an American event. The "Olympic" designation was awarded to everything from a track and field meet between thirteen-year-old schoolboys to Anthropology Days, in which a collection of aboriginal freaks, rumored to have been drafted from sideshows of the concurrent St. Louis Exposition, performed in athletic competition much to the amusement of a handful of gawking spectators. When informed of Anthropology Days as an official Olympic event, Coubertin wrote several years later, "In no place but America would one have dared place such events on the program."[14]

Six-hundred and eighty-one athletes representing twelve NOCs participated in the St. Louis Olympiad. Six women athletes from the United States competed in archery and won all of the events. It should be noted that no other country sent women athletes to the St. Louis Olympic Games. The Olympic Games, for the second time in a row, had been relegated as a mere sideshow, overshadowed by the more prominent and prestigious international exposition. The obvious had been demonstrated. Baron de Coubertin and his beloved Olympic Games had to establish their autonomy and independent identity before they would be accepted on their merit.

The IVth Olympiad: London, 1908

During the 1904 meeting in London, the IOC awarded the 1908 Olympiad to Rome. In 1906 Mt. Vesuvius erupted and caused considerable damage and hardship. The financial burden of attending to the needs of the victims of Vesuvius and staging the Olympic Games was too much for Rome to bear. The Italians asked the IOC to relieve them of the responsibility of holding the games. Great Britain made a proposal to the IOC to host the 1908 games and the IOC promptly accepted. However, once again the Olympic Games would have to share the spotlight. The 1908 London Olympiad was held in conjunction with the Franco-British Exhibition. The arrangement was purely economic, as the exhibition organizers would pay for the construction of the stadium and other facilities that the games required. The British Olympic Committee would receive one-half of the gross receipts.[15] The London Olympiad was the largest yet, with 1,999 athletes representing twenty-two NOCs.

The American team was preoccupied with winning and assumed the posture that "international cooperation was a worthwhile objective as long as America could claim an athletic victory."[16] An enormous athletic rivalry existed between the British and the Americans and was underscored by the headlines of the *New York Times:* "American Athletes Sure of Success," "Britishers Fear Yankee Athletes," and "We Will Knock the Spots Off the Britishers."[17] The English, ever proper and the custodians of the creed of fair play, held to the Olympic ideal of competition. As reported by the London *Times,*

> It is commonly said, and, indeed is put forward as a conclusive argument in favor of the modern Olympic movement, that international athletics encourage international amity. This is only the case if they are organized in so orderly and impartial a manner that every competitor, whether he has won or lost, goes away satisfied and feeling that every opportunity has been given and every courtesy shown to him. That this will be the case at the Olympic Games of London, no Briton, and we feel sure, none of our foreign visitors can doubt; and, if that be so, the games cannot fail to be an immense value both to those who take part in them and to the nations to which they belong.[18]

Unfortunately, the London games became embroiled in political turmoil and nationalism. The athletes from Finland did not display any national flag or banner because the Russians, politically and militarily powerful at this time, were diplomatically able to mandate that if the Finns carried a flag or banner, it would be a Russian one. Likewise, the Irish were told to display and compete under the flag of Great Britain and that all medals won by the Irish athletes would simply add to the prestige of England.[19] In addition, the American team did not like the British scoring system that was used to determine the Olympic victories. American athletes were entered almost entirely in the track and field competition and wanted the "Games Trophy" to be awarded based on track and field victories only. The British insisted that all competitive events be included in the determination of the overall Olympic Championship. The Americans, ever resourceful, devised their own system of scoring that was more favorable to their efforts and by doing so enabled the specter of nationalism to overshadow athletic competition.

The British and Americans were at odds once again concerning the Olympic tug-of-war competition. The British won the event; however, the Americans complained that the British used "illegal footwear." As reported by the London *Times*,

> In the tug-of-war a team of light stalwart policemen easily pulled the great hammer, and discus and weight-thrower of the U.S. over the line. The Americans protested against the results of the first bout on the grounds that their conquerors wore boots, but this objection was, of course, overruled.[20] The British press labeled the American team, as well as the French team, poor sports. The ill feelings between the British and the American teams came to a head over the marathon. Prior to the event the Americans logged a protest against Tom Longboat, the Canadian entry, because the American AAU had declared Mr. Longboat a professional. Much to the dismay of the Americans, the British Olympic Council pointed out that the country of nationality, in this case Canada, was the only authority empowered to determine amateur status. Canada certified Tom Longboat as an amateur. The American protest was disallowed. The Americans would fire yet another protest.

The Italian entrant in the marathon, Dorando, reached the stadium first but was so exhausted and disoriented that well-meaning officials helped him across the finish line. The Americans protested the race on the grounds that Dorando received assistance, which he had. The protest was upheld and the American, Johnny Hayer, was declared the winner. The games ended on July 25, 1908, amid turmoil and bickering among contestants and between nations. Serious doubts were expressed on both sides of the Atlantic concerning the continuation of the Olympics. The British admitted that there had indeed been problems. The American viewpoint was more direct; changes must be made or all American participation would end.[21] In the end the Americans scored more victories in the stadium events (track and field), whereas the British were the victors in the overall competition. The London Olympiad ended with ill feelings between the British and American teams, between Irish athletes and their British counterparts, and between the Finns and the Russians, much to the disappointment of Coubertin and the IOC. However, on a progressive note, thirty-six women representing four countries competed in three sports—tennis, archery, and figure skating. Women athletes also demonstrated their athletic expertise in exhibitions of swimming, diving, and gymnastics.

The Vth Olympiad: Stockholm, 1912

The Stockholm Olympiad is significant for a number of reasons.

1. It was to be the last Olympiad that Russia would compete in until 1952, when the Soviet Union sent its team to the Helsinki Olympiad.

2. Jim Thorpe, perhaps America's most gifted athlete ever, was a member of the U.S. team, which also included George S. Patton, Jr., who later became a famous general in World War II, and Avery Brundage, who later became president of the International Olympic Committee (1952–1972). James E. Sullivan would later strip Jim Thorpe of his two gold Olympic medals because of Thorpe's brief career as a semipro baseball player.

3. The American AAU threatened to boycott the Stockholm Olympics unless American representation in the management of the games was ensured. The Americans were still seething from the blatantly biased officiating and scoring by the British Olympic officials during the London games and therefore demanded to be included in managing the Stockholm games.

4. Finnish athletes demanded to participate as an autonomous team in 1912 and flatly refused to march under the Russian flag. The Russians immediately protested.

5. Bohemia requested that it be allowed to compete as an independent nation, which did not sit too well with the Austro-Hungarian Empire, which included Bohemia.

6. Women's swimming was recognized as an official event.

7. Equestrian competition was held for the first time.

8. Modern pentathlon began.

Ever the diplomat, Baron de Coubertin's efforts assuaged political interests so that serious confrontations were avoided. After some political maneuvering, Swedish Olympic officials allowed foreign Olympic commissioners to be appointed to assist the Swedes. President Taft appointed none other than James E. Sullivan as American commissioner to the 1912 Stockholm Olympics. As the head of the AAU, Sullivan assembled the first truly representative American Olympic team. Olympic trials were held around the country to ensure that the best American athletes would be in Stockholm in 1912.[22]

According to Matthews, there was a total of 111 American track and field athletes on the American team. Of these, thirty-one were undergraduate college students, three were American Indians (James Thorpe, Louis Tewanima, and Alfred Sockalexis), one was Hawaiian (Duke Kohanamaku), and one was African American (Howard P. Drew).[23]

For the first time, women were able to compete in the Olympic Games as swimmers. On April 23, 1912, the decision was made by the American team not to send a team of women swimmers to Stockholm. No reason was given for deciding that America's women swimmers would not be part of the Olympic team.[24]

The Americans and British were eventually able to put the unsavory incidents of the 1908 games behind them. Both the British and the American delegations made sincere efforts to prevent conflict from occurring. The Swedish Olympic Committee did a fabulous job in preparing the facilities and making the necessary arrangements for the hordes of athletes and fans. The games were a rousing success, and Coubertin's hopes and dreams were finally realized. The Stockholm Olympiad hosted 2,490 athletes from twenty-eight nations.[25]

H. P. Drew, the lone African American on the American team, won his qualifying heat in the 100-meter dash. He was accorded much media coverage by the *New York Times* in part because he had a wife and two children to support and was still attending Springfield High School! The students at his high school solicited funds to provide for his family while he was in Stockholm competing for his country. In the later heat of the 100-meter dash, Drew pulled a tendon in his right leg, but he still managed to win the heat and qualify for the finals the next day. His teammates and America hoped and prayed that he would recover to run in the finals, but it was not to be. He could not recover quickly enough, and the high-school student who had equaled the world's record in the 100-meter dash watched as his teammate, R. C. Craig, won the race in 10.8 seconds and the gold medal.[26]

Jim Thorpe won both the pentathlon and decathlon in Stockholm. In the pentathlon, Thorpe won four of the five events and finished third in the javelin competition. One of Thorpe's opponents in the pentathlon was none other than Avery Brundage, who finished fifth behind Thorpe. Brundage later became president of the International Olympic Committee, where he championed the Olympic ideal of purely amateur competition. Brundage was strongly opposed to allowing professional athletes to compete in the Olympic Games.

Less than a year after Thorpe won his Olympic medals, he was accused of playing semipro baseball one summer prior to the 1912 Olympic Games. Jim Thorpe, whom the king of Sweden immortalized as the world's greatest living athlete after his Olympic victories, admitted to the allegation and was stripped of his medals and trophies by James E. Sullivan. What is truly revealing is that the International Olympic Committee did not initiate the investigation of Thorpe; it was the American Olympic Committee.

There were fifty-seven women athletes who represented eleven countries in Stockholm.[27] In addition to women's swimming, equestrian events were held for the first time and the modern pentathlon was inaugurated. The modern pentathlon consisted of running, riding, swimming, fencing, and shooting, and it became popular with military athletes because the skills of the pentathlon were those required of a soldier. The Stockholm Olympic Games were an outstanding success; however, World War I precluded the 1916 Olympic Games. The next Olympics took place in Antwerp, Belgium, in 1920.

Figure 14.2
In a line-up of members of the 1912 U.S. Olympic squad, Jim Thorpe wore a turtle-neck warm-up sweater. Photo by Culver Pictures, Inc. Courtesy of Cumberland County Historical Society, Carlisle, PA.

The VIIth Olympiad: Antwerp, 1920

Eight years after the last Olympiad and amid the rubble and debris of World War I, the Olympic spirit prevailed as the city of Antwerp prepared to host the VIIth Olympic Games. In the aftermath of World War I, the actual decision to award the games to Antwerp was not made until 1919.

The Antwerp Olympiad initiated two Olympic traditions: the athletes took the Olympic oath before the general public, and the five-ring Olympic flag was unveiled at the games. The Olympic flag had actually been displayed in Paris during the 1914 celebration of the twentieth anniversary of the revival of the modern Olympics. The Olympic flag displays five interlocked rings that are colored blue, yellow, black, green, and red. Baron de Coubertin used the interlocking rings to symbolize the coming together of athletes from the five continents.

Paavo Nurmi, the fabulous distance runner from Finland, made his debut at the Antwerp Games and went down in the annals of Olympic history as one of the greatest distance runners of all time. He captured the silver medal in the 5000-meter race and the gold medal in the 10,000-meter race during the VIIth Olympiad. American sprinters were successful and won both gold and silver medals, in both the 100- and 200-meter races. The American Olympic team included women swimmers for the first time, and the American women captured the gold, silver, and bronze medals in the 100-meter freestyle and the 300-meter freestyle, and they won the gold medal in the 400-meter relay. The United States Women's diving team swept the Fancy Diving event by capturing the first four places. The Antwerp Games came to a close, and the International Olympic Committee began preparation for the next Olympiad, which was to be held in Paris in 1924. Baron de Coubertin focused his energy and agenda on addressing an issue that he was not at all comfortable with: the inclusion of more women in the Olympic Games.

The gradual inclusion of women into the Olympic Games is a significant social event that deserves attention. Anita Defrantz is a former Olympic rower and since 1986 has been a member of the International Olympic Committee. Among her many duties is her involvement in the IOC working group on sport and women. According to Defrantz, "The first Olympic Games of the modern era in Athens in 1896 were not open to [women]. The reviver of the Games, Baron Pierre de Coubertin, was a man steeped in the culture of his time, who thought that the Games should traditionally remain "the exaltation of male sport."[28] It is important for students to recognize that although the International Olympic Committee was slow to increase the participation of women in the Games, it did happen. The example set by the IOC relative to opening up the program to more and more women's athletic events served as a catalyst to advance the cause of women's rights and enabled women around the world to experience the joy of sport. The student of history can reflect on the bygone times of the early twentieth century, when women were not accorded equal rights let alone the right to vote. It was during this era that significant growth within the Olympic movement occurred; Baron de Coubertin and the all-male membership of the IOC reflected the social and cultural beliefs of this era. As a result, the process of including and expanding opportunities for women to participate in sport was slow but, nonetheless, continued to move forward.

The post-World War I era ushered in many social and political changes in Europe. European women became interested in track and field, and Mme. Millait established the Federation Feminine Sportive Internationalle (FSFI) to promote sport for women. Prior to the 1920 Antwerp Olympics, the FSFI had conducted international competition in fifteen events with distances up to 1500 meters. Baron de Coubertin was intransigent when Mme. Millait requested that the Antwerp Olympics include track and field events for women. He could support women's swimming, but not track and field.

What Coubertin may have ignored was the fact that eleven women actually participated in tennis and golf during the 1900 Paris Olympiad, but their participation may have been due to accident, oversight, or apathy.[29] The Paris Games were a fiasco, to say the least, especially with regard to organization and administration, and some competition may have been slipped in without the knowledge of Baron de Coubertin.

Baron de Coubertin, according to sport historian Mary Leigh, had no particular objection to women's participation in tennis and swimming. However, "he drew attention to the fact that fencers, horsewomen, and rowers also existed, and that soon, perhaps, there would be women soccer players and runners who would also wish to be included in the Olympics program. Such sports practiced by women, he felt, would not constitute an edifying sight before assembled crowds for Olympic contests."[30] The Baron was indeed a chauvinist.

Because Baron de Coubertin would not cooperate, Mme. Millait organized the First Women's Olympic Games in 1922. The event was successful, and plans were made for a second Women's Olympics when negotiations with the International Amateur Athletic Federation led to a plan to control women's athletics and to recommend an Olympic program of five events for women. Mme. Millait wanted more events but was not successful. The British women athletes stated that they would not compete in the 1928 Amsterdam Olympics to protest the sparse program. Negotiations continued and a five-event Olympic program for women began in the 1928 Olympics.

Baron de Coubertin was disappointed; however, he was able to prevent track and field competition for women in the 1924 Paris Olympiad. Upon retiring as president of the International Olympic Committee in 1925, he did not miss an opportunity to voice his objections against the inclusion of women as Olympic competitors in some sporting events.[31] Some of the Baron's allies were physical educators in the United States. They did not want to lavish cost and attention on a few highly skilled Olympic athletes at the expense of ignoring physical education instruction for a great many women. The United States Women's Physical Education Association protested the inclusion of women athletes in the 1928 and 1932 Olympic Games.[32] The Olympic Games continued to grow. In 1920, 2,686 athletes representing twenty-nine countries took part in the games. Of this total, seventy-seven were women who represented thirteen countries.[33]

The VIIIth Olympiad: Paris, 1924

The 1924 Paris Games were a far cry from the debacle that occurred when Paris hosted the games in 1900. Remembering the results of the 1900 Games, the Paris Organizing Committee worked night and day to insure the success of the games. The number of athletes participating in the 1924 Paris Olympiad was 2,956, representing forty-four nations. Women athletes accounted for 136 of the Olympic athletes. Women competed in swimming (seven events), fencing (one event), and lawn tennis (two events).[34]

The United States won the gold medal in rugby when it beat France 17 to 3. The only other country to enter a team in rugby competition was Rumania, and the Rumanian team was terrible! France beat the Rumanians 61 to 3, and the Americans "edged" the Rumanians by a score of 37 to 0. The championship match was played in front of forty thousand fans who watched the American team take the French entirely by surprise due to the rough, but legal, tactics learned from playing American football.[35]

The athlete who basked in the limelight in Paris was Paavo Nurmi, the magnificent distance runner from Finland who displayed little emotion or joy during the Paris Olympics. The sullen Finn won four gold medals: the 1500-meter, 5000-meter flat race, first in the 3000-meter team race, and in the 10,000-meter cross-country run. Henry said that "without any question Nurmi's performance was the greatest exhibition of distance running ever seen."[36] Grantland Rice, one of America's greatest sportswriters, called Paavo Nurmi "Superman."[37] Between Nurmi and his teammate, Willie Ritola, the two athletes won nine gold and silver medals. The sports world and the press were circulating numerous theories as to how the Finn had become so successful. According to Lucas, "Reams of newspaper and periodical essays were written about the Finnish 'secrets' of athletic superiority. Fascinating claims were made for native foods: raw, dried fish; rye bread 'hard as biscuit'; and sour milk. The magnificent introvert, Nurmi, added mystery by refusing to discuss anything about his private life and training regimen."[38]

The Paris Olympiad, like the Olympic Games before and after, had problems. The Paris organizers took in six million francs at the gate but still ran a deficit of two million francs. The French spectators, much to the chagrin of Coubertin, displayed a general lack of sports knowledge and frequently behaved in a discourteous manner. There were fights in the stands, booing by the crowd during national anthems, and a brawl between the French and Americans during the rugby match. There was still friction between the British and American teams. Several members of the British Olympic delegation demanded that their team withdraw from the Paris Games rather than endure the unfair treatment of the "American Professionals."[39] The issue of professionalism would be a topic that the IOC would have to deal with, and soon!

The Ist Winter Olympics: Chamonix, 1924

The first Winter Olympic Games were held in Chamonix, France, from January 27 to February 5, 1924. The Winter Olympics were initially opposed by Baron de Coubertin because he believed that they would detract from the Summer Games. Once he had become convinced that winter sports were quite popular, he changed his position and joined with the IOC in approving the Winter Games. There were, however, conditions that Coubertin had included. The name "Olympiad" would not be used for the Winter Games, and although the country that hosted the Summer Games could also host the Winter Games, the host cities must not be close to each other.

The program at Chamonix consisted of six sports: speed skating for men, figure skating for both men and women, pairs figure skating, cross-country skiing, bobsledding, and ice hockey. The demonstrating sports of military ski race and shooting and curling were also offered. The United States won the gold medal in the men's 500-meter speed skating, finished second to Canada in ice hockey, and captured the silver medal in women's figure skating. The first Winter Olympics drew 258 athletes representing sixteen countries. Thirteen of these athletes were women who represented sixteen countries.[40] The second Winter Games were held in St. Moritz and featured the American bobsledding team.

The IXth Olympiad: Amsterdam, 1928

The Dutch had campaigned before the IOC to host the Olympics on more than one occasion. Amsterdam had made proposals before the IOC in 1912, 1921, and 1924. The Dutch withdrew their proposals in 1919 in favor of Antwerp, and again in 1921 when Coubertin expressed his desire that Paris be awarded the games. The Dutch had a long and difficult road ahead. The financial burden that the host city and national government must contend with in producing the Olympic Games is enormous, and the officials of the organizing committee have many sleepless nights. Amsterdam was no exception, and even though it was awarded the 1928 Olympic Games way back in 1921, the proper financing of the games was still a problem.

A new stadium was absolutely necessary, as well as the construction of much-needed venues and support facilities. The Dutch officials' first attempt at financing the Olympic Games was through a lottery, but that was not successful. Other creative attempts to finance the games failed, and the mood of the Dutch Olympic Committee was dour when loyal citizens of Holland came to the rescue. Citizens living in the remote Dutch East Indies pledged money, and communities throughout Holland rallied around the Olympic standard with pledges. The press called for support and encouraged every means of raising money. At last, the Dutch Olympic Committee had the financing to insure the success of the Amsterdam Olympiad.[41] The public and financial support of the Amsterdam Olympiad by a myriad of people and groups once again illustrates the social significance that people attach to sport, especially the Olympic Games.

There were 2,724 Olympic athletes representing forty-six nations in Amsterdam; 290 Olympians were women.[42] German athletes participated for the first time since 1912, having been excluded from the Olympic Games because of Germany's involvement in World War I. The Germans quickly asserted their athletic prowess by winning a total of thirty-seven Olympic medals; the United States won fifty-five.

Field hockey was played for the first time, and nine teams entered the competition. British India, known now as India, beat Holland 3 to 0 before forty-two thousand fans to win the gold medal.[43] The American dominance in track and field declined in 1928. With the exception of Ray Barbuti's first-place finish in the 400 meter, U.S. athletes failed to win a single first-place finish in the sprints, middle distance, or distance races. The American 400-meter relay team won the gold medal and followed that with a first-place finish in the 1600-meter relay. Both American relay teams set new Olympic records.

The indomitable Paavo Nurmi, now thirty-two years old, won the silver medal in the 5000-meter race and the gold medal in the 10,000-meter race, where he set a new Olympic record, and he captured another silver medal in the 3000-meter steeplechase. Women's track and field made its appearance for the first time in Amsterdam. The American women won four medals: E. Robinson won the gold medal in the 100-meter race and in so doing set the world record, Mildred Wiley captured the bronze medal in the high jump, Lillian Copeland took second place in the discus throw, and the American 400-meter relay team won the silver medal.

The 1928 Olympiad was a high mark in Olympic competition. More countries competed than ever before; countries that were regarded as "athletically suspect" performed well, and there was a minimum amount of difficulty.[44]

The IInd Winter Olympics: St. Moritz, 1928

The popularity of the Winter Games continued to increase as evidenced by the 464 athletes who competed. Twenty-five countries were represented, and the number of women athletes doubled from thirteen in 1924 to twenty-six in 1928.[45] Norway continued to dominate the Winter Olympics, winning a total of fourteen medals; the United States won six. The Americans won both the gold and silver medals in the two-man and four-man bobsled competition. The other two medals were won by Mr. Farrell, who tied for third place in the 500-meter speed skating competition, and Miss Loughran, who finished third in women's figure skating. The United States did not send an ice hockey team to St. Moritz. However, Canada continued to be the undisputed champion in ice hockey and captured its second consecutive gold medal. Sweden followed in second place and Switzerland won the bronze medal.

The Issue of Amateurism

During the 1924 Paris Olympiad, several members of the British Olympic team demanded that the British withdraw from the Games because the American Olympic team was using professional athletes. The issue of amateurism became such an important topic that after the 1928 Winter and Summer Olympic Games were concluded, the IOC turned its attention to this question. The IOC would have to determine "what is an amateur?" The issue of who is allowed to compete in the Olympic Games became one of the most volatile issues of the twentieth century. The Olympic ideal of amateurism was a noble concept. However, the concept of amateur participation as measured by traditional standards soon became antiquated. The IOC is steeped in the traditions of Olympism, and the amateur ethic was at the foundation of Olympic eligibility. The IOC first addressed the question of amateurism in Prague during the 1925 meeting.

During the Prague meeting, the question of "broken time" was vigorously debated. Broken time was a situation by which athletes were reimbursed for time lost from work when they were traveling and competing.

The prevalent thinking among the IOC was that money given to athletes under the broken-time practice compromised the amateur ethic, and it adamantly opposed the practice of paying athletes via broken-time reimbursement.[46]

In 1930 the IOC convened in Berlin to discuss the amateur issue and once again the payment for broken time, which was supported by the International Football Federation, which controlled soccer. The IOC again opposed outright payments to athletes but ducked the issue of defining the phrase "compensation for loss of salary," leaving the door open for abuse of the amateur ideal and payments to athletes in one form or another.

The Xth Olympiad: Los Angeles, 1932

Southern California welcomed 1,281 of the world's finest athletes from thirty-seven countries with ideal weather conditions and enthusiastic fans. There were 127 women Olympians who represented eighteen countries. The Los Angeles Olympiad would be the most grandiose athletic festival in modern history. Los Angeles was decked out with Olympic banners, and enthusiasm for the games was unprecedented. The Los Angeles Organizing Committee was both well organized and well financed. The Los Angeles Coliseum was designed to hold more than one hundred thousand spectators and was filled to capacity during opening ceremonies. The athletes were housed in a newly constructed Olympic Village. The games featured the most intense competition to date, as nearly every existing record in track and field was broken.

Mildred "Babe" Didrikson of the United States dominated the women's track and field competition, winning gold medals in the 80-meter hurdles and the javelin throw and capturing a silver medal in the high jump. Her efforts in the 80-meter hurdles and javelin throw were world records. The Japanese men dominated the swimming events, although the American Clarence "Buster" Crabbe won the 400-meter freestyle. Of the five gold medals awarded to the victors in men's swimming, the Japanese won four, plus the gold in the 800-meter relay. The American men were still the "toast of the world" in the diving competition and swept the competition, finishing first, second, and third in springboard and high diving.

The American women dominated the swimming events. Helene Madison won the gold medal in both the 100-meter freestyle and 400-meter freestyle in addition to anchoring the gold-medal-winning American 400-meter relay team, which set the world record. Helene Madison set two Olympic records on her way to winning two gold medals.

The Los Angeles organizing committee erected the Olympic Village ten minutes from the Coliseum. Henry describes the village as consisting of "miles of flower bordered streets, vast expanses of lawn, cozy cottages of the Mexican ranch-house type were hidden behind a huge white plaster and red tile administration building, and there, secluded from the public but free to follow their own desires, the athletes mingled in their pleasant fellowship."[47]

The games did have their problems. Paavo Nurmi, still running for Finland, was disqualified from competing because it was determined that he was a professional athlete. He was planning to run in the marathon. In the Parade of Nations, Great Britain, which was alphabetically supposed to follow behind Germany, was mistakenly placed ahead of the Germans, which resulted in a mild protest. There was confusion in the 3000-meter steeplechase that caused the athletes to run an extra lap. Babe Didrikson was penalized in the high jump because she "dived" over the bar (not jumped), which was illegal in 1932. She would have in all probability won the gold medal in the high jump but had to be content with the silver. The no-diving rule was eliminated the next year.

The spirit of Olympism and the cooperation among athletes, officials, and fans during the Los Angeles Olympiad could not have been better. However, the Olympics were soon destined to embark on a journey that would forever cast a dark shadow on Coubertin's dream.

The IIIrd Winter Olympics: Lake Placid, 1932

Seventeen nations sent a total of 252 athletes to compete in the first Winter Olympics held in the United States. There were twenty-one women representing seventeen countries who made the trip to upstate New York. The major problem occurred when the athletes learned that they would have to compete under American rules, which the Europeans were not familiar with. The Americans benefited by the home-field advantage and won gold medals in the men's 500-meter, 1500-meter, and 10,000-meter speed skating. The American team won both the two-man and four-man bobsled races and finished second to the Canadian ice hockey team. Sonja Henie of Norway, who won the women's figure skating for the first time at age fifteen in St. Moritz, won the gold medal again in Lake Placid. The demonstration sports featured women's speed skating in the 500-, 1000-, and 1500-meter along with curling and a 25-mile, cross-country dog-sled race won by Emile St. Goddard of Canada.

The Political Nature of the Olympic Games

In the 1930s, the world was undergoing radical change that was motivated largely by political ideology. The shadowy figures that emerged during this period in history would use any and all means to advance specific political and social agendas. The Olympic Games were not immune to such political manipulation from forces outside the IOC. Beginning with the 1936 Olympiad in Berlin, unsavory politicians exploited the Games for blatant political purposes. Obtrusive politics of regional, national, and international dimensions attempted to partially undermine the noble ideals of Olympic movement. However, the nature of politics, being what it is, attempted to turn the Olympic Games from an athletic arena to a political arena designed to dispense and transmit propaganda and ideology.

Global politics and institutional struggles against social and economic inequality became an unwanted part of the Olympic agenda. Politics became as much a part of the Olympic Games as athletes and sweat. In addition to peace and cooperation, blatant nationalism became a symbol of the Olympics. However, in spite of all this, the members of the IOC dedicated themselves to work even harder to insure that the Olympic Games would persist and persevere. Throughout decades of global strife and tragedy, the Olympic Games came under attack by the press, self-serving politicians, and terrorists. Thanks to the efforts of the IOC, today the Olympic flame burns more brightly than ever as a symbol of peace, unity, and internationalism. However, the struggle to keep both the flame and the spirit of Olympism alive has been an arduous one, as the ensuing chronicles of the Olympic Games will demonstrate.

Up to now, the Summer Olympiads and Winter Olympics have been presented as a series of chronological events that reflect selected athletic, social, and political events. The following discussion of the 1936 Berlin Olympiad is significantly longer and more in depth. The reason for this is that the Berlin Olympics involved a number of significant social, political, racial, and religious issues that became part of the Olympic Games. As a result, the nature of the Olympic Games reflected issues that the Baron de Coubertin never intended to include, and the student of physical education should be made aware of this. In addition, students should understand that the joy of sport can be taken away from athletes. This was the case in Nazi Germany, when Hitler deliberately set about to persecute Jews and people of color by removing their access to sport. In addition, students may ask why the United States sent an Olympic team to participate in the 1936 Games, which historian Richard Mandell refers to as the "Nazi Olympics." Some of these questions will hopefully be addressed in this section. What is important to note is that although the Nazis tried to undermine the ideal of Olympism, the International Olympic Committee refused to let this happen.

The XIth Olympiad: Berlin, 1936

Discussion of the 1936 Olympics begins with one of the most ruthless politicians the world has ever known. The reign of terror initiated by Adolf Hitler was by far the most heinous and hideous imaginable. He was very interested in ensuring the success of the 1936 Olympic Games. Hitler visualized the games as a political-social platform and fashioned a political agenda that utilized the Olympic Games to send his message of Nazi superiority.

Sport and Physical Education in Nazi Germany

Mandell describes Hitler's regard of sport and physical activity:

> While writing Mein Kampf in prison in 1924, Hitler had included some theoretical statements about the value of purposeful physical activity. The views on physical training, however, do not bulk large in Mein

Kampf and are only adjuncts of his reforming schemes for all German education. Characteristically, Hitler viewed the failures of Germany in the past as attributable to a pedagogical regime that was too intellectual, too 'unnatural.'

Hitler states: 'in a race-nationalist state the school itself must set aside infinitely more time for physical conditioning. Not a day should pass in which the young person's body is not schooled at least one hour every morning and evening, and this in every sort of sport and gymnastics.'[48]

Hitler's favorite sport was boxing:

No other sport is its equal in building up aggressiveness, in demanding lightning-like decision, and in toughening up the body in steely agility.[49]

Hitler's consistent seeking of grandeur became apparent in his plans for German sport. Hitler and his compatriots established National Socialist sporting meets which, like the original Olympiads of the classical Greeks, were to be racially exclusive. These new, racially proud athletic festivals were the occasion for expansion of the athletic facilities at Nuremberg, where Hitler produced the massive Nazi spectacles. The Führer felt confident that after 1940, the Olympic Games would, for all time, take place in Germany.

Anti-Jewish legislation was enacted shortly after Hitler became chancellor and was an integral part of Nazi terror. The Nazi master-race ethic permeated all aspects of German life, and sport and physical education were no exception. If an occupant of Nazi Germany was a non-Aryan, that person had virtually all aspects of physical activity cut off. On April 1, 1933, when the national boycott of Jewish business went into effect, the German boxing federation announced that it would no longer tolerate Jewish fighters or referees.[50] During that same year, the new Nazi minister of education proclaimed on June 2 that Jews were to be excluded from youth, welfare, and gymnastic organizations and that the facilities of all clubs would be closed to the Jew. Jewish athletic teams were first forbidden to compete with Aryan teams and later forbidden to go abroad to compete. A police sports association was forced to expel all the members of its ladies' auxiliary who had competed with a team of Jewish women. By the beginning of 1935, all private and public practice fields were denied to Jews.[51]

People of color occupied the same category as the Jew in Nazi thought; however, there were very few blacks in Nazi Germany. Hitler expressed his view on blacks when he said to Balden von Schirach, "The Americans ought to be ashamed of themselves for letting their medals be won by Negroes. I myself would never even shake hands with one of them."[52] Hitler apparently thought that the German track athletes would overwhelm the American Olympic team that had two of the finest sprinters the world had ever seen, Jesse Owens and Ralph Metcalfe, who happened to be African Americans. In fact, not one male or female German athlete won the gold medal in any running event during the 1936 Berlin Olympiad. However, a German, Lt. Handrick, did win the gold medal in the pentathlon, and Anny Steuer, also from Germany, won the silver medal in the 80-meter hurdles.

Preparation for the Berlin Olympiad began during the 1932 Olympic Games held in Los Angeles. Two men were the principal figures in developing, organizing, and staging the Berlin Olympics. Dr. Theodor Lewald, president of the German Olympic Committee, and Dr. Carl Diem, at the time the world's most distinguished sport historian, were the two creators of the Berlin Olympics.[53] Diem and Lewald were apparently blind to the Nazi dogma. They were so caught up in the affairs of staging the Olympic Games that it was too late to stop once they realized what was taking place. Nevertheless, these two men were possibly the closest observers of the 1932 Olympic Games in Los Angeles. Both men were instrumental in developing the 1916 Olympics at Berlin and were grief-stricken when their preparatory work was destroyed by World War I. They were not going to be denied a second time.

Both men were tireless workers and digested every detail of the 1932 Olympic Games. Mandell notes:

> As Lewald filled ceremonial functions in Los Angeles, Diem was behind the scenes, seeking masses of material: sketches, models, addresses, flags, programs, tickets, etc., that had been collected for them. . . . Diem took notes as he chatted with designers of the elevator and telephone system. He photographed garages and workshops and stooped and stretched calibrated tapes to take metric measurements of the cottages in Olympic Village. He recorded in his files the statement of the cooks as to the dietary preferences of the participating nationalities.[54]

The two Germans were compiling an extraordinary volume of information about every conceivable aspect of the Olympic production. It was their task to create the ultimate Olympics. The 1932 games at Los Angeles were the most lavish games in modern times. All the facilities were superb. The stadium held 104,000 spectators, and the technical and logistical expertise was the finest available at the time. It was in Los Angeles that the Olympic Village concept became a reality. The living quarters for the Olympic athletes were modern and comfortable. Everything about the 1932 Olympic Games was first class, and it was the responsibility of Diem and Lewald to make the 1932 Games a second-rate event when compared with the 1936 Berlin Games.

The athletic complex in Berlin was the most complete sporting facility ever built. Construction of the facility progressed rapidly under the direction of Diem, Lewald, and Werner March, the architect of the stadium. There existed a vast complex of arenas, playing and practice fields, schools, offices, parking lots, and subway stations. The main stadium was the largest ever constructed at the time but occupied only one-twentieth of the entire athletic complex or Reichssportfeld.[55] The Berlin Olympics had indeed surpassed the spectacle in Los Angeles four years earlier.

Lewald commissioned a German sculptor to construct a giant Olympic Bell, which was designed as a major symbol of Nazi pageantry.

When the bell was en route to Berlin, each town through which the bell passed held solemn ceremonies of a quasi-religious nature to honor the sixteen-ton bell. Physical Education Director Dunkelberg extolled the bell as a symbol of the staunch will that now characterized the German nation.[56]

The Nazis attempted to ignore and play down their anti-Semitic campaign by directing the pursuits of the visiting journalists to the Olympic Games. The Germans provided almost every imaginable convenience for the visiting press in order for them to "forget" the Nazi racial policies. However, American newspaper readers in 1933 were able to read about the anti-Semitic campaign waged by the Nazis. The American sports executives were shocked at the removal of Dr. Theodor Lewald from his post as president of the German Olympic Committee because of partly Jewish ancestry. During the International Olympic Committee's meeting in Vienna on June 6, 1933, American Olympic officials demanded that the games be removed from Germany if the Nazis did not cease to discriminate against its Jewish athletes. This demand was aired before passage of the Nuremberg Laws in 1935.[57]

The Amateur Athletic Union (AAU) of the United States on November 21, 1933, with but one exception, voted for a boycott of the 1936 Games unless the position of Nazi Germany regarding Jewish athletes be "changed in fact as well as theory." Gustavus T. Kirby of the American Olympic Committee had proposed the resolution and was vigorously supported by Avery Brundage, then president of the American Olympic Committee.

After the anti-Nazi resolution of the AAU, the American Olympic Committee continued to postpone acceptance of the German invitation. The facilities for the games in Berlin became another prime public works project of the Nazis. Germany as well as other nations selected and trained their teams. Well-publicized suggestions appeared that the Americans ought to boycott the Berlin Olympics. Very strong national sentiment supported this. Nervously and with yet another fanfare of international publicity, the German Olympic Committee finally announced in June 1934 that twenty-one Jewish athletes had been nominated for the German training camps. Brundage was suspicious, as were the vast majority of Americans, so the American Olympic Committee sent Brundage to Germany to investigate the situation.

When Brundage returned to America, he revealed himself to be yet one more important personage dazzled by the order, relative prosperity, and joy that most travelers observed in Germany at that time. On the basis of interviews with Jewish leaders (who, as one hostile journalist noted, were always met in cafes and were always chaperoned by Nazi officials), Brundage concluded that the Germans were observing the letter and spirit of Olympicism.[58] On the basis of Avery Brundage's recommendation, the American Olympic Committee voted to participate in the Berlin Games. However, the AAU was still opposed to American participation. Despite Brundage's claims to the contrary, trustworthy stories of religious and racial persecutions continued to leak out of Germany.

For example, it was learned that although twenty-one Jews were "nominated" for the German Olympic training camp, none was "invited" to attend.[59]

By the summer of 1935, most American Olympic officials had accepted Coubertin's commandment that, whatever the obstacles, the regular march of the modern Olympiads must take place.

The Berlin Olympics held opening ceremonies on August 1, 1936, and the magnificent new stadium was filled to capacity. The German Organizing Committee initiated a torch run that originated in Olympia, Greece. Thanks to the efforts of over three thousand relay runners, the sacred flame was transported from Greece across Europe to arrive in Berlin during opening ceremonies. Athletes numbering 3,738 from forty-nine countries arrived in Berlin to take part in the games. Three-hundred and twenty-eight of the athletes were women who represented twenty-six countries.[60] The athletes, coaches, IOC officials, and spectators were treated to a spectacular Olympiad. The Olympic atmosphere was very festive, and the enthusiasm generated by the fans became contagious. Opening ceremonies featured the release of thousands of doves against the backdrop of the massive Olympic flame that burned at the open end of the stadium. The evening ceremonies featured ten thousand dancers and wonderful choreography. They were joined by a chorus of fifteen hundred singers who performed Shiller's "Ode to Joy," which had been specifically requested by Baron de Coubertin.

The superstar of the 1936 Olympics was not a member of the Aryan race from Germany, as Hitler had hoped, but an African American who personified the spirit and ideal of Olympicism. Jesse Owens was one of the most phenomenal track and field athletes in Olympic history. He won gold medals in the 100 meters, 200 meters, running broad jump, and as a member of the 400-meter relay team. In all, Owens set the world record in the 200-meter race and the 400-meter relay and an Olympic record in the running broad jump. The winner in the men's marathon is listed in the official Olympic records as Kitei Son from Japan. In actual fact, he was from Korea, which in 1936 was under control of Japan. The Japanese told the Korean he could run the marathon but would represent Japan and in order to do so was given a Japanese name. The third place finisher in the men's marathon was Shorya Nan, who was yet another Korean running for Japan with a new name.

The Berlin Games were technically the best in history, and nothing had approached the massive scale of the XIth Olympiad. And why not? Hitler was convinced that his Third Reich would last for a thousand years and therefore spared no expense or effort in building the most lavish Olympic facilities history had known. After all, he was positive that all future Olympiads would take place in Berlin. The American team collected a grand total of fifty-six medals and, as usual, were quite strong in men's track and field. The host Germans amassed ninety-nine. The Winter Olympics was also held in Germany, and, as you might expect, the games at Garmisch-Partenkirchen were a success.

Figure 14.3
Jesse Owens setting one of four world records at the Big Ten Meet, May 25, 1935, Ann Arbor, Michigan. Courtesy of University of Michigan.

The IVth Winter Olympics: Garmisch–Partenkirchen, 1936

At Garmisch–Partenkirchen, 1936, Adolf Hitler was on hand to welcome athletes from all over the world, and fifteen thousand fans swarmed into the stadium to join the Führer during opening ceremonies. Close to seventy-five thousand people came to Garmisch–Partenkirchen every day to watch the competition.[61] Twenty-eight nations sent 668 athletes. They were entered in figure skating; fifteen countries sent ice hockey teams; thirteen countries were entered into the bobsledding competition; sixteen nations were entered in speed skating; and twenty-seven nations sent ski teams. There were 143 athletes from Germany alone![62] Eighty women from twenty-eight countries competed in figure skating and skiing.[63]

The American team won both the gold and the silver medals in the two-man bobsled. The bronze medal in ice hockey and the bronze medal in the 500-meter speed skating were the best the United States team could do. The host Germans did not do much better, gathering a total of six medals, as Austria, Norway, Finland, and Sweden dominated the competition.

It was not until 1948 that the Olympic flame would burn in London during the games of the XIVth Olympiad as the world was plunged into yet another world war. As happened in World War I, the Olympic Games were suspended during World War II. The 1940 Olympics had been awarded to Tokyo and then belatedly to Helsinki, which did not give up hope of holding the Olympics until the Russians invaded Finland in 1939.

The international Olympic community mourned the death of Baron de Fredy Pierre de Coubertin who, at age seventy-four, died a few weeks after the close of the Berlin Olympiad. His successor, Count Henri de Baillet Latour, an accomplished diplomat, assumed the duties as president of the IOC in a particularly difficult time. Baillet Latour unexpectedly died, in all probability hastened by the grief he felt over the death of his son, who was killed in a wartime plane crash. The IOC honored J. Sigfried Edstrom as the next president of the IOC during the 1946 London meeting. It was during the London meeting of the IOC that Avery Brundage of the United States was elected as vice-president.

Discussion Questions

1. Was there a political, educational, or social motive for the origin of the modern Olympic Games? If so, who were the individuals involved and how did these political, educational, or social issues manifest themselves?

2. What role did the International Olympic Committee play with regard to the inclusion of women athletes in the Olympic Games? What were some of the cultural barriers that served to limit the participation of women in sport during the early part of the twentieth century? How would you contrast the participation of women Olympians in the era between 1896 and 1936 to that of the 1990s?

3. What were the ideals that Baron de Coubertin wanted to further through the Olympic Games?

4. How would you balance patriotism with internationalism in the Olympic games?

5. Did Hitler use the Olympic Games of 1936 as political propaganda? What political and moral issues were associated with the Berlin Games? Did the American Olympic Committee have concerns about sending a team to the Berlin Games? What were they? What contributions were made by Jesse Owens in the interest of the Olympic ideal?

6. How effective was Baron Pierre de Fredy de Coubertin in promoting the Olympic Games? What were his major victories? What were his major defeats and disappointments?

Notes

1. *The Olympic Movement*, (Chateau de Vidy, Lausanne, Switzerland: The International Olympic Committee, 1993), 8.

2. See John Lucas, *The Modern Olympic Games* (South Brunswick and New York: A. S. Barnes, 1980); Mary Leigh, "Pierre de Coubertin: A Man of His Time," *Quest* XXII (June 1974): 19–24.

3. Thomas Hughes, *Tom Brown's School Days* (Boston: A. W. Elson, 1890).

4. Betty Spears and Richard Swanson, *History of Sport and Physical Education in the United States*, 3d ed. (Dubuque, Ia.: Wm. C. Brown, 1988), 355; Horst Ueberhorst, "Return to Olympia and the Rebirth of the Games," in *The Modern Olympics*, ed.

Peter J. Graham and Horst Ueberhorst (Cornwall, N.Y.: Leisure Press, 1976), 16.

5. Ueberhorst, "Return to Olympia," 15, 16.

6. Spears and Swanson, *History of Sport and Physical Education*, 363.

7. George R. Matthews, "The Modern Olympic Games, 1896–1912" (master's thesis, San Diego State University, 1977), 30–31.

8. Ibid., 37.

9. Pierre DeCoubertin, "The Mystery of the Olympian Games," *North American Review* (June 1900): 806.

10. Anita Defrantz, "The Olympic Games and Women," *Olympic Review*, October-November 1995, XXV-5: 56.

11. Matthews, "Modern Olympic Games," 61.

12. Bill Henry, *An Approved History of the Olympic Games* (Los Angeles: The Southern California Committee for the Olympic Games, 1981), 52.

13. *St. Louis Post-Dispatch*, 7 April 1904.

14. Henry, *Approved History*, 57.

15. Matthews, 83.

16. Ibid., 84.

17. *New York Times*, 12 July 1908, 10.

18. London *Times*, 11 July 1908, 17.

19. John Kieran and Arthur Daley, *The Story of the Olympic Games, 776 B.C. to 1948 A.D.* (Philadelphia: J. B. Lippincott, 1948), 86.

20. London *Times*, 18 July 1908, 9.

21. *New York Times*, 29 July 1908, 9.

22. Matthews, "Modern Olympic Games," 117.

23. Ibid., 118.

24. *New York Times*, 23 April 1912, 11.

25. *The Olympic Movement*, 62.

26. Henry, *Approved History*, 86.

27. Defrantz, *The Olympic Games and Women*, 58.

28. Ibid., 56.

29. *Olympicism* (Lausanne, Switzerland: International Olympic Committee, 1972).

30. Henry, *Approved History*, 98.

31. Leigh, "Pierre de Coubertin," 21.

32. Ibid., 21–22.

33. The Olympic Movement, p. 62; A. Defrantz, *Olympic Games and Women*, 58.

34. Bill Henry, *An Approved History of the Olympic Games*, (Los Angeles: The Southern California Committee for the Olympic Games, 1981), 125–126; Defrantz, Women in the Olympic Games, 58.

35. Ibid., 22.

36. Henry, *Approved History*, 369.

37. Ibid., 115.

38. Ibid., 116.

39. Lucas, *Modern Olympic Games*, 101.

40. *The Olympic Movement*, The International Olympic Committee, 62 & 74; Defrantz, *Olympic Games and Women*, 58.

41. Ibid., 104.

42. Ibid.

43. Ibid., 105–106.

44. Henry, *Approved History*, 133–134.

45. Ibid.

46. Ibid., 134–135.
47. Ibid., 138.
48. Mandell, 234.
49. Ibid.
50. Ibid., 58.
51. Ibid., 59.
52. Ibid., 236.
53. Ibid., 44.
54. Ibid.
55. Ibid., 125.
56. Ibid., 127.
57. Ibid., 70.
58. Ibid., 73.
59. Ibid., 73–74.
60. Ibid.
61. Henry, *Approved History*, 176.
62. Ibid.
63. Ibid.

A Selected Political and Social History of the Modern Olympic Games, 1948–1968

Introduction

The 1936 Berlin Olympiad and the 1936 Winter Games at Garmisch–Partenkirchen were the last for over a decade. The IOC, as did everybody else, endured hardship during World War II. However, the spirit of Olympism prevailed against incredible odds. In 1936, the IOC selected Tokyo as the host city for the 1940 Olympiad. However, Japan later began a military adventure that plunged the United States into World War II. The Tokyo organizing committee worked very hard to bring the Games to fruition but was eventually instructed by the Japanese government to halt preparations for the Tokyo Olympic Games because the Japanese were at war with China. The other city that bid for the 1940 Olympic Games was Helsinki. When Tokyo relinquished the Games, the IOC turned to Helsinki. The valiant Finns faced unprecedented difficulties but persisted in the face of a mounting military threat from the Soviet Union. Unfortunately, Finland was invaded by the Soviet Union in 1939, and the Olympic Games were once again postponed. In a symbolic gesture, the flame that burned brightly above the Los Angeles Coloseum, sight of the 1932 Olympiad, was lit once again during the time when the 1940 Olympiad was to have taken place. As was the case during World War I, the Olympic Games were postponed because of war. The Baron de Coubertin and all of the ensuing IOC presidents believed that the Olympics would promote peace and thus avoid wars. Count Henri De Baillet Latour, president of the IOC from 1925–1942 said that

> May there be an overwhelming response of athletes to this call [to the Olympics]. It can be taken for granted that magnificent contests will result when they measure their strength and suppleness of their bodies against each other; but it is my most earnest desire that from this encounter of their ideals there may grow a more profound understanding of their varying points of view, so that these peaceful combats will give birth to enduring friendships that will usefully serve the cause of peace.[1]

The author notes that the IOC was presided over by two presidents who had seen firsthand the horrors of two world wars, Baron de Coubertin and Count Henri de Baillet Latour. It seemed obvious that the wisdom of these two former IOC presidents and their goal of promoting peace and friendship through an international athletic festival would be an opportunity welcomed by all. However, history shows us that their Olympic ideal was ignored on more than one occasion. We can only speculate what may have happened if the Olympic ideal had prevailed from 1913 to 1919 (World War I) and again from 1937 to 1947 (World War II); where politicians failed, athletes may have prevailed.

The XIVth Olympiad: London, 1948

World War II prevented the Olympic Games from being held during 1940 and 1944. The International Olympic Committee had awarded the 1944 Games to London, which provided justification for the British hosting the 1948 Games. "Hardly had the last shot gone echoing down the halls of time before the International Olympic Committee met in bomb-scarred London in August 1945 to make it official."[2]

The German blitzkrieg had all but devastated London. In addition to rebuilding England, the British agreed to host the 1948 Games. Severe austerity measures were enacted by the government to cope with shortages in food, housing, medical care, and other necessities, so it is understandable if the citizens of London did not embrace the 1948 London Olympiad with enthusiasm. Many questioned the decision of the IOC and the London Organizing Committee for holding the games in London. In the aftermath of World War II, there were much more important issues that needed attention than allocating resources to hold the Olympic Games.

Political Atmosphere

The political atmosphere in post-World War II England revolved around several critical issues that affected the entire global community. Considerable attention by the London *Times* during July 1948 was focused on the following:

1. The Berlin blockade by the Soviets and the formulation and implementation of the state of West Germany occupied the main headlines. International relations were strained almost to the breaking point between the four nations that governed Berlin. Power politics was a means to an end. Britain, France, and the United States were not about to turn West Berlin over to the Communists.

According to the *Times:*

> Mr. Bevin, speaking in the House of Commons yesterday of the events in Berlin, said it was recognized that a grave situation might arise. 'Should such a situation arise,' he said, 'we shall have to ask the House to face it. The British Government and our western allies can see no alternative between that and surrender, and none of us can accept surrender.'[3]

Strong criticism of the action taken by the Russians in Berlin were reiterated on a daily basis. The Berlin airlift was in progress, and the risk of yet another war was a concern for all involved.

2. Britain's evacuation of Palestine, thus creating the new state of Israel, added to the already tense political climate. Both the Jews and the Arabs struggled for control of Palestine; both factions engaged in acts of sabotage against the British during their withdrawal.[4]

During the same day the British evacuated Haifa, Arab kings held a conference in Cairo, Egypt, and "reached complete agreement on national and patriotic objectives." The essence of the meeting was agreement to consolidate forces to gain control of Palestine and eventually make the state of Israel Arab territory.

3. Communism and the atrocious reports from behind the Iron Curtain regarding elimination of freedom and human rights received considerable attention. The development of a fear of communism encompassed the West. Chinese Communists had crossed the Yalu River, and Communist insurgents were causing havoc in the British territories of Malaya and Singapore. The situation was so tragic that Britain outlawed the Communist party in its troubled territories.[5]

Global political issues were at "center stage," which is understandable. As a result, press coverage of the London Games was minimal. The American Olympic contingent was shocked at the lack of media coverage and unconcern for the games by Londoners. Kieran and Daley describe the situation as follows:

> The Americans had just left a country where the newspapers were jam-packed with Olympic news, some 3,000 miles from the spot where they were to be held. The skimpy and threadbare London papers mentioned the Olympics to be sure, but that mention was buried away with the classified ads while their sports columns were filled to overflowing with the real important stuff such as dog race results, hoss [sic] race results and a glowing account of the cricket test match with Australia.[6]

American cities were untouched by World War II, and the United States had a 3,000 mile "buffer zone" of the Atlantic Ocean that separated it from the turmoil that post-war Europe was experiencing. Americans did not have to "dig out" from the rubble created by the German blitz as did the people of London. It stands to reason that the good citizens of London were far more pre-occupied with the events unfolding close by in Europe than most Americans. There was the distinct possibility that Europe would once again be at war with the newly formed countries of the Iron Curtain. This would account for the perceived lack of interest in the London Games by Europeans.

By 1948, the global power struggle was clear cut: East versus West. Two political camps were created and a constant power struggle was underway. Fortunately the political character of the London Games was minimal. However, an interesting political incident did occur during the 1948 Games.

The new country of Israel sent an Olympic delegation to London with the intent of competing in the Olympics. On learning of the wishes of the Israeli delegation, the Arab countries made it clear to IOC officials that if the Olympic team from Israel was allowed to compete, the Arabs would boycott. The IOC denied permission to Israel. The idea of boycotting the Olympic Games is not new. The United States considered boycotting the 1936 Berlin Olympics. However, the Cold War that ensued after the end of World War II gradually embroiled the Olympic movement in political and social issues. Some of these issues were blatant attempts by both the East and West to advance their political agendas. Social issues, such as apartheid, eventually isolated South Africa from the Olympic community for decades.

The 1948 Olympiad is notable for several reasons. After many people had prematurely proclaimed the end of the Olympic Games as a result of the events of World War II, the IOC once again displayed their indomitable spirit, and the Games took place as scheduled. As a matter of fact, there were more countries participating in the London Olympiad (fifty-nine), than in any previous Olympiad. The second largest number of athletes ever, 3,738, took part in the Games. Of these, 385 were women. This was the largest number of women athletes to ever take part in the Olympic Games.[7]

In what would become an almost routine occurrence during the Summer Olympics, the London Olympiad was marked by the threat of a boycott. The irony is that the Baron de Coubertin envisioned the Olympic Games to transcend political and social boundaries and actually bring people together. Instead, some countries threatened to withdraw or boycott the Olympics if certain other countries were invited to participate. This attitude reflects political and social differences that could be resolved if the opposing countries were able to enhance their communication and understanding through a common medium that cuts across most political and social barriers. Sports are this medium, and the Olympics represent an international ideal and opportunity that fosters such communication and understanding. The IOC and many others continue to believe in the message of Baron de Coubertin, that the Olympic Games provide a viable activity that has great potential to promote international understanding and thus contribute to world peace. However, the Cold War and subsequent international disputes would, from time to time, manifest themselves within the Olympics. The London Games demonstrated this fact. In the author's opinion, global politics and related tensions could be removed from the Olympic Games if the individuals and groups who represent various political and social interests heed Baron de Coubertin's message. However, it appears that these same individuals and groups have identified the Olympics as a "political resource" and not necessarily as an instrument or means for promoting the spirit of Olympism and all it represents. The IOC has done a remarkable job, considering the circumstances. True, there have been questionable decisions made by the IOC. However, the intent and integrity of the Olympic ideal remains intact in spite of attempts to undermine the purpose of the Games.

Figure 15.1

This is a replica of the sacred torch that is ignited in Olympia and carried to the site of the Olympic Games. The sun reflects off the gleaming basin to ignite the flame. The torch relay is one of the great symbols of the Olympic Games. Photo courtesy of The Olympic Museum, Lausanne, Switzerland.

The Russians did not compete in the London Games; however, Communist attempts to sabotage the games were reported by the media. A reporter from the London *Times* assigned to cover the progress of the Olympic torch run from Olympia, Greece, to London, filed the following account:

> Special precautions in the form of troops, armored cars, and aircraft were taken at Olympia and along the runner's route (Olympic torch bearer) to Katakolon to prevent any interference in yesterday's proceedings by communist forces. General Markos, the rebel leader, is reported to have broadcast orders for the Olympic ceremony to be wrecked. On Friday a small band attacked Katakolon and killed with machine gun fire a policeman who was defending our party.[8]

Sadly, violence and death occurred during the first Olympiad held during the Cold War era, and it would not be the last time. Two decades later in Mexico City, the 1968 Games were used by student protesters, and many were killed by Mexican authorities. The Munich Olympiad of 1972 saw the massacre of Israeli Olympians by Arab terrorists.

Political defections from East to West occurred during the London Games. Some of the Czeck and Hungarian athletes flatly refused to return. The repressive political and social systems that reflected Soviet "values" were not to their liking. In future Olympiads, Olympic athletes from Eastern Bloc countries would use the Olympic Games as a means to defect to the West. The *Times* offered prophetic insight prior to the opening ceremonies:

> The Olympic oath, taken on behalf of all competitors, speaks of the honour of a country and the glory of sport—not the other way round as some would have it. Probably only two things now could wreck the Games—one, a political-racial use of them by overambitious states, and two, the virtual subsidizing of the athletes which would be bound to follow.[9]

And it came to pass.

The American athletes may have been pleasantly surprised when they participated in the opening ceremonies. Eighty thousand spectators at Wembly Stadium greeted athletes from fifty-nine nations. However, the vile specter of international politics had already been felt. Some officials demanded that German and Japanese athletes be excluded from the games because of their actions in World War II. In addition, there was considerable debate about rescinding the Olympic victories won by Germans and Japanese. The Olympic officials eventually bowed to political pressure and set aside the Olympic title records in the 400- and 1500-meter freestyle swimming races.[10]

Bob Mathias, a seventeen-year-old high-school student from Tulare, California, was the talk of the games as he won the gold medal in the decathlon. Dubbed the "flying Dutchwoman," Fanny Blankers-Koen won four gold medals in women's track. Women's track and field added three new events: 200-meter run, broad jump, and the eight-pound shot put. The only American gold medal winner in women's track and field was Alice Coachman, who won the high jump with an effort of 5′6¼″, which established a new Olympic record. The American men dominated track and field, winning twenty-five medals including eleven gold. Without competition from the traditionally strong Japanese team, the American men won sixteen medals in swimming and diving. In fact, the Americans came in first place in every swimming and diving event. The American team was not "threatened" athletically by the teams assembled for the London Olympiad. However, the level of athletic competition significantly increased during the 1952 Helsinki Olympiad with the return of the Japanese, Germans, and Russians.

The Vth Winter Olympics: St. Moritz, 1948

Six-hundred and sixty-nine athletes from twenty-eight nations arrived in St. Moritz to compete in the first postwar Winter Games. Seventy-seven women athletes representing twenty-eight countries competed in the St. Moritz Winter Games.[11] The amateur question was in the spotlight, and the ensuing scandal involved the International Ice Hockey Federation, the United States Olympic Committee (USOC), and the IOC. The amateur standing of the American ice hockey team was in grave doubt, and the IOC was called on to resolve the issue. It seems that the St. Moritz Organizing Committee and the International Ice Hockey Federation (IIHF) declared that the American team was eligible. The American team did not meet the eligibility requirements at all, even though the IIHF certified them to compete. The IOC was furious with both the St. Moritz Organizing Committee and the IIHF, not to mention the American ice hockey team. The IOC almost decided to ban the ice hockey competition altogether but instead banned the IIHF from any participation with the St. Moritz Organizing Committee.[12] The U.S. team was also barred from competing.

The American men failed to win a single medal in the skiing competition, although Gretchen Fraser won the gold medal in the special slalom and silver medal in the downhill and slalom for the American women's team. Richard "Dick" Button, just eighteen years old, won the gold medal for the United States in men's figure skating. J. Heaton from the United States won the silver medal in the skeleton bobsledding competition. In the four-man bobsledding competition, the Americans won both the gold and bronze medals. In the men's speed skating competition, K. Bartholomew and R. Fitzgerald from America tied with T. Byberg of Norway for second place. The Canadian Olympic Team performed well. In women's figure skating, B. A. Scott won the gold medal, and in pairs figure skating, the team of Suzanne Morrow and W. Distelmyer won the bronze medal. The Canadian ice hockey team once again demonstrated their superiority by winning the gold medal. The next Winter Olympics would be in Oslo, and the American teams would enjoy the success that eluded them in St. Moritz, where the Scandinavian countries were once again overpowering.

The XVth Olympiad: Helsinki, 1952

In 1952 the global political situation continued to manifest itself in the form of ideological differences between East and West. The world was in a precarious situation. Russia and the United States engaged in the Cold War, which eventually brought the world close to war and a possible nuclear confrontation on several future occasions.

The dust had hardly settled from the terror of World War II when the international community was plunged into another war. Korea became the focal point of world attention as the first volatile confrontation between the Iron Curtain nations and the free world. United Nations troops, with the Americans at the helm, waged war against the North Koreans and Chinese Communists, who were trained, equipped, and backed by the Russians.

An era of fear swept over the West during July 1952. The fear of world domination by the "Reds" was evident in the stories published by the *New York Times*. Refugees from East Germany were fleeing to West

Germany at every possible opportunity. The horror stories of Communist brutality and Russian secret police exploits added fuel to the fire in the psychological warfare tactics used by the Russians.[13] In addition to the defections and escapes by the East Germans, North Korean soldiers and peasants sought political asylum in the West and confirmed the accounts of their East German counterparts.[14]

Communists were causing grave problems in India, and the situation was critical in Japan. The French were engaged in the Indochina war with Communist insurgents, which was to entrap the United States in the coming decade. In retrospect, the Finns managed to produce an extraordinary XVth Olympiad in the midst of a seemingly explosive climate. With the exception of the sequestered athletes representing the Soviet Union and its satellite countries, who rarely if ever mingled with athletes from the West, the Helsinki Olympiad was a very successful event. This is not to suggest that it was completely free from political or social issues.

To help the reader understand why certain social and political issues became a part of the Olympics, it is helpful to briefly review the major political and social events that were taking place at the time of the Helsinki Olympiad and each successive Summer and Winter Olympic Game. In this way, the reader can identify with the times and see that a pattern emerges. The pattern illustrates that the Olympic Games may include examples of the social and political climate of the day. We already know that these regional and global political and social entanglements have concerned the IOC and have caused some significant problems. This fact was noted by J. Sigfrid Edstrom, president of the IOC, who, when speaking about the Helsinki Olympics, said:

> International relations improve much too slowly, travel is difficult due to monetary restrictions and other red tape. But nothing can stop young athletes from crossing frontiers to challenge their opponent and get ready for the games. . . . Preparations are developing actively to see that the games are a brilliant success. Lets hope that peace will reign when these games take place.
>
> I invite the youth all over the world to the competition and peaceful combats of the 1952 Olympiad, which can and must prepare the earth so that relations among people may be more friendly and understanding. Because the youth of today will be the leaders of tomorrow their experience in the mastery of international sports may become the ideal ferment that will one day transform into trust the stubborn animosities that nowadays separate nations.[15]

The IOC leadership recognizes that the Olympic Games can be undermined by a number of events that are beyond its control. As best they can, the IOC and associated entities surmount these difficult problems in order to keep the Olympic ideal alive and viable. The social and political horizon is of interest to the IOC and each national Olympic committee because some of these social and political issues may find their way out of the political arena into the arena of sport. When looked at in this context, the words of IOC president J. Sigfrid Edstrom have special meaning. He was keenly aware that although most of the world's countries field Olympic teams, there still exists animosity and mistrust among the participants.

Today, the IOC and the host city continue to work as hard as they can to insure that the Games are successful, but in the end, the words of president Edstrom echo the sentiments of all when he says he "hope[s] that peace will reign when these games take place."

South Africa's apartheid policy garnered media attention in July 1952 and was eventually cause for its removal from the Olympic Games. Headlines in the *New York Times* read: "Negroes Step Up Their Campaign Against South African Race Laws, Original Violators Refuse Bail or to Pay Fines as 88 More Are Arrested—Leaders Say They Hope to Fill Country's Prisons."[16]

The account of civil disobedience reflected a major social issue that divided the people of South Africa according to race. In this particular instance, the civil disobediance resulted in the arrests and detention of about 450 nonwhites, most of them at Johannesburg and Port Elizabeth, where the campaign was well organized. Demonstrators marched through an entrance reserved for whites at a railway station and were arrested by waiting police officers on charges of defying the apartheid laws.

On the home front, the United States entered the era of McCarthyism. Senator Joseph McCarthy had the populace convinced that the Communist "Red Menace" was lurking everywhere, and the ensuing Communist "witch hunt" strained the nation. Americans felt that the possibility of a military attack by the Russians was so probable that drastic precautions were undertaken. The New York City Office of Civil Defense sought nine hundred recruits to act as aircraft spotters. The mistrust and animosity between the United States and the Soviet Union spilled over into the Olympic Games as each nation attempted to demonstrate the superiority of its social and political ideology through victory, by way of medal count, in the Olympic Games.

Cold War of Sports

The media made reference to the 1952 Games as a "Cold War of Sports." Helsinki marked the first time since the Stockholm Games in 1912 that Russia fielded an Olympic team.

The American Olympic Committee and public sentiment was all for assembling the strongest Olympic team possible to insure defeat of the Russians. Economic factors almost ruined the American Olympic team. Two weeks prior to departure, the United States Olympic Committee was short $500,000. However, American ingenuity prevailed. Bob Hope and Bing Crosby staged an around-the-clock Olympic Telethon and raised over one million dollars.[17]

Helsinki was to have an environment of friendship and cooperation among athletes, but the Soviets brought the Iron Curtain to the XVth Olympiad. Instead of mingling with other athletes at the regular Olympic Village, the athletes from the Soviet Union and its satellites were quartered in their own private Olympic Village at Otaniemi on the far side of town, enclosed by barbed wire and near the big Porkkala Naval Base that the Russians grabbed from the Finns in their peace settlement.

The Russians were unapproachable. They spoke to no one and wouldn't even admit the Finns, their hosts, to their camp. Newspapermen, regardless of their nationality, were turned away at the gates.[18]

The Russians were doing all that was possible to discourage political defections by Soviet athletes. When entries were formally filed for the Olympic events, Heino Lipp, the Estonian shot-putter who was among the world's best, as well as several Soviet women, were not among the Soviet contingent. "The rumor was that they were considered 'politically unreliable,' something new and unprecedented in Olympic history."[19]

Since the ancient Olympics, a traditional Olympic truce is declared during the games. The ancient truce allowed the athletes safe passage to Olympia, and wars were suspended. Finland proclaimed an Olympic truce with the hope that the 1952 Olympic Games would proceed without interruption. However, the Associated Press reported that "The games of the fifteenth Olympiad . . . bring together Russia and the United States in direct sports conflict."[20,21,22]

Prior to the opening ceremonies, political disputes marred the games. Gun Son-ho, Olympic representative from Nationalist China (now known as Taiwan), flew to Helsinki from Formosa and insisted that Nationalist China be allowed to compete in the games. The International Olympic Committee stated that neither Nationalist China nor the People's Republic of China would be allowed to enter teams.

After learning of the attempt by the Nationalist Chinese to enter the games, East Germany demanded inclusion in the XVth Olympiad. According to the United Press International,

> The International Olympic Committee received another hot issue in sport's cold war today (July 12, 1952) when it was asked to decide whether both East and West Germany should be admitted to the 1952 Olympic Games.
>
> The executive Olympic Committee had decided last winter that only West Germany should be admitted after efforts failed to organize a combined East-West entry. There was no protest from the East. . . . Thus the I.O.C. will be asked Wednesday to do something the United Nations has been unable to do—reconcile the East and the West. The International Olympic Committee reversed its decision and extended an invitation to Nationalist China to compete in the 1952 Olympics. However, the IOC extended the same invitation to the People's Republic of China. The governing body of the Olympics voted 33 to 20 in favor of a resolution authorizing the athletes of both nations to compete.[23,24]

In response to the authorization by the IOC to allow the two Chinas to compete, the Chinese Nationalists boycotted the games. Once again we are reminded of the words of IOC president Edstrom, which are especially relevant in this case: "Because the youth of today will be the leaders of tomorrow their experience in the mastery of international sport may become the ideal ferment that will one day transform into trust the stubborn animosities that nowadays separate nations."

East Germany was not allowed to compete. Not until 1968 would East Germany field an independent team. However, a new twist developed on the Olympic scene. Rolf Marffly, a Hungarian representing political refugee groups, proposed to the Olympic Committee that refugees be permitted to compete in the games. The refugees could compete under a Red Cross flag, a special Olympic flag, or under the national flag of Switzerland or Greece. No action was taken on the matter.

Propaganda War

Avery Brundage, newly elected president of the International Olympic Committee, was not overlooked by the Soviet press. According to a newspaper account in Moscow,

> *The Young Bolshevik*, the magazine of the youth organization Komsomols, to which most of the Soviet athletes belong, called on athletes everywhere to transform the Helsinki games into a vast demonstration for peace and friendship of peoples.
>
> The journal described United States Olympic leader, Avery Brundage, as 'a Chicago business man and an adventurist,' and accused him of utilizing every possible means of force and pressure at the 1948 games in London to assure 'first places for representatives of the Anglo-Saxon race.' Brundage was charged with having bribed referees and Olympic Committee members in an effort to achieve the desired results. . . .
>
> The Helsinki games, it said, had the greatest significance in the world peace struggle and claimed they would be 'an arena of the struggle of progressive-minded athletes for peace against the rotten propaganda of Warmongers.'[25]

The Russian media called for Russian Olympians to demonstrate superiority over bourgeois nations. *Pravda, Izvestia*, and other Soviet newspapers were quick to attack the United States. According to the Izvestia,

> Sport in bourgeois countries, and especially in the United States, was utilized as a means of 'preparing cannon fodder for a new, aggressive war.' In contrast, in the Soviet Union . . . sports played a role in the 'struggle for friendship and security of the people—of peace of the whole world.' . . . Soviet athletes, said *Izvestia*, provide shining examples of the superiority of Soviet culture over that of bourgeois countries.[26]

Unofficial Olympic scoring was being kept by the world press. The Russians had a commanding lead over the Americans, and the point total was displayed daily in the Soviet Olympic Village. The Soviet press used the Russian lead as a viable and visible propaganda weapon. It appeared that the Soviets would be the "unofficial" victors at Helsinki. The Olympic Committee does not recognize "scoring," but that did not deter the Russians. The Soviets formally proposed to the Congress of the International Athletic Federation that team scoring be recognized. It was quickly voted down.[27]

The Russians were so certain of victory that Radio Moscow announced, "we are certain to win." The games ended with America as the clear-cut victor. The Americans captured the most gold medals: 41 to Russia's 23. The unofficial score showed the Americans over the Russians 614 to 553. The Russian explanation to the Soviet Union was creative.

After the Olympics had ended, *Pravda*, the Soviet's newspaper mouthpiece, hailed the "world superiority" of the Russian athletes and proudly asserted that they had won more medals than anyone else. They offered no figures or substantiation.

Two days more of point juggling in Moscow, an arithmetical juggle that was continued until it added up satisfactorily, brought an official admission. It was that the U.S.S.R. and the U.S.A. had ended in an absolute dead heat, each with 494 points.[28]

The propaganda war engaged in by the United States and the Soviet Union had no boundaries. Both countries continued to use the Olympic Games to exploit their respective political and social agendas in the name of nationalism. The IOC was appalled by this attempt to undermine the purpose of the Olympic ideal and did its best to suppress it. In spite of the feud between the Americans and the Russians, the Helsinki Olympiad was among the best ever. Participating in the games were 4,407 athletes representing sixty-nine countries. For the first time, over one hundred women (109 to be exact) competed in the Games.[29]

The American men made a respectable showing in track and field, winning thirty medals, fourteen of them gold. Bob Mathias once again won the decathlon. The American women athletes won but one medal in the track and field events—a gold medal in the 400-meter relay—and in doing so set a new Olympic record. American swimmers gathered a total of seventeen medals. The men collected ten and the women won seven. The Russians dominated both men's and women's gymnastics and made their presence felt in weightlifting (seven medals), freestyle wrestling (three medals), and Greco-Roman wrestling (seven medals).

The superiority of American athletes were soon put to the test by athletes from the Iron Curtain countries, especially athletes from the Soviet Union and East Germany. The rivalry between the British and American teams paled in comparison to the intense competition between the Americans and the Russians in future Olympiads. It is important to note that even as politicians attempted to manipulate the Olympic Games for their own vile ends, some athletes from the United States and the Soviet Union formed the lasting friendships that would have made the Baron de Coubertin smile.

The VIth Winter Olympics: Oslo, 1952

The Norwegians produced the best-run and best-attended Winter Olympics in history. Although the Soviet Union did not participate, approximately seven hundred thousand people attended the Winter Games to watch the displays of athletic prowess put on by athletes from thirty nations. Once again the Norwegians demonstrated their athletic superiority in winter sports by capturing sixteen medals, followed by the United States with eleven. The athletes from Germany, after an absence of sixteen years, won both bobsled races.[30]

Richard "Dick" Button once again won the gold medal in men's figure skating, and fellow American Andrea Mead Lawrence won the gold medal in the women's giant slalom. Americans Kenneth Henry and D. McDermott won the gold and silver medals, respectively, in the men's 500-meter speed skating competition. The American ice hockey team returned to Olympic competition, after being barred in St. Moritz, to finish second behind—who else—the Canadians!

The XVIth Olympiad: Melbourne, 1956

The Cold War between the United States and its allies and the Soviet Union and its allies continued unabated in 1956. Crisis would be the appropriate term to describe the state of world affairs during the XVIth Olympiad. The Suez Canal crisis brought the world to the brink of yet another war. Rebellion against the Soviet Union, in the form of the Poznan riots in Poland and the short but valiant Hungarian revolution, resulted in enormous destruction of persons and property. The nuclear arms race between the Americans and the Russians terrified the world.

In the Middle East, President Nasser of Egypt instigated the Middle East War by nationalizing the Suez Canal. Nasser was "walking the fence" between Moscow and Washington, receiving economic aid and supplies from both nations. However, the turning point occurred when Nasser asked the United States to construct the Aswan High Dam. Washington agreed, but certain conditions had to be met, the two primary considerations being (1) ending the border war with Israel, and (2) breaking off ever-closening ties with the Russians.

President Nasser closed the canal. The United Nations responded by proposing that the Suez Canal be placed under the operation of an international governing agency. The plan was rejected by Nasser with the support of Syria and Saudi Arabia. During this same time, Arab guerrillas were conducting military operations in Morocco, Algeria, and Tunisia to oust the French. The Arab world was very anti-Anglo-French. However, the Arab states were being equipped and trained by the Russians, and Nasser apparently felt he had the necessary tools at his disposal for such an operation as the closing of the Suez Canal.

As a result of Nasser closing the canal, British, French, and Israeli military launched an offensive against Egypt. Israel attacked on October 29, followed by British and French assaults on October 31. President Eisenhower pledged no direct American involvement. The Melbourne Games were to open twenty-two days later.

The purpose of the military attack on Egypt was twofold. Britain and France needed access to the Suez Canal and therefore needed to seize it to keep it open. Israel's invasion was to prevent Nasser from achieving mastery of the Arab world through a series of palace revolutions in other Middle Eastern states and forming a united Arab crusade against Israel.[31] Revolts in Hungary and Poland kept the Russians occupied militarily, and the consensus was for the invasion to begin while the Soviets dealt with problems on the home front because Eastern Europe was rocked with internal warfare. Eventually the Russians crushed the workers' rebellion at the expense of many lives.

Perhaps the most disheartening event of the year was the tragedy in Hungary. Hungarians were reeling under the yoke of Moscow and sought independence from Soviet control. Premier Imre Nagy asked Moscow to let Hungary withdraw from the Warsaw Pact. The Hungarians, according to reports, wanted to become a neutral state belonging to neither the Eastern nor the Western camp. Nagy's appeal was made on November 1.

On November 3, Soviet troops attacked Budapest along with the entire country. By November 5, the Hungarian freedom fighters realized they could not hold out against the Russians without intervention by the United Nations or the West, help that never came. The rape of Hungary was a brutal warning to Soviet satellites and the rest of the world not to interfere with Communist policy. Stalinism was not dead, Hungary was.

Before the Hungarian revolt, the Hungarian Olympic soccer team withdrew from Olympic competition. *Newsweek* gave this account:

> Hungary's withdrawal from Olympic soccer competition was officially blamed on 'lack of funds' by Moscow following Hungary's victory over the Soviet Olympic team. With Hungary out of the way, Russia expects to win the gold medal.[32]

When the Russians had "control" over the uprisings in East Europe, they turned their attention to the Middle East. Moscow threatened direct military intervention in the Suez Canal crisis on the side of the Arabs. President Eisenhower exclaimed that the possibility of nuclear war existed in Egypt.[33] The announcement by the Russians caused France, Israel, and England to stop short of their military objectives.

Peking and Moscow were ready to send volunteer military units to fight alongside the Arabs against the British, French, and Israelis. The USSR pledged to send several thousand, and Communist China would respond with 380,000 troops.[34] However, the United Nations was able to invoke a cease-fire order.

Elsewhere the Indochina war was still raging, and South Africa continued to suppress the black population. Johannes Gerhardus Strijdom, prime minister of the Union of South Africa, demanded complete white supremacy. He planned to herd South Africa's twelve million blacks into "reservations" no larger than fourteen percent of the nation's territory.[35] Apartheid was not restricted to South Africa. The Mau Mau Rebellion in Kenya was a race war between blacks and whites in which fifteen thousand blacks were killed by British forces and seventy thousand blacks were placed in concentration camps.[36]

The United States reelected the incumbent White House administration, Dwight D. Eisenhower and Richard M. Nixon. A young Massachusetts senator, John F. Kennedy, was starting his climb up the political ladder. A landmark decision by the United States Supreme Court abolished the "separate but equal schools" policy and school integration was ordered. Integration of the nation's schools could not be done easily; violence rocked the southern states, and the National Guard was mobilized to insure school integration. The United States, like South Africa, had serious social problems that eventually manifested themselves in the Olympic Games.

The Aussie Olympics

In spite of a tense world situation, Melbourne was in a festive mood for the XVIth Olympiad. It has often been said that Australia is a sports-loving nation, and the Aussies would not disappoint anyone on that fact. Even though the Australians were in a festive mood, the atmosphere among the Olympic Organizing Committee, and others, would remain guarded but optimistic.

Sir William Bridgeford, chief executive officer of the International Olympic Committee, was quoted as saying, "The Games will definitely go on unless there is a general world war."[37] Bridgeford was saddened by the world political situation but said "we still hope to keep politics and international hatreds out of the games."[38,39] The Associated Press supplied a brief "political" forecast for the games:

> The Olympic Games walked a tight rope today in an atmosphere of outward calm but growing concern over the fighting in Hungary and Egypt. . . . Other tensions marked this amateur sports spectacle scheduled to open Nov. 22 and end Dec. 8. These included:
>
> A. The bitter wrangling between Communist and Nationalist Chinese (Taiwan) groups.
>
> B. Hungarian immigrants in Australia have made one demonstration against Russian participation in the games and plan another tomorrow.
>
> C. There is a strong fear of reaction against the British and French for moving into the Suez Canal area in the Egypt-Israel clash, a move supported by the Australian Government.

Avery Brundage decreed that nations at war were eligible to compete in the Olympic Games.[40]

This was a very difficult decision for Brundage and the IOC. However, perhaps the athletes from these warring countries could put aside their differences for the duration of the Games and compete athletically and not as combat soldiers. There was the hope that athletes could establish a dialogue that would foster international goodwill and assist the peace process. It was clear that the politicians were not succeeding.

It was first reported on November 5 by Radio Budapest that there would be no Hungarian Olympic team due to "interruptions." Reported killed in fighting against Russian troops in Hungary were three of Hungary's top athletes: Jozsef Csermak, 1952 Olympic hammer-throwing champion; Major Ferene Puskas, captain of Hungary's soccer team; and Gabor Benedek, runner-up in the 1952 Olympic pentathlon championship.[41]

The question of South Africa's apartheid policy was brought before the IOC by the Norwegians. Norway's Olympic Committee requested that the International Olympic Committee consider banning South Africa from Olympic participation because of its social policy of discriminating against blacks in sports organizations. Olay Ditlev-Simmonsen of the Norwegian Olympic Committee believed South Africa should not be recognized by the IOC if it continued practicing apartheid.[42]

Olympic Boycott

Once again, nations engaged in an Olympic boycott for political reasons during the 1956 Games. The Associated Press reported:

> The Netherlands, Spain, and Communist China withdrew from the 1956 Olympic Games today (November 6). The Netherlands and Spain decided to withdraw as a protest against Russia's military action in Hungary.
>
> Instead of sending athletes to Melbourne, . . . the Netherlands donated 100,000 guilders ($25,000) to Hungarian relief.
>
> Dr. Homan (president of the Dutch Olympic Committee) criticized Otto Mayer (Chancellor of the IOC) for his recent comment that the Olympic Ideal should prevail over what has happened in Hungary. 'How would we like it if our people were atrociously murdered and someone said that sports should prevail?' Dr. Homan asked.[43]

Five nations, as of November 6, had withdrawn from the Games; they were Egypt, Spain, Netherlands, Communist China, and Iraq. Once again, Communist China withdrew because of the inclusion of Nationalist China (Taiwan), and Iraq quit as a protest against the action by France, Britain, and Israel against Egypt. Two days later, November 8, Switzerland became the sixth nation to quit the Olympics; its reason was the Russian action in Hungary.

Brundage and other members of the International Olympic Committee appealed to the departed nations to reconsider their position and join the XVIth Olympiad. Brundage maintained that

> Every civilized person recoils in horror at the savage slaughter in Hungary, but that is no reason for destroying the nucleus of international cooperation (Olympic Games). . . . In an imperfect world, if participation in sports is to be stopped every time the politicians violate the laws of humanity, there will never be any international contests.[44]

Avery Brundage, like his predecessors, was an idealist and a champion of the Olympic ideal. He saw the Games as an opportunity to bring people together, regardless of their ideological beliefs. To watch in dismay as six countries withdrew their Olympic teams from competition to protest tragic social and political events prevented the Olympic Games from achieving its primary goals of fostering international goodwill and promoting peace. How was the IOC supposed to nurture and extend these ideals if athletes were ordered to return home? These were frustrating and disappointing times for the IOC, who did its best to keep the Olympic Games above politics.

Russia captured the "unofficial" team championship at the XVIth Olympiad amid accusations of prejudicial Olympic judging by Eastern officials against Western nations. The United States protested over the judging by Russian and Hungarian officials, claiming that they had discriminated against American divers. The American complaint was rejected.

Athletes from Eastern bloc countries continued to use the Olympic Games as a means to defect to the West and seek a better life. For example, *Newsweek* reported that

> Forty-five Hungarian athletes who had come out from behind the Iron Curtain to compete in the Olympics were not going back to their ravaged country. Some said they would settle in Australia. Thirty-four asked to enter the U.S. A few, vague about the future, wept.
> Among the defectors was Lavzlo Nadori, Assistant Chairman of the Hungarian Olympic Committee, who had been a leader in Budapest's anti-Soviet revolt last month. Friday, Nadori quietly slipped away from his Olympic Village quarters leaving a terse message. 'God bless you,' it said, 'Farewell.'[45]

The Soviet Union, unlike the United States, allocated significant amounts of money to athletes in both major and minor Olympic sports. The American Olympic effort was in support of athletes who were training for major Olympic competition: swimming, track and field, and later, basketball and boxing. As a result of the decision by Soviet Olympic authorities to spend money and effort on developing both major and minor Olympic athletes, their ability to win Olympic medals was significantly better than that of the United States. Still, the American athletes fared well in the Melbourne Olympics. The men's track and field team won twenty-eight medals, compared to fourteen for the Soviet team. The American women won three medals in track and field but did much better in the swimming competition, winning eleven medals including three gold.

The Melbourne Olympics hosted 2,813 athletes from sixty-seven nations who established thirty-six new Olympic records and eleven world records. The number of women athletes continued to increase, from 109 in 1952 to 132 in the Melbourne Olympiad. Although six nations did boycott the Games, the remaining sixty-seven countries enjoyed a spectacular international athletic festival. The Australian Olympic Committee and the Melbourne Organizing Committee provided a warm reception for athletes and spectators alike. It was the first time that the Olympics were held in the southern hemisphere. Since the seasons are reversed and the Melbourne Olympiad was held from November 22 to December, it was summer in Australia! The Olympic Stadium filled with 104,000 spectators who were there to watch the opening ceremonies. The Melbourne Organizing Committee had planned a program that featured 145 sporting events and two demonstration sports, Australian football and American baseball. Eighty-thousand fans turned out to watch American baseball.[46] In the decathlon, two Americans, Milt Campbell and Rafer Johnson, captured the gold and silver medals, respectively, while Vasily Kouznetsoff of the Soviet Union was a close third and won the bronze medal.

Equestrian events have increased in popularity throughout each Olympiad. The costs associated with mounting a serious equestrian campaign in the Olympics are quite high. The horses, facilities, transportation, and riders all require significant monetary expenditures. For this reason, the equestrian events of the XVIth Olympiad were held in Stockholm, Sweden, during June.

The Olympic Games are not without romance. Olga Fitokova from Czechoslovakia won the gold medal in the discus. She later wed the American hammer thrower Harold Connolly, who won the gold medal in the 1956 Melbourne Olympiad.

The VIIth Winter Olympics: Cortina, 1956

Thirty-two nations sent a total of 820 athletes to compete in the Winter Olympics, which was held in the beautiful Italian Alps. One-hundred and thirty-two women athletes proudly represented thirty-two nations and competed in twenty-four events.[47] The Soviet team won six gold medals: three in men's speed skating, one in ice hockey, the 4×10 kilometer relay, and the 10-kilometer women's ski race. The American team had an absolutely disastrous showing in men's skiing, managing only a fourth-place finish in the slalom. The U.S. women's skiing team could garner no better than a fourth-place finish in the giant slalom. However, the American men swept the first three places in figure skating (ordinals), finished second in ice hockey to the Russians (the Canadian ice hockey team finished third), and captured the bronze medal in the four-man bobsledding competition. The American women won both the gold and the silver in the women's figure skating competition. The Italians were wonderful hosts and very proficient in the bobsled events, finishing first and second in the two-man bob and finishing second in the four-man bobsled competition.

The XVIIth Olympiad: Rome, 1960

The Cold War between the United States and the Soviet Union "heated up" in 1960 and significantly impacted the global political situation. Political ideology in the form of propaganda was "distributed" by both the United States and the Soviet Union. The two Superpowers had learned to utilize every available tool at their disposal in the propaganda war, including sport.

Southeast Asia was in political turmoil. Violence in South Korea over election scandals painted a discouraging picture of a "democratic" nation that was economically and militarily supported by the United States. Ten thousand demonstrators in the North Cholla Province of South Korea destroyed county offices and burned ballot boxes to express their feelings about the election scandals. Elsewhere in Southeast Asia, fighting in Vietnam by Americans against Communists was starting to receive attention. President Eisenhower had stationed military advisers there along with providing military and economic assistance. The war in Vietnam would be the political hot spot in the world during the Mexico City Games in 1968.

The Cuban Revolution and the takeover by Fidel Castro caused concern among members of the Organization of American States (OAS). Communism was now less than one hundred miles from the United States, and the Soviet Union was pouring technicians along with economic and military aid into the island. In Washington, the view was that the Russian military installations on Cuba posed a serious military threat to the United States. Mutual animosity between Cuba and the United States led to accusations and threats by both nations—actions that were to result in the Bay of Pigs and the Cuban Missile Crisis.

Political tensions and international relations between the United States and the Soviet Union reached their peak on May 1, 1960. Francis Gary Powers, a pilot for the Central Intelligence Agency, was shot down in his U-2 spy plane while on a mission over the Soviet Union. Powers was charged as a spy, and the Soviet media utilized every possible avenue of propaganda to condemn the U.S. action. To make matters worse, the Russians shot down an American RB 47 reconnaissance plane that, claimed the Soviets, violated Soviet airspace over the Arctic waters. Powers was found guilty. After the U-2 incident, the Soviets started expelling American students and businessmen from the country as spies. The United States reciprocated by expelling selected Soviet diplomats as suspected agents. The Cold War would not become any "hotter" until the Cuban Missile Crisis.

A noticeable difference in relations between the two Communist giants emerged. Ideological rifts between Moscow and Peking were starting to surface. Russian technicians in China were being called home to Moscow, and Chinese "students" were leaving the Soviet Union. The Chinese were challenging the leadership role of Moscow; divergent methods of achieving world Marxism increased the split between the two nations. This situation was especially significant to Chinese athletes and coaches because they were being helped by Russian coaches who were also told to return home.

In the United States, Senators John F. Kennedy and Lyndon Johnson defeated Richard Nixon and Henry C. Lodge for President and Vice-President, respectively. John F. Kennedy, possibly the most popular U.S. president since Lincoln and Roosevelt, was ushered into the White House as the leader of the free world.

Roman Holiday

It has been said that "all roads lead to Rome," and for several weeks, the world focused on the splendor of the XVIIth Olympiad. This is not to imply that the Cold War was forgotten. Men, medals, and Marxism had an impact on the 1960 Games. The rivalry between the Americans and the Russians drew the most attention. The victors in the Eternal City would reap the coveted rewards of the Cold War: gold medals and new avenues of propaganda.

Italy left nothing to chance when production of the Olympic complex began. A nine-mile "Olympic Road" was constructed on the western edge of Rome. The Olympic stadium and supporting facilities were located in the western sector of the city to enable easy access and promote commercial expansion. The venues were fantastic and the festive atmosphere brought many athletes from different parts of the world together.

East versus West

Although the express purpose of the Olympic Games is to promote peace and international understanding, the political entities who held power in the East and West would attempt to undermine the Olympic ideal in order to serve their own political interests. For example, the announced aim of the Russians was twofold: to win as many medals as possible and to demonstrate the Kremlin's system of mass approach to athletics as superior to all others. Explaining the prowess of Russian athletes, Nikolai Romanov, chairman of the Soviet Sports League, was quoted as saying:

> The first reason is the mass character of the Soviet athletic movement. On August 13 the whole country will be celebrating Athletes Day. The fact that this is celebrated as a national day testifies to the importance to the physical training by the Soviet people, the Communist party, and the Soviet government. . . . 24,000,000 persons in the Soviet Union participate in organized athletics and in the activities of 190,000 physical culture organizations under the direction of 65,000 specialists.[48]

The Soviet Union certainly took athletic competition, both national and international, quite seriously.

The Italian Olympic Committee was not blind to the animosity that existed between athletes from the West and athletes from Eastern bloc nations. They constructed the Olympic Village on a segregated plan. The Russians and their Eastern bloc comrades lived, appropriately, in the eastern section of the Olympic Village. Western bloc nations, particularly the Americans and British, lived near the western area of the village. Between the Russians and the Americans lived the Olympic teams from Switzerland and Liechtenstein to act as a buffer zone. To take it one step further, the Olympic Committee assigned the Russians to eat at restaurant Number V, the Americans at Number III, and again "sandwiched" the Swiss between them at restaurant Number IV.[49] Much to the delight of the IOC and everybody else, when the Soviet athletes arrived in Rome, the majority immediately began to fraternize with athletes from other countries. This is precisely what the Olympic Games are supposed to help foster—international understanding and good will.

Whether the Olympic athletes liked it or not, they were pawns in a hot athletic war that was a phase of the overall political war. The theme of nationalism was running high once again. The emphasis on Americans beating Russians and Russians beating Americans is bred largely by noncompetitors, especially politicians and journalists. Nationalism has always been an integral part of the games, but incitement of inherent political nationalism is nurtured by the mass media and self-serving political organizations. A few days before the American track and field team departed for Rome, Larry Snyder, the head coach, appeared on a television program. "Will we beat the Russians?" asked Bennett Cerf, the publisher. "We'll kill 'em," replied Snyder.[50]

East Germany and West Germany competed as one nation during the XVIIth Olympiad. Both Germanies marched under a common Olympic flag:

> Political squabbling . . . exists strongly on one team—the German squad, combining 200 West Germans with 140 East Germans. . . . 'One team?' Heinz Maegerlein, the leading sportscaster in West Germany, said recently. 'Actually, it is two. They live apart, eat apart, hardly speak to each other. It is no good at all.'[51]

Nationalist China and Communist China continued to display their political differences. The People's Republic of China refused to participate in the 1960 Games as long as the Republic of China (Taiwan) competed. Therefore, the Communist Chinese did not send an Olympic team. However, the Republic of China was ordered to parade not as China but as Formosa. During the opening ceremonies, the Nationalist Chinese Olympic team followed the decree of the IOC. However, the leader of the delegation displayed a placard just before reaching the reviewing stand which said, *Under Protest.* The executives of the IOC maintained that Taiwan does not represent all of China and must carry the banner of its geographical location. This same sensitive political issue surfaced sixteen years later during the Montreal Olympics.

Avery Brundage was up for reelection in Rome as president of the International Olympic Committee, and it was no secret that the Russians wanted to replace the Chicago businessman with their own Constantin Andrianov or another Iron Curtain official. "The Soviet Union is mounting a big propaganda campaign," stated the Associated Press, "among satellites and the smaller nations in an effort to wrest control of the I.O.C. from the West."[52] The Russians were not as successful during the executive meetings as they were in athletic competition. Brundage was reelected for another term.

American Olympic teams have not dipped the flag before the dignitaries of the host nation since 1908, although the other nations do. The United States, however, was not the only nation keeping its flag erect. Russia also chose not to dip its flag.

Political disputes over judging continued, and the Americans were the most disgusted. Dr. Sammy Lee, the diving coach for the U.S. women's team, said that judges had been prejudiced against American athletes for years. The Olympic officials must have taken note; the judging during the boxing competition was so inferior that the International Federation dismissed fifteen judges for incompetence.[53]

Communist nations were also involved in a judging dispute among themselves. Kieran described the following:

Also hitting the headlines was a charge by the International Wrestling Federation that the Communist brothers had been playing a bit of hanky-panky. . . . The villain was a Bulgarian who was accused of letting himself get pinned by a Russian in order to prevent a Yugoslav from winning the gold medal in the lightweight division. Only by getting a fall could the Soviet grappler slide past the Yugoslav, and any adherent of Tito is anathema to a true-blue—or true Red—Communist.

The Russian got his fall and was given the gold medal. The Federation investigated the dive, disqualified the Bulgarian, but weakly permitted the Soviet performer to keep his medal.[54]

Perhaps the most bizarre claim of the games was when Taiwan accused the Soviet Union of having a Red Chinese on its team. Peng Chuan-Kai, chief of the Formosa team, said,

"We know the Russians have a man on their team who is really a Chinese. . . . We should know a Chinese face when we see one." "This man (Peng) is an out and out liar," said Romanov.[55]

However, reporters covering the games recalled seeing a "Chinese-appearing" athlete in a Russian uniform several weeks ago. He has not been seen since.[56]

The games were over on September 8, and many Americans could not accept the fact that the "unofficial" team standings had the USSR in front of the United States for a second consecutive Olympiad. Most Americans did not understand how important sports in general, and the Olympics in particular, were to the Soviet Union. In keeping with communist economic policy, the Soviet Union did not allow any professional sports teams. Instead, they focused their efforts and resources on amateur sports, and the most important athletic event in the minds of the Russians were the Olympic Games. In contrast, Americans prefer professional sports over amateur sports and do not support their Olympic Teams with the attention and resources that other countries do. As a result, although the United States may be the greatest economic and political power in the world, our Olympic athletes are not supported to the same extent as those in other countries. As a result, it becomes very difficult to emerge victorious in the Olympics if an athlete has to struggle financially to prepare for Olympic competition. Nonetheless, Americans continue to be very nationalistic and expect their Olympic athletes to prevail over everybody else. The Russians beat the Americans in total medals and total points, unofficially, of course. The stage had been set for Tokyo. Would the American Olympic team perform better four years later and "beat the Russians"?

The Italian Organizing Committee did a splendid job producing the games. They used both ancient ruins along with modern architecture, which provided an Olympic setting that the 4,738 athletes from eighty-three nations would not soon forget. The number of women athletes continued to increase. In 1960, 143 women athletes competed in twenty-seven events.[57] Americans set two world records and nine Olympic records. For the first time since 1928, Americans failed to win the 100- and 200-meter sprints. A. Hary from Germany won the 100 meters and set a new Olympic record, and L. Berruti from Italy won the 200 meters and set a new world record. To make matters worse, the American men's 4 × 400 meter relay team was disqualified when Ray Norton took the baton from Frank Budd past the legal exchange zone.[58] The U.S. women's track and field team rode the victories of Wilma Rudolph, who won the gold medal in the 100 meter, 200 meter, and anchored the winning 4 × 100 relay team. Perhaps the most popular athlete at the Rome Olympics was Abebe Bikila from Ethiopia. He ran the marathon through the streets of Rome amid the heat of summer barefoot! In doing so he established a new Olympic record. Perhaps the most heartwarming story of the Rome Olympiad was the battle in the decathlon between Rafer Johnson of the United States and C. K. Yang of Taiwan. Both were students at UCLA and best friends. The decathlon came down to the last event, the 1500 meters. Rafer Johnson had to stay within ten seconds of his friend in order to win. Johnson finished two seconds behind Yang and, in doing so, accumulated enough points to capture the gold medal and beat his rival and best friend, C. K. Yang.

The VIIIth Winter Olympics: Squaw Valley, 1960

California hosted the Winter Olympics, and the California Olympic Organizing Committee left nothing to chance. Over $8,900,000 was spent to build four ice-skating rinks, ski runs, dormitories, and housing for athletes and the large crowds of people expected to attend the games. In keeping with the California flair for the big and bold, the ceremonial activities were left to Walt Disney. The Disney production thrilled both the fans and the 665 athletes. Thirty countries sent athletes to the VIIIth Winter Games. There were 143 women athletes who participated in nordic skiing, speed skating, figure skating, and alpine skiing.

The high point for the partisan crowd was the victory by the American ice hockey team over the heavily favored Soviet and Canadian teams. At the end of the championship game between the Russian and American teams, the 8,500 fans in attendance gave both teams a standing ovation.[59] The spirit of Olympicism had come alive at Squaw Valley. The American men captured a silver medal in the 500-meter speed skating event, and the American women won the bronze in the same event. The U.S. team continued to dominate the figure skating events, and both the men and women won the gold medal. In Alpine skiing, the American women won the silver medal in the downhill, the silver medal in the giant slalom, and another silver medal in the women's slalom. The American men did not win a single medal in Alpine skiing.

The XVIIIth Olympiad: Tokyo, 1964

The growing involvement of the United States in the Vietnam War began to receive front-page coverage by the *New York Times* in 1964. Until

September 1964, the Gulf of Tonkin was unknown to most Americans and, for that matter, the world populace. United States warships were engaged in battle with North Vietnamese patrol boats. American naval vessels had been attacked by hostile crafts the previous month. The incidents in the Gulf of Tonkin were only the beginning.

In Japan, the rising sun may have appeared bright and promising to the inhabitants of Nippon, but such was not the case for the remainder of the global community. Although situated in Asia, Japan was far removed from the Vietnam War that was to engulf the United States. The industrious Japanese were hard at work on the games of the XVIIIth Olympiad. During 1964, there were close to eighteen thousand American troops in Vietnam. American casualties were mounting in the wake of an escalating war that was labeled a "police action" by President Johnson. The Southeast Asian "police action" soon became the Vietnam War and would still be underway during the Mexico City Olympiad.

Nikita Khrushchev was removed from the leadership role in the Soviet Union and replaced by Leonid Brezhnev as leader of the Communist party. In addition to the change of leadership in the Kremlin, two other major changes in global leadership took place. Harold Wilson was elected as the new prime minister of Britain, and across the Atlantic, Lyndon B. Johnson was elected president of the United States over Senator Barry Goldwater of Arizona.

Communist China ushered in the atomic age with the detonation of its first atomic bomb. The Peking government issued a statement declaring that "the purpose of developing nuclear weapons was to protect the Chinese people from the danger of the United States launching a nuclear war."[60]

The Perfect Olympiad

Tokyo spent $2 billion in producing the 1964 Games; the Japanese were determined to make their Olympic Games overshadow all the preceding Olympiads.

In planning the Tokyo Games, the Japanese left nothing to chance. Hundreds of observers were dispatched to Rome for the 1960 Olympics. Every detail of the games was scrutinized and noted. Perfection was the main objective of the Japanese, including an analysis of the grass in the infield of the Olympic stadium in Rome.[61] Practice makes perfect, and exactly one year prior to the opening of the Tokyo Olympiad, Tokyo staged an International Sports week. "It was a dry run Olympics of sorts and attracted some 4,000 athletes from 35 countries."[62] The only issues that could draw attention away from the Tokyo Olympiad were political ones.

Olympic Politics

The major political row that erupted during the Tokyo Olympiad was instigated during the Asian Games in 1962. Djokjakarta, Indonesia, was the site of the 1962 Asian Games. President Sukarno of Indonesia was considered a "political leftist" and had close ties with the Arab bloc and with Communist China. For political reasons, the Arabs and Communist Chinese pressured Sukarno to exclude Israel and Nationalist China (Taiwan) from the Asian Games. The Asian Games, which is a Continental Olympiad, received the sanction of the International Olympic Committee provided the games were conducted under the terms of the Olympic charter, which opens them to all certified amateurs regardless of race, creed, color, etc.

However, when the International Olympic Committee received word of the expulsion of Nationalist China and Israel for political reasons, they declared the Asian Games null and void and expelled Indonesia from the Olympic movement.[63] In response, Sukarno organized the Games of the New Emerging Forces (GANEFO). He tried to pass the games off as the underdeveloped and "socialist" world's answer to the "imperialist" Olympic Committee.[64] The International Amateur Athletic Federation, the world governing body in track and field, and the Federation Internationale de Nation Amateur, the world governing body in swimming, deplored the actions of Sukarno. The two international bodies warned Indonesia and all other nations who would compete in GANEFO that it was an "outlaw" meet that would result in the automatic suspension and barring of each participant from the Tokyo Olympics.[65]

Arthur Daley, a prominent sportswriter from the *New York Times,* stated:

> For political reasons, the Soviet Union didn't dare refuse to participate (GANEFO). But the smart Russians were so fully aware of both the rules and the penalties that they sent only clowns to Indonesia. Not one had even the remotest chance of making the team to Tokyo.[66]

Two nations endeavored to enter athletes in the Tokyo Olympiad who had competed in GANEFO. Indonesia tried to enter eleven athletes, and North Korea attempted to include six. "The International Federations in both swimming and track bluntly refused to accept the contaminated seventeen, although they did certify all other entries from Indonesia and North Korea."[67] Once again, the International Olympic Committee deplored the political manipulation of the Games and issued a strong condemnation of political interference in sports.

As the International Olympic Committee was discussing the issue, a delegation of eighty persons presented a petition to Avery Brundage demanding the reinstatement of the ousted athletes of Indonesia and North Korea who were barred from competition. A public rally was attended by several thousand Korean residents of Japan who sympathized with the North Korean government. They protested the expulsion of the Indonesian and North Korean athletes from the Olympic Games. Brundage, who was elected to his third term as president of the International Olympic Committee at a Tokyo meeting, stated:

> It was the disposition of the Committee to be even more firm, if possible, in opposing any political domination or political interference in sports. . . . The organization had acted reluctantly in taking action

that penalized 'innocent athletes for the decisions of others. But when there is open defiance of our rules, we have no other course to take.'[68]

Government officials from Indonesia and North Korea pleaded with the Japanese government to intervene in their behalf and demand that the IOC reverse its decision regarding the suspended athletes.[69] The government of Japan remained true to the IOC and refused to add this dimension to the games. In retaliation to the decision of the International Olympic Committee, Indonesia and North Korea withdrew from the 1964 Games. Ecuador was also forced to withdraw due to internal quarreling among the members of Ecuador's National Olympic Committee. The Indonesian government warned that other nations would follow the decision taken by North Korea and the Djokjakarta government; none did.[70] The Soviet Union attempted to persuade the IOC to lift the ban on the suspended athletes, but it appeared to be a feeble gesture.

President Sukarno was so infuriated over the decision of the IOC that a boycott of all news related to the Tokyo Olympics was instituted throughout Indonesia.[71] Indonesians threatened "all sorts of dire consequences to both a peaceful Olympics and world peace" as they departed Tokyo.[72,73]

The departure of North Korea from the 1964 Games must have been a bitter one for the North Koreans. They had not competed in an Olympiad since 1952; South Korea acted as the "only" Korean representation in the games. The two Koreas had attempted to unify into one team for the Tokyo Olympiad in the same manner as the unified East and West German contingent. However, negotiations broke off after accusations of "treachery and obstructionism." The major difference of opinion revolved around a team name, flag, and anthem. In addition, it was rumored that the South Koreans believed that the North Koreans were better athletes.

United Olympic teams are very difficult to produce, as was the case with East and West Germany. The effort to construct the combined German Olympic team was marred by bitter controversy and recriminations by both nations. On more than one occasion the International Olympic Committee had to step in to resolve differences of opinion between the two sides. During the flag-raising ceremony at the Olympic Village, a dispute erupted between the East and West Germans. The center of controversy was who would carry the black, red, and gold banner with the five Olympic rings on it which was to symbolize the united German team. Agreement could not be reached, so the German Olympic team marched to the flag-raising ceremony without a flag.

The united German team, represented by 199 athletes from the East and 177 from the West, settled their differences and an East German carried the flag during the opening ceremonies. However, the East Germans demanded that they be allowed to enter their own team in future Olympics. Their demand would be met.

The unofficial point scores and medal tabulation has always been a vehicle for inciting nationalism. As in the past, the International Olympic Committee opposed these numerical statistics. Avery Brundage, in addition to acting as president of the International Olympic Committee, was also president of International Business Machines, which runs the Olympic results service. Brundage did his best to discourage the "record race" by discontinuing the compilation and publication of the medals list.

Even though the medal count was discouraged by the powers that be, all eyes were on the "duel meet" between the Americans and Russians. The Russians boasted that they had assembled their best team in history and would destroy the Americans—athletically, that is. The Soviets had accomplished this task in Melbourne and Rome, and most observers felt Tokyo would be no different. "To the victor go the spoils of war," and during the 1964 Olympiad, the spoils are the propaganda value that the two Superpowers obtain as a result of Olympic victories. The Russians were bragging before the games were underway that they would once again emerge victorious over the Americans by a wide margin.

Tokyo witnessed the awakening of American athletic prowess as the U.S. Olympic team came out on top of the Russians thirty-six to thirty in the gold medal race. The American sector in the Olympic Village was referred to as "Fort Knox." Pravda, the Communist party organ, chastised the Soviet track coach and athletes. The paper criticized track and field coaches who "guaranteed" victory but managed to win only five gold medals compared with the American total of fourteen.

Defections

Three Hungarians, one a canoeist on the Hungarian Olympic team, utilized the Olympics as a means to an end. Andras Toro, Denes Kovas, and Karoly Meinar defected to the United States during the Tokyo Olympiad. However, political defections were not a one-way street at Tokyo. "A Chinese Nationalist Olympic pistol marksman, Ma Ching San, 38, . . . defected to the east to join his parents in Mainland (communist) China."[74]

A radical departure, in terms of violence and political protest, lay ahead in Mexico City for the 1968 Olympic Games. Sadly, the use of the Mexico City Olympiad as a political platform would be unprecedented.

Notables

Bob Hayes, who would later star in the National Football League with the Dallas Cowboys, set the world record in the 100-meter dash. Peter Snell, the great distance runner from New Zealand, won the 800 meter for the second time in a row. He followed his victory in the 800 with a gold medal in the 1500 meter as well. Abebe Bikila won yet another marathon title and once again set a new Olympic record. This time he wore shoes. The Russian and Polish athletes dominated in boxing with one exception, the American Joe Frazier won the gold medal in the heavyweight division. He would later become the world's champion. The American men now made a strong showing in swimming, winning nineteen medals; the U.S. women swimmers won eighteen medals, including seven gold.

The IXth Winter Olympics: Innsbruck, 1964

The only major problem with the Winter Games was a lack of snow. The ever pragmatic Austrians brought in three thousand soldiers who were assigned the task of "snow acquisition," which they did in an excellent fashion. The number of athletes increased significantly, from 665 in 1960 to 1091 in 1964! Two-hundred women athletes representing thirty-six nations competed in the IXth Winter Olympics.[75] The Soviet Union's athletes won a total of eleven gold medals, more than any other country.[76] Lydia Skoblikova from the Soviet Union won all the women's speed skating events. In ice hockey, the Soviet team won seven games in a row to win the gold medal; the Canadians finished fourth, followed by the American team in fifth place.

America's Olympic efforts at Innsbruck were modest in comparison to the Soviets. The United States did not win any medals in men's Nordic skiing; in fact, American men did not "place" in the top six of any Nordic skiing event (eight events). The American women also failed to win a medal or to place in Nordic skiing (three events). The American women won two medals in the Alpine skiing; the silver medal in the giant slalom and the bronze medal in the slalom. Both medals were won by J. Saubert. The United States won the bronze medal in men's figure skating, and Richard "Terry" McDermott earned a rare gold medal for the United States in the men's 500-meter speed skating competition, and in doing so he established a new Olympic record.

The XIXth Olympiad: Mexico City, 1968

Political activism, especially among college students, was evident throughout the world in 1968. Regional warfare continued to take its toll on life and property in Southeast Asia, Africa, and the Middle East. Student activism surfaced on the campuses of America, France, Mexico, South Vietnam, England, and West Germany. Moscow's Red Army crushed a rebellion in Czechoslovakia, and death and destruction were widespread. Senator Robert Kennedy, running for the Democratic presidential nomination, was assassinated by an Arab immigrant. Thus, the Kennedy family's death toll was two: a president and a U.S. senator. Militant political activism in the United States was endorsed and utilized by such groups as the Black Panthers and Students for a Democratic Society (SDS). Richard M. Nixon defeated Hubert Humphrey for the presidency and resigned six years later as the result of an administration rocked with scandal. American involvement in Vietnam and race relations in the United States were political and social issues that significantly impacted American society during 1968.

Demonstrations against the Vietnam War were organized by college students and other interested parties. America became divided into "Hawks" and "Doves." The Vietnam War was not the only reason for demonstrations. Major social issues such as education and human rights were crusades that were advanced in America and throughout the world. Colleges were used as a platform to protest "violations."

African-American students demonstrated against alleged human-rights offenses and were, at times, joined by antiwar demonstrators. The Ohio State University experienced such a situation. According to the *New York Times*:

> Indictments were returned today (May 31) by the Franklin County Grand Jury against 34 Ohio State University students in the takeover April 26 of the school's administration building. Members of the Black Student Union had taken charge of the administration building and held top university officials under restraint for hours while presenting a list of grievances involving alleged racial prejudice. The Negroes were later followed by white anti-war demonstrators.[77]

The racial problems that were part of the social fabric in the United States during this era would manifest themselves on the victory platform during the 1968 Olympiad. When Mexico City was awarded the Games, there were a number of people who questioned the decision. The altitude of Mexico City is approximately 7,500 feet. It was believed that the altitude would detract from an Olympian's athletic ability and may even cause serious health problems. None of these dire predictions happened. Olympic teams simply trained at altitude to prepare for the conditions in Mexico City. The other issue was economic. Mexico was a poor country. Why would the International Olympic Committee award the Games to Mexico City? Would this not be an unfair and unreasonable financial burden? Would there be enough money to complete the venues? What benefits would Mexico City derive from hosting the Games? IOC President Avery Brundage responded to these questions by saying:

> There was adverse criticism when the 1956 games were awarded to Melbourne. . . . Prime Minister Menzies told me that they constituted one of the most important events in the history of Australia. Four years of international Olympic publicity, a record of accomplishment and not of disorder, crime, violence, or warfare, brought not only Australia, but also the entire South Seas area . . . tremendous economic, touristic, and social benefits. . . . What was done will now be repeated all over Latin America and Spanish-speaking countries. The games belong to the world, hot and cold, dry and humid, high and low, east and west, north and south.[78]

Student Demonstrations

The IOC and the Mexico City organizing committee invested enormous human capital and resources to help insure a wonderful experience for the 4,750 athletes and spectators in attendance. However, the XIXth Olympiad was among the most controversial and difficult Olympiads ever. The Olympic stadium was built across the street from the National University of Mexico, which enrolls close to 100,000 students. Many of these students questioned why so much money was being spent on a sports festival when other social programs to help the poor were underfunded. There were severe clashes between students and police, which threatened the staging of the games. Six days of rioting involving 150,000 students seeking more "autonomy" for the university scarred the city. According to the *New York Times*:

> Federal troops fired on a student rally with rifles and machine guns tonight (October 2), killing at least 20 people and wounding more than 100. . . . In an inferno of firing that lasted an hour, the army strafed the area with machine guns mounted on jeeps and tanks. The Mexican government was not about to let student activists take anything away from the games. "The nation had become so obsessed by the Olympics and so fearful of anything endangering their success that the crackdown was swift and violent."[79]

Fearful of student activists using the games as a political platform, the government stationed rifle-carrying troops along the main entrance and circulated five thousand military plainclothesmen around the Olympic stadium.[80] The Mexican government's precautions against the students were not needed; the students were quiet. The political demonstrations came from the Olympic athletes.

Olympic Politics

Past Olympiads had been embroiled in politics from the standpoint of East versus West; political propaganda was the main prize, as was the building of nationalism. Political defections and Olympic judges basing their decisions on politics and not athletic ability were among the issues that injected politics into the games. However, the XIXth Olympiad marked a radical departure from past Olympic politics.

During the XIXth and XXth Olympiads, it was sometimes difficult to differentiate between those activities in the political arena and those in the Olympic arena. Political activists and their activities during the games received as much media coverage as the accomplishments of the Olympic athletes. Militant groups employed the Olympic Games of 1968 and 1972 as political platforms to crusade against injustice, and the cost was astronomical. Once again the IOC deplored the actions of a few athletes and outsiders that served to undermine the Olympic spirit, however, there was little they would be able to do.

Aside from the student riots, the second major political impact of the games occurred when U.S. Olympians John Carlos and Tommie Smith staged a demonstration on the victory stand. The demonstration was the end of a long road and added to the political nature of the Olympics.

The planned action undertaken by America's black Olympians during the 1968 Games was organized at the 1967 Black Power Conference in Newark, New Jersey.[81] The initial plan called for all black athletes on the U.S. team to boycott the Olympic Games as "a protest against all forms of American racism and a retaliation for the lifting of Muhammad Ali's heavyweight boxing crown."[82] However, the rules of order during the Black Power Conference mandated that a 75 percent vote was required to carry a particular action; the Olympic boycott received 65 percent. Thus, the boycott was called off. Of the twenty-six black athletes on the American Olympic team, twelve to thirteen "were not willing to boycott under some circumstances," according to Harry Edwards.[83] Among the best-known black athletes to boycott the 1968 Games were basketball players from UCLA, Lew Alcindor (who later changed his name to Kareem Abdul Jabbar), Mike Warren, and Lucius Allen.

The majority of America's black athletes would compete, but two months prior to the opening of the games, Edwards declared:

> Negro Olympians will not participate in victory stand ceremonies or victory marches; some athletes have decided to boycott the Games and lesser forms of protest shall be carried out by others. . . . Protests would also include a sizable contingent of white athletes.[84]

The black athletes who appeared at the XIXth Olympiad had agreed to wear black armbands "and demonstrate their support of the black power movement in some manner during the course of the Olympic Games."[85,86] Tommie Smith and John Carlos did not disappoint Dr. Edwards. Edwards sought to use the Olympics as a political platform, and according to Fraser,

> Other Edwards resolutions asked for support of further disruption 'where deemed necessary' and the use of athletics 'for greater political leverage in all phases of the black liberation struggle. . . .' 'This phase (political demonstrations during the Olympics) of our political movement originating out of the 1967 Black Power Conference has been a success,' Edwards said.[87]

Out of the Black Power Conference emerged the Olympic Project for Human Rights, which was directed by Edwards. Edwards cited the following developments as a result of the project:

A. Exposure of white nationalism and racism instituted in the sports industry,

B. Exposure of the Olympic Games as a white nationalistic racist political tool of exploiting oppressive governments,

C. The banning of Rhodesia and South Africa from the 1968 Olympic Games, and

D. Education of black people as to the degree of racism in the United States.[88]

At the end of the 200-meter dash of the Mexico City Olympics a protest occurred that was unprecedented. Smith was first with a record-setting 19.8 seconds, and John Carlos was third. Smith and Carlos arrived for the awards ceremony "shoeless, wearing knee length black stockings and a black glove on one hand (the right for Tommie, the left for John)."[89] As the American flag was raised and the national anthem played, Smith and Carlos looked at the ground and raised their gloved hands in a black power salute. A *Time* reporter called the demonstration "painfully petty." Observers noted that even the Russians, East Germans, and Cubans stand at attention when the American national anthem is played.

Embarrassed and angry, the U.S. Olympic Committee met for several hours behind closed doors in an effort to decide on a course of action. The U.S. Olympic Committee "issued a strong reprimand to Smith and Carlos, and apologies to the International Olympic Committee, the Mexican Organizing Committee, and the Mexican people."[90] It was not enough. Avery Brundage, 81, perennial Chairman of the IOC, would not tolerate any political or social protests and had warned all competitors that no political demonstrations would be permitted. According to *Time:*

> That challenge helped guarantee the trouble that came, and the I.O.C. bullheadedly proceeded to make a bad scene worse. Unless U.S. officials actually punished Smith and Carlos, the I.O.C. threatened to expel the whole U.S. team from the Olympics. Reluctantly, the U.S. Committee suspended the two athletes from the team and ordered them to leave the American quarters at the Olympic Village.[91]

The social and political issues that surfaced during the games were the most pronounced since the end of World War II. South Africa and Rhodesia were barred from the Olympics because of their apartheid policy. South Africa and Rhodesia responded to the IOC by saying that they would integrate blacks into their Olympic team. The IOC was satisfied that South Africa and Rhodesia would honor their commitments and ordered their reinstatement. However, close to forty African nations and the Soviet Union immediately announced a boycott of the Mexico City Games unless South Africa and Rhodesia were expelled. The Mexican Organizing Committee, already embroiled in student riots and demonstrations by black American Olympians, envisioned total devastation of the XIXth Olympiad.[92]

Pedro Ramirez Vasquez, head of the Mexican Organizing Committee, immediately flew to Chicago to plead with Brundage for reconsideration of South Africa's (and Rhodesia's) readmission. Brundage would not budge. As the games drew nearer, the "Olympic fathers" realized that the survival of the Olympic Games was at stake. What if the Russians "persuaded" their East European satellites to boycott the games? Chances were excellent they could. In the face of disaster, the nine-man executive committee of the IOC met at Lausanne, Switzerland, and changed their minds. Practicality prevailed; South Africa and Rhodesia were expelled from the Olympic Community. South Africa would not compete in the Olympic Games again until the 1992 Barcelona Olympiad.

The invasion of Czechoslovakia by the Soviet Union concerned the Mexican Organizing Committee; would the rape of Czechoslovakia start a tidal wave of revulsion that would affect the games? In reference to the opening ceremonies of the XIXth Olympiad, Kieran states:

> In between they streamed into the arena and marched around the brick-red Tartan track in all sizes, shapes, and colors. No country, not even the Mexicans, received the ovation that the Czechs did, born part of sympathy and part of admiration for the way they had stood up against the bullying tactics of the Soviet Union.[93]

Perhaps taking a cue from Smith and Carlos, Vera Caslavska, a Czech gymnast, lowered her head during the Soviet anthem to protest the invasion of her country by the USSR.

The 1968 Games served as a point of demarcation from past political actions of the games. Political events had sometimes overshadowed athletic events. Violence and political protests became a visible part of the Mexico City Olympiad. Sadly, four years later in Munich, the bitter conflict between Arabs and Jews added a similar chapter to the Olympic Games. These appalling events inflicted serious damage to the spirit of Olympism, however, the indomitable ideal that is emblematic of the Olympic Games would ultimately prevail.

Summary

For the first time since the end of World War II, Germany was represented by two separate teams. The East German team soon dominated the athletes from West Germany in both the Summer and the Winter Olympics. The International Olympic Committee and the German Olympic Officials realized the futility of forcing a "United German team" to compete in the Olympics. Not until 1992 in Barcelona would the Olympic Community watch a Unified German Team compete under the same flag. There were 4,750 athletes from 112 nations entered into the Mexico City Olympiad including 387 U.S. athletes. The American Olympic contingent was the largest in attendance, followed closely by the Soviet Union with 324.[94] Women athletes numbered 211.[95]

The altitude in Mexico City was 7,573 feet and was a concern to the athletes, especially those in the endurance events. World records were set by the American men in the sprints: 100-, 200-, and 400-meter dash. The U.S. men also broke two more world records in the 4×100 relay and the 4×400 relay. Not to be outdone, the U.S. women's track and field team set new world records in the 100-meter dash and the 4×100 relay and set a new Olympic record in the 800 meters as well.

The United States fared well in swimming and diving. The men won eleven gold medals, and the women won twelve gold medals. The American men maintained their dominance in basketball, again winning the gold medal. This would change in Munich. The athletic feat of the games belonged to long jumper Bob Beamon from the United States, who soared to 29 feet, 2.4 inches to win the gold medal. His closest rival was K. Beer from East Germany, who earned the silver medal with a jump of 26 feet, 10.4 inches.

The Xth Winter Olympics: Grenoble, 1968

The games opened on February 6, 1968, as over seventy thousand fans bundled up to ward off icy temperatures. Grenoble greeted 1,158 athletes from thirty-seven countries. Two-hundred and eleven women athletes from thirty-seven countries participated in thirty-five events.[96] President Charles de Gaulle of France presided over the opening ceremonies along with Avery Brundage, the eighty-one-year-old president of the International Olympic Committee.[97]

Jean-Claude Killy of France occupied center stage as he won all the Alpine skiing events: the downhill, giant slalom, and slalom. Peggy Fleming of the United States won the gold medal in women's figure skating, and T. Wood of the United States won the silver medal in men's figure skating. In the men's speed skating, Terry McDermott tied for second place. All in all, the Grenoble Olympics were a disappointment for the American team, which managed to win a combined total of but six medals. The Russians, on the other hand, took home thirteen, including five gold. The East German team won five medals. The Canadian ice hockey team won the bronze medal, finishing behind the team from Czechoslovakia (silver medal) and the mighty Soviet Union team that won the gold medal.

Discussion Questions

1. Why does there seem to be more interest in the Summer Olympic Games than the Winter Olympics? Why do the Summer Olympics attract more political controversy than the Winter Olympics?

2. Describe the political nature of the Cold War Olympics. What political agendas and propaganda "victories" are advanced as a result of Olympic victories? How useful are the Olympic Games to politicians? How can we separate patriotism from nationalism in the Olympic Games?

3. How did politics and social issues manifest themselves during the 1968 Mexico City Olympiad? Should athletes be encouraged to make political statements during the Olympics?

4. Are Olympic athletes used as "political pawns" by politicians? If so, what examples can you draw on to support your position? In relation to the rest of the world, America's Olympic athletes are not supported with the resources that are available to athletes from other countries. Why does this situation exist?

5. In your opinion, what has sustained the Olympic spirit and the International Olympic Committee through difficult periods (e.g., Cold War politics, demonstrations, and boycotts)?

Notes

1. Bill Henry, An Approved History of the Olympic Games (The Southern California Committee for the Olympic Games Los Angeles, California, 1981), 195.

2. John Kieran and Arthur Daley, The Story of the Olympic Games (Philadelphia and New York: J. B. Lippincott, 1973), 184.

3. London Times, 1 July 1948, 4.

4. Ibid.

5. London Times, 24 July 1948, 5.

6. Kieran and Daley, 188.

7. The Olympic Movement. Published by the International Olympic Committee, Chateau de Vidy, Lausanne, Switzerland, 1993, 62; Anita Defrantz, "The Olympic Games and Women," The Olympic Review, XXV-5, October-November 1995, p. 58.

8. London Times, 18 July 1948.

9. *London Times*, 27 July 1948.

10. Bill Henry, *An Approved History of the Olympic Games* (Los Angeles: The Southern California Committee for the Olympic Games, 1981), 205.

11. Defrantz, *Olympic Games and Women*, p. 58.

12. Henry, 202.

13. *New York Times*, 1 July 1952, 2.

14. *New York Times*, 2 July 1952, 3.

15. Henry, *Approved History of the Olympic Games*, 224; The Olympic bulletin at the end of the year 1949 as cited in Henry.

16. *New York Times*, 11 July 1952, 3.

17. Kieran and Daley, 226.

18. Ibid., 227.

19. Ibid.

20. *New York Times*, 11 July 1952, 23.

21. Ibid.

22. *New York Times*, 13 July 1952, 2.

23. *New York Times*, 18 July 1952, 1.

24. Ibid., 1 and 13.

25. *New York Times*, 13 July 1952, 3.

26. *New York Times*, 21 July 1952, 21.

27. Kieran and Daley, 261.

28. Ibid., 265.

29. The Olympic Movement, p. 62; Defrantz, *Olympic Games and Women*, p. 58.

30. Henry, 226–227.

31. *New York Times*, 1 November 1956, 1.

32. "Sport," *Newsweek*, 8 October 1956, 82.

33. "Periscope," *Newsweek*, 19 November 1956, 41–43.

34. Ibid., 43.

35. "Periscope," *Newsweek*, 2 July 1956, 33.

36. "Mau Mau Rebellion," *The New Republic*, 9 July 1956, 8.

37. *New York Times*, 4 November 1956, 3.

38. Ibid.

39. Ibid.

40. *New York Times*, 1 November 1956, 2.

41. "Sports," *Time*, 5 November 1956.

42. *New York Times*, 6 November 1956, 42.

43. *New York Times*, 7 November 1956, 43.

44. *New York Times*, 10 November 1956, 22.

45. "They Won't Go Home Again," *Newsweek*, 17 December 1956, 96.

46. Henry, *Approved History of the Olympic Games*, p. 251.

47. The Olympic Movement, p. 74; Defrantz, *Olympic Games and Women*, p. 58.

48. *New York Times*, 10 August 1960, 40.

49. Curtis G. Pepper and Richard Schaap, "Men-Medals-Marxism, The 1960 Olympics," *Newsweek*, 29 August 1960, 77–81.

50. Ibid., 79.

51. Ibid., 80.

52. *New York Times*, 17 August 1960, 28.

53. Kieran and Daley, 348.

54. Ibid.

55. *New York Times*, 31 August 1960, 21.

56. Ibid.

57. Ibid., p. 62; Ibid., p. 58.

58. Henry, 279.

59. Ibid., 277.

60. *New York Times*, 17 October 1964, 1.

61. Kieran and Daley, 365.

62. Ibid., 366.

63. *New York Times*, 9 October 1964, 24.

64. John C. Pooley and Arthur V. Webster, "Sport and Politics: Power Play," paper presented at a Symposium on Sport, Man and Contemporary Society, Queens College of the City University of New York, March 10–11, 1974, 24.

65. Kieran and Daley, 376.

66. Arthur Daley, "A Word to the Wise," *New York Times*, 6 October 1964, 47.

67. Kieran and Daley, 376.

68. Robert Trumbull, "Brundage Condemns Political Interference in Sports and Olympic Games," *New York Times*, 8 October 1964, 56.

69. *New York Times*, 28 September 1964, 24.

70. *New York Times*, 2 October 1964, 48.

71. *New York Times*, 12 October 1964, 40.

72. Kieran and Daley, 377.

73. *New York Times*, 27 September 1964, 57.

74. *New York Times*, 24 October 1964, 1.

75. Ibid., p. 74; Ibid., p. 58.

76. Henry, 300.

77. *New York Times*, 1 June 1968, 22.

78. Avery Brundage, Address to the International Olympic Committee, 67th Session, October 7, 1968, Mexico City.

79. *New York Times*, 6 October 1968, 16.

80. *New York Times*, 13 October 1968, 83.

81. Gerald C. Fraser, "Negroes Call Off Boycott, Reshape Olympic Protest," *New York Times*, 1 September 1968, 1.

82. Ibid.

83. Ibid., 2.

84. *New York Times*, 13 October 1968, 1.

85. Ibid., 2.

86. Fraser, 1.

87. Ibid.

88. *New York Times*, 13 October 1968, 2.

89. "Black Complaint," *Time*, 25 October 1968, 62–63.

90. Ibid.

91. Ibid.

92. Kieran and Daley, 419.

93. Ibid., 423.

94. Henry, 330.

95. The Olympic Movement, p. 62; Defrantz, *Olympic Games and Women*, p. 58.

96. Ibid., p. 74; Ibid., p. 58.

97. Henry, 327.

A Selected Political and Social History of the Modern Olympic Games, 1972–1996 and Beyond

The XXth Olympiad: Munich, 1972

In 1972, the Cold War mentality that permeated East–West relations was largely responsible for the political and social climate that impacted much of the world. A brief review of the global political situation during 1972 will enable the reader to understand some of the political and social issues that manifested themselves at the Munich Olympiad. One notable change in the political and social scene was that student activism had declined while political terrorism, especially in the Middle East, increased. Sadly, the XXth Olympiad would not be spared from political terrorism.

World View

The United States was still very much involved in the Vietnam War, which had spread to Cambodia and Thailand. The White House believed that American military power was the only salvation to insure the existence of the South Vietnamese government. The People's Republic of China and the Soviet Union supplied military assistance to Hanoi, which prompted the United States to mine Hiphong Harbor to prevent Chinese and Soviet ships from delivering needed materials. The Russians already had vessels in the harbor with more due to arrive, so mining the harbor had the potential to foster an explosive climate between the two superpowers.

The United Kingdom was plagued with the political terrorism of the Irish Republican Army (IRA) and the Ulster Defense League (UDL). The situation in Ireland is actually a combination of social and political issues that evolved into a religious war between Catholics and Protestants. Violence between Catholics and Protestants was so severe that British troops have been called in to restore order and remain in Northern Ireland today. Terrorists were very active in Ireland, and the bombing of public areas resulted in the deaths of many innocent men, women, and children. The IRA, considered the most militant of the terrorist groups, planted explosives in London and carried out attacks against British government officials to force Parliament to recall British troops from Northern Ireland. The axiom "politics and religion don't mix" is the central theme in the hostilities in Northern Ireland. This same theme seems the major cause of conflict in the Middle East, where Jews and Moslems engaged in a political war with religious overtones.

In June 1972, Israeli military assaults against Arab terrorists were striking into southern Lebanon. Lebanon and Syria continued to equip Palestinian guerrillas with arms as well as provide sanctuary for them. The worst was yet to come.

Guerrilla attacks by black nationalist groups in Rhodesia and South Africa against the apartheid policy of the two governments were increasing. The white minority governments of South Africa and Rhodesia and their racist attitudes cultivated sympathy for the black populations of these countries. Racism was not confined to Rhodesia and South Africa. Idi Amin, president of Uganda, expelled all the Asians in Uganda.

Olympic Politics

Before the games of the XXth Olympiad opened, political turmoil had already begun in Olympic circles. Rhodesia sought to participate in the Munich Olympics, but its social policy of apartheid created problems. If Rhodesia were allowed to compete, the nations comprising the Supreme African Sports Council and other sympathetic countries threatened to boycott the games. Rhodesia announced to the International Olympic Committee that the Rhodesian Olympic team would be integrated and pleaded to the IOC for reinstatement in the Olympic community. The IOC, with the support of the Supreme African Sports Council, agreed to allow the Rhodesian Olympic team to compete in Munich if the government of Rhodesia agreed on certain conditions. As reported by United Press International:

> The International Olympic Committee solved the problem of Rhodesia's participation in the Olympic Games today (August 9) by guaranteeing to the Supreme African Sports Council that the Rhodesians would compete as British subjects.
>
> Jean-Claude Ganga, general secretary of the sports council, said his organization had accepted the IOC's guarantee that Rhodesia would participate in the Olympics as 'Southern Rhodesia' and its athletes as 'British subjects.'[1]

Rhodesia also agreed to substitute its national anthem with "God Save the Queen," the anthem of Great Britain. The conditions imposed on Rhodesia would be the equivalent of having the United States participate in the games as a colony of Great Britain and America's Olympic athletes relegated to the status of British subjects marching to "God Save the Queen."

The Rhodesian issue was a political charade. The *New York Times* stated:

> The Supreme Council for Sport in Africa, the sports governing body for the black African bloc, had approved the conditions . . . with the

expectation that Prime Minister Ian Smith's government . . . would refuse such conditions.[2] To the astonishment of the black African bloc, the Rhodesian government accepted the conditions. The plan had failed.

If Olympic politics, instigated by the Supreme Council for Sport in Africa, was designed to make Rhodesia the "goat," the reverse happened. The Rhodesian Olympic contingent, complete with seven black team members, arrived in Munich wearing blazers identifying the team as Rhodesia, not Southern Rhodesia. The leader of the Rhodesian Olympic squad "sneered at the Union Jack and said that they'd march under any flag including the flag of the Boy Scouts or the flag of Moscow."[3]

Rhodesia was not considered a popular nation by the global community. Rhodesia declared independence from Britain in 1965. However, because the country is white controlled and adheres to a policy of apartheid, the nation of Rhodesia has been outlawed by a United Nations resolution since 1968. On August 21, a few weeks prior to the opening ceremonies, the United Nations issued a decree to the effect that there was the "possibility that issuance of Olympic identity cards to the Rhodesians violates Security Council sanctions."[4] The prospect of meddling by the United Nations in the affairs of the IOC potentially served to increase the political nature of the Munich Olympiad.

On the arrival of the Rhodesian team in Munich, token opposition began to surface from the smaller African nations whose athletes did not figure prominently in the games. This was the calm before the storm. Ethiopia and Kenya, the two most prominent African nations to compete in international athletic competition, announced that they would withdraw from the Munich Games unless Rhodesia was expelled. A political snowball developed. Avery Brundage, IOC president, and Willi Daume, the head of the German Organizing Committee, issued strong statements of support for Rhodesia. The lines had been drawn; Rhodesia, with its social policy of apartheid, became an issue of political unity among black African nations.

An unidentified group of black Olympians from the United States also denounced Rhodesia's participation in the Olympics. A statement was issued by the group that read in part:

> In the light of the Rhodesian acceptance into the games, the United States black athletes now in Olympic Park believe it imperative to take a stand concerning the issue. We denounce Rhodesia's participation and if they are allowed to compete, we will take a united stand with our African brothers.[5]

The statement contained no signatures and no direct threats of boycott. However, the implications were clear. Demonstrations similar to the John Carlos and Tommie Smith episode in Mexico City was a possibility if Rhodesia was allowed to compete. The true Olympic spirit envisioned by the IOC was somewhat upheld when Nigeria declined to quit the games if Rhodesia stayed; however, eleven other nations eventually boycotted.

The issue was resolved on August 22 when the International Olympic Committee withdrew its invitation to Rhodesia to compete in the XXth Olympiad. The final vote after two days of deliberation was thirty-six in favor of withdrawal, thirty-one opposed, and three abstentions. "'Political blackmail,' replied Brundage."[6] After the announcement was made, Brundage agreed that political pressure on the Olympics had become intolerable. The political climate of the XXth Olympiad had been set. Thirty-six years earlier, the 1936 Berlin Olympiad were cloaked in Nazi nationalism. The Nazis took significant steps to preclude athletic participation for Jews and people of color. The games of the XXth Olympiad soon became controversial, and Jews were once again political targets on German soil.

Israel and the Arab nations had operated in a climate of hostility and terror since the creation of the Jewish state. A peace settlement in the Middle East during 1972 was very remote. Egypt, the leader of the Arab bloc, had a deep conviction that it could resort to battlefield action and defeat Israel militarily if they (Arabs) were unable to do so politically. The victory of Israel in the 1967 Arab-Israeli war proved otherwise. By 1972, the Arab nations had not attacked Israel. However, Arab guerrilla units continued to operate against Israel, inflicting death and destruction in their path. Israel utilized the "eye for an eye" approach and attacked the Arab terrorists and their bases in Syria and Lebanon. The Black September Arab terrorist organization would escalate the scope of terrorism by launching an attack on Israeli Olympians in Munich that shocked the world.

The Munich Massacre

In the early morning hours of September 5, eight Arab guerrillas equipped with machine guns and hand grenades made their way into the Olympic Village complex occupied by the Israelis "and re-enacted the darkest ritual in German history—the sharp ominous knock on the Jews' door."[7] Nineteen hours later, seventeen people were dead: eleven Israelis, five of the terrorists, and one German policeman. The Arab guerrillas brought their war with Israel to the XXth Olympiad. The Munich Massacre darkened the pages of Olympic history and was the event responsible for the military reprisals carried out by Israel against Arab terrorists.

By dawn on September 5, the terrorists had murdered two Israeli Olympians and captured nine others "as the world watched in horrified fascination on live television."[8] The Arabs secured the remaining nine hostages together in one room and issued demands, an ultimatum, and a deadline. According to *Newsweek*:

> The initial demands included the release of 200 Palestinian guerrillas . . . imprisoned in Israel and safe passage to the Arab world. If the demands were not met by noon, . . . they would begin methodically executing their prisoners—'to show what is what,' the terrorist leader said. But in Israel, the government refused to consider the blackmail; and in Munich the Arabs allowed the noon deadline to pass.[9]

German officials worked frantically in an effort to secure the release of the Israelis. German Chancellor Willy Brandt arrived in Munich to launch rescue efforts through diplomatic channels. However, the Arab guerrillas refused an offer of an unlimited ransom, "and summarily turned down German officials who said they would take the place of the captive Israelis."[10] Brandt appealed to Egyptian President Anwar Sadat to intervene, but the German chancellor could not reach Sadat. Brandt reached Egyptian Premier Aziz Sidky, who told the chancellor curtly, "I cannot pre-empt a decision of the guerrillas. We do not want to get involved in this," and hung up.[11]

In a desperate bid for escape, the terrorists and hostages boarded helicopters that transported them to Furstenfeldbruck Airport, where a plane was waiting for them. With the plane were five German sharp-shooters who ambushed the Arabs, who in turn murdered the remaining Israeli athletes. Three of the terrorists were captured alive.[12,13]

The International Olympic Committee, along with the rest of the world, was shocked and outraged. Israel and the *New York Times* called for an end to the Munich Olympiad. The executive committee of the IOC met to discuss the tragic series of events and to make a decision about continuing with the Munich Olympics. Avery Brundage wanted to continue with the Games, but only after a proper suspension and memorial ceremony was conducted. The IOC conducted a memorial ceremony for the slain Israeli athletes and decided to resume the games. However, for many athletes and Olympic teams, the atmosphere of the Olympic Games changed from celebration to that of anxiety and apprehension.

Fearing reprisals, the Olympic teams from Egypt, Kuwait, and Syria left Munich for their homelands. Mark Spitz, the American Jewish swimmer who was the talk of Olympic swimming circles, left Munich for reasons of safety. Six Arab nations elected to remain for the duration of the games. Those who continued to participate were Lebanon, Morocco, Tunisia, Algeria, Saudi Arabia, and Iran. Norway's Olympic handball team attempted to boycott the remainder of the games to protest the Arab terrorist attack on the Israeli team. However, Norwegian government officials pressured the team into continuing play, because the International Handball Federation threatened to hold Norway responsible for lost gate receipts if their team boycotted. Several thousand deutschemarks were said to be involved.

Several days after the Munich Massacre, scores of Israeli planes struck ten guerrilla bases in a reprisal for Munich. The guerrilla organization of Al Fatah was the target as the Israeli war planes made their deepest penetration into Syria and Lebanon since the Six-Day War in 1967.[14,15]

The IOC and the entire Olympic community remained stunned by the attack on the athletes from Israel. The attack by Israel on Arab guerrilla organizations to avenge the slain athletes brought more pain to the Olympic movement, and the hope for peace in the Middle East dimmed. However, just when it seemed that the Munich Games would once again resume, two other noteworthy incidents occurred during the XXth

Olympiad. The "Troubles" in Northern Ireland spilled over into the Olympic arena when seven Irish Republican Army cyclists deliberately crashed into the Olympic cycle race and caused a pileup of fifteen Olympic competitors. Irish Olympic officials accused the IRA riders of causing the pileup to knock Noel Taggart, the official Irish entry, out of the race. Vince Matthews and Wayne Collett, two black American Olympians who finished first and second in the 400-meter run, were barred from the Olympic Games for life by the IOC for "disgusting behavior" during the victory ceremonies. The United States Olympic Committee objected, saying that no black power protest of any sort was displayed; both athletes were relaxed and were seen talking informally during the Star Spangled Banner. Both athletes also insisted that no protest gestures were involved. Clifford H. Buck, president of the United States Olympic Committee, said he did not believe the athletes had done anything wrong. However, Avery Brundage and the International Olympic Committee members were unmoved. The United States Olympic Committee asked the IOC to rescind its action against Matthews and Collett, but to no avail.

The Munich Olympics prevailed in spite of terrorism, boycotts, and protests. This is not to suggest that the IOC, the Olympic athletes, and the Munich Olympic organizing officials were unfazed by these events. It did not matter what political or social beliefs were represented; millions of people around the world mourned the slain Olympians. However, in the Olympic Village and in Israel, the pain was especially evident. However, once again the Olympic spirit was able to transcend political and social differences as millions of television viewers around the world tuned in to watch the world's most anticipated and most celebrated sports festival.

The Munich Olympiad hosted the largest contingent of Olympic athletes ever! There were 7,123 athletes representing 122 countries. The number of women athletes increased to over a thousand for the first time in history, 1,058 to be exact.[16] The Munich Olympic organizing committee had done a splendid job. The facilities were first class and the citizens of Munich could not have been more helpful.

Notables

Valeri Borzov of the Soviet Union won the gold medal in both the 100- and 200-meter dash, erasing the supremacy long enjoyed by America's black athletes. Frank Shorter of the United States won the marathon. In women's track and field, the East German sprinters won the gold medal in the 100-meter, 200-meter, and 400-meter competition. The West Germans won the 4 × 100 relay, and their sisters from East Germany won the 4 × 400 relay and set a world record. The American women managed three medals in track and field. American swimmers had a sensational meet, with the men taking twenty-seven medals including nine gold. The women won thirty medals including nine gold. The women's team set six world records and one Olympic record in swimming competition. Twenty-four-year-old Nikolai Aviloff from the Soviet

Union set a new record in the decathlon of 8,454 that eclipsed the mark set by American Bill Toomey by 261 points.

In the pole vault, a problem occurred because of the introduction of the fiberglass pole. The 1968 Olympic champion Bob Seagren from the United States had been practicing with a fiberglass pole and set a world record on 18′5¼″ in the U.S. Olympic trials. However, a month before the Munich Olympiad, officials decided to ban the use of fiberglass poles because the rest of the world's pole vaulters did not have the opportunity to use these new poles. Bob Seagren finished second in the pole vault in Munich.

The gold medal performances by Lasse Viren from Finland in the 5,000 and 10,000 meter races were an especially proud moment for Finland as the Finns had not won this event in more than thirty-six years. The reader may recall that for quite some time, Finish athletes had "owned" this event with the likes of Gunnar Heckert (1936 5000-meters champion), Ilmari Salminen (1936 10,000 meters), and the indomitable Paavo Nurmi, who in 1920 won the silver medal in the 5,000 meters and the gold medal in the 10,000 meters. In the Paris Olympiad of 1924, Paavo Nurmi won two gold medals in the 1,500 meters and the 5,000 meters, where he set world records in both events! In the Amsterdam Olympiad of 1928, Paavo Nurmi won the silver medal in the 5,000 meters and the gold medal in the 10,000 meters, where he set yet another world record.[17]

The XIth Winter Olympics: Sapporo, 1972

The success of the 1964 Tokyo Olympiad so favorably impressed the International Olympic Committee that the XIth Winter Games were awarded to Sapporo. This was the second time the IOC had selected Sapporo to host the Winter Olympics; Sapporo was scheduled to hold the games in 1940 before the war.

The amateur question quickly gained the attention of the press and public. The Austrian skier Karl Schranz was disqualified from the Olympics because he had too openly endorsed a ski manufacturer. The Olympic skiers charged that the IOC had unfairly singled him out. The athletes in the Alpine skiing events threatened to withdraw from the games and hold their own championships, although this never happened.

Thirty-five nations sent 1,006 athletes to compete in the games, and in so doing they set seven new Olympic records. Two hundred and six women athletes took part in the Sapporo Winter Games.[18] The best the American men could do in the Nordic events, which consist of nine competitions, was a sixth-place finish in the biathlon relay. The American women, like the men, did not fare well in the Nordic events. Although the men failed to place in Alpine skiing, the American women took the gold medal in the slalom and the silver medal in the women's downhill. The men did not win a single medal in speed skating; however, the U.S. women performed very well, capturing the gold medal in the 500 meters, the bronze medal in the 1,000 meters, another gold medal in the 1,500 meters, and the silver medal in the 3,000 meters. Dianne Holum, who was on the team at the Grenoble Winter Olympics, was a double medal winner. She won the 1,500 meter and placed second in the 3,000 meter. The American ice hockey team won the silver medal, finishing behind the Russians. The U.S. women collected a total of seven medals during the Sapporo Winter Olympics, and the U.S. men came away with a lone silver medal in ice hockey. The Canadian ice hockey team did not finish among the top six.

The XXIst Olympiad: Montreal, 1976

The political character of the Olympic Games continued to manifest itself in Montreal. Avery Brundage had resigned as president of the International Olympic Committee during the Munich Olympiad. Lord Killanin of Ireland replaced Brundage as president of IOC. Lord Killanin's first Olympiad as president of the IOC was truly memorable, but for all the wrong reasons. The political events surrounding the 1976 Games strained diplomatic relations between countries and almost disintegrated the games. International relations, economic considerations, social issues in the form of race relations, and political defections comprised the major factors that embroiled the Montreal Games in political turmoil. The initial political crisis evolved several weeks before the opening ceremonies.

The Taiwan Issue

This problem had been simmering for decades. The reader will remember that in previous Olympiads, the bitter conflict between China and Taiwan surfaced more than once. In late June, 1976, the Canadian government notified the International Olympic Committee that it would refuse to permit a Taiwanese team that identified itself as "Republic of China" to send an Olympic team to Montreal. International relations between Peking and Ottawa were the main consideration for the action against Taiwan by the Canadian government. In 1970, the Canadian government granted diplomatic recognition to the People's Republic of China and severed diplomatic relations with the Republic of China—Taiwan.

Although the government of Canada did not diplomatically recognize Taiwan, it appeared as though the government of Prime Minister Pierre Trudeau was going to allow the Republic of China to compete, until Peking intervened. The International Olympic Committee produced a series of letters indicating that Peking made a direct request to the Canadian government asking that Ottawa bar the Olympic delegation from Taiwan from competing in the Montreal Games.[19] The IOC once again had to deal with international politics and their potential for disrupting the Montreal Olympic Games. The Peking government applied considerable economic leverage against the Canadian government. In 1976, the biggest overseas trading partner Canada had was Communist China. During 1976, the two nations entered into a wheat-exporting agreement that provided new prosperity to farmers in western Canada.[20] Massive political and economic leverage were applied by the Peking government to force the removal of Taiwan from the Montreal Olympiad.

The Canadian government did not capitulate completely to Peking. However, the terms imposed on Taiwan were extreme. The initial stipulations were that the Taiwanese Olympic team:

A. could not march under the name of the Republic of China,

B. could not display its national flag, and

C. would not be permitted to play the national anthem of the Republic of China if it won a gold medal.

Lord Killanin, the new president of the International Olympic Committee, correctly noted that "Canada's decision was in complete conflict with Olympic rules and principles forbidding discrimination on grounds of race, religion or political affiliation."[21] According to a report by Associated Press, "During the period of the Games," he said, "the International Olympic Committee is the supreme authority."[22]

As a result of the actions against Taiwan, the International Olympic Committee considered withdrawing its sanction of the Montreal Games, which in effect would have canceled the Olympics.[23] The United States Olympic Committee and other national Olympic committees indicated that they would withdraw their teams if the International Olympic Committee did not sanction the games. The United States exerted political pressure upon Canada by threatening to withdraw from the XXIst Olympiad in protest over the Canadian government's refusal to allow Taiwan to compete as the Republic of China. Other countries were expected to follow. President Gerald Ford of the United States phoned Phillip Krumm, president of the United States Olympic Committee (USOC), to express his concern over the Taiwan issue and to deplore the actions of the Canadian government.[24]

In an effort to resolve the problem, the International Olympic Committee and the Canadian government engaged in a series of meetings. The IOC and the United States Olympic Committee tried to force Canada into a compromise. The irony of the situation was that the International Olympic Committee had recognized the Taiwan government as the Republic of China, but political squabbles have forced the country to represent itself in the Olympics as something other than the Republic of China.

After five days of nonstop negotiations, not directly involving Taiwan, a compromise accord was reached. Pat Putnam describes the compromise:

> Canadian Prime Minister Pierre Trudeau had relented enough to allow the Taiwanese to use their flag. And if they won a gold medal, he agreed, they could play their anthem. But they still could not participate under the forbidden name. 'They can play whatever tune they want and they can wave whatever flag they want,' he said, 'but they can't use a name that isn't theirs.' A relieved Lord Killanin, President of the IOC, felt that Canada had made important concessions. 'Good

show,' he said. Phillip Krumm, head of the U.S. delegation said . . . 'We feel that our loyalty to the Republic of China and our pledge to it has been fulfilled even with this restriction. We took a tough stand—without those concessions from Canada we could have gone home.'[25]

The compromise was acceptable to all concerned parties except Taiwan. Said Victor Yuen, secretary of the Taiwan delegation, 'Either we are the Republic of China or we go home.'[26] They went home.

Once again the International Olympic Committee found itself in a very difficult position. The Olympic Games were once again being manipulated by politicians whose only interest was to gain the political upper hand. These politicians did not appear to be concerned with the future of the Olympic movement. The credibility of the IOC was called into question by Robert Trumbull of the *New York Times*, who recalled an "earlier" statement by the IOC:

> Olympic officials declared today (July 9), in a formal statement, that the International Olympic Committee 'would have no alternative' but to cancel the 1976 Games, scheduled to open on July 17, unless Canada relented in its decision to prevent Taiwanese athletes from participating as representatives of the Republic of China.[27]

The games were not canceled even though the government of Canada refused to allow Taiwan to represent itself as the Republic of China. The IOC has a commitment to insure that the Olympic Games remain one of the few opportunities left to bring thousands of athletes from around the world to one place where they can not only compete against the best, but also engage each other in conversation and, hopefully, enhance the prospects for peace. The IOC has no other recourse than to compromise from time to time in order to achieve its goals. After all, it is the end result that is important—that the Olympics continue. In achieving this goal, the IOC has done a splendid job in insuring that the youth of the world will be afforded an opportunity to interact with each other and by doing so, can break down the political and social barriers that politicians are so fond of erecting.

Diplomatic relations between Washington and Ottawa were strained as a result of the Taiwan issue. The United States was very critical of the Canadian government's action toward the Republic of China. Canada was upset over the remarks made by President Ford and the criticism leveled against the Trudeau government by the American press. According to a report by Trumbull:

> In an unusually sharp statement, the Canadian Secretary of State for External Affairs, Allan J. MacEachen, accused the United States of intervening in the Taiwan issue in order to further American foreign policy.
> . . . 'The Position we have taken does not affect American interests in anyway whatsoever,' he declared. . . . 'Our position is a reflection of our foreign policy, and I believe it ought to be respected as such. . . .'
> 'We respect a quite different foreign policy on China than is followed in the United States, and which obviously is the basis of the opposition to our position at the Olympics.'[28]

Olympic politics strained relations between the United States and perhaps our "friendliest" ally.

The Boycott

Friday, July 16, was the date on which the Republic of China withdrew from the Montreal Games. Several hours after the Taiwan team had given notice of its departure, Nigeria, Uganda, and Zambia announced they would boycott the XXIst Olympiad if New Zealand was allowed to compete. The three black African nations joined the boycott movement initiated by Tanzania and Mauritius, which had withdrawn earlier.

The black African nations were angry with the New Zealand government because it had permitted one of its rugby union football teams to tour South Africa. Sixteen black nations demanded that the International Olympic Committee ban New Zealand from the XXIst Olympiad, "but the IOC refused even to consider it because rugby is not an Olympic sport."[29] The issue was presented by Abrihim Ordea, head of Nigeria's Olympic Committee:

> We are not talking about rugby. . . . As far as we are concerned, it could have been table tennis, football or cycling. We are talking about relationships with countries which support apartheid sports.[30]

New Zealand was singled out as the "goat" by the black African bloc to call attention to the racial policy of the South African government. The same situation had surfaced during the 1968 and 1972 Olympiads. Once again, the black African bloc would use the Olympic Games as a political tool to attack the government of South Africa. On being informed of the developing African boycott, Lord Killanin, the International Olympic Committee president, stated,

> This is a tragedy. . . . This is the toughest week I have experienced. The athletes must be sick to their back teeth with all the politics.[31]

The government of Tanzania, a prime instigator of the boycott movement, issued the following statement:

> Tanzania has always maintained that political, commercial, and sporting links with the South African apartheid regime strengthen and give respectability to the fascist state. . . . New Zealand's participation in sporting events in South Africa at a time when the whole world was mourning and condemning the barbaric incidents in the apartheid state was an open approval by New Zealand of the murderous acts.[32]

The statement referred to the fact that the New Zealand rugby team had toured South Africa right after the race riots in Soweto "in which more than 170 Africans were killed by the South African police."[33]

An organization was formed with the sole purpose of isolating South Africa from international athletic competition. Known as SAN-ROC (South African Non-Racial Olympic Committee), the organization has its offices in London but is headed by Dennis Brutus. Brutus, a black, was raised in South Africa, where he spent time in six different jails. According to Brutus, SAN-ROC acted as the force that organized the

African boycott and would work to keep governments that believe in the social policy of apartheid, like Rhodesia and South Africa, out of international athletic competition. He maintained that he wanted the Olympic Games to be free of politics. Brutus maintained that "it is the first article of the Olympic Charter that discrimination cannot be permitted. Discrimination is the only issue."[34]

Perhaps New Zealand was singled out as the scapegoat for engaging in a rugby game with South Africa while the memory of the Soweto riots were still very strong. However, a week before the opening ceremonies of the XXIst Olympiad, Canada was entertaining a South African cricket team in Toronto; and France sold military arms to South Africa. Why did the African bloc not boycott the games due to the actions of Canada and France? Brutus responded by saying that "New Zealand plays South Africa more; its government appears to tacitly approve. It's an enormously complicated world."[35]

The black African bloc, consisting of Kenya, Nigeria, Ethiopia, Uganda, Chad, Ghana, Upper Volta, Ivory Coast, Togo, Mali, Morocco, Senegal, Niger, Zambia, and the Congo, signed a pledge to follow Tanzania and boycott the games if New Zealand were allowed to compete. Nigeria was not optimistic; before the pledge was delivered to Lord Killanin, the Nigerian team chartered a plane to return home.

And go home they did. The International Olympic Committee did not force New Zealand out, nor did New Zealand volunteer to withdraw from the games. As a result of the political boycott, 648 athletes representing twenty-five nations withdrew from the Montreal Games.[36] Social issues and politics had once again surfaced to disrupt the games.

Security Concerns

As a result of the terrorism during the XXth Olympiad, the Olympic Village at Montreal took on the appearance of a military fortress. To prevent any terrorist activities during the games, the Canadian government took all the necessary precautions to insure the safety of the athletes and spectators. The Canadians deployed a force of sixteen thousand police and military personnel at a cost of $100 million. Five hundred plainclothesmen and assorted undercover agents operated in and around the Olympic complex.[37]

Trained police dogs capable of sniffing out explosives were stationed at airports and throughout the Olympic Village. Sharpshooters were stationed on rooftops of the Olympic complex. Additional "observers" peered through binoculars as they patrolled the housing areas. Canadian combat troops were highly visible.[38]

Political Defections and Propaganda

The differences in political ideology continued to reflect the tensions between East and West. The first political defection during the XXIst Olympiad was a Romanian rower, Walter Lambertus. He reportedly told an Olympic hostess that he wished to defect to the West. Lambertus was put on a bus for Niagara Falls, where he applied for permanent residence in Canada.[39] The most celebrated political defection was by Sergi Nemtsanov, a seventeen-year-old Russian diver. The Soviet Union claimed he was kidnapped and demanded that Canada return the young diver; "the Canadian government immediately replied that it wouldn't return him."[40] Russian officials issued an ultimatum; either Nemtsanov be returned to Soviet officials immediately, or the Russian Olympic team would withdraw from the last two days of competition.[41]

The next night (July 31), Canadian immigration officials and representatives of Nemtsanov met with Soviet officials. In a monitored phone call, Sergi Nemtsanov told the Russian officials that he was defecting to the West on his own free will and that he did not want to live in the Soviet Union anymore. The Soviet officials immediately replied that Sergi was still immature and was unable to judge life properly. So as not to jeopardize the future of the 1980 Games in Moscow, the Russians backed off from their insistence that the diver be returned and agreed to remain in competition.[42]

Alberto Juantorena, a superb track sensation from Cuba, won the 400- and 800-meter races. He dedicated his gold medals to Premier Castro and the Cuban revolution. Cuba's friend and ally across the ocean was not having an easy time during the games. Sergei Pavlov, head of the Soviet Olympic team, claimed that the Russians were "persecuted right from the start of the Games."[43] According to Pavlov,

> It is not easy for sportsmen from the USSR to perform on the American continent. Our athletes were persecuted from the very first day by forces for whom Olympic ideals are foreign.[44]
>
> The 'persecutions' are interesting to note. The International Olympic Committee censured the Soviet water polo team after trying to pull out of the competition when it appeared it could not win. The reason given for the pullout was 'sickness and injuries to team members.' Dr. Harold Henning, president of the Federation Internationale de Nation Amateur, which governs aquatic sports, said a Soviet representative inquired 'about the feasibility of its team withdrawing from competition inasmuch as they would not be able to finish in the top six teams.' To make matters worse for the Russians, the International Olympic Committee expelled pentathlon competitor Boris Onishchenko from the games because he was caught using an illegally wired foil in fencing that would score 'hits' when he actually missed.[45] Besides the political defection of Nemtsanov, additional embarrassing political activities confronted the Russians. The Soviets were the target of anti-Soviet literature and of demonstrations by Ukrainians living in Canada. They were seeking separation from the Soviet Union. Pavlov complained that piles of anti-Soviet material 'were moved into the Olympic Village almost everyday. . . . How it got there was unknown because a lot of police guard the area.'[46]

As was expected, the Soviet Union captured the unofficial Olympic title, and East Germany came in second, followed by the United States. Pavlov said the results were no surprise to him. "This was predetermined by the social policy of these countries."[47] Moscow would be the host city for the next Summer Olympics in 1980. The Soviets were warned by Lord Killanin that "any attempt at political interference with the 1980 Olympics will not be tolerated."[48] Lord Killanin's mistake was issuing the warning to the Soviets; he should have issued the warning to the United States because it would not be the Russians who mixed sport and politics. Instead, President Jimmy Carter's administration engineered the boycott of the 1980 Moscow Olympiad.

Notables

The Montreal organizers spent over $1 billion on the Olympic Games. The Olympic venues were first class all the way, much to the delight of both the athletes and fans. Queen Elizabeth of England opened the games before a capacity crowd of 72,000 and a worldwide television audience. Eighty-eight nations sent 6,026 athletes to Montreal. The number of women athletes continued to increase, as 1,247 women entered the games. These women represented sixty-six countries and competed in forty-nine athletic events.[49]

Edwin Moses of the United States won the 400-meter hurdles and set a new world record. Teammate Bruce Jenner, after his tenth-place finish in Munich, won the decathlon. Nadia Comaneci, the fourteen-year-old gymnast from Romania, scored a number of perfect tens in gymnastics, which had never before been done in the Olympics. She scored a total of seven perfect tens during the games and won five medals in gymnastics, including three gold.

The American track and field team faced stiff competition in both the men's and women's events. The men won a total of nineteen medals, six of them gold. The women's team won three medals and simply were no match for the powerful East German team, which won nineteen medals, twelve more than the Soviet women were able to collect. In men's swimming the American men dominated the event, winning twenty-seven of thirty-five possible medals. The East German women demonstrated their aquatic superiority by winning eleven of thirteen events and setting eight world records in the process. Sugar Ray Leonard's leadership enabled the United States boxing team to win five gold medals. The American men returned to dominance in basketball by defeating the Yugoslav team to win the gold medal. They were not going to repeat the fiasco of Munich, when they lost the gold medal to the Russians for the first time in Olympic history.

The XIIth Winter Olympics: Innsbruck, 1976

Innsbruck, Austria, had hosted the Winter Olympics in 1964 and agreed to stage the games once again when Denver, Colorado, had to withdraw. The citizens of Denver decided they did not want to pay enormous sums of money to host the games even though the IOC had awarded the Winter Olympics to Denver originally. Less than a year before the start of the 1976 Winter Olympics, one of the most prominent figures in the world of sport, Avery Brundage, died at the age of eighty-seven. He assumed the presidency of the IOC at a time when geo-politics attempted to assert influence and to undermine the spirit of Olympism. He resisted these attempts and steered the Olympic movement through very difficult times.

To ensure the security of athletes and spectators, the Austrian police force was on the scene. The athletes had to accept the unfortunate necessity of having armed guards protect them.[50] There were 1,123 athletes from thirty-seven countries participating in the Winter Olympics, and the number of Austrian police on patrol doubled the number of athletes! Two hundred and thirty-one women athletes competed in thirty-seven events.[51] The American Broadcasting Corporation (ABC) televised almost every event during the Innsbruck Games and was quite popular with the American television audience.

Twenty-five percent of the athletes caught the flu or fell victim to the common, but miserable, cold. Strict drug testing was in place and more than three hundred drugs were on the restricted list. The hockey team from Czechoslovakia came down with the flu and innocently took one of the restricted drugs, unbeknownst to them, to fight off the flu. They were forced to forfeit a game and settle for the silver medal.[52]

Dorothy Hamill won the gold medal for the United States in women's figure skating. Ice dancing was included on the Olympic program for the first time, and the American team of Colleen O'Connor and Jim Millins won the bronze medal. Bill Koch of Vermont was the first American to win a medal in Nordic skiing. He won the silver medal in the 30-kilometer race. The people of Guliford, Vermont, raised money to enable his mother to attend the Winter Olympics to watch her son win the silver medal.[53] The U.S. team came away from Innsbruck with a total of ten medals: four bronze, three silver, and three gold. The Soviet Union ice hockey team did not lose a single game and won the gold medal. The United States ice hockey team finished in fifth place, while the Canadian team did not finish in the top six for the second time in as many Winter Olympics.

The XXIInd Olympiad: Moscow, 1980

The Moscow Olympiad evolved into a microcosm of East–West relations. The animosity between the United States and the Soviet Union and their respective political ideologies severely impacted the XXIInd Olympiad. However, it was not the Soviet Union that undermined the spirit of Olympism but the United States. For the third time since the rebirth of the modern Olympics in 1896, the United States did not send a team to the Olympiad. For the first time in Olympic history, the United States called for and led a boycott of the Olympics. It was not a boycott initiated by the United States Olympic Committee (USOC), but rather a calculated political move by president Jimmy Carter that eventually sabotaged the efforts of the United States Olympic Committee to send a team to Moscow. The political arena would once again spill over into the

Olympic arena, much to the resentment of America's Olympic athletes and the bitter disappointment of the International Olympic Committee.

What Led to the U.S. Boycott?: The Soviet Invasion of Afghanistan

In April 1978, the Soviet Union seized the government of neighboring Afghanistan and set up a puppet government. However, there was continuous rebellion from the Moslem tribesmen who declared a holy war, or jihad, on the Communists.

"Executions, imprisonments, and bitter political rivalries had so undermined the Soviet-backed Kabul government that it was unable to function."[54] On Christmas morning 1979, the Soviets imposed a military dictatorship hoping to restore stability and put Russia in a stronger position to capitalize on unpredictable events in Iran and further long-range Soviet goals in the Middle East. Fifty thousand combat troops were brought into Afghanistan. The move by the Soviet Union was denounced by the United States, Muslim countries, and others throughout the West.

President Hafizullah Amin was murdered and Babrak Karmal was installed, an Afghan who had been in exile in Czechoslovakia and swore allegiance to the Soviet Union. It was the first time since 1945 that the Soviet Union had imposed its will on a nation not formerly under its control.[55] Of major concern to the United States was the danger of Soviet meddling in Pakistan, which shared a long and explosive border with Afghanistan. The United States, by treaty, was committed to defend Pakistan from an outside invasion.

On January 4, 1980, in his address to the nation, President Carter said, "A Soviet-occupied Afghanistan threatens both Iran and Pakistan and is a stepping-stone to possible control over much of the world's oil supplies, the United States, our allies and our friends."[56,57]

As a response to the Soviet invasion of Afghanistan, President Carter had proposed a worldwide boycott of the 1980 Moscow Olympiad. The United States also sought to have the games moved, postponed, or canceled during the spring of 1980, as tension mounted between the two Superpowers. In the ongoing propaganda war between the United States and the Soviet Union, the object was to embarrass and discredit each other. If President Jimmy Carter could influence the decision-making process of the IOC and have the Moscow Olympiad postponed, canceled, or moved to another location, he could punish the Soviet Union and a major victory in the propaganda war would be achieved. The athletes would become mere pawns in a political chess game between the White House, the USOC, and the IOC. To the Carter administration, the opportunity to bring American and Soviet athletes together in Moscow to compete, discuss their differences, foster international understanding, and establish good was not as important as making a political statement. The actions of the White House and the United States Congress would end up debasing the spirit of Olympism in 1980.

Brassy provides the following chronology of events from January to April 1980:

> On January 20, 1980, President Carter set a deadline of February 20 for the withdrawal of troops from Afghanistan as a condition for the U.S. sending its athletes to the Olympics. Two days later, the President issued letters to 100 nations asking for their support of a boycott.
>
> January 24, the House of Representatives voted to support the President 386 to 12. Then on January 26, USOC Executive Board passed unanimously a resolution to support the President's request that the USOC make a presentation to the IOC; the recommendation was that the games be moved or canceled. The USOC added a third option of postponement.
>
> By February 4 the National Olympic Committees had met in Mexico City and rejected the boycott proposal of the Carter Administration.
>
> On February 10, the International Olympic Congresses began at Lake Placid, New York, prior to the start of the 1980 Winter Olympics. Executive Director of the USOC, F. Don Miller, and USOC President, Robert Kane, addressed the IOC General Assembly on February 11 and presented President Carter's proposal to move or cancel the games. The IOC responded with a unanimous rejection of the proposal and confirmed that the games would go on as scheduled in Moscow.
>
> The February 20 deadline arrived. The situation in Afghanistan remained the same. Hodding Carter, the President's Press Secretary, announced that the boycott was "final" and "irrevocable." However, President Carter said the government had made its position very clear and that the question then would address itself to the USOC.[58]

According to the White House, fifty governments were in favor of a boycott, including some African Islamic nations, some European nations, and Canada, New Zealand, and Australia. However, the choice of accepting the Olympic invitation lies in the hands of each country's National Olympic Committee (NOC). The USOC governs the Olympic sports movement in the United States. All other countries have similar governing associations. Technically, it would seem that these committees would make up the International Olympic Committee (IOC); however, that is not how it works.

The IOC is an autonomous body whose members are not elected by the national committees. The IOC selects its own members, and by doing this insures that each IOC member's first duty is to the ideal of Olympism; IOC members do not represent their countries, they uphold the spirit of Olympism. The IOC prides itself in having no national or political connections. Nobody is supposed to be able to tell it what to do. The IOC's only allegiance, according to its own concept, is for an ideal.

Rule 24, Paragraph C of the IOC charter states,

> NOC's must be autonomous and must resist all pressures of any kind whatsoever, whether of a political, religious or economic nature. In pursuing their objectives, NOC's may cooperate with government organizations (i.e., accept moneys to help them support their amateur sports programs). However, they must never associate themselves with any undertaking which would be in conflict with the principles of the Olympic movement and with the rules of the IOC.[59]

When President Carter set up the February 20 deadline, he stated in a letter to Robert Kane, "If Soviet troops do not fully withdraw from Afghanistan within the next month, Moscow will become an unsuitable site for a festival meant to celebrate peace and good will."[60] The government wanted a quick and supportive decision from the USOC, but the USOC postponed it until the House of Delegates was to meet in April.

Ultimately what resulted was a clash between the desires of various Olympic teams around the world (go to Moscow) and the political agenda of their respective governments (support the U.S. led boycott of the Moscow Olympiad). For example, Britain's Olympic Committee stated that not one person from Britain who wanted to go to the games would fail to go to Moscow. They would find a way. However, initially the British government said Britain would not send a team to Moscow.

On March 12, Carter asked U.S. businessmen associated with the Moscow Games to voluntarily stop trade of anything that would support the games. On March 29, he imposed a ban on Olympic-oriented business with the Soviet Union.

On March 23, members of the Athlete's Advisory Council, an advisory and liaison group to the USOC, met in Washington with the president and submitted a proposal. The United States should send a team to compete in Moscow. However, to show the American's feelings about Afghanistan and let the Soviet people know that something was wrong, no athletes would participate in the opening or closing ceremonies. Athletes would stay in the village and only leave for their competitions.

Athletes as Political Pawns

By this point, there was no turning back for the Carter administration. It had taken a hard-line stand and was determined to see it through, right or wrong. For seven months the administration tried desperately to drum up support for its boycott.[61]

April 1980 was a dark month for the USOC. Early in the month, Sears, the giant nationwide retail department store, withdrew its financial support to the USOC as did Southland Corporation, the parent company of the 7-Eleven convenience stores, which was to commence building the new fieldhouse at the Olympic training center. President Carter was killing not only the hope of the United States sending a team to Moscow, but also the hopes and dreams of America's athletes. The USOC is solely supported by private donations from private citizens and American corporations. The government's campaign against the Olympics successfully turned millions of Americans against the USOC. The government told only its side. Almost all donations to the USOC dried up or were withdrawn. The USOC not only sends a team to the Olympics but also develops and helps fund grassroots and development programs, trains athletes, maintains an Olympic training center, and sends athletes to numerous competitions that are held year-round every year.[62]

The Carter Administration's campaign to squelch American support of the Olympics was widespread, reaching into almost every facet of American life. It began as early as January; the Postal Service had issued a series of Olympic stamps for the summer games. For the first time in the history of the Postal Service, a stamp was recalled and taken out of circulation. Corporation after corporation withdrew support of the USOC. The administration began its campaign for votes of the USOC House of Delegates members. Meetings were held at the White House, and mailgrams and briefings were sent to USOC members stating the government's position.[63]

The president dealt the USOC a major setback in April. USOC executives had said that if our participation in Moscow became a threat to our national security, we would not send a team. The administration knew this was a touchy topic because if in fact this was true, much stricter actions against the Soviet Union besides a boycott of the Olympics would be needed. There was a growing desire among amateur athletes and organizations to send a team to Moscow in defiance of the president's demand for a boycott. In a telephone conversation in which the administration tried to stifle this desire, the president's White House council, Lloyd Cutler, said,

> the President has stated it will damage American security. The President has insisted that the United States will not send an Olympic team to Moscow to protest and punish the Soviet invasion and military presence of Afghanistan.[64]

At the White House meeting of the National Governing Bodies (NGB), Warren Christopher, deputy secretary of state, explained the administration's position. "The President will take strong measures to see that we are not represented at the Games." However, no threats were made to sports officials because "we haven't reached that point yet." It was revealed that Carter ordered NBC sports television not to make any more payments to the Soviet Union for television rights and to put a halt to the sale of U.S. equipment to be used during the games. "We have not exhausted the measures we can take," said Christopher.[65] NBC was forced to leave in excess of $10 million worth of equipment in Moscow as a result of President Carter's decision.

Michael Scott, an attorney for the NCAA, said the administration made it clear that it would prefer the USOC House of Delegates to voluntarily vote not to go. Cutler made it clear, saying that the bottom line was "If you vote not to support the President, you are doing the worse thing you can possibly do."[66] A week before the USOC House of Delegates meeting, Carter threatened legal action if necessary to prevent American athletes from participating in Moscow.

On Saturday, April 12, the meeting was held in Colorado Springs. After intimidating speeches by Vice President Walter Mondale and former Secretary of the Treasury, William Simon, a longstanding USOC member, the assembly voted 1,604 to 797 against sending a team to Moscow. In essence, they voted in violation of their own constitution, but considering the monumental pressures of the government, it was not a surprise. In contrast, the NGBs, which are the backbone of the USOC, voted almost unanimously to go. It was all the other member organizations who caved in to the political pressure.[67]

Presidential Pressure and Promises

At one point, the USOC tax-exempt status was threatened. On the other hand, a quick decision by the USOC not to send a team brought promised rewards of tax-exempt status for NGBs, federal funding to make up the $8 million USOC debt, and a push from the administration to allocate the $16 million promised the USOC by law when the Amateur Sports Act of 1978 was passed.[68]

The Carter administration also promised to take a major role in Operation Gold, a post-Olympic fund-raising program, to enable the USOC to get back on its feet. Operation Gold was planned as a series of luncheons all over the country featuring a White House representative to drum up support for the USOC. It was to be a matching-funds program that stipulated that the government would match dollar for dollar any amount it raised in Operation Gold.[69]

Many Olympians who were looking forward to Moscow were angry at President Carter for boycotting the games. Athletes at the Olympic Training Center in Colorado Springs called their own press conference to express their feelings and opinions to the nation. Other athletes all over the country were speaking out. One young woman, rower Anita DeFrantz, a lawyer from Philadelphia, was responsible for organizing many of the athletes. She became such a thorn to the president that the Carter administration offered her a job to keep her quiet. She made herself heard and exploited every weakness in the government's position. Public opinion, which was once estimated as high as 80 percent in favor of the boycott, was evening out but to no avail.[70] She later became a member of the International Olympic Committee.

The Carter administration held firm to its position and on July 21, the Games of the XXIInd Olympiad in Moscow opened as scheduled. Although sixteen countries chose not to participate in the opening ceremonies as a protest to Soviet presence in Afghanistan, 5,217 athletes representing eighty-one nations attended. The number of woman athletes declined because of the boycott, numbering 1,125.[71] Thirty-one nations were part of the U.S. boycott, including Canada, China, Japan, Kenya, and West Germany, whereas twenty-six other nations chose not to compete for their own reasons. Meanwhile, back in Washington, the chosen members of the U.S. 1980 Olympic team were honored in a special ceremony to recognize them. It was the first time in U.S. Olympic history that an entire Olympic team was honored by Congress and allowed to gather together to meet each other outside of the Olympics. Each athlete received a special gold medal struck by Congress and a medal from the USOC. The athletes also received their Olympic apparel from Levi Strauss and Company, one of the only U.S. corporations to continue its support of the team. The city of Washington, D.C., opened its heart to the Olympians and their guests (two each) with parties, dinners, receptions, and tours. To add insult to injury, the USOC was required to organize and pay for the celebration, which was orchestrated by the Carter administration for purely political reasons. It was during those few days that Colonel Miller received a check from the

Department of the Treasury for $4 million, the first installment of the $16 million granted in 1978 by the Amateur Sports Act. Prior to the Washington gathering, the White House was drumming up support for alternate games or international competitions. Almost all the NGBs stated that alternate competitions would be meaningless for the athletes, and most athletes did not want to participate. Nevertheless, the administration ignored the wishes of the athletes and began making commitments to foreign countries that the United States would compete. It was dictating who would attend these games at the virtual expense of the USOC. The USOC had expressly told the White House that if any alternate competitions took place, they would be organized and agreed on by the NGBs and the USOC. The Carter administration then abandoned its plans.[72]

Epilogue

By late August, the USOC was $9 to $11 million in debt due to corporate withdrawal of sponsorships. All USOC funds dried up and there was no money for development programs, the Olympic Training Center, the sports medicine program, World Championships, and other programs. Many NGBs felt the heat at the meetings of the Olympic Congress in Moscow during the Moscow Games. For our role in the boycott, U.S. officials and NGB leaders once again became political victims and lost some voting positions on various international federations.

American citizens and broadcasting and news media people were allowed to go to the games. Although discouraged by the government, they did not come under the great political pressure that descended on the USOC to keep the athletes out of Moscow. The news media and some spectators still went, but in greatly reduced numbers from those who had originally planned to attend. The government realized that it could not win the legal battles that would have ensued had it tried to forcibly keep people from going to the Soviet Union.

To make matters worse, in 1981 the USOC was involved in a legal suit when the Russian Travel Bureau that arranged all travel arrangements for Americans going to Moscow refused to refund deposits to thousands of Americans who had planned on attending the Moscow Olympics. To add to the woes of the USOC, thousands of Americans sued and held the USOC responsible for making the decision not to send a team to Moscow. The USOC opted to settle out of court for $450,000 rather than fight it in court and pay for lengthy court proceedings. Meanwhile, lawsuits filed by various athletes against the USOC for going against their charter were thrown out of court.[73] American athletes lost an intangible object: a chance—for many a once-in-a-lifetime chance—to win a medal doing what they were best at. For many, just the chance to participate and to be a part of the Olympic Games, the greatest peaceful gathering of nations on earth, had passed forever, all in the name of politics.

Lord Killanin, president of the IOC, resigned in 1980. Juan Antonio Samaranch, who was from Spain and who has been a member of the IOC since 1966, was named the new IOC president.

Notables

President Leonid Brezhnev of the Soviet Union opened the games of the XXIInd Olympiad amid the grandeur of the opening ceremonies. The Soviet Union spared no expense, and the facilities were once again first rate. Interestingly enough, Britain did send Olympic athletes to Moscow. The competition was fierce, and thirty-six world records were broken at the Moscow Olympics. The Soviet Union won eighty gold medals, thirty more than they won in Munich. The East German team won forty-seven gold medals. Bulgaria, Cuba, and Italy were the next closest to the Russians and East Germans, capturing eight gold medals apiece.[74] Sebastian Coe and Steve Ovett, world record holders from Britain, engaged in a spectacular dual in the 800-meter and 1,500 meter races. In the 800, Ovett won the gold medal with a time of 1:45.4, edging out Coe, who won the silver medal with a time of 1:45.9. In the 1,500 Coe won the gold with a time of 3:38.4; Straub from East Germany finished second in 3:38.8; followed by Ovett, who captured the bronze medal with a time of 3:39.0. Another Englishman, Allan Wells, won the gold medal in the 100 meters with a time of 10.25.

In the men's 5,000-meter race, Miruts Yifter from Ethiopia won the gold medal and set a new world record with a time of 13:21.0, followed by S. Nyambui from Tanzania, who won the silver medal. Yifter won yet another gold medal in the 10,000-meter race. The pride of Finland, Lasse Viren, finished fifth in the 10,000. In the women's track and field events, it was essentially a dual meet between the Russians and the East Germans. However, the East German women did win the "glamour event," the 4 × 400-meter relay, and set a new world record of 41:60 in the process.

The XIIIth Winter Olympics: Lake Placid, 1980

Since the Winter Olympics occur prior to the Summer Olympiads, the American-led boycott of the Moscow Olympics was several months down the road. Had the Russians known that the boycott of their Olympic Games by the United States was a foregone conclusion, it is highly doubtful they would have sent their Olympic team to Lake Placid. But send the team they did. The "medal count" was essentially a contest between two Communist sports superpowers, East Germany and the Soviet Union. By the time the Lake Placid Winter Olympics were over, the East German team had for the first time won more medals than the Russians, twenty-three to twenty-two. The Russians, however, edged the East Germans in gold medals, ten to nine. The United States had its most productive Winter Olympics since 1932, perhaps due to the home-field advantage of being in upstate New York. The American team won a total of twelve medals, six of them gold. Five of six of the gold medals that the United States won were due to the phenomenal success of speed skater Eric Heiden, who won five gold medals: the 500-, 1,000-, 1,500-, 5,000-, and 10,000-meter races. He set the world record in the 10,000-meter race.

Eric's sister, Beth Heiden, won the bronze medal in the 3,000-meter speed skating competition. Leah Poulos-Mueller from the United States won two silver medals: the 500- and 1,000-meter speed skating competition.

"Miracle on Ice" is what the media called the stunning upset of the Soviet ice hockey team by the American team, which was quite young and had not been given much of a chance by the "experts" to advance into the medal rounds. The victory by the Americans was a true Cinderella story because the Russians were considered virtually unbeatable. After the final period, the Soviet ice hockey team was in shock as the final score read United States 4, Soviet Union 3. The American team went on to beat Finland 4 to 2 to win the gold medal.

The Lake Placid Organizing Committee did a superb job in coordinating the Winter Games with one exception: transportation. Tiny Lake Placid could not accommodate the tens of thousands of fans that descended on the area. Spectators were bussed in from small towns and large cities on a daily basis, which caused massive traffic jams and long delays. It was not at all unusual for many spectators to miss competitions because they were stuck in traffic. Still, the Lake Placid Winter Olympics were a success even amid the grumbling of some of the athletes, who were housed in a newly constructed prison because of the lack of adequate and customary lodging. Corporate sponsorships went into uncharted territory as one of the American bobsled teams was sponsored by a pub, which had painted the establishment name on a specific part of the sled that enabled the pub to get free television advertising when the television cameras televised the race. Another condition of this particular sponsorship agreement was that after each day of the games, the sled, driver, and brakemen had to appear at the sponsoring pub to cash in on the celebrity status.

The XXIIIrd Olympiad: Los Angeles, 1984

The Los Angeles Olympic Organizing Committee (LAOOC), under the leadership of Peter Uberroth, produced the first corporate Olympiad in history, sometimes referred to as the "Spartan Olympics." For the first time in Olympic history, the Olympic Games showed a profit, which the IOC prefers to call a surplus, of over $200 million after the games were over and the bills were paid. It was the astronomical cost of the Olympics and the political nature of the games that deterred prospective cities from submitting proposals to the IOC, which continued to demand complete authority over the financial aspects of the games. Recognizing the difficulty faced by the IOC in attracting bids from prospective host cities, the LAOOC drove a hard bargain and, as a result, gained major concessions from the IOC that nobody had ever obtained before. The two major clauses demanded and received by the LAOOC were:

1. A clause that expressly protected the city of Los Angeles from any financial liability. This allowed the LAOOC to sell corporate sponsorships and corporate advertising to finance major capital improvements, etc. Traditionally the IOC absolutely abhors the commercialization of the Olympics but had no choice under the agreement with the LAOOC.

2. The LAOOC won the right to negotiate the lucrative Olympic television contracts, which account for millions of dollars in revenue.

Historically the IOC had retained all rights and authority where money was involved. However, almost every city that had hosted the Olympic Games acquired enormous debt, which the IOC expected the host city to incur. The delegation from Los Angeles was not about to incur any debt and was not at all interested in "breaking even." Negotiation between Los Angeles and the IOC officials were long and arduous, but in the end the IOC agreed to the demands and subsequent commercialization of the XXIIIrd Olympiad. The only other host city that was serious about hosting the games was Tehran, Iran. What would the 1984 Olympiad have been like if Tehran had been awarded the games by the IOC instead of Los Angeles?

Political Atmosphere

Niccolo Machiavelli, the Italian intellectual who taught the world to think in terms of wielding cold political power ("the end justifies the means"), stated that "whoever considers the past and the present will readily observe that all cities and all peoples are and ever animated by the same desires and the same passions; so that it is easy, by diligent study of the past, to foresee what is likely to happen in the future."[75] Even a cursory study of the Olympics, let alone a diligent study, could predict what was likely to happen in Los Angeles. In 1984, Ronald Reagan was president of the United States and was known as the "consummate Cold War warrior." He managed to fan the flames of the cold war by referring to the Soviet Union as the "evil empire." The invective comments by the American president toward the Soviet Union did not do much to engender goodwill between the two Superpowers or increase the prospects of athletic events between the two countries.

What Goes Around, Comes Around: The Soviet Boycott of the XXIIIrd Olympiad

The Russians remained angry at the Americans for leading the boycott of their Olympic Games. Reports circulating around the LAOOC suggested that the Russians had spent nine billion rubles in producing the Moscow Olympiad and were absolutely outraged at the boycott. Still, most people believed the Russians would come to Los Angeles.

Peter Uberroth and his staff undertook extensive lobbying and diplomatic efforts to assuage whatever concerns the Russians had. Numerous trips were made to Moscow to nurture the cooperation of the Soviets and to pave the way for the Soviet Olympic team. Not surprisingly, the Russians were very difficult to deal with and would not commit themselves one way or another; some days it appeared that they would come, on other days the opposite was true.

During one of Uberroth's trips to Moscow, he encountered a hostile Russian press and Soviet officials. Uberroth was asked to explain the "fact" that the United States had, in the past, assisted in the defection of Soviet athletes. Once more, the hostile Russians claimed that Uberroth knew that the CIA had made plans to encourage and assist in the defection of Soviet athletes in Los Angeles. The propaganda war between the Soviet Union and the United States, as in past years, once again spilled over into the Olympic arena. Although the Russians always seemed to win the "unofficial" Olympic team title, the propaganda they derived from their athletic success paled in comparison to the political propaganda the United States was able to marshal on account of the political defection by Soviet and other East European athletes who risked life and limb to live in the West. The Russians were thoroughly anguished by the potential propaganda bonanza that the United States would reap in Los Angeles on account of potential defections.

Visibly angered at the hostile line of questioning he was receiving, Uberroth responded by saying that if they really believed all those things they were saying about Los Angeles, perhaps they should consider not coming.[76] At that point Mr. Pavlov of the Soviet delegation quickly intervened and, in an attempt to placate Mr. Uberroth, stated that he was anxious to come and that the Soviets do not believe in boycotts; it was only if conditions were not right that they would not participate in the 1984 Olympics.[77]

The Russians could play the cat-and-mouse game relative to attending the Los Angeles Olympiad because it was not until May 24, 1984—only eight weeks before the games were scheduled to begin—that a country had to announce its decision whether to attend or stay home. It is not difficult to imagine the nightmare the LAOOC had relative to logistics. Should it plan for six thousand athletes or ten thousand athletes?

The Soviet Union announced that it would be unable to compete in the 1984 Olympics because of the "lack of compliance with the Olympic ideals by the USA."[78] The fact of the matter was that the Russians were still outraged at the U.S.-led boycott of the 1980 Moscow Olympics, and their boycott of the Los Angeles Olympiad was in retaliation. Once again Olympic athletes had been used as political pawns; last time it was the American athletes, this time the Soviet athletes suffered. With the exception of Romania and Yugoslavia, who sent teams to Los Angeles, the athletes from the Eastern bloc nations stayed home.

Security Concerns

The LAOOC had hired a former agent from the Federal Bureau of Investigation (FBI) to head security. The LAOOC building on the campus of

UCLA was a fortress. Visitors were thoroughly screened and nobody was allowed inside the building without proper authorization. The People's Republic of China (PRC), sometimes referred to as Red (Communist) China during the Cold War, sent an Olympic team to Los Angeles. The People's Republic of China had not sent a team to the Olympic Games for decades because of the inclusion of the Republic of China (Taiwan) in the Olympics. President Carter severed diplomatic relations with Taiwan and formally recognized the People's Republic of China and in so doing formulated a one-China diplomatic policy. The Chinese were pleased at the action of President Carter, but in 1984 it was not President Carter in the White House, it was staunch anti-Communist Ronald Reagan.

To the Chinese, Carter was more sympathetic to them than Reagan; however, George Bush was Reagan's vice president and had been the U.S. ambassador to China. The Chinese liked Vice President Bush. The Chinese were assured of a warm reception in Los Angeles and politely accepted the invitation to compete. In California there resides a large Chinese community who, for the most part, are anti-Communist. There was a concern that demonstration and terrorist activities may be directed against the Chinese team, but fortunately none surfaced.

In addition to the concern for the safety of the athletes from China, elaborate security precautions were in place to protect spectators and athletes alike. In the end, the LAOOC did a spectacular job in staging the most secure and extraordinarily successful Olympiad in the history of the games. The showmanship of the opening and closing ceremonies was magnificent, as were the performances of the athletes. President Reagan was on hand for the opening ceremonies.

Notables

Marching in the most spectacular opening ceremony in Olympic history were 6,797 athletes from 140 nations. The number of women athletes continued to increase, as 1,567 competed during the games of the XXIIIrd Olympiad.[79] The Los Angeles Memorial Coliseum, home to the 1932 Olympiad, was refurbished as a magnificent symbol of Olympic pomp and pageantry. All the talents of Hollywood went into producing a stunning if not moving opening ceremony. Without the participation of athletes from the Eastern bloc nations, U.S. athletes dominated the games.

The U.S. men's volleyball team won its first gold medal under the direction of Coach Doug Beal. The science of coaching has become so sophisticated and technical that Olympic coaches, if they are to be successful, must have advanced training. Coach Beal, who holds a Ph.D. in exercise physiology from Ohio State University, personified the state-of-the-art coach. The American women won the silver medal in volleyball, losing to perennial power Japan. The U.S. men's basketball team, led by Michael Jordan, won the gold medal as did the U.S. women's team. Carl Lewis was clearly the star of the games. The American track and field star won four gold medals and, in an unexpected but welcome surprise, the U.S. men's gymnastics team beat the Chinese to win the gold medal. Mary Lou Retton from the United States beat Ecaterina Szabo from Romania for the gold medal in the all-around competition. Marathoner

Joan Benoit from the United States won the first women's Olympic marathon. For the first time in decades, the U.S. Olympic team won the "unofficial" team title; however, the gold medals shine less brightly when many of the world's best athletes were forced to stay home and therefore could not compete in the Los Angeles Olympics. The Russian, East German, and Cuban athletes were not in Los Angeles. If Machiavelli were alive in 1984, he might have given Olympic athletes the title of "Soldiers of Sport" because in the name of Cold War politics, the end justifies the means.

The XIVth Winter Olympics: Sarajevo, 1984

The Winter Olympics were held in Yugoslavia in weather conditions that made the competition extremely difficult. Athletes and spectators had to put up with fog, snow, ice, and severe wind conditions that made for a difficult time for the 1,274 athletes who competed. There were forty-nine countries represented in the XIVth Winter Olympics. The number of women athletes who participated in the games reached a new high of 313. These women competed in fifty-seven events, surpassing the forty-nine events that marked the 1984 Lake Placid Winter Games.[80] Southern Californian Bill Johnson ignored the hostile conditions and proceeded to win the gold medal in the men's downhill. Johnson's teammate, Phil Mahre, who won the silver medal in the men's slalom in Lake Placid, rebounded and won the gold medal this time in Sarajevo. The two victories by Johnson and Mahre marked the first time in history that the American men won both the slalom and the downhill. Steve Mahre won the silver medal in the slalom, finishing second to brother Phil.

Sensational Katarina Witt from East Germany won the gold medal in women's figure skating, and Scott Hamilton from the United States won the gold in men's figure skating. The United States ice hockey team was unable to make a second Cinderella appearance and was eliminated in pool play. The Soviet Union returned to form and won the gold medal in ice hockey.

Debbie Armstrong and Christin Cooper from the United States won the gold and silver medals, respectively, in the giant slalom. In pairs figure skating, the U.S. team of Kitty Carruthers and Peter Carruthers captured the silver medal. When the Sarajevo Games finished, the United States seemed to be on the comeback trail that would once again enable America's Olympians to compete against the formidable athletes from the Soviet Union and East Germany. Unfortunately, the Americans would not perform as well in the upcoming 1988 Calgary Winter Olympics as they did in Sarajevo.

The XXIVth Olympiad: Seoul, 1988

South Korea has been described as the economic miracle of Asia as compared with Japan, which has become the economic miracle of the twentieth century. When South Korea began digging out of the rubble and

Figure 16.1

Opening ceremonies, 1988 Winter Olympics, Calgary, Alberta. Photo by F. Scott Grant. Courtesy of Athlete Information Bureau and Canadian Olympic Association.

devastation of the Korean War, nobody could have predicted that South Korea would rank as the fifteenth most technologically advanced country in the world less than thirty-five years after the war.[81] In 1945 Korea was divided into two countries: the militant North, which was armed by the Russians, and the South, which was backed by the United States.

The Korean War began with the invasion of South Korea by North Korean troops on June 25, 1950. A cease-fire agreement was put into effect in July 1951, and after two years of sporadic fighting an armistice was signed on July 27, 1953. American forces continue to be stationed in South Korea today to provide security against the hostile North Koreans. The armistice between the two Koreas ended the war but not the hostilities. Peace talks between North and South Korea continue even today. The armistice established a demilitarized zone, or DMZ, just thirty-five miles north of Seoul, the capital of South Korea.

The people of South Korea are very anti-Communist and do not trust the North Koreans. The North Koreans have launched countless terrorist acts against the South Koreans since the end of the war, which places the residents of Seoul on perpetual alert. Soldiers are everywhere in Seoul, and antitank walls line the highway from Seoul to the DMZ. With all the political turmoil in South Korea and the threat of terrorist activities from the North, it must have been a very difficult decision for the International Olympic Committee to award the 1988 Summer Olympiad to Seoul. The IOC did not want a repeat of the 1968 Mexico City Olympiad, when the government had to bring in troops to suppress the students who were opposed to the Olympics.

The South Koreans were looking forward to the Seoul Olympiad and did not want anything to detract from them. To prevent the ugly politics of past Olympiads, the feuding political parties of South Korea agreed to a temporary truce.

Security Concerns and Olympic Politics

After twelve years of political exile, the Russians, Americans, and East Germans were once again going to compete in head-to-head Olympic competition. However, North Korean President Kim Il Sung continued to engage in saber rattling. North Korean agents blew up a South Korean jetliner in November 1987 to discourage other nations from attending the Seoul Olympiad. Sung announced that North Korea would boycott the games and threatened to launch a campaign of terrorism to disrupt the Seoul Olympics. The seventy-six-year-old Sung moved surface-to-air missiles to the DMZ, only twenty-five miles from the Olympic stadium. This did not sit well with the Russian or Chinese, who told their Communist comrades not to interfere in the games or else! The South Koreans had one hundred thousand security forces at the games in case of political demonstration or terrorist attack. It was feared that North Korea would employ the terrorist organization "Red Army" from Japan to ruin the games.

Nationalism

Japan and Korea have a history of confrontation that is over a thousand years old. There were concerns about how the Japanese Olympic fans would be treated in Korea. The focus of the tension between the Japanese and the Koreans was the judo competition. In this event, athletes from Korea and Japan competed in front of thousands of screaming Korean and Japanese fans for the gold medal. The possibility of fan violence between the Koreans and Japanese was a major concern but never did happen. In the end, the Japanese were humbled by the Russians, winning one gold medal; the Japanese believed they would win four. The usually vocal Japanese judo fans were unusually quiet and speculated that their nation's athletes had been softened by affluence and no longer had the commitment to win.

NBC versus South Korea

The Seoul Olympics were, as Olympic Games go, quite peaceful. The only bomb threats were against the National Broadcasting Company

(NBC), which had the Olympic television rights. The South Koreans felt that NBC purposely set out to humiliate and embarrass South Korea in front of a world television audience of over a billion people. It seems that there was a brawl in the boxing arena that involved outraged South Koreans, who jumped into the boxing ring and attacked the referee because he declared that the South Korean boxer had lost the match. The defeated South Korean sulked and pouted in the corner of the ring for sixty-seven minutes; he flatly refused to move. NBC televised the replay of the brawl several times and periodically zoomed in on the brooding South Korean who refused to leave the ring. "Saving face" is a cultural imperative in the Asian world, and the action of NBC thoroughly humiliated the South Koreans. By Korean standards the South Korean boxer was humiliated by NBC as were the South Koreans who jumped into the ring and assaulted the referee. NBC made the South Koreans look bad. The NBC debacle became so inflamed that shop owners displayed signs that said they would not do business with NBC employees. The network sent a memo to all twelve hundred employees in Seoul stating that they should not display the NBC logo or other symbols linking them with NBC.

Banning Performance Enhancing Drugs and Other Illicit Drugs at the Olympics

The International Olympic Committee is adamant about eliminating drugs from the games. Prior to the 1988 Summer Games, IOC President Samaranch declared, "Doping equals Death!"[82] Three million dollars was spent building and equipping the Doping Control Center in Seoul. A staff of eighty analyzed urine samples from the three medal winners in each of the 237 events that were on the Olympic program.[83] Drug testing was also administered to athletes on a random basis. Although the Canadians had the reputation of nailing drug users, it was Canadian Ben Johnson who was found "dirty" after his gold medal win in the 100 meter. Johnson had used steroids and was caught in Seoul. Johnson's use of steroids was a national disgrace to Canada. The gold medal was then awarded to Johnson's arch rival, Carl Lewis of the United States.

The Ultimate Incentive

The last vestige of amateurism all but vanished in Seoul when countries blatantly offered money to athletes who won Olympic medals. The Russians offered the equivalent of $20,200 to each athlete who won a gold medal. Poland offered $10,000 for a gold medal. Hungarian athletes were offered a pay scale ranging from $10,000 for a gold medal to a $4,500 insurance policy for a sixth-place finish. East Germany's payout was $15,000 for a gold medal. China would offer only $2,700 for a gold medal, perhaps explaining to its athletes that it cost much less to live in China than East Germany.[84]

Notables

Athletes from the United States made quite a splash in the Olympics. The spectacular diving of Greg Louganis earned him four gold medals.

Swimmer Janet Evans, a seventeen-year-old El Dorado High School student from Fullerton, California, won three individual gold medals: the 400 freestyle, the 500 freestyle, and 400 individual medley. Matt Biondi, who had recently graduated from the University of California and specialized in the butterfly and freestyle, won five gold, one silver, and one bronze medal to pace the American men's "swimming machine." Not to be outdone, swimmer Kristin Otto of East Germany, who stood over six feet tall, won six gold medals for the always powerful East German women's team. Otto's performance broke the record for the most gold medals won by a woman in any sport at one Olympiad.

The United States men's volleyball team, led by Karch Karily and Steve Timmons, won another gold medal, defeating the Soviet Union 13 to 15, 15 to 10, 15 to 4, and 15 to 8. The U.S. women's volleyball team avoided last place by defeating South Korea. For the second time in Olympic history, the U.S. men's basketball team failed to win the gold medal, losing to the Soviet Union 82 to 76 in the semifinal game. While the Soviets played Yugoslavia for the gold, the United States played Australia for the bronze. The American team destroyed the Australian team 78 to 49.

The U.S. women's basketball team beat Yugoslavia 77 to 70 to win the gold medal. Kay Yow, the American coach, did a fabulous coaching job to neutralize the 6'7" Razija Mujanovic, Yugoslavia's dominant player.

Florence Griffith Joyner of the United States won three gold medals and a silver in track and field. Her UCLA teammate and sister-in-law, Jackie Joyner-Kersee, won the heptathlon and the long-jump competition. The two athletes won or shared five-sixths of the gold medals won by the United States in the track and field competition!

The Seoul Olympics ended on Sunday, October 2. One hundred fifty-nine countries sent 8,465 athletes to Seoul, and most all returned home with fond memories and new friends. For the first time in Olympic history, the number of women athletes exceeded 2,000 as 2,186 participated in the games.[85] The political nature of the games was still in evidence but less so than in previous games; this trend toward the de-politicization of the Olympics would continue. Amateurism was no longer an issue, Olympic athletes could earn huge sums of money from commercial endorsements or their own government, and it is all perfectly acceptable. With the diminishing role of politics, the amateur issue being all but dead, and the entry of professional athletes into the games, it would appear that some of the more controversial issues that have historically plagued the Olympics are either dead or close to dying. Unfortunately this is not the case; ergogenic aides, also known as performance enhancing drugs, have been on the Olympic scene for a long time. Drug testing and the "Dream Team" was in the spotlight as the world turned its attention to Barcelona, Spain, for the Olympiad in 1992.

Prologue

The decade of the 1990s witnessed monumental events that had a significant impact on the world and the Olympics. The fall of the Berlin

Wall that used to separate East Germany from West Germany symbolically proclaimed that the Cold War was essentially over. The Soviet Union soon collapsed and the Iron Curtain fell. The collapse of communism, a united Germany, and autonomy for former Eastern bloc countries were greeted with cheers in both the West and the East.

Although Olympic politics significantly declined as a result of the end of the Cold War, new problems arose that caused great concern within the Olympic community. The two most visible problems are the use of drugs by Olympic athletes and the commercialization of the Olympic Games. Although drug use and the commercialization of the Olympics are indeed alarming, the ensuing Olympic Games would enjoy an atmosphere that was essentially free from political bickering and boycotts. Like a Phoenix, the Olympic Spirit emerged from the shadow of the Cold War stronger than ever. The Olympic flame once again became a symbol of peace and international goodwill; Superpowers no longer looked at the Olympic flame as a "call to arms" where political disputes and boycotts often overshadowed the achievements of Olympic athletes.

The International Olympic Committee made the decision to stagger the Olympic Games on a two-year rotation instead of a four-year rotation. After the 1992 Barcelona Olympiad and 1992 Albertville Winter Olympics had been concluded, the Olympics would occur every two years. The 1994 Winter Olympics were held in Lillehammer, followed by the 1996 Atlanta Olympiad. After the Atlanta Olympic Games were over, the next Olympic Games would take place in Japan, where the city of Nagano would host the Winter Olympics in 1998, followed by the Sidney Summer Olympiad in the year 2000, followed by the Salt Lake City Winter Olympics in 2002. It was a decision that was based partly on economics and partly on public interest. The interest level in the Olympic Games remains very high, and the IOC believes that the citizens of the world will support the Olympics held on a two-year cycle. In addition, there is more of an economic benefit to the IOC and the Olympic movement in general when revenue is generated every two years as opposed to every four years.

The XXVth Olympiad: Barcelona, 1992

Barcelona had bid to host the Olympic Games in 1924 and 1936, which gave Baron de Coubertin the opportunity to visit Barcelona. In 1926 when Baron de Coubertin visited the Catalan capital, he said, "Until I came to Barcelona, I thought I knew what a sporting city was."[86] The home town of IOC president, Juan Antonio Samaranch, did indeed put on a spectacular Olympiad, perhaps the greatest Olympics ever. The financial outlay to insure the success of the games was quite high. It was estimated that the Barcelona Olympiad cost $7.5 billion U.S. dollars to produce. The National Broadcasting Company (NBC) paid $350 million to secure broadcast rights to the game.[87] The Barcelona Olympiad featured the Commonwealth of Independent States, a team made up of athletes from the former Soviet Union, and a unified German team. The traditional and heated political rivalries between athletes from the West and the East were but a memory in Barcelona. There were 9,364 athletes from 170 nations participating in the Barcelona Olympiad. Two-thousand seven-hundred and eight women Olympians from 136 nations competed in eighty-six events.[88]

There were significant geo-political changes throughout the world which showed up in the Barcelona Olympics. For the first time in decades, South Africa sent a team to the Olympic Games. Nambia sent its first Olympic team ever to the games, while the breakup of Yugoslavia was responsible for three new Olympic teams, Croatia, Bosnia-Herzegovina, and Slovenia. When the collapse of the Soviet Union occurred, the Baltic States were able to participate for the first time since World War II as separate countries. As a result, Estonia, Latvia, and Lithuania sent teams to Barcelona. The Barcelona Olympiad was indeed historic, and for all the right reasons!

The opening ceremonies were held in the Montjuic Stadium and were quite a sight for the 70,000 people in attendance. The Barcelona Olympiad did have a social theme, as it was declared "smoke free," which was a first in the history of the Modern Olympics.

The Barcelona Games were the most peaceful in recent history, almost completely void of politics and volatile social issues. However, five athletes tested positive for banned substances, down from the seventeen that tested positive in Los Angeles. There was some concern that Basques who want to separate from Spain would cause some trouble, but this did not occur. The United States team won 108 medals in Barcelona, their most in a nonboycotted Olympiad since the 1908 London Games. Athletes from the old Soviet Union, known as the Commonwealth of Independent States, once again collected the most medals. However, the athletic federation that was represented by the Commonwealth of Independent States was a one-time team, as it was dissolved after the Barcelona Olympiad.

The Barcelona sports program was the most extensive ever offered. There were 25 sports with a total of 257 events. Baseball, badminton, and women's judo were officially included in the Olympic Games. The demonstration sports were rink hockey, Basque pelota (ball) and taekwondo. However, these would be the last demonstration sports as the IOC made the decision in 1989 to no longer include demonstration sports during the Summer Games and Winter Olympics.

Much of the attention of the press and the public was on the basketball team from the United States. Since the issue of amateurism was a moot point, the U.S. team was drawn primarily from the ranks of the National Basketball Association (NBA). The press was quick to note that the combined salary of the U.S. "Dream Team" was in the neighborhood of $100 million. With the likes of Magic Johnson, Michael Jordan, Charles Barkley, Larry Bird, and David Robinson, the U.S. team easily swept through the competition and won the gold medal, defeating Croatia in the championship game 117 to 85. One of the more inspiring moments was in the women's 10,000 meter race. A South African athlete and an athlete from Ethiopia ran together for most of the race and kept on running together after they finished the race. This brought a wide smile to the face of IOC president Samaranch, who personally selected "unity" as the theme for the Barcelona Olympiad. Viatli Chtcherbo from Minsk and representing the Commonwealth of Independent States won six gold medals. Carl Lewis from the United States won his third consecutive gold medal in the long jump and won another gold medal in the 4 × 100 relay. The 4 × 400 relay team from the U.S. (Quincy Watts, Andrew Valmon, Steve Lewis, and Michael Johnson) won the gold medal and set a new world record of 2:55.74, breaking the old record of 2:56.16 in the process. The U.S. men's 4×100 relay team (Mike Marsh, Leroy Burrell, Dennis Mitchell, and Carl Lewis) won the gold medal with a world record time of 37.40. Gail Devers of the United States won the 100 meters. In tennis, the U.S. team of Gigi Fernandez and Mary Joe Fernandez won the gold medal in doubles play, while the men's basketball team from Lithuania upset the team from the Commonwealth of Independent States, 82-78, for third place and the bronze medal. The rivalry between South Korea and Japan went down to the wire in the men's marathon. Hwang Young-Cho of South Korea finished first with a time of 2 hours, 13 minutes and 23 seconds, narrowly edging out Koichi Morishita of Japan, who won the silver medal with a time of 2 hours, 13 minutes and 45 seconds. In volleyball, the U.S. men's team won the bronze medal. In boxing, Cuba once again was the toast of the Olympics, winning seven gold medals. Oscar De La Hoya, a boxer from East Los Angeles, won the gold medal in the 132-pound division, defeating Marco Rudolph of Germany. De La Hoya promised his dying mother he would win the gold medal and on the victory stand waved two flags, one from the United States and one from Mexico in honor of his mother.

On August 9, 1992, the closing ceremonies took place in the magnificent Montjuic Stadium. The head of the Atlanta Committee for the Olympic Games (ACOG) that would play host to the world for the 1996 Olympiad was Billy Payne, who attended the Barcelona Olympics as an observer. He has impressive Olympic credentials, having won the gold medal in the 10,000 meters race in the 1964 Tokyo Olympiad. Mr. Payne assured President Samaranch of the IOC that Atlanta was prepared to produce a splendid Olympiad.

The XVth Winter Olympics: Calgary, 1988

Economics

Calgary, Canada, home of the world-famous Calgary Stampede, was awarded the 1988 Winter Olympics in September 1981 at the XIth Olympic Congress in Baden-Baden, West Germany. Previously Calgary had presented proposals to the International Olympic Committee to host the 1964, 1968, and 1972 Winter Olympics but was unsuccessful. The cost of staging the Calgary Winter Olympics was staggering. The city of Calgary contributed $10 million to the Olympic effort, as did

Figure 16.2

*The Atlanta Olympiad in 1996 celebrates the first
100 years of the modern Olympic Games. Pictured is the
logo of the Atlanta Olympiad. Photo courtesy of the
Olympic Museum, Lausanne, Switzerland.*

Olympics Canada Olympics (OCO '88), the committee organizing the
Calgary Games. The federal government of Canada pledged $200 mil-
lion dollars to insure the success of the Calgary Winter Olympics. The
federal government allocated the money to the following projects:

1. Olympic Saddledome: $27.8 million. The Saddledome was the venue
    for figure skating and ice hockey.

2. Olympic Oval: $35 million. The Oval was the venue for speed
    skating.

3. Father David Bauer Olympic Arena: $2.2 million. The arena was the
    venue for figure skating, compulsory programs, and the demonstra-
    tion sport of short track speed skating.

4. Canada Olympic Park: $60 million. The park was the venue for ski jumping, Nordic combined jumping, bobsled, and luge. The demonstration sports of freestyle skiing and disabled Alpine skiing were also held at the park.

5. Olympic Endowment Fund: $30 million. This fund was to maintain and manage Canada Olympic Park and the Olympic Oval after the completion of the Winter Games.

6. Operational funding for the Calgary Olympic Organizing Committee: up to $45 million.[89]

In addition to the direct funding of $200 million, the Canadian government provided essential federal services such as the Royal Canadian Mounted Police (the legendary Mounties of Canada) for security.

Atmosphere

The hospitality extended to the Olympic athletes from Calgary's citizens was extraordinary. This was clearly a city that had caught "five-ring fever" that signified the enthusiasm and anticipation of Olympic competition. The Calgary Winter Olympics was broadcast to the world courtesy of the American Broadcasting Corporation (ABC), which paid the staggering amount of $309 million for the television rights. Just four years earlier in Sarajevo, ABC paid $91.5 million for television rights to broadcast the XIVth Winter Olympic Games. ABC mesmerized and at times bored Olympic fans with 94.5 hours of both comprehensive and mundane coverage of the Calgary Games. The American team did not perform well, and much of the coverage was considered desperate programming. At one point the programming executives were desperate enough to interview noted sex therapist Dr. Ruth relative to the merits of skiers having sex before competition.

Sixty thousand Olympic fans packed McMahon Stadium on the University of Calgary campus for the opening ceremonies. The Calgary Winter Games took sixteen days to complete, the longest Winter Olympics yet.

Notables

Perhaps at no other time in the history of the Winter Olympics had countries entered Olympic athletes in "unnatural" events. This bizarre occurrence was very much in effect in the bobsledding competition, when the traditional Olympic bobsledding countries of Switzerland, East Germany, Austria, and the United States had to share the track with teams from the Virgin Islands, Mexico, Jamaica (a real mecca for bobsledding enthusiasts), Portugal, Australia, and Taiwan. The Jamaicans were the talk of the games due to the team's ability to negotiate the course on the side of the sled, not upright on the runners which is the preferred way.

The United States won a total of six medals: two gold, one silver, and three bronze. Debi Thomas won the bronze medal in women's figure skating; Bonnie Blair won the gold medal in the women's 500-meter speed skating competition and another bronze in the 1,000 meters as well. Jill Watson and Peter Oppergard won the bronze medal in the pairs figure skating competition, and Brian Boitano won the gold medal in men's figure skating, beating out Brian Orser of Canada. Eric Flaim won the silver medal in the men's 1,500-meter speed skating event. In the unofficial medal count, the United States team placed ninth, as the Soviet Union with twenty-nine medals (eleven gold) and East Germany with twenty-five medals (nine gold) continued to dominate Winter Olympics competition.

The XVIth Winter Olympics: Albertville/Savoie, 1992

When the IOC awarded the Winter Olympics to Albertville/Savoie, it was a milestone of sorts because France was one of two countries that had the opportunity to hold the Winter Olympics on three occasions: 1924 in Chamonix, 1968 in Grenoble, and 1992 in Albertville/Savoie. The other country that was fortunate enough to have the Winter Olympics on its soil three times is the United States: 1932 in Lake Placid, 1960 in Squaw Valley, and Lake Placid once again in 1980.

The organizing committee of the Albertville/Savoie Winter Games was headed up by two people. Jean-Claude Killy, one of the most accomplished skiers in Olympic history, served as co-president along with his friend, Michel Barnier. The XVIth Winter Olympics injected a positive social theme into the games; for the first time in Olympic history, the environment was an integral part of the Winter Olympic Games. Co-Presidents Killy and Barnier were given credit for bringing the theme of environmental responsibility to the Olympic movement. Environmental impact reports were ordered on each project to determine whether or not construction and renovation of facilities would harm the environment. The Albertville/Savoie Organizing Committee recommended that all future cities applying to host the Olympic Games present to the IOC an environmental impact study to show the effects of their projects on the environment.[90]

Economics
The cost of security at the games was 64.4 million francs.[91] The broadcast rights for the Winter Olympics totaled $292 million. The American media giant, CBS, paid $243 million for broadcast rights, followed by the European Broadcast Union (EBU), which paid 27 million Swiss francs, and NHK of Japan, which paid $9 million.[92]

Atmosphere
The Alps provided a magnificent setting for the Winter Olympics, which made for a festive mood among athletes and the thousands of spectators who flocked to see the athletes perform. It was not unusual to see people from Paris attending the games, having caught the high-speed bullet train that makes the journey in about five hours. The trip from Lyon took about an hour, so many spectators were able to return home to

cosmopolitan cities in the evening or stay in the hotels and guest houses in the Alps. The opening ceremonies were conducted on February 8 in Albertville; the closing ceremonies occurred on February 23 in Albertville as well.

Following the geo-political changes that occurred in the late 1980s and early 1990s, a number of new National Olympic Committees (NOCs) had been formed and sent teams to the Winter Games. Germany sent one team composed of athletes from former East Germany (Deutch Democratic Republic—DDR) that were combined with their counterparts in West Germany (Federal Republic of Germany—FRG). The ex-Soviet athletes competed as the Unified Team, while Crotia, Slovenia, Estonia, Latvia, and Lithuania sent their own teams for the first time in decades.

The number of Olympic athletes who competed was 1,801; 488 were women. These athletes represented sixty-four countries and in the end collected a total of 171 medals (gold: fifty-seven, silver: fifty-eight, bronze: fifty-six). The continent of Africa sent four teams; North and South America sent fourteen teams; Asia was represented by nine teams; Europe by thirty-five teams; and Oceania sent two teams. The official program consisted of six sports and fifty-seven events that were broken up as follows; the men had thirty-two events, the women twenty-three events, and there were two mixed events.[93]

Notables

In the United States, the dual between America's two best figure skaters, Tonya Harding and Nancy Kerrigan, received a lot of attention but not as much attention as these two would receive two years later in Lillehammer. However, it was not Kerrigan or Harding who was "golden" in Albertville; that honor fell to twenty-year-old Kristi Yamaguchi of Fremont, California. She won the gold medal in the women's figure skating, the first time an American has won the gold since Dorthy Hamil did it in 1976. Nancy Kerrigan won the bronze medal, while Tonya Harding finished in fourth place.

American football player Hershel Walker attempted to represent the United States as a member of the four-man bobsled team but was removed two days before the competition started. Alberto Tomba of Italy won the gold medal in the giant slalom and a silver medal in the slalom. Paul Wylie of the United States won the silver medal in men's figure skating, losing to Viktor Petrenko of the Unified Team. The U.S. hockey team lost to the Russians/Unified Team in the semi-finals by a score of 5–2 and then lost 6–1 to Czechoslovakia, losing the bronze medal in the process. The team from Czechoslovakia may have had extra incentive because their NOC promised every athlete who won a medal a new car and some money.[94] Kathi Turner of the United States won the gold medal in the 500 meter short track speedskating race, and Bonnie Blair from the U.S. won gold medals in two events, the women's 500-meters speed skating and the 1,000-meters speed skating.

The Olympic movement has experienced enormous growth. The number of NOCs has grown as well, which ironically is causing the IOC serious problems. During the Winter Games, President Samaranch of the IOC stated his belief that modifications must be made to the number of athletes competing in the Olympics, which may preclude the involvement of some countries in the games. Prior to this announcement, the practice has been to allow all of the countries that belonged to the Olympic community the luxury of entering at least one athlete in each event, regardless of whether or not she/he was a world-class athlete. President Samaranch and the IOC are exploring the possibility of increasing the qualifying standards, saying, "That means some small countries will not be able to send athletes to the games. . . . We don't want a situation where an athlete finishes five laps behind the leaders. The Olympic Games are for the most important athletes."[95] This seems to represent a significant departure from the philosophy espoused by Baron de Coubertin, who said that the object of the athlete is not necessarily to win, but to take part. However, the logistical reality of hosting upwards of 15,000 athletes during the 1996 Atlanta Olympiad may serve to alter the longstanding philosophy of Baron de Coubertin.

The XVIIth Winter Olympics: Lillehammer, 1994

The people of Norway and the 23,000 citizens of Lillehammer welcomed the world and 1,737 athletes (including 521 women) from sixty-seven countries to take part in the 1994 Winter Olympics. There were a total of sixty-one events; thirty-four for men, twenty-five for women, and two mixed events. The opening ceremonies took place on February 12, and the closing ceremonies were staged on February 27. The Lillehammer Organizing Committee was headed by Gerhard Heiberg and used the famous northern lights as the logo of the games. The Olympic mascot were two children, Kristin and Hakon. The Winter Games were another great success.[96]

Atmosphere

The Lillehammer Winter Olympics continued with the environmental theme established in Albertville/Savoie and became known as the "white-green" Games based on the respect of the environment. The Norwegians constructed venues that blended in with the natural surroundings. The continent of Africa sent two teams; the Americas sent eleven teams; Asia was represented by nine teams; Europe by forty-one; and Oceania by four. The total number of medals awarded was 815 (gold: 259, silver: 258, and bronze: 298).[97]

The construction of facilities were first rate and very pleasing to the eye. Hamar Olympic Hall was designed to look like an upturned hull of a Viking ship. Gjovik Hall, one of the venues used to hold ice hockey competition, was built completely inside of a mountain! It took nine months and the removal of 29,000 truckloads of rock to complete the hall. The weather was brisk, with the average temperature at 18 degrees. There was no lack of snow; in fact, the Lillehammer Organizing Committee had to remove over 7,000 truckloads of snow because there was so much of the white stuff. The children of Lillehammer got a break from school as the authorities closed down the schools for the two weeks of the Winter Games so the region's 2,000 school buses could be used as shuttle transportation.

Notables

About a month before the start of the Lillehammer Winter Olympics, a despicable incident in the sport of figure skating occurred. Nancy Kerrigan was attacked by a thug allegedly hired by her rival, Tonya Harding and her ex-husband, in an effort to remove Kerrigan from the Olympic Team and insure that Harding would be on it. After the attack, Kerrigan was forced to withdraw from the U.S. Championships in Detroit due to injury. The United States Olympic Committee (USOC) removed Harding from any consideration relative to making the team, but Harding filed suit against the USOC and ended up in Lillehammer along with the woman she ordered crippled, Nancy Kerrigan. Kerrigan won the silver medal, but Harding was not able to win a medal at all, placing eighth. Nancy Kerrigan did not participate in the closing ceremonies and, instead, went to Disney World because she was under contract to the Walt Disney Company.

In the men's short track 5000-meter relay, the U.S. team won the silver medal behind Italy, who set a new Olympic Record. The U.S. bob-sledding team had a very difficult time in Lillehammer. The two-man sled was disqualified because of the sled's runners, while the four-man sled lost to the bobsled team from Jamaica and ended up in fifteenth place. The U.S. bobsled team has not won a medal in thirty-eight years! In ice hockey, Sweden won the gold medal, defeating Canada 3–2, and the U.S. team placed eighth. In the men's downhill, Tommy Moe of the U.S won the gold and also captured the silver medal in the men's super G. In the women's downhill, Picabo Street won the silver medal. Perhaps the most sensational performance was turned in by Bonnie Blair, the speed skater from Milwaukee, Wisconsin. She won gold medals in three events: the 500 meters, the 1,000 meters, and the 1,500 meters. Another speed skater from Wisconsin, Dan Jansen, won the gold medal in the men's 1,000 meters in a time of 1:12.43, setting a world record.

The U.S. team won a total of thirteen medals, while the Russians won twenty-three. Baalentine Sich, head of the Russian sports delegation, was asked why the Russians always seem to do better than the Americans. He replied by saying:

> Let's say you put an American and a Russian together. . . . The American is dressed very nicely, is well fed and has good equipment. The Russian is dressed poorly, is not fed and has no equipment [to speak of]. Now you put $1,000 at the end of 200 meters and you have them run for it. Who do you think will win?[98]

America's Olympic teams have expended great effort to attract corporate sponsorships in order to assemble and train the nation's Olympic athletes. Overall, we do not do as well as other countries in the Winter or Summer Olympics. What do you think is missing from America's Olympic Training Program?

The Lillehammer Winter Games were a splendid success. The next Winter Olympics will take place in Nagano, Japan, in 1998, and in 2002, the Winter Olympics will once again be back in the United States as Salt Lake City plays host.

The Centennial Olympiad: Atlanta, 1996

The XXVIth Olympiad held in Atlanta was a special occasion. It symbolized the first 100 years of the modern Olympic Games. The two primary cities that were considered by the International Olympic Committee (IOC) to host this most important Olympiad were Atlanta and Athens. The Greeks made the forceful argument that Athens should be selected because Greece is the birthplace of the Olympic Games, and the first modern Olympiad was held in Athens in 1896. The symbolism and historic place of Athens in the annals of Olympic history made the decision by the International Olympic Committee (IOC) very difficult. However, Atlanta was selected. Athens later applied to the IOC to host the Olympic Games in 2004.

One of the most significant points that the Atlanta Committee for the Olympic Games (ACOG) made to the IOC in bidding for the Olympics was that the city of Atlanta is primarily populated by minorities; over 60 percent of the citizens of Atlanta are people of color. The IOC was impressed by the commitment and dedication of the ACOG, as well as the fact that the host city was represented by people of all races and creeds. The spirit of Olympicism seeks to bring together athletes from all over the world in order to bring down racial and ethnic barriers that can otherwise be difficult to overcome. Atlanta was the ideal city to host the Olympic Games because the people of Atlanta reflected the spirit of achievement and cooperation—the spirit of Olympicism.

Although terrorist activity at the Olympics had significantly declined in recent years, it remains an issue of enormous concern. Over 30,000 security personnel were assigned to protect athletes and spectators from criminal activity. On July 17, a TWA jumbo jet carrying 229 people exploded over the skies of New York, killing all aboard. Initially it was highly speculated that the crash of TWA Flight 800 was due to a bomb. Security was immediately tightened in Atlanta since the opening ceremonies were scheduled to take place two days later; however, it would not be enough to prevent the explosion of a deadly pipe bomb during the games.

Torch Relay. The Olympic torch relay started in Los Angeles at the Coliseum, the main venue of the 1932 and 1984 Olympic Games, and was carried throughout the United States. In all, the torch relay covered approximately 15,000 miles and visited forty-three states. It was a huge success and drew crowds and cheers in each city and rural town that it passed through. The torch was the subject of media coverage, and almost every day, many of the nation's newspapers showed a map of where the torch was and where it was going on a particular day. The torch was accompanied by a police escort and was carried by people throughout the land, some running, some walking, and some in wheelchairs. It was a stirring sight and brought the Olympic spirit close to home for many Americans who turned out to see the torch.

Opening Ceremonies. The Atlanta Olympiad began on July 19 amid a spectacular opening ceremony. Close to 11,000 athletes from 197 countries took part in the opening ceremonies, which were held in the newly constructed Olympic Stadium. Muhammad Ali, who won the gold medal in boxing at the 1960 Rome Olympic Games as Cassius Clay, carried the Olympic Flame up a flight of stairs and ignited the huge torch in Olympic Stadium. President Clinton was on hand for the opening ceremonies and announced "I declare open the Games of Atlanta celebrating the XXVIth Olympiad of the modern era."

Commercialization. NBC television broadcast the opening ceremonies live to the world to an expected audience of about 3.5 billion viewers. In fact, NBC broadcasted over 170 hours of Olympic coverage. Most of the broadcasts were live, but some events were shown on a delayed basis. The amount paid by television networks to the IOC for broadcast rights to the Olympics have increased dramatically over the years. NBC paid the IOC $456 million dollars for the right to broadcast the Games of the XXVIth Olympiad. In contrast, CBS paid $394 thousand dollars to the IOC to broadcast approximately fifteen hours of coverage during the 1960 Rome Olympiad. In order to broadcast the Sydney Olympiad in 2000, NBC agreed to pay the IOC $715 million dollars.

The commercialization of the Atlanta Olympiad was a topic of discussion not only in Atlanta, but around the world. Especially noted was the seemingly never-ending commercials that NBC ran during the games. However, NBC is a corporate giant and, like other corporations, is in business to make a profit. As a result, NBC sold advertising time during the Olympics to recover the money paid to the IOC in addition to generating additional revenue.

There is an up side to having commercial television involved in broadcasting the Olympic games; although we must contend with what seems to be an overwhelming number of commercial advertisements, it cost us nothing to watch and enjoy the Olympic Games. If and when the IOC begins to sell broadcast rights to the cable networks, we will no longer be able to enjoy the Olympics for free.

The commercialization of the Atlanta Olympic Games went beyond television. If a particular business had enough money to spend on becoming an official Olympic sponsor, its products would be seen by a worldwide television audience. For example, during the opening ceremonies General Motors products were featured in the form of thirty specially decked out Chevrolet trucks used to deliver dancers and other entertainers to the field. General Motors paid the ACOG $40 million dollars to be an official sponsor and to showcase Chevy trucks during the opening ceremonies. In addition to the $40 million General Motors paid to become an official sponsor, General Motors paid NBC over $50 million to advertise cars and trucks during televised events. Atlanta is the corporate home of soft drink giant Coca-Cola. Coca-Cola paid NBC over $60 million to advertise its products during the Olympics.

Centennial Olympic Park was a venue where the spectators could gather and "catch the Olympic Spirit." It was also the location for many commercial interests to set up shop. The IOC and the United States Olympic Committee (USOC) closely guard the "turf" of the Olympics, making sure that there is no infringement on the Olympic name by organizations that did not pay sponsorship fees.

Many independent businesses as well as multinational corporations attempted to increase their product exposure and attendant profits by identifying with the Atlanta Olympiad in some way. Corporations who donated significant sums of money to the ACOG had their corporate logos and products prominently displayed in various venues during the course of the games. Many of the athletes who compete in the Olympics have sizable contracts with shoe companies and apparel companies. These athletes wear particular shoes and attire during competition so the brand name and logo is seen by millions of television viewers as well as those in attendance. Some of the more popular athletes have their own apparel companies and wear their products during Olympic competition, hoping that their fans will buy their product lines.

The commercialization of products like shoes and clothing does not stop with individual athletes. Many of the more recognizable footwear and clothing companies enter into contracts with various Olympic teams around the world. These teams are paid a sum of money to wear particular shoes and other clothing accessories. The commercial message is clear: "if you want to be the best, wear _____ shoes."

The Olympic Games are among the most expensive events to stage in the world. The cost of producing the Olympics continues to escalate, which eliminates many poor cities form hosting them (the Olympic Games are awarded to a city, never a country). Host cities that are located in economically sound countries have turned to the private sector as a source of revenue to finance the Olympics. The private sector provides hundreds of millions of dollars to the host city in return for the commercial use of the Olympic Games. Even though the attention of media and the public are opposed to the commercialization of the Olympic Games, how many cities can afford to bid to host the Olympics if official Olympic sponsorships (generating millions of dollars) can not be sold to commercial enterprises by the host city?

Drugs. Performance-enhancing drugs and, to an extent, recreational drug use are major problems in the Olympic Games. Anabolic steroids that are used to increase strength are used by many athletes and have been a source of frustration for IOC and USOC officials for many years. Athletes who believe in the benefit of using performance-enhancing drugs become very skilled in avoiding detection.

The IOC publishes a list of banned substances, as does the USOC. However, the allure of an Olympic medal and the fame and possible financial rewards that accompany a gold medal can be the reason why athletes have long used performance-enhancing drugs and hope that they are not caught and stripped of their medal.

For example, many Olympians are promised cash prizes and other incentives if they win an Olympic medal. In 1995, the French announced that any Olympian from France who won a gold medal would receive $68,952 tax free; a silver medal would be worth a cash prize of $33,124, and a bronze medal would fetch $21,632. During the 1996 Atlanta Olympiad, Somluck Kamsing from Thailand won a gold medal in boxing—the first medal of any kind for Thailand. When he returned home he was given a cash award of approximately $1.73 million, tax free! Windsurfer Lee Lai-shan from Hong Kong won a gold medal in Atlanta and returned home to claim cash and prizes worth approximately $405,600.[99] These types of cash incentives in addition to securing a place in Olympic history as a medalist tempt athletes to seek an "edge" that the competition doesn't have. Drugs are one method used to gain an edge.

Drugs became an issue in Atlanta when Michelle Smith from Ireland came from out of relative obscurity and shocked the Olympic swimmers by winning the gold medal in the 400 free, the bronze medal in the 200 butterfly, the gold medal in the 200 individual medley, and another gold medal in the 400 individual medley. She married an athlete who once admitted to using performance-enhancing drugs, which caused a great deal of suspicion among the swimmers, especially the Americans who had not considered her a threat before the Olympics. Michele Smith was "clean" and rightfully resented the accusations by the media that she may have used drugs to achieve her Olympic medals.

In order to deter drug use among Olympic athletes, the IOC implemented a very sophisticated drug detection system in Atlanta. The technology that was used enabled the drug testing professionals to detect drugs that were taken into the body several months previous instead of the previous thirty days. Many athletes who use performance-enhancing drugs stopped taking drugs about thirty days prior to competition in order to "wash out" any sign of the drug from their bodies. The new technology enabled the drug tests to "look back" sixty to ninety days using athletes' urine samples.

The drug-testing protocol in Atlanta was set up to take the top four finishers in each event plus others chosen at random. An escort took the athletes to the testing center, where they were required to provide a urine sample to be tested. If the test identifies banned substances in an athlete's urine sample, he/she can appeal to the newly established Court of Arbitration for Sport (CAR), which consists of twelve arbitrators. The CAR was set up to avoid the long and costly legal battles that had taken place when issues of drug use by athletes occurred. Since there were twelve arbitrators on staff, it was hoped that all claims of drug use could be resolved quickly.

Closing Ceremonies. The closing ceremonies on August 4 occurred after sixteen days of competition that featured 271 events. Although many of the Olympic athletes had left Atlanta after their events were over, thousands stayed behind and gathered on the floor of the stadium on a hot August night. Juan Antonio Samaranch, President of the International Olympic Committee, called on the youth of the world to gather in Sydney, Australia, in four years to once again celebrate the Olympic Games. President Samaranch heaped praise upon Billy Payne and the ACOG but stopped short of labeling the Atlanta Olympiad as the "best ever." Perhaps he wanted the "best ever" Olympic Games label to remain identified with the 1992 Barcelona Olympiad, his home town.

Notables

The Atlanta Olympiad was marred with a bomb attack that occurred on July 27 in Centennial Olympic Park. The bomb exploded at approximately 1:20 A.M. by a giant tower near a stage where thousands of tourists and spectators were enjoying a concert. Over 100 people were injured and two people died. Security experts were called in to locate the individual or group responsible for the bombing, and the park was closed for a few days. However, the Olympic Games continued as scheduled. The people of Atlanta, the Olympic athletes, and the tens of thousands of Olympic spectators resolved not to be held hostage by the bombing and continued to uphold the Olympic spirit. Cooperation, good prior to the bombing, was even better afterward because everybody was furious that such a horrible thing could happen. People bonded in the Olympic Spirit. Tourists and spectators were helped by the good people of Atlanta, and although they grieved for the wounded and the dead, they went ahead and celebrated the Olympics. During the closing ceremonies, President Samaranch stated that, "No act of terrorism has destroyed the Olympic movement and none ever will."[100]

In the race for Olympic medals, the United States as expected captured the most, a total of 101. The U.S. won 44 gold medals, 32 silver medals, and 25 bronze medals. In second place was Germany with a total of 65; 20 gold, 18 silver, and 27 bronze. Although the mighty "Soviet Sports Machine" that won more Olympic Medals during the Cold War than any other country was but a memory, the Russian Olympic team finished a strong third in the race for Olympic medals. Many experts believe it is simply a matter of time and money before the Russians will once again compete head to head with the Americans for Olympic dominance. For the record, the Russians won a total of 61 Olympic medals; 26 gold, 21 silver, and 14 bronze.

There were two basketball "Dream Teams" in Atlanta: the NBA-led U.S. men's team and the U.S. women's team. The United States defeated Yugoslavia 95–69 for the gold medal in men's basketball with help from NBA stars David Robinson, Scottie Pippen, Karl Malone, and Shaquille O'Neal. The U.S. women demolished Brazil by a score of 111–87 to win the gold medal. The U.S. women were led by Dawn Staley, Lisa Leslie, and Sheryl Swoopes. The women's basketball team was assembled about a year before the Atlanta Olympics. The team, coached by Tara Van-Derveer, swept through Olympic opponents undefeated. The American women never lost a single game during the year that they prepared for the Olympics, winning sixty straight games.

The men's marathon was won by Josia Thugwane of South Africa. He is the first black South African to win a gold medal in the Olympic Games. Another black South African, Hezekiel Sepeng, won the silver medal in the men's 800, another historic first in South African Olympic history. It should be remembered that South Africa was banned by the International Olympic Committee from participating in the Olympic Games in 1960 due to its policy of apartheid and was not allowed back in to the Olympic movement until 1992. Josia Thugwane dedicated his gold medal to Nelson Mandela, the first black president of South Africa.

In track and field, called "athletics" in Olympic circles, the United States was a dominant force. Michael Johnson of the United States wore gold shoes and won the gold medal in both the 200 and 400, the first man to ever accomplish this amazing feat. Donovan Bailey of Canada won the men's 100 followed by Frank Fredericks of Namibia, who won the silver medal, and Ato Boldoa of Trinidad, who captured the bronze medal.

In the 400 relay, the United States men finished second to Canada but did win the gold medal in the 1,600 relay, beating Great Britain. The title of World's Best Male Athlete was bestowed on American Dan O'Brien from Idaho, who won the decathlon. The amazing Carl Lewis of the United States, perhaps the best athlete ever to participate in track and field, won the long jump and added another gold medal to his collection. Lewis has won nine Olympic gold medals, and there was speculation he might run on the U.S. men's relay team in an effort to capture a tenth Olympic Gold. But he did not run. Nobody in the history of the Modern Olympic Games has won ten gold medals.

The United States women's track and field team was sensational. Gail Devers won the 100, while Gwen Torrence won the bronze medal in this event. In the 200 and 400, Marie-Josie Perec from France was victorious, winning two gold medals. In the 800 and 1,500, Svetiana Masterkova from Russia was unbeatable, winning the gold medal in both events. The American women won gold medals in the 400 relay and the 1,600 relay. Jackie Joyner-Kersee from the United States captured the bronze medal in the long jump. In the discus and shot put, the American women did not win any medals.

Volleyball is a popular American sport, both indoors and on the beach. In 1996, beach volleyball became an official Olympic sport. In 1996 Karch Kiraly was, without question, the greatest volleyball player in the world. He played on the U.S. team that captured the gold medal in 1984 and has since turned his attention to the professional beach tour, where he remains a legend. Kiraly teamed up with Kent Steffes to play in the first Olympic two-man beach volleyball competition. The gold medal match pitted Kiraly and Steffes against the team of Mike Dodd and Mike Whitmarsh. All four players were from California. Kiraly and Steffes prevailed over Dodd and Whitmarsh under a grueling sun and won the gold medal.

In women's beach volleyball, the American teams did not fare nearly as well. Jackie Silva and Sandra Pires from Brazil beat another team from Brazil to win the gold. As a result, the gold and silver medal went to Brazil, while Natalie Cook and Kerri Pottharst Ann from Australia captured the bronze medal.

Apart from the gold and silver medals won by the American men in beach volleyball, the rest of the nation's volleyball teams did not do nearly as well as expected. Both the men's and women's indoor volleyball teams were eliminated and did not medal. In men's volleyball action, the Netherlands captured the gold medal, followed by Italy winning the silver and Yugoslavia with the bronze medal. Cuba won the gold medal in women's volleyball, followed by China, which won the silver, and Italy with the bronze.

In synchronized swimming, the battle was between the United States and Canada for the gold. The Canadians turned in what seemed to be a flawless performance. The United States followed the Canadian team and turned in the best performance possible, edging out Canada for the gold medal.

In the swimming competition, the United States was supposed to be very strong, as was China and Russia. However, there were the usual surprises. Alexander Popov of Russia won both the men's 50 free and 100 free. Danyon Loader from New Zealand won two gold medals in the men's 200 free and 400 free. Gary Hall of the U.S. won the silver in the 50 free and the 100 free, finishing second to Alexander Popov of Russia both times. Denis Pankratov of Russia won the gold medal in the 200 butterfly and 100 butterfly. American Tom Malchow won the silver medal in the 200 butterfly. The American men were victorious in the 400-medley relay, winning the gold medal ahead of Russia and Australia. They repeated as Olympic champions when they also won the 400-free relay, beating Russia and Germany.

The American women did well in swimming. Perhaps the best story in women's swimming belonged to Michelle Smith of Ireland, who dispatched some of the best swimmers in the world by winning four Olympic medals, three gold and one bronze. Amy Van Dyken of the United States won gold medals in the 50 free, 100 butterfly, 400 free relay, and the 400 medley relay.

In baseball, Cuba was the toast of the Olympics, capturing the gold medal once again. Japan won the silver medal, while the United States men's team had to settle for the bronze medal. In softball competition, the U.S. women were fantastic and won the gold medal, followed by China and Australia.

In addition to beach volleyball, mountain biking was added to the Olympic cycling agenda. The U.S. men's team did not medal. The gold medal went to Bart Jan Brentjens of the Netherlands, the silver to Thomas Frishknecht of Switzerland, and the bronze to Miguel Martinez of France. North American women fared better than their male counterparts in this event. Although Paola Pezzo of Italy won the gold medal in mountain biking, the silver medal was won by Allison Sydor of Canada, while American Susan DeMattei of Colorado won the bronze.

One of the more spectacular competitions to occur in Atlanta was in women's gymnastics. The Russians and the Romanians had "owned" the gold medal in the team competition for as long as anybody could remember. In the last night of competition, it came down to the courage and resolute dedication of American Kerri Strug, who was put into a "must do it" situation on the vault if the U.S. women were to capture the team championship. On the previous vault, she suffered a severe sprain to her ankle and limped off the floor in pain. She went to the staging area where her coach, Bela Karolyi, kept saying, "you can do it—you can do it." She did it! She sprinted to the vaulting horse and completed her routine and "stuck" the landing which she *had to do*. She could not waver, could not side-step. After the judges had indicated that her vault was good, she collapsed to the mat in pain and was helped off the floor by her teammates and medical personnel. She made a triumphant entry to the medal ceremony. With her ankle and shin wrapped, she was carried in by her coach to the cheers of the thousands of people in attendance that witnessed her courage and determination. The United States women won the team championship and the gold medal, followed by Russia winning the silver and Romania with the bronze.

During the closing ceremonies, President Samaranch presented Muhammad Ali with a replacement gold medal because Ali had misplaced his 1960 gold medal won as a boxer in Rome. One of the most familiar faces in all of the world, Ali suffers from Parkinson's disease, which leaves him shaking and slow in speech. The ceremony was a touching and tasteful end to a grand Olympiad.

Beyond 1996

Nagano is the host city to the 1998 Winter Olympics. Among the new sports that will debut in this ancient Japanese city will be snowboarding and women's ice hockey. The men's ice hockey competition will be one of the hottest tickets to get, because many of the stars of the National Hockey League (NHL) are expected to represent their countries.

The 1998 Winter Olympics are set to begin on February 7. Olympic spectators will be whisked from Tokyo to Nagano via high-speed bullet trains that will make the journey in about ninety minutes.

Sydney is the host city of the Summer Olympic Games in 2000. The Australians were eager hosts to the Olympic Games of 1956, which were held in the city of Melbourne. Although the IOC and the good people of Sydney are enthusiastically promoting the games, substantial cost overruns have already occurred, which no doubt concerns the Sydney Organizing Committee for the Olympic Games (SOCOG).

The organizers of the Sydney Olympiad had believed that the private sector would supply approximately $35 million for construction of three new venues, cycling, shooting, and tennis. So far, the participation of the private sector is less than expected. In addition to the difficulty in securing sources of capital, there have been significant increases in costs. The *Sydney Morning Herald* (May 24, 1996) reported that there may be a deficit of $375 million (Australian dollars). Like their counterparts in Nagano, the city of Sydney is constructing a high-speed rail line that will carry an estimated 300,000 per day to the Games.

During the Sydney Olympiad, it is quite possible that the baseball team fielded by the United States will be primarily made up of professional players from American and National Leagues. This follows a pattern that was established with the Dream Team (U.S. men's basketball team in Barcelona and Atlanta) and the fact that the National Hockey League (NHL) has suspended play during the Nagano Winter Olympics so the pros can go back home and represent their countries in the Nagano Winter Olympics. Who will be selected as members of the first "Dream Team" the United States fields in Olympic baseball competition? Will there be enough talent on the team to defeat the mighty Cuban baseball team for the gold medal? How strong will the Russian Olympic team be in Sydney?

Salt Lake City is the sight of the Winter Games in 2002. It is an ideal location. Utah advertises that it has "the greatest snow on earth," and most of the venues will be within a 45-minute (or less) freeway commute from downtown. Salt Lake has a very modern airport, and existing transportation systems are quite good. Yet, there is much work to be done and additional venues will have to be constructed. The Olympic organizers from Salt Lake will pay close attention to how the Nagano Winter Games are run.

Summary

In recent years, the amount of research into the Olympic Games has grown at a fantastic rate. Many scholars, but especially John Lucas and David Young, note that there are hundreds of books on the history of the modern Olympic Games. But understanding the complexity of the Games, especially in light of their humanistic mission in these complex times, can sometimes be especially difficult. The Olympic Games, like many modern institutions, have struggled mightily to avoid the corrupting influences of commercialization, drugs, and attacks by the media. To their credit the Olympic Games have remained remarkably true to their original ideals in spite of these detracting influences.

The authors sought to avoid duplicating much of the information already available in contemporary scholarship and instead elected to present a discussion of the modern Olympic Games that focus on selected social and political aspects. Our purpose is to bring to the attention of the reader the complexity and the struggle that has taken place, not only in the athletic arena but also in the political and social arenas. We realize that this approach does limit the discussion of the Olympics in this book and strongly suggest that additional accounts of the Olympic Games be read.

The Olympic Games tend to reflect the day-to-day activities of a large city that can be anywhere in the world. The games, like big cities, are good, bad, glorious, uplifting, hypocritical, inspiring, and memorable.

The Olympic flag waving in the breeze is an inspiring sight. The five interlocking rings are symbolic of the five continents that send athletes to participate in the world's only true international athletic festival. No matter where one travels in this world, the mere mention of the Olympic Games remains one of the few events that generates positive excitement and animated discussions that are focused on the performance of the best athletes in the world. The torch relay that carried the Olympic flame across the United States for the 1996 Games in Atlanta, and the tremendous excitement that this 15,000-mile journey engendered, is a sign that the Olympic spirit is alive and well in the contemporary world. The Olympics represent a belief system that emphasizes the high ideals of personal achievement, understanding, and good will.

The Olympic ideal has survived world wars, terrorist attacks, boycotts, and other meddling by politicians. During the Cold War era the Olympic Games have often deteriorated into competition between nations for the purpose of enhancing national prestige and political ideologies. International relations, social policy, and economic considerations represent elements of political power that sometimes would determine who could compete in the games; power politics, in the form of the boycotts of the XXIst, XXIInd, and XXIIIrd Olympiads, served to undermine, but did not extinguish, the Olympic flame.

It has been demonstrated that political bickering between nations does not confine itself to the political arena of the United Nations. From time to time, the Olympic Games appear to have become a preferred platform for political confrontations. In the past, Olympic athletes have become pawns of their governments and targets of terrorists. Security precautions costing millions of dollars are developed and deployed to deter political terrorists from invading the Olympics. At various times, Olympic athletes who have trained for years have been relegated to the role of soldiers of sport. From 1936 to 1988, it could sometimes be difficult to separate Olympic athletes from the political arena and the Olympic arena. Nationalism has always been a part of the Olympics. How can patriotism be separated from nationalism?

Since the collapse of communism in Eastern Europe, the propaganda war between the United States and the Soviet Union ended, and one of the chief beneficiaries of the end of the Cold War is the Olympic movement. The Olympic Games have entered into a period of prosperity and incredible growth, and the Olympic ideals shine brighter than ever. Within this new atmosphere, the Olympic Games appear to have resumed their goal of bringing people together from different parts of the world in order to foster international understanding and to enhance the prospects for peace. Perhaps this time, the athletes and the Olympics will truly make a difference in promoting good will and international understanding.

The use of drugs by Olympic athletes has replaced politicians as the scourge of the games. Blood doping of distance runners and steroid use among weightlifters and track-and-field athletes have been a plague on the Olympics. The use of ergogenic aids and their detection will no doubt be a recurring story during future Olympics. Still, the use of illicit drugs by unscrupulous athletes is a measure of the importance of an Olympic victory and what athletes will do to achieve it. The ancient Greeks had to deal with cheating in the Olympic Games, and the IOC has inherited this problem as well. Nicco Machieveli, who wrote the classic book, *The Prince*, noted that "the end justifies the means." Drugs have become the means that some athletes resort to in order to achieve their end—an Olympic medal. These athletes are not worthy to be honored as Olympians.

The task ahead for the International Olympic Committee is to continue to instill the Olympic ideal among the athletes of the world that does not place winning over the desire to compete excellently and fairly. Drugs may enhance one's chances of winning, but they have nothing to do with the Olympic spirit that make the games so attractive in which to compete. Athletes must understand this distinction, and it will be necessary for the International Olympic Committee and the National Olympic Committees to educate future Olympians against drug abuse as well as provide the arena in which they can compete.

It has been said that "nothing is forever." If the Olympics once again fall prey to the politicians, the Olympic flame may be extinguished once and for all. The IOC has been very effective in breathing new life into the Olympics in spite of the social and political agendas that have been injected into the games. We can only hope that the IOC will continue to do what many detractors have termed "mission impossible," to keep the Olympic flame burning brightly for a long time to come.

Discussion Questions

1. How have social issues impacted the Olympic Games?

2. To what extent did the issue of apartheid and the political act of terrorism have an impact on the 1972 Munich Olympiad? Did the International Olympic Committee have a moral obligation to make sure the Olympics continued after the massacre of the Israeli athletes? If so, why? Do you believe the International Olympic Committee should have canceled the games after the massacre? Why?

3. With the exorbitant costs associated with holding the Olympic Games, what benefits are derived by the host city and the country?

4. What could be done to remove politics from the Olympics? Do you believe that the end of the Cold War and the breakup of the Soviet Union result in all future Olympiads becoming more peaceful and friendly?

5. What could you suggest to the IOC to ensure that future Olympiads will promote international understanding and goodwill? Should the Olympic Games be permanently located in one place? Where and why? Will American athletes ever again dominate the Olympic Games as they did prior to 1960? With the global changes underway, who will be the dominant Olympic power of the 1990s and into the year 2000?

6. To what extent do you believe that commercialization of the Olympics has a negative impact?

The authors recommend that students interested in the Olympic movement read the critically acclaimed book by John A. Lucas, *Future of the Olympic Games.*

Suggestions for Further Reading

Camper, R. *Encyclopedia of the Olympic Games.* New York: McGraw-Hill, 1972.

Durance, J. *Highlights of the Olympics.* New York: Hastiness House, 1965.

Gray, W., and R. Knight Barony. "Devotion to Whom? German-American Loyalty on the Issue of Participation in the 1936 Olympic Games." *Journal of Sport History,* vol. 17, no. 2 (Summer 1990): 214–231.

Killanin, Lord, and J. Rod, eds. *The Olympic Games 1980.* New York: Macmillan, 1979.

Kretchmar, R. S. "Ethics and Sport: An Overview." *Journal of the Philosophy of Sport* X (1983): 21–32.

Leiper, J. M. "The International Olympic Committee: The Pursuit of Olympicism 1894–1970." Doctoral dissertation, University of Alberta, 1976.

Lucas, J. A. *Future of the Olympic Games.* Champaign, Ill.: Human Kinetics Publishers, 1992.

Mechikoff, R. A. "The Politicalization of the XXIst Olympiad." Doctoral dissertation, Ohio State University, 1976.

Real, M. R. *Super Media: A Cultural Studies Approach.* Newbury Park, Calif.: Sage Publications, 1989.

Notes

1. *New York Times,* 10 August 1972, 43.

2. *New York Times,* 23 August 1972, 47.

3. John Kieran and Arthur Daley, *The Story of the Olympic Games* (Philadelphia and New York: J. B. Lippincott, 1973), 462.

4. *New York Times,* 22 August 1972, 55.

5. *New York Times,* 19 August 1972, 17.

6. Kieran and Daley, *Story of Olympic Games,* 463.

7. "Terror at the Olympics," *Newsweek,* 18 September 1972, 24.

8. Ibid.

9. Ibid.

10. Ibid., 29.

11. Ibid.

12. Ibid., 33.

13. *New York Times,* 8 September 1972, 22.

14. *New York Times,* 9 September 1972, 1.

15. Bill Henry, *An Approved History of the Olympic Games* (Los Angeles: The Southern California Committee for the Olympic Games, 1981), 357.

16. *The Olympic Movement,* published by the International Olympic Committee, Chateau de Vidy, Lausanne, Switzerland, 1993. p. 62; Anita Defrantz, "The Olympic Games and Women," *Olympic Review,* XXV-5 (October-November 1995), 58.

17. Henry, *Approved History.*

18. *The Olympic Movement,* 74; Defrantz, "Olympic Games and Women," 58.

19. *Long Beach Independent Press Telegram,* 8 July 1976, sec. C, 1.

20. *Long Beach Independent Press Telegram,* 12 July 1976, sec. C, 1.

21. *New York Times*, 2 July 1976, sec. A, 20.
22. Ibid.
23. *New York Times*, 4 July 1976, sec. 5, 1.
24. *Whittier News*, 12 July 1976, 1.
25. Pat Putnam, "It Was a Call to Colors," *Sports Illustrated*, 26 July 1976, 17.
26. Ibid.
27. Robert Trumbull, "Threat to Cancel Olympics Made Over Taiwan Dispute," *New York Times*, 10 July 1976, 17.
28. Robert Trumbull, "U.S., Canada: Diplomatic Rift," *New York Times*, 16 July 1976, A17.
29. *Los Angeles Times*, 29 July 1976, sec. III, 1.
30. Ibid.
31. Ibid.
32. *New York Times*, 10 July 1976, 19.
33. Ibid.
34. Putnam, "Call to Colors," 16.
35. Ibid.
36. Ibid., 18.
37. *Long Beach Independent Press Telegram*, 12 July 1976, sec. C, 1.
38. Ibid.
39. *Long Beach Independent Press Telegram*, 19 July 1976, sec. C, 1.
40. *Whittier News*, 31 July 1976, 17.
41. *Los Angeles Times*, 1 August 1976, 1.
42. Ibid., 12.
43. *Long Beach Independent Press Telegram*, 3 August 1976, sec. C, 1.
44. Ibid.
45. *Long Beach Independent Press Telegram*, 19 July 1976, sec. C, 1.
46. Ibid.
47. Ibid.
48. Ibid.
49. Ibid., p. 62; Ibid., p. 58.
50. Henry, *Approved History*, 391.
51. Ibid., p. 74; Ibid., p. 58.
52. Ibid., 393.
53. Ibid., 392.
54. *U.S. News & World Report*, 14 January 1980, 22.
55. Brassy, "Boycott of the 1980 Olympic Games," unpublished paper, San Diego State University, 1983, 3.
56. "Transcript of President's Speech," *New York Times*, 4 January 1980.
57. Henry, 427.
58. Laurel Brassy, "Boycott," 5–6.
59. International Olympic Committee Charter, Rule 24, Parag. C.
60. *Colorado Springs Gazette Telegraph*, 20 February 1980, 1.
61. Brassy, "Boycott," 7.
62. Ibid.
63. Ibid.
64. *Colorado Springs Gazette Telegraph*, 4 April 1980, 1.
65. Ibid.
66. Ibid.

67. Brassy, "Boycott," 8.

68. Ibid., 9.

69. Ibid.

70. Ibid., 9–10.

71. Ibid., p. 62; Ibid., p. 58.

72. Ibid., 10–11.

73. Ibid., 12.

74. Henry, *History of the Olympic Games*, p. 428.

75. Niccolaao Machiavelli, *The Prince and the Discourses* (New York: Random House, 1950), 216.

76. Kenneth Reich, "An Outsiders View of the 1984 Olympic Games Preparations," in *Purposes, Principles, and Contradictions of the Olympic Movement: Proceedings of the United States Olympic Academy VI*, ed. Carolyn Vos Strache (Malibu, Calif.: Pepperdine University, 1982), 99.

77. Ibid.

78. Betty Spears and Richard Swanson, *History of Sport and Physical Education in the United States*, 3d ed. (Dubuque, IA: Wm. C. Brown, 1988), 382.

79. *The Olympic Movement*, p. 62; Defrantz, "Olympic Games and Women," p. 58.

80. Ibid., p. 74; Ibid., p. 58.

81. Barry Hillenbrand, "Breaking into the Big Leagues," *Time*, 12 November 1988, 42.

82. William Oscar Johnson, "The Spirit Flames Anew," *Sports Illustrated*, 26 September 1988, 51.

83. Ibid.

84. Ibid., 52.

85. Ibid., p. 62; Ibid., p. 58.

86. John Huxley, "Barcelona a Searing, Surprising Success," in *The Los Angeles Times*, 10 August 1992, p. 2w.

87. Ibid.

88. *The Olympic Movement*, p. 62; Defrantz, "Olympic Games and Women," p. 58.

89. Media Guide, Calgary 1988 Olympic Winter Games, 26.

90. Official Report of the XVI Olympic Winter Games of Albertville and Savoie—comite d'organization des XVI Jeux Olympiques d'hiver d'Albertville et de la Savoie, 73200 Albertville, France, 1992, p. 124.

91. Ibid., p. 235.

92. Fact Sheet #B-1 from Olympic Museum, Lausanne, Switzerland. 30 June 1995, p. 3.

93. Ibid., p. 2.

94. 23 February, 1992, *The San Diego-Union Tribune*, p. H-13.

95. 8 February, 1992, *The Los Angeles Times*, p. C-9.

96. Fact Sheet #B-3 from Olympic Museum, Lausanne, Switzerland, 30 June 1995, p. 2.

97. Ibid., p. 2.

98. 28 February 1994, *The San Diego Union-Tribune*, p. D-13.

99. 13 August 1996, *The San Diego Union-Tribune*, p. C-2.

100. 5 August 1996, *The Jackson Hole Daily Guide*, p. 21.

Epilogue: Back to the Future: Human Movement as Personal Experience in the Twentieth Century and Beyond

We have argued that the mind/body relationship is important to physical educators because, to a great extent, what we "know" and how we teach is culturally determined by the mind/body relationship.[1] Furthermore, if a given culture considers the mind and body to be integrated and whole, the body will have esteem and value.[2] We have examined the relationship of mind and body from many different philosophical perspectives, all of which were *influential* in Western civilization. These perspectives range from classic Platonic dualism and Descartes' rationalism, which have in common the view that the mind and body are separate and distinct entities, to Hobbes' empiricism, a philosophy that argues that there is only the material world and physical bodies in it. In such a philosophy humans rely on sense perceptions that can be collected and then verified objectively. In Hobbes' empiricism the body is not the enemy of reason or an obstacle to knowledge. Rather, the body is the only mechanism in the process of gathering knowledge. Between Plato and Hobbes we have philosophies that range from only ideas to only matter, from only mind to only body. All of these philosophies have guided, and been guided by, our understanding of embodiment.

Certain philosophies have tried to reconcile these two extremes. Pragmatists argue that experience, and therefore the body, is where one begins to come to know reality. Pragmatists also argue that man is an embodied entity. By embodiment, pragmatists mean that the mind, or spirit, is of the body and that mind and body are integrated into one entity.[3] As Thomas argued,

> Pragmatism was the first position to view the body as having value in and of itself (existential value) rather than just serving the mind. The idea that all knowledge is based on experience of a person suggests an integration of mind and body. This testifies to the value of the body as a source of knowledge.[4]

Several philosophies have been developed in the twentieth century in the West, particularly phenomenology and existentialism, that argue for a monistic view of reality. These philosophies value the body and experience and also treat subjectivity and mind favorably. By looking at these philosophies, we might be able to predict a kind of "future history" of sport and physical education that is based on the philosophies developed in the twentieth century.

This "future history" is not without some basis in history. Since the Reformation, philosophy has become more grounded in the experiences of the "here and now," or of the material world that we experience through our senses. One way of looking at the changes in philosophy since the 1500s is that, to an increasing extent, they seek to understand and explain the experiences we have in the material world. In the Age of Science and the Enlightenment, Galileo, Newton, Descartes, and other philosophers tried to explain the material world. In the nineteenth century the transcendentalists and the pragmatists sought to do the same. Now in the twentieth century philosophers have created still more answers to the questions we ask about the nature of the material world. Phenomenology and existentialism can be seen, in this light, as seeking answers to questions like the following: What is the material world? What is the nature of consciousness and awareness in the material world? How does the awareness of movement fit into this picture?

As we approach the new millennium, the experiential aspects of athletic participation and the resurgence of the Greek idea of pursuing individual excellence appears to be once again in vogue. The ancient Greek concepts of Agon and Arete have emerged once again; many of today's athletes continue their quest for individual excellence with personal satisfaction as the reward, as opposed to medals and other prizes. Personal satisfaction in knowing that "I did my best" is all that's needed for many who participate in physical activity. Sport and physical activity can be a highly personal experience for many of us with no need to explain or analyze our feelings, our personal satisfaction, to anybody else. It may seem odd to us versed in the sports world created in the nineteenth century, but the existential "extreme sports" seen on cable television may well be the model of sport in the future. Although team sports remain as popular as ever, the words of Socrates can be especially helpful in serving as a guide for the millions of individual athletes who engage in sport for the sheer joy of the experience; "know thyself!"

Coming to "know" about one's character, one's nature, can be derived from a number of experiences. Engaging in physical activity through athletic competition or simply by hiking, jogging, playing frisbee, tennis, rock climbing, mountain biking or any number of similar pursuits enables many individuals to "test" their personal "will," their personal physical and psychological limits, which was advocated by Nietzsche. However, many are not interested in being "tested" or testing another, but engage in the activity for personal meaning and enjoyment.

We believe that sport and physical activity are indeed very personal experiences and now present some philosophical ideas that may provide the reader with yet another way to "know thyself."

History of Phenomenology and Existentialism

The beginnings of existentialism and phenomenology can be traced to Soren Kierkegaard (1813–1855). For well over a century the philosophy of Kierkegaard was largely unknown outside Scandinavia because of the inability of most English-speaking people to read Danish. Kierkegaard's philosophy, like that of George Berkeley, argued for the existence of God. Kierkegaard said religion would be absolutely useless if we have the capacity to "reason" our way back to God. God would no longer be omnipotent, the supreme creator, if all knowledge could be completely understood and comprehended by humans.

The essence of his philosophy generally rests on the belief that there are three stages of life experience: (1) aesthetic, (2) ethical, and (3) religious. Kierkegaard's existentialism argues that some of us will progress from one stage to the next, whereas others will remain in the first stage forever. The third stage, however, is superior to the aesthetic and ethical stage. For Kierkegaard, all three stages reflect the attempt to win salvation and achieve satisfaction or "life's greatest good, while it remains in reach to be all you can be in an individual sense."

Shortly after Kierkegaard's philosophy became known, Friedrich Wilhelm Nietzsche (1844–1900) argued that the transcendent ideals of Judeo-Christian ethics, and thus the position of Kierkegaard, was utter nonsense. Nietzsche argued that science had "proven" that there is no spirit or such thing as God. Nietzsche's philosophical approach is generally considered to be one of value theory. He sought a reevaluation of all existing values. Nietzsche viewed the Judeo-Christian system of morality with some disdain and emphatically stated that it should be replaced by returning to the values found in nature.

A proponent of Darwinism, Nietzsche spoke in favor of maximal physical and intellectual development and the expression of animal, or natural, instincts. In *Thus Spake Zarathustra*, Nietzsche described the ideal man, the "Superman," whom he contrasted with the average man of the common herd.[5] The body, to Nietzsche, was a vital component of the Superman. Nietzsche's Superman can be described as one who is "beyond good and evil," who creates his own set of values and rejects any other so-called moral world order. As an individualist, the Superman towers over the "common herd," condemning its slave morality, its conventional behavior, its virtues of meekness and pity, and its cowardly attempts to avoid war and other challenging life situations.

Nietzsche's philosophical position advocated physical fitness as a priority. Physical fitness represented a component of individualism and power. However, Nietzsche's general reasoning rested on the belief that the body occupies a central and important role relative to existence. As a result of Nietzsche's view of the body, he has been described as "the Philosopher of Fitness" by Esar Shvartz:

> When read superficially, [Nietzsche] seems to be an extremist, an anti-Semite and a German nationalist. But for anybody who bothers to understand, his writings reveal that he was an anti-anti-Semite, an anti-German nationalist, and one of the most humane thinkers.[6]

Nietzsche was the major originator of existential thought, and unlike traditional philosophers, he took the body quite seriously. He did not have the dualistic belief in the separation of mind and body, and he claimed that the soul was actually a philosophical invention to undermine the worth of the body. In *The Will to Power*, Nietzsche argued that "the belief in the body is more fundamental than the belief in the soul. The latter arose from unscientific observations of the agonies of the body."[7]

In contrast to his idealistic philosopher contemporaries, Nietzsche strongly advocated that bodily health should become a priority and be taken more seriously. According to Nietzsche, the greatest enjoyment of life is to be had by living dangerously, an approach that necessitates superb health. To live dangerously, Nietzsche was telling individuals to shun the hypocrisy, fear, and mediocrity that are indicative of a conforming "herd" existence.

What Kierkegaard and Nietzsche did was to establish a basis for existential and phenomenological arguments. Both had in common the idea that the experiences of the body are real and important. And both had in common the idea that the experiences of the mind are real and important. What both of these philosophies did was to emphasize experience, which is the starting point for existentialism and phenomenology. What is important to note is that Nietzsche was a proponent of individual excellence in both mind and body. He believed that "to know thy self" one had to engage in physical challenges that would measure the mettle of an individual.

Existentialism

The following is a brief view of existentialism and how this philosophy might be used to approach physical education and sport:

1. Existentialism begins with the belief that the individual is at the center. Everything "outside" the individual is subordinate to, and evaluated by, the individual. In existentialism, the acute interest in the individual is paramount. Existentialism emphasizes this idea because of the belief that "modern" man has become depersonalized in the way described by Nietzsche.

2. "Existence" precedes essence, which accounts for the term existentialism.[8] This means that each individual creates himself or herself through choices and experiences and that a person is the sum total of all his or her choices and experiences. The existing individual is able to perceive an idea, concept, or "essence" of something, such as a new sport, and then bring that essence into being. The existence-precedes-essence formula is valid for the individual because the individual must exist before creation of an essence or idea can occur.

   For everything in the world that is outside the individual, essence precedes existence. For example, the essence of sport preceded the existence of sport. "Sport" was then created and put into operation; that is, it then exists. Only the individual man or woman can create or conceive of the essence of sport. This concept emphasizes once again the acute interest in and importance of the individual. So the hierarchy that describes existentialism is depicted as follows:

EXISTENCE Individual
ESSENCE Idea
EXISTENCE Object/Activity

3. Each and every person should have full opportunity to make choices and decisions. Without the opportunity to make legitimate choices, the individual loses some of his or her existence.[9] Life becomes prefabricated, and in many instances predetermined, when alternatives for thought and action are no longer present. Thus, for an existentialist, there is no recognition of external values because they are determined by the "outside world" and therefore represent conformity. An existentialist would claim that there are no values in sport or physical education other than those of the experience itself. Each individual has the freedom—and responsibility—to determine what value, if any, sport and physical education have, not what the coach or physical education teacher says.

   The freedom to make choices is inherent in existentialism. Individuals will personally determine what value an activity or experience holds. Harold Vanderzwaag argued that

   if any group proceeds to claim the values of sport, the individual has already lost some of his opportunity to make a decision. Values are specific to each individual, and they grow out of the experiences of each person. There are no eternal values so to speak. . . . Consequently, nothing could be worse than to require people to participate in sport.[10]

4. The individual is responsible for his or her actions and behavior. This freedom, however, does not allow the individual to ignore his or her responsibilities. The burden of responsibility that existentialism demands is enormous. Each person is responsible not only for himself/herself, but for other people as well. "The responsibility for others does not mean dictating to others or attempting to limit their freedom in any way. It does mean that one's decisions will also influence and affect others."[11]

   Because existentialism places the individual at the center and demands that each person accept responsibility for his or her behavior, existentialism is concerned with psychological as well as philosophical issues. The difference in values, choices, decisions, and purpose in life that are manifest in existential thought are accounted for by differences in psychological makeup. Therefore, existentialism is not a systematic philosophy or organized body of beliefs. Indeed, most existentialists reject the premise that one should think in terms of a systematic philosophy.[12]

5. The focus on individualism necessitates a commitment to authenticity. The authentic individual is truly an individual, not one who seeks approval from others or who desires to conform to the dress, language, and destination of the "in crowd." An existentialist does not allow others to define what he or she ought to be, but is guided by his or her own existence. If an existential athlete decides to join

a team, that athlete must agree to assume a certain role and function for the benefit of the team; she or he must agree to give up individuality and assume a predetermined, prefabricated role. Not surprisingly, many athletes who would label themselves existential are more comfortable participating in individual sports such as cross country, track and field, and swimming than in team sports such as volleyball, basketball, or football. This is not to say, however, that existentialism determines that one will participate in individual sports, merely that it is easier to be responsible only for oneself.

6. The concept of ambiguity is an essential component in understanding how existentialism operates. Kaplan argued that

existentialism emphasizes . . . possibilities. There must be alternative possibilities of action or choice would be meaningless; and there must be alternative possibilities of existence, or it would be predetermined by essence. This manifold of possibility gives meaning to the final basic existentialist category: ambiguity. . . . Choice is continuous as we go through life, and with each choice some possibilities vanish forever while others emerge for the next choice. We are continuously making something of life, but we can never make it out: life is inescapably ambiguous.[13]

Existential doctrine is highly individualistic and ambiguous, yet as Nietzsche stated, it demands one to 'become who you are!' His philosophy is for the strong and courageous, yet he also advocates an extreme humanism. Nietzsche's existentialism is attractive to sport philosophers, for it calls for 'a doctrine of action,' a refusal to surrender to human weaknesses and falsely human institutions, a call for excellence in every aspect of human endeavor.[14] Although not a systematic philosophy, existentialism demands that we take responsibility for our behavior and actions. Striving to perform at one's very best, refusing to concede defeat, and striving to achieve complete and total victory are existential concepts that were embraced by Nietzsche and no doubt the vast majority of elite coaches and athletes.

Jean-Paul Sartre's (1905–1980) arguments illustrate the monistic view of being that existentialists hold. In *Being and Nothingness*, Sartre argued that there are three dimensions of the body:

1. the body as being-for-itself

2. the body as being-for-the-other

3. my body as body-known-by-the-other

Sartre's three dimensions of the body provide understanding about the nature of movement and the manner in which bodies are viewed. Sartre's three views of the body provide a distinction between the body as an object and the body as a subject. When the body is viewed as an object, having its own laws and defined from the outside, it is difficult to connect or link the material body with a mind or consciousness that is very personal and subjective.[15] However, when the body is experienced or lived on a personal/holistic level (treated not as an object), the subjective "being-for-itself" dimension manifests itself.

The following quote summarizes existential thought on the mind/body relationship:

> In the objective mode, I have a body, I train it, I use it, and in this regard 'IT' can be viewed as separate from me. But this same body in the subjective mode means that I am my body and that my consciousness is embodied, or integrated, in this subjectivity.[16]

Phenomenology

Phenomenology, like existentialism, can be described as a tool or method that can be used to gain insights into questions that arise from "being in the world."[17] As a movement, phenomenology can be traced back to the works of Franz Brentano (1838–1917) and Carl Stumpf (1848–1936). Perhaps the originator of phenomenology was Edmund Husserl (1859–1938). In addition there were a number of Husserl's students who fled to the United States to escape Hitler's Germany in World War II and helped introduce and spread phenomenology throughout the country.

Husserl was very interested in epistemology, the study of how we come to know things. He concluded that current epistemological beliefs, including the methods of science, are not valid. It was Husserl's contention that

> the immediate phenomenon, that which is directly given to us in experience, has been largely ignored by the traditional empiricism of contemporary science. Husserl called for a return to the things themselves. Thus, phenomenology began as a protest which called for a departure from crystallized beliefs and theories handed down by a tradition which only too often perpetuates preconceptions and prejudgements.[18]

Phenomenology, like existentialism, is not comfortable with "preconceptions and prejudgements," because these beliefs and values have been predetermined and have not allowed the individual to decide these things for himself or herself.

From a metaphysical standpoint, the body is viewed monistically as the means of fundamental access to the world, the instrument of communication to the world.[19] The body is not an instrument of the mind or the enemy of reason, but an individual's avenue to the world experience in knowledge. The phenomenologist's view of the body is similar to that of an empiricist, but goes further in that the quality of mind comes into play:

> The empiricists would explain that the reason one becomes aware of himself, or others, is due to a constant stream of data being delivered to the sense organs of the body. The phenomenologist, however, sees no reason to restrict himself to sense data alone. His [the phenomenologist's] experience of the phenomenon itself tells him that there is more involved than that [sense data]. . . . Every experience comes loaded with meanings and qualities, none of which can be explained by a sense organ's reception of stimulus. It is the task of phenomenology to deepen and enlarge the range of immediate experience, which we see to be much richer than the empirical view of it, i.e., experience.[20]

The objective of phenomenology is to go directly to the experience, relish the experience, and take it for what it is. What the experience represents will be decided by each individual. Because each of us experiences things and events differently, our feelings, knowledge, and understanding of a particular event or experience will in all probability vary greatly, even if several people engage in the same activity simultaneously. To the phenomenologist, you are your body and your body is your "being in the world."[21]

From a phenomenological approach, the body and the world of experiences available to the physical/athletic individual has value in and of itself. There is no need to justify or defend bodily, physical experiences and whatever attendant epistemological outcomes that are revealed through human movement pursuits. The body becomes a source of knowledge and personal growth, not the enemy of reason and a hindrance to knowledge as depicted in some dualistic philosophies.

> For the phenomenologist, to understand the body is to see the body not in terms of kinesiological analysis, but in the awareness and meaning of movement. . . . Movement becomes significant not by knowledge about the body, but through an awareness of the self. . . . From the phenomenological view, it becomes the purpose of the physical educator to develop, encourage, and nurture this awareness of, and openness of self—this understanding of self.[22]

Phenomenology and existentialism offer physical educators the opportunity to promote subjective experiences that can enhance the human condition. This can be contrasted to traditional physical education programs that many times encourage conformity. In so doing coaches and teachers can overcome the prevailing philosophical ethos that encourages and promotes conformity and reliability at the expense of responsibility. The question seems to be, are there components of existentialism and phenomenology that are compatible with the activities and purposes of physical education and athletic competition? Put another way, can some of the beliefs of existentialism and phenomenology contribute to the betterment of physical education and sport? The answer to these questions would appear to be yes. And to some extent these philosophies may be used in the future to help improve and better understand our sport and physical education experiences.

Summary

Phenomenology and existentialism represent two of the more powerful philosophical movements of the twentieth century, but they are not the only movements. Logical positivism; Eastern philosophies such as Zen Buddhism, Confucianism, and Taoism; constructivism; deconstruction; and other philosophies are having a radical impact on Western civilization. The effect of these philosophies on American attitudes toward the mind and body, and on sport and physical education, are being experienced even as you read this book, reshaping the kinds of activities and experiences all of us will have in human movement activities. What seems to be the common thread during the twentieth century is the theme of the unified mind and body, a monistic manner of viewing human experiences that include sport and play.

These additions to the philosophical movements that are in place illustrate how quickly America is changing at the end of the twentieth century. Rather than developing a single philosophy that will explain the mind/body relationship and a single consequent approach to sport and physical education, Americans seem to be using more philosophical explanations. And more changes seem to arrive in the academic world every year. What one can expect, then, are more changes than ever in the future. As American culture becomes more culturally diverse, there will be more explanations for this diversity. What will remain consistent will be the desire of these many cultures, in their many ways, to explain in a philosophical way how their playful activities have changed over time.

Discussion Questions

1. What makes existentialism different from empiricism? How does this have an impact on sport and physical education?

2. What makes phenomenology different from existentialism? How does this have an impact on sport and physical education?

3. Given the trends that have developed in the United States since the 1800s, what might be the trend for sport in the twenty-first century with respect to the issue of mind and body?

Suggestions for Further Reading

Kleinman, S. "Pragmatism, Existentialism, and Phenomenology." In *Physical Education: An Interdisciplinary Approach*, ed. Robert Singer, et al. New York: Macmillan, 1972.

Shvartz, E. "Nietzsche: A Philosopher of Fitness." *Quest*, Monograph VIII (May 1967).

Thomas, C. E. *Sport in a Philosophic Context*. Philadelphia: Lea & Febiger, 1983.

Vanderzwaag, H. J. *Toward a Philosophy of Sport*. Reading, Mass.: Addison-Wesley, 1972, 211.

Notes

1. J. R. Fairs, "The Influence of Plato and Platonism on the Development of Physical Education in Western Culture," *Quest* 11 (1968): 12–23.

2. Ibid.

3. Carolyn E. Thomas, *Sport in a Philosophic Context* (Philadelphia: Lea & Febiger, 1983), 31.

4. Ibid., 32–33.

5. Esar Shvartz, "Nietzsche: A Philosopher of Fitness," *Quest*, Monograph VIII (May 1967): 83.

6. Ibid.

7. Friedrich Nietzsche, *The Will to Power* (London: T. N. Foulis, 1913), 18.

8. Harold J. Vanderzwaag, *Toward a Philosophy of Sport* (Reading, MA: Addison-Wesley, 1972), 211.

9. Ibid.

10. Ibid., 212.

11. Ibid.

12. Ibid.

13. Abraham Kaplan, *The New World of Philosophy* (New York: Random House, 1961), 117.

14. Schvartz, "Nietzsche."

15. Seymour Kleinman, "Pragmatism, Existentialism, and Phenomenology," in *Physical Education: An Interdisciplinary Approach*, ed. Robert Singer, et al. (New York: Macmillan, 1972), 353.

16. Thomas, *Sport in a Philosophic Context*, 34–35.

17. Kleinman, "Pragmatism," 352.

18. Ibid.

19. Ibid., 352–353.

20. Ibid.

21. Thomas, *Philosophic Context*, 34.

22. Kleinman, "Pragmatism," 355.

Index